Britain's strike record is the subject of continuous and partisan public debate – never more so than at the present time. Yet serious strike analysis has remained spasmodic, partial and fragmentary. This study provides the first systematic long-run examination of official strike statistics since the war. It is based on a wealth of new material and analysis.

The overall strike pattern is first compared with the relevant data on economic activity rates – e.g. movements in prices, output and employment. Theories linking strikes with variations in all these factors are examined in some detail.

Next, studies of strike prone industries and occupations are analysed and tested against the background of institutional and other changes. Sections follow on the role of government, law and the impact of incomes policy. The role of management and the influence of union militancy are also examined.

A final chapter suggests the way in which these and other factors have combined to produce Britain's varied and varying propensity to strike. An attempt is made to assess the cost and consequences of strikes for management, workers and the British economy.

The result is a standard work which challenges a whole series of assumptions about strikes. Economic factors are found to be less helpful explanations than political change, or legal developments. Bargaining reform and trade union government are shown to have had a significant impact on the form and timing of certain significant changes in the volume of strike activity.

Nobody who wishes to discuss seriously the causes and consequences of Britain's so-called 'strike problem' can afford to remain ignorant of the main conclusions of this book.

J. W. Durcan is a former Research Fellow of Nuffield College who is a Senior Lecturer in Industrial Relations at Oxford Polytechnic.

Lord McCarthy is a Fellow of Nuffield College, Oxford and a leading authority on industrial relations who has published a number of standard works on the subject. He is one of Britain's most experienced mediators and arbitrators, and has served as an adviser to several Governments and public bodies.

G. P. Redman is a Lecturer in Industrial Relations at Southwest London College.

For Mary, Margaret and Jenny

Strikes in Post-War Britain

A study of stoppages of work due to industrial disputes, 1946–73

J. W. Durcan, W. E. J. McCarthy and G. P. Redman
Nuffield College, Oxford University

London
GEORGE ALLEN & UNWIN
Boston   Sydney

George Allen & Unwin (Publishers) Ltd,
40 Museum Street, London WC1A 1LU, UK

George Allen & Unwin (Publishers) Ltd,
Park Lane, Hemel Hempstead, Herts HP2 4TE, UK

Allen & Unwin Inc.,
9 Winchester Terrace, Winchester, Mass 01890, USA

George Allen & Unwin Australia Pty Ltd,
8 Napier Street, North Sydney, NSW 2060, Australia

First published in 1983

British Library Cataloguing in Publication Data

Durcan, J.W.
    Strikes in post-war Britain.
1. Strikes and lockouts—Great Britain—History
I. Title   II. McCarthy, W.E.J.
III. Redman, G.P.
331.89′2941   HD5365
ISBN 0–04–331093–1

Library of Congress Cataloging in Publication Data

Durcan, J. W.
    Strikes in post-war Britain.
Bibliography: p.
Includes index.
1. Strikes and lockouts—Great Britain—
History—20th century.   I. McCarthy, W. E. J.
(William Edward John)   II. Redman, G. P.   III. Title
HD5365.A6D87 1983   331.89′2941   83–5975
ISBN 0–04–331093–1

Set in 10 on 11 point Times by
Media Conversion Ltd, Ickenham, Middlesex
and printed in Great Britain by
Mackays of Chatham

Contents

List of Tables

Acknowledgements

This study was made possible as a result of grants from the Leverhulme Foundation to Nuffield College and the Social Science Research Council to Oxford University. We have to thank these bodies and the Department of Social and Administrative Studies at Oxford for their generous assistance.

The greater part of the data used in the study is drawn from the records of the Department of Employment – both published and unpublished. We have to thank the Department for allowing us to consult their unpublished records, which were of particular assistance in enabling us to undertake a comprehensive study of major stoppages in our period – i.e. those involving a loss of 5,000 or more working days.

In its various stages the study was read by a number of our academic colleagues, who gave us the benefit of their advice and experience. The penultimate draft was read by Professor William Brown, Director of the Social Science Research Council's Industrial Relations Research Unit at the University of Warwick. We would like to thank him for his helpful comments and suggestions.

Our thanks are also due to Lynne Summersbee and Mary Durcan for struggling to understand our successive drafts and for producing versions which printers could use.

All errors, omissions and *non-sequiturs* are to be blamed on us.

J. W. Durcan
W. E. J. McCarthy
G. P. Redman
Nuffield College
January 1983

1 Objectives and Sources

*The striker is unloved, unhonoured, and unsung;
above all he is largely unstudied.*
K. G. J. C. Knowles, *Strikes – A Study in
Industrial Conflict*,1952, p.*xi*

THE REASONS FOR THIS STUDY

This study has three principal objectives: to provide a systematic long–run examination of the pattern of strikes in the UK in the period 1946–73; to account for the level of strike activity and the particular forms it has taken; to contribute to the apparently continuous public debate on strikes. One way of summarising our intentions is to say that we wish to 'up-date Knowles' – to continue and build on his classic study of strike activity for the period 1911–47.

Knowles set out to define the nature of strikes and their relationship to other forms of industrial, social and political action; he considered the general influences that affected the development of industrial militancy and the attempts which had been made to restrain or divert it; he discussed the causes of strikes and their intended and incidental consequences. His methodology involved a mixture of statistical analysis, institutional investigation and appeals to a wide range of textual authorities. Most well informed generalisations concerning the nature and form of strike activity in this country bear evidence of acquaintance with his work.

Of course there has been a considerable increase in the literature of strikes since Knowles wrote. The number of case studies concerned with a detailed analysis of particular strikes has increased significantly (e.g. Lane and Roberts, 1971; Batstone, Boraston and Frenkel, 1978). Several sectional studies have analysed particular parts of the strike pattern in considerable detail (e.g. Goodman, 1967; Turner, Clack and Roberts, 1967). There have been analytical and theoretical studies of strike causation, motivation and justification (e.g. Eldridge, 1968; McFarlane, 1981). Many students have used advanced statistical techniques to investigate various aspects of strike activity that Knowles barely touched (e.g. Pencavel, 1970; Knight, 1972). Even the Department of Employment has published its own factual account of strike trends for the period 1966–73 (i.e. Smith, Clifton, Makeham, Creigh and Burn, 1978). But it remains true that there has been no overall study which has attempted to follow on from Knowles' approach, either in respect of the time span of the data or the depth of the analysis. As a result our picture of the post-war strike pattern has remained both uneven and fragmentary. Islands of light have continued to be surrounded by oceans of ignorance. And yet the debate about what should be done about strikes and strikers has never been more insistent and pervasive.

There appeared to us to be several reasons for seeking to remedy such a deficiency. First, when Knowles produced his study the UK had experienced almost twenty years of relative industrial peace – at least as measured by time lost through stoppages. In consequence Knowles and his immediate contemporaries tended to view strike activity as a phenomenon of declining importance. In that sense his study was not so much about strikes as about the control of strikes – particularly via the provision of effective industry-wide bargaining arrangements which were thought to have 'institutionalised' and 'accommodated' industrial conflict. Yet in the thirty years since the early 1950s there has been an increase in strike activity in most years. In seeking to account for this development we felt that it was imperative that the emphasis should be placed upon the strike pattern and its possible causes, rather than on those mechanisms by which industrial militancy might perhaps be 'accommodated' and 'controlled'. This required our study to have a rather different perspective to that of Knowles.

Secondly, it seemed to us that there had been a major shift in political attitudes towards strikes between the early 1950s and the early 1970s. Thus in August 1951 the Labour government repealed the prohibition on strike action which had been introduced in 1940 by the wartime Coalition government. The Conservative government elected later that same year was content to follow this policy, yet by the late 1960s the two major political parties almost seemed to be vying with each other to see which of them could introduce the most stringent legislative restraints on the use of strikes. One of our aims has been to assess how far these developments could be accounted for by changes in the strike pattern; or whether they should be regarded as the result of a failure to come to terms with other problems.

Thirdly, as has been said, other studies of strikes published since 1952 have all been relatively limited, in the time span of their data, or in their industrial coverage or in their concern with explanatory variables. A long-run, broad sweep study, aimed at accounting for the changes in the level and form of strike activity, seemed likely to be a useful contribution – particularly if it enabled a distinction to be drawn between permanent and transitory features of the strike pattern. Such a distinction seemed particularly useful in identifying different explanatory variables and in evaluating alternative policy options.

Finally, improvements in the quantity and quality of data available and in information handling techniques have been very marked since the post-war period. The amount of information published on strikes has increased gradually over the years until it is now greater than at any time since the First World War. There have also been significant improvements in data handling facilities – in terms of statistical techniques and in machine aids. These developments made it easier to prepare large masses of data for presentation in the descriptive sections of the study and to compare some features of the strike pattern with other variables – the quality of which has also improved during these years.

The period selected for detailed analysis was 1946–73. As we explain in later chapters, it is a central part of our argument that the post-war strike pattern has been significantly affected by political change, especially that which involves a change in the government party. Indeed we believe that it can be shown that each change of party government since the war has been followed by significant and substantial changes in the British strike pattern, although these have often taken some years to emerge, and their full significance has not been apparent at the time. The period 1946–73 encompassed four sub-periods of party government – two Conservative and two Labour – which provided us with a rough degree of balance with which to work. The argument concerning political change is developed in detail in Chapter 11, while its implications for the future are explored in Chapter 12.

It is also the case that 1973 is widely seen as marking the end of a long post-war phase in economic and political policy. Thereafter the problems of worldwide inflation, magnified as they were by the oil crisis, dominated the economic scene in general and government policy in particular. One consequence of this was that public sector stoppages rose to prominence. Another was that the state of full employment which had existed since World War II ended. That end marked the disappearance of what many regarded as a necessary condition for the UK's high incidence of workplace stoppages in private industry. The period 1946–73 was the heyday of private sector stoppages in the UK, and it was the growth of those stoppages which provided the dominant focus for this study. It should perhaps be said that we are now engaged on a study of the period since 1973, in which we seek to apply some of the major findings of this study to the years which followed.

The remainder of this chapter is concerned to outline the methodology adopted in the study and its scope and form. We begin by describing our source data. The sections which immediately follow define and explain the main measures of strike activity which have been extracted from this data and used in our study. Two subsequent sections justify our particular focus. The chapter ends with an outline of the rest of the book and the subject matter of subsequent chapters.

THE AVAILABLE DATA – STRIKE STATISTICS IN THE UK

Virtually all the descriptive material on strikes used in this study was drawn from the records, published and unpublished, of the Department of Employment. (This Ministry went through four titles in the post-war period. We refer to it throughout as the Department of Employment or simply the Department.) The definition of a stoppage which provides the basis for the Department's records is that recommended in the International Labour Organization Resolution on Labour Statistics (ILO, 1926):

The basic unit – the case of dispute – should be defined as a temporary stoppage of work wilfully effected by a group of workers or by one or more employees with a view to enforcing a demand. Disputes affecting several establishments should be considered as one case if they are organised or directed by one person or organisation.

This definition, which also enjoys a wide currency outside the UK, emphasises the essential features of strike action as being temporary collective stoppages in pursuit of specific objectives which serves to distinguish strikes from other forms of industrial, social or political action. The treatment of disputes which result in simultaneous stoppages in several establishments as one stoppage is important because it introduces a strong element of heterogeneity into number of strikes series. The ILO also recommended that a distinction should be drawn between strikes and lockouts: the former being initiated by workers, the latter by employers. This practice was tried in the UK and abandoned as being impracticable as early as 1895. It was never reintroduced. Consequently we were able to follow common usage and use the terms 'strike' and 'stoppage' inter-changeably without implying that all such action results from aggressive action on the part of the workforce.

The Department of Employment has deliberately restricted its coverage of stoppages in two ways which mean that its records are less comprehensive than a literal application of the ILO resolution would require. First, the Department only records those stoppages which arise out of industrial disputes concerning terms and conditions of employment. This means that the Department does not include 'political' strikes in its records. Until recently this policy did not appear to matter a great deal as 'political' strikes were virtually unknown in the UK. This situation was changed by proposals for and the enactment of legislation restricting workers' collective rights, e.g. the Industrial Relations Act 1971 and the statutory incomes policy 1972–4, which were accompanied by a series of protest strikes. The Department ruled that such stoppages did not arise from disputes concerning the terms and conditions of employment and were therefore ineligible for inclusion in its records.

It seems a fine distinction to regard stoppages in support of claims for wage increases in excess of incomes policy limits as industrial stoppages, but to judge stoppages in protest against the introduction of an incomes policy as being 'political'. Strikes against reductions in public expenditure would be classified as 'political', whereas stoppages against redundancies resulting from cuts in public expenditure would be regarded as industrial. This is not to argue that there are no 'political' stoppages – the 1974 Loyalist strike in Northern Ireland to bring down the power-sharing Executive was clearly political – nor that such cases involve very considerable measurement difficulties. Our point is simply that the distinction is not as clear cut as it might appear, so that the decision to include some stoppages and exclude others is rather arbitrary. The effect of the policy was to reduce the level of recorded strike activity. Details of these 'political' stoppages are noted in Chapter 5.

Secondly, the Department excludes from its records those stoppages which involve fewer than ten workers and those which last for less than one day unless the aggregate number of days lost in such stoppages exceeds 100. The precise effects of this decision are impossible to quantify – particularly when we take account, as we do later, of the Department's system for recording stoppages. The decision clearly results in an under-estimation of strike activity. The under-estimation is greatest in relation to the number of strikes. The series for workers involved and working days lost are less adversely affected because large, long stoppages exert a much greater proportionate effect on these series.

But the accuracy and comprehensiveness of the official statistics depends not only on the definitions and criteria employed but also on the system for collecting and recording information. Any such system has two functions: first, to make certain that all stoppages which meet the definitional requirements come to the Department's notice; secondly, to ensure that the information that the Department then gathers is accurate. Doubts exist about the ability of the existing system to fulfil either of these functions.

The Department relies on a system of voluntary reporting. Sources of information include workers and employers making use of the Department's employment services, reports in the local and national press, certain statutory bodies, nationalised industries and the Department's own manpower advisers. In many ways the system has remained unchanged since 1893 when the first paid local labour correspondents were appointed to report on labour disputes. Despite this hallowed tradition it has to be recognised that reliance on voluntary reporting must mean that some stoppages escape the Department's attention. The larger and longer the stoppages the more likely they are to be reported. The smaller and shorter they are the more likely it is that they will pass unnoticed. The difficulty is to assess the amount of strike activity which is unintentionally omitted.

These sources of under-recording are related and principally concern small, short stoppages. Their effects are much greater in relation to the number of strikes series than the number of workers involved or days lost. These latter series are proportionately much more affected by large, long stoppages.

It would be tempting to assume that the only stoppages which are excluded on grounds of size are those which would be overlooked by the recording system. In this way there would only be one problem rather than two. Unfortunately it seems more realistic to suppose that while there is some degree of overlap in these areas the boundaries are not identical. In particular it seems likely that there are some stoppages which fall within the Department's minimum size criteria which are not reported.

From time to time fragmentary evidence is produced to suggest that under-recording is a serious problem, but it is impossible to use such fragments to arrive at any overall estimate. Thus in Turner, Clack and Roberts' study of the car industry they note an instance where management at a particular plant claimed to have experienced 234 stoppages in a given year involving 500 000 man-hours lost (Turner *et al.*, 1967).

Departmental records, when consulted by the same authors, revealed only thirteen strikes leading to a loss of not more than 450 000 man-hours. Unfortunately there is no way of knowing how many of the lost 221 strikes met ILO standards, or what proportion were below the Department's minimum size. Since taken together they only resulted in 50 000 lost man-hours – the equivalent of twenty-eight days each – it is conceivable that they were *all* too small to count.

There is also the problem of how typical the plant in question can be assumed to be. To quote from the Donovan Commission (Donovan, 1968), only twenty-nine plants had more than five recorded strikes in the period 1965–6, which suggests that the plant quoted by Turner *et al.* is in a class apart!

The latest evidence bearing on the problem of under-recording is that provided in a survey confined to manufacturing plants by the Industrial Relations Research Unit at the University of Warwick (Brown, 1981). This post-dates our period, but it is worth mentioning all the same. It suggests that during the period 1976–7 the Department was informed of approximately two-thirds of stoppages eligible for inclusion in the series. It also supports the view that so far as manufacturing is concerned the total number of strikes could be as much as four times as large as the number recorded in the official statistics! But although Brown's figures are illuminating, they remain an imperfect base from which to calculate the *overall* rate of under-recording in our period. Moreover, because of the method of data collection and the assumptions on which it is based, they remain subject to significant margins of error. On the other hand, they do indicate that under-recording should be regarded as a significant defect which is undoubtedly much more marked in terms of strike numbers. Thus Brown (1981) estimated that 94 per cent of actual days lost in his period were included in official statistics.

The other function of the Department's reporting system is to ensure that the information collected is accurate within defined limits. The Department has to rely on the parties to the disputes for detailed information on such matters as size, length, reason given for striking, etc., which it requires for its records. Yet – for the purposes of gaining or maintaining support, sympathy, assistance, etc. – each side may have a vested interest in describing the stoppage in the most favourable terms to itself. Thus union spokesmen might seek to maximise size of stoppage, determination of workforce, issue of principle, etc., whereas employers' spokesmen might try to minimise such aspects. In such circumstances the recording authority could ask both parties for details and attempt to reconcile any conflicts in their reports; or it could conduct its own detailed investigation.

In practice the Department has used a mixture of methods. In respect of major disputes it was customary to approach both parties. But the trade unions' response rate to these enquiries had always been significantly lower than that of the employers, and in the early 1970s trades unions' replies virtually ceased. Consequently the Department relied even more heavily on employers' responses.

In respect of minor stoppages the Department relies on the information gathered by its local offices. The sources of local office information are obscure – some is derived from the local press, some by direct enquiry. Thus it would not seem unreasonable to suppose that at this level too employers constitute the principal source of information. But there is no relevant data available to confirm or deny such a supposition.

Faced by all these difficulties it might be argued that the Department's series are too unsatisfactory to be worth analysing. We rejected this argument on a number of grounds: first, there is no alternative set of records available in the UK; secondly, all other studies of stoppages in the UK have used these records; thirdly, the public debate on policy towards strikes is based on analyses of these series; finally, and most important of all, within their self-imposed limits the Department's records provide a consistent national time series of strike activity; moreover, the use of the minimum size criteria does serve to reduce the scale of the problem of under-recording. We know of no reason to suppose that the series have become more deficient over time; indeed growing public interest in stoppages has probably meant that they have been more widely reported. One needs to be aware of all these difficulties and qualifications but they are not so large as to justify a rejection of the series.

BASIC MEASURES OF STRIKE ACTIVITY

Having considered sources and definitions we turn to the measures to be derived from these and their interpretation. The next few sections of the chapter introduce many different measures of strike activity, describing how they are related to each other and their relative significance. We begin with what may be termed the three basic measures: the number of strikes, the number of workers involved, and the number of working days lost. Each of these refers to a different dimension of strike activity, which is affected by somewhat different causal factors. Partly for this reason variations in each measure can be said to have a different significance.

Most of the data relating to all the measures described has been calculated on an annual basis and derived from the Department's Annual Article on strikes. (This appears in the *Employment Gazette* for May or June of the following year.)Additional material was culled direct from the Department's own records and we have made some use of their published quarterly data. Where this material is employed in association with data from a different source – e.g. economic activity rates – this is noted as the analysis proceeds.

THE NUMBER OF STRIKES

By this measure we mean the total of all those industrial disputes over terms and conditions which result in stoppages of work that satisfy the minimum size criteria of the Department. As such the measure covers a range of stoppages from those which involve ten workers or last one day to those which involve thousands of workers and last many weeks. The smallest and the largest alike have equal weight in the number of strikes series. Given this heterogeneity it is reasonable to enquire what, if anything, the series means.

Knowles (1952) regarded the number of strikes as indicating 'the prevalence of separate outbreaks of discontent'. Our own more prosaic view is that it measures the number of occasions within a given period of time when one or other party to a negotiation adopts a stoppage as a sanction to obtain a satisfactory settlement. One advantage of this definition is that it invites us to view the strike as one possible stage in the collective bargaining process. It follows from this that to be able to evaluate the full significance of variations in strike numbers during a given period one needs to make assumptions about the number of bargains that were negotiated in that period. Otherwise it is impossible to assess whether a change in the number is the result of changes in the attitudes of the parties, the effectiveness of the bargaining machinery or the volume of bargaining itself. Unfortunately there are no measures, nor even any estimates, of the amount of bargaining in particular periods. Consequently it is not possible to assess fully the significance of changes in the number of strikes series. Yet it does not follow from this that no conclusions may be drawn. A very large and rapid change in the number of strikes is more likely to be attributable to changes in the amount of bargaining and the attitudes of the parties than to the efficiency of the bargaining machinery.

In the absence of any direct information on the number of bargains being negotiated per period of time we considered alternative data. We contemplated using the number of establishments as a proxy for the number of negotiations. This produced several problems. In the first place the number of establishments exaggerates the amount of bargaining, in so far as it includes many small establishments where collective bargaining does not exist. On the other hand, it under-estimates the amount of bargaining in that it does not take account of the fact that negotiations usually take place on a much more frequent basis than once a year, plus the fact that a single establishment can cover several bargaining units. On balance it seemed that using the number of establishments as a proxy would substantially under-estimate the number of negotiations taking place and, consequently, over-estimate the incidence of stoppages in the bargaining process.

The Department of Employment study of the distribution and concentration of strike activity (Smith *et al.*, 1978) revealed that 98 per cent of manufacturing establishments were strike free in any one year. Given that manufacturing is more strike prone than the rest of the economy, and our belief that this measure exaggerates the incidence of strike activity, it would not seem unreasonable to suppose that over 99 per cent of bargains negotiated are settled without a stoppage occurring. Even making the most generous allowances for any under-recording of stoppages would not alter such estimates significantly. Thus it can be said that the overwhelming majority of bargains are struck without adding to strike numbers.

THE NUMBER OF WORKERS INVOLVED

This is the second basic measure of strike activity and it may refer to those 'directly' or 'indirectly' involved. Workers directly involved are those who struck, or were locked out, as a result of a dispute. Workers indirectly involved are those laid off as a consequence of the initial stoppage of work because the necessary supplies or orders are no longer available.

Once again there are a host of measurement problems. Should the series relate to the average number of workers involved during the course of a stoppage or to the maximum or to the minimum number – given that the numbers involved may alter during the course of the stoppage? Should all workers indirectly involved be included in the series? If they are, how is a distinction to be made between a shortage of orders or supplies as a result of stoppages and those shortages which occur for all sorts of other reasons? Is the distinction between directly and indirectly involved as clear cut as it seems? Will any of the indirectly involved have their own terms and conditions of employment altered by the settlement of the initial dispute? Are any of the indirectly involved the victims of secondary sanctions – i.e. laid off by their employers in order to put pressure on those on strike, rather than because of a consequential shortage of work. If this is the case then it is arguable that their involvement is similar to those engaged in the primary strike in effect they are the 'victims' of an employer's 'lockout'. (One of the authors was told, by an unattributable source within the Department, that just such a classificatory difficulty was raised by the Government's introduction of the three day week in 1974. The political storm which would have followed this dispute being described as a lockout was averted by classifying it as a voluntary overtime ban.)

In practice the Department has met these largely insoluble difficulties by a series of compromises, which have the effect of providing reasonable amounts of information without requiring undue exertion or expense in the recording system. The number of workers involved in a particular dispute is recorded as the maximum number *ever* involved. Only those workers indirectly involved who are employed in the same establishment(s) as workers directly involved are counted; although the Department has, in exceptional circumstances, made estimates of those indirectly involved at other establishments in the same industry. (Such estimates have not been included in the main statistical series.) The influence of secondary lockouts on the indirectly involved series has largely been ignored. All those laid off in consequence of a stoppage are treated as indirectly involved and not as parties to a lockout.

Although the distinction between directly and indirectly involved workers is drawn clearly in the Department's descriptions of its own statistics, it is not always made in the published data. In particular the important industrial analysis of strike activity only includes a series for all workers involved; it does not distinguish between directly and indirectly involved. The reasons for this blurring of distinctions is not entirely obvious, although it does avoid the necessity of publicly separating those laid off as a consequence of a stoppage from those involved in an unacknowledged lockout. Some information – relating to the economy as a whole and certain broad industry groups – did provide series of the directly involved, but these were not sufficiently detailed for our purposes. In these circumstances we decided, reluctantly, not to pursue the distinction between directly and indirectly involved. All our series for workers involved – except where specifically noted otherwise – relate to *all* workers involved, i.e. to the total of directly and indirectly involved at the same establishments.

However, because we recognised that there has been widespread concern that the processes of technological change and the British system of fragmented bargaining have combined to increase the disruptive power of small groups, we made an attempt to analyse the available data on direct and indirect involvement from this point of view. In particular, we wished to see whether there was any evidence that stoppages were resulting in substantially greater lay-offs than in previous periods. Of course, we were aware that because the series only measured the indirectly involved at the same establishments any analysis based on this data could only be a partial test of the hypothesis, but it seemed worth trying.

Data distinguishing between directly and indirectly involved workers across the whole economy was available for the period 1946–73, and across eight broad industrial groups for the period 1959–73. Analysis of this data revealed substantial changes from year to year and considerable variations between industry groups but no evidence of growing lay-offs in consequence of strike action. Splitting the aggregate data into two sub-periods, pre- and post-1959, revealed that the proportion of workers directly involved was the same in both periods. In summary the available evidence did not support the hypothesis that technological change had substantially increased the power of small work groups to take effective strike action by stopping production over much wider areas. However, as no data was available on lay-offs outside the immediately affected establishments, it should be understood that this cannot be regarded as a complete refutation of the theory.

As in the case of the number of stoppages we felt that it would be more useful if the number of workers involved in strikes were seen in perspective, rather than simply as an absolute total. Following the logic of our earlier argument the most appropriate reference series for workers involved in stoppages appeared to be the number of workers involved in each and every collective bargain negotiated over the same period. Unfortunately, once again, such information was not available. But a possible proxy for such a series would be suitable in that the great majority of trade union members are covered by collective bargaining arrangements. Yet despite the inclusion of a few trade union members who are not covered by collective arrangements, we decided that this series would significantly under-estimate the number of workers involved in collective bargaining over a period of time.

There are two reasons for this. First, except in those few areas where closed shop arrangements are 100 per cent effective, all collective bargains include some non-unionists within their scope. Secondly, and more importantly, some workers are covered by collective bargains which are negotiated more frequently than once a year. If the number of such workers – suitably adjusted for the frequency of bargaining – outweighs the number whose bargains are negotiated at more than annual intervals – again suitably adjusted – then a simple annual count of trade unionists will under-estimate the number involved in collective bargaining over the course of a year. Despite this likelihood of under-estimation we used the number of trade unionists as a reference series where it was appropriate.

Despite the efforts of Bain and Price (1980), finely disaggregated series of trade union membership by Minimum List Heading were not available to match our detailed strike series. Consequently, we were only able to use this reference series in relation to the aggregates of strike activity. To cover the industrial series on strike activity we used the number of employees in employment as our reference series. (This accorded with the Department's practice.) This series, being almost twice as large as that for trade union membership, was less likely to under-estimate the numbers involved in collective bargaining. Indeed, in the absence of the necessary information about bargaining it was impossible to decide whether this series would over- or under-estimate the numbers involved in collective bargaining in any period of time.

Some indication of the frequency of collective bargaining may be gleaned from the data available on repetitive strike acts – i.e. those instances in which the same group of workers takes strike action more than once in a given period. The Department tries to distinguish between those instances in which a series of stoppages arise from a dispute as a result of a tactical decision to mount token stoppages rather than an all-out strike, as against those where several stoppages take place as a result of several different disputes. The first of these could be regarded as a single prolonged stoppage, the second as several different disputes. In terms of workers involved the former would involve the workers being counted once, the latter on each occasion they took strike action.

Until 1967 the Department used to note instances where workers were involved in more than one stoppage a year and to list the main groups affected in a footnote to a table on the industrial distribution of strike activity. The aggregate data for the period 1946–67 revealed that, on average, one strike act in four was repetitive. Unfortunately, the Department seems only to have published data for those industrial groups in which repetitive strikes were important in particular years. From this rather sketchy data it appeared that repetitive strike acts were, unsurprisingly, most common in industries with high levels of strike activity – e.g. coal mining, docks, motor vehicles. Still more unfortunately, the series was discontinued in 1968 and as the industrial data was incomplete we felt we could not make more extensive use of it. However, the available data seems to support our contention that, in some areas at least, collective bargaining was taking place rather more frequently than once a year, but it is too limited to permit us to make estimates of the extent to which this is the case.

THE NUMBER OF WORKING DAYS LOST

This is the third basic measure of strike activity. It is calculated by multiplying the average number of workers involved by the duration of the stoppage. (Adding the number of days lost by each individual would produce a similar result.) Following the practice established in respect of workers involved the Department only calculates the days lost in establishments directly affected by stoppages. It also makes no distinction between days lost by those directly involved and those indirectly involved – an aggregate figure for the affected establishments is all that is produced. Given our aim of maximising comparability between the various strike series we regarded these aggregated figures for working days lost as a further justification for not separating workers involved into directly and indirectly involved. In any case the number of working days lost is difficult to interpret because it is the product of two separate dimensions of strike activity – extent and duration. To explain any shift in this series requires a prior explanation of whether, and in which direction, one or both of these dimensions has altered.

The number of working days lost is sometimes used as an indicator of the economic effects of strikes on production. Knowles (1952, p. 267) remarked that this practice was 'not unlike estimating air-raid damage by reference to bomb tonnage dropped, irrespective of target or type of bomb'. In fact the days lost series may considerably under- or over-estimate the effect on production. In situations where large stocks are available, or where extra working before or after the stoppage is possible, or where suitable spare capacity exists elsewhere, the losses incurred during a stoppage may be offset by increased production at other times or in other places. Alternatively, if a stoppage occurs where stocks are low, or the product is not storeable, or no spare capacity exists, the disruption may spread far beyond the immediately affected area. In practice it is often difficult to distinguish the effects of stoppages from those of the thousands of other changes which are constantly occurring in an economically advanced society. In any case identification of the effects of stoppages on production would not permit an estimation of the *economic* loss involved unless it could be shown that the 'lost' production would have been sold. Indeed, it has been argued that the tendency for large long stoppages to occur during recessions suggests that the production was surplus to requirements – i.e. stoppages provide a means of reducing stocks without reducing capacity (Turner and Bescoby, 1961).

Yet despite all the difficulties of interpretation the number of days lost remains an important indicator of the extent and duration of strike activity. As a reference series against which total working days lost might be evaluated we decided to use potential working time – estimated as the product of the number of working days in the year (after making due allowance for weekends and holidays) and the average number of employees in employment.

One other reference series which we developed to contrast with that of days lost through stoppages was that of days lost through unemployment. Some of the concern over stoppages has been a response to the prospect of valuable resources being left idle. Time lost through unemployment is another measure of resources left idle and one which has frequently been used by post-war governments to restrain the rate of inflation. (Whether this was a wise or successful policy is not discussed in this study.) Strikes are frequently cited as a source of inflationary pressure, although the time lost through stoppages concerning wage increases may perhaps be more accurately described as the price employers pay to try to hold down wage increases (i.e. if employers conceded immediately all wage claims there would not be any time lost through stoppages on this score).

In this sense it can be argued that contrasting time lost through stoppages with unemployment provides a rough indicator of the relative weights given to these two means of combating inflationary pressure. (It should be noted that this is not advanced as an argument in favour of either approach. The fact that all three series have shown a strong upward trend for much of the post-war period may be taken as an indication that they were not particularly appropriate.) In our analyses of the industrial distribution of strike activity we only use the number of employees in employment as a reference series.

GROSS TOTALS AND NET TOTALS – THE CASE FOR EXCLUDING COAL MINING

Throughout the study we have used two different bases for specifying aggregate strike activity, irrespective of which one of the basic measures was being employed. One of these we refer to as the *GROSS TOTAL* and it covers the entire economy. The second is termed the *NET TOTAL* and it covers the entire economy except coal mining – i.e. all coal mining stoppages are excluded from the *NET TOTAL* series.

There were two principal reasons for constructing an aggregate series which excluded coal mining. First, the pattern of strike activity in coal mining was markedly different for most of the period from that in the rest of the economy. Thus in the earlier part of the period coal strikes rose, whilst those elsewhere were falling. In later years coal strikes declined dramatically, whilst those elsewhere were rising. Secondly, for much of the period coal strikes dominated the gross totals of strike activity. Any analyses based on those series were likely to ignore the changes occurring elsewhere.

Table 1.1 shows the share of the gross totals of strike activity attributable to coal mining in each of four sub-periods as well as the period as a whole.

The dominance of coal strikes is seen most clearly in relation to the gross total of stoppages. Over the whole period coal mining accounted for 45 per cent of all stoppages in the UK. The interpretational problems posed by that dominance were made significantly worse by a divergence in trend which appeared in the late 1950s. This arose from a rapid increase in strikes

Table 1.1 *Percentage share of the gross total of strike activity originating in coal mining, 1946–73*

Years	Percentage share of no. of stoppages	Percentage share of no. of workers involved	Percentage share of no. of working days lost
1946–52	63.2	48.6	30.2
1953–59	73.7	30.3	13.8
1960–68	38.5	10.1	9.9
1969–73	6.9	8.5	20.9
1946–73	44.9	17.8	18.0

in most industries and a rapid fall in coal mining strikes. In fact the fall in the latter was so dramatic that it masked the rise elsewhere for a number of years. Figure 1.1 shows the year to year movements in coal mining and in all other industries. It serves to emphasise the divergence between the two.

Coal mining's share of the gross totals of workers involved and days lost tended to be less than its share of the gross total of stoppages. This occurred because, on the whole, stoppages in coal mining were smaller and shorter than those elsewhere. Yet, even this pattern was reversed in the last five years by the incidence of a few large long stoppages which raised the industry's share of workers involved and days lost. The creation of two aggregate series – one of which excluded coal stoppages – does not carry any implication that strikes in coal mining were any less important or less deserving of study. (On the contrary, we devote the whole of Chapter 8 to a detailed case study of changes in the strike pattern of this industry, arguing that it has a general significance for the period as a whole.) It was simply a convenient analytical device to help unscramble some of the more notable complexities of the UK strike pattern.

DISAGGREGATED MEASURES OF STRIKE ACTIVITY

In addition to examining aggregate patterns of strike activity which could be discerned in our three basic measures, we also considered the patterns that emerged at various levels of disaggregation. This section describes the five most important types of data produced as a result.

STRIKES BY INDUSTRY

The content of the Department's Annual Article in the *Employment Gazette* has varied considerably over time. But one of its consistent features has been a table detailing the distribution of stoppages, workers involved and days lost by industry. That table formed the basis for our cross-sectional and time series industrial analysis.

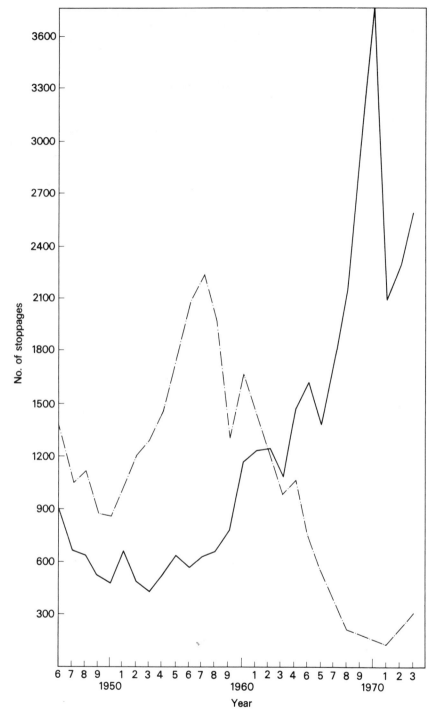

Figure 1.1 Numbers of stoppages in coal mining (—.—) and all other industries (——) in the years 1946–73.

Both kinds of analysis were restricted by certain features of the published data which included its limited industrial reporting and its treatment of workers involved. Unfortunately, the table in the Annual Article only shows some fifty industries and industry groups (compared with 180 industries identifiable by their Minimum List Heading). The information provided covers the whole economy, but it is much more specific for strike-prone industries than for others. (Thus strike activity in coal mining is detailed separately from that in the other four industries in the mining and quarrying industrial sector. These are added together and shown as 'other mining and quarrying'.) This policy is explicable as an economy measure, but it carries certain drawbacks for the serious student. The industrial distribution of strike activity is not static over time. Adjustments in the published data are not made immediately a shift is detected. Consequently, the analysis tends to be somewhat out of date and may not reflect important transitory movements.

Furthermore, in its table of the industrial distribution of strike activity the Department does not distinguish between workers directly and indirectly involved in strike action. This treatment makes it difficult to pursue questions of the relative size of strikes between industries and over time. In our analyses of the industrial strike pattern we used the number of employees in employment as a reference series for the workers involved and the days lost series.

Finally, our time series analyses were further complicated by the introduction of, and subsequent changes in, the Standard Industrial Classification (SIC). Prior to 1949 when the 1948 SIC was first used the Department's industrial analysis only detailed eighteen industries. In 1949 details were reported for thirty-seven industries. This major shift in reporting patterns meant that only one industry – coal mining – could be analysed across the whole period. In all other cases the industrial series are broken in 1948. Decennial revisions of the SIC – to accommodate changes in the industrial structure – further disturbed the strike records time series, but not so seriously.

STRIKES BY CAUSE

The annual article on strikes also carries details of the gross totals of strike activity analysed by so-called 'principal cause'. Separate analyses of the distribution of stoppages and workers directly involved are available for the whole period and for working days lost since 1957. At first sight it might seem that these analyses remove the need for further exploration of the causes of stoppages. Unfortunately the data is marred by reporting, classificatory and interpretational difficulties.

The general failure to consult all parties fully before recording data seems particularly serious in this instance, given the possibility of conflicting views over what was at stake and what had initiated the stoppage. Many stoppages have more than one immediate cause, so that the process of selecting the 'principal cause' is likely to be rather arbitrary and may indeed be biased through partial reporting. Moreover, the Department began in 1946 listing eight principal causes, reduced this to seven in 1953 and then extended it to nine in 1959.

The most serious of the difficulties is that there is a sense in which the 'principal cause' tables are wrongly named. They actually record what is known about the reasons that people give for a strike at the time (see McCarthy, 1959). This is the inevitable result of the way the data is collected and classified. In effect what we have is a rough guide to the main precipitating factors which were quoted at the time, but it is dangerous to assume that what appears is capable of being used as part of a *causal* explanation for particular strike patterns or trends. We are also doubtful whether it is profitable to divide data of this kind under eight or nine separate heads, and we consider that some of the categories chosen make little sense as they stand, e.g. 'other working conditions' and 'trade union status'.

We therefore decided not to rely on the kind of doubtful conclusions to be derived from an exact exploration of variations in the 'principal cause' tables. We did feel, however, that it was worth using the broad distinction between 'wage' and 'non-wage' factors, which is discernible from the Department's data. This distinction has the advantage that it has not been affected by classification changes and that it seems to be the one most likely to reflect substantial differences in precipitating factors or immediate causes.

STRIKES BY REGION

In 1957 the Department began publishing cross-tabulations of the distribution of strikes by region. These refer to workers involved and working days lost during a given year; no information is published relating to the number of strikes. Such data has obvious interest, but it poses severe interpretational problems. What could be the implications of any variations that emerge, and how are they to be explored? Given the size and varied nature of the regions selected, explanation would need to involve a very wide range of factors – e.g. the level and rate of change of unionisation in a given area, its history and traditions, economic record, industrial structure and so on. But to a large extent such factors are dealt with elsewhere in our analysis – particularly in our industrial case studies. Consequently, we decided not to make a major analysis of regional variations in strike activity. However, the data on the regional distribution of strike activity, adjusted for differences in employment levels, is reported in the body of the study. We do make some use of it in our attempts to explain the make-up of the overall pattern.

STRIKES KNOWN TO BE OFFICIAL

To many commentators and some students of the subject this breakdown appears to be of the greatest possible interest and significance – but it is not without its difficulties and defects. It was not until 1960 that the Department began to collect information on whether stoppages were official – i.e. whether they had been sanctioned or ratified by the union or unions involved. Initially the information was collected but not published. Acknowledging this omission, in its submission to the Royal Commission on Trade Unions and Employer's Associations (Donovan, 1966–68), the Department explained that the series had not been published for a number of reasons – including the fact that there was some 'margin of error' attached to the information it contained.

In 1972 this policy was reversed and the data – including historical series from 1960 on – was published under the title 'stoppages known to be official'. The Department's decision to publish was justified, in correspondence with the authors, on the grounds that the information was already being made available through parliamentary questions and that the title 'strikes known to be official' was now accurate. Unfortunately information may be accurate without being comprehensive. What matters is whether the series is reliable as a guide to the total level of and changes in official strike activity.

In part the problem relates to the fact that the union response rate to Departmental inquiries fell off in the early 1970s – which suggests that there may be an increasing number of official strikes that are not included in its net. In part the difficulty lies in the fact that official approval, say in the form of dispute benefit, can be substantially delayed, and is usually paid retrospectively.

There is also the fact that there are significant discrepancies in the estimates made by the Donovan Commission and the Department. Thus the Commission reported (Donovan, 1968, para. 403), that there were nearly 200 strikes where unions paid benefit in 1965 without having given prior approval. In 1966 they recorded over 150 similar cases. But of course in addition to these there must have been some instances, in both years, where prior approval was given. In contrast the Department recorded ninety-seven strikes as known to be official in 1965 and sixty in 1966.

DURATION, EXTENT AND SIZE

The Department also publishes frequency tables showing the distribution of gross totals in relation to the duration, extent and size of strike activity. But although the former is available for our entire period the latter two have only been published since 1950.

These frequency tables are valuable because they allow us to go beyond aggregates and averages and examine stoppages in more detail. Duration data covers a range between those which last one working day or less to those lasting more than sixty working days. Extent data ranges from those involving fewer than twenty-five workers directly and indirectly up to those involving 10 000 or more. Size data ranges from those involving the loss of less than 250 working days up to those involving 50 000 days or more.

We made extensive use of these frequency tables to show the range of strike action and the way in which it had varied over time. Our attempts to account for changes in the frequency distributions were bedevilled by the inclusion of coal mining stoppages in the series – e.g. in the later years of the period the frequency tables suggest that the 'typical' UK stoppage was becoming larger and longer than it had been. This shift coincides with the decline of coal stoppages – which tended to be smaller and shorter than those elsewhere – and the rise of strike activity elsewhere in the economy. It is difficult to assess the extent to which the changes which came about were the product of the shifting industrial composition of stoppages and of 'real' changes elsewhere.

MAJOR STOPPAGES

The available published material provided a substantial base for our studies and a variety of different measures. Its main limitations derive from the high level of aggregation, the incompleteness of certain types of data and the consistency of its coverage. A worrying aspect of this latter problem was that increased concern over stoppages may have resulted in a rise in the number of stoppages reported appearing in the statistics as an increase in strike numbers.

A solution to these problems would be to construct a set of data concerning individual stoppages which would be consistent over time. To overcome the coverage problem these could be made to relate to large stoppages, where reporting worries were least. A check with the Department revealed that, although the published information had undergone major changes, the records from which it was compiled had been very little altered. They were available to us and we therefore decided that it would be worth while making a comprehensive study of all *major stoppages* in our period – i.e. those which the Department considers involve a loss of 5000 working days or more.

It might be supposed that a study of major stoppages would be so limited, in relation to the total level of strike activity, as to be worthless. In fact there were 2429 major strikes in the period 1946–73, which involved 16 000 000 workers and the loss of 106 000 000 working days. In relation to the gross totals of strike activity over the same period major strikes accounted for less than 4 per cent of stoppages, for 56 per cent of workers involved and for 80 per cent of days lost. The results of excluding coal mining from the major strikes series and contrasting the remainder with the net totals of strike activity are shown in Table 1.2.

In relation to the number of stoppages, major strikes are an unusual occurrence, which suggests that explanations of their incidence are unlikely to have much validity if used to account for variations in the number of small, short strikes. But in relation to workers involved and days lost major stoppages are much more important and explanations of their incidence are necessary to account for significant changes in the overall series. While recognising the limitations of a study of major strikes we felt that it was a useful and significant part of our study.

Table 1.2   *Major stoppages as a proportion of all stoppages outside coal mining, 1946–73*

Type of strike activity	No. of strikes	No. of workers involved (000s)	No. of working days lost (000s)
Major strikes	2 243	14 397	88 424
All strikes	35 302	23 385	108 325
Major as a percentage of all	6.4	61.6	81.6

The Department compiles an individual record for each stoppage it includes in the statistics, based on returns made by local offices. They have been maintained on a fairly consistent basis and have included more information than it was practical to publish. Consequently we were able to build a data set showing the values of ten variables for each of the 2400 major stoppages which occurred in the period 1946–73. The ten variables the values of which we recorded were as follows:

occupation(s) of the workers involved
region(s) in which the stoppage occurred
industry(ies) in which the stoppage occurred
month of commencement of stoppage
month of termination of stoppage
number of workers directly involved
number of workers directly and indirectly involved
duration of stoppage
immediate cause of the stoppage
number of working days lost.

Our occupational classification was derived from the list of major occupational groups shown in the Department's *New Earnings Survey 1971*. We made some additions to the list to distinguish particular occupational groups. Full details of this and of our other classifications for the major strikes series are shown in Appendix 1.

THE CASE FOR NOT EXPLICITLY CONSIDERING THE CONSEQUENCES OF STRIKES

We decided against any explicit consideration of the consequences of strike action for a number of reasons. In the first place the methodological problems involved in attempting to assess the direct effects of any particular strike seem to us to be quite insuperable. To begin with one needs to be able to predict the short-run situation if the strike had not occurred for the parties in dispute. But one also needs to know the long-run implications of it both occurring and not occurring. And here it must be stressed that what is involved are both economic considerations – e.g. lost wages, lost production and the impact on costs and employment – and longer term power factors, e.g. the impact on morale and commitment to further collective action.

Secondly, it is arguable that for many kinds of strike (e.g. those affecting transport, or the export industries, or the viability of a government's incomes policy) direct effects are the least important consideration. If one is embarking on an exercise of explicit assessment one needs to know how to judge and total up a whole range of more general factors, which could extend over a decade or more. (In the course of which the totals involved would be likely to reverse direction, moving from debit into credit, according to the viewpoint of the observer.)

Thirdly, our primary concern was with the strike pattern and any substantial diversion of resources and time from this central focus would have been difficult to justify. Fourthly, and finally, we believe that what can be said of any value about the cost and consequences of strikes in the post-war period is best approached via a detailed analysis of the various components of the annual strike pattern. Thus while there is little explicit consideration of the consequence of stoppages, we would argue that our findings in relation to incidence and causes permit the drawing of a number of significant conclusions on this subject in our final chapter.

THE EXCLUSION OF NON-STRIKE SANCTIONS

Our research has focused on describing, analysing and explaining what we have termed the 'pattern' of strike activity. That is to say, we have primarily concerned ourselves with variations in activity levels and changes in the incidence and form of stoppages of work based on the published data of the Department of Employment.

As a result we have not attempted to estimate the size or 'pattern' of other forms of industrial action – either mere threats of strikes, or various types of industrial action which do not involve a complete stoppage of work. (For example, overtime limitations, so called 'go slows' and decisions to 'work to rule'.) It might be argued that a sufficient excuse for this lies in the fact that there are no official figures which relate to the movement over time of any of the phenomena. As a result Knowles (1952) also excluded them from the statistical parts of his study.

Nevertheless, it could be said that the representativeness of what we have been able to analyse does depend, to some extent, on how far it is reasonable to argue that other forms of industrial action are proxies for, rather than alternatives to, strikes. If they are proxies then their incidence will tend to depend on the same sort of factors as those which influence strike activity; so that the exclusion of what might be termed non-strike sanctions need not constitute a serious omission. On the other hand, if non-strike sanctions are to some extent independent alternatives to strikes;

if they are used in areas and by groups that do not use the strike weapon – if they are much more prevalent than strikes – then our enforced exclusion could be more serious. The rest of the section is concerned with what can be said about this question.

There is a small amount of empirical evidence on these matters which is worthy of consideration. A survey of workplace industrial relations was undertaken as part of the research programme of the Donovan Commission in 1966 (McCarthy and Parker, 1968). The survey was not intended to provide a snapshot of the structure, conduct and performance of industrial relations across the whole of the British economy, instead it concentrated on particular areas. It included a series of interviews with shop stewards from a number of the larger unions. Obviously such a survey would reveal a wider experience of the use of sanctions than would be the case for the economy as a whole. The survey revealed that 40 per cent of stewards had experienced at least one stoppage since taking office (on average they had been stewards for six years). Of this 40 per cent four out of five (32 per cent of the total) had also experienced other non-stoppage sanctions. Of the 60 per cent without stoppage experience just less than half (28 per cent of the total) had experienced at least one form of non-stoppage sanction. In short, stewards with stoppage experience were much more likely to have experience of other forms of sanctions than stewards without such experience.

At the same time the use of non-stoppage sanctions appeared quite widespread, with 28 per cent of stewards having such experience compared with the 40 per cent with stoppage experience.

Detailed examination of the incidence of stoppages and other sanctions revealed that threats of stoppages were less widespread than stoppages, although there appeared to be a positive association between the two series. There was also evidence of a positive association between the incidence of stoppages and that of working to rule but there was no evidence of an association between strikes and overtime bans. This was consistent with the view that threats of stoppages were not as widespread as stoppages and that most forms of non-stoppage sanctions were positively associated with the incidence of stoppages.

Further surveys of workplace industrial relations were conducted in 1972 and 1973 by the Social Survey division of the Office of Population, Censuses and Surveys (Office of Population, Censuses and Surveys, 1974, 1975). Unfortunately these surveys were not strictly comparable with that of 1966 because of methodological differences. They covered larger establishments in a restricted sample of industries. (Such a concentration could be expected to reveal a higher incidence of sanctions than would be true across the board.) They also drew a distinction between 'national' and 'non-national' stoppages in order to focus attention on those which arose over workplace issues. Table 1.3 shows the incidence of sanctions as reported by senior managers in the 1973 survey.

Of the 453 senior managers surveyed 54 per cent had not experienced any form of industrial pressure, 27 per cent had experienced non-stoppage

Table 1.3 *The incidence of non-national stoppages and other forms of industrial pressure during the previous two years as reported by senior managers in 1973*

Actions used in last two years	Yes, non-national strike in last two years (%)	No, non-national strike in last two years (%)
Overtime bans	56	19
Threats to strike	48	13
Working to rule	36	13
Go slows	24	5
Other forms of pressure	13	7
No form of pressure other than strikes	28	—
No form of pressure	—	66
(Percentage base, no. of senior managers)	(85)	(368)

sanctions and 19 per cent had had stoppages. Managers with stoppage experience were almost three times more likely to have experienced non-stoppage sanctions than those without such experience, but the use of non-stoppage sanctions was substantially more widespread than the use of stoppages. It also seems that different forms of non-stoppage sanctions were used much more frequently in the stoppage-experienced sector than in the other. The survey did not report the frequency with which such sanctions were used but it seems likely that the rate was substantially higher in the stoppage-experienced sector.

Generalizing from the fragmentary evidence of these surveys is necessarily hazardous. Attention had already been drawn to the partial nature of their coverage and its implications in revealing a higher incidence of stoppages than across the board surveys. However, in the absence of conflicting evidence it is not implausible to suppose that the over-estimation of the incidence of non-stoppage sanctions in these surveys is about the same as the over-estimation of the incidence of stoppages. Moreover, the study by Smith *et al.* (1978) revealed that, in the relatively strike-prone period 1971–3, 98 per cent of manufacturing establishments were strike free in any one year and 95 per cent were strike free throughout the period. Using the survey data reported above, which suggests that the use of non-stoppage sanctions was some two to two and a half times as widespread as that of stoppages, we can make a very rough estimate of the incidence of non-stoppage sanctions. Such estimates indicate that some 4–5 per cent of manufacturing establishments were affected by the use of some form of sanction. The workers involved might have amounted to as much as 20 per cent of the labour force. Outside of manufacturing the incidence of sanctions over workplace-related issues would have been much lower.

Our conclusion is that what evidence there is supports our original contention that stoppages and other sanctions are interchangeable pressures, so that any causal explanation derived from analysis of the former may be said to be relevant to the latter. The extent of use of non-stoppage sanctions, on the basis of the fragmentary evidence we have, may be wider than might have been expected, but they remain a minority interest. We hope that this contention is sufficiently well argued to persuade the reader that their inevitable omission does not deprive our work of all significance.

OUTLINE OF SUBSEQUENT CHAPTERS

The final section of this chapter provides a guide to the order of the rest of the study. It is divided into three sections: the first, covering Chapters 2–6, is largely descriptive; the second, Chapters 7–11, contains our search for explanations; the third, Chapter 12, provides an overall summary of our findings and reports our general conclusions.

Chapters 2–5 divide the strike pattern from 1945 to 1973 into four sub-periods; 1946–52; 1953–9; 1960–8; 1969–73. It is argued that each sub-period marked a substantial shift in the pattern of strike activity. Each chapter begins with an examination of net totals and follows with a review of disaggregated data. Strike activity in mining is discussed in a further section, followed by our findings on major stoppages. Each chapter ends with a summary and a note on the more important questions posed by the strike pattern that has emerged.

Chapter 6 provides an overview of the period as a whole, contrasting one sub-period with another and seeking to identify the most significant long term elements in the strike pattern.

To facilitate comparisons a standard notation is used. To compare details of a particular strike characteristic in different sub-periods one simply notes the suffix of the appropriate statistical table's number and looks for the table with the same suffix in the relevant chapter. In instances where the relevant information was not available for a particular sub-period the table has been omitted.

Chapters 7–11 explore various explanations for different features of the strike pattern. In this part of the study our broad strategy may be described as 'the pursuit of residuals'. Recognising the complexity of strike behaviour, and the difficulty of establishing causation in the social sciences, we proceed to deal with the more obvious explanations, going on to consider the questions they leave unresolved. Thus in Chapter 7 we begin with the role of macro-economic factors – e.g. unemployment, inflation, earnings, etc. These are explored through a consideration of well known theoretical models and statistical techniques drawn from the literature of the subject. They are found to be of limited use and we conclude that a less aggregated approach is required. Yet despite scepticism about its usefulness estimates are made of some of the most likely associations between strikes and macro-economic factors.

Chapters 8–10 contain three case studies of the strike record in particular industries – i.e. coal mining, docks and motor vehicles. This less aggregated approach enables us to combine statistical data with known developments in the industry – e.g. changes in the structure of collective bargaining, employer–union policies, etc. In each case use is made of leading pieces of academic and/or official literature to provide benchmarks against our own research. In doing this we have not sought to provide a comprehensive or comprehensible guide to the literature. Our aim has been to update and, where possible, to extend existing analysis by employing a wider range of economic and institutional factors. These studies complement what can be deduced from our consideration of the role of macro-economic variables. More plausible explanations are advanced for changes in the strike pattern in general, as well as events in the industry concerned. Nonetheless we are left with several questions concerning widespread movements in the pattern which are as yet unexplained. We give reasons for believing that these are best explored via a consideration of the role of the state. The results of this analysis is reported in Chapter 11.

Chapter 12 has three functions: first, to summarise the main features of the strike pattern as it has emerged from the study; secondly, to offer explanations and conclusions concerning its nature, causes and significance; thirdly, to consider what implications, if any, may be drawn from our work concerning the costs and effects of strikes.

2 The Post-war Peace, 1946–52

THE CHARACTERISTICS OF THE PERIOD

To any casual student of post-war British history the suggestion of a seven year peace on the industrial front may sound like a poor case of academic fiction but, in relative and absolute terms, this period was marked not only by a historically low level of strike activity but also by a downward trend.

In absolute terms there were, on average each year, some 525 strikes involving some 228 000 workers and resulting in the loss of approximately 1.3 million working days. In the comparable period immediately following World War 1 the numbers of workers involved and working days lost were much higher, although there were fewer stoppages. Compared with the period of World War II and with the later post-war years the most significant feature of 1946–52 was that there was a more or less continuous downward trend in strike activity.

The comparison with the Ward War II years is perhaps the most appropriate, not only because our period is sequential to those years, but also because the institutional framework created during the war to deal with collective bargaining disputes lasted until 1951. Under these wartime arrangements virtually all strikes and lockouts were illegal. Disputes which could not be resolved through collective bargaining were dealt with by compulsory, legally binding arbitration. It might have been expected that, following the end of the wartime emergency, the social constraints on strike action would be relaxed and that strike activity would increase. In fact strike activity rose sharply during the war years and fell in the years that followed.

The aim of this chapter is to examine these and other characteristics of the period in detail. But before this can be done it is necessary to say a word about the methodology to be employed in this chapter and others which follow in this part of the study. Our aim throughout has been to follow a standard methodology and to use it to describe, in as much detail as was available, the pattern of strike activity in each period. We also wished to emphasise those features of the pattern which most obviously required explanation. In order to do this we needed to examine aggregate series of the three basic dimensions of strike activity: i.e. numbers of stoppages, numbers of workers involved and numbers of working days lost. We also needed to classify separately *gross* and *net* measures of strike activity (i.e. inclusive and exclusive of coal-mining).

We followed this by analysing the industrial distribution of the net totals of strike activity. In addition we looked at various other aspects of strikes:

reported cause, regional distribution, duration, extent, size and whether or not the stoppages were known to be official. Unfortunately, for these latter aspects of strike activity, it was not possible to exclude coal mining strikes from the data. As a result these figures always refer to gross totals.

Having explored the published data as fully as seemed practicable we turned to the series on major strikes, i.e. those involving the loss of 5000 or more working days, which we compiled directly from the Department of Employment's records. Our treatment of these stoppages followed the same pattern as that which we used on the published data. We began with the aggregate data and then examined the distribution of those stoppages by industry, region, cause, occupational group involved, season and duration. One significant difference between these analyses and those for the published data is that in this case we were able to exclude coal mining strikes from all the series.

In using this standard methodology throughout the five chapters which constitute this part of the book we hope to enable readers to check on particular aspects of strike activity in the different periods without undue difficulty. With this aim in mind we also adopted a common numbering system for the various statistical tables: i.e. the suffix of each table number on each particular aspect of strike activity is the same in each chapter. However, it should be noted that in some of the early periods some information was not available. In these instances there is no corresponding table for that chapter.

In conclusion it must be emphasised that our primary intention in this part of the book is descriptive. We have sought to gather and present as much information as we could about what happened to strike activity in the year 1946–73 and pick out those aspects which seemed most to require explanation. We were not centrally concerned to offer explanations – that task is the main aim of Chapters 7–11 of this book. However, the reader will discover that from time to time, some measure of explanation appears in these chapters. In part this was done to enliven the numerical analyses for authors and readers alike, but it principally occurred either because the explanations seemed too obvious to be worth delaying, or because they helped to clarify those features of the strike pattern which most required explanation.

TOTAL STRIKE ACTIVITY: NET AND GROSS

The dominant feature of this period was a decline in strike activity. As can be seen in Table 2.1 the degree of change varied from year to year, in particular 1951 saw a sharp upturn in strikes.

From the net totals it can be seen that by 1952 the number of stoppages had fallen to 56 per cent of the 1946 level, the number of workers involved to 46 per cent and the number of working days lost to 65 per cent. The general downward trend was interrupted in 1951 when all three measures of strike activity showed substantial increases, although they remained below the levels of 1946–7. This upsurge presented us with some difficulties of interpretation. We had to consider whether perhaps 1951 marked the real end of the decline, so that 1952 was merely an 'aberration'. On balance we felt that the events of 1951 were best regarded as the product of a series of particular incidents and that the decline persisted into 1952. We deal with these questions in more detail in Chapter 3.

Table 2.1   *Net and gross totals of strike activity, 1946–52*

Year	No. of strikes		No. of workers involved (000s)		No. of working days lost (000s)	
	Net	Gross	Net	Gross	Net	Gross
1946	876	2205	312.9	529.5	1736	2158
1947	668	1721	314.7	622.6	1521	2433
1948	643	1759	236.9	426.0	1480	1944
1949	552	1426	186.2	434.0	1053	1807
1950	479	1339	161.1	303.0	958	1389
1951	661	1719	244.2	379.0	1344	1694
1952	493	1714	142.5	416.0	1132	1792
Average	625	1698	228.4	444.3	1318	1888

1951 was also the year in which the legal prohibition on strike activity, which had come into force in 1940 with the Conditions of Employment and National Arbitration Order, No. 1305, was abolished. There may have been some positive causal link between these two events, as the government announced a review of the Order in March and the increase began in April. However, it seems unlikely that the link was very strong. Strikes had risen after the Order was introduced in 1940 and fallen again in the period 1946–9. After a rise in 1951 they fell again in 1952, although prohibition was not reintroduced. It seems plausible to suggest that a more important factor was growing dissatisfaction with the effects of the 1948–50 'freeze' coupled with a determination to maintain real living standards in the wake of the 1949 devaluation and Korean War inflation. On the other hand, it is conceivable that the abolition of Order 1305 removed a restraining influence. If this was the case the increase in strike activity was greater than would otherwise have been the case. Despite this the net totals of strike activity remained below the 1946–7 level. At the same time, gross totals, which include coal mining stoppages, also show a general pattern of decline until 1950 and a tendency to increase thereafter.

NET STRIKE ACTIVITY IN PERSPECTIVE

Net totals of strike activity exhibit a clear downward trend but the significance of this in terms of national economic activity cannot be assessed from Table 2.1. However, in Table 2.2 we show the net totals of workers involved and working days lost in relation to some aggregate measures of economic activity and trade union membership.

Table 2.2   *Net strike activity in perspective, 1946–52*

Year	Workers involved as a percentage of employees in employment	Workers involved as a percentage of trade union members	Working days lost as a percentage of potential working time	Working days lost as a percentage of days lost through unemployment
1946	2.3	3.9	0.05	n.a.
1947	2.2	3.7	0.04	n.a.
1948	1.2	2.8	0.03	n.a.
1949	0.9	2.2	0.02	1.2
1950	0.8	1.9	0.02	1.1
1951	1.2	2.8	0.02	1.9
1952	0.7	1.6	0.02	1.1
Average	1.3	2.6	0.03	1.3

1946 and 1947 were years of transition from wartime to peacetime employment patterns. Both the labour force and trade union membership grew by about 15 per cent. This downward trend of strike activity is confirmed by the relative measures. The number of workers involved fell from 2.5 per cent of employees in employment to less than 1 per cent, the number of working days lost from 0.05 per cent to 0.02 per cent of potential working time. Perhaps the most surprising conclusion to be drawn from Table 2.2 is how limited strike activity was in relation to overall economic activity. On average over the period some thirteen workers per 1000 were involved in strikes.

This was not, as it might have been in earlier years, a product of a low level of collective organisation. Measured against the number of trade unionists the average rate was twenty-seven per 1000. If working days lost through strike activity are regarded as an indicator of the shortfall in production it is worth contrasting them with the potential production time lost through unemployment. The latter was some seventy–five times greater than the former. Even after making generous allowance for the possible effect of strikes being concentrated in high productivity sectors, it would seem plausible to assume that unemployment was a much greater source of production loss from the viewpoint of industry as a whole.

NET STRIKE ACTIVITY BY INDUSTRY

Examination of the industrial distribution of strike activity in this period
was complicated by the changes consequent on the introduction of the
Standard Industrial Classification in 1948. In order to overcome this
difficulty we dealt separately with the years 1946–8 and 1949–52. The
industrial groups of the former period were more aggregated than those of
the latter. Our reference series could only be constructed for the years
after 1948.

AVERAGE DISTRIBUTION OF STRIKE ACTIVITY BY INDUSTRY

Table 2.3a shows average strike activity by industry group in the years
1946–8.

Table 2.3a   *Average net strike activity by industry group 1946–8*

Industry groups	No. of strikes	No. of workers involved (000s)	No. of working days lost (000s)
Fishing	2.7	3.9	27.7
Mining and quarrying (exc.coal mining)	10.7	0.8	4.7
Bricks, pottery, glass, chemicals, etc.	27.3	2.8	13.7
Engineering	114.0	59.8	302.7
Shipbuilding	98.3	34.8	251.7
Iron and steel and other metals	123.0	32.2	299.3
Textiles	33.7	8.5	37.3
Clothing	28.3	8.7	50.7
Food, Drink and Tobacco	23.7	6.2	34.3
Woodworking, furniture, etc.	18.0	1.5	6.7
Paper, printing, etc.	9.3	2.9	13.3
Building, etc.	49.3	6.5	25.0
Gas, water, electricity supply	7.7	2.3	7.0
Transport	111.7	91.0	379.0
Public administration	10.7	3.6	28.3
Distribution, commerce, etc.	21.3	11.4	51.0
All others (exc. coal mining)	39.3	11.2	46.7
All industries (exc. coal mining)	729.0	288.2	1579.0

It can be seen that activity by all three measures was highest in transport
and the metal trades – i.e. engineering, shipbuilding and iron and steel.
These groups accounted for 61 per cent of stoppages, 76 per cent of
workers involved and 78 per cent of working days lost. In contrast, fishing,

gas, water and electricity, paper and printing, mining and quarrying and public administration tended to have low levels of strike activity.

After 1948 information about the industrial distribution of strike activity was made available at a more disaggregated level. This information, together with some measures of its significance in relation to the level of employment in the industry, is presented in Table 2.3.

Table 2.3 illustrates the wide diversity of strike experience between industries and the relative insignificance of strikes in most industries during this period. In some industries, most notably the metal trades and the transport sector, the average incidence of stoppages was in double figures. In other industries e.g. tobacco, there was one strike during the whole four year period.

Comparable disparities are apparent when strike activity is measured by workers involved or working days lost. In part these disparities are a product of differences in employment levels between industries. We tried to adjust for this by expressing the numbers of employees in employment in each industry. Such an adjustment allows us to make estimates of the maximum extent of worker unrest in each case. As we pointed out in Chapter 1 the existence of multiple strike acts by individual workers within the time period under comparison biases upwards our estimates of the extent of unrest.

Measured in this way, port and inland water transport was the clear leader in terms of strike-proneness with an average of 20 per cent of its workforce involved in stoppages each year. Only ten out of the thirty-six industries had more than 1 per cent of their workforce involved in stoppages and only two of these had more than 5 per cent so involved. The final column of Table 2.3 shows the number of working days lost per 1000 employees in employment. On the assumption of a standard eight hour working day a level of 125 or over indicates that time lost per employee per year was equal or greater than one hour. Only five industries had losses of more than one hour per employee per year. Only one industry, port and inland water transport, had an average loss of more than one day per employee per year. Of course it may be argued that the use of measures like these understates the impact of stoppages in those areas where they actually occurred, but they do serve to emphasise how unusual such events were.

STRIKE-PRONE AND NON-STRIKE-PRONE GROUPS

Recognising the extent to which strike activity appears to have been concentrated in a minority of industries, we thought it would be useful to estimate the contribution to the net totals of strike activity made by the most strike-prone industries. We also wished to contrast these estimates with those of the contribution made by the least strike-prone industries. Given that rankings of strike-proneness vary with the measure of strike activity used, we had to make an arbitrary judgement as to which measures we should use for selection. We opted for number of workers involved in

Table 2.3 *Average net strike activity by industry group, 1949–52*

Industry group	No. of strikes	No. of workers involved (000s)	Workers involved as a percentage of employees in employment	No. of working days lost (000s)	Working days lost per 1000 employees in employment
Agriculture, forestry etc.	3.0	1.7	0.22	14.7	19.2
Mining and quarrying*	4.7	0.2	0.24	1.0	11.8
Grain milling	0.7	Ø	Ø	Ø	Ø
Bread, flour, etc.	2.7	0.2	0.71	0.5	2.1
Other food	7.2	2.1	0.65	7.0	21.6
Drink	3.0	0.2	0.12	0.5	3.1
Tobacco	0.2	0.1	0.20	6.2	120.0
Chemicals	5.0	0.9	0.19	4.0	8.4
Iron, steel and other metals	43.2	8.7	1.59	39.2	71.4
Non-electrical engineering	56.5	15.8	1.57	90.7	90.7
Electrical engineering	14.5	3.2	0.58	15.2	27.1
Shipbuilding and marine engineering	66.5	13.2	4.28	84.5	272.7
(V1)	46.0	29.5	3.54	222.5	266.2
(V2)	7.5	2.5	1.44	9.0	51.7
(V3)	0.0	0.0	0.0	0.0	0.0
Other metal goods	21.2	2.1	0.33	10.7	17.3
Textiles	15.5	2.9	0.28	20.5	19.1
Clothing	8.5	1.8	0.34	4.7	9.4
Footwear	4.0	0.2	0.14	1.0	6.9
Bricks, pottery, etc.	14.0	0.9	0.27	3.2	9.0
Furniture, wood and cork manufacturing.	15.7	2.4	0.80	18.5	59.8
Paper and board, cartons, etc.	4.2	0.7	0.40	10.0	57.5
Printing and publishing	2.5	3.8	1.12	53.0	156.3
Other manufacturing industries	10.5	2.7	0.82	14.2	42.7
Construction	78.5	16.4	1.24	83.7	63.3
Gas, water, electricity	7.2	3.4	0.94	37.7	105.0
Railways	6.0	4.2	0.78	12.5	22.2
Road passenger transport	20.2	16.6	5.20	33.5	103.4
Road haulage	22.7	7.0	3.78	23.7	129.7
Sea transport†	n.a.	n.a.	n.a.	n.a.	n.a.
Port and inland water transport	22.5	33.6	21.17	267.7	1685.5
Other transport and communications	3.2	0.3	0.05	1.0	1.8
Distribution	11.5	3.7	0.17	18.7	8.8
Insurance, banking, finance	0.0	0.0	0.0	0.0	0.0
Professional and scientific	0.5	0.02	Ø	0.2	0.1
Miscellaneous	9.5	0.8	0.05	6.0	3.6
Public Administration and Defence	8.5	1.5	0.11	5.5	3.6
All industries*	546.3	183.5	0.91	1122.0	56.0

Ø indicated that there was some strike activity during the period but it was too small to be included in the published information or to calculate for the reference series.

* Excludes coal mining.

† Until 1960 strikes in sea transport were included with those in other transport and communications.

relation to the number of employees in employment. Table 2.4 shows the contribution made to the net totals of strike activity by the most and least strike-prone industries.

Table 2.4   *Industry groups' relative shares of net totals of strike activity, 1949–52*

Industry group	Percentage share of no. of strikes	Percentage share of no. of workers involved	Percentage share of no. of working days lost
High strike activity industries			
Port and inland water transport	4.1	18.3	23.9
Road passenger transport	3.7	9.1	3.0
Shipbuilding and marine engineering	12.2	7.2	7.5
Road haulage	4.2	3.8	2.1
(V1) Motor vehicles, aircraft, cycles	8.4	16.1	19.8
Iron, steel and other metals	7.9	4.8	3.5
Non-electrical engineering	10.3	8.6	8.1
(V2) Railway locos, carriages, etc.	1.4	1.4	0.8
Total share of high groups	52.2	69.3	68.7
Low strike activity industries			
Insurance, banking, finance, business	0.0	0.0	0.0
(V3) Carts, perambulators, etc.	0.0	0.0	0.0
Grain milling	0.1	Ø	Ø
Professional and scientific	0.1	Ø	Ø
Other transport and communications	0.6	0.2	0.1
Miscellaneous	1.7	0.4	0.5
Public administration and defence	1.6	0.8	0.5
Drink	0.5	0.1	Ø
Total share of low groups	4.6	1.5	1.1

From Table 2.4 it is clear that the great bulk of strike activity was concentrated in a narrow range of industries which were drawn exclusively from the metal trades and the transport sector. These eight industries accounted for over half of all stoppages and for more than two-thirds of all workers involved and working days lost. The difference between these shares indicates that stoppages in sectors were larger than those elsewhere. These industries only accounted for 17 per cent of all employees in employment. In other words employees in these industries were eleven times more likely to be involved in stoppages than employees in other areas, although even in the most strike-prone areas striking remained a minority activity.

The eight least strike-prone industries accounted for less than 5 per cent of all stoppages and for less than 2 per cent of workers involved and working days lost. In these industries stoppages tended to be smaller and shorter than those elsewhere. The remaining twenty industries accounted for 43 per cent of all stoppages and for 30 per cent of workers involved and working days lost.

In some industry groups a large proportion of strike activity was concentrated into a few large disputes. In shipbuilding, where consistent data was available for the whole period 1946–52, five strikes accounted for 50 per cent of working days lost. The same pattern could be seen in printing and publishing and in road haulage where, in 1949–52, single strikes contributed over 80 per cent and almost 70 per cent of days lost.

DIRECTION OF CHANGE OF NET STRIKE ACTIVITY BY INDUSTRY

One further aspect of the industrial distribution of strike activity which we explored was the extent to which changes in particular industries were consistent with the overall pattern. Our aim was to determine whether the overall movements to which we drew attention at the begining of the chapter really represented the typical pattern of behaviour at the micro-level. In addition we thought it would be useful to identify any industries which were moving strongly against the overall trend.

The change in the system of industrial classification in 1948 meant that we lacked consistent industrial data for the whole period 1946–52, but we did calculate the direction of change of each of the major measures of strike activity for each industry between 1949 and 1952. In so far as the level of strike activity in an industry was atypical in either of these years our estimates will have been affected, but that was unavoidable. It is hoped that such biases cancelled out between industries so that the totals of positive or negative change were not too affected. Our results are shown in Table 2.5.

Table 2.5   *Direction of change of net strike activity in each industry, 1949–52*

	No. of industries experiencing some change in no. of stoppages	*No. of industries experiencing change in no. of workers involved*	*No. of industries experiencing change in no. of working days lost*
Increase in activity	15	15	18
Decrease in activity	17	17	14

Table 2.1 on p.28 indicated that the net totals of strike activity showed, between 1949 and 1952, an 11 per cent fall in the number of stoppages, a 24 per cent fall in the number of workers involved and an 8 per cent rise in the number of working days lost. This is precisely in line with the findings of Table 2.5. This indicates, on balance, an overall decline in the number of stoppages and workers involved and a rise in working days lost. The fine balance between these groups in this period is probably an early indicator of the forces which were to contribute to an overall rise in strike activity in the following period.

This consistent upward trend in strike activity was present in at least five groups – i.e. chemicals; non-electrical engineering; electrical engineering; motor vehicles, aircraft and cycles; and construction. Decreases in strike activity were most noticeable in the transport sector with railways, road passenger transport, and port and inland water transport being well to the fore. Four industries had no change in their strike activity between 1949 and 1952 because they experienced no stoppages in either of these years.

This examination of the direction of change of industrial strike activity exhausts the published information from which coal mining stoppages can be excluded. Consequently the next four tables relate to gross totals of strike activity and are not directly comparable with the preceding analyses.

GROSS STRIKE ACTIVITY BY CAUSE

In Table 2.6 we show the strike activity originating over wage and non-wage issues and the percentage share of the former in the total. (Information on the number of working days lost by cause was not available for this period, the series of workers involved related to workers directly involved not to all workers involved as in previous analyses.)

In the period 1946–52 wage issues accounted for 44.2 per cent of stoppages and 44.6 per cent of workers involved. This implies that, on average, wage issue stoppages were the same size as non-wage issue strikes. Wage issues accounted for 46.9 per cent of stoppages in 1947 and 48.5 per cent in 1951, whereas the peak years in terms of workers directly involved were 1949 (50.1 per cent) and 1952 (55.2 per cent). In terms of absolute numbers wage stoppages fell from 961 in 1946 to 587 in 1950 – a fall of 39 per cent. Non-wage stoppages fell from 1244 to 752 in the same period – a fall of 39.6 per cent. Both wage and non-wage stoppages showed a substantial increase in 1951, but the former fell again in 1952 whilst the latter continued to increase. The number of workers involved in wage stoppages fell by 22 per cent between 1946 and 1950. Yet the pattern is not one of persistent decline. There were year to year fluctuations with the peaks occurring in 1946 and 1952. The number of workers involved in non-wage stoppages fell by 42 per cent between 1946 and 1950, rose sharply in 1951 and then returned to the 1950 level in 1952.

Table 2.6   *Gross strike activity by cause, 1946–52*

Year	No. of strikes	Wage issues		Percentage of total	Non-wage issues	
		Percentage of total	No of workers directly involved (000s)		No. of strikes	No. of workers directly involved (000s)
1946	961	43.6	170.0	42.0	1244	235.0
1947	807	46.9	159.3	32.6	914	329.4
1948	730	41.5	142.1	43.9	1029	181.9
1949	611	42.9	159.5	50.1	815	153.6
1950	587	43.8	132.1	49.1	752	136.8
1951	833	48.5	157.6	46.9	886	178.3
1952	726	42.4	167.3	55.2	988	135.9
Average	751	44.2	155.4	44.6	947	193.0

The inclusion of coal mining in this table makes it difficult to draw conclusions, because of the divergence in the pattern of mining and non-mining industries. It appears that across the economy as a whole the number of stoppages was tending to fall and this was not simply a product of the 1948–50 incomes policy. It both ante- and post-dated that policy and, up to 1950, affected non-wage disputes to the same extent as wage disputes. It might have been expected that as overt conflict over wages declined conflict over non-wage issues would have increased, but this does not appear to have happened.

Information was not available on the regional distribution of strike activity for this period so the next table, Table 2.8, relates to the distribution of gross strike activity by the duration of stoppages.

DIMENSIONS OF GROSS STRIKE ACTIVITY: DURATION, EXTENT AND SIZE

It can be seen that of the 11 883 stoppages which began in the period 1946–52, 9171 (77 per cent of the total) were over within three days. More than 90 per cent were over within six days. These short stoppages were also among the smallest, as may be seen from the fact that those which were over within three days only accounted for 44 per cent of workers involved while those over within six days accounted for 70 per cent. The effect of this combination of extent and duration is reflected in the number of working days lost. Stoppages which were over within three days accounted for 77 per cent of all stoppages but less than 15 per cent of days lost. Those over within six days accounted for 90 per cent of stoppages but only 34 per cent of days lost. Stoppages lasting more than twelve days accounted for less than 5 per cent of strikes, 15 per cent of workers involved and 46 per cent of days lost. Again interpretation of this series is made difficult by the inclusion of some 7511 coal mining stoppages within the total of 11 883.

Table 2.8   *Distribution of gross strike activity by duration of stoppages, 1946–52*

Duration in working days	No. of strikes	Percent-age of total	No. of workers involved	Percent-age of total	No. of working days lost	Percent-age of total
Not more than 1	5 174	43.5	545	17.6	485	3.7
Over 1, not more than 2	2 676	22.5	492	15.9	708	5.4
Over 2, not more than 3	1 321	11.1	318	10.3	738	5.6
Over 3, not more than 4	711	6.0	316	10.2	904	6.8
Over 4, not more than 5	538	4.5	352	11.3	1 075	8.1
Over 5, not more than 6	302	2.5	136	4.4	571	4.3
Over 6, not more than 12	620	5.2	462	14.9	2 687	20.3
Over 12, not more than 18	209	1.8	225	7.3	1 801	13.6
Over 18, not more than 24	125	1.1	139	4.5	2 012	15.2
Over 24, not more than 36	116	1.0	92	3.0	1 380	10.4
Over 36, not more than 60						
Over 60	91	0.8	23	0.7	864	6.5
Total	11 883	100.0	3 100	100.0	13 225	100.0

It may be noted that coal mining stoppages are significantly smaller and shorter than those in other industries. Thus the average coal mining stoppage involved 200 workers with an average loss of 2.7 days per worker involved. Elsewhere in the economy stoppages involved an average 365 workers with a loss of 5.8 days each. Nevertheless it is clear from Table 2.8 that the overwhelming majority of UK strikes were still very small and short.

The fact that larger, longer strikes were atypical in relation to all stoppages, but dominant in terms of workers involved and days lost, is reflected in the next two tables. These show the distribution of strike activity in relation to both measures.

Table 2.9 shows that strikes involving fewer than 100 workers accounted for 68.3 per cent of all stoppages but only 9.9 per cent of workers involved and 7.5 per cent of days lost. Strikes involving 5000 or more workers accounted for only 0.5 per cent of stoppages, 31.3 per cent of workers involved and 37.7 per cent of days lost. If the duration of stoppages were not systematically related to the number of workers involved the share of working days lost in each class interval would tend to be same as the share of numbers of workers involved. In fact there is some tendency for

Table 2.9 *Distribution of gross strike activity by number of workers involved, 1950–2*

No. of workers involved	No. of strikes	Percent-age of total	No. of workers involved (000s)	Percent-age of total	No. of working days lost (000s)	Percent-age of total
under 100	3257	68.3	109	9.9	367	7.5
100 and under 250	738	15.5	117	10.7	405	8.3
250 and under 500	384	8.0	132	12.0	435	8.9
500 and under 1 000	226	4.7	153	14.0	540	11.0
1 000 and under 2 500	124	2.6	179	16.3	908	18.6
2 500 and under 5 000	20	0.4	63	5.7	392	8.0
5 000 and under 10 000	6	0.1	39	3.6	231	4.7
10 000 and over	17	0.4	304	27.7	1611	33.0
Total	4772	100.0	1096	100.0	4889	100.0

Table 2.10 *Distribution of gross strike activity by number of working days lost, 1950–2*

No. of working days lost	No. of strikes	Percent-age of total	No. of workers involved (000s)	Percent-age of total	No. of working days lost (000s)	Percent-age of total
Under 500 days	3854	80.8	253	23.1	403	8.3
500 and under 1 000	380	8.0	121	11.0	266	5.4
1 000 and under 5 000	425	8.9	253	23.1	915	18.7
5 000 and under 25 000	79	1.7	132	12.0	820	16.8
25 000 and under 50 000	17	0.4	104	9.5	587	12.0
50 000 and under 100 000	9	0.2	72	6.6	679	13.9
100 000 and over	8	0.2	161	14.7	1219	24.9
Total	4772	100.0	1096	100.0	4889	100.0

duration to increase with size. The smallest class interval accounted for 9.9 per cent of workers involved but only 7.5 per cent of working days lost, whereas the largest class interval had 27.7 per cent of workers involved and 33 per cent of days lost. This relationship between duration and extent was not a steadily progressive one but the result of a sharp shift when strikes involved more than 1000 workers. It is perhaps curious that duration is positively associated with extent. It might have been expected that larger stoppages would attract greater efforts to keep them short. Part of the explanation may be that there is a two-way relationship between extent and duration with stoppages becoming larger the longer they last. It may also be that issues which attract the support of large numbers of workers are the sort of issues which are difficult to resolve quickly.

The impact of a small number of large stoppages on the totals of workers involved and working days lost is vividly demonstrated in Table 2.10. Large stoppages, i.e. those involving the loss of at least 25000 working days, accounted for less than 1 per cent of all stoppages, 31 per cent of workers involved and 51 per cent of days lost. Within this category eight stoppages accounted for 15 per cent of workers involved and 25 per cent of days lost. It is obvious that although the dominant type of stoppage during this period was small and short the series for workers involved and days lost were very heavily influenced by a handful of stoppages which did not conform to that type. Our analysis of major stoppages allowed us to examine such non-conformists in some detail.

Records of stoppages known to be official were not kept prior to 1960 so we have no direct evidence on this aspect of strike activity. However, there were two sets of factors operating in this period which make it likely that there were few, if any, officially sanctioned stoppages. First, the existence of Order 1305 prohibited strike action and probably made trade unions reluctant to risk prosecution by giving official support to stoppages except in those recognition or jurisdiction disputes which could be argued to fall outside the scope of the Order. Secondly, and perhaps more important, the post-war Labour government enjoyed the close support of most trade union leaders, which made it less likely that strikes would receive official approval. Some of the conflicts of loyalty which arose in these circumstances are reflected in the personal reminiscences of strikers, trade union officials and others (Leeson, 1973).

COAL MINING

Between 1946 and 1952 coal mining experienced 7511 stoppages which involved 1 500 500 workers and the loss of 3 993 000 working days. Outside coal mining there were 4372 stoppages involving 1 598 500 workers and the loss of 9 224 000 days. Comparisons with other industries are complicated by the shift in the system of industrial classification which occurred in 1948, but it is clear that the absolute level of strike activity was substantially greater in coal mining than in any other industry.

The number of stoppages and the number of workers involved in coal mining fell by around 35 per cent between 1946 and 1950 while working days lost rose by 2 per cent. Between 1950 and 1952 stoppages rose by 42 per cent, workers involved by 93 per cent and working days lost by 53 per cent. In other words, although the pattern of stoppages and workers involved in coal mining was not dissimilar from that of all other industries until 1950, there was a sharp divergence thereafter. (For further details of disputes in coal mining see Chapter 8.)

MAJOR STRIKES, 1946–52

This section is concerned with all those stoppages which involved the loss of at least 5000 working days. Once again a distinction is made between net and gross strike activity.

NET TOTALS OF MAJOR STRIKES AND THEIR RELATIONSHIP TO NET TOTALS OF ALL STOPPAGES

The basic magnitudes of major strike activity and their importance in relation to the net totals of all stoppages are shown in Table 2.12.

Table 2.12   *Net totals of major strike activity in absolute terms and in relation to the net totals of all strike activity, 1946–52*

Year	No. of major strikes	As a percentage of all strikes	No. of workers involved (000s)	As a percentage of all workers involved	No. of working days lost (000s)	As a percentage of all working days lost
1946	67	7.6	127.2	40.7	1269	73.1
1947	38	5.7	178.4	56.7	1131	74.4
1948	27	4.2	122.4	51.7	1145	77.4
1949	28	5.1	105.1	56.4	824	78.3
1950	23	4.8	75.7	47.0	664	69.3
1951	38	5.7	126.5	51.8	1026	76.3
1952	26	5.3	68.9	48.4	894	79.0
Average	35	5.6	114.9	50.3	993	75.4

On average there were thirty-five major stoppages a year which involved 115 000 workers and resulted in the loss of almost a million working days. The number of major stoppages followed a general downward trend between 1946 and 1950, rose sharply in 1951 and fell again in 1952. The number of workers involved followed a similar trend except that the peak occurred in 1947. Working days lost followed the same general pattern.

In relation to the net totals of all strike activity major strikes accounted for less than 6 per cent of stoppages, 50 per cent of workers involved and 75 per cent of working days lost. In other words the average major stoppage involved nine times more workers and lasted half as long again as the average minor stoppage. The number of major stoppages tended to decline faster than minor stoppages but no such consistent tendency was apparent in respect of workers involved and working days lost. From Table 2.12 it seems that whatever factors were responsible for the decline in strike activity they affected both large and small stoppages in this period.

NET MAJOR STRIKES IN PERSPECTIVE

Table 2.13 shows major strike activity in relation to a number of appropriate reference series.

Table 2.13 *Net major strike activity in perspective, 1946–52*

Year	Workers involved as a percentage of employees in employment	Workers involved as a percentage of trade union members	Working days lost as a percentage of potential working time	Working days lost as a percentage of days lost through unemployment
1946	0.9	1.6	0.03	n.a.
1947	1.2	2.1	0.03	n.a.
1948	0.6	1.4	0.02	n.a.
1949	0.5	1.2	0.02	0.9
1950	0.4	0.9	0.01	0.7
1951	0.6	1.4	0.02	1.4
1952	0.3	0.8	0.02	0.9
Average	0.6	1.3	0.02	1.0

It can be seen that major stoppages outside coal mining involved, on average, some 3300 workers with an average loss of nearly nine days per worker per strike. Such strikes might be expected to have graver consequences than small short stoppages where disruption elsewhere and internal loss of production could be kept to a minimum, but even if the effect of major stoppages were doubled from that shown above the effect would be minor in relation to the economic life of the nation.

Thus, on average, all major stoppages involved some 0.6 per cent of employees in employment at some time during the year and resulted in the loss of only 0.02 per cent of potential working time. Similarly, time lost through major stoppages was only 1 per cent of that lost through unemployment. Given that the economy was expanding at the same time as strike activity was falling the overall effect of major stoppages may be said to have fallen during this period. Once again this analysis is not intended to imply that such stoppages were quite insignificant: in the areas where they actually occurred they may well have had serious effects. It remains true that in relation to overall economic activity their influence must be considered to be very slight, if only because they were so limited in number and extent.

NET MAJOR STRIKE ACTIVITY BY INDUSTRY

As in our earlier analysis of all strikes we found that the industrial distribution of major strikes was most uneven. Details are shown in Table 2.14.

The industries with the highest incidences of major strikes were non-electrical engineering with twenty-eight stoppages, shipbuilding with twenty-six, motor vehicles with twenty-five, port and inland water transport with twenty-three, and road passenger transport with seventeen. Altogether these five industries accounted for 48 per cent of major strikes. These same five industries accounted for around 36 per cent of the net total of all stoppages. In general those industries which were sizeable contributors to the net strike totals were also sizeable contributors to the major strike series. There were two significant exceptions to this general rule, distributive trades and miscellaneous services. These two industries had accounted for less than 4 per cent of the net total of stoppages but they accounted for over 9 per cent of major stoppages.

Of the thirty-nine industries listed in Table 2.14 fourteen averaged one or more major stoppages per year, seventeen averaged one stoppage per industry per three years and the remaining eight industries did not experience a single major stoppage during this period.

In our analysis of the dimensions of gross strike activity with reference to duration, size and extent we drew attention to the very substantial effect on the series of workers involved and working days lost of a few large stoppages. In the next two tables, Table 2.15 and 2.16, we show the distribution of major stoppages outside coal mining with respect to the numbers of workers involved and working days lost. These tables go beyond the simple distributions relating to all major stoppages and provide cross-tabulations of these dimensions of strike activity by industry. In this way we were able to see whether there was any obvious association between the industry in which the stoppage occurred and the dimensions of that stoppage.

Table 2.15 shows the cross-tabulation of major stoppages by number of workers involved and by the industry in which they occurred. Of the 247 stoppages which occurred in this period only forty-eight (19.4 per cent) could be regarded as small (i.e. involving fewer than 500 workers). There was little tendency for these small stoppages to be concentrated in particular industries: 125 stoppages (50.6 per cent) fell into the medium sized category of 500–2500 workers; there were forty-eight stoppages (19.4 per cent) in the large category of 2500–10 000 workers; and twenty-six stoppages (10.5 per cent) in the very large category of 10 000 or more

Table 2.14 *Number of net major strikes by industry group, 1946–52*

Industry group	No. of strikes	As a percentage of all major strikes
Agriculture, forestry, fishing	5	2.0
Mining and quarrying (exc. coal mining)	1	0.4
Grain milling	0	0.0
Bread, flour, confectionary	1	0.4
Other food	3	1.2
Drink	0	0.0
Tobacco	2	0.8
Chemicals	2	0.8
Iron and steel and other metals	13	5.3
Non-electrical engineering	28	11.3
Electrical engineering	8	3.2
Shipbuilding	26	10.5
Motor vehicles	24	9.7
Aircraft	11	4.5
Cycles	0	0.0
Railway locos, carriages, trams, etc.	2	0.8
Carts, perambulators, etc.	0	0.0
Other metal goods	2	0.8
Textiles	7	2.8
Clothing	1	0.4
Footwear	0	0.0
Bricks, pottery, glass, cement, etc.	0	0.0
Furniture, bedding, wood and cork manufacturing	3	1.2
Paper, board, cartons	2	0.8
Printing and publishing	3	1.2
Other manufacturing industries	7	2.8
Construction	11	4.5
Gas, water, electricity supply	6	2.4
Railways	4	1.6
Road passenger transport	17	6.9
Road haulage	3	1.2
Sea transport	0	0.0
Port and inland water transport	23	9.3
Other transport and communications	1	0.4
Distribution	13	5.3
Insurance, banking, finance, business	1	0.4
Professional and scientific	0	0.0
Miscellaneous	10	4.0
Public administration and defence	7	2.8
Total (exc. coal mining)	247	100.0

workers. There were no stoppages in the massive category of those involving 50 000 or more workers. The medium and large-sized stoppages seemed widely distributed across industries. However, the twenty-six very large stoppages occurred in just seven industries, three of which – motor vehicles, road passenger transport, and ports and inland water transport – accounted for twenty of them (i.e. 77 per cent of very large stoppages). It would appear, then, that although the distribution of most major stoppages was widely spread across industries there was a significant tendency for the very largest stoppages to be concentrated in a minority of industries.

Table 2.16 shows the distribution of major stoppages by industry and number of working days lost. The distribution of major strikes by number of working days lost was heavily skewed towards the smallest size categories: 43 per cent of major stoppages involved the loss of less than 10 000 working days and 74 per cent involved the loss of less than 25 000 working days. There were only fourteen strikes resulting in the loss of more than 100 000 working days, but the combined loss from these (some 2.7 million working days) was 40 per cent of the total due to major stoppages and 30 per cent of the net total of all time lost. Small and medium-sized stoppages were widely spread across industries but the thirty stoppages which resulted in the loss of at least 50 000 working days were confined to ten industries. Three of these (port and inland water transport, motor vehicles, and shipbuilding) accounted for two-thirds of all very large stoppages.

NET MAJOR STRIKES BY CAUSE

As we explained in Chapter 1, our classification of major stoppages by cause differs slightly from that of the Department of Employment. We used the same classification system throughout the whole period 1946–73 whereas that of the Department was subject to a number of minor changes. Yet our series was derived from the original records of the Department and therefore it cannot be regarded as being any more accurate than the official series. Details of our own classification are shown in Table 2.17.

Of the 247 major stoppages, ninety-four were attributed to wage disputes. Of the ninety-four just over one-third arose from claims for wage increases with the remainder occurring over other wage matters. Comparison with the causes of the gross total of stoppages reveals that wage disputes were slightly less common among major strikes (38 per cent compared with 44 per cent), whereas claims for wage increases were rather more frequent (13 per cent compared with 9 per cent). Other frequent causes of major stoppages included issues of trade union principle (20.6 per cent) and other issues (16.6 per cent). The former of these included a number of recognition disputes, particularly in the service sector. The latter, in part, reflected our difficulties in ascribing stoppages to one principal cause. Overall the differences between the causes of major stoppages and those of the gross total of stoppages do not appear to be too great, although it should be remembered that the latter includes a

Table 2.15 *Cross-tabulation of net major strikes by industry group and number of workers involved, 1946–52*

Industry group	No. of workers involved									
	50 and under 100	100 and under 250	250 and under 500	500 and under 1000	1000 and under 2500	2500 and under 5000	5000 and under 10000	10000 and under 25000	25000 and under 50000	50000 and over
Agriculture, forestry, etc.					3	1	1			
Mining and quarrying (exc. coal mining)		1								
Bread, etc.					1					
Other food				1	1	1				
Tobacco			2							
Chemicals			1	1						
Iron and steel and other metals			1	7	1	2	2			
Non-electrical engineering			2	2	8	12	2	1	1	
Electrical engineering	2			2	1	1	2			
Shipbuilding	1	3	2	8	6	4		1	1	
Motor vehicles			2	7	7	2			6	
Aircraft		1	2	1	5	2				
Railway locos, carriages, etc.				1		1				
Other metal goods				1	1					
Textiles			1	1	4			1		
Clothing						1				
Furniture, etc.	1			1		1				
Paper and board		1		1						
Printing and publishing						1	1		1	
Other manufacturing industries				1	1	2	3			
Construction		2	1	3	2	3				
Gas, water, electricity		1			4	1				
Railways				1	2			1		
Road passenger transport				1	1	6	3	2	3	1
Road haulage						1			2	
Port and inland water transport			1	2	1	4	4	1	9	1
Other transport and communication						1				
Distribution				2	2	4	3	2		
Insurance, etc.						1				
Miscellaneous				3	4	1	2			
Public administration					4	3				
Total (exc. coal mining)	4	13	31	50	75	39		9	23	3

Table 2.16   *Cross-tabulation of net major strikes by industry group and number of working days lost, 1946–52*

Industry group	No. of working days lost							
	5000 and under 10000	10000 and under 15000	15000 and under 20000	20000 and under 25000	25000 and under 50000	50000 and under 75000	75000 and under 100000	100000 and over
Agriculture, forestry, etc.	2	1			1	1		
Mining and quarrying (exc. coal mining)	1							
Bread, etc.		1						
Other food	2	1						
Tobacco	1			1				
Chemicals	1	1						
Iron and steel and other metals	7	2	2		2			
Non-electrical engineering	17	5	2	2	1			1
Electrical engineering	1	3	2	1	1			
Shipbuilding	8	8	3		4	1		2
Motor vehicles	8	2	1	2	4	2	3	2
Aircraft	5		1	1	2	1	1	
Railway locos, carriages, etc.	1	1						
Other metal goods	1					1		
Textiles	3	2			2			
Clothing					1			
Furniture, etc.	1	2						
Paper and board			2					
Printing and publishing				1	1			1
Other manufacturing industries	3	3			1			
Construction	7		1		3			
Gas, water, electricity	1	2		1	1	1		
Railways	3			1				
Road passenger transport	5	2	2	3	4			1
Road haulage		1				1		1
Port and inland water transport	7	2	2		2	3	1	6
Other transport and communication	1							
Distribution	8	1	2		2			
Insurance, etc.					1			
Miscellaneous	7	2			1			
Public administration	6				1			
Total (exc. coal mining)	107	42	20	13	35	11	5	14

preponderance of coal mining stoppages which are excluded from the former.

NET MAJOR STOPPAGES BY REGION

The regional distribution of major stoppages is shown in Table 2.18 on next page.

The regions used in the analysis are those described as 'standard' in the Department of Employment *Gazette* in 1966. We have added three categories, various regions of England, Great Britain and the United Kingdom, to allow us to describe those stoppages which affected more than one region. The results shown in Table 2.17 are very heavily influenced by the geographical location of industry and workforce but we felt that they had a certain intrinsic interest and might prove particularly useful in explaining period to period changes.

From Table 2.18 it can be seen that even major stoppages in this period were very localised, at least to the extent of being confined to one region. Some 90 per cent of major stoppages were restricted to the confines of a single region. The remaining 10 per cent were largely restricted to one area, rather than affecting the country as a whole. The predominance of the South East region, 30 per cent of major stoppages, is largely explicable in terms of its share of working population. The same cannot be said of Northern Ireland. This region had 10 per cent of major disputes but only 2 per cent of employees in employment. It might also be noted that the same area has consistently had the worst unemployment record in the UK in the post-war years and that major disputes in Northern Ireland were not confined to one or two 'difficult' industries but affected thirteen different industry groups. For the remaining regions it is difficult to draw conclusions, although type of industry and size of workforce do appear to have influenced their relative rankings.

Table 2.17　*Net major strike activity by cause, 1946–52*

Cause	No. of strikes	Percentage share of the total
Wage increase	33	13.4
Other wage issue	61	24.7
Discipline	16	6.5
Redundancy	18	7.3
Sympathy	15	6.1
Demarcation	12	4.9
Trade union principle	51	20.6
Other	41	16.6
Total	247	100.0

Table 2.18　*Distribution of net major strikes by region, 1946–52*

Region	No. of strikes	Percentage share of the total
South East	74	30.0
East Anglia	0	0.0
South West	3	1.2
West Midlands	22	8.9
East Midlands	1	0.4
Yorkshire and Humberside	9	3.6
North West	27	10.9
Northern	9	3.6
Scotland	37	15.0
Wales and Monmouthshire	15	6.1
Northern Ireland	24	9.7
Various regions in England	18	7.3
Great Britain	6	2.4
United Kingdom	2	0.8
Total	247	100.0

OCCUPATIONAL GROUPS (OTHER THAN COAL MINING) MOST FRE-
QUENTLY INVOLVED IN MAJOR STRIKES

Information published by the Department of Employment during this
period did not cover the occupations of strikers but such details were
included in their unpublished records. When we were compiling our series
of major stoppages we took advantage of this facility. In the period
1946–52 some fifty-six different occupational groups were involved in
major stoppages. Limitations of space prevent us from tabulating the
complete list but the most frequently involved groups are shown in Table
2.19. It should be emphasised that in so far as major stoppages are atypical
of all strikes then the occupational groups involved in them may also be
atypical of the groups involved in all stoppages.

Table 2.19 *Occupational groups (other than coal mining) most frequently
involved in major strikes, 1946–52*

Occupational group	No. of strikes	Percentage share of the total
Engineering workers	38	15.4
Dockers and stevedores	20	8.1
Bus crews	17	6.9
Platers and riveters	11	4.5
Machine operators	10	4.0
Aircraft workers n.e.s.	9	3.6
Shipwrights/shipbuilders	8	3.2
Electricians, wiring/supply, etc.	8	3.2
Textiles knitters, spinners etc.	7	2.8
Fitters	7	2.8
Assemblers	7	2.8
Car and vehicle workers n.e.s.	7	2.8
Boilermakers/boiler shop workers	6	2.4
Van roundsmen, retail sales	5	2.0
Lorry/van drivers	5	2.0
Seamen, boatmen, fishermen, deck/engine room hands	5	2.0
Local government manual workers n.e.s.	5	2.0
39 other occupational groups	72	28.8
Total	247	100.0

n.e.s., not elsewhere specified

It can be seen from Table 2.19 that the occupational group most
frequently involved in major stoppages was that of engineering workers,
who accounted for nearly 16 per cent of the total. Unfortunately this term
was not very specific, was applied to workers in a number of the more
strike-prone industries and was not, therefore, very informative. In
contrast the next two occupational groups, dockers and stevedores and bus
crews, were quite specific in their coverage and between them accounted

Table 2.20 *Major strikes: cross-tabulation of occupational groups most frequently involved by industry (other than coal mining) 1946–52*

Industry	Occupational groups						
	Engineering workers	Machine operators	Aircraft workers n.e.s.	Electricians, building supply, etc.	Assemblers	Car vehicle workers n.e.s.	Boilermakers boilershop workers
Iron and steel and other metal manufacture	1	2		1			1
Non-electrical engineering	20	3			1		1
Electrical engineering	7	1					
Shipbuilding	1	1					3
Motor vehicles	5	1			6	6	
Aircraft	2		8				
Railway locos, carriages, etc.				1		1	
Other metal goods		1					
Furniture, timber, etc.		1					
Construction				2			
Gas, water, electricity	1			4			
Port and inland water transport							1
Other transport and communication			1				
Public administration and defence	1						
Total	38	10	9	8	7	7	6

n.e.s., not elsewhere specified.

for a further 15 per cent of the total. The various shipbuilding trades, platers, riveters, shipwrights, shipbuilders, boilermakers and boiler shop workers, were readily identifiable and accounted for over 10 per cent of the total. Other metal workers accounted for many of the remaining identified occupational groups but, more surprisingly, some service occupations were also prominent. Distributive and transport workers accounted for at least 4 per cent of the total. The significance of Table 2.19 lies not in its identification of particular occupational groups as being strike prone (such a judgement would be invalid in the absence of detailed information on the occupational structure of the whole workforce) but in its indication that major stoppages were not the exclusive province of one or two particularly combative occupational groups.

This point is emphasised by Table 2.20 which presents a cross-tabulation of the most frequently occurring occupational groups by industry.

Limitations on space persuaded us to exclude from this analysis those occupational groups which were completely industry specific (e.g. dockers and stevedores, who only occurred in the port and inland water transport industry). However, it should be appreciated that some occupational groups which straddle more than one industry have titles which are so unspecific that it is likely that the work they do varies substantially from industry to industry, thereby implying even more heterogeneity than was revealed by our count of the number of different occupations.

SEASONAL PATTERN OF NET MAJOR STRIKES

Table 2.21 describes the seasonal pattern of major strike activity by showing the months in which stoppages commenced and terminated.

It can be seen from this table that 60 per cent of major stoppages commenced in the first half of the year, with the months of March, May and June accounting for 33 per cent of the total. Naturally the second half of the year was more quiescent, except in October when 11 per cent of major stoppages began. On this evidence it appears that major stoppages were least likely to begin in holiday periods. There was also a pronounced trough in December and a lesser trough in the months of July, August and September.

Given that many major stoppages were not very prolonged, the starting month was often the month of termination as well. Peak months for the termination of major stoppages were March, April, May, June and October. December also saw a relatively high number of terminations compared with the number of strikes which began in that month. Of the 247 major stoppages which occurred in this period only five continued from one calendar year to the next. Of these one, which began in October, and another, which began in December, ended in January. The remaining three all began in November, two ending in February and one in March.

Table 2.21   *Seasonal pattern of net major strikes, 1946–52*

Month	No. of strikes begining	Percentage share of the total	No. of strikes ending	Percentage share of the total
January	22	8.9	10	4.0
February	23	9.3	17	6.9
March	25	10.1	30	12.1
April	22	8.9	25	10.1
May	31	12.6	24	9.7
June	26	10.5	28	11.3
July	17	6.9	16	6.5
August	16	6.5	18	7.3
September	16	6.5	18	7.3
October	28	11.3	27	10.9
November	18	7.3	20	8.1
December	3	1.2	14	5.7
Total	247	100.0	247	100.0

Table 2.22   *Duration of net major stoppages, 1946–52*

Duration in working days	No. of strikes	Percentage share of the total
Not more than 1	0	0.0
Over 1 but not more than 2	5	2.0
Over 2 but not more than 3	5	2.0
Over 3 but not more than 4	13	5.3
Over 4 but not more than 5	14	5.7
Over 5 but not more than 6	15	6.1
Over 6 but not more than 12	76	30.8
Over 12 but not more than 18	28	11.3
Over 18 but not more than 24	29	11.7
Over 24 but not more than 36	34	13.8
Over 36 but not more than 48	13	5.3
Over 48 but not more than 60	3	1.2
Over 60 but not more than 72	4	1.6
Over 72	8	3.2
Total	247	100.0

Table 2.23 *Cross-tabulation for net major strikes by duration in working days and number of workers involved, 1946–52*

Duration in working days	Number of workers involved									
	50 and under 100	100 and under 250	250 and under 500	500 and under 1000	1000 and under 2500	2500 and under 5000	5000 and under 10000	10000 and under 25000	25000 and under 50000	50000 and over
Over 1 but not more than 2						1	2	1	1	
Over 2 but not more than 3					2	1	1	1		
Over 3 but not more than 4					9	2		2		
Over 4 but not more than 5					5	5	2	2		
Over 5 but not more than 6				3	6	5		1		
Over 6 but not more than 12			3	22	26	15	2	7	1	
Over 12 but not more than 18			5	8	10	2	2	1		
Over 18 but not more than 24		1	7	7	4	5		4	1	
Over 24 but not more than 36		4	12	7	5	3		3		
Over 36 but not more than 48		3	2	3	4			1		
Over 48 but not more than 60	1	1			1					
Over 60 but not more than 72		1	1		2					
Over 72	3	3	1		1					
Total	4	13	31	50	75	39	9	23	3	

THE DURATION OF NET MAJOR STOPPAGES

The final aspect of major stoppages which we examined was their duration as measured in working days. Details for the period 1946–52 are shown in Table 2.22.

No major stoppages lasted as little as one day and only fifty-two (21 per cent of the total) were over within the space of a full working week; 185 (75 per cent) were over within a month; 232 (94 per cent) were over within two months and 239 (97 per cent) were over within three months. Eight stoppages lasted for more than three months; four of these exceeded 100 working days. The two longest major stoppages, one of 181 days involving furniture workers and one of 159 days by electric lamp makers, both arose from disputes over dismissals. The other two, one of 150 days by electricians and one of 110 days by plumbers, were both the result of inter-union disputes. These results on the duration of major stoppages are in sharp contrast to those of Table 2.8 which showed the duration of the gross totals of stoppages. Table 2.8 showed that 90 per cent of stoppages were over within a week and 98 per cent were over within a month.

On this evidence it seems that major stoppages are heavily concentrated at the upper end of the duration distribution scale. Earlier we had suggested that the principal difference between major stoppages and minor stoppages was that the former involved far more workers and were only slightly longer. The apparent contradiction between these findings can be resolved by pointing out that the comparison of major to minor stoppages related only to net totals, whereas Table 2.8 included coal mining stoppages. As coal mining stoppages were significantly shorter than other stoppages their inclusion in Table 2.8 exaggerated the difference between major and minor stoppages.

The extent to which major stoppages were larger as well as longer is reflected in Table 2.23. This shows a cross-tabulation for major stoppages by duration and number of workers involved.

Interpretation of Table 2.23 is complicated by the absence of information on those small, short stoppages which would normally occupy the top left-hand corner of the matrix but failed to meet the qualifying limit of 5000 working days lost. Table 2.23 conveys two immediate impressions. First, the overwhelming majority of major stoppages are large: 80 per cent involved more than 500 workers and 60 per cent more than 1000 workers. Secondly, long major stoppages tended to be small. Stoppages involving very large numbers of workers were less likely to be prolonged than those involving small numbers of workers.

MAJOR STOPPAGES IN COAL MINING

We turn, finally, to the excluded case of coal mining. In the period 1946–52 there were seventy-one major stoppages in this industry: 589 390 workers were involved and 2 250 740 working days lost. In contrast to most other industries the series for workers and days lost were not entirely dominated by major stoppages. Indeed, in relation to all strike activity in the industry major stoppages accounted for 0.1 per cent of strikes, 39 per cent of workers involved and 56 per cent of days lost. There was no discernible year to year trend in major coal mining stoppages in this period.

MAIN FEATURES OF THE STRIKE PATTERN, 1946–52

In concluding this survey of the period we must repeat that the dominant feature of the strike pattern was the downward trend which emerged and persisted with the exception of 1951. Examination of the net totals of strike activity revealed that, overall, stoppages were of minor significance in this period; on average only 1.3 per cent of employees were involved at any time in a year and time lost was equivalent to 0.03 per cent of total potential working time. Unemployment was very low during this period, yet the time lost through unemployment was seventy-five times greater than that lost through stoppages.

But although the impact of stoppages on the whole economy appears to have been very slight this does not imply that those stoppages which occurred did not have serious consequences for the parties concerned. These effects would have been strengthened in so far as stoppages were not evenly spread across the economy. In fact just eight industries, out of the thirty-six for which information was available for the period 1949–52, accounted for over half the net total of stoppages and for nearly 70 per cent of the workers involved and time lost. These same eight industries only employed 17 per cent of the country's workforce. Yet here it is perhaps worth emphasising that even in these eight strike-prone industries only 3.6 per cent of the workforce were involved in stoppages at any time in the year and days lost were equivalent to a mere 0.08 per cent of potential working time.

In order to assess how widespread the decline in strike activity was we examined the direction of change in each industry between 1949 and 1952 (consistent data was only available for this shortened period). This revealed that the number of industries experiencing decreases in strike activity was almost counterbalanced by the number experiencing increases. Industries in which a strong upward movement was detected included chemicals, non-electrical engineering, electrical engineering, motor vehicles, aircraft and cycles, and construction.

The remainder of the analysis of published material was concerned with gross totals of strike activity as we were unable to exclude coal mining stoppages. Examination of the reported principal causes of gross totals of stoppages and workers directly involved revealed that non-wage issues were more important than wage issues. Wage and non-wage stoppages both fell by about 40 per cent between 1946 and 1950, non-wage stoppages continued to increase after the exceptional year of 1951 while wage stoppages fell again. Measured in numbers of workers directly involved non-wage stoppages showed a much sharper fall than wage stoppages between 1946 and 1950. Both series showed an increase in 1951, but non-wage stoppages showed the sharper fall in 1952.

Analysis of the distribution of the gross totals of strike activity by their duration, extent and size showed that the vast majority of stoppages were small and short. It also indicated that there was a minority of stoppages which through their extent, duration (or some combination thereof) exerted a very substantial effect on the numbers of workers involved and days lost.

This minority of stoppages was subject to further detailed analysis. It revealed that stoppages which resulted in the loss of at least 5000 working days accounted for only 6 per cent of the net total. They also accounted for 50 per cent of workers involved and 75 per cent of working days lost. These major stoppages followed the same general downward pattern as the net strikes series, although their movements were slightly more erratic. Industries which had been prominent in the net strikes totals retained their prominence in the major strikes series. We examined the distribution of major stoppages by industry and by number of workers involved and working days lost. These analyses revealed that major stoppages varied greatly in their extent, size and industrial location and that there was a tendency for the very largest stoppages to be concentrated in one or two of the more strike-prone industries.

Wage disputes were the reported principal cause of 38 per cent of major stoppages. Issues of trade union principle accounted for a further 21 per cent of the total. The regional distribution of major stoppages seemed to be explicable largely in terms of location of employment and industry. One significant exception to this general rule was provided by Northern Ireland, which contained 10 per cent of major stoppages affecting thirteen different industries but only 2 per cent of the nation's employment. Even major stoppages were relatively localised; only 10 per cent extended beyond the borders of a single region.

An analysis of strikers' occupations was not as informative as we had hoped but it did reveal that some fifty-six different occupational groups were involved in the 247 major stoppages. Seventeen occupational groups were involved in over 70 per cent of strikes. Major stoppages exhibited a marked seasonal pattern. Four months, March, May, June and October, saw the commencement of 45 per cent of strikes while the four 'holiday' months, July, August, September and December, witnessed only 21 per cent. Only 54 per cent of major stoppages were over within a month compared with 98 per cent of the gross total of stoppages. On the whole major stoppages were both larger and longer than other stoppages.

This outline of the main feature of the post-war strike pattern prompts two obvious questions for further examination. First, why did the overall level of strike activity fall so sharply between 1946 and 1952 – contrary to the wartime period that preceded it and the rest of the post-war period that followed? Secondly, within this overall pattern of a falling level of strike activity, why did some industries – especially those in the metal trades – experience an increasing level of activity, at least from 1949 onwards? We consider both these questions in some detail later in this study.

3   The Return of the Strike, 1953–9

THE CHARACTERISTICS OF THE PERIOD

The chapter derives its title from two significant changes from the previous period. First, the downward trend in strike activity was reversed in the latter part of 1953 and thereafter, despite an isolated fall in 1956, the overall trend was firmly upwards. As a result, by 1959 the net total of stoppages was 786, an increase of 79 per cent over the 1953 level. This increase in stoppages was accompanied by increases in the numbers of workers involved and days lost, but these were much more erratic. Secondly, this period witnessed the reappearance of the 'set piece strike' in both token and total forms – i.e. industry-wide stoppages conducted with the support and approval of the trade unions concerned. This development began in December 1953 with a one day stoppage by over a million workers in engineering. It was repeated over the following six years as a result of national strikes involving train drivers, dockers, busmen and printers. The last stoppage of a similar character had been by textile workers in 1933. The reoccurrence of national level confrontations, after a twenty year absence, is one of the most intriguing features of the whole post-war period.

Although we have laid emphasis on the change in the direction of strike incidence, and on the emergence of a new kind of strike, the scale of the changes involved should be kept in perspective. In comparison with the years 1946–52 the net total of stoppages in 1953–9 was marginally less, 4259 compared to 4372. The numbers of workers involved and working days lost were much more strongly affected by the change in the kind of strike. On average the net total of workers involved rose by 140 per cent and that of working days lost by 160 per cent. However, it should be remembered that these were increases from a very low base so that although the scale of the changes themselves was dramatic it does not necessarily mean that strike activity was having a dramatic impact on the economy as a whole. Once again, these aggregate comparisons indicate the direction of the principal changes, but it is necessary to examine the less aggregated series in order to trace the actual process of change. Using the methodology and format of Chapter 2 we examined the published and unpublished records for 1953–9.

TOTAL STRIKE ACTIVITY: NET AND GROSS

For much of 1953 it appeared as if the downward trend of the previous period was being continued. In fact the net total of stoppages in that year is the lowest of the whole post-war period, as would have been the net totals of workers involved and days lost except for the occurrence of the national engineering stoppage. This involved 1 070 000 workers and an equal number of working days. The net and gross totals of strike activity in this period are set out in Table 3.1.

Table 3.1   *Net and gross totals of strike activity, 1953–9*

Year	No. of strikes		No. of workers involved (000s)		No. of working days lost (000s)	
	Net	Gross	Net	Gross	Net	Gross
1953	439	1 746	1 205.6	1 374.0	1 791	2 184
1954	525	1 989	245.6	450.0	1 989	2 457
1955	636	2 419	317.4	671.0	2 669	3 781
1956	572	2 648	266.6	508.0	1 581	2 083
1957	635	2 859	1 093.6	1 359.0	7 898	8 412
1958	666	2 629	275.5	524.1	3 012	3 462
1959	786	2 093	454.4	645.8	4 907	5 270
Average	608	2 340	551.2	790.3	3 407	3 950

It can be seen that the net total of stoppages rose rapidly between 1953 and 1955, fell in 1956, recovered in 1957 to the level of 1955, rose slightly in 1958 and substantially in 1959. The number of workers involved was heavily influenced by a number of industry-wide stoppages including those in engineering (1953 and 1957), shipbuilding (1957) and printing and publishing (1959). It is, however, possible to discern some upward movement. The working days lost series was also affected by the industry-wide stoppages but in that instance the overall upward movement from less than two million working days in 1953 to almost five million days in 1959 was unmistakable.

In order to discover whether these increases in workers involved and days lost were the result of a widespread upsurge in strike activity, or simply the product of a handful of industry-wide stoppages, we excluded the latter from the net totals. This revealed that between 1953 and 1959 the number of workers involved averaged 270 000 and increased by 147 per cent. The number of working days lost averaged 1 875 000 and increased by 95 per cent. Comparison of these average levels of workers involved and days lost exclusive of industry-wide stoppages with those for the period 1946–52 revealed increases of 18 per cent and 42 per cent respectively.

The gross totals of strike activity, which include stoppages in coal mining, show a sharp rise in the number of stoppages to 1957 and then an even sharper decline. The gross total of workers involved also reached a peak in 1957, although there is some evidence of an upward movement throughout the period. The number of working days lost also peaked in 1957 but there the evidence of a through time increase is stronger. We turn now to the position that emerges when coal mining strikes are excluded.

NET STRIKE ACTIVITY IN PERSPECTIVE

Employment and trade union membership grew very slowly in 1953–9. As a result increases in net strike activity were reflected in an increase in the significance of stoppages in relation to the economy as a whole. The detailed results are shown in Table 3.2.

Table 3.2   *Net strike activity in perspective, 1953-9*

Year	Workers involved as a percentage of employees in employment	Workers involved as a percentage of trade union members	Working days lost as a percentage of potential working time	Working days lost as a percentage of days lost through unemployment
1953	6.0	13.8	0.03	1.9
1954	1.2	2.8	0.04	2.4
1955	1.5	3.5	0.05	4.1
1956	1.3	3.0	0.03	2.3
1957	5.1	12.1	0.14	8.9
1958	1.3	3.1	0.05	2.5
1959	2.1	5.1	0.09	3.8
Average	2.6	6.1	0.06	3.6

In the years 1953–9 an average of 551 200 workers outside coal mining were involved in stoppages each year. This was equivalent to 2.6 per cent of the workforce or 6.1 per cent of trade union members. Two years, 1953 and 1957, exhibited a level of involvement far above the average. In both years there were national engineering stoppages which contributed substantially to the totals of workers involved. Compared to the years 1946–52 each of these measures of worker involvement, both absolute and relative, showed a doubling in 1953–9. Such a change must surely reflect a substantial shift in the attitudes of the parties involved in collective bargaining.

The average number of working days lost per year in 1953–9, 3.4 million, was an increase of 159 per cent over that of the previous period. Yet it still only represented a loss of 0.06 per cent of potential working time, or 3.6 per cent of the time lost through unemployment. The engineering and shipbuilding strikes of 1957 made that year one of exceptionally high strike activity, yet even in that year time lost was only equivalent to 0.14 per cent of potential working time or 8.9 per cent of the time lost through unemployment.

Again we would like to emphasise that the purpose of this analysis is not to deny the significance of stoppages in the areas in which they occurred, but merely to emphasise that the effects of stoppages in relation to the whole productive capacity of the economy were relatively limited.

NET STRIKE ACTIVITY BY INDUSTRY

AVERAGE DISTRIBUTION OF NET STRIKE ACTIVITY BY INDUSTRY

The distribution of the net totals of strike activity between industries is shown in Table 3.3. Where stoppages affected more than one industry we have followed Ministry of Labour practice and ascribed a stoppage to each of the affected industries but only counted it as one stoppage in the total. This practice is only necessary in the case of the number of stoppages and does not affect the numbers of workers involved or working days lost.

It can be seen that in terms of the number of stoppages the most strike-prone industry was construction with an average of 120 strikes per year, almost 20 per cent of the total. After construction the industries with the most stoppages were, in rank order, shipbuilding, motor vehicles, aircraft and cycles, port and inland water transport, and non-electrical engineering. Between them these industries accounted for a further 41 per cent of net stoppages. Two industries, perambulators, carts, etc. and insurance, banking and finance, did not have any stoppages during this period.

Measured by the average number of workers involved the most strike-prone industry was motor vehicles, aircraft and cycles, with 122 500 or 22 per cent of the total. Four other industries, non-electrical engineering, shipbuilding, electrical engineering, and port and inland water transport, had on average a quarter of a million workers involved in stoppages each year, accounting for 47 per cent of the net total of workers involved. When the average number of working days lost was used as the measure of strike-proneness the leading industry was shipbuilding with 594 000 or 17 per cent of the total. Other industries where the number of days lost was high included printing and publishing, motor vehicles, aircraft and cycles, non-electrical engineering, and road passenger transport. Between them these four industries accounted for nearly 50 per cent of the net total of working days lost.

Taking the five most strike-prone industries as indicated by each of these measures we found that three, shipbuilding, motor vehicles, aircraft and cycles, and non-electrical engineering, made three appearances port and inland water transport made two appearances and four other industries, construction, electrical engineering, printing and publishing, and road passenger transport, each made one appearance. In other words, although there was a considerable amount of stability in industry rankings of strike-proneness, these rankings were altered by differences between industries in the type of strikes occurring.

Recognising that differences in industry size affected these comparisons of strike-proneness, we deflated the numbers of workers involved and days lost by numbers of employees in employment. The result was that, measured by workers involved, shipbuilding took over as the most

Table 3.3 *Average net strike activity by industry group, 1953-9*

Industry groups	No. of strikes	No. of workers involved (000s)	Workers involved as a percentage of employees in employment	No. of working days lost (000s)	Working days lost per 1 000 employees in employment
Agriculture, forestry, etc.	1.4	0.5	0.08	6.1	9.0
Mining and quarrying *	2.6	0.2	0.25	1.4	12.3
Grain milling	0.4	0.1	0.24	0.1	2.4
Bread, flour, etc.	1.7	0.7	0.28	1.3	4.0
Other food	4.3	0.8	0.20	3.3	7.7
Drink	2.9	0.7	0.42	1.7	12.0
Tobacco	0.1	0.1	0.21	0.1	2.1
Chemicals	6.4	1.7	0.33	14.3	26.9
Iron and steel and other metals	39.9	31.4	5.56	136.3	240.7
Non-electrical engineering	54.6	107.5	9.77	381.6	347.0
Electrical engineering	16.0	42.3	6.18	138.9	203.2
Shipbuilding and marine engineering	77.6	65.6	21.31	594.4	1928.6
(V1)	65.4	122.5	11.92	406.1	394.9
(V2)	8.6	7.5	4.67	19.9	124.2
(V3)	0.0	0.0	0.00	0.0	0.0
Other metal goods	15.7	13.3	2.04	54.0	82.9
Textiles	17.0	3.5	0.35	23.9	24.2
Clothing	9.3	3.2	0.61	5.7	11.5
Footwear	2.7	0.3	0.22	0.7	7.2
Bricks, pottery, etc.	11.9	2.3	0.68	13.9	41.4
Furniture, wood and cork manufacture	14.6	1.7	0.58	8.9	30.5
Paper and Board, cartons, etc.	2.3	2.3	1.16	42.6	217.2
Printing and publishing	1.3	20.5	5.66	525.6	1453.0
Other manufacturing industries	11.4	5.0	1.43	16.3	45.8
Construction	120.0	21.0	1.52	122.3	88.1
Gas, water, electricity	4.3	1.6	0.42	3.3	7.8
Railways	4.3	11.0	2.16	128.3	253.5
Road passenger transport	21.9	33.4	11.52	372.0	1282.8
Road haulage	16.0	2.5	1.40	22.7	129.2
Sea transport†	n.a.	n.a.	n.a.	n.a.	n.a.
Port and inland water transport	57.3	40.9	14.64	318.3	1139.8
Other transport and communications	2.1	1.1	0.24	4.1	8.8
Distribution	11.3	3.0	0.12	29.0	12.0
Insurance, banking, finance	0.0	0.0	0.00	0.0	0.0
Professional and scientific	1.3	0.7	0.04	0.6	0.6
Miscellaneous	3.9	1.2	0.07	4.4	2.5
Public Administration and defence	7.0	1.1	0.08	4.6	3.7
All industries *	608.0	551.2	2.60	3407.0	162.7

strike-prone industry – i.e. an average of 21 per cent of the workforce involved each year. It was followed by port and inland water transport (14.6 per cent), motor vehicles, aircraft and cycles and road passenger transport (both 12 per cent) and non-electrical engineering (10 per cent). Ranked by working days lost per 1000 employees in employment, shipbuilding retained its premier position with 1929. Other strike-prone industries included printing and publishing, with 1453, road passenger transport, with 1283, port and inland water transport, with 1140, and motor vehicles, aircraft and cycles, with 395. In shipbuilding time lost was equivalent to almost two days per employee per year. Such industries were atypical of the whole economy where, on average, time lost averaged just over one hour per employee per year.

STRIKE-PRONE AND NON-STRIKE-PRONE GROUPS

Table 3.4 shows the percentage contributions to the net totals of strike activity of the eight most and the eight least strike-prone industries.

From Table 3.4 we again found that eight out of the thirty-six industries which we could distinguish accounted for well over half of all strike activity. Of the eight industries with high levels of strike activity six were also in the top eight in 1949–52 but two, electrical engineering and printing and publishing, were newcomers, having displaced road haulage and railway locos, carriages, etc. Compared with 1949–52 the share of total strike activity accounted for by the top eight industries was marginally up in terms of number of stoppages; it rose from 52 to 55 per cent. But it was significantly up in terms of workers involved and working days lost, having risen from 69 to 84 per cent. However, this increased share was not at the expense of the eight least strike-prone industries, who effectively maintained their minimal share of the total, but at the expense of the remaining twenty industries. In these industries stoppages fell from 43.2 to 40.3 per cent, workers involved fell from 29.2 to 14.3 per cent, and working days lost fell from 30.2 to 14.4 per cent.

Two implications may be drawn from these results. First, from the disparity in each group's share of the total it appears that strikes in the top eight industries were, on average, four times larger than those in middle twenty industries and five times larger than those in the bottom eight. Yet average duration was not significantly different, averaging six days in each case. Secondly, although most industries experienced some increase in strike activity between 1949–52 and 1953–9, the rate of increase was far from uniform; both the top and bottom eight industries experiencing increases approximately four times greater than the remaining twenty. However, given that the bottom eight industries accounted for such a small

---

*Excludes coal mining.

†Until 1960 strikes in sea transport were included with those in other transport and communications.

proportion of the net total of strike activity, and that three of the eight were different from those of 1949–52, it might be advisable not to place too much emphasis on a comparison involving those industries.

Table 3.4 *Industry groups' relative shares of net totals of strike activity, 1953-9*

Industry group	Percentage share of no. of strikes	Percentage share of no. of workers involved	Percentage share of no. of working days lost
High strike activity industries			
Shipbuilding and marine engineering	12.7	11.9	17.4
Port and inland water transport	9.4	7.4	9.3
(V1) Motor vehicles, aircraft and cycles	10.8	22.2	11.9
Road passenger transport	3.6	6.1	10.9
Non-electrical engineering	9.0	19.6	11.2
Electrical engineering	2.6	7.7	4.1
Printing and publishing	0.2	3.7	15.4
Iron and steel and other metals	6.6	5.7	4.0
Total share of strike activity	54.9	84.3	84.2
Low strike activity industries			
Insurance, banking, finance, business	0.0	0.0	0.0
(V3) Carts, perambulators, etc.	0.0	0.0	0.0
Professional and scientific	0.2	0.1	∅
Miscellaneous	0.6	0.2	0.1
Public administration and defence	1.2	0.2	0.1
Agriculture, forestry, fishing	0.2	0.1	0.2
Distribution	1.9	0.5	0.9
Other food	0.7	0.1	0.1
Total share of strike activity	4.8	1.4	1.4

∅ indicates that there was some strike activity during the period but it was too small to be included in the published information or to calculate for the reference series.

Moreover, that still leaves the comparison between the top eight and the middle twenty to be considered. From this comparison it might be concluded that although there had been a general increase in strike activity it was particularly marked in a minority of industries – especially the metal trades sector. It is true that a small part of the increase in the share of strike activity accounted for by the top eight industries can be explained away by their increase in employment – i.e. from 17 per cent in 1949–52 to 20 per cent in 1953–9. But even that adjustment still leaves a considerable concentration of strike activity among a minority of the workforce. Employees in the strike-prone industries were seventeen times more likely to be involved in stoppages than workers in other industries.

DIRECTION OF CHANGE OF NET STRIKE ACTIVITY BY INDUSTRY

Table 3.5 shows whether strike activity increased or decreased in each industry for each of the basic measures in the period 1953–9.

It can be noted that in strong contrast to the period 1949–52, when the number of industries showing an increase in the number of stoppages was slightly less than the number showing a decrease, in 1953–9 over twice as many industries showed an increase as showed a decrease. Once again this is consistent with our finding of a strong upward movement in the number of stoppages. When strike activity is measured by workers involved and days lost it appears that industrial changes were more evenly matched. We believe that the situation indicated by the number of stoppages is a more accurate representation of events over the whole seven year period. This is because the 1953 figures for workers involved and working days lost were heavily influenced by the national engineering strike of that year, to which there was no counterpart in 1959. In Chapter 2 we drew attention to the fact that comparisons of the kind shown in Table 3.5 would be adversely affected if either of the years under scrutiny were atypical. We hoped that any atypical industries would cancel each other out. In 1953 seven industries were simultaneously affected by the same distorting factor. In this situation no self-cancelling effect operated. The result was that for all seven industries more workers were involved in 1953 than in 1959 and for six out of the seven more working days were lost in 1953 than in 1959. Consequently, when interpreting Table 3.5, allowance must be made for the fact that 1953 was atypical. If the affected industries were excluded from the analysis Table 3.5 would show a substantial majority of industries experiencing an increase in strike activity on all three measures.

Unfortunately, as was the case in the previous chapter, in the next three sections of this chapter the data relates to gross strike activity – that is to say it includes strike activity in coal mining. As we pointed out in the previous chapter this creates difficulties of interpretation, not least because coal mining, in the years 1953–9, accounted for 74 per cent of the gross total of stoppages, 30 per cent of the gross total of workers involved and 14 per cent of days lost.

GROSS STRIKE ACTIVITY BY CAUSE

Table 3.6 shows gross strike activity analysed by cause in terms of wage and non-wage issues.

It can be seen that the share of stoppages originating over wage issues was very stable throughout the seven years 1953–9, remaining within the range from 44 to 47 per cent for six of the years. The exception was 1955 when it rose to 51 per cent. In contrast the share of workers involved in wage issue stoppages fluctuated widely from 38 to 90 per cent. The peak years for workers involved over wage issues were 1953 and 1957, the engineering

Table 3.5   *Direction of change of net strike activity in each industry, 1953-9*

	No. of industries experiencing change in no. of stoppages	No. of industries experiencing change in no. of workers involved	No. of industries experiencing change in no. of working days lost
Increase in activity	21	15	17
Decrease in activity	9	17	13

Table 3.6   *Gross strike activity by cause, 1953-9*

Year	No. of strikes	Percentage of total	Wage issues No. of workers involved (000s)	Percentage of total	No. of working days lost (000s)	Percentage of total	Non-wage issues No. of strikes	No. of workers involved (000s)	No. of working days lost (000s)
1953	791	45.3	1200.2	90.3	n.a.	n.a.	955	128.9	n.a.
1954	927	46.6	155.4	38.7	n.a.	n.a.	1062	246.1	n.a.
1955	1231	50.9	287.1	48.0	n.a.	n.a.	1188	311.5	n.a.
1956	1208	45.6	240.1	51.7	n.a.	n.a.	1440	224.1	n.a.
1957	1279	44.7	1048.8	82.2	7487	89.1	1580	226.4	912
1958	1208	45.9	212.4	46.6	2453	70.6	1421	243.7	1021
1959	968	46.3	288.3	55.3	4129	78.2	1125	233.3	1151
Average	1087	46.5	490.3	68.0	4690	82.0	1253	230.6	1028

stoppages having a dominant role in both years. Information on the share of working days lost by cause is only available for the years 1957–9, which makes it even more difficult than usual to draw any firm conclusions. From the information which is available there seems to have been a fair amount of variation in the time lost through wage issue disputes but in each year this cause accounted for the majority of time lost. When considered in absolute numbers wage issue stoppages rose by over 50 per cent from 791 in 1953 to 1231 in 1955. They then fell slightly in 1956, rose to exceed the 1955 level in 1957 and fell again in 1958 and 1959. The number of non-wage stoppages followed a fairly similar pattern except that there was no decline in 1956. Unfortunately this series is so dominated by coal mining stoppages that it is quite impossible to draw from it any conclusions concerning stoppages in other industries.

As we mentioned above, the number of workers involved in wage issue stoppages displays two peaks, one in 1953 and one in 1957. In the remaining years there was a considerable amount of fluctuation but little consistency. In contrast the number of workers involved over non-wage issues more than doubled between 1953 and 1955, fell by 28 per cent in 1956 and continued to fluctuate around that level for the remainder of the period.

Contrasting these figures with those for 1946–52 reveals only a marginal increase in the share of stoppages over wage issues, despite a 45 per cent increase in the absolute number of stoppages. This may be taken to indicate that, although there were factors pushing up the number of wage issue stoppages more rapidly than that of non-wage issues, both kinds of strike experienced considerable growth in these years. When measured by workers involved the importance of wage issue stoppages in 1953–9 is much more obvious, having risen from 45 per cent of the total in 1946–52 to 68 per cent in 1953–9. This change is mirrored in the absolute totals, where workers involved over wage issues had risen by over 200 per cent while those involved over non-wage issues had only risen by 19 per cent. Even if the two massive engineering stoppages are excluded from the comparison, workers involved over wage issues still show a 61 per cent increase. From these comparisons it is clear that wage issues became much more important in 1953–9 and resulted in much larger strikes than had occurred in the previous period.

GROSS STRIKE ACTIVITY BY REGION, 1955–9

From 1955 on the Department of Employment published data on the regional distribution of strike activity, measured in terms of workers involved and working days lost. Interpretation of these series has been complicated by changes in the definition of regions over time and by variations in the distribution of employment by industry within regions. To overcome this latter problem would have involved considerable effort in standardising for variations in industrial employment. Given the difficulties of interpreting such information, even after adjustments had been made, we decided simply to present a summary of the Department's published information. Despite the changes in regional definitions we sought to maintain maximum comparability through time and so we aggregated some of the regional data. However, it must be said that our series can only be regarded as approximations. Information for the period 1955–9 is shown in Table 3.7.

Table 3.7   *Regional distribution of gross strike activity as measured by workers involved and working days lost in relation to employees in employment, 1955-9*

Region	Percentage of employees in employment	Average no. of workers involved (000s)	Workers involved as a percentage of employees in employment	Average no. of working days lost (000s)	Working days lost per 1000 employees in employment
South East	35.0	153.7	2.0	1338	175
South West	5.2	17.6	1.5	180	158
Midlands	9.7	58.8	2.8	211	100
North Midlands	6.7	15.6	1.1	137	93
East and West Ridings	8.4	109.9	6.0	520	283
North West	13.4	72.3	2.5	662	226
Northern	5.8	42.7	3.4	316	250
Scotland	9.6	168.0	8.0	830	396
Wales	4.2	76.9	8.3	214	230
Northern Ireland	2.0	26.2	5.9	193	437
UK	100.0	741.5	3.4	4602	210

From the average number of workers involved by region it would appear that the most strike-prone region was Scotland, closely followed by the South East with the East and West Ridings lying third. When a simple adjustment is made for the number of employees in employment in each region this rank order changes, with Wales emerging as the most strike-prone region with an average of 83 per 1000 employees involved in strikes; second is Scotland with 80 per 1000 and third is the East and West Ridings. It should be remembered that each of these regions had substantial coal fields in operation at this time, while Northern Ireland, with no coal mining, was the fourth most strike-prone region. The South East, which had previously ranked second, only ranked eighth out of ten after adjustment for the number of employees.

Using the average number of working days lost as the measure of strike-proneness places the South East firmly at the top of the league, with Scotland and the North West in second and third places respectively.

Adjustment for the number of employees in employment in the region, so that the measure becomes the number of working days lost per 1000 employees, alters the ranking: Northern Ireland emerges as the most strike-prone region, with an average of less than half a day per employee; Scotland and the East and West Ridings occupy the second and third rankings. There is some evidence to suggest that the average duration of stoppages is shorter in the more strike-prone regions but the association is not well defined and probably reflects the influence of coal mining and its tendency towards short stoppages. It is this apparently inverse relationship which explains why the relative measure of working days lost shows less dispersion than the relative measure of workers involved.

DIMENSIONS OF GROSS STRIKE ACTIVITY: DURATION, EXTENT AND SIZE

The distribution of strike activity in relation to the duration of stoppages as measured in working days is shown in Table 3.8.

Table 3.8   *Distribution of gross strike activity by duration of stoppages, 1953-9*

Duration in working days	No. of strikes	Percent-age of total	No. of workers involved (000s)	Percent-age of total	No. of working days lost (000s)	Percent-age of total
Not more than 1	7112	43.4	1825	33.1	1709	6.2
Over 1, not more than 2	4091	25.0	654	11.9	927	3.4
Over 2, not more than 3	2086	12.7	550	10.0	1112	4.0
Over 3, not more than 4	1012	6.2	338	6.1	893	3.2
Over 4, not more than 5	597	3.6	234	4.2	726	2.6
Over 5, not more than 6	259	1.6	103	1.9	425	1.5
Over 6, not more than 12	609	3.7	1036	18.8	6818	24.7
Over 12, not more than 18	239	1.5	350	6.4	4150	15.0
Over 18, not more than 24	118	0.7	24	0.4	378	1.4
Over 24, not more than 36	105	0.6	248	4.5	6067	21.9
Over 36, not more than 60	105	0.6	125	2.3	3529	12.8
Over 60	50	0.3	21	0.4	912	3.3
Total	16383	100.0	5508	100.0	27645	100.0

Most stoppages were of very short duration; 81 per cent were over within three days and 92.5 per cent within six. In addition to being short most stoppages were quite small, those lasting less than six days accounting for 67 per cent of all workers involved, an average of 244 workers per strike. In contrast the 7.5 per cent of stoppages which lasted more than six days averaged 1471 workers each. It was not surprising to find that these same 7.5 per cent of stoppages accounted for 79 per cent of total time lost.

Comparing 1953–9 with 1946–52 reveals that small stoppages became more commonplace; the share of the total accounted for by those lasting less than three days rose from 77 per cent to 81 per cent. This was not true of workers involved and days lost, where prolonged stoppages increased their share of the total. This shift towards larger and longer stoppages was the product of a few major disputes. Given the previously remarked on tendency for coal mining stoppages to be smaller and shorter than those in other industries, one plausible explanation of the increase in the proportion of short stoppages may well be that the proportion of coal mining stoppages also rose from 63 per cent of the total in 1946–52 to 74 per cent in 1953–9.

Table 3.9   *Distribution of gross strike activity by number of workers involved, 1953-9*

No. of workers involved	No. of strikes	Percent-age of total	No. of workers involved (000s)	Percent-age of total	No. of working days lost (000s)	Percent-age of total
Under 100	11003	67.2	356	6.5	997	3.6
100 and under 250	2532	15.5	404	7.3	1114	4.0
250 and under 500	1456	8.9	508	9.2	1436	5.2
500 and under 1000	860	5.2	579	10.5	1589	5.7
1000 and under 2500	398	2.4	575	10.4	2246	8.1
2500 and under 5000	69	0.4	232	4.2	1229	4.4
5000 and under 10000	35	0.2	232	4.2	1847	6.7
10000 and over	30	0.2	2620	47.6	17187	62.2
Total	16383	100.0	5508	100.0	27645	100.0

It can be seen from Table 3.9 that stoppages involving fewer than 100 workers accounted for 67.2 per cent of the total, but only 6.5 per cent of workers involved and 3.6 per cent of days lost. Stoppages involving at least 5000 workers accounted for only 0.4 per cent of the total, but 51.8 per cent of workers involved and 68.9 per cent of days lost. Examination of the relationship between the numbers of workers involved and days lost in stoppages of varying extent revealed that those involving less than 1000 workers averaged 2.8 days lost per worker in each of the four class intervals – i.e. there was no tendency for duration to increase with extent. In stoppages involving more than 1000 workers extent and duration rose together to a peak of eight days per worker for those involving between

5000 and 10 000 workers. Average duration of stoppages involving more than 10 000 workers was reduced by the inclusion of the 1953 national engineering stoppage.

Comparison of these results with those of 1950–2 revealed very little change in the distribution of stoppages by numbers of workers involved but substantial changes in the distribution of workers and days lost. In 1953–9 stoppages involving 5000 or more workers accounted for 0.4 per cent of stoppages, 52 per cent of workers involved and 69 per cent of time lost. In 1950–2 this same class of strike accounted for 0.5 per cent of stoppages, 31 per cent of workers involved and 38 per cent of days lost.

In order to pinpoint the source of this change we calculated the average extent and duration of stoppages in each class interval in each period. We found that in terms of average extent the two periods were virtually identical, except in respect of the largest stoppages which increased from 18 000 to 87 000 workers per strike. The comparison of average durations revealed that stoppages in the earlier period were slightly longer in all cases except the two largest categories. The principal factor behind the change in the distribution of workers involved and days lost was a fivefold increase in the average extent of the largest stoppages, a change which was supplemented by an increase in average duration.

The distribution of gross strike activity by the number of working days lost per stoppage is set out in Table 3.10.

Table 3.10   *Distribution of gross strike activity by number of working days lost, 1953-9*

No. of working days lost	No. of strikes	Percent-age of total	No. of workers involved (000s)	Percent-age of total	No. of working days lost (00s)	Percent-age of total
Under 500 days	13492	82.4	927	16.8	1377	5.0
500 and under 1000	1278	7.8	465	8.4	908	3.3
1000 and under 5000	1329	8.1	993	18.0	2691	9.7
5000 and under 25000	219	1.3	418	7.6	2174	7.9
25000 and under 50000	27	0.2	132	2.4	944	3.4
50000 and over	38	0.2	2573	46.7	19552	70.7
Total	16383	100.0	5508	100.0	27645	100.0

In the years 1953–9 stoppages involving the loss of less than 500 working days accounted for 82 per cent of the total, 17 per cent of workers involved and 5.0 per cent of days lost. At the other end of the scale stoppages involving the loss of at least 50 000 working days accounted for 0.2 per cent of all strikes, 47 per cent of workers involved and 71 per cent of working days. Contrasting the distribution of stoppages by number of days lost per stoppage in 1953–9 with that of 1950–2 revealed an increase in the share of very small stoppages at the expense of all other stoppages. It is difficult to assess the significance of this as small stoppages had an overwhelming share of the total anyway. However, it is clear that stoppages involving the loss of at least 25 000 working days fell from 0.7 to 0.4 per cent of the total in the later period. Yet their share of workers involved rose from 31 to 49 per cent and their share of days lost from 51 to 74 per cent. Calculation of average extent and duration of stoppages in each size category, in order to identify the origin of this change, revealed a strong tendency for the number of workers involved to be positively associated with duration in both periods. It also confirmed our earlier finding that the major factor behind the change was the fivefold increase in the average number of workers involved in the very largest stoppages.

In general then the basic patterns of duration, extent and size of all strikes, including coal mining, did not alter very much between 1950–2 and 1953–9. The majority of stoppages continued to be very limited in extent and duration; if anything the increasing proportion of coal mining stoppages in the total tightened these limits. In so far as changes did occur they were limited to a small number of strikes which exerted a considerable effect on the gross totals of workers involved and days lost because they were far larger than stoppages in the previous period.

Detailed information on stoppages known to be official was not available for this period but contemporary records of the time, i.e. Labour Research Department bulletins, reveal that quite a number of stoppages had official backing. This change was probably strongly influenced by the lifting of the legal prohibition on strike action, the removal of the consequent risk of legal penalties on the unions and by the failure of the government to secure general support for its wages policies.

COAL MINING

Coal mining continued to dominate the gross totals of stoppages and workers involved but lost its pre-eminent position in the working days lost series. In the years 1953–9 coal mining had 12 124 stoppages which involved 1.7 million workers and resulted in the loss of 3.8 million working days. In all other industries taken together there were 4259 stoppages, involving 3.9 million workers and resulting in the loss of 23.8 million working days. The leading industries in these latter totals were construction with 840 stoppages, motor vehicles, aircraft and cycles with 0.9 million workers and shipbuilding with 4.2 million working days.

The number of stoppages in coal mining rose rapidly between 1953 and 1957 but then fell even more rapidly so that the 1959 total was identical with that of 1953. The series for workers involved and working days lost peaked earlier, in 1955, and then tended to decline. There was no obvious relationship between events in coal mining and those in other industries.

MAJOR STRIKES, 1953–9

We turn now to our analysis of major strikes; those involving a loss of at least 5000 working days. Once again it is possible to distinguish between the position in coal mining and elsewhere. We have already noted the disproportionate effect that a relatively small number of stoppages had on the net totals of workers involved and days lost. This section provides an opportunity to examine those stoppages in more detail.

NET TOTALS OF MAJOR STRIKES AND THEIR RELATIONSHIP TO NET TOTALS OF ALL STOPPAGES

The basic magnitudes of major strike activity and their importance in relation to the net totals of all stoppages are shown in Table 3.12.

Table 3.12   *Net totals of major strike activity in absolute terms and in relation to the net totals of all strike activity, 1953-9*

Year	No. of major strikes	As a percentage of all strikes	No. of workers involved (000s)	As a percentage of all workers involved	No. of working days lost (000s)	As a percentage of all working days lost
1953	24	5.5	1127.6	93.5	1600	89.3
1954	22	4.2	136.9	55.7	1766	88.8
1955	31	4.9	175.6	55.3	2352	88.1
1956	28	4.9	115.7	43.4	1232	77.9
1957	34	5.4	957.8	87.6	7524	95.3
1958	34	5.1	131.7	47.6	2652	88.0
1959	48	6.1	248.0	54.6	4454	90.8
Average	32	5.2	413.3	75.0	3083	90.5

Examination of the absolute measures of major strike activity in 1953–9 revealed a weak but discernible upward trend in the number of major stoppages between 1954 and 1959 with the increase in 1959 being particularly marked. Identification of consistent upward movements in the series for workers involved and days lost proved impossible because of the magnitude of year to year fluctuations caused by individual stoppages. Comparing major strike activity in 1953–9 with that of the previous seven year period revealed that the number of stoppages fell by 9 per cent while the numbers of workers involved rose by 260 per cent and working days lost by 210 per cent. This reflected a very substantial increase in the extent but not the duration of major stoppages between the two periods.

In relation to the net totals of strike activity in 1953–9 major strikes accounted for 5 per cent of stoppages, 75 per cent of workers involved and 90 per cent of days lost. In individual years these shares were subject to some variation. In the case of the number of stoppages this was fairly slight, but in terms of working days lost it was rather larger and in terms of workers involved the changes were quite considerable. Contrasting the shares of the net totals of strike activity due to major stoppages in 1953–9 with those for 1946–52 revealed a slight fall when measured in terms of stoppages from 5.6 to 5.2 per cent. However, in terms of workers involved and working days lost there was a substantial rise; from 50 to 75 per cent for the former and from 75 to 90 per cent for the latter.

NET MAJOR STRIKES IN PERSPECTIVE

Table 3.13 shows major strike activity, measured by workers involved and days lost, in relation to a number of appropriate reference series.

Table 3.13 *Net major strike activity in perspective, 1953-9*

Year	Workers involved as a percentage of employees in employment	Workers involved as a percentage of trade union members	Working days lost as a percentage of potential working time	Working days lost as a percentage of days lost through unemployment
1953	5.6	12.9	0.03	1.7
1954	0.7	1.6	0.03	2.2
1955	0.8	2.0	0.04	3.6
1956	0.5	1.3	0.02	1.8
1957	4.5	10.6	0.13	8.5
1958	0.6	1.5	0.05	2.2
1959	1.2	2.8	0.08	3.4
Average	2.0	4.6	0.05	3.3

Outside coal mining major strikes in 1953–9 involved, on average, some 2 per cent of employees at some time each year and resulted in the loss of 0.05 per cent of potential working time. Year by year examination of the data revealed that 1953 and 1957 were the peak years for worker involvement and that 1957 was also the peak year for working time lost. At these peaks major stoppages involved more than 5 per cent of the workforce and more than 10 per cent of trade union members. Yet working days lost still only accounted for 0.13 per cent of potential working time. On average time lost through stoppages was only 3.3 per cent of that lost through unemployment; in the peak year of 1957 this figure rose to 8.5 per cent.

The trough of major strike activity in these years was in 1956. In that year worker involvement and time lost was on a par with the average of the previous period. This indicates that the generally higher levels of 1953–9 were not simply the result of one or two large stoppages, but also the product of a general upward shift in strike activity. Comparing the relative measures of strike activity in 1953–9 with those of 1946–52 revealed a tripling of worker involvement and a 2.5-fold increase in time lost. Yet despite these increases the impact of major stoppages over the economy as a whole was still relatively slight.

NET MAJOR STRIKE ACTIVITY BY INDUSTRY

Table 3.14 shows the industrial distribution of major stoppages outside coal mining in 1953–9.

There were 221 major stoppages outside coal mining in 1953–9 compared with 247 in the previous period. Of the thirty-nine industry groups, eleven were entirely free of major stoppages in this period, eleven had just one such stoppage and seventeen had more than one. Of these seventeen, nine averaged more than one major stoppage per year. Five industries accounted for 61 per cent of all major stoppages. The top three were motor vehicles, shipbuilding and non-electrical engineering, which between them accounted for 43 per cent of the total.

There were a number of similarities between the industrial distribution of major stoppages in 1953–9 and that of 1946–52. Of the nine most strike-prone industries in 1946–52 eight made the top rankings in 1953–9 as well. The exception was distribution, which was replaced by textiles. The same three industries were the most strike prone in both periods, although in 1953–9 their share of the total had increased from 32 to 43 per cent. Detailed comparison of the two periods showed that thirteen industries had an increase in the number of stoppages. There was no change in seven and nineteen experienced decreases. Decreases were particularly noticeable in road passenger transport, distribution and miscellaneous services. Eight industries were strike free in 1946–52 compared with eleven in the later period.

In short, major stoppages fell in number in 1953–9 but increased their share of workers involved and days lost because the stoppages which did occur were much more extensive. Major stoppages were confined to a smaller group of industries. Within that group certain industries, noticeably those in the metal trades, increased their share of the total.

In addition to examining the industrial distribution of major stoppages we also analysed the distributions of major stoppages by number of workers involved per stoppage in each industry and by the number of working days lost per stoppage. Details are shown in Tables 3.15 and 3.16. These analyses allowed us to examine in more detail the dimensions of major stoppages and to assess the extent to which particular kinds of stoppages were associated with particular industries.

From Table 3.15 it is clear that the extent of major stoppages varied considerably: 22.6 per cent of stoppages involved less than 500 workers, 65.1 per cent less than 2500, and 88.2 per cent less than 10 000. Only 3.6 per cent of major stoppages involved as many as 25 000 workers. Contrasting these results with those for 1946–52 showed a decline in the importance of medium-sized stoppages – i.e. those involving between 500

Table 3.14   *Number of net major strikes by industry group, 1953-9*

Industry group	No. of strikes	As a per-centage of all major strikes
Agriculture, forestry, fishing	1	0.5
Mining and quarrying (exc. coal mining)	1	0.5
Grain milling	0	0.0
Bread, flour, confectionery	1	0.5
Other food	1	0.5
Drink	1	0.5
Tobacco	0	0.0
Chemicals	3	1.4
Iron and steel and other metals	13	5.9
Non-electrical engineering	21	9.5
Electrical engineering	5	2.3
Shipbuilding	36	16.3
Motor vehicles	38	17.2
Aircraft	16	7.2
Cycles	3	1.4
Railway locos, carriages, trams, etc.	1	0.5
Carts, perambulators etc.	0	0.0
Other metal goods	3	1.4
Textiles	8	3.6
Clothing	0	0.0
Footwear	0	0.0
Bricks, pottery, glass, cement, etc.	1	0.5
Furniture, bedding, wood and cork manufacture	0	0.0
Paper, board, cartons	0	0.0
Printing and publishing	4	1.8
Other manufacturing industries	2	0.9
Construction	20	9.0
Gas, water, electricity supply	0	0.0
Railways	2	0.9
Road passenger transport	9	4.1
Road haulage	0	0.0
Sea transport	1	0.5
Port and inland water transport	20	9.0
Other transport and communications	1	0.5
Distribution	5	2.3
Insurance, banking, finance, business	0	0.0
Professional and scientific	1	0.5
Miscellaneous	0	0.0
Public administration and defence	1	0.5
Total*	221	100.0

* The total includes two general engineering stoppages which spanned a number of industries and are not included elsewheere.

Table 3.15 *Cross-tabulation of net major strikes by industry group and number of workers involved, 1953-9*

Industry group	No. of workers involved									
	50 and under 100	100 and under 250	250 and under 500	500 and under 1000	1000 and under 2500	2500 and under 5000	5000 and under 10000	10000 and under 25000	25000 and under 50000	50000 and over
Agriculture, forestry, etc.					1					
Mining and Quarrying (exc. coal mining)			1							
Bread, etc.						1				
Other food				1						
Drink					1					
Chemicals				1	1	1				
Iron and steel and other metal		1	4	2		2	2	2		
Non-electrical engineering	3	5	2	6	4			1		
Electrical engineering		1	1	1	2					
Shipbuilding		2	7	7	13	2	3	1		1
Motor vehicles			5	3	11	7	8	4		
Aircraft		1	3	1	6	1	4			
Cycles			1		1		1			
Railway locos, Carriages, etc.						1				
Other metal goods		1	1		1					
Textiles		2	1	3	2					
Bricks, etc.					1					
Printing and publishing			1					2		1
Other manufacturing Industries					1	1				
Construction		2	5	7	3	2		1		
Railways						1				1
Road passenger transport				1	2	1	2	1	1	1
Sea transport					1					
Port and inland water transport				1	3	4	5	6	1	
Other transport and communication						1				
Distribution					4	1				
Professional, etc.					1					
Public administration					1					
General engineering										2
Total	3	15	32	34	60	26	25	18	2	6

Table 3.16　*Cross-tabulation of net major strikes by industry group and number of working days lost, 1953-9*

Industry group	No. of working days lost							
	5000 and under 10000	10000 and under 15000	15000 and under 20000	20000 and under 25000	25000 and under 50000	50000 and under 75000	75000 and under 100000	100000 and over
Agriculture, forestry, etc.					1			
Mining and quarrying (exc. coal mining)	1							
Bread etc.	1							
Other food	1							
Drink	1							
Chemicals	1	1				1		
Iron and steel and other metals	7	3			2			1
Non-electrical engineering	15	5	1					
Electrical engineering	5							
Shipbuilding	12	9	4	2	1	2	1	5
Motor vehicles	19	8		1	6	1	1	2
Aircraft	6	1	2	1	3	1	1	1
Cycles	2	1						
Railway locos, carriages, etc.			1					
Other metal goods	1		1	1				
Textiles	6			1	1			
Bricks, etc.					1			
Printing and publishing			1			1		2
Other manufacturing industries	1			1				
Construction	7	5	2	2	3			1
Railways				1				1
Road passenger transport	5				1		1	2
Sea transport				1				
Port and inland water transport	6	3	1	3	1	2		4
Other transport and communication					1			
Distribution				1	1	2		1
Professional, etc.				1				
Public administration	1							
General engineering								2
Total	98	36	14	15	22	10	4	22

and 5000 workers – from 66.4 to 54.3 per cent. Both small and large stoppages increased in relative importance, with the latter's share rising from 14.1 to 23 per cent. There was little obvious tendency for stoppages of a particular size to be concentrated in particular industries, although non-electrical engineering accounted for 44 per cent of the eighteen smallest stoppages and port and inland water transport had a 27 per cent share of the twenty-six largest stoppages.

Table 3.16 shows the distribution of net major stoppages by number of working days per stoppage by industry. The distribution was heavily skewed towards the smallest size categories: 44 per cent involved the loss of less than 10 000 working days and 74 per cent involved the loss of less than 25 000 working days. Twenty-two strikes resulted in the loss of more than 100 000 days each. The combined loss from these, 18.2 million working days, was 84 per cent of the total time lost through major stoppages and 76 per cent of the time lost through the net total of stoppages. There was no obvious tendency for small and medium-sized major stoppages to be especially concentrated in particular industries. Thirty-six stoppages, which resulted in the loss of at least 50 000 working days each, were spread across twelve industry groups. Of these three industries, shipbuilding, motor vehicles, and port and inland water transport, accounted for 50 per cent. The distribution of major stoppages by number of working days lost in 1953–9 was very similar to that of 1946–52, except that very large stoppages were rather more frequent in the later period and accounted for a much larger share of working days lost, 76 per cent of the net total compared with 30 per cent.

NET MAJOR STRIKES BY CAUSE

Table 3.17 shows the distribution of major stoppages by cause.

Of the eight possible causes which could be ascribed to major stoppages the most frequently occurring was trade union principle; although a 'photo finish' between trade union principle and wage increase with other wage issue running third might be a more accurate description. Between them these three issues accounted for 64.3 per cent of all major stoppages. Of the remaining causes only the miscellaneous category 'other', 14.9 per cent, and redundancy, 10 per cent, were of much importance.

Compared with 1946–52, wage increase stoppages increased in both absolute and relative terms while other wage issues declined on both measures. The effect of combining all wage disputes was to show a small absolute fall and a small relative rise. The change in relative importance of wage increases to other wage issues suggests that attention had shifted from other aspects of wage payment to claims for basic rate increases. Such a change would be compatible with a collapse of government–trade union understanding over wages policy, such as occurred in the mid-1950s, and with the growth in the number of large official disputes over pay. Trade union principle stoppages increased in relative importance and stayed at the same absolute level. Of the fifty-one stoppages which occurred over

Table 3.17 *Net major strike activity by cause, 1953-9*

Cause	No. of strikes	Percentage share of the total
Wage increase	50	22.6
Other wage issue	41	18.6
Discipline	4	1.8
Redundancy	22	10.0
Sympathy	7	3.2
Demarcation	13	5.9
Trade union principle	51	23.1
Other	33	14.9
Total	221	100.0

Table 3.18 *Distribution of net major strikes by region, 1953-9*

Region	No. of strikes	Percentage share of the total
South East	52	23.5
East Anglia	0	0.0
South West	4	1.8
West Midlands	32	14.5
East Midlands	0	0.0
Yorkshire and Humberside	9	4.1
North West	24	10.9
Northern	9	4.1
Scotland	47	21.3
Wales and Monmouthshire	9	4.1
Northern Ireland	10	4.5
Various regions in England	9	4.1
Great Britain	5	2.3
United Kingdom	11	5.0
Total	221	100.0

this issue in 1953–9 only one appears to have been in the public sector, a fact which may not have been unrelated to the growth of shop-floor representation in the private sector during this period. The only other issues which showed increases in this period were redundancy (from 7.3 to 10 per cent) and demarcation (from 4.9 to 5.9 per cent). Of the thirteen demarcation disputes nine were in shipbuilding.

NET MAJOR STRIKES BY REGION

The regional distribution of major stoppages is shown in Table 3.18.

The South East had the highest number of major stoppages with fifty-two. It was closely followed by Scotland with forty-seven and the West Midlands was in third place with thirty-two. These three regions alone accounted for nearly 60 per cent of all major stoppages and for around 52 per cent of employees in employment. Given that the distribution of strikes by region is heavily influenced by the distribution of industry by region the real interest of this table lies in contrasting it with that for 1946–52. On the assumption that the geographical location of industry does not change very rapidly it is possible to draw some conclusions as to whether particular regions were becoming more or less strike prone

Comparing the regional distribution of major strike activity in 1953–9 with that of 1946–52 revealed two regions, East Anglia and the North West, in which there was no change in their share of strike activity. In a further four regions, the South West, the East Midlands, Yorkshire and Humberside and the Northern, the changes were less than 1 per cent of the total. Of the remaining five regions three experienced a decline in strike activity. In Northern Ireland major strikes fell by over a half, in Wales and Monmouthshire by a third, and in the South East by a fifth. Scotland and the West Midlands substantially increased their combined share of major strikes from 23.9 to 35.8 per cent, with the increase being greatest in the West Midlands. Of those stoppages which affected more than one region those which were confined to England or Great Britain declined in importance. Those affecting the UK as a whole increased.

In summary the distribution of major strikes in 1953–9 showed substantial changes from that in 1946–52, but the conclusions which can be drawn from this are far from obvious. The changing industrial distribution of major stoppages was of some importance – e.g. the increase in motor vehicles strikes affected the West Midlands. But other factors might also be expected to play a role – e.g. the local level of unemployment. And how does one explain a simultaneous rise in major stoppages in Scotland and the West Midlands, or a simultaneous fall in Northern Ireland and the South East?

OCCUPATIONAL GROUPS (OTHER THAN COAL-MINING) MOST
FREQUENTLY INVOLVED IN MAJOR STRIKES

Those occupational groups which were most frequently involved in major
stoppages are shown in Table 3.19.

Table 3.19 *Occupational groups (other than coal-mining) most frequently*
involved in major strikes, 1953-9

Occupational group	No. of strikes	Percentage share of the total
Car and vehicle workers n.e.s.	28	12.7
Engineering and electrical engineering workers n.e.s.	21	9.5
Dockers and stevedores	19	8.6
Shipwrights and shipbuilders	12	5.4
Fitters	10	4.5
Aircraft workers n.e.s.	10	4.5
Bus crews	9	4.1
Machine operators	9	4.1
Electricians	7	3.2
Construction n.e.s.	7	3.2
Boilermakers/boiler shop workers	6	2.7
Platers and riveters	6	2.7
Textile knitters, spinners, etc.	5	2.3
Carpenters and joiners	5	2.3
Sheet metal workers	5	2.3
51 other occupations	62	28.1
Total	221	100.0

n.e.s., not elsewhere specified.

In 1953–9 we identified some sixty-eight occupational groups as being
involved in major stoppages; in 1946–52 we only identified fifty-six
occupational groups in 247 stoppages. This change gives the impression
that strike action was becoming more widely dispersed but there are
grounds for supposing that that impression is not necessarily correct. We
have already noted that major strikes were confined to a smaller range of
industries in the later period which suggests that the occupational range
would be more limited. Further, we have already drawn attention to the
inadequacy of the records from which we derived this information and the
tendency to use widely inclusive occupational titles to describe strikers. In
these circumstances even a small improvement in recording practice is
likely to produce a wider range of occupational titles, while reducing the

number of stoppages ascribed to the wider title. Consequently, the apparent increase in diversity of occupational groups involved in major stoppages may or may not be real, but there is no obvious way in which we can distinguish between a real change and an improvement in the quality of the information.

The occupational group most frequently involved in major stoppages during this period was that of car and vehicle workers not elsewhere specified (n.e.s.). The second ranking group, engineering workers n.e.s., has a similarly uninformative job title covering the precise tasks on which the workers were engaged. Various shipbuilding workers, shipwrights, platers, boilermakers, etc., occurred sufficiently frequently to warrant separate inclusion in the table where they accounted for nearly 11 per cent of the total. Of the fifteen occupations identified in Table 3.19 twelve also featured in the corresponding table for 1946–52. The newcomers were construction n.e.s., carpenters and joiners, and sheet metal workers. The ten most frequently occurring occupations were involved in 60 per cent of major stoppages in 1953–9 compared with only 55 per cent in 1946–52. Given that eight out of the ten groups were the same in both periods this increased concentration of activity might be taken to indicate that the increased diversity of occupations involved in the remaining stoppages (fifty-six occupations in 40 per cent of stoppages in 1953–9 compared with forty-six occupations in 45 per cent of stoppages in 1946–52) was the result of a real change, rather than simply improved information. Such a conclusion must, however, remain tentative.

Table 3.20 presents a cross-tabulation of the most frequently occurring occupational groups (which were not industry specific) by the industries in which they occurred.

The occupational groups which were most widely spread across industries were, in general, those with 'catch all' titles which made them generally applicable but not very informative. One exception to this rule were fitters, who were involved in ten major stoppages in six different industries. The seven most frequently occurring non-industry-specific occupational groups were involved in ninety-one major stoppages in fourteen different industries. Compared with 1946–52 six of the seven occupational groups were the same; the exception was fitters, which had displaced assemblers.

SEASONAL PATTERN OF NET MAJOR STRIKES

The seasonal pattern of major stoppages outside coal mining is shown in Table 3.21.

If net major stoppages were evenly distributed across the months of the years then 8.3 per cent of the total would commence in each month. From Table 3.21 it is clear that major stoppages were not evenly distributed in 1953–9. Four months (February, May, September and October) had significantly more than an even distribution would imply, 42.2 per cent as against 33.2 per cent. Three other months, (June, November and

Table 3.20 *Major strikes: cross-tabulation of occupational groups most frequently involved by industry (other than coal-mining), 1953-9*

Industry	Occupational groups						
	Car and vehicle workers n.e.s.	Engineering, electrical engineering workers n.e.s.	Fitters, maintenance, production, etc.	Aircraft workers n.e.s.	Machine operators	Electricians, building maintnce supply	Boilermakers, boiler shop workers and fitters
Iron and steel and other metal manufacture			3		2		
Non-electrical engineering		11	3		2		1
Electrical engineering		1			2		
Shipbuilding		1	1			1	5
Motor vehicles	25	1			1	1	
Aircraft		2	1	9	1		
Cycles	2						
Railway locos, carriages, etc.	1						
Other metal goods			1		1		
Textiles			1		1		
Printing and publishing		1			1		
Construction		2				5	
Other transport and communication				1			
General engineering		2					
Total	28	21	10	10	9	7	6

n.e.s., not elsewhere specified.

Table 3.21   *Seasonal pattern of net major strikes, 1953-9*

Month	No. of strikes beginning	Percentage share of the total	No. of strikes ending	Percentage share of the total
January	18	8.1	16	7.2
February	21	9.5	15	6.8
March	18	8.1	22	10.0
April	17	7.7	21	9.5
May	22	10.0	14	6.3
June	12	5.4	17	7.7
July	19	8.6	13	5.9
August	18	8.1	23	10.4
September	24	10.9	18	8.1
October	26	11.8	28	12.7
November	13	5.9	16	7.2
December	13	5.9	18	8.1
Total	221	100.0	221	100.0

Table 3.22   *Duration of net major stoppages, 1953-9*

Duration in working days	No. of strikes	Percentage share of the total
Not more than 1	3	1.4
Over 1 but not more than 2	9	4.1
Over 2 but not more than 3	13	5.9
Over 3 but not more than 4	8	3.6
Over 4 but not more than 5	5	2.3
Over 5 but not more than 6	11	5.0
Over 6 but not more than 12	43	19.5
Over 12 but not more than 18	36	16.3
Over 18 but not more than 24	12	5.4
Over 24 but not more than 36	30	13.6
Over 36 but not more than 48	18	8.1
Over 48 but not more than 60	15	6.8
Over 60 but not more than 72	5	2.3
Over 72	13	5.9
Total	221	100.0

December) had much less than an even distribution would imply, 17.2 per cent as against 24.9 per cent.

Comparison with the seasonal pattern of 1946–52 revealed that the seasonal distribution of major stoppages had levelled off somewhat and that there had been major shifts in the timing of the commencement of stoppages. In 1946–52 the four most strike-prone months were March, May, June and October, which between them had had 44.5 per cent of the total; the three least strike-prone months were August, September and December, which had had 14.2 per cent of the total. In 1953–9 the most strike-prone months had a smaller share of the total while the least strike-prone had a larger share. Only May and October retained their 'most strike prone' rankings and December retained its 'least strike prone' ranking. September moved from being among the most strike-free months to being among the most strike-prone, while June made the opposite move. It appears that the spring 'strike season' declined in importance while the autumn 'strike season' gained so that the whole distribution was more evenly spread.

The peak months for the termination of major stoppages were of course influenced by these changes in starting dates. The peak months for termination in 1953–9 were March, April, August and October, which between them saw the end of 42.6 per cent of major stoppages. March, April and October had also been peak months for the ending of stoppages in 1946–52.

Eleven major strikes continued from one calendar year to the next, more than twice the number in the previous period. Of the eleven strikes six ended in January, of which three had begun in December and one each in June, September and November; two ended in February having begun in November and December; and the other three ended in March having begun in October, November and December respectively.

THE DURATION OF NET MAJOR STOPPAGES

The duration, measured in working days, of net major stoppages in the period 1953–9 is shown in Table 3.22.

Forty-nine major stoppages (22 per cent of the total) were over within a full working week; 140 (63 per cent) were over within a month; 188 (85 per cent) were over within two months; 208 (94 per cent) were over within three months. Thirteen stoppages lasted for more than three months and five of these lasted for more than 100 working days. Of these the longest, 175 days by clerical workers, was over a disciplinary matter and the second longest, 168 days by surgical instrument makers, was over the lack of consultation on redundancies. Of the other three, two, one of 117 days by textile workers and one of 106 days by construction workers, were over dismissals. The third, of 122 days by steel erectors, was over a pay claim. As in 1946–52 major stoppages tended to be much longer than other stoppages. Of the gross total of stoppages, 92.5 per cent were over within a

Table 3.23   *Cross-tabulation for net major strikes by duration in working days and number of workers involved, 1953-9*

Duration in working days	Number of workers involved									
	50 and under 100	*100 and under 250*	*250 and under 500*	*500 and under 1000*	*1000 and under 2500*	*2500 and under 5000*	*5000 and under 10000*	*10000 and under 25000*	*25000 and under 50000*	*50000 and over*
Not more than 1							2			1
Over 1 but not more than 2						1	7	1		
Over 2 but not more than 3					4	5	2	2		
Over 3 but not more than 4					2	1	2	3		
Over 4 but not more than 5					2	1	1	1		
Over 5 but not more than 6					5	3	3			
Over 6 but not more than 12				11	21	5	2	2		2
Over 12 but not more than 18			7	11	8	3	1	4		2
Over 18 but not more than 24			4	2	5	1				
Over 24 but not more than 36		3	8	3	7	3		4	1	1
Over 36 but not more than 48		5	5	2	2	1	2		1	
Over 48 but not more than 60		2	4	2	3	1	2	1		
Over 60 but not more than 72	1	1	2				1			
Over 72	2	4	2	3	1	1				
Total	3	15	32	34	60	26	25	18	2	6

week and 98.5 per cent were over within a month, compared with 22 per cent and 63 per cent respectively for major stoppages.

Contrasting the duration of major stoppages in 1953–9 with that of 1946–52 revealed a distinct tendency for stoppages to last longer in the later period. In 1946–52 75 per cent of major stoppages were over within a month compared with 63 per cent in 1953–9 and 94 per cent were over within two months compared with 85 per cent. Very short major stoppages, those lasting three days or less, also became more common in 1953–9, increasing their share of the total from 4 to 11.4 per cent. These changes may be interpreted as indicating that large scale token stoppages became more common and that other disputes became more difficult to resolve, perhaps because of the lack of understanding on wages policy, and were therefore more prolonged.

The final table in this chapter is Table 3.23, which presents a cross-tabulation of major stoppages outside coal mining by duration and number of workers involved. Table 3.23 emphasises how many major stoppages were large: 77 per cent involved more than 500 workers and 62 per cent involved more than 1000 workers. The majority of prolonged major stoppages involved relatively small numbers of workers but prolonged strike action was no longer the exclusive province of small stoppages, as it had been in 1946–52. It seems that pressures to bring about a speedy settlement were still more likely to be effective in the case of large stoppages but they were not as effective as they had been in the previous period.

MAJOR STOPPAGES IN COAL MINING

Between 1953 and 1959 there were sixty-two major stoppages in coal mining involving 216 135 workers and resulting in the loss of 1 082 787 working days. On all three measures major strike activity in coal mining reached a peak in 1955 and tended to decline thereafter, although the decline was irregular and not entirely consistent from year to year. Major stoppages accounted for 0.5 per cent of all stoppages in the industry, for 13 per cent of workers involved and for 28 per cent of working days lost. Compared with 1946–52 major strike activity in coal mining in 1953–9 was down, by 13 per cent in the case of stoppages, by 63 per cent for workers involved and by 52 per cent for days lost. This, of course, was in sharp contrast to other industries where major strike activity tended to rise throughout the period and, overall, was much higher than in the previous period.

MAIN FEATURES OF THE STRIKE PATTERN 1953–9

Strike activity in 1953–9 had two principal characteristics which distinguished it from the previous period. First, the general trend was strongly upwards. The net total of stoppages rose by 79 per cent between 1953 and 1959. Movements in the net totals of workers involved and working days lost were rather more erratic but showed on average increases of 140 and 160 per cent respectively over the previous period. This erratic behaviour was due to the second characteristic of the period, the return of the industry-wide stoppage. Between 1953 and 1959 there were four such stoppages, two in engineering, one in shipbuilding and one in printing, which between them involved a total of 1.97 million workers and resulted in the loss of 10.72 million working days. In addition there were a number of other officially supported stoppages in the docks, railways and road passenger transport which did not involve the whole of the industry's workforce but were of sufficient size to leave a distinct impression on the net totals of strike activity. These changes were so large as to double the relative importance of strike activity in 1953–9 compared with 1946–52 to an average of 2.6 per cent of the workforce per year and the loss of 0.06 per cent of potential working time. Unemployment remained at a low level throughout most of this period but even at the peak of strike activity in 1957 time lost through stoppages was only 8.9 per cent of that lost through unemployment.

Of course this strike activity was not uniformly distributed across the economy. The eight most strike-prone industries, which between them had 20 per cent of all employees in employment, accounted for 55 per cent of stoppages and 84 per cent of workers involved and working days lost, leaving the remaining 80 per cent of the workforce with 45 per cent of stoppages and only 16 per cent of workers involved and working days lost. This was a marked increase in the concentration of strike activity compared with 1949–52. Of the eight most strike-prone industries five were in the metal trades sector and two were in transport. Examination of the direction of change of strike activity by industry between 1953 and 1959 revealed that substantially more industries experienced increases than decreases. Although the overall trends were firmly upwards at least a quarter of the industries moved in a contrary direction.

Analysis of the gross totals of strike activity by cause in terms of wage and non-wage issues revealed considerable stability in the share of all stoppages attributable to each issue but the shares of workers involved and working days lost were very volatile due to the influence of the very large stoppages, all of which were concerned with pay questions. Comparison with 1946–52 showed an increase in the relative importance of wage issues, particularly on the workers directly involved series, which reflects the fact that stoppages over pay questions tended to involve far more workers than non-wage issue stoppages.

Analysis of the distribution of workers involved and working days lost through strikes by region for the period 1955–9 revealed that regions with large operating coalfields and relatively high unemployment tended to be prominent in a ranking of regions by strike-proneness, but in the absence of more detailed information on the distribution of industry by region it was difficult to draw firm conclusions from the evidence. The distribution of strike activity by duration showed a tendency for the extremes of short and long duration to increase at the expense of the middle range. In particular the share of stoppages which were over within six days rose compared to 1946–52 and the share of workers involved and working days lost through longer stoppages also rose. Two-thirds of all stoppages involved less than 100 workers but these only accounted for 7 per cent of all workers involved and for 4 per cent of working days lost. Stoppages involving 10 000 or more workers only accounted for 0.2 per cent of stoppages but covered 48 per cent of all workers involved and 62 per cent of working days lost. In summary the conclusion of the previous chapter that 'the great majority of stoppages were small and short but that there was a minority of stoppages which through their extent, duration or some combination thereof exerted a substantial effect on the number of workers involved and days lost' remained true in 1953–9 with, if anything, the latter effect being even more marked.

These major stoppages were the subject of a separate analysis which revealed that they followed a similar pattern to that of all stoppages between 1953 and 1959, but it was more difficult to discern an upward trend in the series of workers involved in and working days lost through major stoppages because of the volatility of these series. In relation to all stoppages in the period 1953–9 major strikes accounted for 5 per cent of the stoppages, for 75 per cent of workers involved and for 90 per cent of working days lost. The industrial distribution of major stoppages was heavily influenced by the industrial distribution of all stoppages and showed surprising constancy, with the same three industries appearing as the most strike prone and with eight out of the nine industries being in the top positions in both periods. Examination of the distribution of major strikes measured by workers involved and by working days lost across industries revealed a wide diversity of experience but little obvious tendency for particular industries to be associated with large or small disputes. Causes of major disputes showed a slight increase in the share of wage issue disputes and a sharp change of emphasis from other wage disputes to wage increase disputes. We suggested that this was not unconnected with the breakdown of the government-union understanding on wages policy. The next most frequent cause of major stoppages were matters of trade union principle. As this was not a period when recognition was a particularly 'live' issue it seems likely that many of these disputes were connected with the growth of shop-floor representation. One might take this analysis slightly further and suggest that the growth of shop-floor representation and bargaining had some influence on the decision of trade union leaders to take a more aggressive stance in relation to pay increases in an attempt to restore their own influence and authority which had been adversely affected by their close co-operation with the government and, in a paradoxical sense, by their inability to continue that co-operative relationship in the mid-1950s.

Other interesting features of major strikes in this period included the shift in the regional distribution of stoppages in favour of Scotland and the West Midlands and away from Northern Ireland, Wales and the South East. The occupations of workers involved in major stoppages showed an increase in diversity compared to 1946–52 but it was not clear whether this was simply the result of more adequate information or whether it marked a real change. (The available evidence slightly favoured the latter argument but was insufficient to support firm conclusions.) The seasonal pattern of major stoppages also showed a shift with the spring 'strike season' diminishing in importance while the autumn 'strike season' became more prominent. Finally, the distribution of major strikes by duration showed a tendency for both extremes of the duration to gain at the expense of the middle, much as happened in the all strikes series.

Three major questions emerge from this period. First, why did the trend of strike activity change so abruptly in 1953? Secondly, was the reappearance of industry-wide official stoppages an inevitable consequence of that reversal of trend, or was it the result of other specific factors? Thirdly, why was so much of the increase during this period concentrated in the metal trades sector? We consider all these questions in some detail later in this study.

4 The Shop-floor Movement 1960–8

The implication of the title of this chapter is not that all strikes in this period arose from shop-floor bargaining. It is not suggested, even more absurdly, that the first effects of the growth in the number of shop stewards were felt in this period. It is rather that the title chosen is appropriate because the principal characteristic of the changes in the pattern of strike activity in these nine years was a growth in the number of stoppages at shop-floor level. Moreover, a further development, which served to emphasise the change, was that for the most part industry-wide stoppages took the form of 'token battles' rather than 'all out conflicts'. Thus in 1953–9 there had been four industry-wide stoppages of which only one was a token protest. In 1960–8 there were six such strikes of which all but one were token protests. The exception was the seamen's dispute of 1966.

Of course it is true that the previous period experienced a substantial growth in the number of shop-floor stoppages. Indeed, in one sense, the events of 1960–8 may be seen as a further development of that trend. But such a view would be misleading in another way because it neglects the dimensions of the change. In 1959 the net total of stoppages was still 10 per cent below the level recorded in 1946, so that it was possible to believe that there had been little fundamental change; that one was merely observing a medium term cyclical fluctuation. But any illusions of this kind were shattered by 1960. In this year the net total of stoppages rose by nearly 50 per cent to 1166. This was the first time ever that it had exceeded the 1000 level. By 1968 it had doubled again to exceed 2000. On average the net total of stoppages in 1960–8 was some 140 per cent higher than in the previous period. This change in the magnitude of strike action played an important role in feeding public concern over the effects of stoppages, a concern which in its turn contributed to the decision to take legislative action to curb the use of strikes as sanctions in collective bargaining.

One of our main concerns in this chapter is to trace these changes in the strike pattern which contributed to the growing clamour for legal intervention (see Donovan, 1966–8). But we are also concerned to examine other less obvious changes and we shall endeavour to keep strike activity in perspective over the period as a whole. We begin, as usual, with the all strikes series.

TOTAL STRIKE ACTIVITY: NET AND GROSS

Our choice of 1960 as a turning point was determined by several considerations. First, the wave of set piece, official, industry-wide stoppages appears to have come to an end with the printing and publishing strike of 1959. Secondly, the 50 per cent increase in the net total of stoppages between 1959 and 1960 (the largest percentage increase at any time in the post-war period), seems to have marked a distinct break with the pattern which had emerged previously. Thirdly, 1959 seems to have marked the peak of a *laissez faire* policy by the government with respect to industrial disputes. We consider the consequences of changes in government attitudes more fully in Chapter 11.

The net and gross totals for strike activity in the period are set out in Table 4.1.

Table 4.1 *Net and gross totals of strike activity, 1960-8*

Year	No. of strikes		No. of workers involved (000s)		No. of working days lost (000s)	
	Net	Gross	Net	Gross	Net	Gross
1960	1 166	2 832	581.4	818.8	2 530	3 024
1961	1 228	2 686	529.9	778.5	2 309	3 046
1962	1 244	2 449	4 268.2	4 422.7	5 490	5 798
1963	1 081	2 068	440.3	592.5	1 429	1 755
1964	1 466	2 524	711.1	883.0	1 975	2 277
1965	1 614	2 354	758.8	876.4	2 513	2 925
1966	1 384	1 937	493.6	543.9	2 280	2 398
1967	1 722	2 116	693.0	733.7	2 682	2 787
1968	2 157	2 378	2 227.8	2 258.0	4 636	4 690
Average	1 451	2 372	1 189.3	1 323.1	2 872	3 189

It can be seen that between 1960 and 1968 the number of net stoppages rose by 85 per cent. Thus within the space of nine years, and for the first time, stoppages exceeded the 1000 and then the 2000 level. Although the average annual rate of increase in number of stoppages was 8 per cent (compared with 10.2 per cent in the previous period), stoppages actually fell in two years, 1963 and 1966, and rose very sharply in the two succeeding years. As in previous periods, trends in numbers of workers involved and days lost were much more difficult to discern because of the effects of occasional large disputes. There also appears to have been some upward movement in the total of workers involved until 1965. This was followed by a fall in 1966 and a further upward movement in 1967–8. The days lost series does not display any similar movement, except perhaps in

1968, because the effect of the increase in the numbers of workers involved is counteracted by a decline in average duration.

This latter effect may be seen most clearly if we compare the four set piece stoppages of 1953–9 with the six of 1960–8. The latter show a 175 per cent increase in the number of workers involved but a 41 per cent decrease in the number of working days lost. Given the influence that a few very large stoppages can exert on the magnitudes of the net totals of workers involved and working days lost, we thought it might be useful to exclude these stoppages from the aggregate series in order to isolate the underlying changes in workers involved and days lost. The adjusted data showed that while the average number of stoppages per year rose by 140 per cent between the two periods, the average number of workers involved per stoppage fell by 9 per cent, while the average number of days lost per worker involved fell by 46 per cent. The principal factor behind the increase in the net totals of strike activity was the increase in the number of stoppages. This more than outweighed a tendency to smaller, shorter stoppages.

The gross totals of strike activity, which include stoppages in coal mining, moved in a very erratic fashion. There was some tendency for the gross total of stoppages to fall, in contradiction of the movement in the net series. There was no discernible trend in the workers involved or the days lost series.

NET STRIKE ACTIVITY IN PERSPECTIVE

The potential impact of these changes on the level of economic activity is reflected in Table 4.2.

Table 4.2   *Net strike activity in perspective, 1960-8*

Year	Workers involved as a percentage of employees in employment	Workers involved as a percentage of trade union members	Working days lost as a percentage of potential working time	Working days lost as a percentage of time lost through unemployment
1960	2.7	6.4	0.05	2.7
1961	2.4	5.7	0.04	2.7
1962	19.1	45.5	0.10	4.8
1963	2.0	4.7	0.03	1.0
1964	3.1	7.4	0.04	2.0
1965	3.3	7.8	0.04	3.0
1966	2.1	5.1	0.04	2.6
1967	3.0	7.1	0.05	2.0
1968	9.8	22.8	0.08	3.2
Average	5.3	12.4	0.05	2.6

Although, on average, 1.2 million workers a year were involved in strike action, such a measure gives a very distorted picture of the period as a whole because two years, 1962 and 1968, accounted for over 60 per cent of all workers involved. In part this distortion arises from a measurement problem. In 1962 an estimated 1.75 million engineering workers took part in two one day token stoppages. Because these were treated as two separate stoppages, rather than as one two day stoppage, all those taking part were 'double counted' making it appear as if some 20 per cent of employees in employment and 46 per cent of trade union members were involved in strike action that year.

In fact, in terms of individuals participating in strike action, no more than 11 per cent of employees in employment or 27 per cent of trade union members were involved. Moreover, apart from these two exceptional years, no more than 3.3 per cent of employees or 7.8 per cent of union members were involved in strikes in any year. Leaving aside 1962 and 1968, the measures of employee and union member involvement both seem to indicate a decline in overall involvement at the beginning of the period. They also show a sharp increase in the mid-1960s. Overall worker involvement appears to have doubled in 1960–8 compared with 1953–9. (But this period also involved a doubling of strike activity in comparison with its predecessor – i.e. 1946–52.)

Although the overall average level of involvement, some 5 per cent of the workforce at any time during a year, remained quite slight, it had increased sharply since the immediate post-war period. There can be little doubt that in those industries where strike activity was concentrated this development was beginning to cause concern.

The number of working days lost was less affected by the token stoppages so that, although 1962 still emerged as the peak year, the relative loss was much closer to that of other years than was the case in respect of the number of workers involved. On average in 1960–8 working days lost through stoppages were equivalent to 0.05 per cent of potential working time and 2.6 per cent of the time lost through unemployment. Moreover, even in the worst year days lost through strikes were only equivalent to 0.1 per cent of potential working time or 5 per cent of the time lost through unemployment. The relative measures show a decline in the significance of working days lost through stoppages compared with 1953–9. The fall in the average duration outweighed the increase in the number of stoppages. In seeking to explain the growing public concern over strikes during this period one cannot easily point to any substantial increase in economic losses. Concern appears to have arisen over the number of stoppages rather than over their impact on the country's productive potential.

NET STRIKE ACTIVITY BY INDUSTRY

AVERAGE DISTRIBUTION OF NET STRIKE ACTIVITY BY INDUSTRY

Table 4.3 shows the less aggregated detail of the distribution of average annual strike activity by industry. This permits us to identify those industries in which strike activity is concentrated and to compare the average distribution in 1960–8 with that in 1953–9. Such a comparison is complicated in this period by the changes consequent upon the revision of the Standard Industrial Classification in 1958 – e.g. employees previously covered by the 'motor vehicles, aircraft and cycles industry' heading were divided into 'aircraft' and 'motor vehicles and cycles'. The motor vehicles and cycles industry was further affected by the removal of garage and garage service station workers, who had a low strike propensity, to the 'miscellaneous services' industry.

In terms of number of stoppages the most strike-prone industry was, again, construction, with an average of 252 strikes per year, some 17 per cent of the total. The other industries with the most stoppages were, in rank order, motor vehicles and cycles, non-electrical engineering, iron, steel and other metals, and port and inland water transport, which between them accounted for a further 37 per cent of the total. There were no industries in 1960–8 which were completely strike free. Of the thirty-two industries which we have not described in detail, three averaged between fifty and 100 stoppages a year, seventeen averaged between ten and fifty, and the remaining twelve averaged less than ten.

Examination of the degree of worker involvement in stoppages revealed that in fourteen out of the thirty-seven industries less than 1 per cent of the workforce had been involved. In a further twelve industries between 1 and 5 per cent were involved; in three industries between 5 and 10 per cent; in four industries between 10 and 20 per cent and in the remaining four more than 20 per cent. When strike activity is measured by the number of working days lost per 1000 employees in employment the majority of industries were to be found in the lower range of strike-proneness. Thus in twenty-three industries time lost averaged less than an hour per employee per year and in a further ten industries it was less than a day per employee. Even in the four remaining industries time lost averaged less than one and a half days per employee.

In terms of strike numbers four out of the five most strike-prone industries in the previous period were also amongst the most strike-prone in 1960–8. The newcomer was iron, steel and other metals which replaced shipbuilding. Analysis of the workers involved and working days lost series provides further evidence of some upward movement, e.g. the number of industries with less than 1 per cent of their workforce involved in stoppages fell from twenty-two to fourteen and the number where time lost averaged less than an hour per employee from twenty-five to twenty-three.

Table 4.3   *Average net strike activity by industry group, 1960-8*

Industry groups	No. of strikes	No. of workers involved (000s)	Workers involved as a percentage of employees in employment	No. of working days lost (000s)	Working days lost per 1000 employees in employment
Agriculture, forestry, etc.	3.2	0.83	0.15	10.3	19.2
Mining and quarrying*	4.6	0.60	0.88	2.0	29.4
Grain milling	1.3	0.43	0.93	1.1	23.3
Bread, flour, etc.	5.0	4.22	2.02	19.4	91.3
Other food	13.9	3.97	1.06	10.0	26.5
Drink	11.2	2.36	1.48	5.2	30.9
Tobacco	0.6	0.14	0.21	0.8	16.7
Chemicals	26.0	8.43	1.62	24.9	48.3
Iron, steel and other metals	102.8	78.27	12.84	234.6	385.2
Non-electrical engineering	179.8	271.13	19.89	440.3	322.8
Electrical engineering	83.9	145.07	16.77	229.0	264.7
Shipbuilding and marine engineering	93.7	64.48	28.06	244.4	1060.9
(V1) Motor vehicles and cycles	159.1	230.74	46.94	559.9	1140.5
(V2) Aircraft	40.1	65.16	24.10	87.7	325.9
(V3) Locos, prams, trams, etc.	14.1	17.72	16.39	23.3	213.0
Other metal goods	62.6	46.54	8.20	79.1	139.3
Textiles	34.3	7.08	0.86	25.6	31.5
Clothing	10.0	1.90	0.42	3.3	6.6
Footwear	4.0	1.01	0.91	2.0	18.2
Bricks, pottery, etc.	28.0	6.72	1.91	29.3	82.4
Furniture, wood and cork manufacture	17.9	3.26	1.10	15.4	50.0
Paper and board, cartons, etc.	8.2	2.67	1.15	6.2	25.5
Printing and publishing	5.6	0.97	0.23	5.6	15.1
Other manufacturing industries	37.6	17.63	4.56	54.4	139.9
Construction	251.7	41.03	2.58	201.3	126.6
Gas, water, electricity	11.3	2.48	0.61	8.1	19.6
Railways	9.9	30.20	7.90	40.4	104.7
Road passenger transport	30.1	20.97	7.74	79.8	295.2
Road haulage	36.8	5.32	2.49	27.8	131.5
Sea transport	2.1	4.68	4.57	108.9	1058.2
Port and inland water transport	97.0	67.53	47.60	206.8	1457.7
Other transport and communications	10.0	17.06	3.13	29.6	54.8
Distribution	30.9	4.68	0.16	16.2	5.5
Insurance, banking, finance	0.7	0.68	0.11	7.2	11.3
Professional and scientific	4.8	6.46	0.27	10.1	4.2
Miscellaneous	19.1	4.06	0.19	12.9	6.1
Public administration and defence	15.6	2.86	0.21	9.0	6.6
All industries*	1451.0	1189.30	5.26	2872.0	127.1

*Excludes coal mining.

STRIKE-PRONE AND NON-STRIKE-PRONE GROUPS

Table 4.4 shows the percentage contributions to the net totals of strike activity of the eight most and the eight least strike-prone industries.

Table 4.4 *Industry groups' relative shares of net totals of strike activity, 1960-8*

Industry group	Percentage share of no. of strikes	Percentage share of no. of workers involved	Percentage share of no. of working days lost
High strike activity industries			
Port and inland water transport	6.6	5.7	7.2
Motor vehicles and cycles	10.8	19.4	19.5
Shipbuilding and marine engineering	6.4	5.4	8.5
Aircraft	2.7	5.5	3.0
Non-electrical engineering	12.3	22.8	15.3
Electrical engineering	5.7	12.2	8.0
Locos, carriages, prams, trams, etc.	1.0	1.5	0.8
Iron, steel and other metals	7.0	6.6	8.2
Total share of high groups	52.5	79.1	70.5
Low strike activity industries			
Insurance, banking and finance	0.1	0.1	0.3
Agriculture, forestry and fishing	0.2	0.1	0.4
Distribution	2.1	0.4	0.6
Miscellaneous	1.3	0.3	0.4
Public administration and defence	1.1	0.2	0.3
Tobacco	Ø	Ø	Ø
Printing and publishing	0.4	0.1	0.2
Professional and scientific	0.3	0.5	0.4
Total share of low groups	5.5	1.7	2.6

It can be seen that the eight most strike-prone industries accounted for 53 per cent of stoppages, 79 per cent of workers involved and 71 per cent of days lost, but less than 18 per cent of employees in employment. Workers in these industries were seventeen times more likely to be involved in stoppages than those in other industries although, on average, only 23 per cent of the workforce in these industries were involved in stoppages. Of the eight only one, port and inland water transport, was not in the metal trades sector. This may reflect some distortion from our use of the degree of worker involvement as the criterion of strike propensity in a period when the metal trades had three national stoppages. Comparing these results with those for 1953–9 reveals that the shares of net strike activity contributed by the most strike-prone industries fell slightly in terms of number of stoppages and workers involved. It fell more sharply in terms of working days lost. This indicates that the increase in strike activity was not simply the product of a handful of industries, but the result of widespread changes in which strike activity increased most rapidly in previously peaceful industries.

It can be seen that the eight least strike-prone industries accounted for 5.5 per cent of stoppages, 1.7 per cent of workers involved, 2.6 per cent of days lost and 46 per cent of employees in employment. Workers in these industries were 117 times less likely to strike than their counterparts in the most strike-prone industries. Yet the share of strike activity accounted for by these relatively strike-free industries had risen on every measure from the previous period. This does not indicate that they were becoming strike prone, but is consistent with the view that strike activity was becoming more evenly distributed. Of the eight least strike-prone industries six were the same as in the previous period. Carts, perambulators, etc. and other food were replaced by tobacco and printing and publishing. (This last had been among the most strike-prone industries in the previous period.)

The remaining twenty-one industries accounted for 42 per cent of all stoppages, 19.2 per cent of workers involved, 26.9 per cent of days lost and 36 per cent of employees in employment. From these relative measures we can estimate that strikes in the top eight industries were, on average, some three times larger than those in the middle range of industries and five times larger than those in the least strike-prone sector. Yet duration of stoppages in the least strike-prone sector was slightly greater than that in the middle range and nearly 70 per cent greater than that of the most strike-prone sector. The size differences between sectors were similar to those of 1953–9 but the duration pattern reflects the extent to which token protests had replaced prolonged stoppages in the most strike-prone sector.

DIRECTION OF CHANGE OF STRIKE ACTIVITY BY INDUSTRY

Table 4.5 shows the direction of change of strike activity in each industry for each of the basic measures in the period 1960–8.

Table 4.5 *Direction of change of net strike activity in each industry, 1960-8*

	No. of industries experiencing change in no. of stoppages	*No. of industries experiencing change in no. of workers involved*	*No. of industries experiencing change in no. of working days lost*
Increase in activity	32	29	26
Decrease in activity	5	8	9

Table 4.5 confirms our conclusion that the strong upward movements in the aggregate series were the product of a general increase in strike activity across the great majority of industries and not simply the result of large upward movements in a minority. Between 1960 and 1968 the number of stoppages rose in 86 per cent of industries, workers involved rose in 78 per cent and days lost in 70 per cent.

In explaining the growth of concern over strikes in this period this industrial analysis is particularly useful for two reasons. First, it serves to emphasise that the number of stoppages tended to grow more rapidly than other measures of strike activity. Secondly, it demonstrates that this growth was particularly rapid in areas which had been relatively strike free. Thus, although it was still true that stoppages were heavily concentrated in a minority of industries, they were no longer as concentrated as they had been.

GROSS STRIKE ACTIVITY BY CAUSE

Having extended its analysis of gross strike activity by cause to include working days lost in 1957 the Ministry of Labour took the process a stage further in 1960 and produced an industrial breakdown. In Table 4.6 we examine the aggregate movements of strikes by cause and in Table 4.6a we look at the distribution by cause within broad industrial groups.

It can be seen that the proportion of stoppages originating from wage issues was again quite stable, remaining within the limits 45–49 per cent of the total in seven out of the nine years. In the remaining two years, 1965 and 1968, over one-half of all stoppages were over wage issues. A number of small patterns may be distinguished in the year by year data. The share of wage issue stoppages fell between 1960 and 1962, rose between 1962 and 1965 and fell sharply in 1966. They then rose again until in 1968 wage issues were more important, in relative terms, than at any time in the post-war years. Over the period as a whole some 48 per cent of stoppages were over wage issues – i.e. slightly more than in 1953–9 when the percentage was 46.5 per cent. The introduction of a statutory wage freeze in 1966, followed by 'severe restraint' in 1967, might appear to provide a simple explanation of the decline in importance of wage issues during this period, but unless one is to credit the Selwyn Lloyd 'pay pause' of 1961–2 with rather more effectiveness than is usually supposed such an argument does not explain the events of 1961–2.

The share of workers directly involved in strikes attributable to wage issue stoppages lacks even the symmetry of these minor cyclical fluctuations, partly because of the effect of the token stoppages of 1962 and 1968 – although there does appear to have been some tendency for wage issue stoppages to decline in importance in 1966–7. Over the period as a whole 73 per cent of workers involved in strike action were involved over wage issues. This was 5 per cent higher than the 1953–9 level. The share of working days lost attributable to wage issue stoppages displays a variability similar to that of the workers involved series, except that there is no obvious decline in 1966 because of the seamen's dispute, which accounted for over half of that year's total of time lost through wage issue stoppages. On average, in 1960–8, there were 1141 stoppages a year over wage issues involving some 750 workers per stoppage and the loss of nearly 1900 working days. In the same period non-wage issue stoppages averaged 1232 per year, involved some 250 workers per stoppage and the loss of 900 working days per stoppage. On the whole there seem to be few marked differences from 1953–9. The share of stoppages and workers directly involved in wage issue stoppages is marginally up and the share of working days lost is down from 82 to 67 per cent, largely because of the reduction in the duration of pay issue stoppages.

We now turn to the industrial distribution of strike activity by cause to examine whether there are any significant differences between industries in the incidence of wage issue strikes. Details are given in Table 4.6a.

It can be seen that the incidence of wage strikes varied from 59.5 per cent in shipbuilding to 44 per cent in construction, with the less affected industry groups being evenly divided between those where wage stoppages were in the majority and those where they were not. Wage stoppages were also more frequent in manufacturing industries. In every industry group, except textiles and clothing, wage stoppages involved, on average, more workers per stoppage than non-wage strikes. This development was particularly marked in the metal trades because of the three national stoppages over pay. There was no consistent relationship between duration and issue: in two industries wage stoppages were shorter than non-wage stoppages, and in four there was little difference, although wage stoppages did tend to be slightly longer. In the remaining two industries duration of wage stoppages exceeded that of non-wage disputes.

Table 4.6a also allowed us to make some estimate of the impact of coal mining stoppages on the distribution by cause of the gross totals of strike activity. The mining and quarrying industrial sector was almost exclusively composed of coal mining stoppages (920 out of the 925 stoppages occurred in coal mining). Consequently, we can use this sector to assess whether there were any significant differences in the distribution of strike activity by cause between coal mining and the rest of the economy. This was done by excluding mining and quarrying from the gross totals and then calculating the share of wages stoppages in the resulting net totals of strike activity. This revealed that 48.9 per cent of the net total of stoppages were over wages (47.1 per cent in mining and quarrying), 76.4 per cent of workers involved (47.4 per cent) and 68 per cent of days lost (53.3 per cent). On this evidence wages stoppages occurred in coal mining to the same extent as in other industries but were significantly smaller and shorter. To a large extent this disparity in size is a product of the token national engineering stoppages; if they are excluded the differences of extent and duration are greatly reduced.

Table 4.6 Gross strike activity by cause, 1960-8

Year	Wage issues						Non-wage issues		
	No. of strikes	Percentage of total	No. of workers involved (000s)	Percentage of total	No. of working days lost (000s)	Percentage of total	No. of strikes	No. of workers involved (000s)	No. of working days lost (000s)
1960	1 391	49.0	400.2	57.0	1 848	60.6	1 446	301.3	1 201
1961	1 306	48.6	329.2	49.0	1 993	65.6	1 380	343.7	1 045
1962	1 125	45.9	3 694.4	86.0	4 352	75.3	1 324	602.2	1 426
1963	956	46.2	247.8	54.4	1 380	69.1	1 112	207.4	617
1964	1 208	47.9	404.7	57.7	1 053	51.9	1 316	296.8	977
1965	1 180	50.1	377.4	56.0	1 645	56.1	1 174	296.1	1 288
1966	883	45.6	197.8	47.6	1 642	68.6	1 054	217.6	753
1967	986	46.5	262.0	47.5	1 607	57.7	1 130	289.8	1 176
1968	1 230	51.7	1 808.9	87.2	3 582	76.0	1 148	265.1	1 137
Average	1 141	48.1	858.0	73.3	2 122	66.5	1 232	313.3	1 069

Table 4.6a   Industrial strike activity by cause, 1960-8

Industry group	Wages issues as a percentage of total in each industry			Annual average of strike activity in each industry		
	No. of strikes (%)	No. of workers involved (%)	No. of working days lost (%)	No. of strikes	No. of workers involved (000s)	No. of working days lost (000s)
Mining and quarrying	47.1	47.4	53.3	925	127	319
Metals and engineering	50.2	86.3	75.5	426	516	982
Shipbuilding and marine engineering	59.5	79.7	67.0	94	60	247
Vehicles	54.0	73.2	65.9	212	229	671
Textiles and clothing	50.8	50.2	51.3	48	9	31
Construction	44.0	53.2	56.0	252	40	201
Transport and communication	45.5	49.9	63.4	186	138	494
All other industries and services	45.2	64.0	66.0	236	67	247
Total	48.2	73.3	66.5	2 372	1 171	3 191

GROSS STRIKE ACTIVITY BY REGION

Table 4.7 shows the regional distribution of strike activity. Unfortunately there was some revision of regional boundaries which makes strict comparison with the previous period impossible. At a slightly less rigorous level some conclusions may be drawn from the changes that took place.

Table 4.7 *Regional distribution of gross strike activity as measured by workers involved and working days lost in relation to employees in employment, 1960-8*

Region	Percentage of employees in employment	Average no. of workers involved (000s)	Workers involved as a percentage of employees in employment	Average no. of working days lost (000s)	Working days lost per 1,000 employees in employment
South East	36.1	256	3.1	622	74
South West	5.6	50	3.9	87	67
Midlands and East and West Ridings	24.7	448	7.8	953	167
North West	12.8	190	6.4	538	182
Northern	5.5	79	6.2	170	133
Wales	4.2	90	9.3	277	287
Scotland	9.1	179	8.4	457	216
Northern Ireland	2.0	32	7.0	87	186
UK	100.0	1 323	5.7	3 189	138

It should be stated that the difficulties of comparison do not arise from the employment data. Consistent estimates of the numbers of employees in employment in each region may be derived for this period. The problem is that strike activity was analysed in accordance with the boundaries prevailing at the time and the figures were not revised along with the boundaries. However, on the available data Wales and Scotland retained their positions as the two most strike-prone regions, together with the new composite area of the Midlands and the East and West Ridings in place of the East and West Ridings which had been third in 1955–9. At the other end of the scale the South East and the South West changed rankings, with the South East emerging as the least strike-prone region of the country.

But these changes in rankings obscure the most interesting change. Strike activity became more evenly distributed across regions. The most strike-prone regions of 1955–9, Scotland and Wales, experienced an increase in workers involved relative to employment of less than 20 per cent. The next lowest increases were in the South East, 55 per cent, and the Northern, 80 per cent. The overall effect of these changes was that, whereas in 1955–9 workers in the most strike-prone region were more than five times more likely to be involved in stoppages than those in the least strike-prone, in 1960–8 they were only three times more likely. One effect of this change was that in the previous period it had been the more strike-prone regions which appeared to be exceptional, in 1960–8 it was the less strike-prone.

Of course some of this 'levelling out' can be attributed to industrial change, but it is doubtful whether a shift of this magnitude is explicable simply in terms of the industrial relocation which occurred between 1955–9 and 1960–8. Some allowance must be made for changes in local attitudes irrespective of industry. Interpretation of time lost per 1000 employees in employment is complicated by the switch from prolonged to token stoppages which meant that time lost fell despite the overall increase in the extent of strike activity. Only one region (the Midlands and the East and West Ridings) actually showed an increase in time lost. All the rest showed decreases with the South East, the South West and Northern Ireland experiencing the largest declines, while Scotland had the smallest decline. There was no obvious relationship between the degree or direction of change and ranking in the previous period.

DIMENSIONS OF GROSS STRIKE ACTIVITY: DURATION, EXTENT AND SIZE

We noted earlier in this chapter that the average duration of stoppages appeared to have fallen relative to that of 1953–9. The dangers of assuming general movements from averages are illustrated in Table 4.8, which shows a widespread tendency for duration to increase.

It can be seen that although 71 per cent of all stoppages were over in three days or less, indicating that the most frequent form of strike action remained the short stoppage, strikes lasting two days or less declined from 68.4 per cent of all stoppages in 1953–9 to 58.3 per cent in 1960–8. The bulk of this change occurred among stoppages lasting one day or less. They declined from 43.4 to 35.3 per cent. Stoppages lasting over two but not more than three days had the same share in both periods. Every other duration category increased its share of the total.

This shift was not detectable in the distribution of workers or working days lost by duration, because both of these series were heavily influenced by the change in the form of national stoppages. In the former case the growth in the number of token stoppages increased the percentage of workers involved in stoppages lasting one day or less from 33 to 61 per cent. This reduced the share in eight out of the ten remaining duration categories. In the latter case the combined effect of token stoppages in 1960–8, and of prolonged struggles in 1953–9, was to increase the share of shorter stoppages at the expense of longer ones. But once again this did not result in a consistent pattern.

In Table 4.9 we show the distribution of stoppages by extent as measured in terms of workers involved.

Table 4.8 *Distribution of gross strike activity by duration of stoppages, 1960–8*

Duration in working days	No. of strikes	Percentage of total	No. of workers involved (000s)	Percentage of total	No. of working days lost (000s)	Percentage of total
Not more than 1	7 532	35.3	7 201	60.7	6 763	23.5
Over 1, not more than 2	4 910	23.0	1 067	9.0	1 504	5.2
Over 2, not more than 3	2 720	12.7	780	6.6	1 613	5.6
Over 3, not more than 4	1 548	7.3	529	4.5	1 339	4.7
Over 4, not more than 5	1 100	5.2	486	4.1	1 664	5.8
Over 5, not more than 6	621	2.9	432	3.6	1 449	5.0
Over 6, not more than 12	1 533	7.2	628	5.3	3 917	13.6
Over 12, not more than 18	515	2.4	284	2.4	2 264	7.9
Over 18, not more than 24	278	1.3	172	1.5	2 155	7.5
Over 24, not more than 36	300	1.4	158	1.3	2 178	7.6
Over 36, not more than 60	174	0.8	95	0.8	2 555	8.9
Over 60	113	0.5	27	0.2	1 318	4.6
Total	21 344	100.0	11,860	100.0	28 721	100.0

It can be seen that Table 4.9 provides more detail than was available in the previous period with a finer breakdown of those stoppages which involved fewer than 100 workers. Of the 21 344 stoppages which occurred in this nine year period almost 24 per cent involved less than twenty-five workers, 42 per cent involved less than fifty and 58 per cent less than 100. At the other end of the scale 0.2 per cent involved 10 000 or more workers but the forty-eight stoppages which fell into this category accounted for over half of all workers involved and over a third of days lost. The 58 per cent of stoppages which involved less than 100 workers each only accounted for 3.8 per cent of workers involved and 6 per cent of days lost.

Table 4.9 *Distribution of gross strike activity by number of workers involved, 1960–8*

No. of workers involved	No. of strikes	Percent- age of total	No. of workers involved (000s)	Percent- age of total	No. of working days lost (000s)	Percent- age of total
Under 25	5 057	23.7	84	0.7	321	1.1
25 and under 50	3 922	18.4	136	1.1	498	1.7
50 and under 100	3 462	16.2	239	2.0	933	3.2
100 and under 250	3 893	18.2	610	5.1	2 095	7.3
250 and under 500	2 302	10.8	792	6.7	2 583	9.0
500 and under 1000	1 471	6.9	996	8.4	3 189	11.1
1000 and under 2500	872	4.1	1 289	10.9	4 381	15.3
2500 and under 5000	220	1.0	753	6.4	2 626	9.1
5000 and under 10 000	97	0.5	641	5.4	2 103	7.3
10 000 and over	48	0.2	6 320	53.3	9 990	34.8
Total	21 344	100.0	11 860	100.0	28 721	100.0

This distribution allowed us to estimate the average duration, measured by number of working days lost per worker involved for each size category, so that we could assess whether or not there was any relationship between extent and duration. We found that duration was inversely associated with extent so that the more workers who were involved the shorter the stoppage tended to be. The differences between the categories were very slight, nine out of ten had average durations of between three and four days. The exception was the very largest category where average duration was less than two days, presumably because of the influence of the token strikes.

Contrasting these results with those for 1953–9 revealed that small stoppages had become less common in the later period – i.e. they accounted for 58 per cent of stoppages compared with 67 per cent. All other size categories increased their share of the total, with the exception of those stoppages involving 10 000 or more which accounted for 0.2 per cent in both periods. The shift was from small to medium-sized strikes. One further interesting change was that in the previous period there had been a positive relationship between duration and size in contrast to the inverse relationship of 1960–8. This seems to indicate a shift in attitudes towards larger stoppages in that they were being settled more quickly than was previously the case.

Table 4.10 brings together the two elements of duration and extent in the distribution of stoppages by number of working days lost per stoppage.

Table 4.10 *Distribution of gross strike activity by number of working days lost*

No. of working days lost	No. of strikes	Percent-age of total	No. of workers involved (000s)	Percent-age of total	No. of working days lost (000s)	Percent-age of total
Under 250 days	13 033	61.1	770	6.5	1 057	3.7
250 and under 500 days	2 822	13.3	623	5.3	985	3.4
500 and under 1000	2 238	10.5	831	7.0	1 557	5.4
1000 and under 5000	2 552	12.0	1 971	16.6	5 202	18.1
5000 and under 25 000	577	2.7	1 259	10.6	5 620	19.6
25 000 and under 50 000	74	0.3	430	3.6	2 453	8.5
50 000 and over	48	0.2	5 976	50.4	11 850	41.3
Total	21 344	100.0	11 860	100.0	28 721	100.0

Stoppages resulting in the loss of less than 250 working days accounted for 61 per cent of the total, 6.5 per cent of workers involved and 3.7 per cent of days lost. Stoppages involving the loss of at least 50 000 days accounted for 0.2 per cent of the total, 50 per cent of workers involved and 41 per cent of days lost. Comparison with 1953–9 has to be made in respect of stoppages involving the loss of less than 500 working days as the finer subdivision was not available in the earlier period. On this basis we found that small stoppages accounted for 82 per cent of the total, 17 per cent of workers involved and 5 per cent of time lost in 1953–9. These figures compare with 74 per cent, 12 per cent and 7 per cent respectively in 1960–8. Very large stoppages – i.e. those involving the loss of at least 50 000 days – had the same relative incidence and the same share of workers involved. Yet their share of working days lost fell from 71 to 41 per cent. Analysis of the average number of workers involved per stoppage and the average number of working days lost per worker involved by each class interval revealed a strong tendency for extent and duration to increase together – except in the largest class interval where the token stoppages substantially reduced the average duration. This finding was in line with those for earlier periods but contradicts our results from Table 4.9 which showed an inverse relation between extent and duration. We have no simple explanation with which to resolve these contradictions but would suggest that, in part, they arise from aggregation difficulties, i.e. Table 4.9 is more finely divided than Table 4.10. Another possible explanation is that Table 4.10 reflects a tendency for stoppages to get bigger as they last longer, either because of sympathetic action or secondary lay-offs.

The reduction in the relative frequency of very small stoppages was no surprise, given that we had already noted a tendency for the frequency of both small and short stoppages to diminish. One explanatory factor in this change is the decline in the relative frequency of coal mining stoppages. In 1953–9 coal mining supplied 74 per cent of all stoppages; in 1960–8 its share fell to 39 per cent. Given that coal mining stoppages, on average, were much smaller and shorter than those elsewhere, a shift of this kind is bound to make the 'typical' strike appear larger and longer than previously. Unfortunately it seems impossible to disentangle the effects of this shift in the industrial location of stoppages from other changes. Exclusion of coal mining stoppages from the aggregate series only allows us to examine averages, not the whole distribution. In consequence there is little that can be done other than to note the change and the likelihood that the decline in coal mining stoppages is the major contributory factor.

NET STRIKE ACTIVITY KNOWN TO BE OFFICIAL

As we mentioned in Chapter 1 (p.18), information as to whether stoppages were officially sanctioned or approved by the trade unions of the workers involved has only been collected in the post-war years since 1960. The decision to begin collecting this series reflects growing concern in official circles about the number of stoppages which were taking place without authorisation from the trade unions concerned and in breach of the agreed bargaining procedures. However, it should be realised that the fact that stoppages took place without union sanction was not a new development and did not necessarily imply union disapproval. We have already noted how many stoppages were over in a very short time. In such circumstances many stoppages would have been terminated before the appropriate union authority had time to pass judgement. Records from the late nineteenth century show that even then the majority of stoppages lacked union approval. Moreover, between 1940 and 1951 virtually all stoppages took place without formal union approval as strikes were illegal. Consequently, it seems unlikely that governmental concern was due to the fact that many stoppages lacked union approval. The concern was really over the growing number of strikes which were said to be taking place outside the agreed bargaining procedures. These stoppages were frequently the result of workplace bargaining, which took place as a supplement to the formal industry-wide negotiations. Given that unions were reluctant to approve stoppages in breach of procedure, a series of stoppages known to be official (i.e. to have obtained official union approval) was taken to be a proxy for a series of stoppages arising from the formal negotiating machinery. It was felt that the vast majority of other stoppages could safely be assumed to have arisen from workplace bargaining outside the formal negotiating machinery.

The available information and the relative importance of stoppages known to be official is shown in Table 4.11.

Table 4.11 *Net strike activity known to be official in relation to the net totals of strike activity, 1960–8*

Year	No. of strikes	As a percentage of total	No. of workers involved (000s)	As a percentage of total	No. of working days lost (000s)	As a percentage of all working days lost
1960	68	5.8	24	4.1	497	19.6
1961	60	4.9	80	15.1	861	37.3
1962	78	6.3	3809	89.2	4109	74.8
1963	49	4.5	80	18.2	527	36.9
1964	69	4.7	119	16.7	648	32.8
1965	97	6.0	94	12.4	607	24.1
1966	60	4.3	50	10.1	1172	51.4
1967	108	6.3	36	5.2	394	14.7
1968	91	4.2	1565	70.2	2199	76.6
Average	76	5.2	651	54.7	1224	42.6

Of the 13 062 stoppages which occurred outside coal mining between 1960 and 1968, 680 (i.e. only 5.2 per cent of the total) are known to have been official in the sense that they received official union approval. Yet these stoppages accounted for 55 per cent of workers involved and 43 per cent of days lost. It is difficult to identify a clear trend in the number of official stoppages but there does appear to have been some upward movement as the number rose by 26 per cent between 1960–2 and 1966–8. There was no such tendency apparent in the series for workers involved and days lost. But both these series were heavily influenced by the national official stoppages, especially those in engineering, which created a very erratic pattern in which no trend was apparent.

Stoppages known to be official varied as a percentage of the net total from year to year within a range of 4.2–6.3 per cent. It is difficult to discern a trend in this movement but, over the period as a whole, official stoppages rose less rapidly than those not known to be official, 26 per cent compared with 45 per cent. Similarly, with the series for workers involved and days lost, it was virtually impossible to determine whether the official series were rising faster or slower than those not known to be official, although the impression is that they were rising somewhat less rapidly.

On average stoppages known to be official were twenty times larger but lasted less than two-thirds as long as other stoppages. If the national engineering stoppages are excluded from this comparison, official stoppages were four times as large and over twice as long as other stoppages.

In Table 4.11a we try to penetrate beneath the level of the aggregate statistics by examining the distribution of working days lost through stoppages known to be official in relation to all working days lost in broad industry groups.

It should be noted that the use of working days lost, given the tendency for official stoppages to be larger and longer than those not known to be official, provides a maximum estimate of the incidence of official action. Of the six industry groups distinguished in 4.11a the metal trades sector had the highest incidence of time lost through official stoppages with 47.5 per cent. Mining and quarrying had the lowest with 1.5 per cent. The remaining four industry groups were in the range 26–37 per cent. With the exception of mining and quarrying, official strike action appeared to be a regular feature of all the industry groups rather than being confined, as one might expect, to occasional industry-wide stoppages. Of the total time lost through official stoppages the metal trades accounted for 73.4 per cent, transport and communication for 13.9 per cent, all other industries and services for 7.3 per cent, construction for 4.2 per cent, textiles, clothing and footwear for 0.7 per cent, and mining and quarrying for 0.4 per cent.

COAL MINING

Measured by number of stoppages coal mining remained the most strike-prone industry in the economy. But in terms of workers involved and working days lost it was no longer pre-eminent. Between 1960 and 1968 there were 8282 stoppages in coal mining involving a total of 1.2 million workers and resulting in the loss of 2.9 million working days. The industry with the next highest total of stoppages was construction with 2265. Three industries, non-electrical engineering, motor vehicles and cycles and electrical engineering, had more workers involved with 2.4 million, 2.1 million and 1.3 million respectively. In terms of working days lost both motor vehicles and cycles, with five million, and non-electrical engineering, with four million, were more strike prone than coal mining.

This change was not simply the result of a more rapid rate of increase of strike activity in other industries. It was also because strike activity in coal mining declined sharply during this period. Between 1960 and 1968 the numbers of stoppages, workers involved and working days lost all declined by more than 85 per cent.

Table 4.11a   *Industrial strike activity known to be official in relation to all strike activity as measured by working days lost, 1960-8*

Year	Mining and quarrying %	Metals, engineering, shipbuilding, vehicles %	Textiles, clothing and footwear %	Construction %	Transport and communications %	All other industries and services %
1960	—	21.9	12.0	13.6	0.2	52.6
1961	—	42.6	63.6	15.4	15.7	46.9
1962	—	80.1	56.7	27.5	63.8	41.5
1963	—	22.1	16.0	78.4	9.7	40.2
1964	13.6	37.4	—	—	37.5	18.1
1965	—	25.8	38.5	11.9	6.6	37.0
1966	—	18.7	33.3	4.1	84.8	50.8
1967	—	14.4	32.3	8.5	16.5	12.9
1968	—	59.8	15.0	13.3	7.3	25.6
Average	1.5	47.5	29.5	25.9	34.7	36.5

Table 4.12   *Net totals of major strike activity in absolute terms and in relation to the net totals of all strike activity, 1960-8*

Year	No. of major strikes	As a percentage of all strikes	No. of workers involved (000s)	As a percentage of all workers involved	No. of working days lost (000s)	As a percentage of all working days lost
1960	69	5.9	287.7	49.5	1926	76.1
1961	65	5.3	247.0	46.6	1678	72.7
1962	81	6.5	3976.8	93.2	4844	88.2
1963	42	3.9	177.3	40.3	1095	76.6
1964	63	4.3	293.3	41.3	924	46.8
1965	85	5.3	312.5	41.2	1635	65.1
1966	48	3.5	129.9	26.3	1544	67.7
1967	89	5.2	239.7	34.6	1749	65.2
1968	117	5.4	1761.4	79.1	3514	75.8
Average	73	5.0	825.1	69.4	2101	73.2

MAJOR STRIKES, 1960–8

NET TOTALS OF MAJOR STRIKES AND THEIR RELATIONSHIP TO NET TOTALS OF ALL STOPPAGES

We have already noted a tendency for the 'typical' UK strike to increase in both extent and duration during this period. Yet we had to conclude that this effect may simply have been the product of a shift in the composition of the gross total of stoppages arising from the decline in the frequency of coal mining strikes.

In addition to the evidence we considered earlier on this point we now add our data on the net totals of major stoppages. If the increase in extent and duration were the product of a 'real' shift in industries other than coal mining one might expect major stoppages to occur more frequently in relation to the net total of stoppages. The relevant details are shown in Table 4.12.

The variability of the major stoppages series makes it difficult to discern a trend but the use of three year averages reveals that the number of major stoppages fell by 12 per cent in 1963–5 and rose by 34 per cent in 1966–8 so that, between 1960–2 and 1966–8, there was an increase of 18 per cent. The series of workers involved and days lost in major stoppages also show considerable variability in the year to year data. Using three year averages again reveals sharp falls in both series in 1963–5 and some recovery in 1966–8, although both are below the 1960–2 levels. These comparisons are heavily affected by the national engineering stoppages. If these are excluded it appears that the numbers of workers involved fell throughout the period whereas days lost fell and then rose again in 1966–8 to exceed the 1960–2 level. This implies that average duration was rising sharply towards the end of the period.

On average major strikes accounted for 5 per cent of the net total of stoppages, 69 per cent of workers involved and 73 per cent of days lost. It appears that major stoppages at first rose less rapidly and then more rapidly than other stoppages, while workers involved and days lost consistently rose less rapidly. Compared with 1953–9 major stoppages were of less importance in 1960–8. In terms of stoppages and workers involved the decline was quite slight, but the share of working days lost contributed by major stoppages fell from 91 to 73 per cent. As to whether or not there was a 'real' increase in the extent and duration of stoppages outside coal mining in this period, this evidence indicates that this was not the case. But the evidence is not conclusive because a shift may have occurred which may also have affected only those stoppages below the qualifying level of 5000 working days. However, taken together with the other evidence, it does suggest that the shift was more apparent than real and owed a great deal to the change in the frequency of coal mining stoppages.

NET MAJOR STRIKES IN PERSPECTIVE

In Table 4.13 we show the major strike activity of 1960–8 in relation to a number of appropriate reference series.

Table 4.13   *Net major strike activity in perspective, 1960–8*

Year	Workers involved as a percentage of employees in employment	Workers involved as a percentage of trade union members	Working days lost as a percentage of potential working time	Working days lost as a percentage of time lost through unemployment
1960	1.3	3.2	0.04	2.1
1961	1.1	2.7	0.03	2.0
1962	17.8	42.4	0.09	4.2
1963	0.8	1.9	0.02	0.8
1964	1.3	3.0	0.02	0.9
1965	1.4	3.2	0.03	1.9
1966	0.6	1.3	0.03	1.7
1967	1.1	2.5	0.03	1.3
1968	7.8	18.0	0.06	2.4
Average	3.7	8.7	0.04	1.9

On average, between 1960 and 1968, major stoppages involved some 3.7 per cent of employees and 8.7 per cent of trade union members. The peak years for involvement were 1962 and 1968 with 17.8 and 7.8 per cent of employees respectively. Apart from these years of national engineering stoppages the peak year was 1965 when 1.4 per cent of the workforce (3.2 per cent of union members) were involved in stoppages. The year of lowest involvement in major stoppages was 1966 with 0.6 per cent. Days lost through major strikes averaged 0.04 per cent of potential working time or 1.9 per cent of time lost through unemployment. The years 1962 and 1968 were again the peak years for major strike activity with 0.09 and 0.06 per cent of potential working time respectively.

Compared with 1953–9 the average absolute level of worker involvement in major stoppages doubled and in relation to employment rose by 90 per cent. At the same time days lost through major stoppages fell by over 30 per cent and in relation to potential working time fell by 20 per cent. Part of the explanation of this pattern is in the number of national official token stoppages, which raised the level of worker involvement and depressed average duration. But that cannot be the whole explanation because 1953–9 was also affected by national official stoppages and even in years when there was no national stoppage worker involvement still tended to be higher in 1960–8. This greater degree of worker involvement is reflected in the fact that the average number of stoppages rose from thirty-two in

1953–9 to seventy-three in 1960–8. At the same time, with the exception of the 1966 seamen's stoppage, prolonged national conflicts were successfully avoided and this helped to keep down the losses from major stoppages. In summary, although major stoppages were still having only a slight effect on the economy as a whole, they had become much more frequent and were therefore much more likely to be causing serious concern in those areas where they actually occurred. It is to the industrial distribution of those stoppages that we now turn.

NET MAJOR STRIKE ACTIVITY BY INDUSTRY

Table 4.14 below shows the industrial distribution of major stoppages in 1960–8.

Of the thirty-nine specific industry groups identified in Table 4.14 five were entirely free of major stoppages in this period, four had just one major stoppage, sixteen had more than one but less than nine, and fifteen averaged at least one major stoppage per year. As in the previous period five industries accounted for 61 per cent of major stoppages, with motor vehicles alone having 173 major stoppages – i.e. 26 per cent of the total. Of the five industries with the most major stoppages four had held the same position in previous period (electrical engineering replaced port and inland water transport). In addition to the 654 stoppages which affected specific industries there were five general engineering stoppages which affected a wide range of industries and are shown separately at the bottom of the table.

Comparing these totals with those for 1953–9 reveals that the number of industries which were entirely free of major stoppages fell from eleven to five. The number of industries experiencing more than one major stoppage per year rose from nine to fifteen. The remaining nineteen industries continued to average less than one major stoppage per year although the number which had just one such stoppage in the period fell from eleven to four. It seems that the increase from 221 major stoppages in 1953–9 to 659 in 1960–8 was not simply the result of very rapid increases in industries like motor vehicles (thirty-eight to 173), but the product of increases in major strike activity in at least three-quarters of all industries.

The distributions of major strike activity, in terms of the number of workers involved and the number of working days lost per stoppage in each industry, are shown in Tables 4.15 and 4.16.

From Table 4.15 we see that 17.6 per cent of major stoppages involved less than 500 workers, 64.6 per cent less than 2500, and 93.8 per cent less than 10 000. Only 1.8 per cent of major stoppages involved as many as 25 000 workers. Comparing these results with those for 1953–9 shows that the share of major stoppages accounted for by small (less than 500) and large (10 000 or more) stoppages declined in the later period. As a result there was an increase in the share of intermediate stoppages (500–9999 workers) from 65.6 to 76.1 per cent. This is the reverse of the change that had occurred in 1953–9 when small and large stoppages had gained at the

Table 4.14   *Number of net major strikes by industry group, 1960–8*

Industry group	No. of strikes	As a percentage of all major strikes
Agriculture, forestry, fishing	2	0.3
Mining and quarrying	0	0.0
Grain milling	1	0.2
Bread, flour, confectionery	3	0.5
Other food	5	0.8
Drink	1	0.2
Tobacco	0	0.0
Chemicals	9	1.4
Iron and steel and other metals	42	6.4
Non-electrical engineering	85	12.9
Electrical engineering	50	7.6
Shipbuilding	51	7.7
Motor vehicles	173	26.3
Aircraft	20	3.0
Cycles	9	1.4
Railway locos, carriages, trams, etc.	3	0.5
Carts, perambulators, etc.	0	0.0
Other metal goods	15	2.3
Textiles	10	1.5
Clothing	0	0.0
Footwear	0	0.0
Bricks, pottery, glass, cement, etc.	5	0.8
Furniture, bedding, wood and cork manufacture	4	0.6
Paper, board, cartons	4	0.6
Printing and publishing	1	0.2
Other manufacturing industries	18	2.7
Construction	43	6.5
Gas, water, electricity supply	3	0.5
Railways	6	0.9
Road passenger transport	20	3.0
Road haulage	5	0.8
Sea transport	3	0.5
Port and inland water transport	40	6.1
Other transport and communications	9	1.4
Distribution	3	0.5
Insurance, banking, finance, business	1	0.2
Professional and Scientific	4	0.6
Miscellaneous	4	0.6
Public administration and defence	2	0.3
General engineering	5	0.8
Total*	659	100.0

*Excluding coal.

Table 4.15   *Cross-tabulation of net major strikes by industry group and number of workers involved, 1960–8*

Industry group	No. of workers involved									
	50 and under 100	100 and under 250	250 and under 500	500 and under 1000	1000 and under 2500	2500 and under 5000	5000 and under 10 000	10 000 and under 25 000	25 000 and under 50 000	50 000 and over
Agriculture, forestry, etc.					1	1				
Grain milling					1					
Bread, etc.					1		1	1		
Other food				2	1	2				
Drink				1						
Chemicals		1	1		6	1				
Iron and steel and other metals		5	5	14	10	3	2	3		
Non-electrical engineering	2	3	12	28	31	6	2	1		
Electrical engineering	1	5	6	7	14	9	7	1		
Shipbuilding	1	5	9	14	16	4		2		
Motor vehicles	1	1	3	18	46	58	34	10	2	
Aircraft	1	3	3	2	5	3	3			
Cycles				1	4	1	3			
Railway locos, carriages, etc.				1	1	1				
Other metal goods		2	2	4	6	1				
Textiles			2	2	5		1			
Bricks, etc.		1	1	1	2					
Furniture, etc.		1	1	1		1				
Paper, board			2	2						
Printing and publishing					1					
Other manufacturing industries		1	1	3	8	3	1	1		
Construction		7	15	13	6		1			1
Gas, water, electricity			2		1					
Railways			1	1	2		1			1
Road passenger transport		1	3	5	5	4		1	1	
Road haulage					2	1	2			
Sea transport						1	1		1	
Port and inland water transport		1	2		7	9	13	8		
Other transport and communication			1	3	2	1		1		1
Distribution				1	1	1				
Insurance, etc.					1					
Professional, etc.				1			2		1	
Miscellaneous			1		3					
Public administration				1	1					
General engineering							1		1	3
Total	6	37	73	126	190	111	75	29	6	6

Table 4.16 *Cross-tabulation of net major strikes by industry group and number of working days lost, 1960–8*

Industry group	No. of workers involved							
	5000 and under 10 000	10 000 and under 15 000	15 000 and under 20 000	20 000 and under 25 000	25 000 and under 50 000	50 000 and under 75 000	75 000 and under 100 000	100 000 and over
Agriculture, forestry, etc.	1						1	
Grain milling	1							
Bread, etc.	1				1			1
Other food	4		1					
Drink	1							
Chemicals	5	2		2				
Iron and steel and other metals	21	10	4		4		1	2
Non-electrical engineering	56	15	4	3	7			
Electrical engineering	29	8	6	2	5			
Shipbuilding	27	8	4	1	5	3		3
Motor vehicles	76	27	17	17	23	8	2	3
Aircraft	14	4	1		1			
Cycles	6	1	1			1		
Railway locos, carriages, etc.	3							
Other metal goods	10	2		2	1			
Textiles	6	2	2					
Bricks, etc.	2		1		1	1		
Furniture, etc.	2	2						
Paper, board	3	1						
Printing and publishing	1							
Other manufacturing industries	10	3	2		3			
Construction	31	4	2	1	3	1		1
Gas, water, electricity	2	1						
Railways	3	1			1			1
Road passenger transport	7	5	3	2	1			2
Road haulage	2			1	1		1	
Sea transport					1		1	1
Port and inland water transport	18	4	4		8	2	1	3
Other transport and communication	5	1			2			1
Distribution	1		2					
Insurance, etc.						1		
Professional, etc.	2				2			
Miscellaneous	1	1	1	1				
Public administration		2						
General engineering					1			4
Total	351	104	55	32	71	17	7	22

expense of the medium sized. Examination of the relationship between the extent of stoppages and their industry of origin revealed little obvious connection. There was some tendency for metal trades stoppages to be slightly smaller than other stoppages and the service industries tended to be over-represented among the very largest stoppages.

Table 4.16 shows the number of working days lost per stoppage in each industry. Of the 659 major stoppages in this period 53.3 per cent involved the loss of less than 10 000 working days and 82.1 per cent less than 25 000 days. Twenty-two strikes (3.5 per cent) involved the loss of more than 100 000 days each. The combined loss from these stoppages (9.6 million working days) was 50.6 per cent of the total time lost through major stoppages and 37 per cent of the time lost through all net strikes. There was little consistent tendency for stoppages of any particular size to be associated with particular industries, except that the metal trades sector had a disproportionate share of smaller stoppages. Comparison with 1953–9 reveals that small stoppages had become more frequent, accounting for 53.3 per cent of the total instead of 44.3 per cent. This increase tended to depress the share of major stoppages attributable to other size categories with the effect being most marked among stoppages of 100 000 working days or more which fell from 10 to 3.5 per cent. This reflects the fact that national confrontations were not a prominent part of the strike pattern in this period. The decline in the relative frequency of very large stoppages also contributed to a decline in their share of working time lost from 76 per cent in 1953–9 to 37 per cent in this period.

NET MAJOR STRIKES BY CAUSE

The distribution of major stoppages by attributed principal cause is shown in Table 4.17.

Table 4.17 *Net major strike activity by cause, 1960–8*

Cause	No. of strikes	Percentage share of the total
Wage increase	247	37.5
Other wage issue	100	15.2
Discipline	46	7.0
Redundancy	41	6.2
Sympathy	14	2.1
Demarcation	23	3.5
Trade union principle	69	10.5
Other	119	18.1
Total	659	100.0

Disputes over claims for wage increases were the single most important cause, accounting for 37.5 per cent of all disputes. In addition disputes over other wage issues accounted for a further 15.2 per cent, so that wage issues were the focus for 52.7 per cent of all major stoppages. Other issues which contributed significantly to the total included the miscellaneous category, 18.1 per cent, and trade union principle, 10.5 per cent. The other four categories, discipline, redundancy, sympathy and demarcation, accounted for less than 19 per cent of the total.

Compared with 1953–9 wage increase strikes rose from 22.6 to 37.5 per cent of the total, an increase which was more than sufficient to offset the decline in importance of other wage issues from 18.6 to 15.2 per cent. Altogether wage issue stoppages rose from 41.2 per cent in 1953–9 to 52.7 per cent in 1960–8. This change was a continuation of one we noted in the previous period with wage increase stoppages becoming relatively more frequent than other wage issues and other causes of disputes. Two other causes became more important in 1960–8, miscellaneous from 14.9 to 18.1 per cent and discipline from 1.8 to 7 per cent. The remaining four categories each declined in relative importance. Trade union principle, which had been the single most important cause with 23 per cent of the total in 1953–9, declined to 10.5 per cent. In the previous chapter we argued that the importance of trade union principle issues was partly due to the struggle to obtain effective recognition of shop-floor representatives. If that was correct then it seems that while that struggle continued, in absolute terms there were more stoppages on the issue, it was increasingly being overtaken by disputes over substantive issues like pay and discipline. This view is given some support by an examination of the year to year data which disclosed that the only strong upward trend in causes was in respect of wage issues. It is surprising that redundancy issues did not figure more prominently in a period which saw two major recessions.

NET MAJOR STRIKES BY REGION

The regional distribution of major stoppages is shown in Table 4.18.

Given the virtual trebling in the number of major stoppages between 1953–9 and 1960–8 it is not surprising that every regional area showed an increase in the absolute number of strikes, but there are interesting variations between the regions. Measured in terms of numbers the West Midlands emerges as undisputed leader with almost 22 per cent of the total. It is followed by Scotland, 17.5 per cent, the South East, 16.2 per cent, and the North West, 12.6 per cent. These four regions alone accounted for 68 per cent of major stoppages and for 65 per cent of employees in employment. The localised nature of even major strikes in the UK is reflected in the fact that 92 per cent of them were confined to a single region.

Comparing these findings with those for 1953–9 reveals that seven regions increased their relative contributions to the total while the share of the other four regions was reduced. The largest increase was in the West

Table 4.18   *Distribution of net major strikes by region, 1960–8*

Region	No. of strikes	Percentage share of the total
South East	107	16.2
East Anglia	3	0.5
South West	15	2.3
West Midlands	144	21.9
East Midlands	29	4.4
Yorkshire and Humberside	34	5.2
North West	83	12.6
Northern	34	5.2
Scotland	115	17.5
Wales and Monmouthshire	26	3.9
Northern Ireland	17	2.6
Various regions in England	23	3.5
Great Britain	16	2.4
United Kingdom	13	2.0
Total	659	100.0

Table 4.19   *Occupational groups (other than coal mining) most frequently involved in major strikes, 1960–8*

Occupational group	No. of strikes	Percentage share of the total
Engineering and electrical engineering workers n.e.s.	199	30.2
Car industry and vehicle workers n.e.s.	135	20.5
Dockers and stevedores	33	5.0
Building workers n.e.s.	27	4.1
Draughtsmen	21	3.2
Electricians – building, maintenance, supply, etc.	21	3.2
Bus crews	19	2.9
Press workers	13	2.0
50 other occupational groups	191	29.0
Total	659	100.0

n.e.s., not elsewhere specified.

Midlands, where the share rose from 14.5 to 21.9 per cent. There was also a strong upward movement in the East Midlands. This region had had no major stoppages in 1953–9 but had twenty-nine in 1960–8, giving it 4 per cent of the total. For four out of the seven regions which had a larger than average increase, this was the second successive period in which their share of strike activity had increased. The affected regions were the South West, the West Midlands, Yorkshire and Humberside and the Northern. Three out of the four regions which had a below average increase in 1960–8 were also repeating their 1953–9 experience. They were the South East, Wales and Monmouthshire and Northern Ireland. Scotland, which had been the most strike-prone region in 1953–9, also had a below average increase so that its share of strike activity fell from 21.3 to 17.5 per cent. Stoppages affecting more than one region declined from 11.4 to 7.9 per cent.

OCCUPATIONAL GROUPS (OTHER THAN COAL MINING) MOST FREQUENTLY
INVOLVED IN MAJOR STRIKES

The occupational groups which appeared most frequently in major stoppages in 1960–8 are listed in Table 4.19.

Although the number of stoppages rose from 221 in 1953–9 to 659 in 1960–8 the number of distinguishable occupational groups involved in those stoppages fell from sixty-six to fifty-eight. This change is most obvious in our listing of the occupational groups which accounted for 2 per cent or more of the total. In 1953–9 there had been seventeen such groups accounting for 72 per cent of all stoppages. In 1960–8 there were only eight such groups which accounted for 71 per cent of the total. In both periods the same two occupational groups (i.e. engineering and electrical engineering workers not elsewhere specified and car industry and vehicle workers n.e.s.) were the most frequently involved in stoppages. But, whereas in 1953–9 these two had accounted for 22.2 per cent of all stoppages, in 1960–8 their share was 50.7 per cent. In contrast the relative frequency of stoppages by dockers and stevedores and by bus crews had declined. Their shares fell from 8.5 to 5 per cent and from 4.1 to 2.9 per cent respectively. Two occupational groups which had not featured on this list in 1953–9 but which made it in 1960–8 were draughtsmen and press operators.

Occupational groups which entered the major strike series for the first time during this period included teachers, actors, actresses and variety artistes, and air and cabin crews employed in civil aviation. Groups which had appeared only once before and staged a comeback included foremen and bank officials. This spread of strike action among white collar and professional groups is one of the interesting features of this period in that it reflects a growing willingness to take strike action.

The contraction of the range of occupational groups involved in major stoppages, and the contraction of so many stoppages on to just two occupational groups, appears, at first sight, to contradict the spread of major strikes which we observed in the industry series and in the appearance of new occupational groups. In Table 4.20 we present a

Table 4.20 *Major strikes: cross-tabulation of occupational groups most frequently involved by industry (other than coal mining), 1960–8*

Industry	Occupational groups						
	Engineering and electrical engineering workers n.e.s.	*Car and vehicle workers n.e.s*	*Building workers n.e.s.*	*Draughtsmen*	*Electricians – building, maintenance, supply*	*Press workers*	*Machine operators*
Iron and steel and other metal manufacture	25		1			2	
Non-electrical engineering	74			2			3
Electrical engineering	38			6			2
Shipbuilding	16			5	4		
Motor vehicles	7	126		1	5	11	1
Aircraft				7			1
Cycles		5					3
Railway locos, carriages, etc.		3					
Other metal goods	13						
Textiles	1						
Bricks, pottery, glass, etc.	2				1		
Furniture, timber, etc.	1		1				1
Other manufacturing industries	4						
Construction	7		25		9		
Gas, water, electricity					1		
Railways		1					
Road passenger transport	1						
Road haulage	1						
Other transport and communications	3				1		
Professional and scientific services	1						
General engineering	5						
Total	199	135	27	21	21	13	11

cross-tabulation of the most frequently occurring occupational groups by the industry in which they appeared.

As in previous periods we excluded from this analysis those occurring in occupational groups which were industry specific, in order to concentrate on those groups which were involved in stoppages in more than one industry. The seven occupational groups which met this criteria were involved in 427 major stoppages (65 per cent of the total) in twenty-one different industries. The seven comparable occupational groups in 1953–9 were involved in ninety-one stoppages (41 per cent) in fourteen different industries. Much of this change was due to stoppages involving engineering and electrical engineering workers n.e.s., who were involved in stoppages in eight different industries in 1953–9 and sixteen industries in 1960–8. Only two of the industries had strikes by these workers and no others in the earlier period. In the later period there were seven such industries.

The apparent paradox of major stoppages occurring in more industries, but affecting fewer occupational groups, derives from the fact that certain occupational groups were tending to strike regardless of the industry in which they were employed. Unfortunately the imprecision of the occupational titles means that we must exercise considerable caution in interpreting these results lest we confuse real changes with the results of changes in recording practice. However, on the available evidence, the spread of major stoppages during this period was more influenced by occupational than by industrial factors.

SEASONAL PATTERN OF NET MAJOR STRIKES

The seasonal pattern of major stoppages is shown in Table 4.21

Table 4.21   *Seasonal pattern of net major stoppages, 1960–8*

Month	No of strikes beginning	Percentage share of the total	No. of strikes ending	Percentage share of the total
January	51	7.7	38	5.8
February	67	10.2	60	9.1
March	61	9.3	61	9.3
April	66	10.0	47	7.1
May	69	10.5	89	13.5
June	53	8.0	57	8.6
July	47	7.1	52	7.9
August	46	7.0	40	6.1
September	63	9.6	46	7.0
October	73	11.1	73	11.1
November	44	6.7	62	9.4
December	19	2.9	34	5.2
Total	659	100.0	659	100.0

It can be seen from this table that major stoppages exhibited their familiar spring and autumn peaks with the months of February, March, April, May, September and October having more than their share of strikes. Peak months for the termination of major stoppages were February, March, May, June, October and November, which between them had 61 per cent of the total. Comparing these results with those for 1953–9 shows that the spring strike season had gained in importance at the expense both of the autumn season and of the other months.

Thirty strikes (i.e. 4.6 per cent of the total) continued from one calendar year to the next. The most extended of these stoppages were three which ended in January, one of these had begun in July and two in August. One ended in February, having begun in September, and one ended in April, having begun in November.

THE DURATION OF NET MAJOR STOPPAGES

The duration of major stoppages, measured in working rather than calendar days, is shown in Table 4.22.

It can be seen that 207 major stoppages (31 per cent of the total) were over within six days; 500 (76 per cent) were over within twenty-four days; 598 (91 per cent) were over within forty-eight days and 630 (96 per cent) were over within seventy-two days. As usual major stoppages were much longer than the gross total of stoppages; 86 per cent were over within six days and 97 per cent within twenty-four days.

Comparing these results with those for 1953–9 shows a shift towards shorter stoppages across the whole distribution. The share of stoppages lasting no more than six days increased from 22.3 to 31.4 per cent, those lasting no more than twenty-four days from 63.5 to 75.9 per cent and those of forty-eight days from 85.2 to 90.8 per cent. The fact that this shift occurred across the whole distribution indicates that the fall in average duration, upon which we remarked previously, was not a product of the large token stoppages but a reflection of a real across the board shift. Major stoppages may have become much more frequent in this period but they did not become more difficult to resolve.

Whether this reduction in duration of major stoppages was accompanied by a change in their size is something that we can examine with the aid of Table 4.23. This shows a cross-tabulation of major stoppages by number of workers involved and duration.

This table confirms our earlier findings that major stoppages tended to be much larger than others – i.e. 82 per cent of major stoppages involved at least 500 workers, 63 per cent involved at least 1000 and 18 per cent involved at least 5000. The corresponding figures for the gross totals of stoppages are 13 per cent, 6 per cent and 1 per cent.

It also confirmed our finding that prolonged major stoppages tended to involve relatively small numbers of workers. Although stoppages involving fewer than 500 workers accounted for less than 18 per cent of major stoppages they accounted for 53 per cent of those lasting more than

Table 4.22   Duration of net major strikes, 1960–8

Duration in working days	No. of strikes	Percentage share of the total
Not more than 1	28	4.2
Over 1 but not more than 2	18	2.7
Over 2 but not more than 3	38	5.8
Over 3 but not more than 4	39	5.9
Over 4 but not more than 5	46	7.0
Over 5 but not more than 6	38	5.8
Over 6 but not more than 12	151	22.9
Over 12 but not more than 18	75	11.4
Over 18 but not more than 24	67	10.2
Over 24 but not more than 36	69	10.5
Over 36 but not more than 48	29	4.4
Over 48 but not more than 60	19	2.9
Over 60 but not more than 72	13	2.0
Over 72	29	4.4
Total	659	100.0

Table 4.23 Cross-tabulation for net major strikes by duration in working days and the number of workers involved, 1960–8

Duration in working days	Number of workers involved									
	50 and under 100	100 and under 250	250 and under 500	500 and under 1000	1000 and under 2500	2500 and under 5000	5000 and under 10 000	10 000 and under 25 000	25 000 and under 50 000	50 000 and over
Not more than 1							13	9	2	4
Over 1 but not more than 2						11	7	1		
Over 2 but not more than 3					8	21	8	1		
Over 3 but not more than 4					18	17	3	1		
Over 4 but not more than 5					18	11	13	3	1	2
Over 5 but not more than 6				1	19	6	6	4		
Over 6 but not more than 12				49	64	20	12	5		
Over 12 but not more than 18			13	20	26	8	6	2		
Over 18 but not more than 24			18	23	13	8	3	1	1	
Over 24 but not more than 36		7	20	19	14	4	2	2	1	
Over 36 but not more than 48		5	8	6	4	3	1	1	1	
Over 48 but not more than 60		11	4	2	2	1				
Over 60 but not more than 72		7	2	2	1	1				
Over 72	6	7	7	4	3		1			
Total	6	37	73	126	190	111	75	29	6	6

twenty-four days and 72 per cent of those lasting more than forty-eight days. No stoppage involving as many as 10 000 workers lasted for more than forty-eight days. Compared with 1953–9 major stoppages appear to have become slightly smaller and shorter with both the extent and the duration distributions showing downwards shifts.

MAJOR STOPPAGES IN COAL MINING

Between 1960 and 1968 there were forty-three major stoppages in coal mining which involved just under a quarter of a million workers and resulted in the loss of just over one million days. Compared with the totals for 1953–9 there was a 30 per cent fall in the number of stoppages, a 13 per cent increase in the number of workers involved and a 4 per cent decline in the number of days lost. This implies that, despite the overall fall in employment levels in this industry, major stoppages were becoming more extensive. If we adjust this data to an annual average basis we find that major strike activity in coal mining was lower on all three measures in 1960–8 than it was in 1953–9 but that the average extent of stoppages had risen by 63 per cent. Examination of the year by year data disclosed a consistent pattern of decline in the number of stoppages but a more volatile picture in terms of workers involved and days lost – strike action being particularly extensive and protracted in 1961 and 1965.

In relation to all stoppages in the industry the frequency of major stoppages remained constant at 0.5 per cent but the contribution of these stoppages to the total of workers involved rose from 13 to 20 per cent and of working days lost from 28 to 36 per cent compared with 1953–9.

MAIN FEATURES OF THE STRIKE PATTERN, 1960–8

The year 1960 marked a turning point for a number of reasons. First, after the upheavals of the previous period there were no official industry-wide stoppages nor even any official stoppages involving a substantial proportion of an industry's workforce. Secondly, 1960 witnessed a quantitative change, with the largest relative increase in the net total of stoppages in the post-war period. It was the first year ever that the net total of stoppages exceeded 1000. Moreover, these two features, a relative absence of national official stoppages and a more or less continuous growth in the net total of stoppages, came to dominate and typify the period as a whole.

Between 1960 and 1968 the net total of stoppages rose by 85 per cent, workers involved by 283 per cent and working days lost by 83 per cent. As an annual average of the period some 5 per cent of employees and 12 per cent of trade union members were involved in stoppages, resulting in the loss of 0.05 per cent of potential working time and equivalent to 2.6 per cent of the time lost through unemployment. Compared with 1953–9 the relative level of worker involvement doubled. But the impact in relation to potential working time was marginally less and in relation to time lost through unemployment substantially less. It is still worth emphasising that even in 1968, at the end of this period of sustained growth, time lost through stoppages was still only 0.08 per cent of potential working time and equivalent to 3.2 per cent of the time lost through unemployment.

But of course strike activity was not evenly spread across the economy. Eight industry groups out of the thirty-seven for which information was available accounted for 53 per cent of stoppages, 79 per cent of workers involved and 71 per cent of days lost, but only 18 per cent of employees in employment. Yet the share of the eight most strike-prone industries in the total of strike activity actually declined between 1953–9 and 1960–8, which indicates that the rate of increase in strike activity was much more rapid in other industries. Indeed, on average, twenty-nine out of the thirty-seven industries experienced an increase in strike activity on all three measures between 1960 and 1968. This tendency was most noticeable in terms of number of stoppages for in this respect thirty-two industries showed an increase. Clearly the overall increase in strike activity in this period cannot be dismissed as the result of changes in a minority of industries. It represents a real dispersal of strike activity across the economy.

The majority of the gross total of stoppages during this period were over non-wage issues except in two years, 1965 and 1968. When measured by workers involved and working days lost wage issues predominated because, on average, wage issue stoppages were three times longer than non-wage ones and only slightly smaller. Compared with 1953–9 the share of strike activity attributable to wage issues rose when measured by stoppages and workers involved but fell when measured by days lost. Wage stoppages had become more frequent, larger, but substantially shorter.

Analysis of the distribution of gross strike activity by region showed that it was becoming much more evenly distributed compared with 1953–9. The most strike-prone regions of the previous period, Scotland and Wales, experienced the lowest rates of increase in worker involvement. The result of these changes was to distinguish the South East and South West regions as areas of low strike propensity compared to the rest of the country. Some of this change may be explicable in terms of changing industrial location but the magnitudes involved make it unlikely that that can be a complete explanation. Some shift in local attitudes must also have been involved.

Although the average number of days lost per worker involved in strike action was lower in 1960–8 than in the previous period, this was largely a product of the large token stoppages. Detailed analysis of the distribution of gross strike activity by duration revealed a tendency for longer stoppages to occur relatively more frequently. We also noted a tendency for stoppages involving very small numbers of workers to decline relative to medium-sized stoppages. This increase in both extent and duration caused a shift towards larger stoppages as measured by number of days lost.

Much of the explanation of these changes lies in the declining frequency of coal mining stoppages, which tended to be smaller and shorter than those in other industries. In 1953–9 coal mining accounted for 74 per cent of the gross total of stoppages, in 1960–8 its share fell to 39 per cent. This change in the industrial composition of the gross totals of strike activity would give the impression that stoppages were becoming larger and longer even if stoppages in industries outside coal retained the same extent and duration. Unfortunately, it is impossible to measure the precise extent to which coal mining influenced the gross totals, so that we cannot know if this is the whole explanation.

Information on stoppages which were known to have received official support from the trade unions of the workers concerned is available for the years since 1960. This series is frequently used as a proxy for the extent to which stoppages occurred after bargaining procedures had been exhausted. It appears that stoppages which were known to be official tended to be larger and longer than other stoppages and that they were more likely to occur in the metal trades than elsewhere. It also appears that stoppages known to be official were increasing less rapidly than other stoppages, from which it may be implied that an increasing proportion of a rising total of stoppages were taking place without bargaining procedures having been exhausted.

Major stoppages increased rapidly between 1960 and 1968 but not as rapidly as other stoppages so that they declined in relative importance. This decline was particularly marked in terms of their contribution to the totals of workers involved and working days lost. In relation to our various reference series workers involved in major stoppages almost doubled but the impact of these stoppages in terms of days lost declined. The average annual number of major stoppages rose from thirty-two in 1953–9 to seventy-three in 1960–8. Examination of the industrial distribution of major stoppages revealed that only five industries had been completely free of major stoppages compared with eleven industries in the previous period. The number of industries averaging more than one major stoppage a year rose from nine to fifteen. There was little obvious association between the numbers of workers involved or days lost per stoppage and the industry in which that stoppage occurred except that service industries had a disproportionate share of the largest stoppages.

Analysis of the attributed principal causes of stoppages showed a sharp rise in the share of wage increase disputes which more than offset a decline in the share of other wage issues so that, for the first time, wage issues accounted for over half of major stoppages. Trade union principle issues declined very sharply in importance as a cause of major strikes. It appears that to some extent the struggle for local bargaining rights of the previous period was overtaken by conflict over substantive issues. Other changing features of major strike activity included a shift in the regional distribution away from the Celtic fringe and the South East towards the Midlands. The number of different occupational groups involved in major stoppages fell, although the frequency of such stoppages almost trebled. It appeared that an increase in the strike-proneness of particular occupational groups was largely responsible for the spread of strike activity across industries, although the inclusive nature of occupational titles made it difficult to be sure about this. Analysis of the duration and extent of major stoppages revealed that smaller, shorter stoppages were becoming more frequent within the total of major stoppages. This evidence, together with the fact that major stoppages had declined in relation to the net total of stoppages, persuaded us that the increase in the extent and duration of stoppages shown in the gross totals was, however, a product of the declining frequency of coal mining stoppages, rather than the result of changes in the magnitudes of stoppages in other industries.

Once again there are several notable features of strike activity in this period which require explanation. What were the factors which made stoppages rise more rapidly in 1960 than in any other post-war year? Were the same factors responsible for the continuing increase in stoppages between 1960 and 1968 or were other forces at work? Why did industry-wide official stoppages decline in importance? Why did stoppages known to be official decline in importance? What caused strike activity to become more widespread across industries?

5 The Formal Challenge, 1969–73

In the previous chapter we described the impact upon the strike pattern of the growth of shop-floor bargaining which resulted in an increasing number of stoppages, especially over wages issues, in an increased range of industries. We also drew attention to the fact that these developments led to growing public concern over the conduct of industrial relations in the UK. That concern resulted, in 1966, in legal controls on pay increases and demands for legal restrictions on the right to strike.

The final five years of our period of study, 1969–73, witnessed the abandonment and the reintroduction of legal restrictions on pay and the introduction of legal restraints on the use of strike action. These moves constituted a formal challenge to organised workers and their representatives. The challenge was met at several levels – the shop floor was one and the trade union movement another. In this sense the resort to legal restraint was countered by the formal exercise of authority within the trade union movement. One of the most interesting features of the period is the effect of that formal exercise on the strike pattern. In addition there were a whole series of other factors acting and interacting upon the strike pattern. Of course, it should be remembered that the aim of this chapter is not to assess the relative importance of all these influences. They will be considered further later. At this stage we simply wish to describe, in as much detail as possible, the pattern of strike activity in this period.

We chose 1969–73 as our final sub-period partly because the debate over and the introduction of legal restraints marked them off from the period as a whole, but also because our preliminary analyses had indicated certain further changes in strike activity during these years. In part, as in the previous period, these changes were ones of magnitude. Compared with the annual averages of the three basic measures of strike activity in 1960–8 the number of stoppages rose by 87 per cent, workers involved by 22 per cent and days lost by 244 per cent. But in part they were also changes in the characteristics of strikes. Strikes known to be official and major strikes increased in relative frequency. Industry-wide stoppages of a non-token kind made a reappearance. The public, rather than the private sector, became the battleground for set piece confrontations. Wage increases became the issue which most frequently led to stoppages. In all these ways the period 1969–73 was marked off from its predecessor.

TOTAL STRIKE ACTIVITY: NET AND GROSS

The choice of 1969 as a turning point was determined by a number of factors. During 1969 the number of stoppages rose very rapidly, the number of workers involved passed the million mark for the first time since the war, without the assistance of a national engineering strike, and the number of days lost exceeded five million for the first time since 1957. During the same period the statutory backed incomes policy collapsed and the government sought to introduce legal restrictions on the right to strike. All these events served to mark off the period that began in 1969 from what had gone before. The totals of strike activity for the period as a whole are shown in Table 5.1.

Table 5.1 *Net and gross totals of strike activity, 1969–73*

Year	No. of strikes		No. of workers involved (000s)		No. of working days lost (000s)	
	Net	*Gross*	*Net*	*Gross*	*Net*	*Gross*
1969	2930	3116	1519.6	1665	5 807	6 846
1970	3746	3906	1683.2	1801	9 890	10 980
1971	2093	2228	1155.4	1178	13 488	13 551
1972	2273	2497	1392.9	1734	13 111	23 909
1973	2572	2873	1481.0	1528	7 107	7 197
Average	2723	2924	1446.5	1581	9 881	12 497

It can be seen that between 1968 and 1969 the number of stoppages rose by 733 (i.e. 36 per cent). In relative terms this was not as large as the increase in 1960 but, given that the number of stoppages in 1968 was already at a record high, it represented a very substantial increase. In 1970 the increase was even greater in absolute terms with an extra 816 stoppages, an increase of 28 per cent. Yet in 1971 this upward spiral came to an abrupt halt. The number of stoppages fell by 1653, or 44 per cent; a fall unequalled since the collapse of the post-war boom in 1921. But even at this level there were more stoppages than at any time prior to 1968. In 1972 and 1973 the number of stoppages resumed its familiar upward path without reaching the 1969 level.

The number of workers involved was lower in 1969 than in 1968, largely because the latter was inflated by the inclusion of the national engineering stoppage involving 1.5 million workers. If that were excluded the series would have shown a 100 per cent increase. After 1969 the series for workers involved followed exactly the same directional pattern as that for stoppages, although the magnitude of the changes tended to be less. The working days lost series followed a pattern all its own, reaching a peak in

1971 and declining thereafter. Yet even in 1973 losses were higher than at any time from 1945 to 1970, with the sole exception of 1957.

The upsurge in strike activity in 1969–73 was the result of an increase in all forms of activity from the very localised to the industry wide. The extent of activity, as measured by workers involved, did not increase so rapidly, partly because the 1960–8 figures were inflated by the inclusion of the three national engineering stoppages involving five million workers. The average duration of stoppages increased markedly, indicating that the parties involved were subject to increasing pressures which made it difficult for them to reach mutually acceptable settlements.

The gross total of stoppages, which included coal mining, followed the same general pattern as the net total. The series for workers involved and days lost showed peaks in 1972 as a result of the prolonged national stoppage in coal mining that year.

NET STRIKE ACTIVITY IN PERSPECTIVE

In Table 5.2 we measure these absolute levels of net strike activity against some indicators of the size and potential of the economy. On average the total of employees in employment in 1969–73 was 2 per cent less than in the previous period, although the average total of trade union membership was 13 per cent higher. As a result the density of trade union membership rose sharply during this period, i.e. from 43 to 49 per cent.

Table 5.2 *Net strike activity in perspective, 1969–73*

Year	Workers involved as a percentage of employees in employment	Workers involved as a percentage of trade union members	Days lost as a percentage of potential working time	Days lost as a percentage of time lost through unemployment
1969	6.7	15.0	0.1	4.2
1970	7.5	15.5	0.2	6.7
1971	5.3	10.7	0.3	7.0
1972	6.4	12.6	0.2	6.1
1973	6.6	13.2	0.1	4.7
Average	6.5	13.4	0.2	5.9

As we pointed out earlier, the number of workers involved in strike action was, on average, only 22 per cent higher than in the previous period. But such a comparison obscures the fairly stable high level of worker involvement which was consistently above that of all but the exceptional years of the previous period. In relative terms an average of 6.5 per cent of employees and 13.4 per cent of trade union members were involved in stoppages, as against 5.3 per cent of employees and 12.4 per cent of union members in the previous period. Worker involvement reached its peak in 1970, when 7.5 per cent of the workforce were involved in strikes. It reached its lowest level the following year, when 5.3 per cent of workers were involved.

It can also be seen from Table 5.2 that time lost through stoppages, which averaged almost ten million working days a year, set new post-war records, being three times higher than in the previous peak period, 1953–9. Yet despite this increase it is worth noting that time lost was only 0.2 per cent of potential working time and equivalent to 5.9 per cent of time lost through unemployment (unemployment was also at its post-war peak). Yet even in the peak year of 1971 time lost was only equivalent to 0.3 per cent of potential working time, or 7 per cent of the time lost through unemployment.

Of course we do not wish to under-estimate the serious effects which strike activity had in particular plants or even in entire industries, during this period. Yet it remains true that in relation to the economy as a whole, it is permissible to question the attention given to strikes, even during the most strike-prone period covered by our study. The point is that there is little evidence to support the view that stoppages were a problem for the economy as a whole. As we have been at pains to point out, the strikes which did occur were concentrated in a narrow range of industries and, within those industries, in a narrow range of plants. Within those plants increases of the magnitudes we have charted must have meant that strikes were causing increasing problems; but this was surely an argument for coming to terms with the situation in those plants, rather than justification for reacting to a 'national' or 'general' strike problem, which could hardly be said to have existed on the evidence available.

NET STRIKE ACTIVITY BY INDUSTRY

AVERAGE DISTRIBUTION OF NET STRIKE ACTIVITY BY INDUSTRY

The Standard Industrial Classification was subject to further revision in 1968. These revisions affected the coverage of the strike series from 1970 onwards. On the whole the changes were quite minor. We have drawn attention to them in the text where we thought they were important. Table 5.3 shows the distribution of average annual strike activity by each of the three basic measures for each industry.

As measured by number of stoppages the most strike-prone industry was non-electrical engineering with an average of 415 stoppages (15 per cent of the total) per year. The other most strike-prone industries were, in rank order, motor vehicles, construction, iron and steel and other metal manufacture and port and inland water transport. Between them these four accounted for a further 37 per cent of the total. The same industries had also headed the list in 1960–8, with 54 per cent of the total, but at that

Table 5.3 *Annual net strike activity by industry, 1969–73*

Industry groups	No. of strikes	No. of workers involved (000s)	Workers involved as a percentage of employees in employment	No. of working days lost (000s)	Working days lost per 1000 employees in employment
Agriculture, forestry, etc.	3.8	0.9	0.23	19.4	47.6
Mining and quarrying *	4.8	0.4	0.73	1.4	18.2
Grain milling	3.8	0.8	2.55	2.6	96.8
Bread, flour, etc.	10.2	6.9	3.54	54.6	282.0
Other food	48.8	16.1	3.89	108.4	261.5
Drink	39.4	9.6	6.60	52.6	365.5
Tobacco	1.0	3.0	6.88	5.2	113.3
Chemicals	61.0	19.8	3.91	92.6	183.8
Iron, steel and other metals	222.6	84.3	15.24	540.4	976.5
Non-electrical engineering	415.4	114.9	9.13	865.6	687.8
Electrical engineering	194.8	106.8	12.36	771.8	893.5
Shipbuilding and marine engineering	84.8	42.3	21.75	445.8	2299.0
(V1) Motor vehicles	273.4	315.5	57.77	1855.6	3399.3
(V2) Aerospace equipment	57.4	38.4	17.31	357.8	1612.6
(V3) All other vehicles†	29.0	17.3	36.19	111.2	2312.5
Other metal goods	133.4	25.5	4.22	202.0	334.4
Textiles	79.2	21.6	3.27	149.2	225.4
Clothing	22.6	11.6	2.99	57.0	146.9
Footwear	5.4	1.5	1.56	6.0	62.5
Bricks, pottery, etc.	56.8	14.5	4.46	139.0	427.7
Furniture, wood and cork manufacture	36.2	5.1	1.73	34.4	114.9
Paper and board, cartons, etc.	30.4	6.7	2.99	35.2	156.2
Printing and publishing	21.0	11.6	2.96	55.4	140.3
Other manufacturing industries	74.4	36.9	9.17	250.6	624.4
Construction	263.4	74.0	5.42	1167.8	855.0
Gas, water, electricity	16.6	10.5	2.80	74.8	200.5
Railways	11.0	13.3	5.32	27.4	108.0
Road passenger transport	47.0	26.9	11.38	111.4	470.3
Road haulage	85.0	8.8	3.49	52.4	206.3
Sea transport	4.8	0.9	1.08	3.0	36.1
Port and inland water transport	212.4	143.8	143.50	450.2	4500.0
Other transport and communications	25.4	89.3	13.89	1325.0	2060.6
Distribution	52.8	5.3	0.20	23.6	8.9
Insurance, banking, finance	3.8	3.4	0.35	55.8	57.1
Professional and scientific	22.8	85.0	2.82	192.6	64.1
Miscellaneous	25.4	3.7	0.19	21.0	10.7
Public administration and defence	46.6	69.7	4.68	302.4	203.0
All industries*	2722.8	1 446.5	6.51	9880.6	444.5

* Excludes coal mining.
† Cycles were included in this group from 1970 onwards, prior to 1970 they were included with motor vehicles.

time the rank order was different, construction and non-electrical engineering having exchanged places. Each of these five industries averaged more than 200 stoppages a year. Of the remaining thirty-two industries two averaged more than 100 stoppages a year, eight more than fifty, fifteen more than ten, and seven less than ten.

But it must be remembered that assessing industrial strike propensity by number of stoppages tends to give undue weight to large industries with fragmented bargaining structures. An alternative measure is the number of workers involved per industry, adjusted for the number of employees in employment. On this basis the five most strike-prone industries were, in rank order: port and inland water transport, motor vehicles, all other vehicles, shipbuilding and aerospace equipment. In the top three of these over a quarter of the workforce was involved in stoppages. In port and inland water transport the level of worker involvement was over 100 per cent, because of multiple strike acts within each year. This serves to emphasise the point which we made in Chapter 1 that levels of worker involvement provide maximum estimates of the degree of individual worker involvement. In the event of multiple strike acts within the period of measurement the degree of individual involvement will be exaggerated. Of the thirty-seven industries shown in Table 5.3, five averaged less than 1 per cent of their employees involved in stoppages, seventeen had between 1 and 5 per cent involved, six had between 5 and 10 per cent, and nine had more than 10 per cent. Compared with 1960–8 these results showed a significant upward movement, particularly among the less strike-prone industries. The number with less than 1 per cent involved in stoppages fell from fourteen to five.

Another measure of industrial strike-proneness is the number of days lost in relation to the number of employees in employment in each industry. On this measure the most strike-prone industries were port and inland water transport, motor vehicles, all other vehicles, shipbuilding and other transport and communication. This list is identical to that for workers involved except that aerospace equipment was displaced by other transport and communication. In eleven industries time lost averaged less than an hour per employee per year; in a further nineteen industries losses were between one hour and one day; in the remaining seven industries losses exceeded a day per employee per year but in no case exceeded one week. It is in this respect that the increase in strike activity in this period is most apparent. The number of industries where losses were less than one hour fell from twenty-three to eleven while the number where losses exceeded one day rose from four to seven between 1960–8 and 1969–73.

STRIKE-PRONE AND NON-STRIKE-PRONE GROUPS

Table 5.4 provides a useful counterpart to this analysis by setting out the contribution to the total of strike activity by the eight most – and least – strike-prone industries. It can be seen that the eight most strike-prone

Table 5.4   *Industry groups' relative shares of net totals of strike activity,
1969–73*

Industry groups	Percentage share of no. of strikes	Percentage share of no. of workers involved	Percentage share of no. of working days lost
High strike activity industries			
Motor vehicles	10.0	21.8	18.8
Port and inland water transport	7.8	9.9	4.6
Electrical engineering	7.2	7.4	7.8
Other transport and communications	0.9	6.2	13.4
Iron and steel and other metal manufacture	8.2	5.8	5.5
Shipbuilding and marine engineering	3.1	2.9	4.5
Aerospace equipment	2.1	2.7	3.6
Other vehicles	1.1	1.2	1.1
Total share of high groups	40.4	57.9	59.3
Low strike activity industries			
Distribution	1.9	0.4	0.2
Furniture, bedding, wood and cork manufacture	1.3	0.4	0.3
Miscellaneous	0.9	0.3	0.2
Insurance, banking and finance	0.1	0.2	0.6
Footwear	0.2	0.1	0.1
Sea transport	0.2	0.1	Ø
Agriculture, forestry and fishing	0.1	0.1	0.2
Mining and quarrying (exc. coal mining)	0.2	Ø	Ø
Total share of low groups	5.0	1.6	1.6

Note: Ø is less than 0.05%

industries accounted for 40 per cent of stoppages, 58 per cent of workers involved, 59 per cent of working days lost and 14 per cent of all employees in employment. Alternatively some 86 per cent of employees accounted for 60 per cent of all stoppages, 42 per cent of workers involved and 41 per cent of working days lost. Six out of these eight industries were also among the most strike-prone in 1960–8. (Non-electrical engineering and railways locos, etc., being replaced by other transport and communications and all other vehicles). Comparing the percentage contribution of the eight most strike-prone industries to the position of comparable industries in 1960–8 reveals a sharp fall in the concentration of strike activity. The proportion of stoppages fell from 53 to 40 per cent, that of workers involved from 79 to 58 per cent and that of working days lost from 71 to 59 per cent. In the earlier period workers in the strike-prone industries were sixteen times more likely to be involved in stoppages than employees in other industries. In 1969–73 they were only eight times more likely to be so involved.

In 1969–73 the eight least strike-prone industries contributed 5 per cent of all stoppages, 1.6 per cent of workers involved and working days lost and 28 per cent of all employees in employment. Employees in these industries were seventy time less likely to be involved in stoppages than their fellows in the most strike-prone industries. Yet only four of these industries were among the least strike prone in 1960–8 – i.e. distribution, miscellaneous services, insurance, banking and finance and agriculture, forestry and fishing. The contribution made to the totals of strike activity by the least strike-prone industries was slightly down for each of the three basic measures. The percentage share of stoppages fell from 5.5 to 5.0 per cent, the share of workers involved from 1.7 to 1.6 per cent and that of working days lost from 2.6 to 1.6 per cent. Most of these changes are quite slight and are not surprising when one takes into account the fact that the share of total employment covered by this group fell from 46 to 28 per cent between two periods.

But the twenty-one industries which do not warrant inclusion in either of these lists, who cover 58 per cent of workers in employment, also increased their share of strike activity. In comparison to the previous period their share of strikes rose from 42 to 55 per cent, while their share of workers involved increased from 19 to 41 per cent and their share of working days lost rose from 27 to 58 per cent.

Measured by reference to the average number of workers involved per stoppage, strikes in this middle range were only half the size of those in the most strike-prone industries but twice the size of those in the least strike-prone industries. Average duration, as measured by number of days lost per worker involved, was roughly similar across all three groups. These measures indicate a levelling out of strike activity in comparison to the previous period where the differences in size and duration between the groups of industries were much more marked.

Overall this analysis confirms the trend we noticed in the previous period, of strike activity becoming less concentrated and more evenly distributed across the economy even though enormous disparities in strike propensities continued to exist.

DIRECTION OF CHANGE OF STRIKE ACTIVITY BY INDUSTRY

Table 5.5 shows the direction of change of strike activity in each industry for each of the basic measures between 1969 and 1973.

Table 5.5   *Direction of change of net strike activity in each industry, 1969–73*

	No. of industries experiencing change in no. of stoppages	*No. of industries experiencing change in no. of workers involved*	*No. of industries experiencing change in no. of working days lost*
Increase in activity	17	18	23
Decrease in activity	19	19	14

As was noted above, 1969–73 lacked the clear-cut and consistent trends of our earlier periods. Detailed evidence on this point is presented in Table 5.5. This shows that just over half of the thirty-seven industries experienced decreases in the number of stoppages and workers involved, while over 60 per cent experienced an increase in days lost. This matches findings in Table 5.1, that in 1973 the net totals of stoppages and workers involved were lower than they had been in 1969.

Table 5.5 may appear to pose major difficulties of explanation, in that almost equal numbers of industries have quite different strike patterns. In fact the dichotomy is not all that sharp, since virtually all industries experienced a fall in the number of stoppages after 1970. A substantial majority experienced increases between 1971 and 1973, but these increases were not sufficient in all cases to exceed the levels established in 1969. Table 5.5 also reflects the variety of conflicting pressures which occurred at different times in this period and which produced different effects in different industries.

GROSS STRIKE ACTIVITY BY CAUSE

As usual at this stage in the analysis we turn from consideration of net totals to gross totals because of the difficulties of excluding coal mining stoppages. We begin by examining the distribution of gross strike activity by cause in terms of wage and non-wage issues.

Table 5.6 *Gross strike activity by cause, 1969–73*

Year	Wage issues						Non-wage issues		
	No. of strikes	Percentage of total	No. of workers involved (000s)	Percentage of total	No. of working days lost (000s)	Percentage of total	No. of strikes	No. of workers involved (000s)	No. of working days lost (000s)
1969	1782	57.2	810	56.8	4 506	65.1	1334	617	2419
1970	2465	63.1	1033	70.7	9 237	84.7	1441	427	1671
1971	1155	51.8	594	68.7	12 286	90.4	1073	270	1303
1972	1477	59.2	1010	69.7	21 661	90.5	1020	440	2262
1973	1462	50.9	749	67.9	5 147	72.0	1411	354	1998
Average	1668	57.0	839	66.6	10 567	84.6	1256	422	1931

It can be seen that on average, in the years 1969–73, wages issues accounted for 57 per cent of all stoppages, 67 per cent of workers involved and 85 per cent of days lost. Within this period wages issues, measured both in absolute terms and as a percentage of the total, had peaks of stoppages and workers involved in 1970 and 1972. The level of worker involvement was virtually identical in both years at just over one million, while the number of stoppages fell from 2465 in 1970 to 1477 in 1972. The peak year for working days lost was 1972, both in absolute and relative terms, when nearly twenty-two million days were lost.

The difference between 1970 and 1972 mirrors the complexity of this period and the forces which were at work within it. The years 1970 and 1969 have a parallel in 1951. In all three years the Labour government's incomes policy was in the process of collapsing. Its operation had led to widely perceived anomalies, which groups of workers sought to resolve through larger pay increases, if necessary backed by strike action. At the same time the 1967 devaluation, like the 1949 devaluation, was contributing to domestic inflation. These forces, operating in a much enlarged context of shop-floor bargaining, gave rise to a whole host of disputes. Yet as in 1951 the process of adjustment was quite short. In early 1970 the rate of increase in the number of stoppages was already slackening and in the second half of the year the number of stoppages was falling significantly. The mechanics of this adjustment process are far from clear but two factors may be guessed at. First, in so far as stoppages succeed in achieving workers' aims, and providing that they do not provoke a further series of claims, then the cause of the increase in strikes will be removed. It is arguable that this was the case during 1970. Secondly, the cost of stoppages, as measured by average duration, rose sharply in this period. The longer stoppages last the more costly they are likely to become for the parties involved; yet the average number of days lost for each worker directly involved in wage stoppages rose from 5.6 in 1969 to 8.9 in 1970 and 20.6 in 1971.

Unlike 1952 the incoming Conservative administration did not seize this opportunity to reach some sort of understanding with the unions on wages policy in 1970. Instead they sought to impose their own form of incomes restraint, the 'n − 1' policy, and accepted increased industrial conflict as a consequence. At the same time they sought (through legislation) to restrict the right to strike. The aims and consequences of that legislation, and of this form of incomes policy, are explored more fully in Chapter 11. At this stage it is sufficient to note that the government's policies appear to have facilitated some kind of 'understanding' between the workers' representatives in both the formal and informal bargaining systems. This understanding allowed them to combine and eventually defeat the government's aims. One manifestation of the understanding was that the average number of workers involved in wage stoppages rose by over 60 per cent between 1970 and 1972, as action was taken on a wider basis in order to meet the government's challenge.

Although the character of the years 1969–73 is dominated by wages stoppages we should not overlook strikes over non-wage issues; 1969–73 was the first period when non-wage issues had not been the cause of the majority of stoppages. In 1969–73 the average number of such stoppages was 1256, in 1960–8 it was 1232, and in 1953–9 it was 1253. Yet this constancy in the number of non-wage stoppages was accompanied by a steady growth in the average number of workers involved, but this may simply have been another reflection of the decline in the frequency of coal mining stoppages. On this supposition it seems that if we wish to explain changes in the number of stoppages our explanation should relate primarily to wage stoppages. If we wish to explain the overall frequency of stoppages our explanation must account for the apparent constancy in the number of non-wage stoppages as well.

Table 5.6a gives details of the distribution of strike activity by cause for eleven broad industry groups. (In 1960–8 only eight industry groups had been distinguished in this table.)

Table 5.6a   *Industrial strike activity by cause, 1969–73*

Industry group	Wage issues as a percentage of total in each industry			Annual average of strike activity in each industry		
	No. of strikes (%)	No. of workers involved (%)	No. of working days lost (%)	No. of strikes	No. of workers involved (000s)	No. of working days lost (000s)
Mining and quarrying	24.8	66.4	90.6	206	131.5	2 617
Metals	65.2	58.9	75.4	356	74.7	743
Engineering	64.8	61.0	80.3	610	176.6	1 641
Shipbuilding and marine engineering	62.7	72.1	91.6	85	31.1	444
Motor vehicles	55.0	58.1	81.0	273	158.2	1 853
Other vehicles	64.4	62.6	84.5	87	45.0	471
Textiles and clothing	65.0	68.4	80.0	106	26.9	212
All other manufacturing industries	58.6	65.3	73.1	384	105.0	830
Construction	48.7	63.9	87.4	263	69.7	1 028
Transport and communication	55.4	60.7	86.0	386	268.0	1 968
All other non-manufacturing industries	56.6	94.1	93.5	172	174.0	690
Total	57.0	66.6	84.6	2 924	1 261.0	12 498

It can be seen that all industry groups, with the exception of mining and quarrying and construction, had between 55 and 65 per cent of their stoppages over pay issues. In mining and quarrying less than a quarter of stoppages were over pay, which is probably a reflection of the dominant role of coal mining within that sector and of the effectiveness of that industry's industry-wide wage negotiations. These effectively excluded local bargaining over pay in the years 1969–73. The share of workers directly involved in stoppages lay within the range 58–72 per cent for all industry groups with the exception of the all other non-manufacturing industries and services sector which covered many public sector employees. Employees in this sector, like those in coal mining, tend to be covered by centralised bargaining arrangements. This means that pay disputes, when they occur, tend to encompass large sections of the industry's workforce in contrast to the more fragmented bargaining systems of the private sector. The share of working days lost attributable to wage stoppages was subject to considerable inter-industry variation, ranging from 73 per cent in all other manufacturing to 94 per cent in all other non-manufacturing. In eight out of the eleven industry groups wage stoppages were larger than non-wage stoppages. In ten out of the eleven wage stoppages were more prolonged than non-wage stoppages.

GROSS STRIKE ACTIVITY BY REGION

The regional distribution of gross strike activity is presented in Table 5.7. In the absence of any further major changes of regional boundaries we have been able to provide rather more detailed information than in the corresponding table of the previous chapter.

Overall the rate of worker involvement in strike action was 7 per cent of employees in employment. Between individual regions the rate varied from 3.1 per cent in East Anglia to 11.5 per cent in the West Midlands. Using worker involvement in relation to employment as a measure of strike proneness indicates that the most strike-prone regions, in order, were the West Midlands, Wales, the North West and Scotland. The least strike-prone regions were the South East and East Anglia. Scotland and Wales had been the most strike-prone regions in 1960–8 while the South East, including East Anglia, had been the least strike-prone. In the previous period there was some evidence that strike activity was becoming more evenly distributed across regions. Any such tendency disappeared in this period. In 1960–8 workers in the most strike-prone region were three times more likely to be involved in stoppages than those in the least strike-prone. In 1969–73 they were four times more likely to be involved, which indicates that the increase in strike activity had been greater in the more strike-prone regions than in the less strike-prone.

Using working days lost per 1000 employees as a measure of strike-proneness produces a different ranking. The most strike-prone regions, in order, were Wales, the North, Scotland and the West Midlands. The North West has been replaced by the North and Wales has taken over from the West Midlands as the most strike-prone region. The least strike-prone regions continued to be the South East and East Anglia. Average time lost

Table 5.7 Regional distribution of strike activity as measured by workers involved and working days lost in relation to employees in employment, 1969–73

Region	Percentage of employees in employment	Average no. of workers involved (000s)	Workers involved as a percentage of employees in employment	Average no. of working days lost (000s)	Working days lost per 1000 employees in employment
South East	33.4	273	3.6	1 925	255
East Anglia	2.8	19	3.1	206	328
South West	5.9	62	4.6	420	315
West Midlands	9.9	257	11.5	1 627	729
East Midlands	6.1	64	4.6	767	555
Yorkshire and Humberside	8.6	170	8.8	1 441	743
North West	12.3	290	10.4	2 100	755
North	5.6	115	9.2	1 175	938
Wales	4.3	104	10.8	949	986
Scotland	9.0	215	10.0	1 717	840
Northern Ireland	2.1	24	5.1	169	354
United Kingdom	100.0	1581	7.0	12 497	554

per employee in the South East was just over two hours, in Wales it was just less than one day. There seemed to be some tendency for the most strike-prone regions to have shorter stoppages than other regions but the association was not strong.

Northern Ireland, which in 1955–9 was among the more strike-prone regions, slipped steadily down the rankings thereafter. This process was accentuated in 1969–73, when the actual number of workers involved fell at a time when all other regions were experiencing increases. Various hypotheses might be offered to explain this development, including some reference to the other forms of social and political conflict manifest in the province during these years. But a much more detailed study would be required before any firm conclusions could be drawn.

DIMENSIONS OF GROSS STRIKE ACTIVITY: DURATION, EXTENT AND SIZE

We have already noted that the massive increase in the total of days lost was largely a product of an increase in the duration of stoppages; detailed information on duration is set out in Table 5.8. Of the 14 620 stoppages which occurred between 1969 and 1973, 53.6 per cent were over within three days, 73.2 per cent in six days and 89.4 per cent in twenty-four days. Although the majority of stoppages remained short, they were not as short as they had been. In 1960–8 some 71 per cent of stoppages were over within three days and 80 per cent were over within six.

Table 5.8   *Distribution of gross strike activity by duration of stoppages, 1969–73*

Duration in working days	No. of strikes	Percent-age of total	No. of workers involved (000s)	Percent-age of total	No. of working days lost (000s)	Percent-age of total
Not more than 1	3 502	24.0	1941	24.7	1 657	2.7
Over 1, not more than 2	2 492	17.0	1018	12.9	1 463	2.3
Over 2, not more than 3	1 841	12.6	653	8.3	1 483	2.4
Over 3, not more than 4	1 187	8.1	447	5.7	1 462	2.3
Over 4, not more than 5	1 040	7.1	427	5.4	1 662	2.7
Over 5, not more than 6	636	4.4	230	2.9	1 082	1.7
Over 6, not more than 12	1 897	13.0	761	9.7	5 120	8.2
Over 12, not more than 18	754	5.2	407	5.2	4 988	8.0
Over 18, not more than 24	403	2.8	454	5.8	5 448	8.7
Over 24, not more than 36	423	2.9	833	10.6	17 916	28.7
Over 36, not more than 60	291	2.0	418	5.3	13 688	21.9
Over 60	154	1.0	272	3.5	6 518	10.4
Total	14 620	100.0	7863	100.0	62 490	100.0

The decline in the percentage of short stoppages was most noticeable among those lasting one day or less, although those lasting between one and two days also declined in relative frequency. The percentage share of every duration category over three days increased, with many of the longer durations doubling their shares. This would seem to support the contention that the increase in duration in this period was a result of a change affecting many stoppages rather than just a few.

This conclusion is supported by the distributions of workers involved and days lost, both of which show marked shifts towards longer stoppages. Compared with 1960–8 the share of workers involved in stoppages lasting more than twenty-four days rose from 2.3 to 19.4 per cent and the share of days lost from 21 to 61 per cent.

Changes in the extent of strike activity are portrayed in Table 5.9.

Table 5.9   *Distribution of gross strike activity by number of workers involved, 1969–73*

No. of workers involved	No. of strikes	Percentage of total	No. of workers involved (000s)	Percentage of total	No. of working days lost (000s)	Percentage of total
Under 25	2 115	14.5	35	0.5	289	0.5
25 and under 50	2 256	15.4	80	1.0	519	0.8
50 and under 100	2 545	17.4	178	2.3	1 099	1.8
100 and under 250	3 231	22.1	509	6.5	2 705	4.3
250 and under 500	1 909	13.1	652	8.3	3 404	5.4
500 and under 1000	1 273	8.7	858	10.9	4 521	7.2
1000 and under 2500	842	5.8	1253	15.9	7 101	11.4
2500 and under 5000	259	1.8	883	11.2	5 338	8.5
5000 and under 10 000	128	0.9	893	11.4	5 930	9.5
10 000 and over	62	0.4	2522	32.1	31 584	50.5
Total	14 620	100.0	7863	100.0	62 490	100.0

Stoppages involving fewer than 100 workers accounted for 47.3 per cent of the total, for 3.8 per cent of workers involved and for 3.1 per cent of days lost. Stoppages involving less than 250 workers accounted for 69.4 per cent of the total, 10.3 per cent of workers involved and 7.4 per cent of days lost. At the other end of the scale stoppages involving 10 000 workers or more amounted to only 0.4 per cent but had 32 per cent of workers involved and 51 per cent of days lost.

Contrasting these findings with those for 1960–8 discloses a very sharp decline in the relative frequency of stoppages involving fewer than twenty-five workers – i.e. from 23.7 to 14.5 per cent. There is also a lesser decline in the relative frequency of those involving less than fifty workers. The shares of all other categories rose. This implies a substantial shift away from smaller stoppages. In fact, stoppages involving 2500 workers or more almost doubled their share of total stoppages.

Finally, in the previous period we noted an inverse relationship between extent and average duration. That relationship was not fully maintained in 1969–73. It remained true among small stoppages – i.e. those involving fewer than 500 workers. But among larger stoppages duration increased with the extent of the stoppage.

Table 5.10 provides details of the distribution of gross strike activity by number of days lost per stoppage.

Table 5.10   *Distribution of gross strike activity by number of working days lost, 1969–73*

No. of working days lost	No. of strikes	Percent-age of total	No. of workers involved (000s)	Percent-age of total	No. of working days lost (000s)	Percent-age of total
Under 250 days	6 301	43.1	448	5.7	665	1.1
250 and under 500 days	2 414	16.5	440	5.6	851	1.4
500 and under 1000	2 044	14.0	586	7.5	1 430	2.3
1000 and under 5000	2 735	18.7	1742	22.2	5 839	9.3
5000 and under 25 000	883	6.0	1755	22.3	8 882	14.2
25 000 and under 50 000	115	0.8	496	6.3	4 271	6.8
50 000 and over	128	0.9	2395	30.5	40 554	64.9
Total	14 620	100.0	7863	100.0	62 490	100.0

Of the 14 620 stoppages which occurred between 1969 and 1973 some 6301, or 43 per cent of the total, involved the loss of less than 250 working days. Some 8715 stoppages, or 60 per cent of the total, involved the loss of less than 500 working days. They also accounted for 11.3 per cent of workers involved and 2.5 per cent of days lost. There were only 128 stoppages involving the loss of 50 000 working days or more. These accounted for less than 1 per cent of stoppages, 31 per cent of workers involved and 65 per cent of days lost. Comparison with 1960–8 showed that stoppages involving the loss of less than 250 working days had declined from 61 to 43 per cent of the total. The relative frequency of all other stoppages rose, with increases being greatest for the largest stoppages.

As in 1960–8 this analysis of gross strike activity indicates that stoppages were becoming larger and longer, even though the majority remained quite small and short. In the previous period we pointed out that this change might reflect the changing industrial composition of the gross total of stoppages or it might reflect a 'real' shift in the size of UK stoppages. The change in the industrial composition of stoppages was largely occasioned by the fall in the incidence of coal mining stoppages. In 1953–9 coal mining accounted for 74 per cent of the gross total; in 1960–8 its share fell to 39 per cent; in 1969–73 it was down again to 7 per cent. As coal mining stoppages tend to be smaller and shorter than those in other industries their decline tended to raise the average size. In 1960–8 we concluded that the changing industrial composition was in fact the major cause of the change because we also observed that major stoppages declined in relative frequency and that the major stoppages which did occur tended to be smaller and shorter than previously. Consequently, we cannot pass judgement on the further changes which took place in 1969–73 until we have considered the major stoppages data. However, it should be noted that the tendency to larger, longer stoppages is much more marked in this period, which makes it unlikely that the decline in the frequency of coal mining stoppages can provide a complete explanation.

NET STRIKE ACTIVITY KNOWN TO BE OFFICIAL

The final aspect of strike activity for which published data was available was that relating to stoppages known to be official. The absolute totals of known official strikes outside coal mining and their contribution to the net totals are shown in Table 5.11. On average there were 142 stoppages a year

Table 5.11 *Net strike activity known to be official in relation to the net totals of strike activity, 1969–73*

Year	No. of strikes	Strike activity known to be official				
		As a percentage of all strikes	No. of workers involved (000s)	As a percentage of all workers involved	No. of working days lost (000s)	As a percentage of all working days lost
1969	98	3.3	283	18.6	1 613	27.8
1970	162	4.3	296	17.6	3 320	33.6
1971	161	7.7	376	32.5	10 050	74.5
1972	159	7.0	326	23.4	7 502	57.2
1973	132	5.1	396	26.7	2 009	28.3
Average	142	5.2	335	23.2	4 899	49.6

which were known to be official involving 335 000 workers and resulting in the loss of 4 899 000 days. The number of stoppages rose sharply in 1970, remained at this level for a further two years and then declined. The number of workers involved rose sharply from 1969 to 1971, fell in 1972 and then rose again in 1973. The number of working days lost increased rapidly up to 1971 and then decreased almost as rapidly until 1973.

In relation to the net totals of strike activity, stoppages known to be official accounted, on average, for 5.2 per cent of stoppages, 23 per cent of workers involved and 50 per cent of working days lost. On all three measures strikes known to be official reached a peak in 1971 and then declined, although there was a secondary peak in terms of workers involved in 1973.

Comparing the average absolute levels of strikes known to be official in 1969–73 with those of 1960–8 reveals an 87 per cent increase in the number of stoppages, a 49 per cent decrease in number of workers involved and a 300 per cent increase in the number of days lost. The decrease in workers involved may seem surprising until it is recalled that in the previous period there were three national engineering stoppages which involved five million workers. There was no counterpart to these in 1969–73. In relation to the net totals of stoppages there was no change in relative frequency of stoppages known to be official. They accounted for 5.2 per cent of the total in both periods. In terms of workers involved their share fell from 55 to 23 per cent while for days lost the share rose from 43 to 50 per cent. In the previous period strikes known to be official had declined relative to other stoppages. In this period they increased sharply in relation to other stoppages up to 1971 and then declined. On average strikes known to be official were more than five times as large and three times as long as other stoppages.

Finally, the consequences of excluding coal mining stoppages from our series of known to be official stoppages should be noted. In 1960–8 this policy made little difference as there was only one official stoppage in coal mining which involved a one day stoppage of 42 000 workers. In 1969–73 only one stoppage was excluded but that involved 309 000 workers and the loss of almost eleven million days in 1972. If that stoppage had been included, it would have made 1972 the peak year for official action in terms of workers involved and days lost, and thereby contributed substantially to the impression of confrontation which characterises this period. The origins of this stoppage are further discussed in Chapter 8 and its national consequences are explored in Chapter 11.

In the previous chapter we examined the proportion of days lost attributable to official stoppages in several broad industry groups, similar information in respect of 1969–73 is shown in Table 5.11a.

Once again the most obvious feature of this table is that strike action in mining and quarrying rarely receives official sanction, although the stoppage that had official backing involved the whole of the coal mining industry's manual workforce and lasted seven weeks. As a result it accounted for more than four-fifths of total time lost by that sector over five years. Industry-wide official stoppages also played a major role in several other industrial sectors. In the transport and communication section two national docks disputes and the postal workers' stoppage accounted for 96 per cent of the time lost in the sector. The widespread official action by building workers in 1972 accounted for three-quarters of all time lost in construction over five years.

Table 5.11a   *Industrial strike activity known to be official in relation to all strike activity as measured by working days lost, 1969–73*

Year	Mining and quarrying (%)	Metals, engineering, shipbuilding, vehicles (%)	Textiles, clothing and footwear (%)	Construction (%)	Transport and communications (%)	All other industries and services (%)
1969	–	32.9	5.0	4.3	11.5	31.8
1970	–	12.9	15.1	4.1	44.9	60.9
1971	–	58.9	14.1	8.2	95.5	38.4
1972	99.3	40.0	47.1	91.7	65.8	26.5
1973	–	19.2	42.5	8.5	30.8	55.2
Average	81.9	34.7	26.9	75.9	77.2	49.5

Only two sectors, metals and textiles, showed a decline in the relative importance of officially sanctioned stoppages compared with the previous period – i.e. from 48 to 35 per cent and from 30 to 27 per cent respectively. In the metal trades the absence of official industry-wide stoppages was a significant contributory factor in this decline. In the textile trades officially sanctioned action was low in 1969–71, but it rose sharply in the last two years of the period. Of the total time lost through official stoppages mining and quarrying accounted for 31 per cent, metal trades for 25 per cent, transport and communication for 22 per cent, construction for 11 per cent, all other industries and services for 11 per cent and textiles for 1 per cent.

COAL MINING

In the previous period we remarked that coal mining had lost its pre-eminent position in the industry ranking in respect of workers involved and working days lost; but we also noted that it had retained its pre-eminence in the case of stoppages. In this period the situation altered again. The industry recaptured the premier position for days lost while improving its ranking in terms of workers involved and sliding sharply down in respect of stoppages.

Between 1969 and 1973 there were at least 1006 strikes in coal mining (indeed there may have been more as no information has been made available on stoppages for December 1973). These involved 674 000 workers and resulted in the loss of thirteen million working days. Five industries (i.e. non-electrical engineering, motor vehicles, construction, iron and steel and other metals and port and inland water transport) had more stoppages than coal mining. Two industries (motor vehicles and port

and inland water transport) had more workers involved. No industry had
more days lost.

The decline in the number of stoppages in coal mining, which had been
evident since 1957, continued until the first half of 1972. Then the trend
was reversed with the result that the number of stoppages rose by over 60
per cent between 1969 and 1973. The numbers of workers involved and
days lost fell, but that merely reflects the occurrence of a very large
unofficial stoppage in 1969 which had no parallel in 1973.

MAJOR STRIKES, 1969–73

NET TOTALS OF MAJOR STRIKES AND THEIR RELATIONSHIP TO NET TOTALS
OF ALL STOPPAGES

We have already demonstrated that stoppages in 1969–73 tended to be
larger and longer than those of the previous period. Some effect of those
changes is evidenced in Table 5.12.

Table 5.12   *Net totals of major strike activity in absolute terms in relation to
the net totals of all strike activity, 1969–73*

Year	No. of major strikes	As a percentage of all strikes	No. of workers involved (000s)	As a percentage of all workers involved (000s)	No. of working days lost (000s)	As a percentage of all working days lost (000s)
1969	181	6.2	729.0	48.0	4 238	73.0
1970	261	7.0	820.6	48.7	7 547	76.3
1971	171	8.2	713.8	61.8	12 297	91.2
1972	278	12.2	917.4	65.9	11 575	88.3
1973	225	8.7	924.4	62.4	5 323	74.9
Average	223	8.2	821.0	56.8	8 196	82.9

The number of major stoppages followed a most erratic pattern, rising
and falling in alternate years. The number of workers involved followed a
broadly similar pattern, although the magnitude of the fluctuations was
much less and the expected downturn did not materialise in the final year.
The number of working days lost followed a simpler pattern, almost
trebling between 1969 and 1971 and then falling by over half by 1973.
Averaging across these various fluctuations reveals that there were 223
major stoppages involving 821 000 workers and resulting in the loss of 8.2
million working days. In relation to the net totals of strike activity both
stoppages and workers involved reached a peak in 1972 and then fell.
Working days lost reached its relative peak in 1971 and declined thereafter.

Compared with the annual averages of major strike activity in 1960–8 the number of stoppages in 1969–73 rose by 150 a year, or just over 200 per cent. On average workers involved fell by 4000, although if national engineering stoppages are excluded from the previous period this decline is transformed into an increase of just over 552 000 a year – i.e. just over 200 per cent. Working days lost rose by just over six million days per year if engineering strikes are included, or 6.7 million if they are excluded. In relative terms these changes imply increases of 290 per cent and 430 per cent respectively. If comparisons are made of major strike activity relative to net totals, we find that major stoppages rose from 5 to 8.2 per cent in the later period, while workers involved fell from 69 to 57 per cent and days lost rose from 73 to 83 per cent. Once again, if the national engineering stoppages are excluded, the workers involved measure shows an increase rather than a decrease.

In the previous chapter, in our examination of the gross totals of strike activity distributed by duration, extent and size, we observed a tendency for stoppages to become larger and longer. Because this tendency was not reflected in an increase in the relative frequency of major stoppages, we were inclined to dismiss it as a product of the decline in coal mining strikes. In this chapter we again observed a tendency for stoppages to become larger and longer, but in this instance there was also an increase in the relative frequency of major stoppages. This suggests that the change in the size of strikes was due to factors other than the continued decline in the frequency of coal mining disputes.

NET MAJOR STRIKES IN PERSPECTIVE

Some measures of the significance of the massive increase in major strike activity of 1969–73 are shown in Table 5.13.

Table 5.13　*Net major strike activity in perspective, 1969–73*

Year	Workers involved as a percentage of employees in employment	Workers involved as a percentage of trade union members	Working days lost as a percentage of potential working time	Working days lost as a percentage of time lost through unemployment
1969	3.2	7.2	0.08	3.0
1970	3.6	7.6	0.14	5.1
1971	3.3	6.6	0.23	6.4
1972	4.2	8.3	0.22	5.4
1973	4.1	8.2	0.10	3.5
Average	3.7	7.6	0.15	4.8

Over the period as a whole 3.7 per cent of employees, or 7.6 per cent of trade union members, were involved in major stoppages each year. This resulted in the loss of 0.15 per cent of potential working time, or 4.8 per cent of the time lost through unemployment. On a year by year basis the rate of employee involvement fluctuated between 3.2 and 4.2 per cent; involvement of trade union members ranged from 6.6 to 8.3 per cent. Working days lost, which experienced the largest increase of the three basic measures both within this period and relative to the previous period, increased from 0.08 to 0.23 per cent of potential working time between 1969 and 1971. In relation to time lost through unemployment this was equivalent to an increase from 3 to 6.4 per cent.

Compared with the previous period the rate of worker involvement in major stoppages in 1969–73 was the same, while the rate of trade union member involvement fell from 8.7 to 7.6 per cent. This comparison reflects the overwhelming effect of the national engineering stoppages in the previous period. It also reflects some of the problems we faced in trying to decide whether or not to exclude particular stoppages or industries from our analysis. If we exclude them we risk being accused of not taking all the facts into account. If we include them we risk being accused of drawing inappropriate comparisons because of differences in the nature of the strikes under consideration. If the national engineering stoppages are excluded from the previous period's figures then the rate of worker involvement falls to 1.2 per cent and that of trade union members to 2.8 per cent. On the basis of these revised figures there was a very substantial increase in worker involvement in major stoppages in 1969–73.

But it must also be noted that on the basis of these revised figures 1960–8 was much less strike prone than 1953–9, contrary to the analysis of the last chapter. Time lost through major strikes in relation to potential working time showed almost a fourfold increase between the two periods. In relation to time lost through unemployment the increase was only 2.5-fold because the level of unemployment itself rose very substantially.

Major strike activity rose very sharply in both absolute and relative terms during this period but even at its peak it remained of little consequence in terms of the total level of economic activity. Indeed in relation to time lost through unemployment major strike activity was of less consequence in 1971 than it had been in 1957. On these grounds we might well wonder why the increase in strike activity between those years attracted quite so much attention in contrast to the greater rise in the level of unemployment.

NET MAJOR STRIKE ACTIVITY BY INDUSTRY

Between 1969 and 1973 there were 1116 major stoppages in the UK, an increase of 70 per cent over the total in the previous nine year period. The industrial distribution of those stoppages is shown in Table 5.14. Of the forty industries and industry groups listed in Table 5.14 twenty-five had an increase in their total of stoppages between the two periods, eight had a

Table 5.14 *Number of net major strikes by industry group, 1969–73*

Industry group	No. of strikes	As a percentage of all major strikes
Agriculture, forestry, fishing	2	0.2
Mining and quarrying (exc. coal mining)	–	–
Grain milling	–	–
Bread, flour, confectionery	6	0.5
Other food	24	2.2
Drink	11	1.0
Tobacco	2	0.2
Chemicals	22	2.0
Iron and steel and other metals	90	8.1
Non-electrical engineering	153	13.7
Electrical engineering	131	11.7
Shipbuilding	44	3.9
Motor vehicles	247	22.1
Aircraft	48	4.3
Cycles	5	0.4
Railway locos, carriages, trams, etc.	2	0.2
Carts, perambulators, etc.	–	–
Other metal goods	53	4.7
Textiles	26	2.3
Clothing	6	0.5
Footwear	–	–
Bricks, pottery, glass, cement, etc.	10	0.9
Furniture, bedding, wood and cork manufacture	8	0.7
Paper, board, cartons	6	0.5
Printing and publishing	7	0.6
Other manufacturing industries	33	3.0
Construction	50	4.5
Gas, water, electricity supply	4	0.4
Railways	5	0.4
Road passenger transport	18	1.6
Road haulage	5	0.4
Sea transport	1	0.1
Port and inland water transport	56	5.0
Other transport and communications	12	1.1
Distribution	3	0.3
Insurance, banking, finance, business	1	0.1
Professional and scientific	11	1.0
Miscellaneous	5	0.4
Public administration and defence	9	0.8
General engineering	–	–
Total (exc. coal mining)	1116	100.0

decrease and seven experienced no change. Of these seven, three were strike free in both periods. Eighteen industries had above average rates of increase in strike activity with those industries which had previously experienced very few stoppages having the highest rates of increase.

Of the five industries with the largest numbers of major strikes in 1960–8 three, motor vehicles, non-electrical engineering and electrical engineering, retained this status in 1969–73. The other two industries, shipbuilding and construction, were displaced by iron and steel and other metal manufacture and by port and inland water transport. In both periods the top five industries accounted for 61 per cent of major stoppages. Among the industries which experienced below average rates of increase were motor vehicles, construction and port and inland water transport. As all these industries featured prominently in the major strikes league in previous periods this might be taken as an indication that such action was becoming more evenly spread across industries. In fact that does not appear to be the case. We have already noted that the share of the total accruing to the five most strike-prone industries was the same in 1960–8 as in 1969–73, while the share of the ten most strike-prone industries fell from 82 to 81 per cent in the later period.

The distributions of major stoppages by numbers of workers involved and working days lost per stoppage by industry are shown in Tables 5.15 and 5.16.

Of the 1116 major stoppages which occurred between 1969 and 1973, 22 per cent involved less than 500 workers, 70 per cent involved fewer than 2500 and 95 per cent less than 10 000. Twenty-two stoppages, or 2 per cent of the total, involved as many as 25 000 workers. Compared with 1960–8 these results show a distinct shift towards smaller stoppages. The share of those involving less than 500 workers rose from 17.6 to 22.3 per cent, while those involving less than 2500 increased from 64.4 to 70.5 per cent. This increase was at the expense of the middle range of stoppages. The very largest stoppages also slightly increased their share of the total.

The industrial distribution of these stoppages reveals, as usual, that virtually all industries which experienced more than one major stoppage also experienced major stoppages of varying sizes. The smallest stoppages were spread across the metal trades and construction. In the previous period they had all occurred in the metal trades. Of the ten largest stoppages nine occurred in the public sector and one in construction. The predominance of public sector strikes in this group reflects both the centralised bargaining structures of these industries and the problems produced by the government's attempt to implement an incomes policy by 'standing firm' in the public sector. (This is discussed further in Chapter 11.) In general the metal trades tended to be over-represented in the middle range of strikes, i.e. those involving between 500 and 5000 workers, and under-represented at the two extremes of the distribution, particularly in respect of the very largest stoppages. In contrast, the services sector was under-represented in strikes involving between 500 and 2500 workers and over-represented among the largest stoppages. The remaining industries,

Table 5.15   *Cross-tabulation of net major strikes by industry group and number of workers involved, 1960–8*

Industry group	No. of workers involved									
	50 and under 100	100 and under 250	250 and under 500	500 and under 1000	1000 and under 2500	2500 and under 5000	5000 and under 10 000	10 000 and under 25 000	25 000 and under 50 000	50 000 and over
Agriculture, forestry, etc.					2					
Bread, etc.			2	1	1	2				
Other food			1	8	13	2				
Drink		1	1	3	5	1				
Tobacco		1						1		
Chemicals			4	6	8	2	2			
Iron and steel and other metals		6	23	19	23	8	8	3		
Non-electrical engineering	2	22	33	34	49	7	5	1		
Electrical engineering	1	7	18	33	43	21	7	1		
Shipbuilding			11	12	8	6	4	2	1	
Motor vehicles		5	12	24	74	64	53	12	3	
Aircraft	1	5	3	11	17	7	4			
Cycles			1	1	3					
Railway locos, carriages, etc.			1	1						
Other metal goods		6	16	21	10					
Textiles			5	7	11	1	2			
Clothing			1	1	2	1		1		
Bricks, etc.		1	2	1	3	1	1	1		
Furniture, etc.			1	4	1	2				
Paper, board			2	3	1					
Printing and publishing		1	1		2	1	1		1	
Other manufacturing industries		2	2	6	11	5	7			
Construction	5	7	20	6	7	2	1		1	1
Gas, water, electricity			1			1		1	1	
Railways		1		1	1			2		
Road passenger transport				7	2	7	1	1		
Road haulage		1		1	2		1			
Sea transport				1						
Port and inland water transport		1	5	6	16	8	12	5	3	
Other transport and communication			1		1	2	1	3	1	3
Distribution			2		1					
Insurance, etc.							1			
Professional, etc.			1			1	3	2	1	3
Miscellaneous		1	1	2		1				
Public administration		1	1			2	2			3
Total	9	70	170	220	318	153	119	35	12	10

Table 5.16 *Cross-tabulation of net major strikes by industry group and number of working days lost, 1969–73*

Industry group	No. of working days lost							
	5000 and under 10 000	10 000 and under 15 000	15 000 and under 20 000	20 000 and under 25 000	25 000 and under 50 000	50 000 and under 75 000	75 000 and under 100 000	100 000 and over
Agriculture, forestry, etc.					1	1		
Bread, etc.	3				2			1
Other food	10	5	4	2	2	1		
Drink	8	1	1			1		
Tobacco	1	1						
Chemicals	14	4	2		1	1		
Iron and steel and other metals	44	18	7	2	8	5	2	4
Non-electrical engineering	78	25	11	8	19	4	4	4
Electrical engineering	63	29	10	4	8	11	1	5
Shipbuilding	16	8	4	1	4	1	1	9
Motor vehicles	103	46	22	15	30	9	8	14
Aircraft	22	8	3	1	6	2	2	4
Cycles	5							
Railway locos, carriages, etc.		1	1					
Other metal goods	33	10	5	1	4			
Textiles	14	5	1	2	2		1	1
Clothing	1	3			1			1
Bricks, etc.	4	1	2		1	1		1
Furniture, etc.	4	2	1		1			
Paper, Board	3	1	2					
Printing and publishing	2	2			2			1
Other manufacturing industries	15	7	2	1	4	1		3
Construction	30	7	6		5			2
Gas, water, electricity	2		1					1
Railways	2		1	1	1			
Road passenger transport	10	2		2	1	1	2	
Road haulage	1	1	2			1		
Sea transport	1							
Port and inland water transport	26	14	4	6	4			2
Other transport and communication	3	1	1	1	3	1	1	1
Distribution	2	1						
Insurance, etc. Professional, etc.	3	1		1	2		2	2
Miscellaneous	3	1		1				
Public administration	4	1		1				3
Total	530	206	93	50	112	41	24	60

which were drawn from the manufacturing and primary sectors, were over-represented in stoppages involving between 500 and 2500 workers and under-represented elsewhere – especially in the smallest and largest categories. These results are similar to those for 1960–8.

From Table 5.16 we find that 48 per cent of major stoppages involved the loss of less than 10 000 working days, 66 per cent less than 15 000 and 79 per cent less than 25 000. Sixty strikes, or 5.4 per cent, involved the loss of at least 100 000 working days each. Compared with 1960–8 these results show a shift away from small stoppages (i.e. from 53.3 to 47.5 per cent) and an increase in the relative frequency of very large stoppages. Those involving the loss of at least 50 000 increased their share of the total from 7 to 11.2 per cent. This is in marked contrast to our findings on the numbers of workers involved in major stoppages which showed an increase in the proportion of smaller stoppages. It implies that the duration of major stoppages must have increased.

As in previous periods these stoppages were very widely spread across industries. We examined once again their distribution in the broad sectors of metal trades, services and others. We found that in stoppages involving the loss of less than 20 000 days the distribution was quite stable and close to each sector's share of the total. The metal trades were over-represented in stoppages involving the loss of between 50 000 and 100 000 days and services were over-represented among stoppages involving the loss of more than 75 000 days.

NET MAJOR STRIKES BY CAUSE

Earlier in this chapter we showed that pay issues had become a more common cause of stoppages in the gross totals of strike activity. In Table 5.17 we present the results of our analysis of the causes of major stoppages. In 1969–73 some 51.4 per cent of stoppages were over claims for wage increases, 16 per cent were over other wage issues and 11.2 per cent were over such miscellaneous issues as hours, procedures, etc., which are covered by 'other causes' category. The remaining five cause classifications accounted for the other 21 per cent of the total.

Comparing these results with those of 1960–8 reveals that three cause categories increased their shares of the total. These were wage increases (from 37.5 to 51.4 per cent), other wage issues (from 15.2 to 16 per cent) and sympathy stoppages (from 2.1 to 2.4 per cent). The largest rise was in wage increase strikes, which rose from an average of twenty-seven per year in 1960–8 to 115 per year in 1969–73. The sharpest falls involved issues such as trade union principle, miscellaneous and demarcation. Demarcation disputes actually fell slightly when measured as an annual average.

The increase in the number of stoppages over wages followed a similar shift in the previous period and must be seen as very largely the product of the failure to obtain any general agreement on wages policy in these years. The slight rise in the importance of sympathy stoppages is interesting for two reasons. First, it reverses a trend which had been apparent since the immediate post-war years. Secondly, it reflects an increase in concern, albeit at a minor level, with matters other than direct self-interest. It should also be noted that this change occurred at the same time as legal action was being taken, via the 1971 Industrial Relations Act, to restrict the right to use sanctions of this kind. The decline in the number of demarcation disputes was no doubt due to a number of factors, including the decline of the shipbuilding industry and the craft union amalgamations which had taken place in the early 1960s. It is, however, plausible to suppose that these developments were encouraged by TUC pressure following its 'solemn and binding undertaking' to the government in exchange for the withdrawal of the 1969 White Paper *In Place of Strife*.

NET MAJOR STRIKES BY REGION

The regional distribution of major stoppages is given in Table 5.18.

The most strike-prone regions were the West Midlands, 19.9 per cent of the total, the North West, 18.2 per cent, Scotland, 15.9 per cent, and the South East, 13.8 per cent. These four regions were also the most strike-prone in 1960–8, although the ranking was different since the North West moved up from fourth to second place. As in the previous period these four regions accounted for 68 per cent of major stoppages. Three of them – i.e. the West Midlands, Scotland and the South East – experienced a decrease in their share of major strike activity, but the increase in the North West's share was sufficient to offset these declines and maintain the same overall degree of concentration. Changes in the remaining regions were quite slight. Four regions experienced increases in their shares of the total. Three of them, the South West, Yorkshire and Humberside and the Northern, also had increases in each of the previous periods. Two regions, Northern Ireland and the East Midlands, had decreases. (For Northern Ireland it was the third successive decrease.) One region, East Anglia, had no change in its share of major strikes. Even in this period major strikes remained very localised and only 5.7 per cent extended beyond one region. In 1960–8 some 7.9 per cent of major strikes involved workers in more than one region.

OCCUPATIONAL GROUPS (OTHER THAN COAL MINING) MOST FREQUENTLY INVOLVED IN MAJOR STRIKES

The occupations of workers most frequently involved in major stoppages in the years 1969–73 are shown in Table 5.19.

Sixty-four identifiable occupational groups were involved in the 1116 stoppages. One group, engineering and electrical engineering workers not elsewhere specified, were involved in 460 stoppages, 41 per cent of the total. At the other end of the scale, fifteen occupational groups were involved in one stoppage each. Of the nine occupational groups shown in Table 5.19 four had also appeared in the corresponding table for 1960–8. It is interesting to note that of the nine groups shown in this table only one,

Table 5.17 *Net major strike activity by cause, 1969–73*

Cause	No. of strikes	Percentage share of the total
Wage increase	574	51.4
Other wage issue	179	16.0
Discipline	68	6 1
Redundancy	55	4.9
Sympathy	27	2.4
Demarcation	12	1.1
Trade union principle	76	6.8
Other	125	11.2
Total	1116	100.0

Table 5.18 *Distribution of net major strikes by region, 1969–73*

Region	No. of strikes	Percentage share of the total
South East	154	13.8
East Anglia	6	0.5
South West	32	2.9
West Midlands	222	19.9
East Midlands	43	3.9
Yorkshire and Humberside	82	7.3
North West	203	18.2
Northern	61	5.5
Scotland	178	15.9
Wales and Monmouthshire	50	4.5
Northern Ireland	21	1.9
Various regions in England	23	2.1
Great Britain	21	1.9
United Kingdom	20	1.8
Total	1116	100.0

stevedores and dockers, could be considered to be very specific. Groups such as bus crews, draughtsmen and electricians, who featured in previous periods, have disappeared. This either reflects a change in recording practice by the Department of Employment, which obscures the precise nature of the occupational groups involved, or a change in the form of strike action. The first of these possibilities seems unlikely in view of the Department's efforts to improve the quality of its records, especially as it had begun publishing this information in 1969. If the second reason is correct, this would seem to suggest a shift away from sectional to more widely based bargaining. A change of this kind would also help to explain why a 70 per cent increase in the number of major stoppages in this period was accompanied by a rise of only 10 per cent in the number of identifiable occupational groups involved.

Table 5.19   *Occupational groups (other than coal mining) most frequently involved in major strikes, 1969–73*

Occupational group	No. of strikes	Percentage share of the total
Engineering and electrical engineering workers n.e.s.	460	41.2
Car and vehicle industry workers n.e.s.	192	17.2
Dockers/stevedores	46	4.1
Building workers n.e.s.	41	3.7
Clerical workers	36	3.2
Aircraft workers n.e.s.	34	3.0
Food manufacturing workers n.e.s.	32	2.9
Assemblers	26	2.3
Textile spinners, doublers, twisters, etc.	23	2.1
55 other occupational groups	226	20.3
Total	1116	100.0

n.e.s., not elsewhere specified.

Table 5.20 shows the most frequently involved occupational groups by industry.

It can be seen from this table that the seven most frequent non-industry-specific groups were involved in 801 major stoppages across twenty-five industries. One occupational group, engineering and electrical engineering workers not elsewhere specified, was involved in stoppages in sixteen industries. The range of industries covered by the seven most frequently occurring occupational groups increased from fourteen in 1953–9 to twenty-one in 1960–8 and to twenty-five in 1969–73. In 1960–8 virtually the whole of this increase could be attributed to one occupational group: engineering and electrical engineering workers not elsewhere specified. This group increased its range from eight to sixteen industries. As there was no similar increase by this group in 1969–73 we have to conclude that

Table 5.20 *Major strikes: cross-tabulation of occupational groups most frequently involved by industry (other than coal mining), 1969–73*

Industry	Occupational groups						
	Engineering and electrical engineering workers n.e.s.	*Car and vehicle industry workers n.e.s.*	*Dockers and stevedores*	*Clerical workers*	*Food manufacturing workers n.e.s.*	*Assemblers*	*Fitters*
Bread, etc.					2		
Other food	5				19		
Drink					11		
Tobacco	1						
Chemicals							1
Iron and steel and other metal manufacture	75			5			1
Non-electrical engineering	139			3			
Electrical engineering	111			3		7	1
Shipbuilding	32						2
Motor vehicles	8	190		8		19	
Aircraft	1	1		5			1
Cycles	3						
Railway locos, carriages, etc.	1	1					
Other metal goods	51						
Textiles	2						
Other manufacturing industries	25						
Gas, water, electricity							2
Railways	2						
Road passenger transport	2			1			
Road haulage				2			
Sea transport			1	4			
Port and inland water transport			45				
Other transport and communications	2						
Miscellaneous				1			
Public administration and defence				4			1
Total	460	192	46	36	32	26	9

the change was due to other groups widening their industrial range. In this context it is worth noting that of the seven occupational groups listed in Table 5.20 only two were listed in the corresponding table for 1960–8.

As in the consideration of similar tables in previous chapters, our interpretation of this table is weakened by our knowledge that changes in recording practices may have affected the results. However, despite these doubts, increases in the range of industries covered from twenty-one to twenty-five, and in the share of the total of stoppages from 65 to 72 per cent, do suggest that occupational factors were of considerable importance in contributing to the rise in strike activity during this period.

SEASONAL PATTERN OF NET MAJOR STRIKES

The seasonal pattern of major strikes in this period is set out in Table 5.21.

The seasonal pattern of the commencement of major stoppages exhibited its now familiar spring and autumn peaks with a slight variation from previous periods. January has not usually been an above average month for major stoppages, but in 1969–73 this was the case. This had the effect of creating two strike seasons in the first half of the year, one of January and February, and one of April, May and June. The autumn season covered the months of September and October.

As usual the summer and winter holiday periods saw below average numbers of major stoppages. The peak months for the termination of major stoppages were May, June, October and November. Thirty-four strikes continued from one calendar year to the next. The three most extended included two which began in June and ended in January and February respectively and one which began early in September and ended on the last day of February. Overall, by comparison with 1960–8, there was a distinct shift towards major stoppages commencing in the first half of the year.

THE DURATION OF NET MAJOR STOPPAGES

The information we have already considered on numbers of workers involved and days lost implied that duration of major stoppages had increased. Direct evidence on this point is available in Table 5.22.

In this period 25.8 per cent of major stoppages were over within six days, 68.1 per cent within twenty-four days, 90.1 per cent within forty-eight days and 97.1 per cent within seventy-two days. As usual the duration of major stoppages was much greater than that of the gross total of stoppages, 73.2 per cent of which were over within six days and 94.1 per cent within twenty-four days. Of the thirty-two most prolonged major stoppages eight lasted for over 100 days. These included five pay disputes, two stoppages over the dismissals of shop stewards and one combined pay and redundancy dispute. Six of these strikes were in engineering and the other two in construction.

Compared with 1960–8 we find a marked shift towards longer stoppages

Table 5.21   *Seasonal pattern of net major strikes, 1969–73*

Month	No of strikes beginning	Percentage share of the total	No. of strikes ending	Percentage share of the total
January	110	9.9	68	6.1
February	100	9.0	93	8.3
March	93	8.3	93	8.3
April	129	11.6	85	7.6
May	109	9.8	131	11.7
June	119	10.7	132	11.8
July	66	5.9	69	6.2
August	89	8.0	83	7.4
September	103	9.2	84	7.5
October	102	9.1	126	11.3
November	73	6.5	101	9.1
December	23	2.1	51	4.6
Total	1116	100.0	1116	100.0

Table 5.22   *Duration of net major stoppages, 1969–73*

Duration in working days	No. of strikes	Percentage share of the total
Not more than 1	42	3.8
Over 1 but not more than 2	35	3.1
Over 2 but not more than 3	45	4.0
Over 3 but not more than 4	55	4.9
Over 4 but not more than 5	63	5.6
Over 5 but not more than 6	48	4.3
Over 6 but not more than 12	234	21.0
Over 12 but not more than 18	136	12.0
Over 18 but not more than 24	102	9.1
Over 24 but not more than 36	157	14.1
Over 36 but not more than 48	88	7.9
Over 48 but not more than 60	49	4.4
Over 60 but not more than 72	30	2.7
Over 72	32	2.9
Total	1116	100.0

Table 5.23 Cross-tabulation of net major strikes by duration in working days and the number of workers involved, 1969–73

Duration in working days	Number of workers involved									
	50 and under 100	100 and under 250	250 and under 500	500 and under 1000	1000 and under 2500	2500 and under 5000	5000 and under 10 000	10 000 and under 25 000	25 000 and under 50 000	50 000 and over
Not more than 1							25	11	2	4
Over 1 but not more than 2						20	9	4	1	1
Over 2 but not more than 3					12	20	11	1	1	
Over 3 but not more than 4					27	16	9	2	1	
Over 4 but not more than 5					30	19	11	3		
Over 5 but not more than 6				1	36	4	7			
Over 6 but not more than 12			7	77	102	31	11	6		
Over 12 but not more than 18			30	51	26	16	7	3	3	
Over 18 but not more than 24			41	20	20	5	14			
Over 24 but not more than 36		21	47	42	27	9	8	1	1	1
Over 36 but not more than 48		17	22	14	21	7	4	2		2
Over 48 but not more than 60		14	14	7	10	1	1	1	1	1
Over 60 but not more than 72	1	12	4	2	3	3	1	1	2	
Over 72	8	6	5	6	4	2	1			1
Total	9	70	170	220	318	153	119	35	12	10

in virtually all but the longest duration categories. Stoppages lasting no more than six days accounted for 31.4 per cent of the total in 1960–8 but only 25.8 per cent in 1969–73, and those lasting no more than twenty-four days fell from 75.9 to 68.1 per cent. In 1960–8 there had been a marked shift towards shorter stoppages across the whole range of the distribution. In 1969–73 there was a shift towards longer stoppages which was most marked at the short end of the distribution.

Table 5.23 shows a cross-tabulation of major stoppages by duration and number of workers involved.

Table 5.23, with its empty space in the top left-hand corner marking the exclusion of 12 500 stoppages which do not meet the qualifying limits, serves to emphasise the extent to which major stoppages are larger and longer than other strikes. Of major stoppages, 78 per cent involved at least 500 workers, 58 per cent involved at least 1000 and 16 per cent involved at least 5000. The corresponding figures for the gross totals are 18 per cent, 9 per cent and 1 per cent. Of the thirty-two longest stoppages 78 per cent involved less than 1000 workers. Of the sixty-two strikes which lasted for more than sixty days 71 per cent involved less than 1000 workers but four stoppages (6.5 per cent) involved more than 10 000 workers and one involved more than 50 000. Although prolonged major stoppages tended to involve relatively small numbers of workers, this period was also distinguished by an eightfold increase in the number of large, long stoppages, i.e. those involving at least 10 000 workers and lasting for more than thirty-six days. This increase occurred at a time when the total of major stoppages did not even double and reflects the widespread and bitter conflicts which characterised the period.

MAJOR STOPPAGES IN COAL MINING

Between 1969 and 1973 there were ten major stoppages in coal mining which involved a total of 535 000 workers and resulted in the loss of 12.8 million working days. In our count of the number of stoppages we followed the Department of Employment's lead in treating the unofficial stoppage of 1970 as three separate stoppages in England, Scotland and Wales, although on the common cause criterion there were good grounds for treating it as one stoppage, particularly as bargaining in the industry is conducted at national level. Compared with the totals for 1960–8 there was a 76 per cent fall in the number of major stoppages, a 119 per cent increase in workers involved and a staggering 1100 per cent rise in working days lost – despite the fact that the later period was four years shorter than the former. These increases in workers involved and days lost reflect the influence of the widespread unofficial stoppages of 1969 and 1970 plus the industry-wide official strike in 1972.

In relation to the total of strike activity in the industry, major strikes accounted for 1 per cent of stoppages, 79 per cent of workers involved and 98 per cent of days lost. On all three measures major strikes continued the trend of the previous period by increasing their share of the total.

MAIN FEATURES OF THE STRIKE PATTERN, 1969–73

The period 1969–73 is set apart from the rest of the post-war period by substantial changes in both the magnitude and type of strike activity. Measured by annual averages the net totals of stoppages rose by 87 per cent, workers involved by 22 per cent and days lost by 244 per cent. Wage issues became the principal precipitating cause of strike action; official stoppages were declared more frequently than at any time in the post-war period; while the shop-floor disputes of the previous period continued and were supplemented by a revival of the kind of industry-wide stoppage that had been common in the late 1950s. In addition these industrial stoppages were accompanied by a wave of political strike activity of a level never previously witnessed in the United Kingdom. In later chapters we will argue that the industrial strike history of these years cannot be adequately explained without reference to the factors which provoked these overtly political stoppages. In this section we review briefly the main changes in industrial strike activity in the year 1969–73 and seek to highlight those features which most obviously require an explanation. We also give a very brief review of the political strike activity in the period.

Industrial strike activity outside coal mining in the years 1969–73 involved, on average, 6.5. per cent of employees in employment and 13.4 per cent of trade union members. Days lost through these stoppages amounted to about 0.2 per cent of potential working time and were equivalent to 5.9 per cent of the time lost through unemployment. In terms of worker involvement these rates were only slightly above those of the previous period, but days lost in relation to potential working time had quadrupled and in relation to unemployment had more than doubled. However, this activity was not evenly distributed across industries. There were three industries in which more than a quarter of the workforce was involved in strike action and twenty-two industries in which less than 5 per cent of the workforce was so involved. The eight most strike-prone industries accounted for 40 per cent of all stoppages, 58 per cent of workers involved, 59 per cent of days lost and 14 per cent of employees in employment. This represented a marked lessening in the concentration of strike activity. In the previous period employees in the most strike-prone industry were sixteen times more likely to be involved in a stoppage than other employees. In 1969–73 they were only eight times more likely to be so involved.

Prior to 1969 it had only been in exceptional years that more than half of the gross total of stoppages were concerned with wage issues. Every year in 1969–73 was exceptional. The share of the total of working days lost attributable to wage issues was also very high in this period but the share of workers involved was only on a par with that of the two previous periods. The number of wage stoppages was much more volatile than the number of non-wage stoppages. To explain changes in the gross total of stoppages we need to concentrate on factors affecting pay disputes. In order to account for the overall level of the gross total of stoppages we must also take into account factors affecting non-pay issues. Wage issue stoppages, on average, directly involved one and a half times as many workers as non-wage issues and resulted in the loss of four times as many working days. Examination of the industrial distribution of strike activity by cause appeared to reveal more about differences in bargaining arrangements between industries than about differences in workers' attitudes.

Analysis of the regional distribution of strike activity showed that the West Midlands, Scotland, the North West and Wales were the most strike-prone regions, with rates of worker involvement three times higher than the South East and East Anglia. The only region to experience a decline in its strike-proneness was Northern Ireland.

The distribution of the gross totals of strike activity in relation to duration, extent and size revealed that very short stoppages, i.e. those lasting two days or less, had again declined in frequency. Longer stoppages had increased, with the gains being most marked among the most extended stoppages. Stoppages involving fewer than fifty workers declined in relative frequency while larger stoppages increased their share of the total. Not surprisingly the frequency of stoppages involving the loss of less than 250 working days declined from 61 per cent of the total in 1960–8 to 43 per cent in 1969–73. Strikes involving the loss of at least 50 000 working days increased from 0.2 per cent of the total to 0.9 per cent.

Part of this change was due to events in coal mining. In the previous chapter we observed that the frequency of coal mining stoppages had declined from 74 per cent of the gross total in 1953–9 to 39 per cent in 1960–8. This trend continued, with coal mining's share of the total falling to 7 per cent in 1969–73. Much of the decline in the frequency of small, short stoppages was due to the virtual disappearance of the typical, very small, short coal mining strike. It is unlikely that this is a complete explanation as the magnitude of the changes were so large and were accompanied by an increase in the relative frequency of major stoppages in the net totals.

Strikes known to be official accounted for 5 per cent of the net total, 23 per cent of workers involved and 50 per cent of days lost. They were more than five times as large and three times as long as other stoppages. The proportion of total time lost due to stoppages known to be official varied widely between industries depending on whether or not there had been any industry-wide stoppages. In general there seems to have been a greater willingness by the unions to sanction stoppages during this period.

Major strikes increased sharply both in absolute terms and as a percentage of the net total of stoppages. This pattern was paralleled by the number of days lost through major stoppages, but workers involved were fewer than in 1960–8 when the total was inflated by the inclusion of three national engineering stoppages. In relation to our various reference series workers involved showed no increase over the previous period but time lost almost quadrupled to 0.15 per cent of potential working time, equivalent to 4.8 per cent of time lost through unemployment. Of the forty industries for which major stoppage data was available, twenty-five had more stoppages in 1969–73 than in 1960–8, seven had less and eight had the same, including three which had no major stoppages in either period. There was no apparent tendency for major stoppages involving relatively small numbers of workers to increase their share of the total at the expense of medium-sized stoppages. Analysis of major stoppages by number of working days lost per stoppage revealed that small stoppages had become less frequent while very large stoppages had increased their share of the total. Examination of the attributed principal cause of major stoppages revealed that wage increases rose very sharply to account for over half of the total of 1116 strikes. Other wage issue and sympathy disputes also increased in relative frequency.

At regional level major strikes remained heavily concentrated in the West Midlands, the North West, Scotland and the South East. These four accounted for 68 per cent of all stoppages and 65 per cent of employees in employment. Some sixty-four occupational groups were identified as being involved in major stoppages in this period. One group, engineering and electrical engineering workers n.e.s., was involved in 41 per cent of major stoppages. There was a considerable change in the rankings of the most strike-prone occupational groups with the specific occupations which had dominated earlier periods being replaced by more inclusive occupational groups. We felt that this development could not simply be dismissed as a change in recording practice. It was more likely that it indicated a real shift in the kinds of workers most frequently involved in major stoppages. The familiar spring and autumn strike peaks were observed with the first half of the year apparently becoming more strike-prone than usual. Holiday periods appeared to exercise their customary depressing effect on major strike activity. Short major stoppages declined in relative frequency while moderately long ones increased.

In addition to this industrial strike activity the years 1969–73 saw some fifteen or sixteen political stoppages in which nearly six million workers took part and which resulted in the loss of at least six million working days. Details of these stoppages are provided in Appendix 2. The majority of time lost occurred as a result of protests against proposals for the legal reform of the conduct of industrial relations and against judicial interventions in industrial relations after the proposals had become law. Most of the remaining time was lost in a protest against the Conservative government's introduction of a statutory incomes policy.

It should be clear that the final period of our study raises many questions which we will need to consider further below. Why did the number of stoppages rise so rapidly in 1969 and 1970? Why did it fall so rapidly in 1971? Why were pay issues so important in this period? Why did the number of workers involved increase so much more rapidly than the number of stoppages in the early 1970s? Why did stoppages become so much more prolonged? Was there change in unions' willingness to sanction strike action or was it that more stoppages met the requirements of official approval? Why did industry-wide stoppages of the kind which had been common in the later 1950s stage a comeback? Why did major stoppages become so much more frequent? What caused the levelling out in the industrial distribution of strike activity? Why did this period witness such extensive political stoppages? Was there a connection between these upsurges of industrial and political strike activity? These and other questions are dealt with more extensively in the chapters which follow.

6   An Overview, 1946–73

In the previous four chapters we have concentrated on identifying the special characteristics of each sub-period and how they differed from one another. Our purpose in this chapter is to stress the characteristics of the period as a whole: to point to continuities and consistencies, rather than differences and atypical developments.

Clearly the most notable development which emerges is the overall rise in various measures of strike activity since the early 1950s. In this sense the overall pattern which we need to interpret and explain is fundamentally different from that which went before – i.e. in the form presented by Knowles (1952) in his study of strike activity from 1911 to 1947. Knowles was concerned, above all, to explain an overall reduction in activity; especially in comparison with the levels which existed in the second decade of the twentieth century.

Thus he devoted much of his attention to explaining the development of more effective 'controls' over the pace and duration of strikes. In contrast, in the second part of our study, we shall need to consider how far the overall rise in activity in our period can be said to be due to a lessening of effective 'controls', or whether it was due to other factors. Meanwhile, the layout of this chapter mirrors that of the preceding four.

TOTAL STRIKE ACTIVITY: NET AND GROSS

Over the years 1946–73 the net total of stoppages averaged 1261, workers involved averaged 835 000 and working days lost averaged 3.9 million. Yet the interest of this period lies not only in its absolute levels but also in the extent of its changes. These can be measured in a variety of ways. Using beginning of period to end of period comparisons reveals that the number of stoppages rose by 194 per cent, workers involved by 373 per cent and days lost by 309 per cent. Alternatively, by estimating the change between the trough and peak of each basic measure series, we can derive maximum estimates of the change in strike activity. This shows that the peak year for stoppages was 1970 with 3746; for workers involved it was 1962 with 4.3 million; for working days lost it was 1971 with 13.5 million. The trough year for stoppages was 1953 with 439; for workers involved 1952 with 143 000; for days lost 1950 with 958 000. Between trough and peak stoppages rose by 753 per cent; workers involved by 2895 per cent and days lost by 1308 per cent.

Of course, it can be argued that any comparison relying on a single pair of years will be distorted to the extent that those years are atypical. One way of meeting that argument is to estimate the change between the averages of a number of years. Thus, between 1946–52 and 1969–73 stoppages rose by 336 per cent, workers involved by 533 per cent and days lost by 650 per cent. Full details of net and gross totals of strike activity are shown in Table 6.1.

This table also permits us to identify those periods when each measure of strike activity rose fastest and to assess the extent to which similar movements occurred simultaneously across all three measures. We have already observed that the troughs and peaks of the various series did not coincide precisely, so it is not closely co-ordinated. Strike numbers, like the other two series, fell from the beginning of the period until the early 1950s. It then rose continuously: slowly in the mid-1950s; most rapidly in the late 1950s and early 1960s; more slowly in the mid-1960s; rapidly again in the late 1960s; slowly again in the 1970s. Movements in the workers involved series were dominated by the national engineering stoppages, particularly those of 1962. Underlying these peaks was a strong upward movement similar to that of the number of stoppages. The working days lost series was dominated by the effects of occasional large stoppages. The confrontations over pay policy in the late 1950s and early 1970s were especially prominent with the underlying trend moving upward.

A further question prompted by Table 6.1 is the extent to which particular dimensions of strike activity contributed to the overall increase. We have already observed that workers involved and days lost tended to increase faster than stoppages over the period as a whole. But this does not necessarily imply that the principal cause of the overall increase in strike activity was a change in the extent or duration of stoppages. Between 1946–52 and 1969–73 the average net total of stoppages rose by 336 per cent, the average number of workers involved per stoppage rose by 45 per cent and the average number of days lost per worker involved rose by 42 per cent. If the averages provide a reliable indicator of the distribution by extent and duration, this implies that the principal cause of the overall increase in strike activity in this period was the increase in strike numbers.

NET STRIKE ACTIVITY IN PERSPECTIVE

Increases in strike activity of the magnitude outlined above, even starting from the very low levels of 1946–52, were bound to attract a good deal of attention. In Table 6.2 we summarise our attempts to put these increases into perspective.

On average, between 1946 and 1973, 4 per cent of employees, or 9 per cent of trade union members, were involved in strike action at some time during the course of each year. Strike action resulted in the loss of 0.07 per cent of potential working time, equivalent to 3.8 per cent of the time lost through unemployment.

Within the period the rate of worker involvement rose persistently, but not steadily. Thus it doubled between 1946–52 and 1953–9, and doubled again in the following period – i.e. 1960–8. It rose rather more slowly in the

Table 6.1   *Net and gross totals of strike activity, 1946–73*

Year	No. of strikes		No. of workers involved (000s)		No. of working days lost (000s)	
	Net	*Gross*	*Net*	*Gross*	*Net*	*Gross*
1946	876	2205	312.9	526	1 736	2 158
1947	668	1721	314.7	623	1 521	2 433
1948	643	1759	236.9	426	1 480	1 944
1949	552	1426	186.2	434	1 053	1 807
1950	479	1339	161.1	303	958	1 389
1951	661	1719	244.2	379	1 344	1 694
1952	493	1714	142.5	416	1 132	1 792
Average 1946–52	625	1698	228.4	444	1 318	1 888
1953	439	1746	1205.6	1374	1 791	2 184
1954	525	1989	245.6	450	1 989	2 457
1955	636	2419	317.4	671	2 669	3 781
1956	572	2648	266.6	508	1 581	2 083
1957	635	2859	1093.6	1359	7 898	8 412
1958	666	2629	275.5	524	3 012	3 462
1959	786	2093	454.4	646	4 907	5 270
Average 1953–59	608	2340	551.2	551	3 407	3 950
1960	1166	2832	581.4	819	2 530	3 024
1961	1228	2686	529.9	779	2 309	3 046
1962	1244	2449	4268.2	4423	5 490	5 798
1963	1081	2068	440.3	593	1 429	1 755
1964	1466	2524	711.1	883	1 975	2 277
1965	1614	2354	758.8	876	2 513	2 925
1966	1384	1937	493.6	544	2 280	1 428
1967	1722	2116	693.0	734	2 682	2 787
1968	2157	2378	2227.8	2258	4 636	4 690
Average 1960–8	1451	2372	1189.3	1323	2 872	3 189
1969	2930	3116	1519.9	1665	5 807	6 846
1970	3746	3906	1683.2	1801	9 890	10 980
1971	2093	2228	1155.4	1178	13 488	13 551
1972	2273	2497	1392.9	1734	13 111	23 909
1973	2572	2873	1481.0	1528	7 107	7 197
Average 1969–73	2723	2924	1446.5	1581	9 881	12 497
Average 1946–73	1261	2294	835.5	1016	3 869	4 681

final period, 1969–73, but the trend was in the same direction. Yet in the final sub-period the rate of worker involvement was still only 6.5 per cent of employees per year, implying that, on average, less than 0.2 per cent of the workforce were on strike at any one time.

Numbers of workers involved, as a percentage of trade union members, followed a very similar pattern to that of worker involvement, except that the rate of increase was slightly faster in the first part of the period and slightly slower in the latter. This was partly because trade union density fell and then rose sharply during the period as a whole.

Table 6.2   *Net strike activity in perspective, 1946–73*

Years	Workers involved as a percentage of employees in employment	Workers involved as a percentage of trade union members	Working days lost as a percentage of potential working time	Working days lost as a percentage of time lost through unemployment
1946–52	1.3	2.6	0.03	1.3
1953–59	2.6	6.1	0.06	3.6
1960–68	5.3	12.4	0.05	2.6
1969–73	6.5	13.4	0.20	5.9
1946–73	4.0	8.9	0.07	3.8

Days lost in relation to potential working time doubled between 1946–52 and 1953–9, fell slightly in 1960–8 and then quadrupled in 1969–73. In relation to unemployment days lost rose very sharply in 1953–9, fell sharply in 1960–8 and then rose 2.5-fold in 1969–73. However, the upward trend in unemployment since the late 1950s tended to reduce the significance of the rise in working days lost.

NET STRIKE ACTIVITY BY INDUSTRY

DISTRIBUTION OF NET ANNUAL AVERAGE STRIKE ACTIVITY BY INDUSTRY

The industrial distribution of the net totals of strike activity for the period 1949–73 is shown in Table 6.3. In order to achieve the maximum comparability over this long period we were forced to aggregate various sections of the vehicles industry under one heading and to incorporate strikes in 'sea transport' with those in 'other transport and communication'.

The differences in strike-proneness between industries are clearly evident in Table 6.3. Across the economy as a whole the average rate of worker involvement in stoppages was 4 per cent. Out of the thirty-four

Table 6.3   *Average net strike activity by industry group, 1949–73*

Industry groups	No. of strikes	No. of workers involved (000s)	Workers involved as a percentage of employees in employment	No. of working days lost (000s)	Working days lost per 1000 employees in employment
Agriculture, forestry, etc.	2.8	0.9	0.2	11.7	23.4
Mining and quarrying (exc. coal mining)	4.1	0.4	0.5	1.6	22.3
Grain milling	1.5	0.3	0.8	1.0	24.9
Bread, flour, etc.	4.8	3.1	1.4	18.4	82.7
Other food	17.1	5.2	1.4	27.3	72.0
Drink	13.2	3.0	1.9	13.0	81.2
Tobacco	0.5	0.7	1.5	2.4	51.1
Chemicals	24.2	7.6	1.5	32.1	63.0
Iron and steel and other metals	99.6	55.2	9.6	237.0	411.7
Non-electrical engineering	172.1	153.2	12.7	453.0	374.1
Electrical engineering	76.0	85.9	11.2	278.1	363.8
Shipbuilding and marine engineering	83.0	52.1	20.3	357.1	1388.4
(V1, V2, V3)	178.0	229.0	23.5	863.0	886.0
Other metal goods	57.0	25.9	4.3	85.7	140.7
Textiles	35.4	8.3	0.9	49.0	56.0
Clothing	12.1	4.2	0.9	15.0	31.8
Footwear	3.9	0.8	0.7	2.3	19.0
Bricks, pottery, etc.	27.0	6.1	1.8	42.8	126.1
Furniture, wood and cork manufacture	20.3	3.1	1.0	17.9	60.0
Paper and board, cartons, etc.	10.4	3.1	1.4	22.8	107.1
Printing and publishing	7.0	9.0	2.4	168.7	448.2
Other manufacturing industries	33.3	15.6	4.2	76.6	207.3
Construction	189.4	38.1	2.6	325.7	225.4
Gas, water, electricity	9.8	4.0	1.0	24.8	64.1
Railways	7.9	17.3	4.2	58.0	139.6
Road passenger transport	29.6	25.0	9.0	160.5	579.0
Road haulage	38.4	5.4	2.6	30.6	148.2
Port and inland water transport	97.0	69.9	49.7	296.4	2106.6
Other transport and communications	11.5	26.2	4.8	316.8	577.0
Distribution	26.7	4.2	0.2	21.7	8.3
Insurance, banking, finance	1.0	0.9	0.1	13.8	22.1
Professional and scientific	6.7	19.5	0.9	42.4	19.5
Miscellaneous	14.6	2.7	0.1	11.0	5.9
Public administration and defence	18.2	15.5	1.1	65.9	47.5
All industries (exc. coal mining)	1324.8	901.2	4.0	4143.2	184.3

industries for which information was available, twenty had rates of worker involvement of less than 2 per cent. In three industries worker involvement was between 2 and 4 per cent; in six between 4 and 10 per cent and in five more than 10 per cent.

Similar disparities were evident in the amount of time lost per employee. Twelve industries had averages of less than half an hour per employee per year; seven averaged between half and one hour; ten between one and four; three between four and eight, and two more than one day. The five where strike losses were heaviest were port and inland water transport, shipbuilding, vehicles, road passenger transport and other transport and communication.

In terms of the number of stoppages the most strike-prone industries were construction (189.4 stoppages), vehicles (178), non-electrical engineering (172.1), iron and steel and other metal manufactures (99.6) and port and inland water transport (97). Between them these five industries accounted for 55.6 per cent of stoppages but only 19.4 per cent of employees in employment.

Despite the very substantial overall increase in strike activity which took place within the period, only six industries showed an increase on all three basic measures of strike activity in every sub-period – i.e. chemicals, vehicles, textiles, other manufacturing industries, construction and professional and scientific services.

It would obviously be of considerable interest if it were possible to identify those industries which contributed most to this increase in strike activity. But there are certain difficulties in so doing. If we simply identify those industries in which strike activity increased fastest, we are likely to find that they include a significant number where strike activity was very slight at the beginning of the period so that, without the industries becoming particularly strike-prone, they register very large increases in activity. Alternatively, if we concentrate on those where the absolute increase was greatest, we may overlook some where the increase was more rapid. In these circumstances any decision is bound to be somewhat arbitrary. We decided to concentrate on those industries where the absolute increases were largest after adjusting, where appropriate, for the employment level of industry. Further, in order to overcome the problems created by atypical years, we compared average levels of strike activity in 1949–52 with those of 1969–73.

Between 1949–52 and 1969–73 the average net total of stoppages rose from 546.3 to 2722.8, an increase of 2176.5. Over the same period seven industries experienced increases of more than 100 stoppages per year in their average totals. They were non-electrical engineering, 359; vehicles, 306; port and inland water transport, 190; construction, 185; electrical engineering, 180; iron and steel and other metal manufacture, 179; and other metal goods, 112. Between them these industries accounted for 69 per cent of all increases in stoppages between the two periods. Their combined share of the total rose from 53 per cent in 1949–52 to 66 per cent in 1969–73.

The average rate of worker involvement also rose from 0.91 per cent of employees in employment in 1949–52 to 6.51 per cent in 1969–73; an increase of 5.60 per cent. In eleven out of the thirty-four industries the rate of worker involvement increased by more than 5.6 per cent. The eight industries which had the largest were port and inland water transport, with a staggering 122.33 per cent increase; vehicles, 42.36 per cent; shipbuilding, 17.47 per cent; iron and steel and other metal manufacture, 13.65 per cent; other transport and communication, 12.35 per cent; electrical engineering, 11.78 per cent; other manufacturing industries, 8.35 per cent; and non-electrical engineering 7.56 per cent. Between 1949–52 and 1969–73 the average number of workers involved in stoppages rose from 184 000 to 1 446 000, an increase of 1 263 000. These eight industries contributed to 70 per cent of the increase. Their combined share of the net total of workers involved rose from 60 to 68 per cent.

Days lost per 1000 employees in employment across all industries net of coal mining also rose from fifty-six in 1949–52 to 444.5 in 1969–73, an increase of 388.5. Ten industries had increases greater than this and in nine out of the ten the increases exceeded 500 per 1000 employees. This was equivalent to an increase of at least half a day per employee. The nine industries were as follows: port and inland water transport, with an increase of 2815 per 1000; vehicles, 2622; shipbuilding, 2026; other transport and communication, 1827; iron and steel and other metal manufacture, 905; electrical engineering, 866; construction, 792; non-electrical engineering, 597; and other manufacturing industries, 582. Of the net total increase in working days over this period these nine industries accounted for 84 per cent. Their own combined share of the total increased from 74 to 82 per cent.

It would appear from this analysis that most of the increase in strike activity over this period was a product of increases within the more strike-prone industries. Thus industries which accounted for a substantial proportion of strike activity at the beginning of the period accounted for an even greater proportion at the end. Five industries, non-electrical engineering, vehicles, port and inland water transport, electrical engineering and iron and steel and other metal manufacture, appeared on all three lists. This is not to deny the dispersion of strike activity, which we remarked in Chapters 4 and 5, but merely to emphasise that any explanation of the overall growth of strike activity in this period still needs to concentrate on the industries listed above.

STRIKE-PRONE AND NON-STRIKE-PRONE GROUPS

Shares in the net totals of strike activity accruing to the eight most and least strike-prone industries are shown in Table 6.4 (strike-proneness was measured by the number of workers involved relative to the number of employees in employment).

The eight most strike-prone industries accounted for 56 per cent of all stoppages, 77 per cent of workers involved and 71 per cent of days lost, but

Table 6.4　*Industry groups' relative shares of net totals of strike activity, 1949–73*

Industry groups	Percentage share of no. of strikes	Percentage share of no. of workers involved	Percentage share of no. of working days lost
High strike activity industries			
All vehicles industries	13.3	25.4	20.8
Non-electrical engineering	13.0	17.0	10.9
Electrical engineering	5.7	9.5	6.7
Port and inland water transport	7.3	7.8	7.2
Iron and steel and other metal manufacture	7.5	6.1	5.7
Shipbuilding and marine engineering	6.2	5.8	8.6
Other transport and communication	0.9	2.9	7.6
Road passenger transport	2.2	2.8	3.9
Share of most strike-prone industries	56.1	77.3	71.4
Low strike activity industries			
Public administration and defence	1.4	1.7	1.6
Distribution	2.0	0.5	0.5
Miscellaneous	1.1	0.3	0.3
Agriculture, forestry and fishing	0.2	0.1	0.3
Insurance, banking and finance	0.1	0.1	0.3
Footwear	0.3	0.1	0.1
Mining and quarrying (exc. coal mining)	0.3	Ø	Ø
Grain milling	0.1	Ø	Ø
Share of least strike-prone industries	5.5	2.8	3.1

Ø, less than half of 0.1 per cent.

only 17 per cent of employees in employment. Four of these featured in each of the sub-periods – i.e. port and inland water transport, shipbuilding, vehicles, and iron and steel and other metal manufacture. Strike activity was most heavily concentrated in 1953–9. Since then it has tended to become more widely distributed, especially in the 1969–73 period.

The eight least strike-prone industries accounted for less than 6 per cent of stoppages, 3 per cent of workers involved and days lost, but 35 per cent of employees in employment. Of these only two consistently ranked among the least strike-prone – i.e. insurance, banking and finance and miscellaneous services. The share of total strike activity in this group increased up to 1960–8 but fell in 1969–73. Changes in the industrial composition of this group pose considerable problems of interpretation. But it seems likely that at least some of the decline was due to a reduction in the number of employees.

The remaining eighteen industries had 38 per cent of stoppages, 20 per cent of workers involved, 26 per cent of days lost and 49 per cent of employees in employment. This group comprised the principal beneficiaries of the decline in the concentration of strike activity in 1969–73.

It seems that throughout most of the post-war period strike activity in the United Kingdom has been heavily concentrated in a number of relatively small industries. But the concentration has lessened in the most recent years. The composition of the most strike-prone group has altered during the course of time, with industries like road haulage and road passenger transport being replaced by electrical engineering and other transport and communication.

It is also clear that some industries gained their ranking on the basis of one or two large stoppages. This suggests two conclusions. First, the forces which led to an increase in strike activity were not uniform in their operation across the economy – otherwise the rankings would have remained constant. Secondly, despite the changing industrial composition of the most strike-prone group the majority of strike activity remained confined to a minority of employees in a minority of industries. These observations are supported by the experience of the least strike-prone industries, which have had even greater changes in their industrial composition and only account for a tiny fraction of total strike activity despite employing a substantial proportion of the workforce.

DIRECTION OF CHANGE OF STRIKE ACTIVITY BY INDUSTRY

Table 6.5 shows the direction of change of strike activity for each basic measure between 1949 and 1973.

This confirms what has been said above about the widespread nature of the increase in activity. Of the thirty-four industries for which information is available, thirty-two had an increase in the number of stoppages. In one there was no change, and in the other, railways, there was a decrease. In respect of workers involved the situation was very similar; thirty-one industries had increases, in one there was no change, and in two (agriculture, forestry and fishing and road passenger transport) there was a decline. In respect of working days lost only three industries (agriculture, forestry and fishing, mining and quarrying (exc. coal mining) and port and inland water transport) experienced decreases.

Table 6.5   *Direction of change of net strike activity in each industry, 1949–73*

	No. of industries experiencing change in no. of stoppages	No. of industries experiencing change in no. of workers involved	No. of industries experiencing change in no. of working days lost
Increase in activity	32	31	31
Decrease in activity	1	2	3

In so far as 1949 and 1973 are atypical years these results understate the extent of the increases in strike activity. Comparison of the annual averages for 1949–52 with those of 1969–73 reveal that all industries had increases in the number of stoppages; thirty-three had increases in worker involvement in relation to the level of employment. The exception was road haulage, where there was a slight decrease. In terms of working days lost per 1000 employees only two industries (tobacco and printing and publishing) had decreases, the rest had increases.

The rates of increase were far from uniform between industries but the range of industries affected serves to remind us that industry-specific factors are unlikely to provide a complete explanation.

GROSS STRIKE ACTIVITY BY CAUSE

The distribution of gross strike activity by cause is shown in Table 6.6.

Presenting the information in this way emphasises the fact that conflict over wages has been much greater in some periods than in others. Wage stoppages reached particularly high levels in 1955–8, 1960–1, 1964 and 1968–73. However, if we examine the percentage of the total number of stoppages attributable to wage issues we find that 1951, 1955, 1960–1, 1964–5 and 1968–73 were the exceptional years, in the sense that the factors affecting the number of wage stoppages did not simultaneously affect the number of non-wage stoppages in the same way. Thus the number of wage stoppages varied within the range from 587 to 2465, while non-wage stoppages were more closely confined, varying within the range from 752 to 1580. This implies that the factors affecting the number of wage stoppages are subject to much greater fluctuation than those affecting non-wage stoppages.

Table 6.6   *Gross strike activity by cause, 1946–73*

Year	No. of strikes	Wage issues Percentage of total	No. of workers directly involved (000s)	Percentage of total	No. of working days lost (000s)	Percentage of total	Non-wage issues No. of strikes	No. of workers directly involved (000s)	No. of working days lost (000s)
1946	961	43.6	170.0	42.0	n.a.	n.a.	1244	235.0	n.a.
1947	807	46.9	159.3	32.6	n.a.	n.a.	914	329.4	n.a.
1948	730	41.5	142.1	43.9	n.a.	n.a.	1029	181.9	n.a.
1949	611	42.9	159.5	50.1	n.a.	n.a.	815	153.6	n.a.
1950	587	43.8	132.1	49.1	n.a.	n.a.	752	136.8	n.a.
1951	833	48.5	157.6	46.9	n.a.	n.a.	886	178.3	n.a.
1952	726	42.4	167.3	55.2	n.a.	n.a.	988	135.9	n.a.
1953	791	45.3	1200.2	90.3	n.a.	n.a.	955	128.9	n.a.
1954	927	46.6	155.4	38.7	n.a.	n.a.	1062	246.1	n.a.
1955	1231	50.9	287.1	48.0	n.a.	n.a.	1188	311.5	n.a.
1956	1208	45.6	240.1	51.7	n.a.	n.a.	1440	224.1	n.a.
1957	1279	44.7	1048.8	82.2	7 487	89.1	1580	226.4	912
1958	1208	45.9	212.4	46.6	2 453	70.6	1421	243.7	1021
1959	968	46.3	288.3	55.3	4 129	78.2	1125	233.3	1151
1960	1391	49.0	400.2	57.0	1 848	60.6	1446	301.3	1201
1961	1306	48.6	329.2	49.0	1 993	65.6	1380	343.7	1045
1962	1125	45.9	3694.4	86.0	4 352	75.3	1324	602.2	1426
1963	956	46.2	247.8	54.4	1 380	69.1	1112	207.4	617
1964	1208	47.9	404.7	57.7	1 053	51.9	1316	296.8	977
1965	1180	50.1	377.4	56.0	1 645	56.1	1174	296.1	1288
1966	883	45.6	197.8	47.6	1 642	68.6	1054	217.6	753
1967	986	46.5	262.0	47.5	1 607	57.7	1130	289.8	1176
1968	1230	51.7	1808.9	87.2	3 582	76.0	1148	265.1	1137
1969	1782	57.2	810.0	56.8	4 506	65.1	1334	616.6	2419
1970	2465	63.1	1032.7	70.7	9 237	84.7	1441	427.4	1671
1971	1155	51.8	593.8	68.7	12 286	90.4	1073	270.0	1303
1972	1477	59.2	1010.8	69.7	21 661	90.5	1020	439.6	2262
1973	1462	50.9	749.1	67.9	5 147	72.0	1411	354.1	1998
Aver.	1124	49.0	587.1	64.9	5059	79.4	1170	317.6	1315

It is sometimes argued that there is little real difference between wage and non-wage stoppages – the latter may be seen as proxies for the former. But if that were true it would be difficult to explain why the wage series is so much more volatile than the non-wage series. Another argument, which is sometimes put forward, is that the two kinds of disputes are substitutes for each other, so that there are more non-wage stoppages when overt conflict over wages is reduced, e.g. by the operation of an incomes policy. There is some evidence to support this view in the early part of the period, but even that is far from clear cut, and over the period as a whole the two series appear to have a positive rather than an inverse relationship.

The series for workers directly involved in wage stoppages is dominated by national engineering stoppages, most of which lasted a day or less. Underlying these peaks there is a general upward movement, with changes being most noticeable in 1955, 1960, 1964 and 1968–73. On average almost two-thirds of all workers directly involved were engaged in wage stoppages. Throughout the period there was a steady upward trend in the share of workers directly involved attributable to wage issues. The number directly involved in wage stoppages varied from 132 000 to 3 694 000 (or 1 033 000 if years affected by national engineering stoppages are excluded). In contrast workers directly involved in non-wage issues only varied from 129 000 to 617 000.

Information on the number of working days lost through strikes with different causes only became available in 1957. Between 1957 and 1973 some 79 per cent of time lost was due to wage stoppages. There was little obvious trend in this share over the whole period, although it dipped in the mid-1960s. Annual losses through wage stoppages varied from just over one million days to more than twenty-one million. Losses from non-wage stoppages varied from just over half a million to two and a half million days. On average wage stoppages resulted in the loss of four times as many working days as non-wage stoppages.

The industrial distribution of strike activity by cause for eight broad industrial groups is shown in Table 6.6a.

The industry with the highest proportion of wage stoppages was shipbuilding, where they accounted for 61 per cent of all strikes. It was followed, in order, by textiles and clothing, metals and engineering, vehicles, all other industries and services, transport and communication, construction and mining and quarrying. When ranked by share of workers directly involved in wage stoppages shipbuilding again led the field with 78 per cent. It was followed by all other industries and services, metals and engineering, vehicles, textiles and clothing, mining and quarrying, construction and transport and communication. In terms of share of days lost through wage stoppages, mining and quarrying was the leader with shipbuilding and construction in joint second place followed by transport and communication, all other industries and services, metals and engineering, vehicles and textiles and clothing.

With the exception of shipbuilding, which was among the top rankings on all three measures, there was little obvious consistency in the

Table 6.6a Industrial strike activity by cause, 1960–73

Industry group	Wage issues as a percentage of total in each industry			Annual average of strike activity in each industry		
	No. of strikes	No. of workers involved	No. of working days lost	No. of strikes	No. of workers directly involved (000s)	No. of working days lost (000s)
Mining and quarrying	44.6	58.5	83.9	668	119.5	1140
Metals and engineering	58.4	69.0	77.4	619	492.8	1483
Shipbuilding and marine engineering	60.6	78.0	79.3	91	49.6	318
Vehicles	55.6	68.5	76.3	265	219.5	1261
Textiles and clothing	58.6	61.5	74.1	69	15.5	95
Construction	45.7	58.4	79.3	256	50.7	496
Transport and communication	50.8	55.5	79.0	257	184.5	1020
All other industries and services	52.5	77.5	78.7	351	142.6	702
All industries and services	51.8	66.8	78.9	2569	1274.8	6515

importance of wage stoppages in each industry. In part this reflects the interrelationship between type of bargaining structure and type of stoppage. For example, in coal mining, for much of this period, there was no local bargaining over wages. In consequence, when stoppages did occur, they involved the whole of the industry's workforce. Such stoppages tended to push coal mining up the rankings of workers directly involved.

GROSS STRIKE ACTIVITY BY REGION

As we pointed out in earlier chapters, regional boundaries were subject to major revisions during this period. In order to overcome the most serious of the comparability problems which this created, we aggregated some of the data. The results are shown in Table 6.7.

It can be seen that on average, during the period 1955–73, 5.5 per cent of employees in employment were involved in strike action at some stage during the course of each year. Time lost was equivalent to 265 days per 1000 employees per year, or just over two hours per employee per year. Of the eight regional areas identified in Table 6.7 the most strike-prone were Wales, with a rate of worker involvement of 9.4 per cent, and Scotland, with a rate of 8.7 per cent. Four regions, the Midlands, Yorkshire and Humberside, the North West, the North and Northern Ireland, appeared as moderately strike prone, with rates of worker involvement ranging from 6.9 to 6.2 per cent. The least strike-prone regions were the South West and South East, with worker involvement rates of 3.5 and 2.9 per cent respectively. Time lost per 1000 employees followed a similar pattern to that of worker involvement. The most strike-prone regions, in rank order, were Wales, with 545 days per 1000 employees; Scotland, 384; the North, 372; the North West, 337; the Midlands, Yorkshire and Humberside, 301; Northern Ireland, 297; the South West, 157; and the South East, 149.

Between 1955–9 and 1969–73 the average annual rate of worker involvement in stoppages more than doubled. The three regions with the highest levels of worker involvement in 1955–9 (Wales, Scotland and Northern Ireland) had the lowest rates of increase thereafter. Indeed the rate of worker involvement in Northern Ireland actually fell. The only other region where the rate of increase was below the national average was the South East, which makes it difficult to ascribe much influence to the prevailing level of unemployment. The other four regions all had rates of increase above the national average, with that of the North West quadrupling between 1955–9 and 1969–73.

Examination of changes in time lost per 1000 employees revealed some interesting differences from changes in the rate of worker involvement. Overall time lost per 1000 employees rose by 164 per cent. Only one region had a fall in time lost – Northern Ireland. Other regions, where the increase was less than the national average, were the South East, the South

Table 6.7   Regional distribution of strike activity as measured by workers involved and working days lost in relation to employees in employment, 1946–73

Region	Percentage of employees in employment	Average no. of workers involved (000s)	Workers involved as a percentage of employees in employment	Average no. of working days lost (000s)	Working days lost per 1000 employees in employment
South East	35.8	238.6	2.9	1207	149
South West	5.6	44.8	3.5	199	157
Midlands, Yorkshire and Humberside	24.7	389.6	6.9	1689	301
North West	12.8	185.1	6.4	982	337
North	5.6	79.1	6.2	473	372
Scotland	9.2	182.5	8.7	802	384
Wales	4.2	90.1	9.4	522	545
Northern Ireland	2.0	28.7	6.2	136	297
UK	100.0	1238.5	5.5	6010	265

West and Scotland. The largest increases were in the Midlands, Yorkshire and Humberside, Wales, the North and the North West. Differences between these changes and those of worker involvement reflect differences in the rate of change of duration between regions. There appeared to be some tendency for regions with low rates of worker involvement to have smaller than average increases in duration.

In seeking to explain these changes it must be remembered that the regions themselves are far from homogeneous and that only a small minority of employees in each region was involved in stoppages – e.g. even in Wales 90 per cent of employees were not, on average, involved in stoppages at any time in the course of each year. In these circumstances it may be that some of the industrial location changes which took place significantly affected the region's strike record – e.g. to what extent can the increase in strike activity in the North West be attributed to the development of the motor vehicles industry on Merseyside? One conclusion that emerges from this analysis is that high local levels of unemployment are not necessarily associated with low levels of strike activity. Nor are low local levels of unemployment associated with high levels of strike activity.

DIMENSIONS OF GROSS STRIKE ACTIVITY:
DURATION, EXTENT AND SIZE

We have already indicated that the principal element in the overall increase in net strike activity was the rise in the number of stoppages and that changes in the extent and duration of strikes appeared to be of secondary importance. However, we did caution that such a conclusion would only be valid if one accepts that averages of extent and duration are reliable indicators of the whole distribution. Unfortunately we lack information on the distributions of net total strike activity by extent and duration. Our information relates to gross strike activity. Consequently, in using this information to trace movements of duration, extent and size we must constantly make allowances for the changing contribution of coal mining to total strike activity.

Table 6.8 gives details of the duration of all stoppages which took place in the UK between 1946 and 1973.

In the years 1946–73 there were 64 320 stoppages of which 36 per cent lasted a day or less, 58 per cent lasted two days or less and 71 per cent lasted three days or less. Only 1.5 per cent of stoppages lasted for more than 36 days and only 3 per cent for more than twenty-four days. Very short stoppages – i.e. those lasting three days or less – accounted for 60 per cent of workers involved but only 15 per cent of days lost. Very long stoppages – i.e. those lasting for more than twenty-four days – accounted for only 8 per cent of workers involved and 43 per cent of time lost.

Examination of sub-period averages shows that the share of the total

Table 6.8 Distribution of gross strike activity by duration of stoppages, 1946–73

Duration in working days	No. of strikes	Percentage of total	No. of workers involved (000s)	Percentage of total	No. of working days lost (000s)	Percentage of total
Not more than 1	23 320	36.3	11 512	40.6	10 614	8.0
Over 1, not more than 2	14 169	22.1	3 231	11.4	4 602	3.5
Over 2, not more than 3	7 968	12.4	2 301	8.1	4 946	3.7
Over 3, not more than 4	4 458	6.9	1 630	5.8	4 598	3.5
Over 4, not more than 5	3 275	5.1	1 499	5.3	5 127	3.9
Over 5, not more than 6	1 818	2.8	901	3.2	3 527	2.7
Over 6, not more than 12	4 659	7.3	2 887	10.2	18 542	14.0
Over 12, not more than 18	1 717	2.7	1 266	4.5	13 203	10.0
Over 18, not more than 24	924	1.4	789	2.8	9 993	7.6
Over 24, not more than 36	944	1.5	1 331	4.7	27 541	20.8
Over 36	978	1.5	981	3.5	29 384	22.2
Total	64 230	100.0	28 331	100.0	132 081	100.0

accounted for by stoppages lasting two days or less rose from 66 per cent in 1946–52 to 68.4 per cent in 1953–9. It then fell to 58.3 per cent in 1960–8 and 41 per cent in 1969–73. In contrast the share of stoppages lasting more than twenty-four days fell from 1.8 to 1.5 per cent and then rose in successive periods to 2.7 and 5.9 per cent. This latter pattern of increase was not confined to very long stoppages but was shared by all categories of stoppage lasting more than three days. No such consistent patterns emerged for shares of workers involved and days lost, partly because the occurrence of one or two large stoppages in any category affects the share of all the others.

Table 6.9 gives details of the distribution of gross strike activity by number of workers involved per stoppage in the period 1950–73.

Table 6.9   *Distribution of gross strike activity by number of workers involved, 1950–73*

No. of workers involved	No. of strikes	Percent-age of total	No. of workers involved (000s)	Percent-age of total	No. of working days lost (000s)	Percent-age of total
Under 100	33617	58.9	1217	4.6	5023	4.1
100 and under 250	10394	18.2	1640	6.2	6319	5.1
250 and under 500	6051	10.6	2084	7.9	7857	6.3
500 and under 1000	3830	6.7	2586	9.8	9839	8.0
1000 and under 2500	2236	3.9	3296	12.5	14636	11.8
2500 and under 5000	568	1.0	1931	7.3	9585	7.7
5000 and under 10000	266	0.5	1805	6.9	10111	8.2
10000 and over	157	0.3	11766	44.7	60372	48.8
Total	57119	100.0	26327	100.0	123745	100.0

Of the stoppages which occurred between 1950 and 1973, 59 per cent involved less than 100 workers, 77 per cent involved less than 250 workers and 88 per cent less than 500. Stoppages involving less than 500 workers only accounted for 19 per cent of workers involved and 16 per cent of working days lost. There were only 157 stoppages which involved 10 000 or more workers, a mere 0.3 per cent of the total, but they accounted for 45 per cent of workers involved and 49 per cent of days lost.

Examination of the sub-period data shows that stoppages involving less than 500 workers declined in relative frequency. Thus they were 68 per cent of the total in period two (1950–2), but this figure was reduced to 67 per cent, 58 per cent and 47 per cent in subsequent periods. Every other size category showed a consistent tendency to increase its share of the total with the sole exception of the very largest stoppages. Strikes involving at least 10 000 workers fell from 0.4 per cent in 1950–2 to 0.2 per cent. They remained at this level in 1960–8 and then reverted to 0.4 per cent in

1969–73. There appears to have been some tendency for the proportion of total workers involved attributable to the larger stoppages to rise over time. This effect was most marked among stoppages involving between 2500 and 10 000 workers whose share of workers involved rose erratically from 9.3 per cent in 1950–2 to 22.6 per cent in 1969–73. No such pattern was apparent in the shares of working days lost.

The distribution of gross strike activity by number of working days lost per stoppage is shown in Table 6.10.

Table 6.10   *Distribution of gross strike activity by number of working days lost, 1950–73*

No. of working days lost	No. of strikes	Percent- age of total	No. of workers involved (000s)	Percent- age of total	No. of working days lost (000s)	Percent- age of total
Under 500 days	41 916	73.4	3 461	13.1	5 338	4.3
500 and under 1000	5 940	10.4	2 003	7.6	4 161	3.4
1000 and under 5000	7 041	12.3	4 959	18.8	14 647	11.8
5000 and under 25 000	1 758	3.1	3 564	13.5	17 496	14.1
25 000 and under 50 000	233	0.4	1 162	4.4	8 255	6.7
50 000 and over	231	0.4	11 177	42.5	73 854	59.7
Total	57 119	100.0	26 327	100.0	123 745	100.0

Of the gross total of stoppages between 1950 and 1973, 73 per cent involved the loss of less than 500 working days, 84 per cent the loss of less than 1000 days and 96 per cent the loss of less than 5000 days. Stoppages involving the loss of less than 500 working days only accounted for 13 per cent of workers involved and 4 per cent of days lost. Stoppages involving the loss of 50 000 days or more accounted for 0.4 per cent of stoppages, 43 per cent of workers involved and 60 per cent of days lost.

Our usual sub-period analysis revealed that the share of all stoppages accruing to those involving the loss of less than 500 days rose initially from 81 to 82 per cent. It then fell to 74 per cent and again to 60 per cent. Every other size category followed a pattern of an initial fall followed by a substantial rise. The largest relative gains occurred among stoppages involving the loss of between 1000 and 25 000 days. Their share rose from 10.6 to 24.7 per cent. No similar consistent patterns emerged for shares of workers involved or days lost.

In explaining the increases in the duration, extent and size of these stoppages, stress must be placed on the effect of changes in the frequency of strikes in coal mining. More than 99 per cent of stoppages in coal were not major stoppages – i.e. they involved the loss of less than 5000 working days each. On average these minor coal mining stoppages involved 121 workers and lasted less than two days. Non-major stoppages in all other industries involved an average of 247 workers and lasted for nearly two and a half days. In these circumstances a change in the ratio of coal mining stoppages to the gross total of stoppages could make it appear in the gross aggregate series as if they were substantial changes taking place in the characteristics of the 'typical' strike. In fact coal mining's share of the gross total of stoppages rose from 63 per cent in 1946–52 to 74 per cent in 1953–9. They then fell to 39 per cent in 1960–8 and to 7 per cent in 1969–73. This pattern matches the rise in the proportion of small, short stoppages in 1953–9 and the falls in the following sub-periods. Such a change in the industrial composition of the gross strike series does not provide anything like a complete explanation of all the changes which have taken place, but it must play an important role in explaining why the typical UK strike is no longer as small and short as it used to be. For the rest the changes which occurred are quite consistent with some slight general upward movement in extent and duration across the whole spectrum of strike activity. This confirms that the principal element in the overall increase in net totals was the rise in the number of stoppages.

NET STRIKE ACTIVITY KNOWN TO BE OFFICIAL

Series for the net totals of stoppages known to be official, and their share of the net totals of all strike activity, are shown in Table 6.11.

Between 1960 and 1973 there were, on average, ninety-nine stoppages a year known to be official. They involved 538 000 workers and resulted in the loss of 2 536 000 days. In relation to the net totals of strike activity these strikes accounted for 5.2 per cent of stoppages, 42 per cent of workers involved and 47 per cent of days lost. There seems to have been some tendency for the share of net strike activity known to be official to fall in the late 1960s and then rise sharply in the early 1970s, so that overall no clear trend is discernible.

Two conclusions may be drawn from this data. First, stoppages known to be official were much more important in terms of workers involved and working days lost than their relative frequency would suggest. On average strikes known to be official involved thirteen times as many workers and lasted rather longer than other stoppages. Secondly, there is little evidence to support the view that strikes not known to be official were increasing at a much faster rate than those known to be official. Consequently, it cannot be assumed that the sole cause of the growth in the UK's strike record in this period was the growth in the number of unconstitutional stoppages. As unconstitutional stoppages accounted for around 95 per cent of the increase they clearly bulk large in any explanation of the period. But some attention must also be devoted to stoppages known to be official, particularly in the light of their contribution to the workers involved and days lost series.

Table 6.11 Net strike activity known to be official in relation to the net totals of strike activity, 1960–73

Year	No. of strikes	As a percentage of all strikes	Strike activity known to be official		No. of working days lost (000s)	As a percentage of all working days lost
			No. of workers involved (000s)	As a percentage of all workers involved		
1960	68	5.8	24	4.1	497	19.6
1961	60	4.9	80	15.1	861	37.3
1962	78	6.3	3809	89.2	4109	74.8
1963	49	4.5	80	18.2	527	36.9
1964	69	4.7	119	16.7	648	32.8
1965	97	6.0	94	12.4	607	24.1
1966	60	4.3	50	10.1	1172	51.4
1967	108	6.3	36	5.2	394	14.7
1968	91	4.2	1565	70.2	2199	76.6
1969	98	3.3	283	18.6	1613	27.8
1970	162	4.3	296	17.6	3320	33.6
1971	161	7.7	376	32.5	10050	74.5
1972	159	7.0	326	23.4	7520	57.2
1973	132	5.1	396	26.7	2009	28.3
Average	99	5.2	538	42.0	2536	47.2

Table 6.11a   *Industrial strike activity known to be official in relation to all strike activity as measured by working days lost, 1960–73*

Year	Mining and quarrying (%)	Metals, engineering, shipbuilding, vehicles (%)	Textiles, clothing and footwear (%)	Construction (%)	Transport and communications (%)	All other industries and services (%)
1960	—	21.9	12.0	13.6	0.2	52.6
1961	—	42.6	63.6	15.4	15.7	46.9
1962	—	80.1	56.7	27.5	63.8	41.5
1963	—	22.1	16.0	78.4	9.7	40.2
1964	13.6	37.4	—	—	37.5	18.1
1965	—	25.8	38.5	11.9	6.6	37.0
1966	—	18.7	33.3	4.1	84.8	50.8
1967	—	14.4	32.3	8.5	16.5	12.9
1968	—	59.8	15.0	13.3	7.3	25.6
1969	—	32.9	5.0	4.3	11.5	31.8
1970	—	12.9	15.1	4.1	44.9	60.9
1971	—	58.9	14.1	8.2	95.5	38.4
1972	99.3	40.0	47.1	91.7	65.8	26.5
1973	—	19.2	42.5	8.5	30.8	55.2
Average	67.5	39.8	27.5	62.9	64.0	46.6

Table 6.11a shows the share of working days lost in each industry group which can be attributed to stoppages known to be official.

In terms of their contribution to the total of working days, lost stoppages known to be official were most important in mining and quarrying, 68 per cent; transport and communication, 64 per cent; construction, 63 per cent; and all other industries and services, 47 per cent. Yet in mining and quarrying stoppages known to be official occurred only twice in the fourteen year period whereas every other industrial sector experienced official action in at least thirteen out of the fourteen years. The share of working days lost due to official action was usually particularly high in years of a single large stoppage – e.g. in transport and communications the high levels of 1962, 1966 and 1971 were the products of stoppages by railwaymen, seamen and postal workers respectively. As we have remarked previously, centralised bargaining systems are much more likely to produce high shares of time lost through official action than decentralised systems.

COAL MINING

Between 1946 and 1973 there were 28 923 stoppages in coal mining involving more than five million workers and the loss of twenty-three million working days. Of the gross total of strike activity coal mining accounted for 45 per cent of all stoppages and 18 per cent of workers involved and days lost. The number of stoppages in coal mining followed the economy-wide pattern of decline until 1950 but then rose consistently to a peak of 2224 strikes in 1957. It fell to a trough of 135 in 1971 before rising again. The numbers of workers involved and days lost followed broadly similar patterns to that of stoppages, except that both peak and trough occurred two years earlier. These patterns are so different, particularly in respect of the fall in strike activity from 1955–7 to 1969–71, that, as has been said, we made coal mining the subject of special study. The results are reported in Chapter 8.

MAJOR STRIKES, 1946–73

NET TOTALS OF MAJOR STRIKES AND THEIR RELATIONSHIP TO NET TOTALS OF ALL STOPPAGES

Table 6.12 provides details of those stoppages which involved the loss of at least 5000 working days each.

On average, between 1946 and 1973, there were eighty major strikes a year involving over half a million workers and the loss of more than three million days. In relation to the net totals of strike activity, major stoppages accounted for over 6 per cent of stoppages, 65 per cent of workers involved and 82 per cent of days lost. In most years major strikes were less

Table 6.12   *Net totals of major strike activity in absolute terms and in relation to the net totals of all strike activity, 1946–73*

Year	No. of major strikes	As a percentage of all strikes	No. of workers involved (000s)	As a percentage of all workers involved (000s)	No. of working days lost (000s)	As a percentage of all working days lost (000s)
1946	67	7.6	127.2	40.7	1269	73.1
1947	38	5.7	178.4	56.7	1131	74.4
1948	27	4.2	122.4	51.7	1145	77.7
1949	28	5.1	105.1	56.4	824	78.3
1950	23	4.8	75.7	47.0	664	69.3
1951	38	5.7	126.5	51.8	1026	76.3
1952	26	5.3	68.9	48.4	894	79.0
1953	24	5.5	1127.6	93.5	1600	89.3
1954	22	4.2	136.9	55.7	1766	88.8
1955	31	4.9	175.6	55.3	2352	88.1
1956	28	4.9	115.7	43.4	1232	77.9
1957	34	5.4	957.8	87.6	7524	95.3
1958	34	5.1	131.7	47.8	2652	88.0
1959	48	6.1	248.0	54.6	4454	90.8
1960	69	5.9	287.7	49.5	1926	76.1
1961	65	5.3	247.0	46.6	1678	72.7
1962	81	6.5	3976.8	93.2	4844	88.2
1963	42	3.9	177.3	40.3	1095	76.6
1964	63	4.3	293.3	41.3	924	46.8
1965	85	5.3	312.5	41.2	1635	65.1
1966	48	3.5	129.9	26.3	1544	67.7
1967	89	5.2	239.7	34.6	1749	65.2
1968	117	5.4	1761.5	79.1	3514	75.8
1969	181	6.2	729.0	48.0	4238	73.0
1970	261	7.0	820.6	48.7	7547	76.3
1971	171	8.2	713.8	61.8	12297	91.2
1972	278	12.2	917.4	65.9	11575	88.3
1973	225	8.7	924.4	62.4	5323	74.9
Average	80	6.4	543.9	65.1	3158	81.6

important than this, but outstanding events dominated a few exceptional years.

In terms of the direction of change the number of major stoppages generally followed a pattern similar to that of the net total of stoppages, but there were some differences in the rate of change. Major stoppages fell more rapidly between 1946 and 1954, rose more rapidly up to 1962, more slowly up to 1967 and then much more rapidly than the aggregate series.

The number of workers involved series was much more volatile in both absolute and relative terms. The average number of workers involved was 544 000 but it fluctuated from 69 000 in 1952 to nearly four million in 1962. As a percentage of the aggregate series workers involved in major strikes averaged 65 per cent but fluctuated from 94 per cent in 1953 down to 26 per cent in 1966. Workers involved in major strikes in relation to those involved in all stoppages appear to have suffered a decline in the 1960s but to have made a more than adequate recovery in the 1970s. Working days lost through major stoppages varied from 664 000 in 1950 to 12 297 000 in 1971 and from 47 per cent of the total in 1964 to 95 per cent in 1957.

The volatility of these series makes it difficult to discern overall movements. Using the annual averages of the four sub-periods reduces this volatility although there is a risk that it may obscure other features. On this basis the absolute number of major stoppages fell in 1953–9 and then rose at an accelerating rate. In relative terms it fell and fell again before rising to an all-time high in the last sub-period. The number of workers involved more than trebled, then doubled, then fell very slightly. In relative terms this became a substantial rise followed by two falls. The number of days lost trebled, fell sharply and then quadrupled to finish eight times greater than its original level. In relative terms there was a moderate rise, a moderate fall and a small rise. Between the first and last sub-periods the number of stoppages rose by 537 per cent, workers involved by 615 per cent and days lost by 725 per cent. In relation to the net totals all three measures were higher in the last sub-period than the first, although workers involved and days lost had peaked in the second.

NET MAJOR STRIKES IN PERSPECTIVE

Table 6.13 shows the average numbers of workers involved and days lost in perspective.

On average major stoppages involved 2.5 per cent of employees or 5.8 per cent of trade union members at some time in the course of each year. Days lost through these stoppages amounted to 0.6 per cent of potential working time and were equivalent to 3 per cent of the time lost through unemployment. But such averages mask the very sharp increase which occurred in major strike activity. Between 1946–52 and 1960–8 the rate of worker involvement in major stoppages rose sixfold from 0.6 to 3.7 per cent of employees. Days lost showed a sevenfold increase, from 0.02 to 0.15 per cent of potential working time between 1946–52 and 1969–73. The rise in relation to trade union membership was slightly less marked because

Table 6.13   *Net major strike activity in perspective, 1946–73*

Year	Workers involved as a percentage of employees in employment	Workers involved as a percentage of trade union members	Working days lost as a percentage of potential working time	Working days lost as a percentage of time lost through unemployment
1946–52	0.6	1.3	0.02	1.0
1953–59	2.0	4.6	0.05	3.3
1960–68	3.7	8.7	0.04	1.9
1969–73	3.7	7.6	0.15	4.8
1946–73	2.5	5.8	0.06	3.0

trade union membership rose faster than employment. Similarly days lost in relation to time lost through unemployment showed a smaller increase, because unemployment itself was also rising rapidly. Yet despite these very rapid increases major strike activity remained of minor significance in relation to the capacity of the economy as a whole. Even in the last sub-period, when major strike activity was at its highest, on average 0.15 per cent of employees were engaged in strike activity at any one time and 0.15 per cent of potential working time was lost in the course of a year.

NET MAJOR STRIKE ACTIVITY BY INDUSTRY

The distribution of major stoppages by industry is shown below. The most strike-prone industry, in terms of number of stoppages, was motor vehicles with 482. It was followed by non-electrical engineering, 287; electrical engineering, 194; iron and steel and other metal manufacture, 158; and shipbuilding, 157. Between them these five industries accounted for 57 per cent of all major stoppages and averaged more than five major stoppages a year each. Of the remaining thirty-five industries, two experienced no major stoppages at all, twenty-four averaged less than one major stoppage a year and nine averaged between one and five stoppages a year.

Examining each industry's share of the total on a sub-period by sub-period basis revealed little consistent movement. Three industries had had increases in each sub-period – i.e. iron and steel and other metal manufacture, other metal goods and professional and scientific services. Four had industries that had decreases in their share of the total in each sub-period – i.e. agriculture, forestry and fishing, road passenger transport, port and inland water transport and distribution. Comparing annual averages in the first and last sub-periods showed that in thirty-two industries major strike activity had increased, in five it had fallen, and in three there had been no major stoppages in either sub-period. The average number of major stoppages rose from thirty-five a year in 1946–52 to 223 per year in 1969–73. Major contributors to this increase of 188 stoppages a

Table 6.14   *Number of net major strikes by industry group, 1946–73*

Industry group	No. of strikes	As a percentage of all major strikes
Agriculture, forestry, fishing	10	0.4
Mining and quarrying (excl. coal mining)	2	0.1
Grain milling	1	Ø
Bread, flour, confectionery	11	0.5
Other food	33	1.5
Drink	13	0.6
Tobacco	4	0.2
Chemicals	36	1.6
Iron and steel and other metals	158	7.0
Non-electrical engineering	287	12.8
Electrical engineering	194	8.6
Shipbuilding	157	7.0
Motor vehicles	482	21.5
Aircraft	95	4.2
Cycles	17	0.8
Railway locos, carriages, trams, etc.	8	0.4
Carts, perambulators, etc.	—	—
Other metal goods	73	3.3
Textiles	51	2.3
Clothing	7	0.3
Footwear	—	—
Bricks, pottery, glass, cement, etc.	16	0.7
Furniture, bedding, wood and cork manufacture	15	0.7
Paper, board, cartons	12	0.5
Printing and publishing	15	0.7
Other manufacturing industries	60	2.7
Construction	124	5.5
Gas, water, electricity supply	13	0.6
Railways	17	0.8
Road passenger transport	64	2.9
Road haulage	13	0.6
Sea transport	5	0.2
Port and inland water transport	139	6.2
Other transport and communications	23	1.0
Distribution	24	1.1
Insurance, banking, finance, business	3	0.1
Professional and scientific	16	0.7
Miscellaneous	19	0.8
Public administration and defence	19	0.8
General engineering	7	0.3
Total (exc. coal mining)	2243	100.0

Table 6.15   *Cross-tabulation of net major strikes by industry group and number of workers involved, 1946–73*

Industry group	No. of workers involved									
	50 and under 100	100 and under 250	250 and under 500	500 and under 1000	1000 and under 2500	2500 and under 5000	5000 and under 10 000	10 000 and under 25 000	25 000 and under 50 000	50 000 and over
Agriculture, forestry, etc.					7	2	1			
Mining and quarrying (exc. coal mining)		1	1							
Grain milling					1					
Bread, etc.			2	3	2	3	1			
Other food			1	12	15	5				
Drink		1	1	4	6	1				
Tobacco		1	2					1		
Chemicals		1	6	8	15	4	2			
Iron and steel and other metals		13	39	36	35	15	12	8		
Non-electrical engineering	7	32	49	76	96	15	8	3	1	
Electrical engineering	4	13	27	42	60	32	14	2		
Shipbuilding	2	10	29	41	43	16	7	6	2	1
Motor vehicles	1	6	22	52	138	131	95	32	5	
Aircraft	2	10	11	15	33	13	11			
Cycles		1	2	1	8	1	4			
Railway locos, carriages, etc.			1	3	1	3				
Other metal goods		9	19	26	18	1				
Textiles		2	9	13	22	1	4			
Clothing			1	1	2	2		1		
Bricks, etc.		2	3	2	6	1	1	1		
Furniture, etc.	1	1	2	6	1	4				
Paper, board		1	4	6	1					
Printing and publishing		1	2		4	2	1	3	1	1
Other manufacturing industries		3	4	10	22	12	8	1		
Construction	5	18	41	29	18	7	2	1	1	2
Gas, water electricity		1	3		6	1	1	1		
Railways		1	1	3	5	1	2	2		2
Road passenger transport		1	4	14	15	15	5	6	3	1
Road haulage		1		1	5	1	3	2		
Sea transport				1	1	1	1		1	
Port and inland water transport		3	9	8	30	25	31	28	5	
Other transport and communication			2	3	4	4	1	4	1	4
Distribution			4	3	10	5	2			
Insurance, etc.					2		1			
Professional, etc.			1	1	1	1	5	2	2	3
Miscellaneous		1	5	6	4	3				
Public administration		1	1	5	5	2	2			3
General engineering							1		1	5
Total	22	135	306	430	643	329	228	105	23	22

year included motor vehicles, non-electrical engineering, electrical
engineering, iron and steel and other metal manufacture and other metal
goods. These five industries accounted for 55 per cent of the total increase.

Table 6.14 only shows one measure of strike activity by industry. Tables
6.15 and 6.16 show the distribution of major stoppages by the numbers of
workers involved and days lost per stoppage.

Of the 2243 major stoppages which occurred between 1946 and 1973,
20.6 per cent involved less than 500 workers, 68.5 per cent less than 2500
workers and 93.4 per cent less than 10 000 workers. Only 2 per cent of
major stoppages involved more than 25 000 workers and only 1 per cent
more than 50 000. The most frequently occurring size of stoppage was that
involving between 1000 and 2500 workers. These accounted for 28.7 per
cent of the total.

Our usual sub-period by sub-period analysis adds little to our understanding of this pattern. Only two size categories displayed a constant direction
of change throughout the period. Stoppages involving less than 100
workers and those involving between 10 000 and 25 000 stoppages both
experienced continuous declines in their shares of the total. We even tried
aggregating across several categories of size to produce small, medium and
large stoppages but still could not find any consistent movement. In
summary over half of all major stoppages involved between 500 and 4999
workers. Very large major stoppages (involving more than 50 000 workers)
and very small major stoppages (involving less than 100 workers) were
equally uncommon. There does not appear to have been any consistent
shift to any particular size of strike.

The industrial distribution of these stoppages yielded few surprises. All
industries which experienced more than one major stoppage also experienced stoppages of varying sizes. The infrequency of major stoppages in
many industries made detailed comparisons rather meaningless, but
analyses over broad sectors proved to be of some value. We divided the
industries into three groups, 'metal trades', 'services' and 'other industries'. Metal trades accounted for 65.9 per cent of major strikes, services
21.4 per cent and other industries 12.8 per cent. Metal trades were
under-represented amongst the largest stoppages, those involving 10 000
workers or more accounting for only 44 per cent of the total and slightly
over-represented in virtually all the other size categories. Services were
over-represented among the largest stoppages, having 49.3 per cent of the
total. But they were under-represented among small stoppages, those
involving between 500 and 2500 workers. Other industries were under-
represented among the largest stoppages, only having 8.9 per cent, and
slightly over-represented in all the other categories. The most plausible
explanation of these differences is that they reflect differences in bargaining structures and employment levels between industries.

Table 6.16 shows that 48.4 per cent of major stoppages involved the loss
of less than 10 000 working days, 65.7 per cent less than 15 000 and 78.7
per cent less than 25 000. At the other end of the scale 5.3 per cent of
major stoppages involved the loss of 100 000 days or more. Comparison of

Table 6.16 *Cross-tabulation of net major strikes by industry group and number of working days lost, 1946–73*

Industry group	No. of working days lost							
	5000 and under 10 000	10 000 and under 15 000	15 000 and under 20 000	20 000 and under 25 000	25 000 and under 50 000	50 000 and under 75 000	75 000 and under 100 000	100 000 and over
Agriculture, forestry, etc.	3	1			3	2	1	
Mining and quarrying (exc. coal mining)	2							
Grain milling	1							
Bread, etc.	5	1			3			2
Other food	17	6	5	2	2	1		
Drink	10	1	1			1		
Tobacco	2	1		1				
Chemicals	21	8	2	2	1	2		
Iron and steel and other metals	79	33	13	2	16	5	3	7
Non-electrical engineering	166	50	17	14	27	4	4	5
Electrical engineering	98	40	18	7	14	11	1	5
Shipbuilding	63	33	15	4	14	7	2	19
Motor vehicles	206	83	40	35	63	20	14	21
Aircraft	47	13	7	3	12	4	4	5
Cycles	13	2	1			1		
Railway locos, carriages, etc.	4	2	2					
Metal goods	45	12	6	4	5	1		
Textiles	29	9	3	3	5		1	1
Clothing	1	3			2			1
Bricks, etc.	6	1	3		3	2		1
Furniture, etc.	7	6	1		1			
Paper, board	6	2	4					
Printing and publishing	3	2	1	1	3	1		4
Other manufacturing industries	29	13	4	2	8	1		3
Construction	75	16	11	3	14	1		4
Gas, water, electricity	5	3	1	1	1	1		1
Railways	8	1	1	3	2			2
Road passenger transport	27	9	5	7	7	1	3	5
Road haulage	3	2	2	1	1	2	1	1
Sea transport	1			1	1		1	1
Port and inland water transport	57	23	11	9	15	7	2	15
Other transport and communications	9	2	1	1	6	1	1	2
Distribution	11	2	5		3	2		1
Insurance, etc.					1	1		1
Professional, etc.	5	1	1	1	4		2	2
Miscellaneous	11	4	1	2	1			
Public administration	11	3		1	1			3
General engineering					1			6
Total	1086	388	182	110	240	79	40	118

the shares of the total of stoppages occurring in each size category in each of the four sub-periods revealed no consistent pattern of change. Comparison of shares in the first and last sub-periods disclosed a tendency for stoppages involving the loss of less than 20 000 working days to increase their share of the total, from 68 to 74 per cent. Stoppages involving the loss of 100 000 working days or more showed a decline from 5.7 to 5.4 per cent of the total.

It was again impossible to make detailed industry comparisons of the incidence of stoppages of various sizes because many industries had so few stoppages. Therefore we followed the same practice as before – i.e. grouping industries into metal trades, services and others. There was little difference between these groups in terms of the distribution of stoppages by number of days lost per stoppage. Metal trades were slightly under-represented among the largest stoppages (involving the loss of 75 000 days or more) and slightly over-presented among the rest. The reverse was true for the services sector whilst other industries followed the metal trades pattern. These differences were quite slight and again appear to reflect differences in bargaining arrangements.

NET MAJOR STRIKES BY CAUSE

The distribution of major stoppages by attributed principal cause for the period 1946–73 is shown in Table 6.17.

Altogether 57.3 per cent of major stoppages were concerned with wage issues. Of these 40.3 per cent were over claims for wage increases and 17 per cent were over other wage issues. Of the remaining cause classifications the 'miscellaneous' category (hours, procedures, etc.) was the most important with 14.2 per cent of the total. Issues of trade union principle came next with 11 per cent. This was followed by redundancy and demarcation, 6 per cent each, and sympathy and demarcation, less than 3 per cent each.

Examination of the share of the total attributable to each cause in each sub-period revealed only one category with a consistent pattern of change. Wage increase issues rose from 13.4 per cent in 1946–52 to 51.4 per cent in 1969–73. All pay issues did not grow as rapidly as this, because the share of other wage issues fell from 25 to 16 per cent. Beginning and end of period comparisons of shares for the remaining cause categories showed a general pattern of decline, although the changes were not consistent across each sub-period. The largest changes affected issues of trade union principle (down from 20.6 to 6.8 per cent), miscellaneous (from 16.6 to 11.2 per cent) and demarcation (from 4.9 to 1.1 per cent).

It must be emphasised that these were relative and not absolute declines. Every cause category showed an increase in the annual average number of stoppages between the first and last sub-periods. The rate of increase varied from 41 per cent for demarcation disputes to 2340 per cent for wage increase issues. Of necessity any attempt to explain the increase in the

Table 6.17　*Net major strike activity by cause, 1946–73*

Cause	No. of strikes	Percentage share of total
Wage increase	904	40.3
Other wage issue	381	17.0
Discipline	134	6.0
Redundancy	136	6.1
Sympathy	63	2.8
Demarcation	60	2.7
Trade union principle	247	11.0
Other	318	14.2
Total	2243	100.0

Table 6.18　*Distribution of net major strikes by region, 1946–73*

Region	No. of strikes	Percentage share of total
South East	387	17.3
East Anglia	9	0.4
South West	54	2.4
West Midlands	420	18.7
East Midlands	73	3.3
Yorkshire and Humberside	134	6.0
North West	337	15.0
Northern	113	5.0
Scotland	377	16.8
Wales and Monmouthshire	100	4.5
Northern Ireland	72	3.2
Various regions in England	73	3.3
Great Britain	48	2.1
United Kingdom	46	2.1
Total	2243	100.0

number of major stoppages must focus heavily on those factors likely to affect the number of wage increase disputes.

NET MAJOR STRIKES BY REGION

The distribution of major strike activity by region is shown in Table 6.18.

Four regions, the West Midlands, the South East, Scotland and the North West, accounted for 68 per cent of all major stoppages. The other ten classifications (seven regions and three multi-region areas), shared the remaining 32 per cent of the total. As we have pointed out in previous chapters, the regional distribution of strike activity is heavily influenced by such factors as the industrial structure of the area and the collective bargaining arrangements in those industries. Consequently analysis of this kind can offer little guidance as to the impact of local attitudes on regional strike patterns.

However, changes in the regional distribution of strike activity over time are of some interest, particularly if the changes do not obviously correspond to changes in other variables. Bearing this in mind we examined changes in the share of the total of major stoppages in each region in each sub-period. Almost half of the fourteen areas experienced consistent patterns of change. Three regions, the South West, Yorkshire and Humberside and the Northern, increased their shares of the total in each sub-period. As a result their combined share rose from 8.4 per cent in 1946–52 to 13.4 per cent in 1969–73. Three areas, the South East, Northern Ireland and various regions in England, experienced a consistent decrease with their combined share of the total falling from 47 to 17.8 per cent. Beginning to end of period comparisons revealed that nine areas increased their share of the total and five areas experienced decreases. In absolute terms all areas experienced an increase in the average annual number of stoppages between 1946–52 and 1969–73. Between 1946–52 and 1969–73 the average annual total of major stoppages rose from thirty-five to 223, an increase of 188. The principal contributors to that increase were the West Midlands, with major stoppages up by forty-one a year; the North West, up by thirty-seven; Scotland, up by thirty; and South East, up by twenty. Differences in the rates of increase of major stoppages between regions were substantial and require explanation. But without more information on the other changes which have taken place one can do little more than note them as part of the pattern which requires explanation.

OCCUPATIONAL GROUPS (OTHER THAN COAL MINING) MOST FREQUENTLY INVOLVED IN MAJOR STRIKES

Altogether ninety-three different occupational groups were involved in major stoppages during these periods. Details of those most frequently involved are shown in Table 6.19.

One occupational group, engineering and electrical engineering workers not elsewhere specified, was involved in 32 per cent of all major strikes. A further 16 per cent of major stoppages involved car and vehicle industry workers not elsewhere specified. This group reflects the large number of major strikes which took place in the motor vehicles industry. A further eight occupational groups, each with a share of at least 2 per cent of the total, had a combined share of 22.5 per cent. In all the ten most frequently occurring occupational groups accounted for 70.6 per cent of major strikes. The remaining 29 per cent was spread across eighty-three occupational groups which averaged eight stoppages each. Of these eighty-three, eighteen were involved in one stoppage each and a further eleven in two stoppages each.

Table 6.19　*Occupational groups (other than coal mining) most frequently involved in major strikes, 1946–73*

Occupational group	No. of strikes	Percentage share of total
Engineering and electrical engineering workers n.e.s.	718	32.0
Car and vehicle industry workers n.e.s.	362	16.1
Dockers/stevedores	118	5.3
Building workers n.e.s.	79	3.5
Aircraft workers n.e.s.	64	2.9
Bus crews	60	2.7
Clerical workers	47	2.1
Assemblers	47	2.1
Food manufacturing workers n.e.s.	45	2.0
Electricians – building, maintenance, supply, etc.	44	2.0
83 other occupational groups	659	29.4
Total	2243	100.0

n.e.s., not elsewhere specified.

The overwhelming impression obtained from Table 6.19 is that major stoppages were very heavily concentrated in a handful of occupational groups. Unfortunately some of the occupational titles were so imprecise that they covered a wide range of occupational tasks. This point is emphasised by Table 6.20, which shows the industrial location of major stoppages involving the most frequent non-industry-specific groups – i.e. occupations like bus crews, which only occurred in road passenger transport, are excluded.

Of the seven occupational groups shown in Table 6.20, four are largely concentrated in single industries, although there is some 'spillover' into related trades. The other three groups, engineering and electrical engineering workers n.e.s., clerical workers and assemblers, seem far less industry specific. Of the ten most frequently occurring occupational groups shown in Table 6.19 only three, engineering and electrical engineering workers n.e.s., car and vehicle workers n.e.s. and dockers and stevedores, achieved a similar prominence in each sub-period.

Table 6.20 *Major strikes: cross-tabulation of occupational groups most frequently involved by industry (other than coal mining), 1946–73*

Industry	Occupational groups						
	Engineering and electrical engineering workers n.e.s.	Car and vehicle industry workers n.e.s.	Dockers and stevedores	Building workers n.e.s.	Aircraft workers n.e.s.	Clerical workers	Assemblers
Other food	5						
Tobacco	1						
Iron and steel and other metal manufactures	101			1		7	
Non-electrical engineering	244					4	1
Electrical engineering	157					4	8
Shipbuilding	50						
Motor vehicles	21	347				9	36
Aircraft	5	1			62	5	
Cycles	3	7					
Railway locos, carriages, etc.	1	6					
Other metal goods	64					1	1
Textiles	3						
Bricks, pottery, glass, cement	2						
Furniture, timber, etc.	1			1			
Printing and publishing	1						
Other manufacturing industries	29					1	1
Construction	9		77			1	
Gas, water, electricity	1						
Railways	2	1					
Road passenger transport	3					1	
Road haulage	1						
Sea transport			1				
Ports and inland water transport			117			2	
Other transport and communication	5				2	6	
Professional and scientific	1						
Miscellaneous						2	
Public administration	1					4	
General engineering	7						
Total	718	362	118	79	64	47	47

In summary the occupational groups which have been most often involved in major stoppages varied a good deal from sub-period to sub-period although, over the period as a whole, major strikes have been concentrated in a handful of occupations. Doubts over the job contents implied by these occupational titles makes us cautious about attributing too much to occupational factors, but the possibility that they may be important must be admitted.

SEASONAL PATTERN OF NET MAJOR STRIKES

The seasonal pattern of the commencement and termination of major stoppages in 1946–73 is shown in Table 6.21.

Table 6.21   *Seasonal pattern of net major strikes, 1946–73*

Month	*No. of strikes beginning*	*Percentage share of total*	*No. of strikes ending*	*Percentage share of total*
January	201	9.0	132	5.9
February	211	9.4	185	8.3
March	197	8.8	206	9.2
April	234	10.4	178	7.9
May	231	10.3	258	11.5
June	210	9.4	234	10.4
July	149	6.6	150	6.7
August	169	7.5	164	7.3
September	206	9.2	166	7.4
October	229	10.2	254	11.3
November	148	6.6	199	8.9
December	58	2.6	117	5.2
Total	2243	100.0	2243	100.0

Spring and autumn are the two periods in the year when major stoppages are most likely to begin. The months of April, May, June, September and October witnessed the commencement of 49.5 per cent of major stoppages. In addition there was a third minor peak, in January and February. Our customary sub-period by sub-period analysis revealed no consistent pattern of change in the share of any particular month or even group of months. We also examined shares in the first and last sub-periods without detecting any obviously significant shifts.

Major stoppages were most likely to end in the months of May, October, June and March. These four witnessed the termination of 42.4 per cent of major stoppages. Again through time analysis revealed few consistent patterns, except that the share of stoppages ending in March fell from 12.1 to 8.3 per cent. The timing of major stoppages is obviously influenced by many variables, but it would be unreasonable to suppose that the settlement dates for major bargaining units and the occurrence of holiday periods were unimportant.

THE DURATION OF NET MAJOR STOPPAGES

The distribution of major stoppages by their duration in working days is set out in Table 6.22.

Table 6.22　*Duration of net major stoppages, 1946–73*

Duration in working days	No. of strikes	Percentage share of total
Not more than 1	73	3.3
Over 1　but not more than 2	67	3.0
Over 2　but not more than 3	101	4.5
Over 3　but not more than 4	115	5.1
Over 4　but not more than 5	128	5.7
Over 5　but not more than 6	112	5.0
Over 6　but not more than 12	504	22.5
Over 12 but not more than 18	275	12.3
Over 18 but not more than 24	210	9.4
Over 24 but not more than 36	290	12.9
Over 36 but not more than 48	148	6.6
Over 48 but not more than 60	86	3.8
Over 60 but not more than 72	52	2.3
Over 72	82	3.7
Total	2243	100.0

Over the period as a whole 26.6 per cent of stoppages were over within six days; 70.7 per cent were over within twenty-four days; 90.2 per cent within forty-eight days and 96.3 per cent within seventy-two days. This contrasts sharply with the gross totals of stoppages, where 85.6 per cent were over within six days and 97 per cent within twenty-four days. Examination of the sub-period data revealed no consistent patterns among the various duration categories, or even among groups of categories. Beginning and end of period comparisons show that stoppages of less than six days increased their share from 21.1 to 25.7 per cent. Those lasting between twenty-four and seventy-two days increased from 21.9 to 29.1 per cent. It seems that there was a simultaneous shift to very short and moderately long stoppages at the expense of moderately short and very long stoppages.

The association between duration and extent of major stoppages is portrayed in Table 6.23.

Table 6.23 gives the impression that there is a strong inverse relationship between extent and duration, because 33 000 stoppages which did not meet

Table 6.23   Cross-tabulation for net major strikes by duration in working days and the number of workers involved, 1946–73

Duration in working days	Number of workers involved									
	50 and under 100	100 and under 250	250 and under 500	500 and under 1000	1000 and under 2500	2500 and under 5000	5000 and under 10 000	10 000 and under 25 000	25 000 and under 50 000	50 000 and over
Not more than 1							40	4	9	
Over 1 but not more than 2						33	25	6	2	1
Over 2 but not more than 3					26	47	22	5	1	
Over 3 but not more than 4					56	36	14	8	1	
Over 4 but not more than 5					55	36	27	9	1	
Over 5 but not more than 6				5	66	18	16	5		2
Over 6 but not more than 12			11	159	213	71	27	20	1	2
Over 12 but not more than 18			55	90	70	29	16	10	3	2
Over 18 but not more than 24		1	70	52	42	19	17	5	3	1
Over 24 but not more than 36		35	87	71	53	19	10	10	2	3
Over 36 but not more than 48		30	37	25	31	11	7	4	2	1
Over 48 but not more than 60	1	28	22	11	16	2	3	2	1	
Over 60 but not more than 72	2	21	9	4	6	4	2	1	2	1
Over 72	19	20	15	13	9	4	2			
Total	22	135	306	430	643	329	228	105	23	22

the qualifying limit are omitted from the top left-hand corner of the matrix. Some 79 per cent of major stoppages involved over 500 workers; 60 per cent involved over 1000 and 17 per cent more than 5000. Yet of stoppages lasting more than seventy-two days only 2 per cent involved more than 5000 workers while 66 per cent involved less than 500. Of stoppages lasting more than forty-eight days only 6 per cent involved more than 5000 workers and 62 per cent involved fewer than 500 workers. In general Table 6.23 supports our earlier conclusion that very large stoppages, once started, are more difficult to stop in the very short term. But the pressures for a settlement mount, so that such stoppages are rarely very prolonged. Small stoppages seem more amenable to rapid settlement in the first instance, but pressure to force an eventual settlement does not necessarily increase to the same extent as in the large strike case.

MAJOR STOPPAGES IN COAL MINING

In the period 1946–73 there were 186 major stoppages in coal mining involving 1 584 846 workers and the loss of 17 161 308 working days. In relation to total strike activity in the industry major strikes accounted for 0.7 per cent of stoppages, 31 per cent of workers involved and 73 per cent of days lost. By and large major strikes, although quite volatile, followed a pattern similar to that of other strikes in the industry, except that they peaked in 1955 and fell until 1969. In the last five years of the period there was a significant shift towards longer major stoppages.

MAIN FEATURES OF THE STRIKE PATTERN, 1946–73

Although we divided the period 1946–73 into four separate parts the most important division is between 1946–52 and the rest of the period. In the years 1953–73 there were important changes in the kind of strike action that took place and in the rate at which it increased, but the whole period was one of increasing strike activity. By contrast 1946–52 was a period of decreasing strike activity. The turning point in this process was 1953. Thereafter the changes which occurred were those of pace and kind. They were not fundamentally changes of direction.

On average, over the whole twenty-eight year period, some 4 per cent of employees in employment, or 8.9 per cent of trade union members, were involved in stoppages each year. This activity resulted in the loss of 0.07 per cent of potential working time, equivalent to 3.8 per cent of the time lost through unemployment. Of course these period averages conceal the wide range of year to year experiences. The rate of worker involvement varied from 0.7 to 19.1 per cent; the rate of trade union membership involvement varied from 1.6 to 45.5 per cent. Working time lost through these stoppages varied from 0.02 to 0.26 per cent of potential working time.

Yet strike action never involved more than a small minority of the workforce for a small part of the year. Of the thirty-four industries for which information was available in the period 1949–73, twenty averaged less than 2 per cent of their workforce involved in strikes, while only three averaged 20 per cent or more. As we have emphasised above, the number of workers involved provides a maximum estimate of the extent of individual involvement. In so far as some individuals were involved in more than one strike a year, it overstates the extent of individual involvement in strike action.

When time lost through strikes was measured against the size of the industry's workforce, nineteen industries averaged losses of less than an hour per employee per year; only two industries had losses averaging more than a day per employee per year. In these circumstances it is scarcely surprising that eight industries, employing 17 per cent of the workforce, accounted for 56 per cent of the net total of stoppages, 77 per cent of workers involved and 71 per cent of days lost. On the other hand, between 1949 and 1973 over 90 per cent of industries experienced an increase in the number of stoppages, workers involved and days lost. And although the more strike-prone industries accounted for the bulk of the overall increase, the fact that increases were so widely spread must be taken as an indication that factors other than industry-specific ones were important.

Over the period as a whole less than half the gross total of stoppages were concerned with wage issues, but these accounted for almost two-thirds of workers involved and four-fifths of working days lost. There was no clearly distinguishable relationship between the number of wage and non-wage stoppages, but wage issues were much the more volatile. Over the period as a whole there was a strong tendency for wage stoppages to grow in relative importance, a tendency which also affected the shares of workers involved and days lost. On average wage stoppages involved twice as many workers and resulted in the loss of four times as many days as non-wage strikes.

The regional distribution of strike activity, measured by the numbers of workers involved and days lost in relation to employees in employment, disclosed that the most strike-prone regions were Wales and Scotland. The least strike-prone regions were the South East and the South West. (It is worth emphasising that even in Wales, which was three times more strike prone than the South East, on average less than 10 per cent of the workforce were involved in stoppages at any time in the course of a year and that time lost was equivalent to just over half a day per employee.) We believe that in general these differences reflect variations in industrial structure, although local traditions, customs and economic factors no doubt played a part.

One surprising feature is the extent to which regional strike-proneness varied over the period. The most strike-prone regions of 1955–9 were amongst those experiencing the lowest rates of increase thereafter. It might

be thought that marked changes in regional strike-proneness are incompat-
ible with our assumption that the industrial structure was a major
explanatory factor because the industrial structure changes slowly.
However, we would argue that, as only a minority of the workforce were
involved in stoppages anyway, even small changes could have significant
effects on a region's strike-proneness – e.g. the development of the motor
vehicles industry in the North West as a contributory factor to that region's
growing strike-proneness, or the decline of coal mining in explaining the
relative decline in Scotland and Wales.

Analysis of the dimensions of strike activity revealed that, over the
period as a whole, 71 per cent of the gross total of stoppages lasted no more
than three days, 77 per cent involved less than 250 workers and 73 per cent
the loss of less than 500 working days. This characteristic of strikes was
enhanced in 1953–9 and diminished thereafter. The pattern of change
coincided with changes in the relative importance of coal mining stoppages
in the gross total. Given that coal mining stoppages, on average, were
smaller and shorter than those in other industries, this would appear to be
a major explanatory factor in influencing gross changes. It is, however,
unlikely that it provides a complete explanation, particularly of events in
1969–73, when the increase in frequency of larger, longer stoppages was
especially strong.

Information on stoppages known to be official was only available for the
period 1960–73. In Chapter 2 we drew attention to the likelihood that there
were virtually no official stoppages in the period 1940–50, because of the
legal prohibition on strike action. Between 1951 and 1959 we know that
there were a number of official stoppages but the available information is
too scanty to provide anything approaching a comprehensive series.
Between 1960 and 1973 there were, on average, ninety-nine stoppages a
year which were known to be official. They involved 538 000 workers and
resulted in the loss of 2.5 million days. In relation to the net totals of strike
activity stoppages known to be official accounted for 5.2 per cent of strikes,
42 per cent of workers involved and 47.2 per cent of days lost. Over these
fourteen years it appears that stoppages known to be official increased less
quickly than other stoppages in the middle of our period and more quickly
towards this end. There was no evidence to support the view that stoppages
known to be official were increasing less rapidly than other stoppages. The
implication of this is that it cannot be said that unconstitutional stoppages
accounted for an increasing proportion of UK stoppages, although it is true
that such stoppages made up the great bulk of the increase in strike activity
in the post-war period.

Over the period as a whole major strikes outside coal mining averaged
eighty a year, involved 544 000 workers and resulted in the loss of 3.2
million working days. In relation to the net totals of strike activity these
stoppages accounted for 6.4 per cent of strikes, 65 per cent of workers
involved and 82 per cent of days lost. However, in most years major strikes
were not as important as these average figures suggest. In general the
pattern of major strikes was similar to that for all strikes, although on

occasion the rate of change differed between the two series. The industrial distribution of major stoppages showed a marked concentration: motor vehicles alone accounted for 21.5 per cent of the total and the metal trades as a whole for 65.6 per cent. Of the forty industries and industry groups for which we have information, two had no major strikes at all, twenty-four averaged less than one stoppage a year; nine averaged between one and five, and five more than five per year. Some 80 per cent of industries experienced increases in the annual average number of stoppages between the first and last sub-periods. On the whole the rates of increase were greatest in the manufacturing sector. The most important causes of major stoppages were as follows: wage increases, 40 per cent of the total; other wage disputes, 17 per cent; miscellaneous, 14 per cent; trade union principle, 11 per cent. The share of the total attributable to wage increase issues rose in each sub-period, from 13 per cent in 1946–52 to 51 per cent in 1969–73. In consequence the share of all other cause classifications was reduced, although they all increased in absolute terms. Any explanation of the increase in major stoppages must concentrate on factors affecting wage issues.

Judged on their regional location even major stoppages were very localised, only 7.5 per cent extended across regional boundaries. The most strike-prone regions, judged by their share of the total of stoppages, were the West Midlands, 19 per cent; the South East and Scotland, 17 per cent each; and the North West, 15 per cent. Three regions, the South West, Yorkshire and Humberside, and the Northern, each experienced consistent increases in their share of the total: their combined share rose from 8.4 to 13.4 per cent.

Although ninety-three occupational groups were involved in stoppages in this period, two groups accounted for 48 per cent of all stoppages. A further eight groups accounted for 22.5 per cent of the total, leaving the remaining eighty-three groups to share 29 per cent. Of these eighty-three, eighteen were involved in one stoppage each and eleven in two stoppages. This concentration of major strikes in certain occupational groups might be taken to indicate that occupational as well as industrial factors were of considerable importance, but our reservations about the quality of the information are such as to prevent us from pressing this view very strongly. The timing of major stoppages within the year revealed three strike 'seasons', January–February, April–June, and September–October. The periods when strikes are less frequent appear to coincide with holiday times.

Major stoppages were much larger and more prolonged than other stoppages. Only 26.6 per cent were over within six days compared with 85.6 per cent of the gross total. Shares of the total attributable to each duration category in each sub-period showed no consistent pattern of change. Beginning and end of period comparisons showed a shift to very short and to moderately long stoppages, largely at the expense of moderately short stoppages. Cross-tabulation of number of workers involved per stoppage by the duration of that stoppage indicated that large stoppages were less amenable to very rapid resolution than small stoppages, but were less likely to become very protracted.

By way of concluding this section of our study we should note that over the whole of our period there has been a considerable degree of stability in terms of the institutional and economic background against which strikes occur. Collective bargaining structures and forms have remained relatively stable, while levels of unionisation have remained higher than at any time in the past. Full or nearly full employment has been maintained for much of the period, albeit within the context of a persistent and increasing problem of rising prices. Yet within this framework there have been substantial changes in the use made of industrial sanctions, both in general and within and between different groups of employees. In the five chapters of this section of the study we have mainly tried to record and summarise the changing nature of the British strike pattern since the war. In the next five chapters we aim to examine a wide variety of explanatory factors in an attempt to explain what has happened in more detail and depth.

7   Strikes and the Economic Environment

THE AIMS OF THE CHAPTER

The most frequent of academic explanations for strikes is that the level and form of the strike pattern are likely to be related, in some way, to the factors in the economic environment that surrounds a given system of industrial relations. It follows from this proposition that one should seek to explain particular variations in the pattern over a given time period by relating appropriate strike measures to suitable economic variables over the same period – for the most part those used in analysing variations in economic activity rates and the business cycle.

In practice this usually involves attempts to answer a number of more or less standard questions: Are there fewer strikes at higher levels of unemployment? Is an increase in the rate of inflation usually accompanied by a rise in strike activity? Do strikes last longer in recessions, or are they relatively unaffected by these and other macro-economic changes?

In this chapter we examine some of the more important and suggestive studies which have been based on assumptions of this kind, to see how far they are likely to help us in our task of interpreting the post-war strike pattern of the United Kingdom. We go on to argue that none of them is entirely satisfactory for our purposes. One reason for this is that they have tended to treat strike activity as if it were a *general* phenomenon. In fact, as we have seen, it is extremely limited in its occurrence. Another is that those who explore the assumed relationships between strike statistics and other economic series usually fail to distinguish between the determinants of strike activity and the factors producing changes in the volume and form of collective bargaining: in effect the explanations they offer for strikes usually fail to take their role in relation to collective bargaining into account. This is partly because the separation and identification of bargaining influences cannot be adequately achieved at the macro level – which is the level of most studies and economic series. In consequence, although it can be shown that strike activity has some sensitivity to business cycle fluctuations, we conclude that the relationship between strikes and the economic environment is best examined at a less aggregated level than that of the national economy. (In the chapters that follow we seek to explore this approach by means of special studies of three contrasting industries with different strike patterns.)

OTHER STUDIES OF STRIKES AND THE ECONOMIC ENVIRONMENT

Of the various studies which have been made of the relationship between strike activity and changes in the economic environment we picked out five which we thought were of particular interest. The first two were rather early studies by Knowles (1952) and Rees (1952). The other three were published after 1970 and reflect not only the changes in ideas but also the changes in research methods which occurred in the post-war period. These later studies were by Pencavel (1970), Knight (1972) and Wilkinson and Turner (1972).

We began by looking at Knowles' analysis of the relationship between strikes and a variety of economic indicators. Knowles' work was of particular interest because he discussed the problems involved in making such analyses as well as the results he obtained. Assuming that there is some relationship between strike activity and the economic environment, there are two areas of difficulty in conducting any analysis. The first area relates to the choice of the measure of strike activity to use, the second to the choice of macro-economic variables.

We have already pointed out in Chapter 2 that there is no single measure of strike activity which adequately represents the whole pattern – that each of the basic measures defines a different dimension of strike activity. This point is reinforced if one measures the degree of correlation between the three basic series (net totals of strike activity excluding the national engineering stoppages of 1953, 1962 and 1968). Although the series show substantial similarities, they do not move in the same way at the same time. The degree of correlation between the number of strikes and workers involved was measured as $r = 0.90$, between strikes and days lost as $r = 0.66$, and between workers involved and days lost as $r = 0.81$. Strikes and workers involved followed similar paths between 1946 and 1973 but the relationship between strikes and duration was much weaker. These differences are not particularly surprising. The factors which affect the decision to initiate strike action are likely to be different from those which affect the decision to continue the strike.

In these circumstances there is a real choice to be made as to which measure of strike activity should be used in the analysis as it cannot be assumed that one is a reasonable proxy for the others. Knowles was unusual in that he recognised this problem and discussed it briefly. Unfortunately, he went on to use the number of strikes in his own analysis because it was the measure of strike activity which seemed most sensitive to trade cycle fluctuations in the period. But of course using a measure as the dependent variable simply because it gives better results than the alternative is unlikely to contribute to the explanatory power of the model. What it did do was encourage others to do likewise. Thus Bean and Peel (1974) justified their use of the number of strikes by reference to Knowles, in this case with no explanation or discussion. Indeed, all the studies we examined focused on the number of strikes, usually without any consideration of the meaning of the measure and without any appraisal of alternatives.

A more logical method of selecting between strike measures, which ought to commend itself to economists, might be to choose that method which appears to relate most closely to the hypothesis one is seeking to test. Thus if the decision to take strike action is assumed to be some function of the individual workers' utility function (defined in respect of the relationships between future real income and expected effort), the most appropriate measure would seem to be the number of workers involved in strikes. Alternatively, if strike activity is viewed as a function of both the workers' utility function and that of the employer (defined in respect of the relationship between future real labour costs and anticipated loss of output), one presumably wishes to include a prediction of strike duration. In this case the number of working days lost would appear to be a more appropriate measure. Curiously enough it is not easy to see how strike numbers, as such, can be assumed to relate to the customary assumptions of economic theory in respect of strike motivation; the fact remains that they are frequently used as if this was self-evidently the case.

Knowles was also unusual in that he appreciated that there are problems in deciding which economic indicators to use to represent the economic environment and establish the causal nature, if any, of the relationships observed. The suitability of particular indicators will also be influenced by the extent to which fully specified models of strike activity are being tested, or whether the aim is simply to test the degree of association between strike activity and other variables. If fully specified models are involved, then the economic variables should be those which most closely approach the theoretical constructs. If the association between variables is being examined then the choice will be largely determined by the judgement, arbitrary or otherwise, of the investigator. In the former instance the nature of the causal relationship becomes of paramount importance. In the latter it may be left either partly or entirely unresolved.

Knowles himself opted for the latter course – selecting those economic indicators which seemed most interesting and describing observed relationships without specifying the form or direction of causality. His graphical evidence indicated that the number of strikes varied inversely with the level of unemployment and directly with prices and wage rates in the period 1911–47. It was not possible, on the basis of such evidence, to estimate the strength or stability of these relationships.

Rees's analysis, published at the same time as Knowles's, was based on US rather than UK data. However, his work is of particular interest to us because he attempted to identify causes of cyclical fluctuations. Rees argued that:

'A cyclical fluctuation in the number of strikes could occur for any of three reasons: (1) The propensity to strike of workers in a given unit (department, plant or company) could vary with the cycle. (2) The number of units organised by unions could fluctuate with the cycle. (3) The scope of strikes could change during the cycle, so that during expansion strikes took place in small units while during contraction they took place in large units.'

This argument is interesting for several reasons. First, it assumes that strikes are always initiated by the worker-union side and never by the employer. Secondly, it relates quite specifically to the number of stoppages rather than any of the other measures of strike activity. Thirdly, the distinction drawn between the various factors which could lead to changes in the number of strikes appear to be important. Fourthly, the argument is only concerned with cyclical fluctuations and not with the overall level of strike activity.

It must also be said that whereas Knowles focused primarily on the effects of changes in the collective bargaining machinery, and rather neglected the potential impact of changes in the business cycle on the attitude of the parties to that machinery, Rees sought to make explicit allowance for both sets of factors. Given the comprehensive nature of this approach we thought it worth examining his arguments in detail.

The assumption that only workers' attitudes vary with changes in the business cycle implies that employers' attitudes are quite unaffected. Such an *a priori* assumption seems far too strong. It is not plausible to suggest that employers' attitudes on such questions as wage increases, or job security, would be the same if they were facing a falling market or a rising market (see Mayhew, 1979). It might be more plausible to suppose that employers' attitudes varied inversely with those of their workers over the course of a cycle. In which case – assuming equal capacity to start a strike – one might predict that there would be no discernible cyclical pattern. If workers used the upturn of a cycle to press for higher wages or greater job security, while employers used a downturn to press for lower wages or less job security, the result might be that the same number of stoppages would occur in the upturn as in the downturn. Alternatively, employers' attitudes could vary directly with those of their employees over the cycle. Employers might be willing to concede workers' claims during the upturn without stoppages, whereas employees would concede employers' demands in the downturn. In such circumstances there would again be no discernible cyclical pattern. However, in the more likely circumstances that such perfect symmetry of attitudes does not prevail, it is surely necessary to produce some explicit account of how employers' attitudes might be affected by a changing economic climate.

Rees's other propositions, concerning the potential importance of changes in the number of bargaining units and the extent of stoppages, emphasise the necessity of understanding the structure of collective bargaining and its determinants as well as the attitudes of the parties to that machinery. By concentrating on the number of bargaining units Rees comes close to justifying his use of the number of strikes as the principal indicator of strike activity. But the justification is not complete, because the number of stoppages is not simply a function of the number of bargaining units. It is also affected by such factors as the frequency of bargaining within those units and the attitudes of the parties concerned. On the other hand, as Rees argues, changes in the number of bargaining units organised will affect the number of bargains being negotiated in any period of time, and this, in turn, will have some affect on the probability of strikes occurring.

As direct evidence on the number of bargaining units was lacking, Rees used changes in trade union membership as a proxy variable. This measure is not entirely satisfactory, for trade union membership and the number of bargaining units could vary independently. Except in conditions of a fully effective universal closed shop system it is possible that trade union membership could increase or decrease, while leaving the collective bargaining structure unaffected. If there were non-members working within the scope of a collective bargaining unit, it would be possible to increase trade union membership by enrolling them without increasing the number of bargaining units. Alternatively, it is possible for workers to leave a trade union without that union necessarily forfeiting bargaining rights. It is also possible, within the context of a given level of union membership, that the collective bargaining structure itself could be changed – by moves to a more centralised or a decentralised system.

This latter point was taken up by Rees in his discussion of the possibility of the extent of strike action altering over the course of the business cycle. If, as he suggested, strikes took place in small units during expansion and in large units during contraction, it means that during economic upturns there is a shift towards more decentralised bargaining. This should result in more frequent but smaller stoppages. Conversely, during economic downturns there should be a shift towards more centralised bargaining, resulting in less frequent but larger stoppages.

Rees tested this hypothesis by examining the number of establishments affected per stoppage, and concluded that there was no evidence to support it. Unfortunately, comparable data for the United Kingdom has not been published for the post-war period. (The Ministry of Labour recorded such information for a while after 1945 but the practice was discontinued in the 1960s.) However, an alternative test would be to examine whether the number of workers involved per stoppage had altered at different points in the cycle. We made a crude test of this kind by examining the average size of the net total of stoppages at successive peaks and troughs of post-war UK business cycles. We found that stoppages tended to be smaller in the troughs (with the sole exception of 1971). We recognise that this test is somewhat crude and that our dating of peaks and troughs might be subject to objection, but the finding was quite consistent. Of course it may be due to the fact that wage stoppages were more frequent in peak years and wage stoppages tended to be larger than non-wage stoppages.

Finally, it should be noted that Rees, by concentrating on cyclical movements in the number of stoppages, avoids the problem of explaining the overall level of strike activity. Implicitly he is assuming that, while changes in the economic environment may have some impact on the number of stoppages, a much wider range of variables is required to account for the overall level.

After this early work of Rees relatively little attention was paid to the relationship between strike activity and the economic environment until the advent of Ashenfelter and Johnson (1969). Their study presented a formally specified model of strike activity in the USA, buttressed by the use of multivariate regression analysis. This model and methodology was adapted for application to the UK by Pencavel (1970). We decided to focus on the Pencavel study because it dealt with UK data. (It is, in fact, entitled 'Industrial strike activity in Britain', but appears to include stoppages which occurred in Northern Ireland.)

Pencavel's work is based on a view of trade unionism which has as its object the pursuit of the economic welfare of union members, plus the survival and development of the union and the fulfilment of the leaders' personal preferences. In this context the strike is seen as a leadership control device, designed to maintain the hold of the leaders over the membership while depressing the workers' expectations to a level where agreement can be reached. To explain the frequency of strikes, Pencavel uses an optimising model. In this model the employer is faced by a trade-off between meeting the union's demands or incurring a strike which will reduce the increase in wage costs. Pencavel argued that this model, although it was developed to explain strikes in the USA, is applicable to the UK situation because shop stewards fulfil the trade union leadership role.

Pencavel tested his model for the period 1950–67. He used quarterly data with the number of non-coal strikes beginning in each quarter as the dependent variable. The independent variables in the estimation included unemployment, profits, real wage rate changes, wage rates, prices, incomes policies, changes of government, a time trend and a number of dummy variables to catch the effects of seasonal variations. All the independent variables were statistically significant with the exception of the third quarter seasonal adjustment, incomes policies and changes of government. Pencavel estimated three versions of the equation without noticeably affecting the overall degree of correlation ($R^2 = 0.87$ in all three cases). The estimated coefficients of some of his variables did not appear to be very stable. To check this point he split the data into two equal sub-periods and estimated the same equation for each. The results indicated that the estimated coefficients were not stable over time. Pencavel suggested that this instability might have reflected an aggregation problem, when the composition was shifting. But it might also have derived from a changing structure within a given composition, or some combination of both these two effects.

Using four industrial sectors (construction, metals, transport and communication and coal mining), Pencavel also tested his model at a less aggregated level. Data limitations reduced the period of analysis and excluded the profits variable. The relevant industry unemployment series was used in each equation together with the aggregate unemployment series. The model worked much less well at this level.

Many of the explanatory variables were not statistically significant in one or more equations, although the trend term and some of the seasonal dummies remained important. (Pencavel noted that in the metals sector the trend term and the seasonal dummies removed 69 per cent of the variance in the dependent variable.) In his conclusions he laid stress on the difficulty of interpreting the trend term but argued that, although there was scope for improvement, the model represented a step forward from the vague formulations which had preceded it.

In assessing a paper of this kind there are two questions which must be asked. First, is the model a reasonable theoretical representation of reality? Secondly, does the statistical analysis support the theory? In response to the first question we would argue that the model is not appropriate to the UK. The view of trade unionism on which it is based does not fit the situation in this country. This is not to argue that strikes are never used as a control device by union leaders, but that it is not a common phenomenon. In part this is because most British strikes occur in decentralised bargaining systems where negotiations are conducted by shop stewards. Shop stewards are not so separated from their members, as Ashenfelter and Johnson assume that union leaders are in the USA. They are subject to much greater shop-floor control. In these circumstances we would argue that strikes are best seen as a means by which negotiators and members put pressure on employers. A steward who cynically encouraged his members to take strike action in order to *reduce* their expectations, would be likely to be speedily removed from office.

In situations of more centralised bargaining the division between workers and negotiators may be more obvious, but strong elements of membership control, through ballots and conferences, remain. In any case strikes are less frequent in these circumstances than in the decentralised systems and it is difficult to think of any evidence to support the view that national leaders in Britain have used stoppages as a control device. It would be more plausible to argue they have tended to eschew strike action for fear that control would pass away from them.

A further point is that the model envisages all stoppages as occurring over wage demands. But we have already noted that the majority of the gross total of stoppages (figures for the net totals are not available) in the period 1950–67 were not over wage issues. We have also noted that there is little evidence to support the view that non-wage issues may be regarded as proxies for wage issues. This implies a serious mis-specification in the Pencavel model.

A related point is the assumption that all strikes are initiated by workers and that the employers' role is confined to responding to those initiatives. It may be true that in regard to wage increases workers tend to take the initiative, otherwise in an inflationary situation they would suffer real wage cuts. But, as we have seen, the majority of stoppages took place over non-wage issues – e.g. manning levels, discipline, redundancy, etc., issues on which it is equally plausible to suppose that many initiatives came from employers. In these circumstances it seems grossly inadequate to ascribe nothing more than a reaction function to employers.

Finally, it is not clear why the number of strikes is used as the dependent variable. The model seems to view strikes as a product of individual workers' utility-maximising behaviour, which is determined by expectations of future wage increases subject to constraints imposed by the state of the labour market. Even if it is legitimate to aggregate these utility functions, which seems doubtful, the model seems more suited to explaining the number of workers involved in strike action than the number of strikes.

The statistical analysis was also less than satisfactory. The independent variables in the equation included a linear time trend. Indeed, in the studies of industrial sectors the only variable which was satisfactory in every equation was the time trend. This raises the question of the extent to which the time trend was important in the aggregate equation. To answer this question we estimated an equation using quarterly data with the net total of strikes beginning in each quarter as the dependent variable, plus a time trend and seasonal dummies as the independent variables for the same period. In effect we estimated the same equation as Pencavel, except that we excluded the explanatory variables derived from the Ashenfelter–Johnson model. The result was a relationship where the trend term and the seasonal dummies, except that of the third quarter, were significant and the estimated equation had an R^2 of 0.78.

This compares favourably with the R^2 of 0.87 that Pencavel obtained by the addition of the unemployment, profit and real wage rate change variables. On this evidence it appears that a major cause of the high degree of correlation which Pencavel found was not the explanatory power of the modified Ashenfelter–Johnson model, but the existence of a strong upward trend in the number of stoppages since the early 1950s together with a marked seasonal pattern. Of course the degree of correlation is not the only criterion by which an estimation may be judged but these findings, taken together with instability of the estimated coefficients which Pencavel himself found, cast considerable doubt on the usefulness of this approach.

Unfortunately, Knight's paper, which was concerned with strikes and wage inflation in the UK, shared the Pencavel approach of formal model building and multivariate statistical analysis. However, it did meet some of our objections. Knight began by rejecting the appropriateness of the Ashenfelter–Johnson model, because of the high level of unofficial strikes in Britain. Instead, he offered a model 'which seeks to explain the actions of groups of workers, rather than trade unions'. For this purpose he specified a utility function for a group of workers which derives from the real wage level and the value expected to accrue to their employer from their labour in the next period. By explicitly assuming that the utility function is a product of group consciousness, rather than the aggregation of individual preferences, Knight neatly side-stepped the aggregation problem and focused attention on the bargaining unit rather than the individual. His model assumes that one can expect diminishing marginal utility of real wages and increasing marginal disutility of the value to accrue to the employer. Collective bargaining takes place to raise the level of utility from the initial level and the degree of aggressiveness exhibited by workers is inversely related to their level of utility. *Ceteris paribus,* lower paid workers are expected to be more militant than higher paid workers. The employer's utility function is specified in terms of the level of real profits expected to prevail in the next period. Consequently, employer resistance to workers' efforts to raise their utility is a negative linear function of the level of real profits expected to prevail in the subsequent period – i.e. employer resistance is founded on the belief that workers can only raise their level of utility by reducing that of their employers. Knight, like Pencavel, includes an unemployment variable to catch the effects of the state of the labour market on the two parties.

Apart from these differences Knight's work is also distinguished from that of Pencavel by his choice of dependent variable. Knight used the rate of change of the number of strikes in manufacturing divided by the corresponding labour force. By using rate of change rather than absolute totals he tried to focus on cyclical fluctuations in the number of strikes to the exclusion of secular trends. The labour force adjustment, we assume, was intended to allow for changes in the number of bargaining units, but it was an inadequate device as many factors affect this variable.

The equation was estimated on half-yearly data for the period 1950–68. With the exception of unemployment all the variables were expectational in character. Expectations were based on the experience of the previous eighteen months. Problems of multi-collinearity caused Knight to estimate three forms of the equation, each specifying a different form of the relationship between strikes, prices and output. Despite these different formulations expected money wage increases consistently emerged as the single most important factor. Knight himself commented 'The coefficient in (9′a) suggests, for example, that a fall in the expected rate of money wage increase from 6 per cent to 5 per cent induces an increase in the rate of change of strikes of 12 per cent'. Of the other independent variables neither prices nor unemployment were statistically significant, output was positively related to the rate of change of strikes and the profits variable was not particularly well defined. Overall the fit of the various estimated equations was quite high, accounting for over two-thirds of the variation in the rate of change of the number of strikes.

To evaluate this study we asked the same two questions as we raised in respect of the Pencavel paper: How adequate is the model? Does the statistical analysis support the theory? The model appeared to be a more realistic approximation of the situation in the UK than Pencavel's model but we retain some doubts. As was pointed out above, many strikes occur over issues other than wages, and there is little statistical evidence to support the view that wages are a suitable proxy for non-wage issues. This lack of evidence is not surprising since it seems – to us at least – that the factors affecting workers' attitudes towards wage issue stoppages would be quite different from those affecting their attitudes on issues of personal or collective job security or the exercise of 'managerial prerogatives'. We also find it difficult to accept that bargaining should be seen exclusively as a zero-sum game, in which one party can only gain at the expense of the other. The exclusion of any form of productivity bargaining appears unnecessarily restrictive. While the specification of a group utility function avoids the aggregation problems which occur when individual utility functions are specified, it is not clear that this is anything more than a sleight of hand which fails to explain why group decisions are likely to be different from individual decisions.

In respect of the statistical analysis our reservations are restricted to the use of the rate of change of strikes as the dependent variable. By focusing on the possibility of conflict between a group of workers and their employer Knight is closer to justifying his use of number of strikes, rather than number of workers involved. But there is still no explanation of the size and number of worker groups – i.e. their bargaining structure. For this reason alone this remains an incomplete model.

The work of Wilkinson and Turner, which constituted our final study, is based on a rather different approach to that of both Pencavel and Knight. This study is more in the Knowles–Rees style of imprecise formulations supported by graphical and tabular evidence. It is of interest because of the factors which it identifies as being important in the determination of strike activity, and because of its implications for the results of collective bargaining.

The study drew attention to two apparent changes of recent years. It pointed out that inflation had increased at the same time as unemployment and that this rise was also accompanied by a rise in strike activity. The positive association between unemployment and inflation contradicted much existing academic theory – especially the vast literature based on the notion of the 'Phillips' curve (see Phillips, 1958). The positive association between unemployment and strike activity reversed Knowles' findings. The problem – as Turner and Wilkinson saw it – was to explain why inflation and strike activity, which historically had varied inversely with the level of unemployment, began in the late 1960s to vary directly with unemployment. These changes appeared to have affected most of the economically advanced nations outside the Socialist bloc. Therefore, the authors argued, it required an explanation which was not specific to the UK but was capable of international application. Various explanations were considered and rejected – many of the more plausible on grounds of national specificity.

The Turner–Wilkinson hypothesis was that previous explanations of workers' behaviour, which relied on responses to changes in money or real (money adjusted for prices) wages, had been rendered inadequate because of the increase in importance of deductions from earnings in the form of income tax and social security contributions. Workers' behaviour had become a function of net real earnings.

Post-war trends in net real incomes were described in some detail by reference both to male manual workers' earnings and those of all employees. The evidence presented showed that the effects of income tax and social security deductions rose very sharply in the years just prior to 1970. The effect of these changes was larger amongst male manual workers but, relative to earlier periods, it was marked amongst all employees.

Certain features of this piece of analysis did not appear to us to be entirely satisfactory. The data on manual workers related to a 'typical' family, whereas the data for all employees was derived from aggregate series of wages, salaries and deductions. Although a married couple with two children may be a 'typical' family, it does not follow that manual workers as a group were affected by changes of the same magnitude, direction and timing in respect of real net earnings as the 'typical' family. In so far as the 'typical' family is not representative of manual workers as a whole then the conclusions drawn by Wilkinson and Turner about how they suffered relative to all employees may be invalidated.

Secondly, the retail price index was used to deflate manual workers' earnings whereas the consumer price index was used for all employees' earnings. This differential treatment was justified by the authors on the grounds that 'all employees' covers the whole range of social groups and the consumer price index reflects the expenditure of those groups, whereas manual workers' households were more heavily represented in the retail price index. There is no simple solution to problems of this kind but we would argue that the differential treatment was unnecessary. All employees includes a majority of manual workers whilst the consumer price index also reflects the expenditure of some large non-employee groups – i.e. pensioners and self-employed. The retail price index is not based exclusively on manual workers' expenditure but covers many non-manual workers as well. If the same price index had been used to deflate both earnings series the differences between them would not have been so marked.

The authors also examined the impact of these changes on the distribution of personal taxation between families of different size. They considered the possible offsetting effects of indirect tax changes and personally attributable welfare benefits. Movements in personal and corporate income after tax were also examined.

Having presented this evidence Wilkinson and Turner returned to their original question: 'Why did British strike liability rise so sharply at the end of the 1960s, despite increased and increasing unemployment?' They drew attention to a number of factors in their search for an answer. First, the strike experience in the UK in 1969–71 was unusual in that the number of stoppages did not move inversely to the level of unemployment. Secondly, strikes for wage increase were particularly responsive to changes in the level of unemployment. (It should be noted that the evidence they produce on this point is also consistent with the view that effective incomes policies reduce wage stoppages.) Thirdly, there was a positive relationship between the number of strikes and changes in net real earnings until 1967, when stagnation of net real earnings was accompanied by a sharp rise in the number of strikes. Fourthly, there was a positive relationship between the number of working days lost and changes in net real earnings. From this evidence the authors argued that the events of the late 1960s were the product of the frustration of expectations derived in the 1950s and early 1960s when net real earnings had grown at a fairly consistent though moderate rate. This general effect was exacerbated by the discriminatory impact of inflation and a progressive tax structure between groups of workers who had different levels and rates of increase in earnings.

It was also shown that different rates of increase of industrial earnings in the period 1964–9 probably resulted in a situation in which some groups enjoyed substantial increases in their real living standards whereas others, despite having substantial money wage increases, had their standard of living cut. The groups who lost out in this process were subject to double pressures. The expectations they had derived from earlier experience were frustrated, whilst other groups, with whom they might compare themselves, were fulfilling, or perhaps more than fulfilling, those same expectations. It is worth noting that the Wilkinson–Turner data related to industries, but it seems probable that the same process also occurred within industries.

This analysis was particularly interesting because it divided industries into three broad groups in the period 1964–9. At one extreme were those industries where consistently high rates of increase in earnings had resulted in substantial improvements in real living standards. At the other extreme were those industries where low rates of increase in earnings resulted in cuts in living standards. In between were those where experience ranged from those where there was some improvement to those where there was little change. One might have expected that Wilkinson and Turner would use this evidence to generate and test some further hypotheses about the level and rate of change of strike activity between industries but this was not done. However, there were practical difficulties because Wilkinson and Turner analysed 126 different industries and strike data is only available for some 40 industries and industry groups. Yet the failure to tie these differential changes in earnings to differential changes in strikes at the industry level forces us to regard the hypotheses as not fully proven.

In summary, Wilkinson and Turner showed that net real earnings diverged markedly from real earnings in the latter half of the 1960s. They also demonstrated that inflation and a progressive tax structure had a marked effect on the distribution of net real earnings between industries. They indicated that the general stagnation of net real earnings in the late 1960s was paralleled by a sharp rise in strike activity despite the higher level of unemployment which existed at that time. They did not show that manual workers as a group were more affected by these changes than other workers. As manual workers were more frequently involved in stoppages than other groups it might have been expected that they would have been more severely affected. It was not demonstrated that those industries which were most severely affected by the redistribution of net real earnings in the late 1960s were those which experienced the greatest increase in strike activity.

On balance it seems reasonable to conclude that, although Wilkinson and Turner were persuasive on the importance of net real earnings, their hypothesis that this factor was the principal determinant of the increase in strike activity was not conclusively established. Our doubts arise not only from the flaws and omissions in their analysis, to which we have already drawn attention, but also from a basic scepticism about mono-causal explanations. Wilkinson and Turner have provided – at best – a partial explanation of strike activity. It is one which ignores the possible role of employers, incomes policies, bargaining structures, etc. In these circumstances more work is required before one can decide whether the substitution of net real earnings for real or money earnings would improve current explanations of strike activity.

COMMON FEATURES OF OTHER STUDIES

Despite the obvious differences between them, these five studies had a number of features in common. In the first place each of them tended to concentrate on the number of stoppages as the principal indicator of strike activity. This was usually done without any discussion of the alternative measures or of the appropriateness of the measure in use. Secondly, in all the studies workers were seen as the initiating agents in the strike. Employers – if they were considered at all – were seen as reacting to the demands placed upon them rather than as taking an active role in the bargaining process. Thirdly, in those cases where an explicit causal relationship was posited, wages or earnings (defined in money, real or net real terms) were seen as the motivating factor.

We have argued that objections can be raised to each of these features. In Chapter 1 we discussed in some detail the meaning of each of the basic measures of strikes and showed how each related to a different aspect of strike activity. Despite the high degree of correlation between these measures one cannot be used as a proxy for the others because they measure different aspects and the correlation, although high, is not complete. In some of these studies, e.g. that of Pencavel, it appeared that the number of strikes was less appropriate than the number of workers involved as the dependent variable.

Viewing workers as the initiating agents of strike action may reflect accurately the situation in many strikes – but this means little more than that employers tend to benefit from the maintenance of the *status quo* in periods of inflation. Such a view ignores the fact that management has the power and responsibility for introducing changes in the work situation. In these circumstances workers are left to react against management's initiatives.

Finally, as we argued earlier, wage rates or earnings are not the sole cause of strike activity. Over the whole period 1946–73 just less than half of the gross total of stoppages arose over wage issues. If models are constructed solely to explain workers' actions over wages it would be more realistic to confine the dependent variable to strike activity which arose from wage disputes (see Bean and Peel, 1974, for an attempt to do this). Alternatively, the models could be extended to encompass those strikes which arise over other issues. The simplest solution might be to recognise this heterogeneity and attempt to develop different models for strikes over different issues.

But the studies also differed from each other in a number of important respects. The most obvious differences were those of methodology, where the incomplete specifications and graphical techniques employed by Knowles, Rees and Wilkinson and Turner contrasted strongly with the more sophisticated and specified models of Pencavel and Knight which made use of multivariate regression techniques. In terms of methodological elegance and precision the latter writers appeared to have improved on the more rough and ready devices of their predecessors – but it was by no means obvious that this resulted in a more plausible and acceptable explanation for strike activity.

The main reason for this was that in their search for methodological rigour and precise model building Pencavel and Knight narrowed their variables to the point where they excluded any consideration of the impact of the bargaining process itself. Strikes, in their models, were viewed as exogenously determined phenomena, which responded to the indirect impact of those half dozen or so macro-economic variables that could be fitted into models. This meant that no consideration was given to phenomena for which there were no appropriate series available – most notably the more directly related factors that arose out of mutations in accepted bargaining structures.

Yet changes in the extent and form of bargaining can have a very significant impact on the strike pattern. If new groups are brought into the bargaining process, or the frequency of bargaining increases, there is likely to be some increase in strike activity. If bargaining is focused on different levels this will have an impact on the size and duration of strike activity – and is likely to affect the question of whether or not strikes are known to be official. If established groups are able to extend the frontier of bargaining – so that matters outside the area of wages and basic conditions come to be jointly determined – this development will make itself felt in the causal breakdown of strikes.

Moreover, considerations of this kind constitute more than theoretical objections to theories that set out to 'explain' strikes without reference to the bargaining process from which they derive. We have already noted that there were significant changes in bargaining structure and behaviour in the period under review – especially since the mid-1950s. It is generally agreed that during this time the established system of relatively high centralised and restricted industry-wide bargaining was supplemented and even replaced by a more fragmented and diverse system of informal bargaining by workshop-based shop stewards. This 'informal system' concerned itself with an additional range of questions – e.g. manning, discipline, safety, productivity, overtime and so on. It also added to the frequency of disputes over pay and payment systems. At the same time, the spread of forms of plant and company bargaining to white collar groups in private industry added a further dimension to the British bargaining system, giving rise to a new form of industrial action.

It seems to us that to provide explanations for the British strike pattern which ignore factors of this kind is like trying to understand why a ship moves in a given direction at a given speed by reference to the constraints set by the tide and the weather! No doubt these factors are important; but one also has to have some regard to what the captain and crew think they have been trying to do. The problem is that their behaviour cannot really be observed with any precision above a certain level; it is also impossible to calculate from any known statistical series.

That is why, in our next three chapters, we concentrate on a sectoral or industry-wide approach, seeking to combine what can be learnt about changes in the bargaining structure and behaviour with relevant economic data that are likely to have had some impact on the partners to the bargaining process.

THE STRIKE PATTERN AND MACRO-ECONOMIC VARIABLES

In our final chapter, we return to the question of how far macro-economic variables may be said to have had some impact on the overall strike pattern. To this end we need to complete this chapter by returning, if only briefly, to a consideration of the questions listed at the outset. In particular, we wish to examine how far it was possible to establish satisfactory significant relationships between macro-economic variables and the three basic measures of overall strike activity. (Yet it should be noted that this was not attempted to prove a particular theory or model; merely to try to establish what the historical pattern had been, and whether it had altered over time.) Consequently, using multiple regression techniques, we examined some of the more obvious relationships to see what form they took, and whether they were stable.

We used both quarterly and annual data in the analysis. The strike data was the net totals with the token national engineering stoppages of 1953, 1962 and 1968 excluded. We did not adjust the other macro-economic variables to exclude coal mining. The quarterly data covered the period 1949–73 and related to the number of strikes, the number of working days lost, the level and rate of change of the number of wholly unemployed, the rate of change of retail prices, a trend term and three dummy variables to catch the seasonal pattern of strike activity. The annual data covered the period 1946–73 and related to the three basic measures of strike activity, the level and rate of change of the number of wholly unemployed, the rate of change of retail prices, the rates of change of both money and net real earnings for male manual workers, and a trend term. Equations were estimated for whole periods and for various sub-periods.

Some of our results, for the period 1949–73, using quarterly data with the number of strikes as the dependent variable, are shown below:

$$S = -33.09 + 6.56T + 67.89D_1 + 55.88D_2 + 7.92D_3,$$
$$\qquad\quad (15.63) \quad (1.98) \qquad (1.63) \qquad (0.23)$$
$$\text{D.W.} = 0.32, \bar{R}^2 = 0.71; \tag{7.1}$$

$$S = -98.43 + 0.90U + 8.61D_1 + 60.21D_2 + 29.56D_3,$$
$$\qquad\quad (8.90) \quad (0.18) \qquad (1.26) \qquad (0.62)$$
$$\text{D.W.} = 0.25, \bar{R}^2 = 0.44; \tag{7.2}$$

$$S = -69.23 + 0.91U - 3.25\dot{U} + 16.23D_1 - 18.91D_2 - 16.92D_3,$$
$$\qquad\quad (9.09) \quad (1.81) \qquad (0.34) \qquad (0.28) \qquad (0.31)$$
$$\text{D.W.} = 0.26, \bar{R}^2 = 0.45; \tag{7.3}$$

$$S = 207.83 + 82.75\dot{P} + 55.48D_1 + 5.36D_2 + 53.99D_3,$$
$$\qquad\quad (3.46) \quad (0.91) \qquad (0.09) \qquad (0.86)$$
$$\text{D.W.} = 0.21, \bar{R}^2 = 0.08; \tag{7.4}$$

$$S = -111.38 + 85.91U - 2.83\dot{U} + 50.77\dot{P} + 21.96D_1 - 31.81D_2 + 19.87D_3,$$
$$\qquad\quad (8.70) \quad (1.62) \qquad (2.78) \qquad (0.48) \qquad (0.51) \qquad (0.37)$$
$$\text{D.W.} = 0.34, \bar{R}^2 = 0.49. \tag{7.5}$$

Key: The numbers shown in parentheses are t statistics. S is the number of strikes, excluding those in coal mining beginning in each quarter. T is the linear time trend. D_1, D_2 and D_3 are dummy variables to catch seasonal effects. U is the average number of wholly unemployed in each quarter. $\dot{U}$ is the rate of change of average number of wholly unemployed. $\dot{P}$ is the rate of change of retail prices. D.W. is the Durbin–Watson statistic. R^{-2} is the corrected regression coefficient.

Equation (7.1) consists of a linear time trend and the seasonal dummies. The time trend and first quarter seasonal adjustment were statistically significant. The positive sign on the time trend reflected the strong upward movement of stoppages through most of this period. The overall correlation was quite high and implied that about 71 per cent of the variance in the number of stoppages could be accounted for simply by a positive trend and seasonal adjustments. This finding, of course, left open the question as to what caused the trend and the seasonal movements. The Durbin–Watson statistic was very unsatisfactory, implying a serious mis-specification in the model.

This latter finding was confirmed when we estimated the equation for the sub-periods shown in Chapters 2–5. These estimations confirmed our earlier findings of a negative trend in the first sub-period, positive trends in the second and third sub-periods and a negative trend again in the fourth sub-period. The simple assumption of an upward trend was inadequate to describe the first and fourth sub-periods and resulted in a serious mis-specification.

The second equation showed the relationship between unemployment and the number of strikes. It revealed a positive, statistically significant relationship. One possible explanation of this finding would be that both unemployment and strikes exhibited upward trends in the post-war period and the positive correlation shown here reflects that fact. This view was supported by our analysis of the sub-periods. The relationship between strikes and unemployment followed the same pattern as that of the trend term and strikes. It was negative in the first and fourth sub-periods and positive in the other two. On this evidence the Wilkinson–Turner hypothesis was based on a false premise, since the number of strikes was positively related to unemployment between 1953 and 1968 and negatively related thereafter. They had assumed that the reverse relationships held.

In an attempt to separate the possible trend effects of the level of unemployment from the cyclical changes we added the rate of change of unemployment to the equation. The result is shown in equation (7.3). The level of unemployment remained positive and statistically significant with very little change in the size of the estimated coefficient. The rate of change of unemployment was negative and statistically significant. These findings might be interpreted to indicate that the level of unemployment did act as a proxy for trend factors while the rate of change variable reflected the expected cyclical response to changes in unemployment. Alternatively, they could be taken at their face value, which would imply that higher levels of unemployment, when reached, resulted in more stoppages than would have occurred at lower levels. Yet when unemployment was rising the number of strikes would be depressed. It should, however, be pointed out that the equation accounted for less than half of the variance in the number of stoppages and that the Durbin–Watson statistic again implied the existence of strong positive serial correlation. This latter finding was again supported by the coefficient of the rate of change variable which varied from sub-period to sub-period.

Our estimation of the relationship between the rate of change of retail prices and the number of strikes is shown in equation (7.4). Prices were positively related to the number of strikes and were significant. However, the overall correlation was very low and the Durbin–Watson statistic unsatisfactory. Again the sub-period analysis revealed changes in the sign and size of the estimated coefficient.

We included all of these independent variables except the trend term in equation (7.5). They all retained their signs from the earlier equations; unemployment and prices were statistically significant, the rate of change of unemployment variable almost so. The magnitudes of the two unemployment variables were not too sharply affected by this combination. However, the overall correlation remained well below that of the trend equation and the Durbin–Watson statistic remained obstinately unsatisfactory. Again the sub-period analyses revealed considerable variations in the size and sign of the estimated coefficients with none of them being significant in all four sub-periods.

The other measure of strike activity for which we had quarterly data, number of working days lost (DL), was analysed in a similar fashion. The results are shown below:

$$DL = -363.26 + 20.55T + 525.48D_1 + 396.65D_2 + 283.47D_3,$$
$$ (5.02) \quad\;\; (1.57) \qquad\;\; (1.19) \qquad\;\; (0.85)$$
$$\text{D.W.} = 1.54, \bar{R}^2 = 0.19; \tag{7.6}$$

$$DL = 1027.85 + 3.84U + 295.07D_1 + 429.95D_2 + 383.17D_3,$$
$$ (5.56) \quad (0.90) \qquad\;\; (1.32) \qquad\;\; (1.17)$$
$$\text{D.W.} = 1.61, \bar{R}^2 = 0.23; \tag{7.7}$$

$$DL = 1029.90 + 3.84U + 0.23\dot{U} + 294.54D_1 + 435.45D_2 + 386.37D_3,$$
$$ (5.52) \quad (0.02) \quad\;\; (0.89) \qquad\;\; (0.98) \qquad\;\; (1.03)$$
$$\text{D.W.} = 1.61, \bar{R}^2 = 0.22; \tag{7.8}$$

$$DL = 210.33 + 408.28\dot{P} + 499.77D_1 + 171.02D_2 + 522.59D_3,$$
$$ (2.90) \qquad (1.39) \qquad\;\; (0.47) \qquad\;\; (1.41)$$
$$\text{D.W.} = 1.38, \bar{R}^2 = 0.06; \tag{7.9}$$

$$DL = 1268.70 + 3.54U + 2.65\dot{U} + 287.62\dot{P} - 326.98D_1 - 358.25D_2 - 594.82D_3,$$
$$ (5.10) \;\mid\; (0.22) \quad (2.24) \qquad (1.01) \qquad\;\; (0.82) \qquad\;\; (1.57)$$
$$\text{D.W.} = 1.17, \bar{R}^2 = 0.25. \tag{7.10}$$

Equation (7.6) shows the estimated relationship between the number of days lost and the time trend and the seasonal dummies. The trend term was statistically significant and positive. None of the seasonal dummies were significant in this or any of the quarterly equations in respect of days lost. The overall correlation was much less than in the corresponding equation for the number of strikes. This probably reflects the much greater volatility of the days lost series. The Durbin–Watson statistic was much more satisfactory although it still implied some serial correlation. On the sub-period analyses the usual problems of variation in the sign and size of the estimated coefficient were apparent and the trend term was only significant in the period 1953–59.

Equation (7.7) shows a positive relationship between the number of days lost and the level of unemployment. The overall correlation was quite low but better than that of equation (7.6). This was in marked contrast to the situation in respect of the number of strikes where the trend term persistently outperformed the other variables. The unemployment variable was statistically significant and the Durbin–Watson statistic was satisfactory. In the sub-period analysis the unemployment variable was not statistically significant in any of the sub-periods.

The effect of including the rate of change of unemployment variable in equation (7.7) is shown in equation (7.8). The rate of change variable was not statistically significant, added nothing to the overall correlation and had a positive sign. Analysis of the various sub-periods revealed little of interest except that the rate of change of unemployment was positive and significant in 1953–9.

The relationship between days lost and the rate of change of retail prices is shown in equation (7.9). Prices were positively and significantly related to days lost but the degree of correlation was small and the Durbin–Watson statistic unsatisfactory. The sub-period analysis revealed little except that the size of coefficient rose sharply in the last period.

These independent variables, excluding the trend term, were brought together in equation (7.10). The level of unemployment and the rate of change of prices were statistically significant and positively related to the number of days lost. The rate of change of unemployment was not significant although it was positively related. It appears that the phenomenon observed by Wilkinson and Turner – days lost rising at a time when unemployment and prices were rising – was not inconsistent with the experience of the whole post-war period. It might be suspected that the overall relationship was heavily influenced by events in recent years but our sub-period analyses revealed that the level of unemployment and the rate of change of prices variables had had positive signs in each of the sub-periods prior to 1968 as well as in the post-1968 period. It would seem that recent experience was not as paradoxical as Wilkinson and Turner believed. Overall these variables accounted for 25 per cent of the variance in the number of days lost and the Durbin–Watson statistic was satisfactory.

The equations we estimated using annual data are shown below. It should be recognised that we had far fewer observations at our disposal and that this restricted our ability to make sub-period analyses. We did in fact make estimations for the periods 1946–59 and 1960–73. We also had a greater range of independent variables available in this analysis so that the results shown here are our selection of those which appeared most interesting. The equations estimated with the number of strikes as the dependent variable are shown below:

$$S = -456.06 + 3.86U,$$
$$(5.31)$$
$$\text{D.W.} = 1.34, \bar{R}^2 = 0.50;$$
\hfill (7.11)

$$S = 1118.53 + 84.86DE,$$
$$(1.31)$$
$$\text{D.W.} = 0.33, \bar{R}^2 = 0.03;$$
\hfill (7.12)

$$S = -565.11 + 3.78U + 90.56L\dot{E} - 101.19L\dot{P},$$
$$(5.35) \quad (2.42) \quad (2.03)$$
$$\text{D.W.} = 1.52, \bar{R}^2 = 0.58;$$
\hfill (7.13)

$$S = -268.81 + 69.02T + 1.56U - 2.65\dot{U} - 20.15L\dot{E} - 3.04L\dot{P},$$
$$(2.99) \quad (1.48) \quad (0.66) \quad (0.41) \quad (0.06)$$
$$\text{D.W.} = 1.25, \bar{R}^2 = 0.68;$$
\hfill (7.14)

$$S = -435.29 + 67.47T + 37.85\dot{E} + 0.79U + 2.17\dot{U} + 17.68\dot{P},$$
$$\qquad\qquad (3.70) \quad\ (0.71) \quad\ (0.70) \quad (0.42) \quad (0.40)$$

D.W. $= 1.15$, $\overline{R}^2 = 0.69$. $\hspace{5cm}$ (7.15)

Key: S is the annual net total of strikes. U is the number of wholly unemployed. $\dot{U}$ is the rate of change of U. $D\dot{E}$ is the rate of change of real disposable earnings of male manuals. $\dot{E}$ is the rate of change of male manual workers' average earnings. $L\dot{E}$ is $\dot{E}$ lagged one year. $\dot{P}$ is the rate of change of retail prices. $L\dot{P}$ is $\dot{P}$ lagged one year. T is the linear time trend.

Equation (7.11) shows a positive statistically significant relationship between the number of strikes and the level of unemployment. The correlation was higher than in the quarterly estimate but that may be a reflection of the inadequacy of the seasonal adjustment used in the latter. Comparison of estimates for the two sub-periods revealed that it was weaker and not statistically significant in the first half of the period.

The second equation was estimated in the hope of throwing some light on the Wilkinson–Turner hypothesis that real disposable earnings had become the key variable in the determination of workers' attitudes and hence of the level of strikes. The estimate shows a positive but not statistically significant relationship. The correlation between the two variables was very low and the Durbin–Watson statistic unsatisfactory. Estimates for the two sub-periods did not provide any evidence that the relationship strengthened in the latter half of the period. On this evidence it appears that net real earnings were not a major influence on strike activity although it is possible that less aggregated data might produce counter-evidence.

Following Knight's argument that strike activity was heavily influenced by expectations derived from recent experience, but evaluated with regard to current labour market conditions, equation (7.13) shows an estimate of the relationship between the number of strikes, the level of unemployment and earnings' and prices' movements in the previous year. The unemployment and earnings variables were positive and statistically significant, the prices variable was negative and almost significant. The correlation was reasonable and the Durbin–Watson statistic satisfactory. The estimate of the unemployment variable was close to that of equation (7.11). The signs of the lagged variables were difficult to interpret. They indicate that the higher the level of earnings in the previous year the higher the level of strikes in the current year, whilst the higher the rate of price increase in the previous year the lower the number of strikes in the current year. One interpretation might be that the signs of the variables reflect employers' responses – a high rate of earnings increase in the previous year leading to greater cost-consciousness and a greater willingness to resist wage claims in the current year whilst a high rate of price increase in the previous was taken as an indication of an 'easier' climate in which to pass on cost increases, thereby reducing the need for conflict.

Equation (7.14) shows the effect of adding the trend term and the rate of change of unemployment variable to equation (7.13). It appears from the sign of the trend term and the fall in the size of the coefficient of the unemployment level variable that we were correct in supposing that part of the relationship between the level of unemployment and the number of strikes was the result of trend factors, but we were mistaken in attributing the positive sign to that cause. However, none of the independent variables, with the exception of the trend term, are statistically significant. All the rate of change variables have negative signs including the earnings variable which was positive in the previous equation. The degree of correlation has risen, but this merely reflects the strength of the trend term. The Durbin–Watson statistic was again satisfactory.

Equation (7.15) was the same as equation (7.14) except that the lagged forms of the prices and earnings variables were replaced by current values. Only the trend term was statistically significant in this equation. On this evidence it appears that the apparent significance of the other variables in the earlier equations was largely the result of strong upward movements in all the variables. All the rate of change variables changed signs in equations (7.13)–(7.15); this probably occurred because the variables were closely correlated so that the estimated coefficients were not well defined.

The equations estimated in respect of the net total of workers involved (*WI*) are shown below:

$$WI = -302.98 + 2.07U,$$
$$(5.22)$$
$$\text{D.W.} = 1.69, \bar{R}^2 = 0.49;$$
(7.16)

$$WI = 523.18 + 56.72D\dot{E},$$
$$(1.64)$$
$$\text{D.W.} = 0.61, \bar{R}^2 = 0.06;$$
(7.17)

$$WI = -404.60 + 1.95U + 57.77L\dot{E} - 50.49L\dot{P},$$
$$(5.25) \quad (2.93) \quad (1.92)$$
$$\text{D.W.} = 2.26, \bar{R}^2 = 0.60;$$
(7.18)

$$WI = -280.61 + 29.26T + 0.97U - 0.40\dot{U} + 14.55L\dot{E} - 10.72L\dot{P},$$
$$(2.21) \quad (1.60) \quad (0.17) \quad (0.52) \quad (0.35)$$
$$\text{D.W.} = 2.00, \bar{R}^2 = 0.64;$$
(7.19)

$$WI = -315.85 + 34.13T + 44.57\dot{E} + 0.20U + 2.92\dot{U} + 2.10\dot{P},$$
$$(3.43) \quad (1.54) \quad (0.33) \quad (1.04) \quad (0.09)$$
$$\text{D.W.} = 1.79, \bar{R}^2 = 0.69.$$
(7.20)

The number of workers involved was positively and significantly related to the level of unemployment in equation (7.16). The degree of correlation was quite strong but the Durbin–Watson statistic was not very satisfactory. The sub-period analysis demonstrated that the relationship was stronger in the latter half of the period although it was positive in both.

Equation (7.17) shows that the relationship between number of workers involved and changes in net real earnings was positive and almost statistically significant. However the degree of correlation was very low and the Durbin–Watson statistic unsatisfactory. The sub-period analysis revealed that the relationship strengthened in the second half of the period but did not become statistically significant.

The effect of including lagged values of the prices and earnings variables to equation (7.16) is shown in equation (7.18). All three variables were statistically significant, unemployment and earnings having a positive effect on workers involved and prices having a negative one. These signs are the same as those in the corresponding equation for the number of strikes. The degree of correlation was quite high but the Durbin–Watson statistic was unsatisfactory.

Equation (7.19) shows the effect of including a trend term and the rate of change of unemployment in equation (7.18). Only the trend term was significant, although the level of unemployment variable was close to significance. The rate of change of unemployment variable was negative; the other variables retained their signs from equation (7.18). The magnitudes of the estimated coefficients for the level of unemployment and the prices and earnings variables were substantially reduced compared with equation (7.18). Again it appears that much of the apparent significance of variables in the earlier equations was simply a product of strong upward movements in all the series.

In the last equation (eqn 7.20) which we estimated in respect of number of workers involved we substituted current values for the lagged values of prices and earnings in equation (7.19). The principal effect of these changes appears to have been to reduce the estimated coefficient and the significance of the level of unemployment variable whilst increasing the size and significance of the earnings and rate of change of unemployment variables. Despite these changes the trend term remained the only significant variable although the earnings variable was quite close. All the independent variables in equation (7.20) had positive signs whereas in equation (7.19) the prices and rate of change of unemployment variables were negatively signed. Overall the degree of correlation was quite high and the Durbin–Watson statistic was satisfactory.

The equations estimated in respect of the number of workers involved turned out to be quite similar to those estimated for the number of strikes – at least in respect of the signs and significance of the independent variables. This was not wholly surprising for we had already noted a high degree of correlation between the two dependent variables. However, the results were not identical. In particular the trend term appeared to be slightly less important in respect of workers involved whereas the other independent variables were marginally more significant. These are aspects of the strike pattern which require further examination at a less aggregated level.

Finally, the equations we estimated in respect of the number of working days lost disclosed a slightly different picture. The results are shown below:

$DL = -4005.20 + 17.23U,$
$$(6.33)$$
D.W. $= 1.25, \bar{R}^2 = 0.59;$ (7.21)

$DL = 2606.33 + 622.78D\check{E},$
$$(2.51)$$
D.W. $= 1.60, \bar{R}^2 = 0.16;$ (7.22)

$DL = -5007.72 + 15.69U + 347.42L\dot{E} - 131.87L\dot{P},$
$$(6.00)(2.51)\phantom{L\dot{E} - }(0.71)$$
D.W. $= 1.60, \bar{R}^2 = 0.66;$ (7.23)

$DL = -5239.83 - 51.37T + 17.02U + 7.15\dot{U} + 456.15L\dot{E} - 218.00L\dot{P},$
$$(0.50)(3.65)(0.40)(2.12)\phantom{\dot{U} + 45}(0.93)$$
D.W. $= 1.80, \bar{R}^2 = 0.64;$ (7.24)

$DL = -4667.12 + 68.05T + 534.85\dot{E} + 7.87U + 33.06\dot{U} - 46.35\dot{P},$
$$(0.85)(2.29)(1.60)\phantom{\dot{E} + }(1.46)(0.23)$$
D.W. $= 1.40, \bar{R}^2 = 0.65.$ (7.25)

Equation (7.21) falls into the established pattern of showing a positive significant relationship between strike activity – in this case number of working days lost – and the level of unemployment. The degree of correlation was higher than for the corresponding equations for the other measures of strike activity and the Durbin–Watson statistic was almost satisfactory.

Similarly equation (7.23) matched our earlier findings. The variables all had the same signs and were significant, with the exception of prices variable. The correlation was slightly higher than in the corresponding estimates and the Durbin–Watson statistic satisfactory.

However, our estimate of the relationship between days lost and net real earnings was different from our earlier estimates for the other measures of strike activity. The estimated relationship was positive and significant. The degree of correlation was higher than for the other estimates and the Durbin–Watson statistic not too unsatisfactory. Analysis by sub-period revealed that, although the relationship was stronger in the second half of the period, it was not significant in either. The positive sign, unless it is interpreted as reflecting effect rather than cause, appears to be at odds with the Wilkinson–Turner explanation of recent events.

Equation (7.24) also differed from our earlier findings. The trend term was negatively related to the number of days lost and not significant. The level of unemployment and the earnings variable remained significant. The rate of change of unemployment was positively related but not significant. In respect of the earlier estimates we argued that the positive relationship between strike activity and unemployment was largely a result of trend factors so that it tended to disappear when an explicit trend factor was included in the equation. In respect of days lost this does not appear to be true. The implication is that the duration of stoppages increases with unemployment (see Turner and Bescoby, 1961b, for a parallel finding in respect of the motor vehicles industry).

In equation (7.25) we replaced the lagged values of prices and earnings of equation (7.24) with current values. This change produced several effects. The trend term changed its sign and became positive but not significant. The earnings variable was positive and significant whilst the two unemployment variables were both positive and close to significance. The magnitude of the estimated coefficient for the level of unemployment variable fell sharply compared with equation (7.24) whilst that of the rate of change of unemployment variable rose substantially. The degree of correlation was no higher than in equation (7.23) but still quite reasonable while the Durbin–Watson statistic was satisfactory. Although not so clear cut as the earlier equations in respect of number of days lost, equation (7.25) confirms the impression that trend factors were of little importance and other variables rather more important. The most likely explanation of this finding is that the duration of stoppages is more influenced by these factors than either the frequency or the extent of stoppages.

SUMMARY AND CONCLUSIONS

We have seen that, despite the apparent importance of this subject, it has not been the object of frequent study. Of the studies which have occurred the early ones were characterised by imprecise formulations of relationships and an interest in the effects of institutional change. The later studies were characterised, for the most part, by their more precise formulations, their use of multivariate regression analysis and their concentration on economic variables to the exclusion of institutional factors. Yet they all shared a tendency to attribute phenomena which were limited in their incidence to general factors, and to concentrate on the role of wages in motivating workers to take strike action. They also tended to assume that the influence of employer attitudes and objectives could be ignored in explanations of strike activity. Most important of all, the later studies of Pencavel and Knight, although much improved by their use of specific models and regression analysis, were weakened by their neglect of institutional factors – most notably recent changes in bargaining structure.

The solution would seem to be to combine strike data at a less aggregated level with a more flexible approach that allows for the interpretation of a wider range of explanatory variables. Within this context it should be possible to reach more meaningful conclusions concerning the relationship between strikes and changes in the economic environment.

Meanwhile it seemed worthwhile making limited use of multiple regression techniques to examine the relationships between measures of strike activity and the more obvious macro-economic variables. This analysis produced few surprises. Trend terms appeared to be important in accounting for the number of strikes and workers involved, but not working days lost. The level of unemployment was positively, not negatively, related to all three measures of strike activity – which contrasts with the findings of Knowles for his period (i.e. 1911–47). Current changes in money earnings also frequently appeared to be strongly related to all three measures of strike activity. We now turn to our industry studies, to see if these factors were also important at less aggregated levels.

8 Coal Mining – The Traditional Battleground

THE AIMS OF THE CHAPTER

Out of the forty or so industries for which we had strike data we decided to select three as subjects for more detailed study. We felt that coal mining had to be one of these for a number of reasons. First, there was the massive contribution that the industry had made to the total of strike activity. (Between 1946 and 1973 coal mining accounted for 45 per cent of stoppages and 18 per cent of workers involved and days lost.) Secondly, we wanted to account for decreases as well as increases in strike activity and coal mining provided the sole example of an industry with a proven capacity for strike action where stoppages actually fell at a time when many other industries were experiencing sharp increases. Thirdly, coal mining was a relatively homogeneous industry with a clearly recognisable product and subject throughout to the same sort of external pressures. Fourthly, the industry provided an interesting test case for some widely canvassed proposals to reduce the level of strike activity, e.g. alteration of the payment system. Finally, there was a wealth of material available which was not always the case with other industries.

Consequently the aim of the chapter is to trace the way in which the pattern of strike activity altered in coal mining between 1946 and 1973, and to try to account for both the level and form of changes. We begin by examining the strike pattern in detail, by which we mean the number of stoppages, workers involved, days lost, duration, cause and the distribution between large and small stoppages. In particular, we seek to draw attention to these features which are relatively constant through time as well as to the changes that have taken place. We go on to assess the influence of a wide range of factors which it is reasonable to assume has an impact on various aspects of the pattern – i.e. the economic environment, the composition and turnover of the labour force, movements in earnings and the payment system, dispute procedures, industrial structure and trade union organisation. In a final section of the chapter we seek to summarise what we have discovered and draw a number of conclusions which are of relevance to the study as a whole.

THE STRIKE PATTERN IN COAL MINING

Table 8.1 shows the totals of strike activity as measured by the three basic series in each year from 1946 to 1973. In addition there are three reference series, two of which relate to the number of workers involved and one to

Table 8.1　*Basic measures of strike activity in coal mining, 1946–73*

Year	No of strikes	No. of workers involved (000s)	No. of working days lost (000s)	Workers involved as a percentage of employees in employment	Workers involved as a percentage of average no. of wage earners	Working days lost as a percentage of potential working time
1946	1329	216.6	422	n.a.	31.1	n.a.
1947	1053	307.9	912	n.a.	43.3	n.a.
1948	1116	189.1	464	23.8	26.1	0.22
1949	874	247.8	754	31.3	34.4	0.35
1950	860	141.9	431	18.4	20.4	0.21
1951	1058	134.8	350	17.4	19.3	0.17
1952	1221	273.5	660	34.7	38.7	0.31
1953	1307	168.4	393	21.2	23.8	0.18
1954	1464	204.4	468	25.9	29.1	0.22
1955	1783	353.6	1 112	45.1	50.6	0.52
1956	2076	241.4	502	30.9	34.6	0.24
1957	2224	265.4	514	33.5	37.7	0.24
1958	1963	248.6	450	31.8	35.9	0.21
1959	1307	191.4	363	25.1	29.1	0.18
1960	1666	237.4	494	34.0	39.4	0.29
1961	1458	248.6	737	37.4	43.6	0.45
1962	1205	154.5	308	24.0	28.1	0.20
1963	987	152.2	326	24.7	29.4	0.22
1964	1058	171.9	302	29.1	35.0	0.21
1965	740	117.6	412	21.0	25.8	0.30
1966	553	50.3	118	9.8	12.0	0.09
1967	394	40.7	105	8.3	10.4	0.09
1968	221	29.8	54	7.0	8.9	0.05
1969	186	145.1	1 039	37.9	47.6	1.13
1970	160	117.5	1 090	32.7	40.9	1.26
1971	135	22.8	63	6.6	8.1	0.08
1972	224	341.5	10 798	103.5	127.4	13.58
1973	301	46.6	90	14.8	18.5	0.12

the number of working days lost. The former compare the number of workers involved with the total of employees in employment and with the number of wage earners on colliery books (until 1963–4 this series related to calendar years, thereafter it related to financial years April to March). The latter contrasts the number of working days lost with the total of potential working time.

As has been noted, the pattern of strike activity in coal mining was quite different from that of other industries. It is true that the industry shared the common pattern of declining activity in the late 1940s, but between 1950 and 1957 the number of strikes rose by nearly 160 per cent from 860 to 2224, a change which began earlier and occurred much more rapidly than in other industries. More remarkable still, after 1957 the number of strikes began to fall and an erratic downward trend continued until 1971. At this point the pattern again reversed itself and the number of strikes began increasing.

The other basic measures of strike activity were much more volatile than the number of strikes but they showed a similar pattern, except that it was in advance of the number of strikes series. (That is to say, workers involved and days lost peaked in 1955 and reached their trough in 1968.) In 1969 there was a widespread unofficial stoppage which led to a sharp increase in the numbers of workers involved and days lost. This action was repeated in 1970 and followed in 1972 by an official industry-wide strike. Following its conclusion the number of stoppages began to rise again.

The high level of strike activity in coal mining is perhaps best illustrated in columns 4 and 5 of Table 8.1, which show the number of workers involved in relative terms. Column 4 shows workers involved as a percentage of employees in employment in the industry. This measure may slightly understate the incidence of strike activity because it includes some workers who never went on strike (e.g. management), although it also includes those involved in multiple strike acts within the same year. According to this measure the percentage of workers involved in strikes exceeded 10 per cent in twenty-two out of the twenty-six years considered; 20 per cent in nineteen years and 30 per cent in eleven. Wage earners, the relative measure used in column 5, covers all industrial staff up to first line supervision but excludes management and clerical workers. This measure indicated a similar pattern to that of column 4, although the proportion of workers involved was higher. As a result, more than 10 per cent were involved in every year but two, over 20 per cent in every year but six, and over 30 per cent in fourteen out of the twenty-eight years. Both measures indicate that 1955 and 1968 were peak years of strike activity and that there was a decline from 1964 to 1968. It is possible that the decline began in the early 1960s but the series were too volatile for that to be clearly established.

The most surprising column of the whole table was that which related working days lost to potential working time. Although the assumptions required to calculate this series were quite strong, the orders of magnitude which resulted suggested that weaker assumptions would not have yielded

Table 8.2   *Small strikes in coal mining, 1946–73*

Year	No of strikes	No. of workers involved (000s)	No. of working days lost (000s)	Average no. of workers involved per small strike	Average no. of working days lost per worker involved per small strike	Workers involved as a percentage of average no. of wage earners
1946	1320	97.8	303.2	74	3.1	14.0
1947	1037	149.1	273.2	144	1.8	21.0
1948	1103	125.1	237.6	113	1.9	17.3
1949	867	93.6	176.4	108	1.9	13.0
1950	852	88.5	171.9	104	1.9	12.7
1951	1052	116.9	231.8	111	2.0	16.7
1952	1209	166.9	348.2	138	2.1	23.6
1953	1297	151.4	313.1	117	2.1	21.4
1954	1454	187.8	363.2	129	1.9	26.8
1955	1768	246.8	492.4	140	2.0	35.3
1956	2067	221.4	421.3	107	1.9	31.8
1957	2218	253.3	451.8	114	1.8	36.0
1958	1956	235.8	403.7	121	1.7	34.0
1959	1302	160.5	273.8	123	1.7	24.4
1960	1657	220.9	412.1	133	1.9	36.7
1961	1451	164.2	313.8	113	1.9	28.8
1962	1199	139.4	264.1	116	1.9	25.3
1963	982	127.9	244.5	130	1.9	24.7
1964	1053	118.3	213.7	112	1.8	24.1
1965	736	75.5	142.7	103	1.9	16.6
1966	549	45.3	92.4	83	2.0	10.8
1967	391	37.4	84.2	96	2.3	9.5
1968	221	29.8	54.0	135	1.8	8.9
1969	185	24.2	59.6	131	2.5	7.9
1970	156	17.3	34.7	111	2.0	6.0
1971	133	20.7	48.3	156	2.3	7.4
1972	222	31.0	59.7	140	1.9	11.6
1973	300	45.5	85.0	151	1.9	18.0

radically different results. Days lost only accounted for more than 0.5 per cent of potential working time in four years out of the twenty-six; three of those were in the last five years. The only occasion when days lost seem to have been really important was in 1972, when there was an official industry-wide stoppage which lasted for almost seven weeks. For the rest this series emphasises the fact that the majority of stoppages in coal mining were small, short and of little consequence in terms of lost production.

Our major strikes series allowed us to depict the pattern of small strikes by excluding major strikes from an industry series. The results of such an analysis for coal mining are shown in Table 8.2 which relates to those stoppages which involved the loss of less than 5000 working days each.

Because there were few major strikes in coal mining the number of small strikes followed a pattern very similar to that of all strikes. Workers involved followed a similar pattern to that of strike numbers except that it began to rise in 1971 rather than 1972. The number of working days lost reached its peak in 1955 and its trough in 1970. The number of strikes at its trough was only 6 per cent of its peak value; workers involved and working days lost only 7 per cent. It is, of course, true that the industry had contracted substantially during this period but the decline in small strike activity was considerably greater than the decline in the size of the industry.

The range of the average size of small strikes was from seventy-four workers in 1946 to 156 in 1971, but in a majority of the years considered the average size was in the range of 100–130 workers. Average duration of small strikes, measured by the days lost per worker involved, was fairly constant – i.e. less than two days in eighteen out of the twenty-eight years. Expressing the number of workers involved in small strikes as a percentage of the average number of wage-earners serves to emphasise the increase in strike activity after 1950 and the fluctuations around a high level between 1955 and 1960; 1960 was revealed as the peak year for small strike activity, by a short head from 1957. It also pointed to a continuous decline until 1971.

By 1973 strike activity had reached its highest level since 1965. Table 8.3 is similar to Table 8.2, except that it covers major strikes rather than small ones, i.e. those which involved the loss of at least 5000 working days.

In the period 1946–73 there were 186 major stoppages in coal mining, less than 0.7 per cent of all stoppages in the industry. However, major strikes in coal were still relatively small. On average, in fifteen of the years, fewer than 5000 workers were involved. Similarly, less than 5 per cent of employees were involved in major stoppages in over half the years. The number of working days lost fluctuated a good deal but, when the industry was expanding, never amounted to as much as one day per employee per year. That situation changed dramatically in later years as losses from major strikes rose very significantly.

We also analysed the characteristics of major strikes in coal mining. As expected miners accounted for the great majority of major strikes although under-officials, clerks and craftsmen were also involved. Regional shares

Table 8.3   *Major strikes in coal mining, 1946–73*

Year	No. of strikes	No. of workers involved (000s)	No. of working days lost (000s)	Average no. of workers involved per major strike	Average no. of working days lost per worker involved in major strike	Workers involved as a percentage of average no. of wage earners
1946	9	34.4	118.8	3820	3.5	4.9
1947	16	158.8	638.8	9930	4.0	22.3
1948	13	64.0	226.4	4920	3.5	8.8
1949	7	154.2	577.6	22030	3.7	21.4
1950	8	53.4	259.1	6679	4.8	7.7
1951	6	17.9	118.2	2989	6.6	2.6
1952	12	106.6	311.8	8885	2.9	15.1
1953	10	17.0	79.9	1697	4.7	2.4
1954	10	16.6	104.8	1657	6.9	2.4
1955	15	106.8	619.6	7122	5.8	15.3
1956	9	20.0	80.7	2219	4.0	2.9
1957	6	12.1	62.2	2016	5.1	1.7
1958	7	12.8	46.3	1835	3.6	1.9
1959	5	30.9	89.2	6171	2.9	4.7
1960	9	16.5	81.9	1828	5.0	2.7
1961	7	84.5	423.2	12064	5.0	14.8
1962	6	15.1	43.9	2510	2.9	2.7
1963	5	24.3	81.5	4868	3.3	4.7
1964	5	53.6	88.3	10713	1.6	10.9
1965	4	42.1	269.3	10528	6.4	9.2
1966	4	5.0	25.6	1238	5.2	1.2
1967	3	3.3	20.8	1114	6.2	0.8
1968	—	—	—	—	—	—
1969	1	120.9	979.4	120938	8.1	39.6
1970	4	100.2	1055.3	25050	10.5	34.9
1971	2	2.1	14.7	1071	6.9	0.8
1972	2	310.5	10738.3	155269	34.6	115.8
1973	1	1.2	5.4	1230	4.4	0.5

were influenced by the distribution of the workforce, but it was not possible to adjust our series to reflect this. Three regions (Yorkshire and Humberside, Wales and Monmouthshire and Scotland) consistently had a greater share of strike activity than other regions. Yorkshire and Humberside was the clear leader, accounting for seventy-eight strikes (41.9 per cent of the total). Strikes affecting all areas of Great Britain were a very rare event. There were only three of these – in 1948, 1969 and 1972. The first was a relatively minor affair involving workers in coke and by-product plants. The other two were of rather more importance and are further discussed below.

Other wage issues were the single most frequent cause of major stoppages, but this predominance reflects their pre-1958 importance when they accounted for 50 per cent of stoppages. In the last five years this issue only accounted for 10 per cent of strikes. Stoppages over claims for wage increases have grown in importance and accounted for 40 per cent of major strikes in the last five years. Sympathy strikes were also of importance in the early part of the period but then declined.

Further evidence of changes in major strikes in recent years may be seen in their extent and size. Measured by workers directly involved the predominant pattern has been for major strikes to be quite small; over 30 per cent involved less than 1000 workers and 76 per cent less than 2500 workers. In contrast there have been four strikes involving more than 50 000 workers – all since 1957. Workers indirectly involved in strike action, as measured by the Department of Employment, were not usually very numerous in coal mining, so that the distribution of all workers involved was very similar to that of workers directly involved. In terms of working days lost major strikes again looked fairly small – 63 per cent involved the loss of less than 10 000 days and nearly 80 per cent the loss of less than 20 000. Only 7 per cent, thirteen strikes in all, involved the loss of more than 100 000 days. Five of those occurred in the last five years. In the period up to 1968 strikes involving the loss of 100 000 days or more accounted for 4.4 per cent of major strikes (0.03 per cent of all coal mining strikes), since then such strikes have accounted for 50 per cent of major stoppages (0.5 per cent of all coal mining strikes).

SUMMARY

Essentially coal mining has had two strike patterns since the war. The first may be conveniently termed the *micro strike*. Micro strikes are small, short stoppages arising from workplace disputes that rarely extend much beyond those directly involved. Coal mining has been characterised by a very high incidence of this form of stoppage for much of the period 1946–73. Most of the 186 major strikes which we distinguished are really outgrowths from the predominant pattern. They arose over workplace issues and involved either small numbers of workers in strategic positions (e.g. deputies who were able to affect large sections of the workforce and consequently turn a small strike into a major one) or sympathetic action on behalf of those involved in workplace disputes. The micro strike pattern went through four phases; decline in the late 1940s, increase from 1950 to 1957, decline again from 1957 to 1972 and, apparently, increase from 1972 – although two years is a rather short period on which to judge a complete reversal of such a trend.

The second strike pattern in coal mining has only become clearly distinguishable in recent years and arises from those extensive and lengthy strikes involving national rather than workplace issues. There have only been a small number of these, but they have been important and quite different in character to the great majority of micro strikes. It seems reasonable to characterise them as *macro strikes*.

The aim of the rest of the chapter is to explain both micro and macro activity in relation to their 'typical' characteristics and incidence. We begin by considering a number of the more obvious explanations – such as the economic environment, the composition of the labour force and so on – before going on to evaluate a number of less immediately apparent factors which we feel are not without significance, especially in relation to changes in the micro pattern.

Obviously we appreciate that both patterns cannot be completely separated, yet we feel it is useful to recognise that strikes in coal mining and elsewhere have not been homogeneous. (Indeed, we shall go on to argue that the relevance of the distinction made here between micro and the macro is not confined to coal mining.)

THE ECONOMIC ENVIRONMENT

The economic record of the coal mining industry revealed four distinct phases in the period 1946–73. The first, from 1946 to 1951, saw a rapid expansion of output to meet the demands of a recovering economy. The second, from 1951 to 1957, saw production stabilised at a high level to meet the high level of demand. The third, from 1957 to 1970–1, saw coal no longer so competitive with other fuels and responding to a declining market by a substantial reduction in output. The fourth, from 1970–1 onwards, has seen coal's competitive position improved by the increase in oil prices, which has led to some stabilisation of its output level. These four phases coincided closely enough with changes in the incidence of stoppages in the industry to require further investigation. Some relevant information is set out in Table 8.4.

In the first phase, from 1946 to 1951, production of deep-mined coal rose by 17 per cent; distributed coal stocks rose sharply in 1947 and then tended to fall (it is not possible to make comparisons between 1951 and 1952 because of a change in the method of compilation). Coal stocks at collieries fluctuated without any clear pattern while employment fell slightly between 1948 and 1951. Using production, less any change in stocks, as an indicator of the sales of domestically produced coal reveals that between 1946 and 1951 sales rose by around 13 per cent. In summary 1946–51 was a

Table 8.4 *Economic record of the coal mining industry, 1946–73*

Year	Employees in employment (000s)	Production of deep-mined coal (million tons)	Distributed coal stocks (million tons)	Coal stocks at collieries (million tons)
1946	n.a.	181.2	8.3	1.4
1947	n.a.	187.2	16.4	1.2
1948	794.3	199.8	14.4	1.4
1949	792.9	202.7	14.7	1.5
1950	772.7	204.1	12.4	1.3
1951	775.2	211.3	16.2	1.1
1952	791.0	212.7	16.1	1.5
1953	794.8	211.8	17.4	1.0
1954	788.1	213.6	15.6	0.9
1955	784.7	210.2	18.3	1.5
1956	782.6	209.9	18.0	1.8
1957	792.0	210.0	18.8	4.7
1958	781.5	201.5	17.5	13.7
1959	761.6	195.3	14.3	28.8
1960	697.6	186.0	13.4	23.6
1961	664.9	181.9	15.7	17.7
1962	643.9	189.3	15.1	22.2
1963	616.9	189.7	16.5	17.7
1964	591.3	186.8	17.3	18.2
1965	559.2	180.2	16.6	18.6
1966	512.7	167.6	18.4	15.3
1967	487.9	165.0	18.6	23.4
1968	427.5	157.2	17.1	23.8
1969	383.1	144.2	15.4	15.3
1970	359.4	134.5	14.4	5.3
1971	346.0	134.3	20.9	7.0
1972	329.9	107.3	21.9	7.6
1973	315.4	118.1	16.8	7.6

period of rising sales, production stocks and of declining strike activity; employment reduction caused mainly by workers leaving the industry voluntarily.

The second period, 1951–57, was one of stability: employment averaged 787 000, production remained in the range 209–213 million tons and coal stocks rose marginally. Sales of domestically produced coal rose slightly between 1951 and 1954 and then fell by 5 per cent. This apparently aroused little concern at the time as it provided some opportunity to build up stocks. The only exception to stability was strike activity, which rose very substantially over the period.

After 1957 stability was replaced by decline. Between 1957 and 1970 employment fell by 55 per cent and production by 36 per cent, while output per man-shift rose by 76 per cent. Distributed stocks fell by 23 per cent and colliery stocks rose by 13 per cent. But these end of year comparisons conceal the way in which changes occurred. Between 1957 and 1959 sales fell by about 18 per cent. Production could not be reduced as rapidly without causing widespread economic and social dislocation, so the excess production was stockpiled at collieries where stocks rose by 1500 per cent between 1956 and 1959. However, demand and production remained roughly stable between 1959 and 1964, while stocks and employment fell by 18 and 22 per cent respectively. Between 1964 and 1970 all indicators showed a decline; employment fell by 39 per cent, production by 28 per cent, demand by 24 per cent and stocks by 45 per cent. Thus the period 1957–70 encompassed three stages of decline: rapid decline between 1957 and 1959, slow decline between 1960 and 1964 and a further rapid decline between 1965 and 1970.

Throughout the years 1957–70 stocks were higher than in 1946–56, despite the reduction in production and demand. In 1946–56 total stocks averaged 16.6 million tons a year. In 1957–70 they averaged 34.1 million tons. This change was most pronounced in colliery-held stocks, which rose, on average, from 1.3 million to 17.7 million tons. In relation to average production this represented an increase from 0.6 to 10.0 per cent.

The final phase of the industry's economic record, from 1970–1 onwards, is more difficult to describe because the crucial changes were potential rather than real. In real terms, between 1970 and 1973, employment fell by 12 per cent, production by 12 per cent and demand by 18 per cent. At the same time stocks rose by 24 per cent. One interesting feature of the stock position was the increase in distributed stocks as against stocks at collieries. In all but two of the years between 1958 and 1969 colliery-held stocks were greater than distributed stocks. In every year since 1969 the reverse has been true. On average distributed stocks have been three times as large as those at collieries.

It is difficult to explain this switch in terms of market requirements, given the substantial reduction in sales and the experience of the previous twelve years. Even if one took the view that the National Coal Board (NCB) had been able to reduce its stocks to a more appropriate level, this would not explain the increase in distributed stocks which occurred, in both absolute terms and in relation to the level of sales.

The change in the industry's potential was caused by oil price increases which made coal more price-competitive than it had been for over a decade and a half. This improvement meant that the case for continuing to rundown the industry was substantially weakened and there was some scope for an improvement in the relative earnings of mineworkers. The former possibility was not acted upon immediately, so that the industry continued to decline. However, the efforts of the mineworkers to seize the latter opportunity contributed to the occurrence in 1972 of the first national mining strike since 1926.

If we contrast the four phases of economic development with those of strike activity we find that there are some indications of causal links. Yet any explanation entirely based on the industry's economic record would be far from complete. There seems to have been little causal link between the first two phases, when economic activity expanded rapidly and strike activity tended to decline. (It is worth remembering that in this respect coal mining exhibited the same tendency as most other industries.) Between 1951 and 1957 demand for the industry's products was high but relatively constant, whereas strike activity rose rapidly. Under these circumstances the increase in strike activity cannot simply be attributed to the pressure of demand within the industry. It could be attributed, in part at least, to the high level of demand acting as a 'necessary' condition for strike action.

Thus it could be argued that the workers realised that in a situation of high demand and limited stocks stoppages were likely to produce a more rapid managerial response than the reference of disputes were through procedure. Through time realisation of this fact grew and stoppages became more common. Of course it can be replied that such an argument is highly speculative, but it must be said that it does help to explain the situation post-1957, when the slackening of demand and the increase in coal stocks coincided with a reduction in strike activity. On balance we would argue that the decline in strike activity in this period was significantly influenced by the shift in market conditions, and in particular by the change in the stock position. We consider that after 1957 the high level of stocks combined with greater cost consciousness on the part of management to produce a situation where stoppages could no longer be relied upon to secure rapid results. We also think that the acceleration in the rate of decline in strike activity after 1965 may have been influenced by the rapid decline in industry size. However, the large unofficial stoppages of 1969 and 1970 represent a break in this pattern. Moreover, this break antedates the oil price rise so that, although that factor may have been of some importance in the 1972 strike, it cannot account for the shift.

Although our evidence appears to support the view that changes in the industry's economic position directly influenced the level of strike activity, such changes cannot hope to provide anything like a complete explanation. To concentrate solely on the level of demand, production, stocks and employment is to ignore the impact of other kinds of changes – e.g.

increasing use of capital equipment and changes in the payment system. It also does not take into account the manner in which these changes were brought about. We attempt to remedy these omissions in the sections which follow.

THE COMPOSITION OF THE LABOUR FORCE

The overall size of the labour force in coal mining was discussed in the previous section. The aim of this section is to examine its composition and the way in which it has altered over time, to see which groups have been most affected by change and to see how change was brought about. Many of the series in this section relate to NCB employees, which means that they are not strictly comparable with official series which include those working at non-NCB pits. In practice this distinction probably makes very little difference as the NCB dominates the coal mining industry.

Examination of the composition of the labour force reveals, as one might have expected, that it was dominated by male manual workers. From the official employees in employment series it appears that women have increased their relative share of the labour force, but that it remains at a very low level. In 1948 there were 11 000 women employees, 1.5 per cent of the total. By 1973 there were only 10 000 but they accounted for over 3 per cent of the total. In terms of absolute numbers the peak year for women's employment in the industry was 1959, when there were 19 500. The peak year in relative terms was 1970 when women accounted for 3.6 per cent of total employment.

The NCB only publishes data relating to industrial workers – i.e. manual workers and first-line supervisory staff up to but excluding under-managers. Consequently, information on the number of non-industrial staff is not readily available, but it may be estimated. Assuming that the number of employees in coal mining who are not employed by the NCB is very small, the number of non-industrial staff may be estimated by subtracting the NCB figures for industrial workers from the official series of employees in employment; this covers all occupational grades. These estimates provide only a rough approximation of the actual situation and should be seen as a guide to the principal changes of the period, rather than as a firm indicator of minor fluctuations. The estimates suggest that in the period 1948–57 non-industrial workers accounted for 10 per cent of employees in employment. From 1958 until the mid-1960s non-industrial staff tended to increase their relative share of the labour force until it again stabilised – this time at around 20 per cent of the total. After the mid-1960s the number of non-industrial staff fell in line with the total number of employees, so that their relative share of the labour force remained at around 20 per cent.

It is somewhat difficult to provide explanations for change after 1957 without a great deal more information on the occupational composition of non-industrial staff. Part of the explanation probably is that the rundown of the labour force was facilitated by the adoption of more productive processes by industrial workers, an option which was not available for non-industrial staff. Another factor seems to have been that the administrative structure was not immediately streamlined to match the fall in productive capacity, so that the structure became increasingly 'top-heavy'. This view is supported by the fact that from 1967 onwards, when the administrative structure was reformed, non-industrial workers' relative share of the labour force ceased its expansion. However, despite these changes in relative shares the industry remained overwhelmingly composed of male industrial workers, with long traditions of conflict and strike action.

The occupational composition of these workers also appears to have been the subject of some change, but our findings are somewhat impressionistic because of the comparative lack of data for much of the period. Only two occupational groups can be distinguished, underground officials and craftsmen. Underground officials appear to have increased their share of the industrial workforce from 5.5 per cent in 1956 to over 8 per cent at the end of the period. Craftsmen accounted for some 15 per cent of the workforce in recent years and it appears that they too may have been increasing their relative size. This would be consistent with the increasing mechanisation of the pits. There seems to have been little change in the relative shares of surface and underground workers, the latter accounting for between 77 and 80 per cent of all workers during the whole period from 1950. It is difficult to draw firm conclusions from such slender evidence, but these changes are consistent with an increase in the skill level of the industrial workforce – a change, *ceteris paribus,* which one might have expected to be accompanied by changes in relative earnings.

Considering the experience of other industries the most surprising feature of the coal mining industry in this period was that it was able to reduce its labour force so sharply without producing the sort of resistance that occurred elsewhere. This is particularly surprising since the history of the mineworkers bears ample witness to their willingness to take collective action when their interests are threatened. Consequently, we felt that it was important to examine how this rundown was brought about. Some relevant information is set out in Table 8.5.

On this evidence it would seem that any simple view of the labour force in coal mining as a stock, which has been gradually rundown since 1957, omits some important features of the actual process. Thus in the period 1949–57 recruitment averaged 9 per cent per annum; in 1958–73 it fell to 6.5 per cent per annum. Even at this lower rate the total number of workers recruited between 1958 and 1973 – i.e. about 480 000 – was considerably larger than the total workforce in 1973. This must have influenced mineworkers' attitudes towards the rundown of the industry, since there was plenty of opportunity to work in coal mining, although it might have involved moving to a different part of the country.

The 2.5 per cent reduction in recruitment would have allowed a slow rundown of the industry if wastage had remained at its pre-1958 rate of 9

Table 8.5   *Recruitment and wastage in coal mining, 1949–73*

Year	Average manpower (000s)	Recruitment as a percentage of average manpower	Wastage as a percentage of average manpower	Final wastage (%)	Dismissals and redundancies (%)	Voluntary wastage (%)
1949	712.5	7.3	9.6	2.2	1.4	6.0
1950	690.8	8.0	11.0	2.1	0.9	8.0
1951	692.6	10.5	9.2	2.4	0.6	6.2
1952	709.7	10.9	7.7	2.5	0.7	4.5
1953	707.4	7.3	8.8	3.2	0.6	5.0
1954	701.8	8.7	8.7	2.9	0.5	5.3
1955	698.7	8.7	9.5	3.0	0.4	6.1
1956	697.4	9.4	9.0	2.8	0.5	5.7
1957	703.8	10.1	9.2	2.6	0.6	6.0
1958	692.7	5.7	9.0	2.9	0.7	5.4
1959	658.2	4.0	11.5	3.1	1.4	7.0
1960	602.1	7.0	15.5	5.2	0.7	9.6
1961	570.5	9.2	13.0	3.3	0.6	9.1
1962	550.9	6.5	11.0	3.3	1.3	6.4
1963	544.3	5.5	10.5	3.5	1.4	5.6
1964	517.0	5.1	10.4	4.0	1.3	5.1
1965	491.0	6.9	12.6	4.1	1.0	7.5
1966	455.7	6.9	15.9	4.7	1.0	10.2
1967	419.4	8.2	14.5	4.6	1.5	8.4
1968	391.9	4.9	15.9	4.3	4.3	7.3
1969	336.3	5.6	19.3	4.0	7.1	8.2
1970	305.1	7.6	15.1	3.4	3.9	7.8
1971	287.2	10.3	13.6	3.2	3.0	7.4
1972	281.5	6.3	10.7	2.9	2.9	4.9
1973	268.0	6.6	10.4	2.9	3.4	4.1

per cent. In fact the rate rose to an average of 12.8 per cent per annum after 1957. Three types of wastage may be distinguished: (a) final wastage, i.e. those who are leaving the workforce as well as the industry; (b) dismissals and redundancies; (c) voluntary wastage, i.e. those who leave the industry voluntarily to seek alternative work. The last three columns of Table 8.5 show the wastage from each of these sources as a percentage of the average manpower for that year.

This shows that the largest single source of wastage throughout the period has been voluntary. Pre-1958 the annual rate was 5.9 per cent; post-1957 it rose slightly to an average rate of 7.2 per cent, although it fell sharply in the last two years of the period. Since 1957 voluntary wastage alone has exceeded recruitment, which means that the size of the labour force would have fallen even if no further wastage had occurred.

Final wastage may arise from death, retirement or workers leaving the industry for medical reasons. The first and last of these would not seem to be particularly susceptible to NCB control, although the latter did increase somewhat after 1957. This change was probably due to a combination of factors including the ageing of the working population. Wastage through retirements appears to have been more influenced by NCB policy, since it almost doubled between the earlier and later periods to reach an average annual rate of 1.6 per cent. To some extent this latter rate will also have been influenced by the ageing of the working population, as well as the NCB policy of encouraging premature retirement.

So far we have considered those types of wastage which do not involve any degree of compulsion, consequently they are less likely to be resisted. The remaining forms – i.e. dismissals and redundancy – are not of this kind and are much more likely to provoke hostility. Yet it is this form which shows the greatest relative increase after 1957, rising from 0.7 to 1.9 per cent. In fact there appear to have been three phases in their growth. The first, which was pre-1958, had a rate of 0.7 per cent; the second, from 1958 to 1966, had a slightly higher rate of 1 per cent; the third, from 1967 to 1973, had a rate of 3.7 per cent. The first of these phases coincided with a period when employment in the industry was fairly stable, despite the closure of some worked-out collieries. As a result it seems likely that the bulk of wastage was due to dismissals. (Unfortunately the NCB has not distinguished in its series between redundancy and dismissal, so it is impossible to be precise on this point.) But there seems no plausible reason for supposing that the rate of dismissal increased after 1957. If anything, given the tendency for the rate of dismissals to be related to the rate of recruitment, we might have expected it to fall. Consequently it does not seem unreasonable to attribute the whole of the post-1957 increase to redundancies. But even on this assumption the rate of wastage through redundancy remained very low until 1967 – indeed it may have been as low as 0.3 per cent per annum. After 1967 the rate rose very sharply to approximately 3 per cent per year. It seems reasonable to suggest that this accelerated rate contributed substantially to the conflict which became manifest in the coal fields at the end of the decade.

If proposals to reduce substantially the level of employment in an industry are not to provoke conflict it is necessary that the workers who leave go voluntarily and are able to find suitable alternative employment. Otherwise, particularly in tightly knit mining communities, the failure of those leaving the industry to find work will become widely known and prejudice further attempts to reduce the labour force. Unfortunately, for the NCB, the increase in the rate of redundancy came at a time when the rest of the economy had entered a recession, so that alternative employment became progressively more difficult to obtain.

The industrial classification of the unemployed is determined by the industry in which they last worked. Those who left coal mining, but were unable to find alternative work, would be shown as unemployed in coal mining. The conventional relative measure for unemployment expresses the number unemployed as a percentage of the labour force. The use of such a measure in coal mining reveals that unemployment was very low for much of the period – only exceeding 1 per cent in one year between 1948 and 1966. After 1966 it rose rapidly to 6 per cent in 1970 and fell back to 5 per cent in 1973. However, a measure of this kind is not particularly useful in coal mining because those registered as unemployed either left their jobs because they wished to leave the industry or because they were made redundant. A more interesting measure would be to express the number of unemployed as a percentage of those leaving the industry each year to find alternative work – i.e. those leaving voluntarily or for reasons of redundancy or dismissal. In a rough sort of way this measure could be used to indicate the employment prospects of those leaving the industry. If the series showed a sharp deterioration in employment prospects one might expect increased conflict over the policy of reducing the labour force. Using this series it appears that, between 1949 and 1957, 3 per cent of those leaving the industry had difficulty in finding alternative employment. In the period 1958–66 this rate quadrupled to an average of 12 per cent, although it tended to vary directly with the overall level of unemployment. In the period 1967–73 the rate quadrupled again to average 52 per cent. It reached a peak of over 80 per cent in 1972–3. We would not claim that the rates indicated by this analysis are necessarily accurate, but we are confident that the very substantial deterioration in employment prospects which it reveals occurred, and that the situation became worse after 1966.

In summary it would seem reasonable to suggest that up to 1966 the first phase of the rundown of the industry was largely acceptable, mainly because the great majority of those leaving did so without compulsion and without undue difficulty in finding alternative work. After 1966 the situation altered radically, with the number of redundancies increasing sharply while employment prospects deteriorated. In these circumstances it would be surprising if there had not been rather more hostility to the rundown of the industry. Yet such hostility could not easily be directed against the rundown policy, if only because that policy had longstanding union support. Consequently, it seems plausible to argue that it was likely to manifest itself in relation to some other bargainable issue – i.e. in the view that miners had been inadequately rewarded in financial terms for their co-operation in the rundown and deserved higher wages. But to be able to establish the extent to which the large strikes which occurred towards the end of the period were influenced by these more general feelings of hostility, we must examine earnings' movements in coal mining and the change in the payment system which also took place at this time. These are the subjects we consider in the next section.

EARNINGS PATTERNS AND THE PAYMENT SYSTEM

During the last few years there has been a good deal of argument (see Hughes and Moore, 1972; Stewart, 1977) over the measurement of miners' earnings. It would seem that the NCB's figures and those of the Department of Employment are inadequate, at least until the advent of the *New Earnings Survey* in 1968. The reasons for this include defects of coverage, in the sense that they are based on supervisory as well as manual workers, and their treatment of holiday pay. In order to match our strike series as closely as possible we opted to use the NCB's series. The NCB's figures cover the period from 1947 and specify average earnings for the year rather than just for one point in a year.

In view of various arguments about which series best measures the level of mineworkers' earnings, and how that level related to the earnings of other workers, we decided to avoid most of the difficulties by using rates of change rather than levels of earnings. Our analysis concentrated on changes in miners' earnings and is shown in Table 8.6. We distinguished between surface workers and underground workers and three measures of the rate of change of earnings. These were (a) gross percentage change in average earnings from one year to the next; (b) real percentage change in earnings (calculated by adjusting the gross changes by price changes); (c) net real percentage changes in earnings (calculated for a 'typical' family of a married couple with two children under 11, claiming only standard personal tax allowances) by estimating the real percentage changes after making allowance for tax and social security deductions. The series are those of cash earnings excluding allowances in kind.

Between 1948 and 1957 underground miners received average gross increases of 7.5 per cent per annum. In 1958–9, when the first effects of the decline in the demand for coal were felt, average gross earnings actually fell because of the reduction in overtime and the ending of Saturday working. In the decade following 1958 they rose at an average annual rate of just over 4 per cent per annum. After 1968 there was a very substantial acceleration in the rate of increase and the average annual rate was 10 per cent. Price increases absorbed slightly more than two-thirds of these increases. Between 1948 and 1957 the average annual real rate of increase was 2.5 per cent; between 1958 and 1968 it was 1.3 per cent; after 1968 it rose to 3.2 per cent. For the typical family, after making allowance for tax and social security contributions, the net real rates of increase were 1.6 per

Table 8.6 *Changes in the earnings of surface and underground workers, 1948–73/4*

Year	Underground workers			Surace workers		
	Percentage change in cash earnings	Real percentage change in cash earnings	Real percentage change in disposable cash earnings	Percentage change in cash earnings	Real percentage change in cash earnings	Real percentage change in disposable cash earnings
1948	17.7	7.7	n.a.	19.3	9.3	n.a.
1949	7.3	4.5	2.9	3.7	0.9	0.8
1950	4.5	1.4	1.3	3.2	0.1	0.1
1951	11.3	2.2	1.0	13.8	4.7	3.9
1952	10.5	1.3	–0.6	9.9	0.7	0.4
1953	2.5	–0.6	3.3	4.0	0.9	0.8
1954	5.0	3.1	2.2	8.6	6.7	6.1
1955	5.7	1.2	1.6	7.6	3.1	3.1
1956	8.3	3.4	2.0	10.2	5.3	4.6
1957	7.2	3.5	2.2	6.5	2.8	1.8
1958	–1.8	–4.8	–5.4	–4.1	–7.1	–7.8
1959	–0.2	–0.8	–0.2	–0.3	–0.9	–0.6
1960	3.7	2.7	2.3	3.5	2.5	2.3
1961	6.0	2.6	0.2	7.2	3.8	1.8
1962	4.2	–0.1	–0.9	2.9	–1.4	–1.9
1963/4	5.8	4.2	4.4	7.3	5.7	6.6
1964/5	4.4	0.4	–0.3	4.4	0.4	–0.3
1965/6	6.5	1.8	0.1	7.3	2.6	0.7
1966/7	5.1	1.4	0.3	6.4	2.7	1.1
1967/8	5.1	2.8	1.5	4.0	1.7	0.8
1968/9	5.5	0.0	–2.3	7.9	2.4	0.5
1969/70	2.5	–2.7	–4.3	5.8	0.6	–0.9
1970/1	18.5	11.2	7.5	14.3	7.0	3.9
1971/2	12.7	3.4	4.1	19.7	10.4	9.2
1972/3	14.3	7.2	7.8	19.3	12.2	11.7
1973/4	5.3	–5.1	–5.9	5.3	–5.1	–6.0

cent, 0.5 per cent and 2.6 per cent respectively.

The earnings of surface workers followed a similar pattern but, on the whole, they had a marginally higher rate of increase so that the differential between the two groups was substantially reduced. At the beginning of the period surface workers' earnings were only 75 per cent of underground workers, by 1973 they had become 88.5 per cent. Between 1948 and 1957 average gross earnings rose by 7.8 per cent per annum; between 1958 and 1968 they rose at an annual average rate of 4.6 per cent; since then they have risen at a rate of 11.4 per cent a year. Taking account of price rises these rates are reduced to average increases of 3.1 per cent, 1.8 per cent and 4.7 per cent respectively. For the typical family the average rates of increase in net real earnings were 2.2 per cent, 1.0 per cent and 3.6 per cent.

In addition to this reduction in the differential between surface and underground workers' earnings the latter part of the period witnessed a substantial reduction in the differences in earnings between areas. This change was chronicled in the National Union of Mineworkers' evidence to the Wilberforce Inquiry (see Hughes and Moore, 1972). We see little point in repeating that evidence. The implication of these changes is that the highest paid workers in the industry – i.e. underground workers in the productive Midlands pits – accepted lower rates of increase than other workers. In these circumstances it is not surprising to find considerable pressure for a higher general rate of increase as a way of ensuring that all workers receive sufficient increases, whilst enabling the new structure of differentials to be preserved.

A good deal of attention has been given – particularly in the course of the national strikes – to the relationship between mineworkers' earnings and those of other manual workers. Because of the difficulties previously alluded to in comparing levels of earnings we decided to limit our comparisons to rates of change. In the period before 1958 the increase in mineworkers' earnings was closely comparable to that of all manual workers – implying that the relative position of mineworkers remained the same. However, between 1958 and 1968 the earnings of manual workers in other industries rose by approximately 5.5 per cent per annum, whilst in coal mining underground workers' earnings rose by 4.1 per cent and surface workers' by 4.6 per cent, as a result miners lost ground relative to other groups. The bulk of this change took place in 1958–9. Thereafter the rates of increase moved much more closely together, with surface workers' earnings increasing at approximately the same rate as other workers' and underground workers' by about 0.5 per cent per annum less. In the period since 1969 there have been further slight changes. Surface workers' earnings increased by approximately 11.4 per cent per annum; other manual workers' by about 10.5 per cent and underground workers' by 10 per cent. The net result of these changes was that underground workers continued to lose ground but surface workers improved their relative position.

So far we have examined the changes in mineworkers' earnings from two angles – i.e. those of mineworkers themselves (by examining their real purchasing power over time) and those of other manual workers. The aim of both analyses was to assess the extent to which events in coal mining supported the widely held belief that a reduction in the rate of increase of real disposable earnings, or a decline in earnings relative to other groups, would create such conflict that strikes were bound to occur.

Real disposable earnings of underground workers fell sharply in 1958, 1968–70 and 1973/4. Those of surface workers fell in 1958, 1962 and 1973. Comparison of mineworkers' earnings with those of other manual workers suggests that mineworkers lost ground relatively in 1958–60, 1969 and 1973. The coincidence of these dates is not surprising, since the low rate of growth in real earnings in the post-war period has meant that any group which received noticeably lower increases than the average was likely to suffer a reduction in real disposable earnings. This effect has been increased in recent years with the acceleration in inflation. Both analyses suggest that there was likely to be a great deal of conflict over earnings in the late 1950s and 1960s and in 1973. The analysis may be somewhat misleading about the situation in 1971–2, if only because the settlement following the 1972 strike was backdated.

On this evidence it is tempting to argue that the cause of the change in the trend of strike activity in 1969, and of the national strikes in 1972 and 1974, was a conflict over pay resulting from a reduction in both real and relative earnings. The difficulty with this argument is that it also implies that there should have been extensive strikes in the late 1950s. Yet they did not occur. There was an increase in the number of small disputes in 1960, but widespread strikes over pay, similar to those later years, did not emerge.

To account for this apparent contradiction we need to consider several other factors that are likely to have exercised a differential impact at varying points in time. We begin with the payment system in the industry, and how it changes through time.

Throughout the post-war period the majority of mineworkers were paid on a daily or weekly basis, although faceworkers, for much of the time, were paid on a piecework system. Unfortunately little detailed information is available until late in our period about how many workers were on piecework, or to what extent their total earnings were made up from timework and piecework components. An earlier study of conflict in coal mining (Scott, Mumford, McGivering and Kirkby, 1963) showed that the piecework system was the major cause of disputes in the pits they studied and that these disputes frequently resulted in strike action. In 1966 a National Power Loading Agreement was reached which allowed the great majority of faceworkers to be transferred from piecework to daywork. It is widely accepted that this helped to avoid the disputes which used to arise under the old system. Indeed it seems plausible to suggest that this new agreement was largely responsible for the progressive decline in strike activity after 1966. The National Agreement cannot explain the reduction in strike activity before then, but as Clegg (1970) points out, 'the powerloading agreement was the culmination of a long process of mechanisation and of adjustment in the traditional methods of wage settlement'. This process had lead to area agreements before 1966 and, as Clegg goes on to suggest, such 'agreements led to a progressive reduction in the propensity of face-workers to strike by diminishing the range of fluctuations in earnings and the scope for fragmented bargaining over pay at the colliery'. We feel this agreement most persuasive, particularly as an explanation of the progressive reduction in the number of strikes since the mid-1950s.

The change in the payment system also contributes to the explanation of the change in the form of strike activity which took place in 1969. Under the National Power Loading Agreement the time rate, although not uniform across the coal fields, was fixed by industry-wide negotiation. Prior to 1966, while some mineworkers had their rates determined by national bargaining, the majority had rates fixed below this level. This made it unlikely that industry-wide action would be taken to support any particular pay claim. The change in the payment system after 1966 meant that *all* mineworkers were dependent on the national negotiations which covered both faceworkers and surface workers. If mineworkers were to use sanctions to try to improve their rates it was now necessary for those sanctions to be applied on a much wider scale. Of course the change in the payment system did not make it inevitable that larger strikes would occur in coal mining. What it meant was that in any future dispute over pay, if sanctions were adopted, they were likely to result in a macro-strike. But so far we have mainly been concerned with the substantive factors which were likely to produce disputes over pay and related matters. Whether disagreements of this kind result in strike action or not is influenced by the adequacy and acceptability of the machinery for avoiding disputes. In effect it is a matter of procedural arrangements. For that reason we must now turn to consider the operation of disputes procedures in the industry.

DISPUTES PROCEDURES

There are three sets of disputes machinery in coal mining, each of which covers a different group of employees – i.e. industrial workers, non-industrial staff and ancillary workers. In this section we consider only the machinery relating to industrial staff, because this covers those groups who have been involved in the greater part of strike action.

The formal machinery for the resolution of disputes involving industrial workers operates at three levels – national, district and pit. At the national level there are two bodies, the Joint National Negotiating Committee (JNNC) and the National Reference Tribunal (NRT). The former, as its title implies, is a negotiating body and consists of sixteen representatives from each side. The latter is a permanent arbitration body of three part-time members and four assessors. When these arrangements were originally made, any disputes which were not resolved at the JNNC were bound, within an agreed time limit, to be referred to the NRT. In 1961 this agreement was varied so that the parties were no longer bound to use the NRT to resolve national disputes.

The district level dispute machinery parallels that of the national level with one important exception – in the event of a failure to agree district disputes are subject to automatic binding arbitration. Each district has a District Conciliation Board, which is the negotiating body, and a three-man panel of referees which deals with arbitration cases. District negotiations are constrained by the national agreement to the extent that (a) each district shall negotiate a district conciliation agreement; (b) such agreements must provide for arbitration on all questions upon which district conciliation boards are unable to agree; (c) agreements of district boards and decisions of district referees must be binding on all parties; (d) all questions arising at the district level which ought to be transferred to the national level shall be transferred.

A pit level conciliation scheme was introduced in 1947. It has six steps:

(a) An issue must be discussed by the workman or workmen concerned with his or their immediate superior, i.e. deputy, overman or under-manager.

(b) If agreement is not reached within three days, the workman must see the colliery manager or his appointed representative.

(c) If there is no agreement after a further three days, the workman must see his union official who, if he feels the issue to be of minor importance, will then discuss it with the colliery manager.

(d) If there is no agreement after a further three days, a pit meeting is arranged at which representatives of both union and management are present. When it is decided to invoke this stage of the procedure the party wanting the meeting must inform the other side in writing. Meetings must be held as soon as possible and in no case later than five days after they are requested.

(e)If the pit meeting cannot reach agreement within fourteen days from the date it is requested, the issue is referred to the district disputes committee.

(f) If, after a further fourteen days, the case is still outstanding, the issue goes to an umpire whose decision is final and binding.

It can be seen that the pit conciliation scheme provides for a progressive escalation of the level of hearing, a quick and rigid timetable and for arbitration for virtually the whole of our period during which the great majority of strikes have been confined to a single pit. Yet between 1950 and 1957 the number of strikes rose by 160 per cent and in the following thirteen years fell by 90 per cent. It is tempting to conclude from this that whatever else may have caused the variation in the pattern the effectiveness of existing pit conciliation machinery had little to do with it. On the other hand, one detailed study of the operation of the pit machinery in two contrasting pits (Scott *el al.*, 1963) concluded that in the opinion of its authors the machinery they studied was not without effect on the volume and scope of strike action. As they put it:

> Although the amount of conflict arising may not have been affected the existence of disputes machinery did reduce the day-to-day impact of conflict on the running of the collieries. Had there been no disputes machinery, it is probable that there would have been considerably more stoppages of work.

In view of our evidence on changes in the number of strikes this conclusion may seem rather surprising, but a closer look at some of the other findings of that study may help to explain the apparent contradiction. Scott *et al.* found that the actual operation of the conciliation machinery was subject to considerable modification at pit level. In particular the early stages of the machinery were frequently bypassed at one of the two collieries they studied. Disputes at that colliery were dealt with by the colliery manager and the branch secretary as a matter of course. They were invariably settled at pit rather than at district committee or umpire level. From this evidence it appears that although the formal procedures were not subject to alteration throughout our period, the way in which they actually operated probably varied from pit to pit.

In addition to examining the way in which the machinery was used Scott *et al.* also examined those groups of workers who used the machinery and the principal causes of disputes. They found that use of the machinery was confined to a number of occupational groups and that these groups were also more likely to take strike action. Other groups which experienced conflict but lacked the cohesion or the bargaining power to express their feelings effectively, either through the disputes machinery or through strike action, tended to resort to individual forms of protest – e.g. absenteeism or quitting. This distinction was important because those groups that used the disputes machinery were more likely to receive management attention in resolving their problems than those which did not, although in all cases there was a tendency for disputes to be 'papered over' rather than resolved because forces external to the colliery were responsible for the conflict, e.g. the existence of a piecework payment system was the product of national not local negotiations and could only be resolved at that level. Scott *et al.* found that the piecework system was the major cause of disputes. Strikes resulted because although many disputes were dealt with entirely in procedure there were so many disputes that even a small fraction not dealt with in this way resulted in a considerable number of disputes. In these circumstances a policy objective of reducing the number of strikes is only achievable if the number of disputes can be reduced, e.g. by reform of the payment system; a wider policy objective of improving industrial relations is only likely to be met if all groups of workers can be encouraged to make use of the machinery.

Scott *et al.* argued that the existence of the conciliation machinery did not affect the level but only the form of conflict in the sense that some conflict was diverted into the procedural machinery while some of the rest was expressed in strike action. We would go further than this and argue that the conciliation machinery also influenced the form of strike action. This influence was manifest in two ways, both of which contributed to keeping strikes in the industry small and short: first, the system of pit, district and national negotiations is 'watertight' in the sense that disputes which properly belong at one level cannot be extended beyond their place of origin; secondly, the system of compulsory binding arbitration at pit and district level meant that virtually all strikes in coal from 1947 up to the national stoppage of 1972 were in breach of procedure and, in consequence, not only unofficial but discouraged by the union officials who would have to seek to have the dispute handled by the appropriate machinery.

But in seeking to explain changes in the strike pattern in coal mining there are two further variables which we must consider at this point: the structure of the industry and its trade union organisation. We turn to the first of these in the next section.

INDUSTRIAL STRUCTURE

Prior to nationalisation on 1 January 1947 the coal industry consisted of over 800 independent enterprises. Following nationalisation it became a single organisation under the National Coal Board with a pyramidical structure of eight divisions, forty-eight areas and 958 collieries. In 1955 this structure was amended to include another level, the group, between area and colliery level. Initially there were some 200 groups. This revised structure lasted, despite some reductions, until 1967, when there was a very considerable reorganisation. As a result areas took over most of the functions of divisions and groups and the five-tier structure was replaced by three tiers: headquarters, area and colliery.

Our primary interest in this structure is with collieries. The predominant feature of strike activity in mining has been a high incidence of very small and short stoppages – the kind which would be confined to a single colliery or part of a colliery. But of course collieries in themselves are at the peak of a structure of pits and faces. In this kind of organisation work groups tend to be small and isolated. The shift system contributes to this isolation by ensuring that even groups on the same face have little contact with each other. To some extent this isolation at work may be overcome by a tight knit social community of mining villages, but it does mean that conflicts which involve one group are unlikely to 'spill over' unless they last for some time. It is not easy to show the influence of these factors because we lack information on the number of pits, and have only partial information on the number of faces. But we do have a series for the number of producing collieries.

Between 1947 and 1957 the number of collieries fell from 958 to 822, while the total workforce remained roughly constant. As a result the average number of wage-earners per colliery rose from 740 to 860. Until 1957 collieries only tended to be closed if they were worked out, but after 1957 there was much greater pressure to close down unprofitable pits. By 1970 the number of collieries had fallen to 299, less than a third of the 1947 total. The labour force also fell after 1957, but not to the same extent, so that the average number of wage-earners per colliery rose to 960.

However, one cannot invoke a simple explanation, to the effect that the number of strikes fell after 1957 because the number of collieries fell. The number of collieries had been falling since 1950 while the number of strikes was rising. But the structure of the industry, with its small isolated work groups, must have had an influence on the size of strikes. It also seems likely that the rapid fall in the number of collieries after 1957, in conjunction with other factors, was of some influence in reducing the number of points of conflict. It is also worth noting that the number of faces tended to fall faster than the number of collieries, so that the reduction in the number of separate work groups was greater than might at first appear. In a context of work organisation of this kind a pattern of very small disputes, as measured by the number of workers involved, is not very surprising, particularly when the earnings of faceworkers are dependent on piecework payments that vary from face to face according to changing technological and geological conditions.

The modification in the organisational structure of the industry in 1967 is also of some interest because it may be seen as the product of two influences. One was the need to streamline the administrative structure to match a reduction in productive capacity. Another was a desire to centralise the organisational structure in line with the centralised system of pay negotiations, which had emerged the previous year with the National Power Loading Agreement. The same drive towards centralisation can be seen in the trade union organisations which we consider below.

TRADE UNION ORGANISATION

The creation of one employing authority in 1947 had been preceded, to some extent, by a similar change in trade union organisation in 1945. The Miners' Federation of Great Britain, which dated from 1888, was replaced by the National Union of Mineworkers (NUM). The new organisation was a mixture of area unions, which formed the basis of the administrative structure, and constituent associations, which paid a *per capita* affiliation fee to the NUM but retained responsibility for friendly benefits.

The NUM attempted to establish itself as the industrial union for coal mining by reaching agreements with the other unions that had membership in the coal fields. Its attempt met with considerable success. The various craft unions agreed that their members working at collieries should become members of the NUM providing that the individuals concerned had the option of retaining membership of their original unions as well. The two biggest general unions, the Transport and General Workers Union and the

General and Municipal Workers Union, were reluctant to yield their members to the NUM. Instead they agreed on a standstill on further recruitment and that their existing membership should have dual membership and be organised within the NUM in two power groups.

Among clerical, supervisory and managerial staff the NUM was less successful. Two other unions, the National Association of Clerical and Supervisory Staffs and the Clerical and Administrative Workers Union, had clerical members in the industry. It proved possible, with TUC assistance, to secure a good measure of agreement on future recruitment. At the supervisory level the NUM clashed with the National Association of Colliery Overmen, Deputies and Shotfirers (NACODS). At higher levels of management the NUM's recruiting efforts were contested by the British Association of Colliery Management. At supervisory and managerial levels the NUM's attempts to secure exclusive rights were to no avail.

This pattern of greater opposition to the NUM's industrial union pretensions from organisations within the industry than from those without was repeated among a key group of manual workers – the windingmen. These workers were involved in several attempts to secure separate bargaining rights. Opposition to these claims by the NUM and the NCB resulted in several quite large stoppages, notably in 1949 (225 000 working days lost), 1952 (105 000 days lost) and 1964 (42 000 days lost).

Some information on the size and relative strength of the TUC-affiliated unions in mining is shown in Table 8.7. (Since this table was compiled the BACM has affiliated to the TUC.) The NUM recruits some workers in coke and by-product plants. Where these plants are attached to collieries their employees will be included in the coal mining employment series, otherwise they will be included in chemicals. This means that our estimate may overstate the extent of the NUM's membership in coal mining, but the effect will be slight.

From Table 8.7 it can be seen that the NUM's membership appears to have grown in two distinct phases, the first in 1946–8 and the second in 1950–4. This growth could result from two factors: growth in employment in the industry or increasing union density among the existing workforce. Unfortunately for the period 1946–8 information on employment in the industry is lacking so we cannot establish the relative contributions of these two factors. In 1950–4 the increase in membership was largely due to increased density as employment only rose by 15 000 while membership rose by 73 000. Membership as a percentage of employees in employment rose from 78 to 86 per cent.

NUM membership reached its peak in 1957 and has fallen in every year since then. This decline was a product of the fall in employment of coal miners in the industry. The other TUC-affiliated union which was confined to coal mining was the National Association of Colliery Overmen, Deputies and Shotfirers (NACODS) which recruited supervisory workers. Membership of NACODS rose fairly steadily up to 1959 and has declined fairly steadily since then. Despite this long period of decline the union still has more members than it had in 1946 (the NUM's membership in 1973

Table 8.7 *Number and degree of trade union membership in coal mining, 1946–73*

Year	NUM members (000s)	NACODS members (000s)	NUM members as a percentage of employees in employment	NACODS members as a percentage of employees in employment	NUM and NACODS members as a percentage of employees in employment
1946	537.5	16.0	n.a.	n.a.	n.a.
1947	572.3	20.9	n.a.	n.a.	n.a.
1948	610.6	24.6	76.7	3.1	79.8
1949	608.9	26.5	77.8	3.4	81.2
1950	602.3	28.3	77.8	3.7	81.5
1951	613.1	30.5	78.3	3.9	82.2
1952	640.8	32.0	80.8	4.0	84.8
1953	669.1	33.7	84.5	4.3	88.8
1954	675.4	34.4	85.9	4.4	90.3
1955	674.5	34.7	86.1	4.4	90.5
1956	673.6	35.3	85.6	4.5	90.1
1957	680.7	36.1	86.5	4.6	91.1
1958	674.1	36.5	87.4	4.7	92.1
1959	639.0	37.3	87.6	5.1	92.7
1960	586.4	37.0	86.1	5.4	91.5
1961	545.3	35.8	83.3	5.5	88.8
1962	529.0	34.6	83.9	5.5	89.4
1963	501.6	33.5	83.3	5.6	88.9
1964	479.1	33.5	83.3	5.8	89.1
1965	446.5	31.5	83.3	5.9	89.2
1966	412.9	29.9	82.5	6.0	88.5
1967	379.6	28.2	82.9	6.2	89.1
1968	344.0	27.1	84.9	6.7	91.6
1969	297.1	24.6	80.0	6.6	86.6
1970	279.5	23.4	79.3	6.6	85.9
1971	276.4	22.7	81.8	6.7	88.5
1972	271.1	22.7	84.0	7.0	91.0
1973	261.2	22.2	84.9	7.2	92.1

was less than half its 1946 level) because it raised its share of employees in employment in membership from 3.1 per cent in 1948 to 7.2 per cent in 1973. This relative growth was probably the result of two factors: NACODS had a low level of organisation among the workforce at the beginning of the period and this gave it scope for growth and the occupations covered by the union have suffered less from the general cutbacks than those of the NUM so that relatively they have risen.

Overall Table 8.7 confirms the popular view of coal mining as a highly organised sector with the NUM the dominant union. The NUM has undergone considerable change during the period, not only in terms of total membership, but also in organisational terms as it has tried to create a more unitary structure through merging constituent associations into their area unions. This change may have been related to the development of a more centralised system of wage bargaining which required a more cohesive approach than the NUM's original structure was able to produce.

CONCLUSIONS

We began this chapter by examining the level and form of activity in the industry. We found that the predominant form of strike activity was that of small short stoppages. These stoppages tended to fall in the late 1940s and rise sharply thereafter until 1957. Then they embarked on a long process of decline which was only reversed in 1972. Overlaying this pattern of small short stoppages was one of occasional major stoppages. These accounted for 0.7 per cent of strikes in the industry, 31 per cent of workers involved and 73 per cent of time lost. When these patterns are taken together they indicate that a sizeable minority of the industry's workforce undertook strike activity in most of the years under consideration, but that, in relation to potential working time in the industry, the effect of these strikes in most years was very small. The most significant exceptions have all occurred in recent years.

In our attempts to account for this pattern we examined a large number of factors, including the economic record of the industry since the war. This seemed to fall into four phases which roughly coincide with shifts in the strike pattern, although it was not at all clear that there was any consistent relationship between strikes and economic activity. In the first phase, 1946–50, economic activity rose strongly while strike activity tended to fall. In the second phase, 1950–7, economic activity was high and stable while strike activity rose sharply. In the third phase, 1957–70, both economic and strike activity fell for much of the period. In the fourth phase, 1970–3, strike activity rose while economic activity continued to decline although the industry's prospects improved. We drew attention to the general decline in strike activity in 1946–50 and suggested that it was the product of factors external to the industry which more than outweighed any internal pressure created by the increase in economic activity.

For the period 1950–7 we argued that the existence of a high pressure of demand, coupled with low stock levels, meant that stoppages were a very effective means of gaining attention for particular disputes and that over time workers increasingly took such action. After 1957 these conditions were reversed. Stock levels were substantially higher than earlier in the post-war years and demand was falling so that small, short stoppages were unlikely to attract so much attention. In addition the price-competitive position of the industry was such that managements were less likely to be willing to concede claims that would increase costs. Faced by this change in circumstances workers came to use strikes less. Of course part of the decline in strike activity was simply a result of the reduction in the size of the industry, but this effect was not sufficient to account for the whole of the decline in strikes. The improvement in the industry's prospects in 1970–1 following the rise in oil prices was antedated by an increase in strike activity from 1969 onwards. We felt that the oil price rise had some impact on the decision to stage a national strike in 1972 but had little effect prior to that.

Apart from changing the conditions in which strike action would be more or less effective the shift in the industry's fortunes also had important implications for the size of the workforce in the industry and for its composition. We felt that this needed particular consideration as the reduction in the size of the labour force occurred without any of the overt conflict apparent in other industries. We argued that the acquiescence of the workforce in the rundown of the industry was strongly influenced by the manner in which that rundown was achieved. For the most part those who left the industry did so voluntarily and with reasonable prospects of finding alternative employment if they desired it. This happy state of affairs ended in the late 1960s, when the combination of a massive rise in the rate of redundancies and a sharp deterioration in the external labour market meant that alternative employment became much more difficult to secure. In these circumstances it seems likely that the continued rundown of the industry provoked a good deal of resentment which contributed in no small part to the conflict which became manifest in 1969–70. Although this conflict was ostensibly about pay, it does not seem entirely implausible to suggest that part of it was inspired by conflict over redundancies which could not be directly expressed.

After 1957 not only did the total labour force in coal mining decline but it also changed in occupational composition. Non-industrial staff appear to have increased their share of employment substantially between 1957 and the mid-1960s. Among the industrial workforce it appears that under-officials and craftsmen also increased their shares of the total. The distribution of employment between surface and underground work does not appear to have altered very much. Although much of this information is incomplete or based on rather rough estimates, the principal conclusions are quite clear. Coal mining remains predominantly an industry of male manual workers and the skill-mix of the labour force has tended to rise. These changes occurred for a number of reasons including the adoption of a more capital-intensive production process and a change in the payment system.

We also examined changes in mineworkers' earnings and spending power and the change in the payment system. For much of the period we found that changes in miners' earnings were similar to those of workers in other industries, which implies that they were not a major influence on the unique strike record of the mining industry. However, there was some evidence to suggest that adverse movements in earnings, both in real terms and relative to those of other workers, had contributed to the increase in conflict in recent years. These changes were not a sufficient explanation of that conflict as similar adverse movements occurred in the late 1950s without provoking such widespread reaction. The change in the method of payment of faceworkers from piecework to time rate, a process which culminated in the National Power Loading Agreement of 1966, seems to have had a more significant effect on strike activity, particularly on the number of small strikes, although this effect does not appear to have been strong enough to survive the aftermath of the 1972 national strike.

The industrial staff employed by the NCB are covered by a three-tier structure for collective bargaining. There have been only minor formal changes in this structure since 1947. This absence of change implies that the structure has not been a significant influence in any of the major changes in the strike pattern. But having examined the results of a study of the operation of the pit level conciliation machinery we concluded that the disputes machinery may still have been important because its structure was changed by informal agreements and practices. We also agreed with the conclusion of the earlier study (Scott *et al.*, 1963) that the disputes machinery succeeded in resolving a large number of disputes which would otherwise have resulted in stoppages. We also argued that the collective bargaining structure tended to keep those stoppages which did occur small and short. There were two reasons for this. Disputes which properly belonged at pit level had to be settled at that level so that the scope for extending disputes was limited. The system of compulsory binding arbitration meant that virtually all stoppages were unconstitutional and unofficial. Consequently there would be substantial pressure – not least from union officials – to end stoppages quickly so that the dispute might be returned to procedure where it could be dealt with.

Other factors we considered as possible explanatory variables included the structure of the industry and its trade union organisation. The structure of the industry, with a large but declining number of collieries and an even larger and even more rapidly declining number of faces, influenced the number of work groups and, indirectly, the number of small stoppages. Yet this influence on the number of stoppages may not have been very great because the number of collieries fell between 1947 and 1957 while the number of stoppages rose. The management structure of the industry was revised in 1955 and again in 1967. The 1967 change may have been of some consequence in that it produced a more centralised structure which was likely to be less responsive to worker pressure at local level, thereby encouraging the use of pressure at national level.

Employee organisation in coal mining is, of course, dominated by the National Union of Mineworkers (NUM). The NUM, which was formed in 1945, tried to become the complete industrial union in the period immediately after nationalisation but failed to make significant inroads in the supervisory and managerial grades. It also encountered difficulties in its dealings with colliery windingmen who felt that their craft interests were insufficiently recognised within the larger union. Although the time lost through strikes arising from this source was minor in relation to that due to other causes, it is indicative of the difficulties which can arise within industrial unions.

In general coal mining has been free from the problems which can arise from inter-union rivalries. If this freedom meant, as is sometimes argued, that the union had more influence over its members than would have been the case in a multi-union situation, it appears to have been more confined to securing agreement on and support for general policy issues – e.g. attitudes to technological change and the rundown of the industry, rather than to restraining the responses of individual work groups in particular workplace situations. The NUM has also undergone a gradual process of organisational change with constituent associations being absorbed into area unions to provide a more uniform structure. This change may have facilitated the process of obtaining agreement on national wage claims towards the end of the period. The other sizeable union in coal mining is the National Association of Colliery Overmen, Deputies and Shotfirers which, although it has increased its share of the workforce in membership, remains much smaller than the NUM and does not appear to have been much involved in the overall level of strike activity.

Before trying, very briefly, to fit together all these various elements we would like to draw attention to one factor which we have so far ignored in our analysis – tradition. Coal mining is an industry with a long history of conflict and strike action. This history undoubtedly influenced the pattern of events in the post-war years as men's attitudes and responses were shaped by their own experiences and those of their predecessors. Unfortunately we have no way of quantifying such effects. As we pointed out in Chapter 1, this is a study based entirely on published sources. Consequently all we can do is draw attention to our omission and point out that our study should be seen against the background of the industry's history as perceived by those involved in it.

In order to assess the contribution of each of these factors to the determination of the strike pattern in the industry it is useful to draw a distinction between those factors which are internal to coal mining and those which are external. Using this perspective the increase in strike activity between 1950 and 1957 may be seen as the result of both internal developments and external circumstances – i.e. a change in attitudes operating in an economic context which appeared to favour the use of industrial sanctions to maintain and improve wages. After 1957 these favourable circumstances disappeared and it became accepted that wage levels could affect employment opportunities. At the same time the reform of the payment system helped to reduce the level of strike activity by removing the single most important source of disputes at pit level. Moreover, by securing agreement in advance, and by careful internal planning, the NCB was able to adjust to changes in the external demand for coal and secure the reduction of the labour force without this producing overt conflict.

But in the end the failure to maintain this reduction in strike activity was largely the product of external forces which were too strong to be overcome by internal adjustment. Thus the rate of deterioration of the external labour market, a result of the government's efforts to secure a surplus on the external trade account, prevented the absorption of redundant miners and soured the prospects for a further agreed reduction in the size of the labour force. Relations between the parties began to deteriorate as the relative position of miners in relation to other groups came to be more fully appreciated and resented. At this point external circumstances underwent a further significant modification; the development of the Organization of Petroleum Exporting Countries (OPEC) as an effective and aggressive force in the field transformed the industry's prospects more rapidly than any of the internal reforms promoted by the NCB and the NUM over the last decade. In this situation it was perhaps inevitable that the union and its members should seek to recover lost ground. When they did the reforms of the payment system made it inevitable that the dispute which resulted should be fought out at national level. But of course the strike that resulted was prolonged and made more difficult to settle because the aims of the union so clearly transgressed the externally fixed parameters of the goverment's incomes policy.

From the viewpoint of the serious student of industrial relations this account of the many different factors which affected the post-war strikes in mining can only reinforce the dangers of seeking explanations for the strike patterns in terms of macro-economic variables alone. The record indicates that although both product and labour market factors were an essential part of the story, they interacted with political, organisational and cultural influences which sometimes affected quite crucially the form and extent of strike action. But from the viewpoint of the practical reformer or practitioner it is possible to argue that the history of the industry suggests a no less cautionary moral. One can accept that the prolonged decline in strike activity in the industry stands as a lasting tribute to the efforts of both sides; but it must also be admitted that its resurgence on a larger scale than at any time since 1926 serves as a reminder of the limits of internally motivated change, however well managed and thought out. It indicated how easily sustained and imaginative reforms can be challenged by external forces.

9 Docks – Another Traditional Battleground

THE AIMS OF THE CHAPTER

To choose the docks as the subject for our second case study may seem like too much of a good – or bad – thing. Our reasons for doing so were several. In the first place, when considered against the criteria we used in selecting coal mining the docks had a good case in their own right. It was a highly strike-prone, traditionally conflict-ridden industry which had been the subject of a good deal of reforming zeal in the post-war period. Of course, in relation to total strike activity, docks were a much smaller contributor than coal mining. It accounted for 4 per cent of strikes and 6 per cent of workers involved and days lost. However, in relation to the size of the industry, the degree of strike activity in the docks was much higher – 50 per cent of employees were involved compared with 28 per cent in coal mining. Of course this figure was affected by multiple strike acts by individual employees, particularly in recent years. Nevertheless, an average of one strike act per two employees per year undoubtedly made the docks the most strike-prone industry in the United Kingdom in our period.

Another similarity with coal mining was that the industry also experienced a sharp decline in its demand for labour. But the interesting feature of the change was that the response of the workforce in the docks was markedly different to that of mineworkers. It was this contrast, as much as the other similarities, which persuaded us to choose docks for our second case study.

In layout the chapter follows the same pattern as that on coal mining. It begins with a detailed examination of the industry's strike record and then compares movements in that record with changes in factors similar to those we looked at in the previous chapter.

STRIKE ACTIVITY IN THE DOCKS, 1949–73

The period under consideration in this chapter is somewhat shorter than that of most of our analyses because of the impossibility of unscrambling strikes in the docks from the wider sector of transport and communications in the years 1946–8. This difficulty does not arise in our examination of major strikes. Table 9.1 shows the broad pattern of activity each year from 1949 to 1973.

Table 9.1   *Basic measures of strike activity in the docks, 1949–73*

Year	No. of strikes	No. of workers involved (000s)	No. of working days lost (000s)	Workers involved as a percentage of employees in employment	Workers involved as a percentage of total of registered dockers	Working days lost as a percentage of potential working time
1949	29	54.8	485	35.4	73.1	1.16
1950	21	21.3	119	13.7	28.3	0.28
1951	26	55.0	452	34.0	68.7	1.03
1952	14	3.5	15	2.2	4.4	0.03
1953	21	16.4	33	10.6	21.8	0.08
1954	69	80.0	787	51.3	106.8	1.87
1955	68	63.6	763	38.8	78.8	1.72
1956	68	14.2	21	8.8	18.0	0.05
1957	70	51.6	200	32.1	67.3	0.46
1958	49	38.0	355	24.3	51.3	0.84
1959	55	20.6	44	13.5	28.7	0.11
1960	107	94.1	421	61.6	129.6	1.12
1961	66	35.6	159	23.7	49.7	0.43
1962	66	49.8	147	34.1	74.6	0.41
1963	80	27.8	46	19.6	43.0	0.13
1964	102	114.8	129	82.3	179.1	0.38
1965	81	63.0	105	45.7	96.8	0.31
1966	81	65.4	134	48.0	104.6	0.40
1967	97	78.3	606	57.7	130.3	1.82
1968	193	79.0	114	57.9	139.6	0.34
1969	368	194.6	424	163.0	369.3	1.48
1970	259	197.9	727	186.2	422.0	2.85
1971	151	73.7	173	74.1	162.0	0.73
1972	137	180.5	773	196.0	437.6	3.48
1973	147	72.1	154	90.6	209.0	0.81

It is difficult to discern any clear trends in Table 9.1. The strike number series is particularly erratic. The number of stoppages tripled in 1954 and fluctuated around this new level until the early 1960s. It then began to rise, first slowly and then quickly – i.e. in 1968–9. After this strike numbers tended to fall, although in 1973 they were still much higher than at any time prior to 1968.

Workers involved followed an even more erratic course, but the same upward tendency was apparent from the early 1960s. Working days lost was highest in the early and later years, with relatively low losses in the intervening period. This change came about because there was a tendency for average duration to fall, but this development was 'overpowered' by the increase in the number of workers involved towards the end of our period.

Relative measures of strike activity also showed considerable volatility, but it was a little easier to identify trends. It will be remembered that in relation to the number of employees in employment the number of strike acts has been rising since the mid-1950s. When the same comparison is made with the number of 'registered' dock workers a similar pattern emerges, although the tendency was slightly steeper because registered dock workers have declined as a proportion of the total workforce. (Registered dock workers are those in, or in the vicinity of, a port whose work is connected with the loading, unloading, movement or storage of cargoes, or with leaving port where that port is covered by the National Dock Labour scheme. These workers are often regarded as comprising the total labour force in the port transport industry. In fact they accounted for less than half of the employees in employment throughout the period.)

Working days lost in relation to potential working time was much higher for most of the period than in coal mining. Thus in nine years out of twenty-five time lost exceeded 1 per cent and in 1972 was almost 3.5 per cent. In view of the importance of the docks for handling imports and exports this suggests that the effects on the rest of the economy may well have been of some significance.

As in the previous chapter we analysed strike activity further by drawing a distinction between larger and smaller stoppages – i.e. those involving the loss of less than 5000 days. Details of the latter are shown in Table 9.2.

The number of small strikes followed a pattern very similar to that of all strikes, because the great majority of the latter were small. Among the outstanding features of this pattern were the sharp increases in 1954, 1960 and 1968–9, and the fall-back since that time.

It has been suggested (Turner, 1969) that the increase in 1967–8 was, in part at least, a product of 'double counting' by employers after decasualisation. This increased the recorded number of strikes because the 'common cause' rule was not followed. (The 'common cause' rule for treating stoppages affecting more than one establishment as one stoppage is described in Chapter 1.) If this were the explanation one would expect the average number of workers per stoppage to fall sharply. There is no substantial evidence of this. On balance it seems likely that the effect of

Table 9.2   *Small strikes in the docks, 1949–73*

Year	No. of strikes	No. of workers involved (000s)	No. of working days lost (000s)	Average no. of workers involved per small strike	Average no. of working days lost per worker involved per small strike	Workers involved as a percentage of employees in employment
1949	25	9.8	17.7	392	1.8	6.3
1950	19	5.9	10.8	311	1.8	3.8
1951	20	11.2	17.2	560	1.5	7.0
1952	13	3.3	7.8	254	2.4	2.0
1953	20	10.2	12.4	510	1.2	6.6
1954	65	21.8	25.5	335	1.2	14.0
1955	64	17.3	28.0	266	1.6	10.6
1956	68	14.2	21.0	209	1.5	8.8
1957	65	16.2	35.5	249	2.2	10.1
1958	46	11.0	15.1	239	1.4	7.1
1959	53	12.0	17.6	226	1.5	7.8
1960	100	36.0	18.7	360	0.5	23.6
1961	63	17.1	51.0	271	3.0	11.4
1962	61	25.3	40.2	415	1.6	17.3
1963	78	19.6	31.6	251	1.6	13.8
1964	96	54.5	57.1	568	1.0	39.1
1965	78	42.6	32.9	546	0.8	30.9
1966	75	35.7	33.5	476	0.9	26.2
1967	92	37.4	39.3	407	1.1	27.6
1968	190	65.8	86.5	346	1.3	48.2
1969	348	140.3	189.5	403	1.4	117.5
1970	251	105.7	139.9	421	1.3	99.4
1971	143	46.8	59.6	327	1.3	47.1
1972	124	38.5	54.4	311	1.4	41.8
1973	140	36.1	56.0	258	1.6	45.4

such a factor was considerably exaggerated by Turner and that strike activity really did increase sharply in 1967–8.

The number of workers involved tended to move in the same direction as the number of strikes but not always to the same extent. The differences in movement of the two series are reflections of changes in the average size of stoppages. But although average size was very volatile (fluctuating in the range 209–568) certain broad trends can be discerned. Thus average size fell sharply in the mid-1950s, rose until the mid-1960s and fell again afterwards. Comparing workers involved in small stoppages against the number of employees shows that strike movement increased from 5 to 6 per cent at the start of the period to 40 per cent at the end. In 1969–70 it reached 100 per cent. This indicates an unusually high level of involvement in local disputes and an unprecedented increase in workers affected.

Numbers of working days lost tended to increase after 1952, but the rate of increase was quite slow also, apart from 1968–9. After 1969 days lost fell sharply at first and then levelled off. Average duration of small strikes was very low throughout the period – less than one and a half days in thirteen years and less than two days in the remaining twenty-two. The years of highest duration were 1952, 1957 and 1961.

Although all three basic measures revealed a persistent upward trend for most of the period, the dominant factor appears to have been the increasing incidence of stoppages, since neither average size nor average duration showed any consistent upward movement. It might have been expected that the average number of strikes would fall, because the labour force was declining, but the size of work groups must also be taken into account. We look more closely at these aspects later in the chapter.

Details of major strikes in the docks are shown in Table 9.3.

It can be seen that major strikes displayed the same kind of volatility as we found in coal mining. Consequently, it was difficult to draw any firm conclusions, except that strike activity rose substantially towards the end of the period. For the purpose of analysis we decided to divide the period into two parts – from 1946 to 1968 and from 1969 to 1973. In the earlier period there were, on average, less than four major stoppages a year; in the later period there were eleven. Stoppages in the first period tended to be slightly larger and longer but this was mainly a product of the first decade.

During the period 1946–73 there were 138 major strikes in the docks: eighty-two occurred in the period 1946–68 and fifty-six in 1969–73. Dockers and stevedores accounted for around 80 per cent of the total. The remainder were shared among a number of occupational groups in which tally clerks (6.5 per cent of the total) and lightermen (8.7 per cent) were the most prominent. There was little change in the occupations of strikers between the two sub-periods, except that lightermen increased their share and tally clerks decreased.

The regional distribution of major strike activity showed a marked concentration for the period as a whole; the South East, the North West and Yorkshire and Humberside accounted for nearly three-quarters of the total. This, of course, reflects the location of the major ports of London,

Table 9.3   *Major strikes in the docks, 1946–73*

Year	No. of strikes	No. of workers involved (000s)	No. of working days lost (000s)	Average no. of workers involved per major strike	Average no. of working days lost per worker involved in major strikes	Workers involved in major strikes as a percentage of employees in employment
1946	3	6.2	19.0	2 067	3.1	n.a.
1947	3	32.9	220.0	11 000	6.7	n.a.
1948	4	37.1	220.5	9 275	5.9	23.9
1949	4	45.0	467.3	11 250	10.4	29.1
1950	2	15.4	108.2	7 700	7.0	9.9
1951	6	43.8	434.8	7 300	9.9	27.0
1952	1	0.2	7.2	200	36.0	0.1
1953	1	6.2	20.6	6 200	3.3	4.0
1954	4	58.2	761.5	14 550	13.1	37.3
1955	4	46.3	735.0	11 575	15.9	28.3
1956	0	0.0	0.0	0	0.0	0.0
1957	5	35.4	164.5	7 080	4.6	22.0
1958	3	27.0	339.9	9 000	12.6	17.3
1959	2	8.6	26.4	4 300	3.1	5.6
1960	7	58.1	402.3	8 300	6.9	38.0
1961	3	18.5	108.0	6 100	5.8	12.3
1962	5	24.5	106.8	4 900	4.4	16.8
1963	2	8.2	14.4	4 100	1.8	5.8
1964	6	60.3	71.9	10 100	1.2	43.2
1965	3	20.4	72.1	6 800	3.5	14.8
1966	6	29.7	100.5	4 950	3.4	21.8
1967	5	40.9	566.7	8 180	13.9	30.1
1968	3	13.2	27.5	4 400	2.1	9.7
1969	20	54.3	234.5	2 715	4.3	45.5
1970	8	92.2	587.1	11 525	6.4	86.7
1971	8	26.9	113.4	3 363	4.2	27.1
1972	13	142.0	718.6	10 923	5.1	154.2
1973	7	36.0	98.0	5 143	2.7	45.2

Liverpool and Hull. Between the sub-periods the South East's share fell from 33 to 23 per cent, that of the North West rose from 26 to 48 per cent and that of Yorkshire and Humberside increased from 9 to 11 per cent. The combined share of these regions rose from 67 to 82 per cent. Other changes included a decline in the number of strikes affecting various regions of England and the emergence of national strikes which accounted for 5 per cent of the total in 1969–73. The seasonal pattern was similar to that in the rest of the economy with spring and autumn peaks. The autumn peak became increasingly prominent.

The causes of major strikes changed significantly between sub-periods. Wage strikes increased their share from 30 to 48 per cent while stoppages over redundancies rose from 3 to 14 per cent. Discipline and sympathy strikes declined in importance, while those over trade union principle remained constant at 16 per cent. A complicating factor in this analysis was the fact that stoppages in the miscellaneous category fell from 26 to 7 per cent. This may have reflected a real narrowing of the areas of conflict, or merely a simplification of recording practice. In these circumstances it seemed best to exercise even more than our usual caution in dealing with causal movements and not draw any firm conclusions.

The extent of major strikes, as measured by workers involved, also showed marked changes between sub-periods. In general the extent of stoppages tended to fall. Strikes with fewer than 1000 workers directly involved increased their share from 16 to 22 per cent. Strikes involving less than 10 000 workers directly raised their share from 75 to 88 per cent. This shift was even more marked when workers indirectly involved were included – i.e. those laid off at the same establishment because of the stoppage. On this basis stoppages affecting less than 1000 workers increased from 10 to 21 per cent and those affecting less than 10 000 rose from 70 to 86 per cent. One exception to this tendency occurred amongst the largest stoppages – i.e. those involving between 25 000 and 50 000 workers. Here the share rose from 2 to 5 per cent of the total.

One other interesting change which affected the extent of strikes was a decline in the *relative* importance of the number of workers indirectly affected by stoppages. Prior to 1969 these accounted for 10 per cent of all workers involved; after 1968 they accounted for only 4 per cent. This was probably a result of the decline in the prevalence of strike action among tally clerks. In general strikes by dockers do not result in other workers being laid off at the same establishment, since dockers are at the end of the production process. Tally clerks, on the other hand, are an intermediate strategic group whose strike action may often result in dockers being unable to work.

The size of major strikes as measured by the number of days lost, also showed a marked tendency to fall in the later of the two sub-periods. Those strikes involving the loss of between 5000 and 10 000 working days increased their share of the total from 37 to 46 per cent. Those involving less than 25 000 days increased their share from 60 to 90 per cent. This movement appears to have been quite general; even the largest category of strike, involving 100 000 days and over, fell from 16 to 4 per cent.

The length of major strikes, as measured by their duration in working days, also showed a shift towards shorter stoppages in the second sub-period. This change was not uniform in its effect, but was greatest among fairly short strikes. The share of major stoppages lasting one day or less rose from 9 to 25 per cent while that of strikes lasting more than six days fell from 56 to 50 per cent. This decline in duration combined with the reduction in the number of workers involved to produce a marked downward shift in the number of days lost.

Finally, we looked at the location of strikes between different ports. This information was only available from 1965 onwards when the National Ports Council began publishing the results of a special analysis of strikes made by the Department of Employment. Details are given in Table 9.4.

Table 9.4 *Percentage share of strike activity by port, 1965–73*

Port	Strikes (%)	Workers involved (%)	Working days lost (%)	Average labour requirement in men per turn (%)
London	11.6	21.8	28.8	37.2
Liverpool	35.5	40.2	38.2	23.4
Hull and Goole	8.5	17.4	9.9	7.0
Southampton	3.1	4.5	4.5	4.5
Manchester	12.3	5.5	5.0	3.8
Aberdeen	1.5	0.4	0.3	1.2
Other ports	27.5	10.2	13.3	22.9

The analysis relates to the port transport industry and excludes stoppages in inland waterways, which are included in the other series. The number of employees affected by this change is very small and it does not appear to be significant. The published analysis provided a breakdown of strike activity as measured by number of strikes, workers involved, days lost and duration by port. We summarised the information available for the first three measures for those ports which had stoppages in every year between 1965 and 1973. Three ports, London, Liverpool and Hull and Goole, accounted for over two-thirds of the average labour requirement during this period. These three ports also accounted for 55 per cent of stoppages, 80 per cent of workers involved and 77 per cent of days lost. This implies that stoppages in these ports were substantially larger than those in other ports, but slightly shorter. Compared to its share of labour requirements London had less strike activity whilst Liverpool, on every measure, had considerably more. Hull and Goole, particularly in relation to the number of workers involved, also emerged as relatively strike prone. Manchester was involved in an abnormally large proportion of stoppages.

Southampton does not appear to have been particularly strike prone but its labour requirements were unavoidably exaggerated by the inclusion of Weymouth and Poole. The residual category of 'other ports' was also involved in a disproportionate number of stoppages, but this strike-proneness did not carry over to workers involved and days lost.

Of course the information presented in Table 9.4 was limited in two important respects. First, it only covered nine out of the twenty-five years. Secondly, in showing the average pattern of strike activity over those nine years it may have concealed changes in its distribution between ports. In order to overcome this latter difficulty we examined the shares of strike activity attributable to each of the ports shown in Table 9.4 on a year to year basis. This analysis revealed a great deal of volatility in the distribution of strike activity between ports but few consistent changes. Among the shifts which did appear were a marked fall in London's involvement in the number of strikes from 1969 onwards, a rather less marked fall for Hull and Goole from 1968 and a marked rise in Liverpool's involvement. Workers involved and days lost did not show any consistent shifts, but a great deal of year to year change. This suggests that it might be unwise to place too much emphasis on changes in strike number – e.g. Manchester's high level of involvement in strike number was largely a product of one year, 1970, when a great number of stoppages were common to the ports of Liverpool and Manchester. On the whole Table 9.4 does not appear to misrepresent the pattern of strike activity over the nine years as a whole because there were few fundamental changes.

In summary the number of strikes in the docks seems to have been affected by a series of sudden shifts with a general tendency to increase until 1969 and a downward movement since that time. The series for workers involved and days lost displayed even more volatility, but shared the same upward trend, particularly when compared to the level of employment in the industry. The typical small strike in the docks involved between 200 and 400 workers and lasted less than a day and a half. Such disputes became much more frequent in the later years of the period and this pushed up the level of worker involvement. Major strikes are more difficult to typify because of variations in the numbers of workers involved and days lost. However, it was clear that the incidence of such stoppages rose sharply in the last five years of the period. Again this increase in frequency raised the level of worker involvement but the impact in terms of days lost was limited by a decline in average duration.

The features of strike activity in the docks which would seem to demand explanation include the high level of activity in the immediate post-war years, the upsurge in 1954–5 and 1960 and the events since 1967. Less dramatic events which also require explanation include the decline in activity in 1952–3, and 1959, and the relatively low level of losses through strike action during most of the early and middle 1960s. We now examine some of the possible explanations for these events.

COMMUNITY ISOLATION

As a strike-prone industry port transport has been the subject of much study, both historical and international; much of this work has sought to establish a connection between the relative isolation of the dockers community and his readiness to take collective action. One of the most well known and influential studies of this kind was that by Kerr and Siegal (in Kornhauser, Dubin and Ross, 1954). They examined the characteristics of a number of strike-prone industries – e.g. coal mining, lumber jacking and docks – in different countries. They concluded that all these industries were affected by their position as tightly knit communities, isolated both socially and economically from the wider society. This isolation was seen as an important factor in developing group awareness and a disposition to react to common problems by taking collective action.

Given that the major ports in Britain were situated in large cities it might be expected that dockers' communities would be affected by the changes in the distribution of urban population in the post-war years. In particular the programmes of slum clearance in the inner city areas and the transfer of population to overspill estates are widely believed to have destroyed much of the integration and isolation which used to characterise such communities (Young and Willmott, 1957). However, as the strike pattern in docks showed little sign of any weakening it is surely reasonable to suggest either that past authors have exaggerated the impact of the changes which have occurred or that these factors were never all that important as explanations of strike proneness amongst dockers. With the evidence at our disposal it was difficult for us to reach any decisive conclusions on this point, but we did note that in 1973 over 40 per cent of the direct intake to the dock labour register was made up of dockers' sons. (Changes in recording practice made it difficult to make comparisons, but in 1953–5 approximately 24 per cent of entrants to the main register could be identified as dockers' sons.) This evidence is consistent with the fragmentary evidence showing that many workers continued to travel back to their original inner city areas even after they were rehoused, which suggests that the workforce may have retained at least some of the old community attitudes long after the community itself had been dispersed.

THE ANALYSIS OF THE DEVLIN REPORT

Among more recent studies by far the most important was that of the Devlin Committee (Devlin, 1965). This was established by the Minister of Labour to investigate and report on labour relations in the docks after national negotiations aimed at securing a series of far-reaching reforms had broken down. The Devlin Report was an unusually ambitious document. It sought to explain the high strike propensity of the industry and to advance proposals to reduce strike activity. Its analysis was founded on the premise that throughout the post-war period the docks had been significantly more strike prone than other industries. Consequently it sought for an explanation which was unique to the industry and operative throughout the post-war years. The report listed no less than nine features of dock work which had contributed to strike-proneness. They were (a) the dockers' lack of security; (b) the preferential treatment given to 'blue-eyed boys'; (c) lack of responsibility amongst dockers; (d) defects in management; (e) time-wasting practices; (f) piecework; (g) overtime; (h) welfare amenities and working conditions; (i) trade union organisational difficulties.

The accuracy of Devlin's analysis may be assessed in two different ways. First, the analysis itself can be examined in more detail. Secondly, since most of the prescriptions suggested by Devlin were implemented, so far as was practicable at the time, it is reasonable to ask whether this led to a reduction in strike activity.

On the first count it must be appreciated that central to the Devlin analysis was the post-war system of employment. It was argued that this had contributed significantly to the development of several of the nine features set out above. In order to understand how the post-war system worked it is necessary to describe briefly the pre-war system from which it developed.

Prior to 1940 employment on cargo handling in the industry had, for the most part, been on a casual basis. Men were employed by the half day on specific tasks, as and when the conditions of trade demanded. This system resulted in significant under-employment among dockers, resulting in poverty for them and their families. It also produced inconvenience and inefficiency since a man might work for a different employer every turn and have to collect his money from each of them. These problems were widely recognised amongst employers, but it was argued that fluctuations in trade due to seasonal factors, weather conditions, tides and the state of world markets were such that it would be impossible for employers to operate without the existence of a large pool of surplus labour to meet maximum demands.

The necessities of war resulted in an abrupt change in this position. Employers and dockers alike were required to register: employment was restricted to those on the register. Dockers could be transferred between ports and a system of 'maintenance' – payment for those who proved attendance but were unable to find work – was introduced. In some ports the registers were the subject of joint control.

After the war there was general agreement that there should be no return to the old system. However, it proved impossible to secure voluntary agreement on a new scheme as the employers were adamantly opposed to joint control of the registers and discipline. However, these objections were over-ridden by the government through the Dock Workers (Regulation of Employment) Order which came into force in mid-1947. The scheme embodied in the Order provided for registration, maintenance and joint control of both registers and discipline. This system applied to the eighty-six most important ports in England, Scotland and Wales, which handled 94 per cent of the United Kingdom's foreign trade. It covered 78 000 dock workers.

The scheme was administered through a system of joint boards at national and local level. The responsibilities of the National Dock Labour Board (NDLB) included control of the size of the register. They were also responsible for training, welfare arrangements and amenities. The costs were to be met by a levy on employers of up to 25 per cent of the wages bill.

Local boards, of which there were twenty-two, were responsible for carrying out the decisions of the NDLB and for discipline.

When the scheme was first introduced it was widely welcomed as a way of ending 'casualism' in the docks. In fact the employment relationship it created was not permanent. The casual element persisted, albeit in a modified form. The dock labour board became a 'holding' employer – responsible for maintenance payments when work was not available. Private employers remained the 'operational' employers – although they only acknowledged an employment relationship with the worker for the duration of a specific task. In effect the old casual system persisted in a new form, softened only by a permanent 'fall-back' relationship with the dock labour board.

Devlin argued with some plausibility that this persistence of casualism was, in large measure, responsible for the continued strike-proneness of the docks. He said it was this system which caused the dockers' lack of security, gave the employers power to discriminate between sections of the workforce and resulted in the absence of a sense of responsibility from both dockers and employers. It also encouraged the adoption of restrictive practices and the mal-utilisation of labour. Devlin's analysis seemed to be confirmed by the fact that labour relations appeared to be much better in those areas of the industry where permanent employment had been established.

Turning to the other factors Devlin cited as of some importance, we may say that piecework has been generally recognised as a potential contributory factor to a high level of disputes in a number of British industries. Similarly, overtime has been a persistent source of conflict in the docks and elsewhere. This is because it is an area where differences in the aims of employers and workers are most obvious. For employers overtime is a necessary part of dock operations if they are to provide a seven day service and cope with the maximum demands that the trade places upon them. For dockers, on the other hand, overtime in one week is likely to result in unemployment the next. In this kind of situation the persistence of casual employment does little to reconcile the claims of the two sides.

Welfare amenities and working conditions were considered to be important by Devlin not because they had been the immediate cause of many strikes, but because they had had a 'souring' effect on relationships. Again it was plausible to argue that the continuance of casual employment contributed to this development, if only because the responsibility for improvements in this area was not clearly established.

Finally, Devlin drew attention to the influence of 'trade union organisational difficulties'. This heading covered relations between as well as within the unions, of which there were five – i.e. the Transport and General Workers' Union (TGWU), the National Amalgamated Stevedores and Dockers Union (NASDU), the Watermen Lightermen Tugmen and Bargemen's Union (WLTBU), the Scottish Transport and General Workers Union (STGWU) and the General and Municipal Workers Union (GMWU). However, the last three had relatively few members in the docks and each was geographically concentrated – the GMWU in the North East ports, the STGWU in Glasgow and the WLTBU in London. All three tended not to be involved in inter-union disputes. Any legacy of bitterness arising from the fact that the STGWU and the WLTBU originated as breakaways from the TGWU does not appear to have led to strike action. In recent years the situation has been simplified by the STGWU and the WLTBU rejoining the TGWU, in 1971 and 1972 respectively.

Nevertheless, as Devlin stressed, in our period serious inter-union conflict occurred between the TGWU and the NASDU. The TGWU was by far the largest union in the industry, with members in all ports except Glasgow and the North East coast. The NASDU, although much smaller, was the second largest union but was initially confined to London, where it was still overshadowed by the TGWU. Conflict between these unions was of long standing. In 1923 the Stevedores' Union had taken in a breakaway group of dockers from the TGWU. This conflict flared up in 1954 when the NASDU tried to expand beyond its traditional location by recruiting TGWU members in Hull, Liverpool and Manchester. For this action they were expelled from the TUC in 1959. Despite expulsion the NASDU held on to some of its recruits in the northern ports, although estimates of its effective strength varied widely (see Devlin, 1965, para. 104).

The TGWU also experienced considerable difficulty with some sections of its own membership. These arose from the operations of various unofficial committees which at times exercised considerable influence, especially in London. The existence of these committees has been blamed on sinisterly motivated political activists, but it seems more reasonable to suggest that more important causes lay in the structural weakness of the TGWU – i.e. its eighty branches based on the pre-war pattern of dockers' residences and its three-tier London structure – plus the lack of a clearly outlined policy and a determination to pursue it. (For example the Devlin Committee's Interim Report was concerned with a national pay claim in the industry. The TGWU failed to make any written submission in support of their claim, other than copies of the minutes of past meetings of negotiating committees.)

In contrast the NASDU operated on a much simpler and more effective basis. Policy was decided by mass meetings of the membership and negotiations were subject to constant reporting back. This structure was successful in providing much more information to the members and it encouraged a higher level of involvement. Yet it also created problems – especially after the union's expansion into the northern ports (see Wilson, 1972, p. 208).

It seems reasonable to suggest that all these factors were present, in varying degrees of strength, throughout the post-war period. The interrelations between them may be best seen by examining in some detail two of the major stoppages in the period before the establishment of the Devlin Committee.

In 1948 the NDLB ordered the local labour boards to review their registers with a view to excluding those workers who were unable or unwilling to meet their obligations under the scheme. When this review was carried out in London, thirty-three men (out of approximately 25 000) were listed for exclusion from the register. Despite the fact that their General Secretary was a member of the NDLB and the London Labour Board, and thus a party to their decisions, the Executive of the NASDU recommended an official strike against these exclusions. The recommendation was approved at a mass meeting. The strike was supported by many members of the WLTBU and some members of the TGWU. However, it lasted less than a week and secured no concessions from the NDLB. As a result of its repudiation of the Board's decisions the NASDU was deprived of its place on the NDLB. The vacancy went to the STGWU.

A number of the elements identified by Devlin may surely be seen in this dispute. The casual system of employment engendered very strong feelings about job rights in the industry, which provided the mainspring for strike action. The structure of the NASDU allowed those feelings to determine policy, despite its representation on the official decision-making bodies. At the same time the TGWU's official position was repudiated by at least some of its members. Finally, in the decision to exclude the NASDU from NDLB representation, one might conclude that the old rivalry between the two biggest unions had some influence. The exclusion of the second largest union from the process of joint control cannot have been calculated to make it adopt a less intransigent attitude.

The 'Overtime Ban' strike of 1954 was a more complicated affair because of the events which occurred simultaneously in the northern ports. Overtime had been a contentious issue in the London docks since the inception of the scheme. The employers contended that there was an obligation on dockers to work 'reasonable' overtime while the unions maintained that they were opposed to 'compulsory' overtime and argued that all overtime working should be 'voluntary'. The issue was skirted for a number of years, but at the beginning of 1954 the conflict became apparent.

A number of men were disciplined for refusing to work overtime. The NASDU and the WLTBU imposed an overtime ban. The employers retaliated by refusing to discuss matters of general policy until the ban was lifted. Both the TGWU and the NASDU opposed this decision. At the beginning of March the workers' side of the National Joint Council (NJC) for the industry expressed their resentment at the NASDU having taken unilateral action and called for the ban to be lifted but without effect. Other initiatives to resolve the dispute also failed.

Then, in August 1954, there were developments in London and Hull. In London a dispute arose over the piecework rate to be paid for meat sorting. In Hull, following an unofficial dispute over working arrangements, the NASDU accepted an invitation from some dissident dockers to start recruiting there. Unfortunately the dissidents were already members of the TGWU. In September the NASDU refused to attend a meeting in London to fix rates for meat sorting until the employers agreed to discuss overtime. The meeting went ahead without the NASDU, and the TGWU agreed a scale of rates. Meanwhile the NASDU had extended its recruitment from Hull to Birkenhead – another TGWU port. At the end of September some NASDU members in London were engaged for a meat sorting operation but, as their union had not been involved in fixing the rates, they stopped work. At the beginning of October a mass meeting of the NASDU decided on an all-out strike to force discussions on all outstanding issues. Two weeks later the WLTBU took similar action. The strikes ended with the publication of the Interim Report of a Court of Inquiry set up to look into the dispute.

Echoes of these disputes continued for a considerable period. Late in October 1954 the NASDU was suspended from membership of the TUC for breach of the Bridlington agreement. In December the NASDU was excluded from the NJC of the industry. In May 1955 it began an official strike to secure recognition. This ended when the TUC Disputes Committee found against it for recruiting in the northern ports.

From our point of view the interest of these disputes lies not in their consequences but in their causes, which included so many of the factors to which Devlin drew attention – e.g. overtime, union rivalry, piecework, etc. On the basis of both major stoppages which we examined it appears once again as if the factors isolated by Devlin were in fact of some importance. However, it does not necessarily follow that the Devlin analysis provided a complete explanation of the strike pattern in the docks. This point is dealt with more fully below when we attempt to assess the effectiveness of Devlin's proposals for reducing strike-proneness in the docks.

Essentially Devlin's solution consisted of further moves towards decasualisation. In exchange for being given full-time contracts with particular port operators dockers were asked to agree to more flexible systems of work and the introduction of mechanical aids. At the same time the wage structure of the industry would be reviewed, along with existing negotiating provisions. In this way dock workers would be offered the prospect of greater job security and the chance of a more equitable payment system. It was hoped that the result would be greater efficiency and fewer industrial disputes.

In broad terms it can be said that all the major parties involved accepted the terms of the Devlin Report and did their best to carry them out (see Mellish, 1972). Most important of all, in September 1967, the National Dock Labour Board assigned permanent dockers to individual employers in the sector in which they usually operated. The number of employers was significantly reduced and strenuous efforts were made in all major ports to negotiate more equitable payment systems based on improved basic rates.

The major union involved, the TGWU, introduced new methods of representation based on the creation of a system of locally elected shop stewards. Table 9.5 records the strike pattern which followed up on all these changes. It shows the calculations which Devlin used to assess strike-proneness in the docks and contrasts them with our own calculations for the post-Devlin period. The figures for 1947–55 are taken from Devlin's 1965 Report.

Unfortunately Devlin appears to have mistakenly inflated his estimates by excluding employees in inland waterways – whose actions were included in the appropriate strike series for 1947–55. This mistake has not been repeated in the figures set out in Table 9.5 for the 1956–64 period, when the basis of comparison changes. We estimate that the true figure for strike-proneness during the period 1947–55 should have been 2180 man-days per 1000 employees (which seems to strengthen the conclusions drawn below).

Table 9.5   *Strike activity in the docks, 1947–73*

Years	Average no. of man-days lost through disputes	Average no. of man-days lost yearly in disputes per 1000 employees in employment
1947–55	344 400	3 134
1956–64	169 100	1 117
1965–67	281 700	2 061
1968–73	394 200	3 736

Nevertheless, even from the table as it stands it is obvious that strike activity in the docks, especially when measured against the level of employment, rose sharply after 1964 – i.e. after the implementation of Devlin. For the period 1965–7 the increase might be explained away by reference to the difficulties surrounding the negotiation and implementation of decasualisation. But for the period 1968–73 such an explanation seems implausible.

By this time decasualisation had been achieved and some benefit might have been expected. Given that one of the main aims of the Devlin Report was to reduce the level of strike activity in the docks, it would seem to have been a comparative failure.

Of course it might be argued that, in the absence of the Devlin-inspired reforms, the situation would have been much worse. But this view receives little support from evidence for the rest of the economy. It is true that in all other industries (excluding coal mining) the number of days lost per 1000 employees rose by 155 per cent between 1956 and 1964 and 1968 and 1973; if coal mining is included the increase becomes 187 per cent. Yet in the docks it was 235 per cent. Thus although there was a general increase in strike activity between the two periods, it was more marked in the docks than in the rest of the economy. This indicates that there continued to be specific factors at work in that industry with which further decasualisation failed to deal.

Of course there are a number of propositions which could be put forward to explain the conflict between Devlin's aim and its apparent consequences. First, it could be argued that the Devlin analysis was incorrect or incomplete. Secondly, it could be argued that the analysis was correct but the prescriptions were inappropriate and, consequently, ineffective or even damaging to the aim of reducing strike activity. Thirdly, it could be argued that the analysis and the prescriptions were correct, but were not fully implemented, or were implemented in a way that provoked rather than reduced strike action. Fourthly, it could be argued that the situation worsened after 1965 because new factors came into play which could not reasonably have been foreseen by Devlin. In the remainder of the chapter we look at each of these arguments in turn, bearing in mind the possibility that each may contribute only a part of the explanation.

DEVLIN – INCORRECT OR INCOMPLETE?

The first explanation – that the Devlin analysis was incorrect or incomplete at the time it was written – seems improbable, given its intuitive appeal and the evidence summoned to support it. Yet a close examination of the strike pattern from 1947 to 1964 raises one major question. Why did the level of strike activity, measured by days lost in relation to the workforce, fall so sharply after 1955? On our estimates there was a reduction of nearly 50 per cent. On the Devlin figures it was over 60 per cent. Yet the factors spotlighted by Devlin operated throughout the period, which would imply a more constant level of strike activity during a time when in the rest of the economy strike losses were rising. This suggests that external factors were not responsible. Closer examination of the period 1947–55 reveals that major losses through strikes occurred in two phases, 1947–51 and 1954–55.

The strikes in the period 1947–51 were the subject of three official inquiries, two of which were conducted by the Ministry of Labour and one by a Committee of Inquiry chaired by Sir Frederick Leggett. The Ministry of Labour's inquiries were concerned with the strikes in connection with the Canadian seamen's strike and with the strike in Manchester and Salford in 1951. The reports are most notable for the emphasis laid on the role of Communists in fomenting and organising these disputes. The Leggett Inquiry was concerned with the major disputes in the London docks between 1947 and 1950 and took a wider view of the causes of the conflict. In many ways the Leggett Inquiry provided an analysis similar to that of Devlin, except in its discussion of the role and future of the National Dock Labour Board scheme.

Despite the effort put into these investigations it can be argued that they were incomplete. Some of this deficiency was remedied by Kenneth Knowles (1951). Moreover, in addition to commenting on the continuation of casual employment and the internal difficulties of the TGWU, he drew attention to the shift of traffic between ports and to the threat of redundancies.

We considered that both factors were worthy of further investigation. Of course they are interrelated, but they will not necessarily move in the same direction at the same time. Within the total of cargo there are likely to be significant differences in handling requirements for different types of commodities. Further, productivity, and hence manning requirements, are very likely to vary between ports depending on the capital equipment available, the working methods adopted and the degree of utilisation achieved. Of course it may be felt that it is not necessary to examine the pattern of cargo traffic as a separate entity, since it makes it impact on labour relations with its consequences for labour requirements. We rejected that view for two reasons. First, knowledge of the physical volume of traffic allowed us to calculate productivity. Secondly, changes in the volume of traffic would be observed by the dockers concerned and might be expected to affect their behaviour, irrespective of actual redundancy decisions.

Some impression of the changing pattern of traffic is given by the volume of arrivals and departures with cargo (measured in thousands of tons net) at United Kingdom ports. Knowles showed that between 1938 and 1942 arrivals with cargo fell by 75 per cent and that the northern and western ports benefitted relatively at the expense of the eastern and southern ones. We also noted that from 1944 onwards the distribution of traffic began to revert to its pre-war pattern, but the overall growth in trade helped to safeguard employment in those ports whose relative share was declining.

He noted that between 1946 and 1951 the volume of traffic more than doubled. The impact on dock work was probably less than that because the aggregate figures included fuel cargoes, which rose particularly rapidly but which were subject to bulk handling techniques that minimised labour requirements. Virtually all ports gained from this increase in trade, although Liverpool's share of the total fell from 18 per cent in 1946 to 14 per cent in 1951.

This increase in traffic was reflected in an increase in the demand for labour, details of which are shown in Table 9.6.

On this evidence it seems that the increase in activity was met, initially at least, by fuller utilization of existing manpower, so that the number 'proving attendance' (available for work but not employed) was reduced. It also appears that there was a sharp increase in demand in 1951, which was largely met by the recruitment of temporary workers who could be laid off if demand fell. Even at this time of peak demand 7 per cent of those available for work were, on average, unemployed because of fluctuations in demand between ports and through time.

In these conditions of rising employment opportunities and declining underemployment, it may seem surprising that Knowles (1951) suggested that the threat of redundancies was a contributory factor to the strikes of the time. But in fact redundancies were more than a threat, they were a reality. Between 1947 and 1951 a total of 1237 men were discharged as redundant and a further 1532 were dismissed as 'ineffective' – i.e. unable to carry out their obligations under the scheme. These dismissals took place over a five year period and averaged less than 1 per cent of the labour force. But, in an industry which had experienced chronic unemployment in the inter-war period, the occurrence of any compulsory dismissals was likely to increase tensions, particularly when they occurred under the aegis of a scheme to regularise employment in the industry.

Table 9.6   *Labour requirements of the National Dock Labour Board scheme, 1948–51*

Years	Average no. in employment	Average no. proving attendance	No. proving attendance as a percentage of employed	Others on dock register	Total no. on dock register
1948	57 419	9 322	16.2	11 593	78 334
1949	56 735	7 129	12.6	11 183	75 047
1950	58 330	6 924	11.9	10 010	75 264
1951	63 542	4 789	7.5	11 757	80 088

In short, despite the increase in the volume of traffic and the introduction of a scheme to regularise employment, old insecurities were revived through the discharge of redundant and ineffective workers. The 'acid test' of the importance of these factors rested on their ability to explain the situation after 1951, when the level of strike activity dropped sharply, although all the factors mentioned by Leggett and by Devlin were operative.

Measured by arrivals and departures at British ports the volume of trade rose by approximately 20 per cent between 1951 and 1956. In terms of handling requirements the increase was probably less because much of the increase was due to petroleum imports on which bulk handling methods were used. The impact of these changes in terms of labour requirements is shown in Table 9.7.

The 1951 increase in employment was sharply reversed in 1952. The average number in employment fell by 6700 and those proving attendance rose by 7000 so that, on average, one in six of those seeking work was unsuccessful. This turndown in employment prospects was not met by mass dismissals. Only twelve men were declared redundant and a further 242 discharged as ineffective. At the same time the register fell by over 5600, through a combination of restricted recruitment and high voluntary wastage. The employment situation stabilised in 1953, rose to another peak in 1955 and then fell again. After 1952 separate figures were not provided for the numbers declared redundant or discharged as ineffective. They were included under the general heading of dismissals. However, comparison of the number of dismissals pre-1953 (excluding redundancies and dismissals) with the post-1952 totals showed that the latter was lower. Consequently it seemed reasonable to assume that there were few, if any, redundancies after 1952.

Table 9.7 *Labour requirements of the National Dock Labour Board scheme, 1952–6*

Years	Average no. in employment	Average no. proving attendance	No. proving attendance as a percentage of those available	Others on dock register	Total no. on dock register
1952	56 832	11 834	17.2	11 132	79 798
1953	56 888	7 441	11.6	10 831	75 160
1954	57 724	4 406	7.1	12 807	74 937
1955	62 248	4 598	6.9	13 828	80 874
1956	59 167	8 045	12.0	11 510	78 722

In summary then, it seems that, although the rate of increase in activity in the docks slowed down markedly during this period and labour requirements were subject to considerable fluctuations, after 1952 compulsory mass discharges were not required and more emphasis was placed on voluntary severance. Use was made of a temporary release register, by which dockers could seek work in other industries without immediately forfeiting their rights under the National Dock Labour Board scheme. Thus the relatively low level of strike activity in 1952, 1953 and 1956 may be taken as an indication that Knowles' analysis of the post-war period was not without force: fluctuations in labour requirements arising out of changes in traffic flow were partly met by more positive manpower policies.

The high level of strike activity in 1954–5 required separate explanation. We have already discussed in some detail the major strike of 1954 and shown how it was a product of a conflict over overtime obligations exacerbated by the rivalry between the TGWU and the NASDU. The major strike of 1955, which involved the loss of more than 600 000 days also arose from the TGWU–NASDU conflict. It was an official NASDU strike designed to obtain recognition in the northern ports where it had recruited members in the previous year. It can therefore be argued that both the major strikes of these two years were closely related to the inter- and intra-trade union difficulties and do not constitute a refutation of our argument concerning the importance of changes in demand for dock services and dock labour.

One further factor seems to have influenced the pattern of strikes in these early years – the introduction of the National Dock Labour Board scheme itself. When the scheme was first introduced it was viewed with a good deal of suspicion by the dockers. In particular its disciplinary provisions, which involved joint committees of union officials and employers, created considerable antagonism and mistrust. Other difficulties, including those concerning overtime, arose from disagreements over the interpretation of the wording of the scheme. Such difficulties were eventually 'ironed out' and the scheme won a much more widespread acceptance. These developments have two implications. First, part of the strike activity in the early part of our period may be attributed to the NDLB scheme itself. Secondly, the early resistance to the scheme suggests that the docks was deeply conservative work environment where employees were suspicious of all change; consequently, the introduction of change, no matter how benign in intention, was likely to produce an adverse reaction in the first instance.

The next stage of our analysis was to examine the extent to which changes in cargo traffic and labour demand offered an explanation of the strike pattern in the remainder of our period. The principal changes in traffic after 1955 are summarised in Table 9.8.

Table 9.8   *Type and volume of cargo, 1956–72 (in millions of tons)*

	1956	1960	1964	1968	1972
Total dry cargo (exc. fuel)	75.0	84.4	90.3	94.1	101.3
Total petroleum	46.1	67.9	87.0	119.5	145.7
Total coal and coke	16.7	6.9	7.5	3.7	7.7
Total traffic	137.8	159.2	184.8	217.3	254.7

It can be seen that total traffic through British ports rose by 85 per cent between 1956 and 1972. But this figure conceals marked differences in the rate of increase between fuel cargo and other cargoes. Petroleum traffic rose by over 200 per cent, other dry cargoes (excluding fuel) by 35 per cent. Because petroleum traffic was subject to bulk handling techniques which required only minimal handling it was the increase in dry cargoes (excluding fuel) which was important for our purposes. Traffic in coal and coke was also subject to bulk handling techniques at a small number of specialised ports so we excluded that from the main analysis as well. On average, dry non-fuel cargo grew at an annual rate of 1.9 per cent with the increase being somewhat faster between 1956 and 1964. Such a growth rate was unlikely to place an undue strain on the industry's capacity.

In 1965 information became available about total traffic excluding fuels on a port by port basis. Table 9.9 shows this information for six of the more important ports. The totals in this table are lower than those in Table 9.8 because they relate to Great Britain whereas the previous table was for the United Kingdom.

Table 9.9   *Traffic through major ports, 1965–73 (Great Britain only)*

	1965	1967	1969	1971	1973
London	17 320	16 003	16 397	16 230	17 356
	(19.73)	(18.34)	(17.49)	(16.97)	(15.46)
Liverpool	14 296	12 890	12 726	12 145	10 222
	(16.28)	(14.77)	(13.58)	(12.70)	(9.11)
Hull	4 436	4 645	4 668	4 005	4 100
	(5.05)	(5.32)	(4.98)	(4.18)	(3.65)
Southampton	1 173	1 406	1 506	2 147	3 585
	(1.34)	(1.61)	(1.61)	(2.24)	(3.19)
Manchester	5 202	5 069	4 896	5 207	5 357
	(5.93)	(5.81)	(5.22)	(5.44)	(4.77)
Bristol	3 457	3 473	3 319	2 899	2 922
	(3.94)	(3.98)	(3.54)	(3.03)	(2.60)
Other ports	41 912	43 756	50 220	52 987	68 694
	(47.74)	(50.15)	(53.58)	(55.41)	(61.20)
Total traffic	87 796	87 242	93 732	95 620	112 236

The numbers in parentheses in Table 9.9 are the percentage shares of the total. Total trade increased by 28 per cent between 1965 and 1973 with two-thirds of the increase occurring in the last two years of the period. Only one port, Southampton, significantly increased its trade in both absolute and relative terms. London and Manchester just about maintained their absolute levels of trade but their shares of the total fell substantially. Liverpool, Hull and Bristol all witnessed declines in their absolute levels and their relative shares. The net beneficiaries of these changes, in addition to Southampton, were other ports, whose trade increased by 64 per cent to raise their share of the total from 48 per cent to 61 per cent. The ports hardest hit by these changes were Liverpool and London. The effect on London was 'masked' because the Port of London and Tilbury are included under the same heading. There was a substantial shift from the former to the latter. The predominant pattern of traffic in these nine years was one of change between ports, with no overall increase in trade until the end of the period. These changes resulted in a decline in importance for five of the major ports.

The implications of these changes for labour requirements in the industry are discussed below. We begin by examining the aggregate situation for registered dock labour, before looking at the distribution of these changes between ports and the situation of non-registered employees. Table 9.10 shows the aggregate situation for registered dock labour between 1956 and 1973.

The year 1967 is divided into two parts because of decasualisation which resulted from the Devlin reforms. Decasualisation was introduced late in 1967, so that thirty-seven weeks of the year were in the pre-decasualisation period. The practice of proving attendance ceased at the same time.

Thereafter the series relates to those who were not attached to particular employers.

Despite a 20 per cent increase in traffic between 1956 and 1964 average labour requirements fell by 8000 workers, 13 per cent of the total. There was also a considerable improvement in the utilisation of labour so that the number proving attendance fell by nearly 5000. The net effect of these and other changes was that the total register fell by approximately 14 500, or 19 per cent of the total. This decline in employment and employment opportunities was not accompanied by overt resistance of the kind common in the 1940s.

Table 9.10   *Total registered dock labour, 1956–73*

Years	Average no. in employment	Average no. proving attendance	No. proving attendance as a percentage of no. available	Others on dock register	Total no. on dock register
1956	59 167	8 045	12.0	11 510	78 722
1957	58 070	7 309	11.2	11 312	76 691
1958	53 691	8 451	13.6	11 990	74 132
1959	54 085	7 221	11.8	10 540	71 846
1960	56 466	4 658	7.6	11 426	72 550
1961	52 512	8 136	13.4	11 031	71 679
1962	49 621	6 895	12.2	10 295	66 811
1963	49 966	4 767	8.7	9 864	64 597
1964	51 209	3 134	5.8	9 740	64 083
1965	51 770	3 575	6.5	9 783	65 128
1966	48 529	4 452	8.4	9 541	62 522
1967	45 024	5 173	10.3	9 947	60 144
1967	38 205	3 649	8.7	15 651	57 505
1968	43 104	3 340	7.2	10 119	56 563
1969	38 923	3 964	9.2	9 845	52 732
1970	34 373	2 336	6.4	10 203	46 912
1971	33 542	4 700	12.3	7 249	45 491
1972	28 427	3 137	9.9	9 683	41 247
1973	26 625	1 938	6.8	5 946	34 509

The pace of change quickened after 1964. By 1973 the number of registered dockers had fallen by a further 30 000, 46 per cent of the total. Average labour requirements declined to almost half the 1964 level. These changes, particularly those which occurred at the end of the period, were marked by considerable conflict. The way in which this reduction was accomplished by variations in recruitment and wastage is shown in Table 9.11. Again 1967 is divided into pre- and post-decasualisation weeks. Column six of the table includes those who left the main register voluntarily together with those who left the probationary and temporary registers, which would include some who were compelled to leave.

Table 9.11 Composition of changes in the size of the total dock register, 1956–73

Years	Net intake as a percentage of total register	Net outflow as a percentage of total register	Deaths as a percentage of total register	Retired as a percentage of total register	Dismissed as a percentage of total register	Outflow from the industry as a percentage of total register	Voluntary severance as a percentage of total register
1956	4.2	9.0	0.8	1.0	0.6	6.5	—
1957	5.3	6.8	0.9	0.9	0.5	4.4	—
1958	2.4	6.8	1.0	1.2	0.6	4.1	—
1959	4.1	6.4	1.0	1.0	0.5	3.9	—
1960	11.1	7.1	1.0	0.5	0.6	5.1	—
1961	7.2	14.3	1.0	5.4	1.0	6.9	—
1962	3.9	9.3	0.8	2.6	0.7	5.2	—
1963	6.6	8.3	0.9	2.5	0.6	4.3	—
1964	10.9	10.8	0.9	2.2	1.1	6.7	—
1965	12.1	12.4	0.8	2.0	1.6	8.1	—
1966	6.2	10.2	0.8	2.0	1.3	6.2	—
1967	2.1	5.3	0.6	1.3	0.7	2.7	—
1967	0.6	5.0	0.2	3.3	0.1	1.4	—
1968	4.8	7.6	0.8	1.8	0.6	4.4	—
1969	2.7	14.1	0.7	3.0	0.4	4.2	5.7
1970	3.1	11.0	0.7	1.1	0.3	1.3	7.6
1971	5.0	9.2	0.6	0.9	0.3	2.4	5.0
1972	4.1	20.5	0.4	0.3	0.3	0.8	18.7
1973	7.1	13.8	0.3	—	0.2	1.9	11.3

However, despite the overall reduction in the size of the labour force which took place in this period there was also a good deal of recruitment, although the rate of recruitment tended to fall over the period. In all but two of the eighteen years net wastage exceeded net recruitment. The difference between these two rates was particularly marked in the last five years of the period. The make-up of that net outflow is shown in the remaining columns of the table.

The death rate fluctuated in the range 0.8–1 per cent for most of the period before falling in the most recent years. This latter fall reflects the success of efforts to retire the more elderly and unfit members of the workforce. These efforts are reflected in the next column, which shows the numbers retiring. There was no pension scheme nor any active policy on retirement before 1960, so losses through retirement remained quite low. In 1960 agreement was reached on a pension scheme and on a policy of compulsory retirement with progressively reducing age limits. This scheme was implemented in 1961 for men aged seventy and over. In the two succeeding years the maximum age limit was reduced to sixty-eight. There were no further changes until 1969, when the age limit was reduced to sixty-five, although a voluntary retirement scheme for those in the age range sixty-five to sixty-seven was operated in 1967–8. When the first scheme was introduced in 1961 the retirement rate quintupled to 5.5 per cent, or more than one in twenty of those on the register. Thereafter it declined initially before stabilising at around 2 per cent per year – twice the pre-scheme rate. It rose sharply again in 1967, with the introduction of the voluntary retirement scheme, but fell from 1970 onwards until 1973 when it was negligible. This latter development reflected the fact that those who were approaching retirement age opted to leave the industry through the voluntary severance schemes which operated from 1969 onwards.

The rate of dismissal fluctuated widely, from a high of 1.6 per cent in 1965 to a low of 0.2 per cent in 1973. One possible explanation of this pattern is that dismissals for reasons of misconduct, which one would not expect to vary much from year to year, were overlaid by changes in dismissals due to unsuitability. These, in turn, were related to fluctuations in recruitment – the higher the rate of recruitment the higher the rate of dismissals. After 1967 it seems that decasualisation, with its creation of permanent employment relationships, also reduced the rate of dismissals.

The outflow of labour from the industry shown in column six was difficult to interpret because it included voluntary and non-voluntary leavers and its coverage varied over time. We were able to make some minimal estimates of voluntary wastage which indicated that, for the period as a whole, it averaged 3 per cent per year. Separate estimates for the pre- and post-decasualisation periods showed a fall from 3.5 to 1.4 per cent. Part of this decline can be attributed to the reduced rate of recruitment which cut the number of short service workers who tend to feature prominently among voluntary leavers. It also probably reflects some influence from the voluntary severance schemes which were picking up some workers who would have left anyway.

The effect of these voluntary severance schemes is depicted in the last column of Table 9.11. Altogether more than 20 000 workers left the industry under these schemes, it is likely that some would have left the industry anyway. The 'buying out' of jobs on this scale was bound to have raised significant antagonisms.

It appears that before 1964 the industry was able to shed labour at the required rate by going beyond natural wastage and limited recruitment and taking active steps to encourage men to leave the industry – e.g. the compulsory retirement scheme and the release register. Using these techniques it was able to reduce its labour force by an average of 2.2 per cent per year. But in the following ten years the rate of reduction more than doubled and conflict in the industry increased in parallel. We examined the employment prospects of those who left the industry using the techniques outlined in the previous chapter. The results were not as clear cut as in the coal mining case, but they did indicate a substantial deterioration after 1967. Once again we had a situation where workers were confronted by a lack of security in their existing employment and a lack of employment opportunities elsewhere.

The distribution of the reduction in employment between ports is shown in Table 9.12.

Table 9.12   *Average register at different ports, 1957–73*

	1957	1961	1965	1969	1973
London	30 273	28 749	25 484	19 570	11 710
Liverpool	16 532	15 098	14 033	11 885	7 629
Hull and Goole	4 667	4 810	4 808	4 019	2 452
South Coast	2 278	2 398	2 235	2 081	2 190
Manchester	2 980	2 800	2 412	2 043	1 213
Bristol and Severn	2 194	2 257	2 141	1 829	1 378
All other ports	17 767	15 567	14 015	11 305	7 937
Total	76 691	71 679	65 128	52 732	34 509

The labour force reduction appears to have seriously affected all the major ports except those of the south coast group, which included Southampton, where the reduction was less than 4 per cent in sixteen years. The most important implication to be drawn from this table is that the reduction in the demand for labour was, effectively, an industry-wide phenomenon. In this docking was unlike the coal mining case, where demand varied between areas. It seems likely that the industry-wide nature of the rundown was a significant factor in producing the industry-wide reaction evident in the 1972 national strike.

Although registered dock workers were the worst affected by the reduction in the demand for labour between 1964 and 1973, the rest of the industry's labour force did not escape unscathed. Employees in employment, excluding registered dock workers, fell from 75 000 to 45 000, a reduction of 40 per cent. In part this might be accounted for by non-registered dockers (those working in non-scheme ports) who were subject to the same kind of technological change as the registered workers. But another explanation would be that ancillary workers left the industry as the tasks with which they were concerned (e.g. container groupage, cold store operations, storage, etc.) were moved outside dock areas.

The other potential source of conflict which Devlin failed to explore in sufficient depth was the distribution of earnings. It is true that the final report drew attention to the existence of instability in weekly earnings, which were found to be dependent on the amount and type of work available under a casual system of job allocation. Changing from piecework to a system of day rates was seen as one way out of this problem. What Devlin failed to see was that moves away from piecework were unlikely to be uniform in all ports. Consequently, by 1973, according to the *New Earnings Survey* of April of that year, 40 per cent of dock workers covered by the NJC agreement still received piecework payments. On average these amounted to 14 per cent of their gross weekly earnings. But the Inquiry also tended to neglect the possible role of earnings comparisons at a time when earnings enter a period of relative decline. In our coal mining case study we observed that a fall in relative earnings was widely canvassed as the cause of a great deal of the upsurge in strike activity in that industry. Although the evidence was not conclusive, we felt that the relative fall in the more recent years had played a contributory role. With this in mind we thought it would be useful to examine comparable movements in the relative position of dockers' earnings, to check whether there was any obvious connection with changes in strike activity.

We used two measures of earnings in our comparisons – average weekly gross earnings and average weekly disposable earnings (calculated for a married man with two children under 11). Dockers' earnings for each year were estimated by averaging the quarterly data reported by the NDLB. Earnings in other industries were estimated as the average of the Ministry of Labour's April and October surveys for male manual workers.

Throughout the period 1948–73 dockers consistently had higher earnings, on the gross and the disposable measures, than workers in other industries. Within the overall pattern three phases could be distinguished. In the first phase, 1948–51, the dockers' advantage was 18 per cent on gross earnings and 14 per cent on disposable. In the second phase, 1952–67, the dockers' relative advantage was 9 per cent on gross and 6 per cent on disposable. Most of the reduction occurred in 1952, but there was a slight downward trend throughout. In the third phase, 1968–73, the position changed again. The dockers' advantage on gross earnings rose to 35 per cent and on disposable to 24 per cent. This change came about in two stages, in 1968 and 1970. After 1970 the dockers' 'lead' was slightly eroded.

Thus with the exception of the individual years already indicated, and 1960 when the relative advantage fell sharply before recovering in the following year, earnings increases in the docks seem to have kept up fairly well with those in other industries. This suggests that relative earnings movements were not an important factor in influencing the industry's strike record, over the period as a whole. Moreover, the years when there were exceptional relative earnings movements revealed no consistent association with changes in strike activity. Thus relative earnings fell sharply in 1952 and 1960, but strike activity fell sharply in 1952 and rose sharply in 1960. The position improved in 1968 and 1970, but strike activity in 1968 was not exceptional and 1970 comes second in a ranking of years by strike activity. We concluded that on balance there was no evidence of any firm relationship, positive or negative, between changes in strike activity and those in relative earnings.

In summary, our first proposition that the worsening of the strike record in the docks post-Devlin might, in part at least, be explicable in terms of an inadequacy in the Devlin analysis, seems to be supported by at least some of the evidence available to us since they wrote. Most importantly the Inquiry failed to consider the reasons for the reduction in strike activity post-1951. Consequently they overlooked the possibility of conflict arising from changes in the pattern of traffic, and the large scale loss of job opportunities. Whether, even if the historical analysis had been more comprehensive, it is reasonable to suggest that the Committee should have recognised the possible impact of future changes in the pattern of trade, plus the very substantial technological changes which occurred simultaneously, is a question which must be left until we have considered the three other propositions outlined above.

DEVLIN – INAPPROPRIATE PRESCRIPTIONS?

Our second proposition was that, although the Devlin analysis was correct, the recommendations which were made to deal with the situation were inappropriate. Indeed they may even have contributed to the post-Devlin increase in strike activity. The Devlin recommendations were set out briefly at the end of the Final Report and have been summarised above. They have to be considered against the background of the failure of the earlier negotiations in the industry, and against the aim of the Committee to resuscitate those negotiations and bring them to a successful conclusion. With this aim in mind the Committee recommended measures to strengthen both parties at the bargaining table. The employers were to accept a reduction in their numbers in order to remove the 'casual' employers. The TGWU was to regain its authority in London, Liverpool and Hull by winning back the allegiance of its members and reaching an understanding with the NASDU. The latter was to be involved in the new round of negotiations providing that it respected the usual bargaining conventions.

The starting point for a new round of negotiations was to be the introduction of a system of regular employment for all dock workers. This was to be accompanied by guarantee payments and a sick-pay scheme and to be matched by the abolition of those restrictive practices 'which were essentially a feature of the casual method of employment'. A further round of negotiations were to deal with the following: (a) revision of the wage structure; (b) abolition of time-wasting practices, in so far as they were not covered by the basic settlement; (c) acceptance of firmer discipline; (d) review of manning scales to take account of increased mechanisation and changing methods. The decision to advocate two rounds of negotiations followed from Devlin's conclusion that one of the reasons for the failure of the earlier negotiations was that they tried to cover too much and became too complicated.

On balance these recommendations appear to have been well matched to the diagnosis of the industry's problems. That analysis had focused strongly on the effects of the casual system of employment on both employers and workers. The first substantive step in the negotiations must be the abolition of that system. But before even that could be negotiated it was recognised and stipulated that there would have to be considerable changes in the attitudes of the parties to the negotiations – otherwise even if an agreement could be reached it would be effective only on paper. It was hoped that after decasualisation a better atmosphere would prevail which would facilitate negotiations on the remaining items.

The most serious weakness of this approach was that it relied on representatives of the parties at local level to carry through the negotiations and implement the necessary agreements. The Committee did not see their role as one of putting forward a cut and dried plan for the parties to follow slavishly; they wished only to provide a blueprint which would form the basis for negotiations. They recognised that such negotiations might not result in agreement, and urged the Minister of Labour to be prepared to enforce a settlement through legislation if necessary, as had been done with the National Dock Labour Board scheme in 1947. Yet they relied heavily on the self-interest and good intentions of the parties to ensure that the negotiations were brought to a speedy conclusion and implemented effectively. In doing so they could be said to have ignored the fact that those same self-interested and well intentioned parties had put up with the existing arrangements for the best part of twenty years, without feeling that they were so intolerable that they had to be changed. In reality both parties were internally divided on the need for reform, and on the price they were willing to pay to achieve it.

It can be argued that this reliance on the goodwill and common sense of the parties left the Committee reluctant to lay down precise guidelines – except on the need for decasualisation. One consequence of this was that while ports like London were abandoning piecework other ports, notably Liverpool, began to make more extensive use of it. The subsequent rise in Liverpool's share of the strike action may not have been unconnected with this fact. Similarly, the lack of clear guidance on the removal of restrictive practices inevitably resulted in a situation where progress varied from port to port. These various difficulties are chronicled in the next section which examines in some detail the problems which arose in implementing the recommendations.

DEVLIN – IMPLEMENTATION OR EVISCERATION?

Our third proposition was that, even if the Devlin diagnosis and prescription were broadly correct, the implementation of their recommendations covered was so mishandled as to contribute significantly to the increase in strike activity after 1965. We have already pointed out that Devlin saw reform within each of the two parties as a precondition of the successful negotiation and implementation of the recommendations. Most importantly, the number of employers had to be reduced so that those who remained would be large enough to be economically efficient, provide adequate welfare facilities and accept a reasonable quota of men from the labour pool when it was brought to an end. They also had to be large enough to give their workers constant daily employment for a reasonable proportion of their time. It was hoped that this process of rationalisation would squeeze out those smaller employers who had been most resistant to the need for reform.

Unfortunately, the recommended reductions were not met, in the majority of cases, by the date of decasualisation, although there were further reductions later. Yet the results of a failure to meet Devlin's targets in this report should not be exaggerated. In Manchester the port authority had been the sole 'operational' employer for years, but the port was far from strike free.

On the trade union side Devlin's recommendations concerned the TGWU and the NASDU. The TGWU was to undertake a 'great campaign' to re-establish its position in the ports of London, Liverpool and Hull. The NASDU was to co-operate in resolving the jurisdictional problems in those ports. In part the recommendations were dependent on achieving decasualisation. It was hoped that in the stable employment situation which would result it would be possible to set up a well developed shop steward system – casual employment made such a system unviable.

It must be admitted in this respect that the TGWU made strenuous efforts. In London far-reaching propositions were put forward to reform the antiquated branch structure, and to incorporate shop stewards into the constitutional machinery. But these met with considerable opposition. Some reorganisation of the branches was achieved but the existence of NASDU stewards, who could not be incorporated into the TGWU machinery, proved to be a considerable obstacle. The TGWU's other aim in London – to overcome the challenge of the 'unofficials' – was largely unmet. Despite these setbacks relations with the NASDU were improved. A demarcation dispute in London between the two unions was settled amicably.

In Liverpool there was little improvement prior to decasualisation. After that a shop steward system was organised which strengthened the position of the TGWU without reducing the area's considerable local autonomy. In Hull the situation was much improved in 1966 following a series of changes which included the sacking of three local full-time officials. These reforms also helped to create a better atmosphere with the NASDU. It would seem that both parties made progress towards meeting Devlin's recommendations, but both fell short of full implementation.

The best account of the negotiations which followed the publication of the Devlin Report, and of the difficulties which ensued, is that given by David Wilson (1972). In the analysis which follows we draw heavily on his material. The negotiations for Devlin Stage One were marked by a series of difficulties. Agreement could not be reached on the payment which was to accompany decasualisation, largely because of divisions among the employers. Eventually the Devlin Committee was recalled and came up with a complex formula which included a 'modernisation payment', a high guarantee and a sick pay scheme. This was worth an estimated 16 per cent at a time when a statutory wages 'freeze' was in force. Considerable pressure was exerted on the National Modernisation Committee – the body set up by the NJC to handle the negotiations – to ensure that this increase in payments was matched by the removal of enough restrictive practices to meet the terms of the incomes policy. The position was further complicated when the London employers succumbed to pressure and gave a further increase in the guarantee. This led to a round of similar claims from other ports. Government pressure in support of incomes policy secured the deferment of this payment, but at a probable cost of a further souring of negotiating climate. All the outstanding problems were eventually overcome or evaded and decasualisation came into effect on 18 September 1967.

The immediate result was strike action in London, Liverpool, Hull and Manchester. Most of these disputes collapsed within a week but the stoppage at Liverpool remained total. The Liverpool dispute was largely over higher earnings. The TGWU had agreed to stop the practice of spinning work out into overtime and the dockers were demanding higher incentive payments to maintain (or increase) their earnings. The strike was settled after six weeks with a guarantee of £4 per week bonus. In London the port initially settled down after decasualisation but was disrupted by a dispute over the operation of the 'continuity rule' for transferred men. At the height of this strike it involved a third of the labour force. It was eventually settled after the transfer arrangements were modified.

Despite these various difficulties and setbacks Stage One had been accomplished – even if its implementation did not fully live up to Devlin's expectations. Casual employment had been replaced by a scheme which promised permanent employment to the whole of the registered dock labour force. Stage One negotiations over restrictive practices varied in content from port to port. In some substantial improvements were reported; in others very little changed. Devlin Stage Two was supposed to see the abolition of all remaining restrictive practices, the fullest possible use of mechanical equipment and a review of the wages structure. The conflict of responsibility between national and local negotiations which had accompanied Stage One was again apparent. The National Association of Port Employers (NAPE) was keen to keep control of negotiations in order to prevent leap-frogging local settlements. In the absence of a substantial measure of agreement about objectives, and in the presence of widely differing local requirements, this aim was unrealistic. Local negotiations were almost bound to become paramount.

In some cases local employers realised the need for a comprehensive deal if the foundation provided by Stage One was to be built on to provide a modern port industry. Consequently, they began negotiations almost as soon as Stage One was accomplished to ensure that the end of casual employment was matched by the end of all other casual practices. In other ports conflicts of interests and objectives slowed the pace of negotiations and made employers less willing to consider the problems of implementation until a substantial measure of agreement had been reached.

All the new agreements featured a minimum weekly wage which was higher than the national time rate. Otherwise there were substantial differences. Some ports opted for shiftwork while others did not. Some replaced piecework by a high basic wage system; others opted for simple tonnage bonuses in place of more complicated piecework arrangements. One exception to this general pattern was Liverpool, where piecework was adopted more extensively than previously and shiftwork introduced on a greater scale than at any other major port. The Stage Two negotiations tended to be more protracted than those of Stage One, with the delays varying between ports. Middlesborough implemented Stage Two in January 1970, London in September 1970 and Liverpool in October 1971.

Perhaps the most surprising feature of the Stage Two negotiations was the national dock strike of 1970. In 1968, when the possibility of national negotiations over Stage Two still existed, a claim had been lodged at the NJC for a substantial increase in the national time rate. This claim was partially met in 1969 with the concession of a third week's holiday, improved pensions and the conversion of the guarantee from a weekly to a daily basis. The employers were still hoping that the negotiation of local agreements would remove the pressure for further increases. Unfortunately for them the local negotiations were prolonged. By mid-1970 the situation reached crisis point and, despite a last minute offer by the employers, a national dock strike began. The strike lasted three weeks and included the major non-scheme ports. A Court of Inquiry headed by Lord Pearson was set up. Its award (estimated to be worth 7 per cent) did not improve the national time rate but raised the guarantee to £20 per week, improved overtime premia and added a £1 'modernisation' payment across the board.

Some difficulty arises in explaining why the first national dock strike since 1926 should have occurred at a time when local negotiations were making the national time rate more and more irrelevant for most dockers. In part it may be explained as an act of solidarity with the 7000 or so dockers at the smaller ports who were excluded from the Stage Two negotiations. In part it may have been an attempt to raise the cost of the locally negotiated Stage Two settlements. It may have been, as Wilson suggested, an attempt to create a sense of unity in the face of the threat to jobs created by the introduction of new technology. (This development is further discussed in the next section.) But it does not seem to us that these reasons, even taken together, offer a complete explanation. A further possiblity which suggests itself to us is that the 1970 dock strike was, in part, a reflection of the mood of the times.

After all, the breakdown of the incomes policy from 1969 onwards had been accompanied by a very rapid rise in strike activity. The usual restraints on such action seemed, temporarily at least, to have disappeared. Perhaps then the dockers' strike of 1970 was partly imitative of similar action elsewhere.

In summary, it would seem that there is some evidence to support our third proposition – that the manner of implementation of the Devlin proposals contributed to the increase in strike activity. Apart from the rash of strikes which greeted decasualisation, which might have been predicted from the upheaval associated with the previous major change, there were two situations where strikes were directly related to the Devlin reforms – Liverpool and the national docks strike. In Liverpool the introduction of piecework, at a time when most other ports were trying to opt out of that type of payment system, probably contributed to the rise in Liverpool's share of strike activity over the last few years of the period. The starting point for the national dock strike was the NAPE's attempt to keep control of the Devlin negotiations at national level, rather than concede the over-riding importance of local negotiations. In turn the 1970 national dock strike, by demonstrating a degree of solidarity previously unrecognised in the industry, probably contributed to the 1972 dispute. Yet despite these difficulties the bulk of the Devlin proposals were introduced and, in so far as they were well founded, must have contributed to some improvement in relations in the industry.

DEVLIN – OVERWHELMED BY THE UNKNOWN?

Our fourth proposition to explain the post-Devlin increase in strike activity was that factors came into play after 1965 which could not reasonably have been foreseen at the time of the Inquiry. The obvious example of a factor of this kind is technological change. Technological change in the docks in the form of containerisation, roll-on roll-off traffic, palletisation, etc., accelerated rapidly after 1965. In the absence of an equally rapid growth in traffic it resulted in a substantial reduction in labour requirements. We have already drawn attention to the role of employment insecurity in contributing to strike activity. The aim of this section is twofold: to consider the extent to which the Committee was aware of the impending changes and to establish what relationship, if any, existed between these changes and the increase in strike activity.

In a remarkable passage Wilson (1972, p. 290) argues that the Devlin Committee was to some extent misled on this issue by their terms of reference. As he says it was unfortunate that

> the forward-looking purpose of the Devlin Inquiry was never explicit in the Committee's terms of reference. Lord Devlin was asked to make good the legacy of the past, but it was fundamentally the pressures of transport technology which directed the attention of the Government, employers and trade unions to the reform of labour relations in the 1960s. Imminent containerisation was implicit in the *timing* of the Inquiry . . . the casual system, with attendant casual attitudes, could not have coped with the container.

In other words decasualisation was realised by the parties to be the *sine qua non* for imminent technological change; yet for some reason they failed to point this out to Devlin.

It is not clear what evidence was available to persuade Wilson of this view. Elsewhere he admits that the only people who were in a position to make detailed estimates of future labour requirements were the ship-owners, and they were not called to give evidence. In fact there are no indications that either the unions or the employers fully realised the implications of the changes which shipowners planned to introduce in the foreseeable future.

The timing of the Inquiry is much more easily accounted for by the breakdown of negotiations over decasualisation and the national pay claim. Indeed, the initial spur to negotiations over decasualisation in 1961 undoubtedly was concern over the industry's strike record, rather than foresight with regard to potential reductions in the demand for labour.

Of course technological change, on a smaller scale, had been a feature of the industry throughout the post-war period. In the decade prior to Devlin traffic had risen while the register had fallen by 14 000, nearly 20 per cent of the total. That this change had taken place without any overt resistance from the workforce must have encouraged the parties' belief that they could cope with further changes, especially if they continued at about the same rate. One evidence of this is that the employers felt able to offer a 'no redundancy' pledge which was accepted.

On this basis, the orientation of the Inquiry towards seeking to explain and ameliorate the industry's relatively high level of strike activity and low level of labour utilisation is consistent with the negotiations which preceded it. It also explains why the Inquiry did not consider the problems raised by the definition of dock work. It seems to us that the alternative to accepting such an 'ignorance' hypothesis is to postulate a much less plausible 'collusion' assumption, in which both the parties involved and the Committee recognised the difficulties but deliberately chose not to consider them, perhaps because they believed that any suggestion of redundancies would lead to a rejection of the decasualisation proposals. There seems to be no evidence to support such a view.

But if it is accepted that those giving evidence to the Inquiry did not recognise the full implications of technological change, one may still ask whether the members of the Devlin Committee might reasonably have done so? With the benefit of hindsight the warning signals, particularly from the United States of America, were unmistakable. They might, at the very least, have prompted some questions. Wilson argues with some force that all such matters were regarded as being outside the terms of reference, particularly as there had been a major inquiry into other aspects of the industry in 1962 (Rochdale, 1962). It is also true that the Inquiry was not equipped to carry out the kind of research necessary if the implications of changes in cargo-handling techniques were to be explored in any detail.

Its methodology was traditional and largely involved taking submissions from the parties. Consequently, unless the parties involved drew attention to the matter, the Inquiry would tend not to consider it. Indeed, as the Committee itself pointed out in its Final Report, they were not required to make positive recommendations in *any* form by their terms of reference.

Our conclusion is that while the lack of consideration given to problems of imminent technological change by Devlin mitigated against the realism of their conclusions, this casts more doubt on the quality of the submissions of the parties, and the foresight of those who drew up the terms of reference, than anything else.

Given that our concern is with the pattern of strike activity in the docks, it is also necessary for us to trace the relationship between these changes in technology and the level of strike activity. Between 1967 and 1973 the demand for labour in the industry fell by 40 per cent and the number on the register by 43 per cent. There were two elements in this reduction in the demand for labour. New techniques of cargo-handling raised productivity faster than traffic growth, so that less labour was required. The new techniques also permitted still more operations to be carried out away from the docks and outside the scope of the National Dock Labour Board scheme. This movement of work away from traditional dock areas was seen by dockers as an attempt by some employers to avoid their responsibilities. The dockers retaliated by picketing the new premises and by 'blacking' cargoes from them. In 1972 this conflict resulted in legal action against several groups of dockers under the Industrial Relations Act 1971 and in some dockers being sent to prison for contempt of court. It also ended in a further three week national strike aimed at securing more work for registered dockers. The conflict engendered by lack of job security could not be better exemplified, although the events of 1972 were inextricably caught up in the operation of the Industrial Relations Act 1971, which is further discussed in Chapter 11.

One final factor which may have affected the post-Devlin level of strike activity was the government's announcement in 1969 of its intention to nationalise the major ports. Coming as it did during the Stage Two negotiations, this announcement did nothing to persuade employers to press forward with their plans and may have contributed to the delays which helped to bring about the 1970 national dock strike.

On balance we feel that our fourth proposition, that the post-Devlin increase in strike activity was due to the operation of factors which could not reasonably have been foreseen by the Inquiry, has considerable support. The Inquiry failed to recognise the full implications of the impending technological changes. Consequently, the employers' pledge of 'no redundancy' was accepted without question, so that the problems raised by a massive reduction in employment opportunities and the legal definition of dock work went unconsidered. With hindsight the warning signals were quite clear but, three years prior to Devlin, the Rochdale Report commented on the rate of progress towards containerisation and the relative importance of other less labour-saving forms of technological change. In part the warnings went unheeded because neither the Inquiry nor, apparently, the industry was organised in such a way that it could easily conduct research into matters of this kind.

Finally, it should be noted that, although the process of adjustment to the effects of technological change caused considerable conflict in the industry, it does not follow that the potential benefits of the Devlin reforms have been permanently lost. It may be that once the painful process of adjustment has come to an end relations in the industry will show substantial improvement.

SUMMARY AND CONCLUSIONS

In the period 1949–73 the docks was the most strike-prone industry in the United Kingdom with an average of one worker in two involved in strike action each year. This average was almost twice as high as in coal mining. Comparing average strike activity at the beginning of the period, 1949–53, with that at the end of the period, 1969–73, showed increases of 857 per cent in the number of stoppages, 376 per cent in workers involved and 104 per cent in days lost. The industry became much more dispute prone, but the average dispute fell dramatically in extent and duration.

Disaggregation of total strike activity into small and major stoppages revealed significant differences. For most of the period small stoppages increased much more rapidly than major ones, but this pattern was reversed in the last few years. The average size of small stoppages, measured by extent and duration, fell by 13 per cent, whereas the average number of workers involved in major stoppages fell by 21 per cent and the average duration by 47 per cent.

Our search for an explanation of this pattern of strike activity began with the report of the Devlin Committee of Inquiry into labour relations in the docks. The Inquiry found that most of the immediate causes of the high level of strike activity were related to the form of the employment relationship. Since the introduction of the National Dock Labour Board scheme in 1947 there had been two kinds of employers: 'operational' employers, who required labour and paid for it as and when they used it, and 'holding' employers – local dock labour boards – with whom dockers registered when there was no work available and from whom they received 'fall-back' payments. Contrasting this employment relationship with those in other industries, and with those situations in which dockers were in permanent employment, Devlin concluded that this was the major cause of the poor labour relations in the industry. He proposed that it should be abolished and replaced by permanent employment with the 'operational' employers. A number of other recommendations were made to deal with other sources of conflict in the industry and to guide both parties in the implementation of such far-reaching proposals.

One of the main aims of the Devlin Report was to reduce strike activity in the docks. If strike activity had fallen following the implementation of the Report's proposals it would have provided substantial evidence that the analysis and proposals were correct. Unfortunately implementation took several years, which makes it difficult to assess their impact, but decasualisation was brought in in 1967. This allowed us to make some assessment of its effectiveness.

In relation to the number of employees in employment all three basic measures showed substantial increases in 1968–73 compared with 1956–64. (We excluded the years 1965–7 because they coincided with the negotiation and implementation of the decasualisation proposals which might in themselves have been expected to cause conflict.) The number of strikes rose by 308 per cent, workers involved by 284 per cent and days lost by 234 per cent. On this evidence the proposals did not have any beneficial effects in terms of reducing strike activity. The increase in strike activity in the docks was greater than that in all other industries (excluding coal mining) so that the post-1967 experience cannot be explained away in terms of some 'macro' influences overpowering specific industry improvements.

While recognising that this evidence was too limited to be construed as constituting a refutation of the whole Devlin analysis, it did suggest that four propositions, which were not mutually exclusive, should be explored. These were that the Devlin analysis was incorrect or incomplete, that the recommended reforms did not match the analysis, that the reforms were inadequately implemented, and that factors arose after the report had been completed which invalidated, in whole or in part, its conclusions.

With regard to the first of these we noted that time lost through strikes was much lower in 1956–64 than in 1949–55, although the factors listed by Devlin had been operative throughout the period. Consequently we looked for sources of conflict which had been operative in the earlier years and then declined in importance. We noted that the immediate post-war years had been marked by substantial changes in the volume of traffic and, to a lesser extent, in its distribution by port. We also noted the introduction of the National Dock Labour Board scheme and attempts to remove men compulsorily from the dockers' register. Each of these appeared to be of some significance. After 1951 they became much less important. Traffic grew quite slowly and there do not appear to have been major changes in its distribution between ports. At the same time the size of the labour force was adjusted through control of recruitment, wider use of temporary registrations and the introduction of compulsory retirement. The NDLB scheme and its disciplinary provisions gradually came to be accepted. The overlooking of these factors by Devlin was unfortunate as some of them returned to prominence in the later years of the period. In recent years there have been marked changes in the distribution of traffic. This in turn has severely affected labour requirements in some ports. In addition a number of technological changes – e.g. containerisation, roll-on roll-off traffic, etc., have contributed to an increasing rate of decline in the demand for labour. In these circumstances the gradual method of labour force adjustment developed in the 1950s proved to be inadequate. Although compulsory redundancies were largely avoided, the rate of decline in job opportunities created considerable uncertainty and inevitable conflict.

It is worth noting at this point that there were several differences between the situation in the docks and that in coal mining. In the latter the industry was in decline and the demand for its product was falling. In the docks demand for the industry's services was rising and this helped to support the workers' bargaining position despite the decline in demand for labour. In coal mining there was a centralised structure on both sides of the industry which meant that decisions could be taken about the industry as a whole. In the docks the NJC had declined in importance as earnings rose faster than the national time rate. This process was encouraged by Devlin with the development of local port-wide negotiations on working practices and time rates. Inter-union rivalries left the workers' side divided and weakened. At the same time the introduction of new expensive capital equipment led to competition among the employers as they fought for more traffic in order to obtain maximum utilisation. These develoments, coupled with the changing pattern of traffic, resulted in some sections of the labour force finding themselves in a much more favourable position than others. In part the conflict of the later years was a result of the workers' efforts to use their combined strength on behalf of those worst affected by these changes.

Our second proposition, that the recommended reforms were not suited to the analysis, found little support. However, we did note that the proposals relied heavily on the self-interest and good intentions of the parties to carry through successfully the voluntary negotiations. Given that the earlier negotiations had failed and that the situation they were attempting to reform had existed for almost twenty years, this reliance seemed somewhat misplaced. In retrospect it seems plausible to suggest that the Inquiry could usefully have given firmer guidance on some issues – e.g. the way in which the wage structure and the payment system was to be reformed.

Our third proposition, that the implementation of the reforms actually created conflict, received rather more support. Decasualisation itself was greeted by strikes in the major English ports, in a manner reminiscent of the response to the earlier introduction of the National Dock Labour Board scheme. This may be taken to indicate that in an industry which is as traditionally conflict-ridden as the docks virtually all change is likely to be met with hostility because of fear of its consequences.

Despite Devlin's proposals to strengthen the position of negotiators on both sides of industry with respect to their own members the negotiations met with considerable difficulty. Stage One negotiations over decasualis-ation broke down when the employers failed to agree among themselves about what was to be offered and were only rescued by a reconvened Devlin Inquiry which proposed a complicated and expensive package. The Stage Two negotiations also met with difficulty. The National Association of Port Employers tried to keep control of negotiations to avoid leap-frogging claims at local level. In pursuit of this aim they admitted a claim for a national increase to the bargaining arena in 1968. They hoped that local negotiations would proceed swiftly enough to render the claim redundant. The local negotiations were protracted and in 1970 there was a three week national strike in support of the claim. This was an unprecedented display of solidarity by the dockers, involving scheme and non-scheme ports, and was a foretaste of the 1972 national strike over the temporary unattached register. If the national negotiations had been more effective, or the local negotiations more rapid, both of these national strikes might have been avoided.

One further difficulty which arose during implementation was a clash between the Devlin recommendations and the requirements of incomes policy. Devlin had dismissed the employers' argument that decasualisation could only be delivered as a *quid pro quo* for changes in working arrangements. He recommended that decasualisation be introduced with-out conditions in order to so improve relations. He said that negotiations on other matters could take place in Stage Two. The government insisted that the cost of decasualisation be met from higher productivity, in order to conform with the incomes policy. Eventually sufficient changes were agreed to obtain government approval. But it meant that an important part of the Devlin strategy had been abandoned and that decasualisation could not fill the role which had been designed for it.

Our fourth proposition, that factors came into play after 1965 which could not reasonably have been foreseen by the Inquiry and which caused the increase in activity, centres on the technological change in the industry. Should Devlin have foreseen it and to what extent did it contribute to the post-1967 increase in strike activity?

Here we decided that the orientation of the Inquiry was towards the industry's past, not its future. Its brief was to reduce the level of strike activity, not equip it for the coming changes. Even if it had considered the possible problems it would probably have underestimated the pace and extent of change. Three years earlier the Rochdale Report had commented on the slow progress towards containerisation and the relative importance of other less labour-saving innovations. It is true that the warning signs were available in North America, but they were not brought to the Inquiry's attention. The shipowners were the best informed about the likely scale of changes, but they were not called to give evidence. This reflects a weakness of this form of inquiry. It was set up to seek a settlement of the outstanding issues between the parties. It was dependent on the quality of their submissions. It had neither the resources nor the authority to conduct its own investigation of wider issues. Consequently, it was unlikely to see much further than the parties themselves. This was not far enough.

The damage caused by this lack of foresight was considerable. The Devlin reforms had been designed to eliminate that insecurity of employment which was thought to have had such a deleterious effect on relations in the industry. In fact the reforms were accompanied by a loss of jobs on a scale unprecedented in the post-war years. The new technology not only raised productivity faster than traffic growth, it also permitted and required shifts of traffic between ports and allowed the removal of traditional dock work away from the ports. The conflict which ensued was inevitable, although the 1972 national strike might have been avoided if the National Industrial Relations Court had not become embroiled in the struggle over dock work. But the failure of Devlin to contribute to the solution of this conflict should not blind us to the value of his reforms over the longer term. We accept his central premise, that the casual employment relationship was largely responsible for the poor state of labour relations in the docks; it follows that the abolition of that relationship should have a beneficial effect. This may be more in evidence when the problems caused by technological change are resolved.

In conclusion it should be said that the story of the docks after Devlin reinforces and underscores two points made in our previous chapter. It is at once again clear that micro-economic factors, such as variations in labour demand or fluctuations in trade at particular ports, can have their import magnified, or rendered relatively unimportant, by a complex of 'institutional' or 'cultural' factors – e.g. payment systems changes, inter-union rivalries, deep-seated resistance to all forms of change and the exigencies of the government's incomes policies. We need to appreciate all the factors before we can hope to explain particular stoppages, or general movements in the strike pattern.

Secondly, it is once again illuminating to draw the distinction between factors 'internal' to the industry and those which derive from outside. In this sense one must surely regard the attempts to decasualise as internally rooted – although they partly came about as a result of the appointment of an 'external' committee. On the other hand, reductions in labour demand, and the problems of job security which result, are essentially external. They derive from the revolutionary technology adopted by owners of bulk handling ships the world over. As in the case of the miners, the events which followed remind us how easily useful and worthwhile internal reforms can be challenged and rendered nugatory by external forces.

10 Motor Vehicles – An Odd Case?

THE AIMS OF THE CHAPTER

Motor vehicles, like our other case studies, made a sizeable contribution to the total of strike activity in the post-war years. Overall figures for motor vehicles were only available after 1948, but these show that in the period 1949–73 the industry accounted for 5 per cent of stoppages, 15 per cent of workers involved and 13 per cent of days lost. On average 41 per cent of employees in motor vehicles were involved in stoppages every year. (The effects of the national engineering stoppages of 1953, 1957, 1962 and 1968 are included in these figures, but excluded from our averages in the rest of the chapter, since their origins were very largely external to the industry itself.)

Yet despite its high level of strike activity, motor vehicles was unlike coal mining or the docks in several respects. It lacked a pre-war history of strike activity. Its demand for labour has not been subject to substantial secular decline. There was little fundamental change in the post-war work technology. It did not feature prominently in international comparisons of highly strike-prone industries. Consequently, one of our main reasons for choosing motor vehicles for our final case study was that in all these respects it provided a substantial contrast with other studies. But, in addition, there were two further reasons for our choice.

First, car assembly plants were the subject of an influential and detailed study (Turner *et al.*, 1967) some years ago. We thought it would be a valuable cross-check on our own methodology to contrast that study's findings with our own. We also wished to assess the extent to which the explanations offered by the earlier study accounted for more recent events. Secondly, motor vehicles has attracted a good deal of public attention because of its strike record and the alleged shortcomings of its industrial relations. In the light of this attention we felt that the industry required more than summary treatment.

The structure of this chapter is similar to that of the previous two. We begin with a detailed examination of the industry's strike record in order to identify those features which seem most to require explanation. We consider the explanations offered by earlier studies and evaluate their ability to account for events over the whole period. In .so far as those explanations appear less than adequate we consider the role of other factors.

STRIKE ACTIVITY IN MOTOR VEHICLES

Analysis of strike statistics for motor vehicles is complicated by two factors – changes in the Standard Industrial Classification and Department of Employment policy on the level of disaggregation at which information was made available. The Standard Industrial Classification, after its introduction in 1948, was revised decennially. The most important revision in respect of motor vehicles occurred in 1958, when the manufacture of cycles (which had previously been included in the series) was excluded while the manufacture of parts and accessories (which had previously been excluded) was included. A further revision in 1968 led to the exclusion of wheeled tractor manufacture. Strictly speaking these revisions render invalid comparisons based on the 1948, 1958 and 1968 series – only comparisons within the time periods covered by each series are really valid. In practice the manufacture of cars, commercial vehicles, vehicle bodies and engines dominates this series throughout the period. This means that some broad comparisons are possible, but undue weight should not be attached to minor variations between periods.

We have already described the Department of Employment policy of publishing detailed information on strike-prone industries and of 'lumping together' other industries into broad industrial groups. As motor vehicles only rose slowly to prominence in the strike activity tables information relating solely to that industry was only published from 1970 onwards. Fortunately, however, the Department kept unpublished records of strike activity at industry level from 1960 onwards and kindly agreed to make details of strike activity in motor vehicles available to us.

For the period 1960–73 we had a consistent series (if the exclusion of wheeled tractor manufacturing from 1970 onwards is ignored) of strike activity in motor vehicle manufacturing. For the period 1946–59 we were faced by two broad choices – either to make some use of the published series, despite their high level of aggregation, or to try to compile our own series directly from the Department's records of individual strikes. We opted for the latter. Our next problem was to decide the basis on which we should compile our own series – should it conform to the 1948, 1958 or 1968 SICs? We decided to compile it on the basis of the 1948 SIC because that would allow us to match it up to other reference series e.g. employment, earnings, labour turnover, etc. We also decided to restrict our series to the period 1949–59, as most of the other reference series were also not available for the period 1946–48.

In summary then the strike statistics set out below relate to motor vehicle manufacture. For the period 1949–59 they were compiled in accordance with the 1948 SIC (Minimum List Heading 80), for the period 1960–9 in accordance with the 1958 SIC (MLH 381), and for the period 1970–3 in accordance with the 1968 SIC (MLH 381). It should also be noted that, as we compiled the series for 1949–59 ourselves, there is the possibility of some minor errors as it was not always clear to which industry establishments belonged. However, we are confident that the overall picture shown by the 1949–59 data is accurate, although we would stress that the significance of minor variations should not be exaggerated.

Table 10.1 shows our series for total strike activity in motor vehicles in the period 1949–73.

The overall impression is of a very substantial rise over the period as a whole. Using five year averages to smooth out year to year fluctuations reveals that between 1949–63 and 1969–73 the number of strikes rose by 990 per cent, workers involved by 1440 per cent and days lost by 990 per cent. Part of these increases can be explained away by the increase in the level of employment in the industry but, even allowing for this, we are left with a ninefold increase in worker involvement and a sevenfold increase in time lost.

Close examination of the number of stoppages reveals no consistent upward movement in the first five years, but thereafter there is a rapid escalation. This accelerated to a peak in 1959–63 and then decelerated, although the overall movement continued in the same direction. Workers involved and days lost series followed a similar pattern although both had a secondary spurt in 1969–73. Indeed, the working days lost series grew more rapidly at this time than at any other. The implication of these changes was that the average size of stoppages – measured by number of workers involved – rose in 1954–63 and 1969–73 but fell in the mid-1960s. On the other hand, average duration fell until 1963 and rose thereafter. This pattern was quite similar to that of the net series of strike activity.

The inclusion of the two reference series in this table serves to confirm the impression of strong upward movement and to place it in perspective. Worker involvement in stoppages in motor vehicles rose from an average of 7 per cent of the workforce per year at the beginning of the period to 62 per cent at the end. The largest increases were in the mid- and end-years of the period. To some extent this measure exaggerates the degree of individual worker involvement in stoppages because of the occurrence of multiple strike acts. Yet it also under-estimates – particularly in an industry as integrated as motor vehicles – because it excludes those workers who are laid off at establishments other than those where the strikes occur.

Days lost in relation to potential working time rose from 0.2 per cent at the beginning of the period to 1.5 per cent at the end. Again there is a degree of under-estimation in that losses at establishments not directly involved are excluded. Such secondary losses might have pushed the total of time lost at the end of the period to as much as 2–3 per cent of potential working time. It should also be noted that attention has been drawn to the tendency for heavy losses to occur at times of depressed demand and high stocks, when manufacturers might have found it very difficult to sell the 'lost' output (Turner and Bescoby, 1961a). This is not to under-estimate the seriousness of the stoppages which did occur, particularly in the more strike-prone plants of some of the major companies. But it is important to keep such stoppages in perspective in relation to the industry as a whole

Table 10.1 *Total strike activity in motor vehicles, 1949–73*

Year	No. of strikes	No. of workers involved (000s)	No. of working days lost (000s)	Workers involved as a percentage of employees in employment	Working days lost as a percentage of potential working time
1949	24	3.6	14	1.2	0.02
1950	30	14.7	112	4.9	0.14
1951	29	38.3	105	12.7	0.13
1952	28	31.5	371	10.4	0.45
1953	16	14.3	250	4.8	0.31
1954	16	15.5	35	5.0	0.04
1955	36	34.7	70	10.5	0.08
1956	26	70.6	293	21.6	0.33
1957	44	43.2	102	14.0	0.12
1958	55	54.5	128	17.2	0.15
1959	85	128.9	327	39.3	0.37
1960	124	183.0	513	42.0	0.48
1961	93	111.4	403	25.8	0.38
1962	109	112.6	347	26.4	0.33
1963	120	137.2	298	30.4	0.27
1964	159	149.1	367	31.0	0.31
1965	159	215.0	857	43.3	0.70
1966	164	119.4	340	23.9	0.28
1967	219	194.9	486	41.5	0.42
1968	227	181.0	670	38.1	0.57
1969	272	271.0	1624	53.9	1.35
1970	336	271.4	1105	52.9	0.90
1971	241	340.3	3100	67.5	2.56
1972	217	247.3	1355	50.5	1.15
1973	297	442.6	2082	86.8	1.70
Average	125	137.0	614	33.9	0.60

and to be aware of the fact that management has some degree of flexibility to make good the losses which occur through stoppages. It must also be stressed that, even in the peak year of 1971, when one of the major car assembly firms experienced an eight week total stoppage, the great majority of the industry was at work for the great majority of the year.

Table 10.1 gives a good impression of the overall change in strike activity in the industry and of the way in which each of the three basic measures altered over time. Before trying to draw any conclusions as to the causation behind this pattern we followed our usual practice of disaggregating the series into small and major stoppages. Details of the small stoppages are shown in Table 10.2

Use of the five year average technique revealed that, between 1949–53 and 1969–73, the number of small strikes rose by 930 per cent, workers involved by 1440 per cent and days lost by 1290 per cent. The trend in all three basic measures was upwards throughout the period. For the number of stoppages the rate of increase was largest in the middle of the period and smallest at the beginning and end. The number of workers involved rose most rapidly in 1954–63 and more slowly in the later years. The rate of increase in days lost was rather more steady, although 1959–63 did emerge as the period of most rapid change.

Column 4 of Table 10.2, which shows the average size of stoppages as measured by workers involved, indicates that small stoppages rose rapidly in size in the mid-1950s but tended to decline thereafter. This may not be a completely accurate impression. Column 5, which shows the average duration of small stoppages as measured by days lost per worker involved, indicates that average duration declined up to 1959–63 and then rose. Given that our definition of small stoppages is simply 'those involving the loss of less than 5000 working days' a reduction in duration could result in stoppages which would previously have been excluded from the series being included so that average size would tend to rise. Statistical quirks of this kind probably do not account for the whole of the change, but the possibility of their existence suggests that caution should be exercised in the interpretation of an increase in average size when duration was falling and a decrease in average size when it was rising. It could even be argued that the fall in average duration was a statistical quirk resulting from an increase in the average size of small stoppages. On the whole it is probably true that small stoppages in motor vehicles increased in size and decreased in duration in the 1950s and that the reverse was true in the 1960s, but the numbers in Table 10.2 exaggerate the scale of the changes.

The final column in Table 10.2 shows workers involved as a percentage of employees in employment. Worker involvement rose from 2 per cent in 1949–53 to 23 per cent in 1969–73, with the most rapid period of change being 1954–63. This indicates that the frequency of small stoppages increased so rapidly that the chances of any individual worker being involved in such a stoppage in a particular year fell from one in fifty to one in four. The principal reason for this was not that such stoppages became

Table 10.2   *Small strikes in motor vehicles, 1949–73*

Year	No. of strikes	No. of workers involved (000s)	No. of working days lost (000s)	Average no. of workers involved per strike	Average no. of working days lost per worker involved	Workers involved as a percentage of employees in employment
1949	24	3.6	14.0	150	3.9	1.2
1950	26	10.8	24.5	415	2.3	3.6
1951	23	10.4	16.8	452	1.6	3.4
1952	24	6.7	20.6	279	3.1	2.2
1953	15	5.3	11.0	353	2.1	1.8
1954	15	4.3	12.1	287	2.8	1.4
1955	33	17.4	31.7	527	1.8	5.3
1956	21	23.8	25.3	1133	1.1	7.3
1957	39	26.5	44.8	679	1.7	8.6
1958	47	30.9	48.9	657	1.6	9.8
1959	71	74.1	85.9	1044	1.2	22.6
1960	98	60.0	95.5	612	1.6	13.8
1961	83	42.7	46.9	514	1.1	9.9
1962	95	44.2	45.7	465	1.0	10.3
1963	102	67.6	88.0	663	1.3	15.0
1964	141	80.4	103.8	570	1.3	16.7
1965	138	71.3	114.8	517	1.6	14.4
1966	155	75.6	142.4	488	1.9	15.1
1967	199	102.2	152.8	514	1.5	21.7
1968	193	74.9	147.6	388	2.0	15.8
1969	239	128.0	371.0	536	2.9	25.4
1970	291	125.6	251.6	432	2.0	24.4
1971	200	99.0	172.5	495	1.7	19.6
1972	171	92.0	163.3	538	1.8	18.8
1973	232	125.7	248.8	542	2.0	24.6
Average	107	56.1	99.2	524	1.8	13.9

Table 10.3   *Major strikes in motor vehicles, 1946–73*

Year	No. of strikes	No. of workers involved (000s)	No. of working days lost (000s)	Average no. of workers involved per strike	Average no. of working days lost per worker involved	Workers involved as a percentage of employees in employment
1946	5	19.8	228.0	3 960	11.5	n.a.
1947	1	0.7	13.5	700	19.3	n.a.
1948	2	35.3	488.0	17 650	13.8	12.6
1949	0	0.0	0.0	0	0	0
1950	4	3.9	87.5	975	22.4	1.3
1951	6	27.9	88.2	4 650	3.2	9.3
1952	4	24.8	350.4	6 200	14.1	8.2
1953	1	9.0	239.0	9 000	26.6	3.0
1954	1	11.2	22.9	11 200	2.0	3.6
1955	3	17.3	38.3	5 800	2.2	5.2
1956	6	46.8	267.7	9 360	5.7	14.3
1957	5	16.7	57.2	3 340	3.4	5.4
1958	8	23.6	79.1	2 950	3.4	7.5
1959	14	54.8	241.1	3 914	4.4	16.7
1960	26	123.0	417.5	4 731	3.4	28.2
1961	10	68.7	356.1	6 870	5.2	15.9
1962	14	68.4	301.3	4 886	4.4	16.0
1963	18	69.6	210.0	3 867	3.0	15.4
1964	18	68.7	263.2	3 817	3.8	14.3
1965	21	143.7	742.2	6 843	5.2	28.9
1966	9	43.8	197.6	4 867	4.5	8.8
1967	20	92.7	333.2	4 635	3.6	19.7
1968	34	106.1	522.4	3 121	4.9	22.4
1969	33	143.0	1253.0	4 333	8.8	28.4
1970	45	145.8	853.4	3 240	5.9	28.4
1971	41	241.3	2927.5	5 885	12.1	47.9
1972	46	155.3	1191.7	3 376	7.7	31.7
1973	65	316.9	1833.2	4 875	5.8	62.1
Average 1949–73	18	80.9	514.9	4 486	6.4	20.0

larger and involved more workers. It was simply that they became much more frequent.

Details of major stoppages are shown in Table 10.3.

Over the period 1949–73 major strikes accounted for 14 per cent of all stoppages, 59 per cent of workers involved and 84 per cent of days lost. On average major strikes involved nine times as many workers as small strikes and lasted four times as long, resulting in an average of thirty-one times as many days lost per stoppage!

Using five year averages for the period 1949–73 revealed that the number of stoppages rose by 820 per cent, workers involved by 1430 per cent and days lost by 950 per cent. Compared with the small stoppages series the number of major strikes and days lost rose less rapidly and workers involved at almost the same rate. In general the small and major strike activity series followed broadly similar patterns – both displayed their most rapid growth in 1959–63 – except that the major strikes series showed a secondary growth peak in 1969–73. In fact days lost through major stoppages grew more rapidly at this time than at any other.

The series shared other characteristics as well. The average size of major stoppages rose very rapidly in 1954–8 and then tended to decline while remaining well above the 1949–53 level. Average duration fell sharply in 1954–8 and rose in the final decade. The increase was particularly sharp in the last five years, although it did not match the 1949–53 peak. These changes were very similar to those which occurred in the small strikes series. In our discussion of this series we suggested that some of the changes observed might be explicable in terms of a statistical quirk associated with our definition of a small stoppage. It is difficult to reconcile such an explanation with the simultaneous occurrence of similar changes in the major strike series. Consequently, it appears that there was, in the mid-1950s, a marked shift towards larger, shorter stoppages and that, although the effects of this shift were eroded, stoppages at the end of the period were considerably larger and shorter than those at the beginning.

Workers involved in major stoppages rose from 4 to 40 per cent of employees in employment between 1949–53 and 1969–73. This change took place in two phases – in the 1950s and in the early 1970s – there was little consistent upward movement in the 1960s. Again the principal reason for this increase in worker involvement was the growth in the frequency of major stoppages, although the increase in the average size of such stoppages also played a substantial role.

As usual we also examined the characteristics of major stoppages. Between 1946 and 1973 there were 460 major stoppages in motor vehicles. In order to keep the analysis reasonably simple we examined the group as a whole but, recognising the possibility of inter-temporal shifts, we cross-checked for consistency by splitting the period into two parts – 1946–68, when there were 230 strikes, and 1969–73, when there were 230. Where there were substantial differences between the strike characteristics in the two sub-periods we draw attention to them in the text.

Our analysis identified twenty-four occupational groups as being involved in stoppages between 1946 and 1973. The dominant group was that of car and vehicle workers, who accounted for 73 per cent of the total. Their share rose from 67 per cent in 1946–68 to 79 per cent in 1969–73. Other groups with a significant share of strike activity included assemblers with 7.6 per cent, engineering workers with 3.7 per cent, press workers with 3.2 per cent and sheet metal workers and clerks with 1.9 per cent each. Comparison of the two sub-periods revealed that clerks increased their share from 0.4 to 3.5 per cent whilst the shares of the other groups either remained constant or tended to fall. It is difficult to draw any firm conclusions from this except to note that, apart from the clerks, the increase in strike activity in the final five years cannot be attributed to the more specialised groups.

The timing of strikes in the industry exhibited a marked seasonal pattern with a major peak in April and May and lesser peaks in August and October. There was also a pronounced trough in December with lesser troughs in March, July and November. Comparison of the sub-periods revealed that while the July and December troughs and the August peak became more marked the May peak was little changed and the other prominent features became less noticeable. Troughs appeared to be related to holiday periods and peaks to production requirements – particularly the pattern of new model launches in the autumn. The timing of the termination of stoppages was obviously influenced by the date at which they started, but it also seemed comparatively rare for strikes to straddle holiday periods.

As has been pointed out in earlier chapters we are reluctant to place much emphasis on the attributed causes of strikes – except in respect of the wage non-wage breakdown. However, for what it is worth, 35 per cent of major stoppages concerned wage increases, 20 per cent other wage disputes, 8 per cent issues of trade union principle, 7 per cent redundancy, 6 per cent discipline, 2 per cent demarcation and sympathetic action and 20 per cent other miscellaneous issues. In the final years of the period other wage disputes and disciplinary questions increased in relative frequency while redundancy and trade union principle issues declined. Stoppages over wage increases, sympathy, demarcation and miscellaneous matters showed little change in their share of activity.

Some of these features are more easily explained than others. In the first place the relative stability of strikes over wage increases, taken together with the small increase in other wage disputes, was rather surprising. It would not have seemed unreasonable to suppose that in the more recent period, with high rates of inflation and earnings' growth, strikes over wages would have become more predominant. On the other hand, the decline in the relative frequency of disputes over trade union principles probably reflects the growth in acceptance by management of trade union organisation, and, more importantly, trade union representation by shop-floor representatives. There had been a number of bitter struggles on this question early in the period.

The decline in strikes over redundancy may reflect an improvement in procedural arrangements compared with an earlier situation, where some managements refused to discuss such matters with the unions on the grounds that it was outside the scope of their existing bargaining rights. But it may also reflect the influence of the 1965 Redundancy Payments Act, or it could be a consequence of rising production in the final years of the period which reduced the likelihood of redundancies.

The increase in the frequency of stoppages over discipline might reflect a struggle over whether such matters are appropriate to collective bargaining, or, if they do come within the scope of collective bargaining, whether disciplinary decisions in particular cases were acceptable. In either instance the widespread changes in payment systems which have resulted in more management-enforced discipline are likely to have contributed to the volume of conflict.

Measured by the numbers of workers directly involved, major strikes tended to be fairly small: 30 per cent involved less than 250 workers; 46 per cent less than 500; 61 per cent less than 1000; 95 per cent less than 10 000. Comparison of the two sub-periods showed little change other than a tendency for there to be more very small strikes. Strikes directly involving less than 100 workers increased their share of the total from 9.1 to 15.6 per cent. But strikes involving less than 250 workers remained roughly constant at around 30 per cent of the total. If the measure of size is extended to all workers involved, so that it includes those indirectly involved, the effect is to increase the number in the middle size range. Some 34 per cent of strikes involved between 1000 and 10 000 workers directly, but if those indirectly involved are taken into account 75 per cent of strikes came into this category.

Measuring major strikes by the number of days lost revealed that 44 per cent resulted in the loss of less than 10 000 working days, 50 per cent less than 15 000, 68 per cent less than 20 000, 75 per cent less than 25 000 and 95 per cent less than 100 000. Comparison of the two sub-periods disclosed an increase in the relatively small and large strikes at the expense of the middle range. One consequence of this was that there were fourteen stoppages involving the loss of more than 100 000 days in 1969–73 compared to seven such stoppages in the preceding twenty-three years.

Most major strikes were quite short but a substantial number lasted much longer. Some 50 per cent of major stoppages were over within six days, 69 per cent within eleven days, 78 per cent within seventeen days and only 2 per cent lasted for sixty days or more. Analysis of the sub-periods showed that very large and very small strikes increased in relative frequency at the expense of middle range strikes. If smaller strikes were also shorter ones, this would explain part of the shift in the pattern of working days lost. But cross-tabulation of all workers involved by duration revealed an inverse association between the two variables – the smaller the strike the longer it lasted. The explanation of the shift in the pattern of days lost would appear to lie elsewhere.

The last characteristic of major stoppages which we examined was their regional distribution. This was heavily influenced by the regional distribution of employment which itself altered during the period with the opening in the early 1960s of new plants away from the traditional areas of the South East and the West Midlands. In order to take account of these changes we examined three sub-periods, 1946–62, 1963–8 and 1969–73 as well as data for the whole period. Overall the West Midlands dominated the major strikes league with 48 per cent of the total. Runners-up included the South East with 21 per cent, the North West with 12 per cent and Scotland with 7 per cent. Other regions accounted for 9 per cent and strikes affecting more than one region amounted to less than 3 per cent of the total. Analysis by sub-periods disclosed a consistent decline in the West Midlands share and a consistent rise in the North West's. Scotland's share rose in the mid-1960s and then fell. The South East's share fell and then rose. In terms of actual numbers of stoppages, comparison of the last two sub-periods disclosed that major strikes in Scotland rose by 13 per cent, in the West Midlands by 49 per cent, in the South East by 135 per cent and in the North West by 400 per cent. The variation in these rates requires explanation and is a matter to which we shall return.

This description of the industry's strike record may be summarised by drawing together the more obvious questions which it poses: Why did the number of stoppages rise 10-fold within twenty-five years? Why, when adjusted for the size of the industry, did the number of workers involved rise ninefold and days lost sevenfold? Why was 1959–63 the period of most rapid change in all three basic measures of strike activity? Why was there such a widespread tendency for stoppages to increase in average size and decrease in average duration in the 1950s? Why were these shifts in average size and duration eroded in later years? Why was there a further sharp rise in major strike activity in 1969–73? Why did the regional distribution of major stoppages change so markedly? These and other questions relating to year to year variations in strike activity should be borne in mind as we consider various explanations of the pattern of events in motor vehicles.

EXPLANATIONS FOR THE STRIKE PATTERN

Our starting point was with the work of Turner, Clack and Roberts (*Labour Relations in the Motor Industry*, 1967). Their study was, in fact, limited to major car assembly firms, rather than embracing the whole of the motor industry. They made extensive use of inter-firm and inter-plant comparisons and tested many theories of strike causation by attempting to isolate those factors which appeared to contribute to the relative freedom from strike activity of particular plants and firms. This methodology was of considerable interest to us, because it contrasted sharply with our own. We felt that if our own methodology were to produce similar results it could be taken as an indication that the level of aggregation at which we were working was not so high as to destroy the explanatory power of the analysis used in this case study and its predecessors above.

Turner *et al.* concluded that their evidence did not support most of the more popular theories of strike causation in the British car industry which they examined. Among these were technology, technological change, geographical isolation of plants, working conditions, 'tensions of the track' and agitators. Factors which were held to be important were equally varied. To begin with, irregularity of employment, both cyclical and seasonal, resulting from fluctuations in production requirements, was held to be an important contributory factor. Attention was also drawn to the tendency for working days lost to rise in recessions and it was suggested that strikes were used as a means of reducing production to its desired level without widespread lay-offs. That much of the industry's labour was supplied by adult recruitment from other industries was seen as a further contributory factor. The combination of high average earnings and marked anomalies between groups within the industry, plus considerable instability of earnings because of variations in hours and employment, was said to add substantially to the overall level of conflict.

But to some extent these influences were all viewed as indirect or background factors. A more direct determinant was held to be a change in worker expectations. These concerned two separate but related issues. One was an expectation of 'fair wages' – i.e. that earnings from a particular job should be 'fair' relative to other earnings. Of course Turner *et al.* accepted that such expectations were not exceptional. After all, comparisons of 'fair' wages are a major determinant of earnings in the public sector. But in motor vehicles, according to Turner *et al.*, expectations were under continual pressure as a result of the operation of the piecework system in association with frequent changes in product and work organisation. This led to frequent changes in the relative pay levels of different groups. In the absence of any agreed overall structure such changes were bound to generate frequent sectional claims, many of which ended in strike action.

The other expectation concerned 'job rights'. This did not simply consist of an expectation of continuing employment with a particular firm, although that was important. It also took the more demanding form of an expectation of the continuation of a particular job in a particular location. Such expectations were especially important at the workplace because that was where the effective decisions were taken. They were likely to be reflected in the development of workplace representation, which was a further source of conflict.

But workplace conflict was also related to another major factor of a more novel kind – 'obsolescence in institutions'. In an argument subsequently broadened and made familiar through the Donovan Report, the failure of the formal institutions of collective bargaining to adapt themselves to issues which had become important to the workforce was said to be a major factor leading to an increase in strike activity. In effect this was a criticism of the practices and procedures adopted by employers, unions and their associations in both vehicles and engineering generally – i.e. in companies and plants covered by the Engineering Employers'

Federation (EEF) and the Confederation of Shipbuilding and Engineering Unions. Their failure was said to be reflected in the absence of a large proportion of the 'new' issues processed through the Federation's formal conciliation procedure, and by the lack of quick or final settlements. Institutional obsolescence was also reflected in the relative independence of much shop steward activity from the formal decision-making processes of the unions and in the EEF's continuing formal refusal to countenance bargaining except on matters relating to wages and hours. The effects of this failure were said to be particularly marked in motor vehicles, because of the rapid pace of change in the industry and the growth of employment had contributed to inter-union tensions over recruitment of members.

The final set of factors picked out by the analysis were certain acts and omissions of particular firms. It was argued that in an industry where employment was as concentrated by firm and establishment as it was for motor vehicles, events of this kind could have an effect on the overall situation. Such acts included Standard's 1949 agreement and Ford's response to the initial pressure for unionisation and to later claims for negotiations over workload and effort. Outstanding omissions included over-reliance on membership of the EEF as a means of handling labour relations and a lack of awareness of the likely impact of mergers on those relations. Finally, the attempt by the authors to identify those features of management action which contributed to relative industrial peace in two car firms produced little in common between the two. That which was common was also shared by at least one strike-prone firm.

It should be evident that certain strands of this wide-ranging analysis have shown up in our earlier case studies – in particular the difficulties which can arise over uncertainty of employment and earnings, the importance of workers' attitudes and expectations and the significance of management's role in influencing not only the scope and structure of collective bargaining but also the climate in which it is conducted. In this sense at least our work lends general support to the direction taken by Turner *et al.*'s conclusions in respect of motor vehicles.

We begin our own analysis of the industry by looking at fluctuations in employment and hours of work. We consider the causes of these changes and their relationship to the strike pattern. We go on to review the influence of these and other factors on earnings in the industry. We consider how earnings have varied over the years and how they compare with those in other industries. We then turn to the institutional structure of the industry and the likely effect of changes. Finally, we look at some of the specific events in recent years and consider their implications for the strike pattern.

FLUCTUATIONS IN EMPLOYMENT AND HOURS OF WORK

Some information on the level of employment, the way in which it changed and the rate of unemployment in the industry is set out in Table 10.4. All the series relate to Great Britain only because UK data was not available for some of the series. The difference is only slight because there was little motor industry employment in Northern Ireland, but the strike series are for the UK.

Table 10.4   *Employment fluctuations in motor vehicles, 1949–73*

Year	Total of employees in employment in GB (000s)	Average annual rate of labour engagements per 100 employees	Average annual rate of labour losses and discharges per 100 employees	Average annual net rate of labour turnover per 100 employees	Wholly unemployed per 100 employees in June each year
1949	295.2	35.4	31.5	3.9	0.9
1950	298.8	35.1	30.2	4.9	0.8
1951	301.1	30.6	29.9	0.7	0.4
1952	303.3	29.3	31.5	−2.2	0.8
1953	294.6	33.8	27.0	6.8	0.8
1954	310.7	38.0	28.3	9.7	0.4
1955	329.3	37.7	29.9	7.8	0.3
1956	319.5	20.8	29.6	−8.8	0.8
1957	309.0	32.8	24.7	8.1	0.7
1958	314.5	20.8	20.8	0.0	0.9
1959	382.1	32.2	18.5	13.7	0.6
1960	434.8	28.3	25.0	3.3	0.3
1961	412.7	20.2	15.9	4.3	0.4
1962	426.4	23.1	19.2	3.9	0.6
1963	449.7	24.4	17.9	6.5	0.7
1964	480.8	23.1	19.8	3.3	0.4
1965	495.8	26.3	23.1	3.2	0.4
1966	499.8	21.8	32.2	−10.4	0.4
1967	469.5	19.8	23.7	−3.9	1.4
1968	473.8	23.7	20.8	2.9	1.3
1969	501.6	26.7	22.8	3.9	1.1
1970	512.4	23.4	23.4	0.0	1.3
1971	501.9	13.0	20.8	−7.8	2.1
1972	487.7	15.0	19.5	−4.5	2.4
1973	508.1	20.8	18.9	1.9	1.2

A number of points are immediately obvious from Table 10.4. Between 1953 and 1966 employment in the industry rose by 72 per cent, although, to some extent, this is an over-estimate because the 1958 SIC revision added 55 000 workers (a quarter of the total increase) to the official series. Since 1966 there has been little consistent tendency for employment in the industry to increase. The average annual rate of labour engagements ('hire rate') has tended to fall throughout the period. The average annual rate of labour discharges and other losses ('quit rate') fell very sharply at the beginning of the period, rose again in the mid-1960s and then declined again. The combined impact of these changes in labour turnover rates is shown in the average annual net rate of labour turnover. In the first fifteen years the overall tendency was for the labour force to increase, although there were reductions in the recessions of 1952 and 1956. In the last ten years the upward tendency was much less marked and there were reductions in four of the years.

If Turner, Clack and Roberts were correct in their argument that irregularity of employment was an important background influence on the increase of strike activity up to 1965, it seems likely that its effects have been much greater since then. The changing circumstances of more recent years are also reflected in the final column of Table 10.4. This shows the number of wholly unemployed in June each year who were previously employed in the motor industry in relation to total employees in the industry. Throughout the period this rate has been markedly lower than the national unemployment rate, which may be taken to indicate that those leaving employment in motor vehicles found it easier to obtain alternative employment than those from other industries. In relation to the numbers leaving the industry it would seem that employment prospects worsened markedly in recent years, although ex-motor vehicle workers continued to be better placed than ex-miners or ex-dockers. This is not surprising in view of the geographical location of the industry and the more transferable skills of its workforce. Taking the industry's unemployment rate together with the net rate of labour turnover suggests that if loss of employment were resisted it was because its expectations over job rights and earnings were violated rather than because of fears over the lack of alternative employment.

There is one further aspect of employment fluctuations in motor vehicles which we felt was worth some consideration – the long term decline in the hire and quit rates and the differences between the two series. The two rates are, of course, closely related in the sense that, if the labour force is to remain at a constant level, the hire rate must equal the quit rate. They are also related because of the tendency for workers to quit most readily soon after taking up employment. Other factors – alternative employment prospects, age of labour force, etc. – also affect the rates of labour turnover. The curiosity on our part arises because between 1954 and 1963 the quit rate tended to fall faster than the hire rate. This tendency was particularly marked in 1959–63, which also marked an upsurge in strike activity. Was this association purely coincidental, or was there some causal connection between the increase in strike activity and the decrease in the quit rate?

We noted in the coal mining study that occupational groups with low strike records tended to have higher than average turnover and absentee rates, whilst groups with low turnover and absentee rates were more dispute prone. In evidence to the Donovan Commission it was noted that although strike activity in the Ford plant at Dagenham had fallen sharply after the events of 1962 the labour turnover rate had trebled. In a National Economic Development Office (NEDO) report on the motor industry (NEDO, 1973) it was reported that

> The labour stability/turnover picture in the UK motor manufacturing industry is in general significantly better than in other countries. It is reported that turnover in a typical Swedish car manufacturing plant is of the order of 75%; the Japanese motor industry is experiencing growing problems with labour turnover which is currently around 20% as against virtually nothing five years ago. Absenteeism in the Turin area is running at over 14% (well above any comparable UK area) and West German motor factories have reported up to 20% absenteeism rates.

The same report stated that time lost through absenteeism in the UK motor industry was of the order of 5 per cent of total working time. Thus the UK industry's good record in relation to labour turnover and absenteeism relative to other countries was in marked contrast to its relative position in respect of strike activity. These fragments of evidence cannot be regarded as in any sense conclusive, but they certainly do not contradict the assertion that an association of falling quit rates and increasing strike activity was not coincidental. Unfortunately it was not possible, on the available evidence, to ascertain the direction of any causal link between the two variables. But the association does support the suggestion made by Scott and his colleagues in relation to the mining industry (Scott *et al.*, 1963). This was that there is often a trade-off between what they termed 'informal' and 'formal' types of conflict – i.e. that in situations where workers are discontented or 'in conflict' with management norms and/or policies they may respond either collectively (through the use of dispute procedures, or the employment of sanctions) or individually (via an increase in absenteeism or quit rates).

It will be remembered that one conclusion which may be drawn from the 'alternative conflict' theory is that the weakening or even the destruction of the worker's collective organisation is not likely to lead to a reduction in overall levels of conflict – it will merely channel it into more 'individualistic' forms.

This analysis also raises a number of interesting questions as to whether it is in the interests of the various parties to the employment relationship (e.g. workers, management, government and public) to have conflict expressed in an overt or a covert form. It seems to us that the quality of the public debate over 'Britain's strike problem' could only be improved by a wider recognition of the possible existence of such a trade-off. We do not wish to labour the point, particularly as the evidence is far from conclusive, but it does serve to draw attention to the manifestations of all forms of industrial unrest.

The use of total employment series and related measures tends to

Table 10.5   *Motor vehicle employment (000s) by region, 1959–73 (figures in parentheses show percentage of share of Great Britain total)*

Year	South East and East Anglia	South West	East Midlands, West Midlands, Yorkshire and Humberside	North West	Northern	Scotland	Wales
1959	150.6	9.3	176.9	29.4	2.1	7.3	6.4
	(39.4)	(2.4)	(46.3)	(7.7)	(0.5)	(1.9)	(1.7)
1960	174.8	10.0	199.3	33.1	2.7	6.1	8.9
	(40.2)	(2.3)	(45.8)	(7.6)	(0.6)	(1.4)	(2.0)
1961	167.1	9.7	184.5	34.5	2.6	6.8	7.5
	(40.5)	(2.4)	(44.7)	(8.4)	(0.6)	(1.6)	(1.8)
1962	171.9	10.4	188.5	36.0	2.4	8.8	8.4
	(40.3)	(2.4)	(44.2)	(8.4)	(0.6)	(2.1)	(2.0)
1963	176.9	11.4	190.2	41.1	2.9	17.3	9.9
	(39.3)	(2.5)	(42.3)	(9.1)	(0.6)	(3.8)	(2.2)
1964	178.8	11.5	203.4	51.9	3.3	20.5	11.5
	(37.2)	(2.4)	(42.3)	(10.8)	(0.7)	(4.3)	(2.4)
1965	190.0	11.5	203.7	53.7	3.9	20.5	12.5
	(38.3)	(2.3)	(41.1)	(10.8)	(0.8)	(4.1)	(2.5)
1966	188.4	14.1	199.9	56.7	5.0	21.4	14.3
	(37.7)	(2.8)	(40.0)	(11.3)	(1.0)	(4.3)	(2.9)
1967	168.8	12.5	189.8	61.1	5.2	18.8	13.3
	(36.0)	(2.7)	(40.4)	(13.0)	(1.1)	(4.0)	(2.8)
1968	165.5	13.7	188.5	68.3	5.5	18.0	14.2
	(34.9)	(2.9)	(39.8)	(14.4)	(1.2)	(3.8)	(3.0)
1969	177.2	14.3	198.0	69.4	6.3	20.0	16.4
	(35.3)	(2.9)	(39.5)	(13.8)	(1.3)	(4.0)	(3.3)
1970	173.6	14.8	198.0	76.1	8.9	22.5	18.5
	(33.9)	(2.9)	(38.6)	(14.9)	(1.7)	(4.4)	(3.6)
1971	158.4	13.9	203.9	76.1	8.7	21.2	19.6
	(31.6)	(2.8)	(40.6)	(15.2)	(1.7)	(4.2)	(3.9)
1972	154.9	13.2	196.2	74.1	9.5	19.9	19.9
	(31.8)	(2.7)	(40.2)	(15.2)	(1.9)	(4.1)	(4.1)
1973	160.4	14.6	202.6	75.5	10.4	21.7	22.9
	(31.2)	(2.9)	(39.9)	(14.9)	(2.0)	(4.3)	(4.5)

understate the degree of employment fluctuation in particular plants and firms because, to some extent, the changes are self-cancelling; e.g. if one firm grew at the expense of another it might result in substantial employment changes which would not be reflected in the total employment series. Information on employment in particular plants or firms was not available, but details of the distribution of employment by region were and we thought those worth consideration. These are shown in Table 10.5.

The total number employed in motor vehicle manufacture in Great Britain rose by 33 per cent between 1959 and 1973. The distribution of this increase between regions was very varied. In general those regions with the largest number of motor vehicle employees at the beginning of the period had the smallest increase, whilst those with the smallest number exhibited the biggest rise. It can be seen that the South East and East Anglia fell from 39.4 per cent of the total in 1959 to 31.2 per cent in 1973 and the Midlands, Yorkshire and Humberside from 46.3 to 39.9 per cent. All other regions gained: the changes were most noticeable in the North West, Wales and Scotland. One effect of this dispersion of employment was that regions in which employment was concentrated suffered more severely from recessions than would be supposed from the total series. Had employment not been dispersed it seems likely that the overall upward trend in the demand for labour would have smoothed over many localised difficulties. In other words the dispersion of employment worsened the irregularity of employment in those areas where production had previously been concentrated.

Another facet of employment within the industry was its distribution by establishment size. If there were changes in the distribution of total employment between establishments of varying size, while total employment remained constant, it would indicate further changes in individual employment patterns. Table 10.6 shows the percentage shares of total employment accounted for by establishments of varying size. The information was culled from the censuses of production data for the years 1951, 1954, 1968 and 1972. Unfortunately the data for 1958 and 1963 was not in a comparable form.

Table 10.6   *Distribution of motor vehicle employment by establishment size, 1951–72*

Average no. employed per establishment	Percentage of total by establishment size			
	1951	*1954*	*1968*	*1972*
11–99	7.4	5.8	5.5	5.3
100–399	12.9	11.8	10.8	8.1
400–999	13.5	12.9	13.0	10.2
1000–1999	17.7	14.7	14.2	12.7
2000–4999	21.0	26.5	19.7	12.4
5000 and over	27.5	28.3	38.7	51.3
Total of employees (000s)	361.2	376.1	448.3	476.3

Table 10.6 shows that the employment share of the two smallest categories has fallen consistently through the period and that the shares of the five smallest categories were subject to a long-run irregular downward trend. In contrast the largest category of establishments almost doubled their share of the total. These changes were a result of employment growing faster in the largest establishments as well as a shift in the distribution of employment between plants. The development was interesting for two reasons: first, because it indicated a further irregularity of employment; secondly, because the concentration of employment in larger establishments may itself have contributed to the increase in strike activity. The prior arguments on this latter point are fairly evenly balanced but some recent evidence suggests that large establishments are disproportionately more likely to experience strike activity (Prais, 1978).

The other source of employment fluctuations concerns the number of hours of work. Both overtime and short-time can have significant effects on earnings and both are substitutes for adjustments in the number of jobs. Table 10.7 shows series for the incidence and extent of overtime and short-time working per week.

Table 10.7 illustrates the importance of variations in working hours as well as variations in employment levels as a means of adjusting productive capacity. The number of operatives engaged on overtime work was subject to much more variation than was the average number of hours per worker so engaged – the latter measure varied between 5.9 and 8.4 hours per week, whilst the proportion of the labour force engaged in overtime working varied between 18.4 and 50.2 per cent. The same pattern appeared in the series for short-time working, although the much smaller numbers involved makes drawing firm conclusions somewhat hazardous. This means that variations in the total number of hours worked were achieved largely through varying the actual number of workers on overtime or short-time, rather than through varying the number of hours across the board.

One consequence of this was that the earnings of those so affected were subject to considerable variation, as the cash effect of working or not working between six and eight hours overtime was substantial. In general the industry appears to have been reluctant to use short-time working as a means of scaling down production. With the exceptions of 1956 and 1958 the percentage of operatives on short-time has never exceeded 5 per cent. It would appear that the industry preferred to respond to a fall in production requirements by cutting the number of workers on overtime and by reducing the size of the labour force than by short-time working. The last column of Table 10.7 shows the average number of hours worked per male manual employee in October of each year. From this we may note the effect of reductions in the standard working week and that, despite the tendency for the incidence of overtime working to increase, the overall effect has been that the average number of hours worked per week has fallen.

Our analysis has concentrated on levels of employment, the manner and

Table 10.7 *Overtime and short-time working in motor vehicles, 1951–71*

Year	Operatives working overtime			Operatives working short-time			Average no. of hours per male manual in industry
	No. of operatives (00s)	Percentage of all operatives	Average no. of overtime hours worked	No. of operatives (000s)	Percentage of all operatives	Aver no. of hours lost	
1951	48.0	21.5	7.5	7.1	3.2	6.2	46.0
1952	42.0	18.4	8.0	5.5	2.4	6.2	45.3
1953	61.9	28.3	6.9	0.8	0.4	8.6	46.0
1954	75.9	33.4	7.3	0.2	0.1	7.0	46.9
1955	75.4	29.9	7.1	0.2	0.1	10.0	46.9
1956	65.7	26.6	7.0	14.6	5.9	8.8	44.3
1957	65.7	30.2	6.5	5.6	2.6	6.0	46.1
1958	54.0	23.0	7.7	25.9	11.0	20.5	44.0
1959	110.5	45.3	6.8	2.1	0.9	7.1	47.2
1960	150.8	44.5	5.9	4.6	1.4	10.2	43.4
1961	144.6	42.9	6.7	13.1	3.9	14.9	43.8
1962	137.3	41.4	6.7	8.2	2.5	7.5	43.6
1963	147.3	41.5	7.3	4.7	1.3	7.6	45.3
1964	173.7	46.7	7.7	12.1	3.2	8.6	44.3
1965	181.8	47.1	8.4	6.8	1.8	12.8	43.1
1966	156.1	40.1	7.4	3.7	1.0	8.1	39.7
1967	131.5	38.8	6.7	14.2	4.2	8.5	43.1
1968	182.4	50.2	6.9	9.1	2.5	9.2	43.8
1969	176.6	45.8	7.5	9.9	2.6	22.9	43.5
1970	168.2	43.8	7.2	3.6	0.9	10.0	42.1
1971	139.9	36.5	6.7	11.5	3.0	8.9	41.2
1972	132.5	34.8	7.2	3.5	0.9	8.4	42.3
1973	154.2	38.8	6.9	4.8	1.2	11.1	43.0

*Relates to survey week nearest the mid-year; in 1951–60 this fell in May and in June thereafter.

magnitude of changes in those levels, the distribution of employment by region and establishment size and on the incidence and extent of variations in working hours. This evidence supported the view of Turner *et al.* that there was substantial irregularity of employment in the industry and that this irregularity, besides being an important background influence on the level of strike activity through promoting – in the Devlin phrase – 'casual attitudes on both sides of the industry' was also likely to be a source of conflict in its own right because it violated workers' expectations about 'job rights'. Such conflict would have been made more acute by the tendency for major adjustments in productive capacity to take place through variations in the number of employees and the availability of overtime working to certain groups. As a result adjustment costs were concentrated on relatively small sections of the labour force.

These changes had implications for earnings and we examined these next. Details are shown in Table 10.8.

It can be seen that average gross weekly earnings (AGWE) of male manual workers in motor vehicles rose by slightly less than 440 per cent between 1949 and 1973. (Over the same period AGWE of male manuals in all industries and services rose by 475 per cent.) This implied an average annual increase of 6.1 per cent but actual movements varied wildly around this rate. In four out of the twenty-five years earnings actually fell; in four years the increase was less than 5 per cent; in nine years it was in double figures. Although the rate of increase quickened in later years it is worth noting that three of the double figure years occurred prior to 1960. Given the degree of irregularity observable in the average earnings series, it follows that some workers experienced even greater changes in their individual earnings.

In Chapter 7 we discussed the argument that workers were primarily concerned with real disposable earnings rather than gross earnings. We noted that there was little evidence to support this proposition at the aggregate level, but concluded that it might be better examined at the industry level. Column 3 of Table 10.8 shows the rate of change of real disposable earnings for a 'typical' family man (married, two children under eleven, claiming just the standard personal allowances). Between 1949 and 1973 his real disposable earnings rose by 47 per cent – in eleven of these twenty-five years the rate of change was negative. It is difficult to imagine that such experiences would have generated very firmly held expectations of real increases. Consequently it is also difficult to believe that the non-fulfilment of such expectations was a major contributory factor in the increase in strike activity. This scepticism was supported by a comparison of the three major measures of strike activity with the annual average rate of change of real disposable earnings, which failed to reveal any consistent relationship. On the other hand, it is not implausible to suppose that the frequent falls in living standards were contributory factors in the worsening relationships within the industry.

The last two columns of Table 10.8 are relativity measures – showing gross and disposable earnings in motor vehicles in relation to those of all

Table 10.8 *Average weekly earnings of male manuals in motor vehicles, 1949–73*

Year	AGWE in October £	Annual percentage change in AGWE	Annual percentage change in real NDE	AGWE in motor vehicles as a percentage of AGWE in all industries	NDE in motor vehicles as a percentage of NDE in all industries
1949	8.76	4.0	-0.5	123	119
1950	9.41	7.4	4.2	125	120
1951	10.00	6.3	-5.4	120	117
1952	10.55	5.5	0.6	118	116
1953	11.38	7.9	5.9	120	118
1954	12.65	11.2	6.3	124	120
1955	13.90	9.9	4.3	121	121
1956	13.61	-2.1	-5.6	114	112
1957	15.78	15.9	8.7	125	121
1958	15.76	-0.1	-3.0	123	119
1959	18.01	14.3	12.2	133	127
1960	17.65	-1.6	-3.3	121	118
1961	18.36	4.0	-1.7	120	116
1962	19.10	4.0	0.5	120	117
1963	21.03	10.1	7.4	126	121
1964	21.75	3.4	-1.5	120	116
1965	23.01	5.8	-1.0	117	114
1966	21.70	-5.7	-8.5	107	106
1967	25.03	15.3	9.7	117	113
1968	27.32	9.1	0.7	119	115
1969	29.58	8.3	-0.4	119	114
1970	33.30	12.6	3.7	119	115
1971	36.68	10.2	1.5	119	114
1972	43.38	18.3	9.5	121	116
1973	47.18	8.8	-2.2	115	112

AGWE, average gross weekly earnings; NDE, net disposable earnings.

industries and services. It is unlikely that such information was much used within motor vehicles – because of the generally fragmented bargaining structure. But we thought it was worth including because of the external attention which was often paid to motor vehicles earnings. The gross earnings relativity reveals that in 1949–59 earnings in motor vehicles were, on average, 21 per cent higher than those elsewhere. In 1959–63 this advantage increased to 24 per cent and fell to 16 per cent in 1964–8 before returning to 19 per cent in the final years of the period. The fall in 1964–8 is heavily influenced by the inclusion of the October 1966 figure when overtime earnings were adversely affected by the onset of recession. If 1966 is excluded the relativity was 18 per cent, which indicates a sizeable reduction. The relativity measured by disposable earnings displayed smaller fluctuations although the overall pattern was similar to that of gross earnings. Between 1949–53 and 1959–63 the relative advantage increased from 18 to 20 per cent, fell in 1964–8 to 13 per cent (15 per cent if 1966 is excluded) and averaged 14 per cent in 1969–73. The effect of taxation and national insurance contributions was to reduce motor vehicles' relative advantage – especially in the later years. Thus there is no evidence to support the view that the higher level of strike activity in motor vehicles raised the relative wages of that industry; if anything the reverse would appear to be the case, although there was not necessarily any causal connection.

Turner *et al.* were not so much concerned with fluctuations in earnings, or with external relativities, as with the difficulties which arose within the industry as a result of comparisons of earnings and workloads. Such effects are difficult to discern in an industry-level study but we did examine the distribution of earnings within the industry and some of the more important components in the make-up of pay. The distribution of gross weekly earnings of male manual workers showed some variation in the period 1960–73, but the changes were greater for those above the median. There was no evidence of any consistent tendency for differentials to widen or contract. The short-term fluctuations which occurred are consistent with the view that, in the absence of any general agreement about appropriate differentials, there were continuous shifting pressures which had immediate, but not lasting effects. Comparison of the earnings distribution in motor vehicles with those of other industries indicate that the upper end of the distribution was more compressed while the lower end was not very different.

Information on the make-up of pay does not appear to have been made available prior to 1968. Information for 1968, 1970 and 1973 is shown in Table 10.9.

The importance of overtime pay and shift premia varied little; the dramatic change was in PBR payments. Between 1970 and 1973 PBR payments fell from 24 to 12 per cent of total pay. Given that a large section of the workforce was not on PBR prior to 1970, this implies a very substantial change in the composition of pay for some groups of workers. This change coincides with the efforts of two major car assemblers to change their payments systems away from piecework. Unfortunately it was not possible to estimate how many workers were affected by this change as the form in which the information was collected was altered between 1970 and 1973.

Table 10.9   *Make-up of average gross weekly earnings of male manuals in motor vehicles, 1968, 1970 and 1973*

	Overtime pay	Shift, etc., payments	PBR, etc., payments	All other pay
As a percentage of total pay				
1968	13.1	5.2	23.5	58.2
1970	11.0	6.0	24.0	59.0
1973	11.4	5.5	12.1	71.0
Percentage of employees in receipt				
1968	62.7	39.8	n.a.	n.a.
1970	59.5	38.0	n.a.	n.a.
1973	54.9	31.7	39.1	n.a.

The management-inspired payment system changes of this period arose, in part at least, from the belief that piecework payment systems were more dispute prone than other payment systems. Consequently it was hoped that there would be a reduction in strike activity. Alternatively, it might be argued that it was not piecework systems *per se* but variations in products and production techniques which created bargaining opportunities. In these circumstances the suppression of pay bargaining – as a result of changes in the payment system – might be met by an increase in effort and wage structure bargaining, particularly by well-established shop steward organisations. In addition the process of change itself was likely to generate conflict. On balance there was little evidence up to 1973 that the payment system changes had improved the industry's strike record, although later years would need to be taken into consideration before a final judgement could be reached.

PRODUCT MARKET INFLUENCES – OUTPUT, DEMAND AND COMPETITION

Up to this point our analysis has concentrated on such factors as the changes in employment, hours of work and earnings and their influence on employee attitudes. In this section we examine likely causes of those changes because they reflect some of the pressures on management and some of the problems with which the industry was confronted. Information on production levels, national and international demand for cars, and overseas competition is set out in Table 10.10.

Table 10.10   *Production of and demand for UK motor vehicles, 1949–73*

Year	Car production (000s)	Commercial vehicle production (000s)	New car registrations in UK (000s)	UK share of car exports by leading producer countries* (%)	Imported cars as a percentage of new car registrations in UK†
1949	412	216	155	49.4	1.3
1950	523	261	134	55.4	0.7
1951	476	258	138	44.0	2.9
1952	448	242	191	44.1	1.0
1953	595	240	301	41.3	0.7
1954	769	269	394	39.5	1.3
1955	898	340	511	33.1	2.2
1956	708	297	407	28.3	1.7
1957	861	288	433	29.3	2.1
1958	1052	313	566	27.4	1.9
1959	1190	370	657	26.1	4.1
1960	1353	458	820	25.2	7.0
1961	1004	460	756	18.5	3.0
1962	1249	425	800	21.9	3.6
1963	1608	404	1031	21.3	4.7
1964	1868	465	1216	21.7	5.4
1965	1722	455	1149	19.9	4.9
1966	1604	439	1091	17.0	6.1
1967	1552	385	1143	15.6	8.1
1968	1816	409	1144	15.7	8.9
1969	1717	466	1013	16.0	10.1
1970	1641	457	1127	12.9	13.8
1971	1742	456	1335	11.5	21.0
1972	1921	408	1702	9.9	26.4
1973	1747	417	1688	9.1	29.9

Source: Society of Motor Manufacturers and Traders.
* Includes UK, France, West Germany, Italy, Sweden, Japan, USA and Canada, but excludes intra-continental trade between USA and Canada.
† This is not the same as imported cars' share of UK sales because, particularly in recent years, imported cars have been stockpiled prior to sales drives.

Between 1949 and 1964 car production in the UK rose by 350 per cent. Since 1964 car production fluctuated around a level of 1.7 million cars a year without displaying any consistent trend. Commercial vehicle production followed a somewhat similar pattern with 110 per cent increase in production between 1949 and 1961 and no substantial upward movement thereafter. But cars and commercial vehicles are not the only products of the motor vehicles industry. The manufacture of parts and components is also important, not only for inclusion in UK vehicle assembly but also for direct sale to non-UK manufacturers and as replacements. In 1974 it was estimated that direct sales of parts and accessories accounted for nearly a third of the industry's sales. Unfortunately we were unable to obtain time series information of the value of these products in constant prices so we were unable to make comparisons with the production of cars and commercial vehicles. One other point which should be noted is that although the number of units produced showed no consistent upward trend in the later years, this does not necessarily imply that the real value of production was unchanged. If the value of the individual unit or the composition of the total altered the real value of the level of production may have been affected.

Changes in production levels of motor vehicles in the UK can, for the most part, be explained in terms of changes in demand and the degree of competition from overseas producers. Demand for UK motor vehicles may be divided into domestic and overseas markets. Domestic demand is reflected by the series for new car registrations. Between 1949 and 1964 domestic demand for new cars rose by almost 700 per cent. In 1964–70 it fluctuated around a level of 1.1 million cars per year. After 1970 it rose sharply to 1.7 million in 1972–3. In the 1949–64 period domestic demand was very largely met from domestic sources. Production rose only half as rapidly as demand, but a switch from exports to home sales enabled domestic producers to maintain their market share. After 1970 a considerable part of the increased demand was met through imports. In summary the UK car industry has been faced, throughout the post-war period, by rising demand in its domestic and overseas markets, but has been unable to maintain its share of either. The reasons for this failure are no doubt complex, but in large measure they must reflect a failure by the industry to maintain its competitive position.

Until 1964 the failure to maintain competitiveness was largely disguised by the growth of domestic demand which permitted production levels to rise. After 1964 domestic demand was static and motor vehicles ceased to be a growth industry. There was a brief resurgence of exports following the 1967 devaluation, but it had petered out by 1970. One curious feature of this experience was that the lack of competitiveness was not widely recognised until much later on. On our analysis 1965 was the year in which the failure became manifest but, at the time, the lack of growth in production was explained away by reference to government restriction of domestic demand and the difficulties of exporting when saddled with an over-valued currency. This response was in sharp contrast to that of coal mining where, from 1959 onwards, the fall in demand for coal was seen to be the result of the industry's uncompetitiveness, compared with other energy sources. In our analysis of coal mining, we argued that the perception of the lack of competitiveness significantly affected the attitudes and actions of all parties as measures were taken to improve the industry's position. In motor vehicles the problem went unrecognised and responsibility for the industry's difficulties was attributed to external economic forces.

This situation was of interest for two reasons. First, it focused attention on the possibility that responses to problems might be different if the problems were seen as continuing rather than merely temporary. Secondly, it seemed likely that the potential for conflict among the parties would be greater in situations where a common perception of the nature of and solutions to difficulties was absent. Unilateral responses to common problems are more likely to cause conflicts of interest than multilateral responses. In specific terms Turner *et al.* suggested that when falls in demand in the motor industry have necessitated cut-backs in production management allowed stoppages to drag on, or become more extensive than would normally have been the case in periods of relative boom. In this way production was reduced without management having to indulge in such conflict-ridden activities as announcements of redundancies or short-time working. Such developments had advantages for negotiators on both sides – according to Turner *et al.* not the least of which was that they did not require any explicit acknowledgement.

But measures of this sort, of course, are likely to be effective when the required production cutbacks are only temporary. Post-1964 cyclical movements continued to be apparent – providing scope for such temporary palliatives – while obscuring the long-term difficulties with which the industry was faced. In other words, the industry's tacit arrangement covered situations where there was a temporary fall in demand due to cyclical factors, but was inappropriate for conditions where the loss of demand was due to overseas competition. Ironically, one explanation of the failure to recognise the industry's competitive problems may well have been the very success of the temporary measures to reduce production. In coal mining the post-1956 loss of demand was accompanied by a rapid rise in stocks which helped to concentrate attention on the industry's problems. In motor vehicles the manufacturers were under greater pressure not to stockpile because of the physical and marketable perishability of their products, but their very success in avoiding undue stocks distracted attention from the real problems.

Despite these temporary successes the underlying situation remained unsatisfactory. Production failed to resume its strong upward path. Export market shares continued to fall and imports began to make serious inroads on the domestic market. These failures were reflected in the financial difficulties which beset some of the major firms. Management's recognition that these were not merely temporary difficulties was reflected in a twofold response. First, there was a series of mergers and take-overs. In

1965 the British Motor Corporation bought out Pressed Steel Fisher, the major independent body-supplier in the industry. In 1966 BMC took over Jaguar. In the same year Leyland, which had entered the volume car market in 1961 through its acquisition of Standard–Triumph, absorbed Rover and Chrysler took a controlling interest in Rootes. In 1968 Leyland merged with BMC to form British Leyland. In the space of three years the number of major independent car firms had been halved. Of the four survivors three were American owned. In part this process reflects the difficulties in which some of the firms found themselves when the demand for UK produced cars ceased to expand. But it also reflects a belief that only large firms could survive in the international car markets, because they alone could exploit economies of scale, carry a sufficient range of products to meet dealer demands and have access to the capital sums necessary to remain competitive.

It is impossible, even in hindsight, to judge whether those responsible for these mergers and take-overs saw them primarily as a means of reducing competition, or as a way of coming to terms with the industry's fundamental problems. What is certain is that the mergers and take-overs in themselves did nothing to improve the industry's prospects – all they did was to create certain opportunities. What is also true is that there were costs attached to both the creation and the seizure of those opportunities. The cost of the creation lay in the uncertainty which the mergers and take-overs provoked among the managements and workers involved. The seizure of opportunities required changes in plant utilisation, the type and level of production, cost control systems and management styles. Such changes were likely to produce additional problems and conflicts. Turner *et al.* have drawn attention to the problems which accompanied the Austin–Morris merger, particularly in respect of 'fair wages' claims. In many ways that experience provided only a mild foretaste of what was to come. Even at the time of writing BL continues to struggle with the difficulties created by past mergers – both those undertaken in the 1960s and those of earlier decades.

It is interesting to note that in Graham Turner's apparently comprehensive account of the factors leading to the Leyland–BMC merger (Turner, 1973) there is no mention of the likely effect on industrial relations, or any discussion of how it might contribute to a solution of labour difficulties. One is tempted to conclude either that industrial relations were not seen as a particular problem or that it was believed that the merger would have little effect on them.

The second management response to the underlying difficulties was to try and change its style – at least in those firms where the financial difficulties were greatest. Among the car assembly firms, Ford had had a consistently superior financial performance. Recognition of this encouraged emulation of Ford in both style and practice. Ford-trained management were recruited by British Leyland. The decision by British Leyland and Chrysler to replace piecework by measured daywork was influenced by the fact that Ford used measured daywork. A significant part of the Ford style was to make every effort to keep costs at a minimum. In so far as this was copied by other firms both the change and its implications were fruitful sources of conflict – particularly in the absence of any general agreement as to the nature of and solutions to the industry's problems.

One further point worth noting, before we leave this analysis of the influence of the product market, is that the fall in the size of the differential in earnings between motor vehicles and all other industries and services occurred in 1965. The most plausible explanation of this change is that it was the result of cyclical factors but that thereafter conditions never improved sufficiently for it to be made up. However, this development does support our view that from 1965 onwards the industry was subject to substantial competitive pressures.

'OBSOLESCENCE IN INSTITUTIONS' – A REAPPRAISAL

In addition to factors specific to the motor industry, which we have examined, Turner *et al.* (1967) developed a further range of arguments of more general applicability. Here they suggested that motor vehicles represented something of an extreme case. These arguments were brought together under the umbrella title 'obsolescence in institutions'.

Much of their argument was repeated in the report of the Donovan Commission, but we felt that the original case was worth re-examination. Turner *et al.* began by questioning why so much of the growth in stoppages had been concentrated in the engineering and metal working sectors of economy. They argued then that workers' expectations about 'job rights' and 'fair wages' were under persistent threat from the changes in technology and products. This threat had encouraged the development of the traditional engineering shop steward system to articulate such expectations. Unfortunately the shop steward system had been unable to influence satisfactorily the formal collective bargaining in the sector. The multiplicity of trade unions, coupled with outdated internal organisations which failed to provide adequate representation for specialist interests, or adequate recognition of the importance of workplace organisations, meant that the formal negotiating bodies had not responded to the changes in workers' expectations and attitudes. One example of the unions' inability to develop and pursue co-ordinated policy, which was quoted, was the continued operation of the procedural arrangements imposed by the employers after their successful lockout in 1922. Those arrangements persisted despite widespread criticism of their effectiveness and despite the *de facto* bargaining power which the unions had possessed since 1940.

But the failure to adapt was not confined to the unions. The Engineering Employers' Federation had maintained its traditional structure of local associations, rather than develop specialist groups attuned to the requirements of different sections of the industry. Its membership of large and small firms with different products, technologies and problems compounded the unions' difficulty of overcoming conflicting interests and was equally likely to resolve them by adopting the lowest common denominator. More importantly perhaps, the EEF had, formally, stuck to the terms of the 1922 agreement and refused to bargain over matters other than those related to wages and hours. Such attitudes, and the procedural arrangements they maintained, were nineteenth century in origin. They belonged to an industrial structure which had passed. In a competitive situation of many small firms producing similar products it was in the interests of the unions and the firms which they had organised to ensure that all firms in the industry paid the same rate. Where the collective bargaining unit was the whole industry it made sense for the final settlement level to be at the industry level. But, in a situation where products had become much more differentiated, creating separate markets, and where those markets were dominated by a small number of large firms, such general arrangements were no longer capable of responding to the different problems which arose.

Turner *et al.* further argued that, while the formal bargaining machinery had failed to respond to the changes which had occurred, the workplace representatives, despite their growth in number and sophistication, had been unable to sustain the kind of wider organisation necessary to handle company or industry matters. In other words there were parallel sets of failures; the formal machinery failed to accommodate to the changes taking place below its level, whilst workplace representatives were unable to take over higher level functions. The resulting situation was one in which many of the problems were left unarticulated at levels at which they could be resolved, whilst the decisions which were taken at those levels were unlikely to be made known in any adequate fashion to those most affected by them.

This analysis had a solid intuitive appeal and brought together many of the salient facts. Our reappraisal was confined to an examination of some of the foundations of the analysis and an assessment of events post-1964. The analysis was founded on the premise that the growth in the number of stoppages had been heavily concentrated in the engineering and metal trades. In Table 10.11 we present the available evidence.

Table 10.11 confirms the view that much of the growth in the number of stoppages was concentrated in the engineering and metal trades sector. The sector accounted for less than 20 per cent of total employment and more than 50 per cent of strike activity. Between 1954–8 and 1964–8 stoppages in the sector increased more rapidly than in other industries. Over the period as a whole strike activity in the engineering and metal trades increased more rapidly than in other industries.

But Table 10.11 does not offer unqualified support for the view that the causes of the increase in strike activity in the UK can be discerned solely by reference to the engineering and metal trades. If our concern is with the increase in strike activity and not just the relative levels of strike activity, then we must note that in 1954–8 and in 1969–73 the rate of growth was faster outside engineering and metal trades. Even in the period 1959–68, when the engineering and metal trades led the field, other sectors still

Table 10.11   A comparison of average annual strike activity in the engineering and metal trades* with that of all other industries (exc. coal mining), 1949–73

Year	No. of strikes in engineering and metal trades	No. of strikes in others	No. of workers involved in engineering and metal trades (000s)	No. of workers involved in others (000s)	No. of working days lost in engineering and metal trades (000s)	No. of working days lost in others (000s)
1949–53	245	279	69	106	469	573
1954–58	268	338	120	165	696	1504
Percentage change	9%	21%	74%	56%	48%	162%
1959–63	535	566	295	259	1158	1475
Percentage change	100%	67%	146%	57%	66%	–2%
1964–68	869	800	407	270	1451	1066
Percentage change	62%	41%	38%	4%	25%	–28%
1969–73	1411	1312	752	694	5150	4732
Percentage change	62%	64%	85%	157%	255%	344%
Overall Percentage change	476%	370%	990%	555%	998%	726%

*Because we were principally interested in workplace developments in making this comparison, we excluded the national engineering stoppages of 1953, 1957, 1962 and 1968 from these series.

experienced very substantial increases in strike activity.

Finally, the 'obsolescence in institutions' hypothesis was developed to explain the rise in the number of stoppages. Yet it is in terms of the number of stoppages that the least difference is apparent between the two sectors. The most marked difference is in terms of workers involved and working days lost. These conclusions remain valid, except in respect of working days lost, even if the analysis is restricted to the period up to 1964 when the hypothesis was first developed.

An inter-sector comparison at this level of aggregation is fairly crude material on which to speculate about the causes of a limited amount of strike activity, but it does throw up a number of questions. Can the rapid growth in the number of stoppages outside the engineering and metal trades be explained by an extension of the 'obsolescence in institutions' hypothesis? Or is it possible that the two sectors were simultaneously exposed to a variety of social and economic changes which produced overt conflict almost regardless of their respective procedural arrangements? The most significant difference between the engineering and metal trades and other industries in terms of strike activity was the growth in the number of workers involved, which reflected a substantial increase in the average size of stoppages. Yet one might have expected the average size of strikes to fall as sectional bargaining became more common. How can the relatively greater increase in strike activity in other industries in the later years of the period be accounted for? Was it because the factors leading to strike activity had become more widespread in the later years and that, at the same time, the engineering and metal trades had become less responsive to such factors?

On this last point there have been a number of institutional changes in the engineering and metal trades sector in recent years. These may have served to reduce the sector's sensitivity to strike-producing influences. In the first place let us consider the multiplicity of union organisations in the vehicles sector. In 1965–6 it was estimated that the two major unions, the Transport and General Workers Union and the Amalgamated Engineering Union, had 66 per cent of union membership. By 1975 it was estimated that these two accounted for 90 per cent of the total – with some fifteen other unions sharing the remaining 10 per cent. This change might have been expected to reduce inter-union rivalry and lead to some improvements in internal union communications. (Alternatively, it could simply have heightened union rivalries, as it became apparent that further membership gains could only be secured at the expense of other unions.)

Secondly, the Engineering Employers' Federation and the Confederation of Shipbuilding and Engineering Unions began a series of discussions with the aim of reforming the procedural arrangements through which bargaining was conducted. These talks became deadlocked in 1971 over the '*status quo*' question. Unable to break the deadlock the unions withdrew from the existing arrangements in December 1971, although they had not reached any agreement on an alternative. Since that time agreements have been reached with a number of companies, including

British Leyland (in February 1972), on domestic procedural arrangements. These have been followed by the development of more formal contracts at plant level, and even by the development of plant-site negotiations along the lines suggested by both the Donovan Report and Turner *et al.* Thus fragmented piecework bargaining at shop-floor or departmental level has to some extent been replaced by plant-wide agreements on systems of measured daywork and other conditions of service. Attempts to restart national negotiations on procedure arrangements have been unsuccessful, and industry-wide agreements on pay have come to be confined to the establishment of engineering industry 'minima': these have little or no impact on pay structures in the car industry, except in so far as they affect shift and overtime premia.

Then there is the fact that in 1965 government concern over strike activity in the industry resulted in tripartite discussions which led to the setting up of the Motor Industry Joint Labour Council, consisting of six members from each side of the industry and an independent chairman, Sir Jack Scamp. The functions of the Council were to include the following: (a) to inquire into particular disputes leading to serious unofficial strikes or lockouts in breach of procedure; (b) to review the state of industrial relations within particular firms; (c) to keep the general state of relations in the industry under review and to examine matters of general significance for relations in the industry.

According to the third general report issued by the Council the majority of its time was taken up with the first of these functions. The Council had a semi-official status, drawing its Secretary from the Ministry of Labour and being given Court of Inquiry powers on the occasions when it was felt that these were necessary. Despite providing a fast and effective service in terms of dispute settlement, the Council's activities rapidly declined. There were two inquiries in 1965, nine in 1966, three in 1967 and one in 1968. In 1969 Scamp resigned; the Council became a 'talking shop' for the industry and faded into obscurity.

The creation of the MIJLC was due to government pressure rather than an internal industry initiative, but at its inception the Council appeared to be a potentially radical departure. It brought together all the major car firms, including Ford and Vauxhall who were not members of the EEF, and provided both a new means of resolving unofficial stoppages within the industry and a forum for discussion of ways of improving relations. In practice, however, the Council found it increasingly difficult to provide more than *ad hoc* temporary fire-fighting services. It is true that in his last general report Scamp sketched out a whole number of ideas for the reform of relations within the industry. (These included the establishment of a National Joint Industrial Council for the industry, the formation of national negotiating committees for each of the major companies, the institution of domestic procedure agreements and a modification of employers' relations with the EEF.) But nothing came of any of these proposals. Despite the many common problems within and between the two sides, no joint action was forthcoming on the Scamp reforms.

Finally, in our brief review of some of the major institutional changes since the mid-1960s, we would like to draw attention to events in Ford. Ford has a system of national negotiations over wages and other conditions of employment. In 1969 a new national agreement was reached in the National Joint Negotiating Committee but rejected by mass meetings and by shop-floor representatives who called for an all-out strike. This strike was made official by the TGWU and the AEU. After three weeks and further negotiations a new agreement was reached and accepted by the membership. In the wake of the strike the trade union side of the NJNC was reconstituted. In the past Ford had been unwilling to recognise trade unions and when it eventually did so, during the war, recognition was arranged through the TUC. In consequence every TUC affiliate with any members at Ford was included in the recognition deal and was given a place on the NJNC. Prior to the 1969 strike the trade union side consisted of eighteen delegates, one for each union recognised. Each union had one vote so that the TGWU and the AEU, which between them had a majority of the membership, had only two votes compared with the sixteen of the other minority unions. Following the events of 1969 the TGWU proposed a dramatic reshaping of the NJNC so that voting strength would be proportionate to union membership in the company, with the additional representatives for the big unions being lay delegates elected by the members. Six months of negotiations followed before agreement was reached on an expanded trade union side which would include lay representatives and preserve the voting rights of smaller unions. This involvement of lay delegates was later supplemented by having the convenors on hand to discuss the negotiations as they proceeded. Such a policy was not sufficient to end 'parallel unionism' but it serves to illustrate that improvements in representative arrangements are possible if the parties desire to move in this direction, although in forms which lack national negotiations the operation is likely to be rather more difficult to imitate.

SUMMARY AND CONCLUSIONS

Total strike activity in the motor vehicles industry, measured by five year averages, revealed that between 1949–53 and 1969–73 the number of stoppages rose by 540 per cent, workers involved by 1075 per cent and days lost by 870 per cent. Disaggregating these totals into major and minor stoppages disclosed interesting differences within the overall pattern. Minor stoppages rose only half as rapidly as major stoppages – 490 per cent as compared to 1100 per cent – but grew more rapidly in terms of average size and duration. All stoppages experienced a marked increase in average size in the mid-1950s and a tendency for average duration to fall up to the early 1960s and increase again thereafter. This analysis of the strike data provoked a number of questions: Why had the number of minor stoppages risen so rapidly in 1959–60 and why had the rate of increase declined since then although it remained positive? Why had the number of major strikes increased so rapidly in 1959–60 and again at the end of the period? Why had the average number of workers involved per stoppage risen so rapidly in the mid-1950s, but not increased thereafter? Why did average duration tend to fall in the middle of the period and why was that trend reversed?

Our starting point in seeking an answer to these questions was the work of Turner, Clack and Roberts. Their study suggested a number of avenues of investigation: irregularity of employment and the development of workers' expectations concerning 'fair wages' and 'job rights'; the failure of the formal collective bargaining institutions to reflect those expectations or to adapt their machinery to accommodate their articulation; and, in an industry as concentrated as motor vehicles, the possibility that certain acts or omissions might have had an influence far beyond their immediate areas. Their study was concerned with the car assembly plants in the post-war years prior to 1965. We wished to see how far, working at a higher level of aggregation, we could support their analysis of that period and whether their explanations were adequate for the period.

We began by examining the levels of employment and unemployment and the rates of labour turnover within the industry. We found substantial growth in employment up to 1966 and stability in the later years of the period. The unemployment rate among ex-motor vehicle industry workers was consistently below the national average. In general employment in the industry has been subject to quite sharp fluctuations; the effects of these fluctuations have been more severe in recent years. Turner *et al.* drew attention to the possibility that the recruitment of adult workers from other industries was a contributory factor to the level of strike activity. We noted that in 1959 net recruitment reached its highest ever level and strike activity rose very substantially. Of course that was not the whole explanation as labour demand was related to production requirements which were influenced by cyclical factors, but it is indicative.

Another feature to which we drew attention was the apparent inverse association of labour turnover with strike activity. This association appears in international comparisons as well and had been noted in our coal mining case study. We tentatively drew the conclusion that there was a trade-off between these variables as indicators of industrial conflict. The existence of such a trade-off implies that attempts to suppress overt manifestations of conflict without dealing with its causes are likely to produce covert manifestations of conflict. It also appears that if, in the words of the Central Policy Review Staff report, 'There are three classic indicators of poor labour relations, high absenteeism, high labour turnover and a large number of disputes' (Central Policy Review Staff, 1975), the UK motor industry performs reasonably well on the first two if poorly on the third.

We also examined the distribution of employment by region and plant size. The regional analysis indicated that the dispersion of employment had made the areas where motor vehicle manufacture had previously been concentrated more susceptible to adverse movements in employment. Over the period employment of motor vehicle workers had become significantly more concentrated in very large plants. Recent findings that large plants tend to be disproportionately more strike prone than small plants suggest that part of the increase in strike activity may be attributable to this concentration. It may also help to explain the increase in the average size of strikes in the mid-1950s and the increase in the number of large strikes in more recent times. These shifts in the distribution of employment by region and plant must have created further employment irregularities for the individuals concerned.

But the industry's labour requirements were not simply measured in terms of number of employees – variations in the number of hours worked provided another means of labour force adjustment. We examined overtime and short-time working in the period 1951–73 and found that overtime was a much more important form of labour supply adjustment than short-time. The number of employees engaged on overtime varied much more than the average number of hours worked. One consequence of this was that employees affected by any change in overtime working experienced much greater earning fluctuations than would have been the case if the adjustment had been made through an across the board change in the number of overtime hours worked. In other words the burden of any adjustment was carried by a minority of the workforce.

Examination of average gross weekly earnings in the industry, a measure which was bound to under-estimate the volatility of individual earnings, revealed substantial variations in the direction and magnitude of the annual rate of change through time. A series for average real net disposable earnings disclosed even greater volatility. On average, earnings in motor vehicles were significantly higher than those in other industries throughout the post-war period, although a reduction in the size of the industry's advantage could be discerned in the mid-1960s. This fall in the industry's relative earnings position seems to have passed largely unremarked, probably because comparisons within the industry were much more common than external comparisons. It does indicate though that the industry's relative strike-proneness has not had a demonstrably beneficial effect on its relative earnings position in recent years.

The distribution of earnings for male manual workers in the industry displayed some short-term changes but no long-term trends. Such findings are consistent with a situation in which groups are constantly jockeying for position, but are unable to sustain any relative advantage which they may gain. Examination of the make-up of earnings in the industry revealed that the importance of piecework payments was halved between 1970 and 1973. This reflected the change in payment systems which had taken place in some of the major car assemblers during this period. Given that piecework systems are frequently alleged to be associated with high levels of strike activity it might have been expected that this shift in payment systems would have been accompanied by a fall in this activity. Such a fall did not occur. There are several possible explanations for this. It is possible that the process of change itself created conflict. Alternatively, it might be argued that it was not the payment system but the frequent changes in product and production process which created the scope for bargaining which in turn led to more disputes. In these circumstances a change in payment system may simply lead to a shift from bargaining over earnings to bargaining over effort requirements and manning levels. It may be that the change from one payment system to another requires greater supervision of the work operations by management, that in itself might be a source of conflict. It may be that the conflicts arose not from the payment system but from the structure of earnings. Unless the change in payment system was accompanied by the negotiation of an agreed structure of earnings the problems will not have been resolved. In short, if piecework bargaining is simply the means through which conflicts are expressed rather than the cause of those conflicts, then the abandonment of piecework will not reduce the number of disputes – it may in fact exacerbate the situation if conflicts cannot be articulated in their usual manner.

In order to understand why employment, hours and earnings had fluctuated so much we examined production levels in the industry and the demands for its products. We found that between 1949 and 1964 production of cars rose by 350 per cent but that there had been little consistent upward growth since then. The explanation of this pattern appeared to lie in the demand for UK cars, both at home and abroad, and in the degree of competition from overseas producers. Throughout the post-war period the UK's share of world car exports has tended to fall – partly indicating a lack of competitiveness by the UK industry. Until 1964 this failing was disguised by the growth of demand in the protected home market in which the UK producers were dominant. When the UK market ceased to expand after 1964 the motor industry became a static rather than a growth industry. This change was not immediately perceived as reflecting the industry's competitive failings, instead the difficulties were attributed to the government's restriction of domestic demand and an over-valued exchange rate.

This lack of perception contrasted sharply with the situation in coal mining where, after 1959, the need to restore the industry's competitiveness against other fuels was widely recognised and agreement was reached within the industry on the action necessary to secure its survival. The lack of perception in the motor industry may be explained away by several factors: the companies had successfully adjusted production and stocks to the new situation by using the means they had employed in previous years when the downturns had proved temporary, consequently there was no permanent reminder of the industry's problems in terms of stocks; the existence of competing companies with differing success records focused attention on the shortcomings of individual companies rather than on the industry's difficulties; the fragmented organisation of both employers and unions was not conducive to industry-wide discussions; and because demand was initially static rather than declining there were grounds for believing that the difficulties were temporary.

One important consequence of this lack of awareness was that later in the decade, when the companies began to recognise the necessity for change, their actions and initiatives were often decided unilaterally and were unsympathetically received by the workers. These management initiatives took two forms – first, there was a series of mergers and take-overs; secondly, greater efforts were made to reduce or at least contain costs. In 1965 there were eight major companies in the car industry of which two were American-owned subsidiaries. By 1968 there were only four companies of which three were American-owned subsidiaries. This change was interesting for two reasons. First, it was a unilateral response by the companies to the difficulties in which they found themselves – a response which appears to have been made without any discussion with the trade unions and with apparently little concern as to how they would view the situation. Secondly, the mergers were likely to lead to further industrial conflict. If they were to be successful they required changes in plant utilisation, in the type and level of production, in cost control systems and in management style. All such changes carried the risk of clashing with workers' expectations about 'job rights' and 'fair wages'; the latter was also likely to be affected by the extension of the area of legitimate comparisons within the same company. We are not seeking to argue that these reorganisations were unnecessary or undesirable, we are simply drawing attention to the fact that the decisions to reorganise were taken unilaterally and that the changes which they necessitated were likely to produce further conflict unless they were subject to prior agreement. Employers' efforts to contain costs, which became more evident after the mergers and take-overs had taken place, contributed to the shift away from piecework as well as exacerbating the already existing conflicts over earnings. The increase in the demand for cars in 1971–3 tended to divert attention from the competitive problems to production problems so that the acute nature of the former did not become fully apparent until 1974–5 – a decade after the unmistakable emergence of the warning signals.

We also examined the contention of Turner *et al.* that the growth in the number of stoppages had been particularly concentrated in the engineering and metal trades sector and that this was substantially due to its specific institutional arrangements. We found that, up to 1964, the growth in the number of stoppages in that sector was only slightly higher than in all other industries excluding coal mining – 118 per cent as compared to 102 per cent. From this we concluded that there were three possible explanations, which were not mutually exclusive: the institutional arrangements were not significantly different to those elsewhere; they were not as important as Turner and his colleagues believed; they were both as different and as important, but other factors were at work in the non-engineering sector which had increased their relative liability to strikes. On reflection it seems to us that there may well be something in both of the first two explanations. Subsequent experience indicates that many of the defects which Turner and Donovan criticised in the procedures and practices of the engineering industry also existed elsewhere. Both in the private and the public sector procedural inadequacy and an inability to come to terms with rising expectations on the shop floor have continued to cause problems, disputes and strikes. (Examples are provided in the General Reports of the

National Board for Prices and Incomes and in the Annual Reports of the Commission on Industrial Relations.) The period since the mid-1960s has seen a very considerable growth in shop steward numbers and a spread of shop-floor bargaining to many other trades and industries apart from engineering (Boraston, Clegg and Rimmer, 1975). It seems reasonable to assume that these developments often resulted in similar forms of 'institutional obsolescence'. Yet having said this it also seems reasonable to wonder whether, in the light of subsequent developments, both Turner and the Donovan Report tended to place rather too much emphasis on the role of defective procedures in generating strikes; certainly the evidence of our three case studies indicates that internally motivated change to improve industrial relations systems may be unable to effect or maintain an improvement in the strike pattern unless reforms of this kind are introduced against a background of other changes which assist the process of reform rather than frustrate it.

All this is not to deny that there have been some improvements in procedural arrangements and systems of representation, both within car manufacture and in the wider engineering industry. In this respect we noted the development of plant and company bargaining, the concentration of union membership in the TGWU and the AUEW and the considerable reforms of the trade union side of the National Negotiating Committee at Fords. On the other hand, we also had to record the abortive negotiations over a new national disputes procedure and the decline and demise of the Motor Industry Joint Labour Council. On balance the changes which have been introduced scarcely amount to an institutional revolution. It is true that the period 1969–73 was the first since 1954–8 when the increase in strike activity in engineering and metal trades was less than in other industries, but we would not like to say that this was the direct result of procedural and institutional reform. In broad terms, in our period at least, there has been little sign of a major decline in strike activity in engineering and metals since the publication of the Donovan Report, and this is bound to make one entertain a certain degree of scepticism about the effectiveness of proposals for institutional reform which leave the mainsprings of conflict untouched.

In summary our view must be that Turner's analysis still contains much that is valid about the continuing causes of conflict in car manufacture, but that it placed too great an emphasis on the relative importance of institutional obsolescence. It is clear that problems continued to arise out of the irregularity of employment; indeed in some ways the failure of the industry to maintain its market share, and the decision to open up new points of production, only served to exacerbate these difficulties. There remained instabilities and inequities in earnings opportunities, despite the removal of many of the more chaotic systems of piecework. Worker expectations of and demands for 'fair wages' were still being frustrated; disputes still arose over the application of the new payment systems – most notably in terms of their impact on manning levels and output targets. And all this took place against the background of a decline in the comparative earnings position of car workers and periodic reductions in the real value of disposable income.

Given the tradition of strikes in many motor vehicles plants it is not surprising that the result was a maintenance of overall strike activity. Given the changes in the payment system, and the development of wider bargaining units, this was bound to take the form of a shift towards larger and longer strikes. In this context, it seems to us, the weight one decides to place on institutional obsolescence depends on how far one believes that it was institutional inadequacies that prevented both management and unions from coming to terms with the most important single fact that faced them both – i.e. the long-run implications of a hardening product market and a loss of international competitiveness. It was in this respect, it will be remembered, that we sought to contrast the record and initiatives of the NCB and the NUM.

In conclusion we may note that once again our analysis demonstrates the importance of seeking to trace the interaction between economic and non-economic variables; just as it confirms what we have said earlier about the importance of factors largely beyond the control of would-be reformers of systems of industrial relations. We return to both these matters in our final chapter.

11 Strikes and the State – the Changing Role of Government

THE AIMS OF THE CHAPTER

In the first section of this study we sought to describe and measure variations on the post-war strike pattern. In the chapter which followed we considered how far economic variables – especially those that operate at the national level and exert an overall impact – provided the key to explaining and interpreting the magnitude, form and distribution of strikes. In broad terms we concluded that data of that kind, together with the models so far based on their use, did not take us very far; we also gave our reasons for believing that a sectoral approach, explored through a series of case studies, would constitute a more promising methodology.

In the last three chapters we used this methodology to account for the strike pattern in three of the most important and interesting strike-prone industries. These analyses served to emphasise the localised nature of most strikes, and the importance of specific factors in determining the level and rate of change in strike activity. (In our final chapter we seek to draw together a number of general comments based on this evidence.)

But the methodology of the sectoral approach left us with a number of unresolved questions: For example, what accounts for the overall movements we noted in the first section – and especially in the overview we sought to provide in Chapter 6? Is it reasonable to suggest that these apparent trends were simply the product of innumerable small and independent influences – or did they reflect some change in the general climate of the times? More particularly, why did the level of strike activity fall between 1946 and 1952? Why was there a rash of major strikes in the mid- and late 1950s – was this simply the product of a number of factors peculiar to the industries involved? Why did the number of strikes rise so rapidly in 1960, and again in 1969–70? Why did time lost through strike action increase so fast and so far in the early 1970s?

It should be appreciated that it is part of our argument that if there are common threads to be discovered, which are running through all these events, then they are unlikely to be found in factors of more general application, which are likely to have affected all sectors of the economy more or less equally: we found this to be part of the problem when seeking plausible reasons for particular strike movements in terms of some of the more general macro-economic indicators beloved of model builders. What we were searching for were factors which were likely to fall more heavily on some sectors of the economy than others – i.e. those where strike activity was concentrated. In this respect there can be little doubt that the major influence which we had so far failed to examine in any detail was the role of the state – i.e. government attitudes, policies and legislative initiatives. In this chapter, therefore, we examine such activities to see how far they provide clues to any or all of the questions listed above.

In broad terms there would seem to be at least three areas of government activity which might be said to affect the strike pattern: First, there is the government's traditional role of industrial peacemaker through conciliation, arbitration and inquiry; secondly, there are governments' attempts to influence the substantive terms of collective agreements through incomes policy (under this area we include discussion of the government's role as employer); thirdly, there is the initiation of new legislation which may affect the substantive or the procedural terms of agreements or both. We examined each of these areas in turn.

CONCILIATION, ARBITRATION AND INQUIRY

The Conciliation Act 1896 gave powers to the Board of Trade to conciliate, appoint arbitrators and inquire into industrial disputes. The powers in respect of arbitration and inquiry were strengthened by the Industrial Courts Act 1919. In addition the Minister of Labour (now the Secretary of State for Employment), by virtue of his office, is held to have general powers to set up inquiries.

CONCILIATION

Conciliation was defined by the Ministry of Labour (1961) as

> the adjustment of differences by agreement between the parties or their representatives. Under Section 2(1)(b) of the Conciliation Act, 1896, it is within the discretion of the Minister of Labour to take such steps as may seem expedient to enable the parties to a difference to meet together by themselves, or through their representatives, under the chairmanship of an individual selected by the Minister of some other agreed authority.

Conciliation work was undertaken by full-time officials who were organised on a regional and national basis. The records of this work, particularly prior to 1961, are very incomplete but there is a series for the number of conciliation cases settled. Details are shown in Table 11.1.

The number of cases settled doubled between 1946 and 1949 and fluctuated around a somewhat lower level in the following four years. A downward trend emerged in 1953 which was not reversed until 1961; thereafter there was slow rise such that the 1949 peak was not bettered

Table 11.1   *Number of conciliation cases settled and some relative*
             measures, 1946–73

Year	No. of conciliation cases settled	Conciliation cases settled as a percentage of all conciliation cases	Conciliation cases settled as a percentage of all stoppages	Conciliation cases settled as a percentage of all non-coal stoppages
1946	200	n.a.	9.0	22.8
1947	227	n.a.	13.1	33.9
1948	362	n.a.	20.5	56.2
1949	403	n.a.	28.2	73.0
1950	300	n.a.	22.4	62.6
1951	330	n.a.	19.1	49.9
1952	320	n.a.	18.6	64.9
1953	353	n.a.	20.2	80.4
1954	255	n.a.	12.8	48.5
1955	243	n.a.	10.0	38.2
1956	276	n.a.	10.4	48.2
1957	217	n.a.	7.5	34.1
1958	190	n.a.	7.2	28.5
1959	173	58*	8.2	22.0
1960	162	54*	5.7	13.8
1961	200	59	7.4	16.2
1962	195	58	7.9	15.6
1963	206	58	9.9	19.0
1964	281	69	11.1	19.1
1965	288	71	12.2	17.8
1966	310	69	16.0	22.3
1967	281	68	13.2	16.3
1968	301	73	12.6	13.9
1969	393	75	12.6	13.4
1970	473	73	12.1	12.6
1971	456	70	20.4	21.8
1972	506	70	20.2	22.3
1973	676	78	23.5	26.2

*These figures are approximations calculated from rounded estimates of the number of conciliation cases shown in the Ministry of Labour Annual Reports of 1959–60.

until 1970. Assessment of the significance of this series is complicated by the need to distinguish between changes in the number of cases being conciliated and changes in the settlement rate of those cases. Column 2 of Table 11.1 reveals a marked upward shift in the settlement rate in 1964 but this change must be treated with caution as the figures for the period prior to 1964 were the product of a retrospective analysis by the Ministry. Even if the early figures are accurate it appears that changes in the number of cases have been much greater than changes in the settlement rate. This suggests that the post-1953 fall in cases settled resulted from a diminishing use of the Ministry's services rather than because the cases were more difficult to settle.

Our use of the number of stoppages as a reference series was designed to indicate changes in the volume and difficulties of bargaining through time. Obviously such series are very crude indicators by which the significance of changes in the number of cases settled might be assessed but they appear to be the only ones available. It seems unlikely that any disputes in coal mining would have been referred outside the industry for settlement but, in the absence of any information on the industrial make-up of cases settled, we felt we had to include both the gross and the net totals of stoppages. Comparisons of cases settled with gross total of stoppages confirmed our initial impression that use of the conciliation services declined in the 1950s and recovered in the 1960s. Comparison of cases settled with the net total of stoppages produced a rather more complicated picture. Up to 1960 there appeared to be an inverse relationship between cases settled and the net total of stoppages. After 1960 the two series tended to rise together. Within this overall pattern the comparison indicates two troughs in the successful utilisation of the conciliation services, one in 1959 and another in 1969–70.

Further information on conciliation activities post-1960 is available. Some of these details are shown in Table 11.2

After 1960 a distinction was drawn between conciliation cases where stoppages had occurred and cases where they had not. Cases involving stoppages followed a very similar pattern to that of the net total of stoppages. This association is highlighted in the final column of Table 11.2 which shows cases involving stoppages as a percentage of the net total of stoppages. The percentage was subject to a certain amount of year to year fluctuation and some upward movement was apparent in the later years. This upward movement implies that cases involving stoppages were increasing more rapidly than the number of stoppages itself, although even at the 1973 peak conciliation was invoked in less than one in ten stoppages. The settlement rate of stoppage cases also showed a slight upward shift in the later years of the period. The number of non-stoppage cases exhibited little association with the net total of stoppages.

There was some growth up to 1966, a decline until 1968 and then sustained growth up to 1973. Between 1961 and 1973 the number of conciliation cases involving stoppages rose by 310 per cent and non-stoppage cases by 120 per cent. This suggests perhaps that stoppages rose faster

Table 11.2　*Details of conciliation cases, 1961–73*

Year	No. of conciliation cases which involved stoppages	Percentage of conciliation cases involving stoppages which were settled	No. of conciliation cases not involving stoppages	Percentage of non-stoppage conciliation cases which were settled	Conciliation cases involving stoppages as a percentage of all non-coal stoppages
1961	58	72.4	281	56.2	4.7
1962	74	78.3	261	52.4	5.9
1963	75	76.0	283	52.6	6.9
1964	98	69.3	310	68.7	6.7
1965	95	78.9	311	68.4	5.9
1966	78	79.4	369	67.2	5.8
1967	91	69.2	322	67.7	5.3
1968	128	77.3	284	71.1	5.9
1969	171	80.1	345	74.2	5.8
1970	246	76.8	401	70.8	6.6
1971	166	77.1	484	67.7	8.0
1972	156	75.0	560	69.4	6.9
1973	239	82.8	627	76.2	9.3

than other disputes during these years. The relative trough in conciliation service utilisation which we noted in relation to Table 11.1 appears to have resulted from the slow growth of non-stoppage conciliation cases rather than because stoppage case conciliation failed to keep pace with the 'strike explosion' of these years. The settlement rate of non-stoppage cases exhibited a marked upward shift in 1964 but little other persistent change. In the absence of any compelling explanation of this sudden shift we are inclined to regard it as a product of the Ministry's retrospective analysis.

Further information on the work of the conciliation service post-1963 was made available to us by the Ministry. In the period 1964–73 63 per cent were initiated by trade unions, 19 per cent by employers, 13 per cent jointly and 5 per cent by the Ministry itself. Between 1964 and 1973 the union's share of initiated cases fell from 71 to 53 per cent while the employers' share rose from 18 to 20 per cent. Joint initiation rose from 9 to 22 per cent and that by the Ministry from 2 to 5 per cent. Although these shares fluctuated from year to year there is no evidence that an end-year comparison of this kind presents a distorted picture. In 1969–70 the Ministry's share of conciliation initiation rose to 10 per cent but declined again in the following year. On this evidence it seems that the Ministry, despite the growing number of stoppages, preferred to retain its traditional passive role of responding to requests from the parties rather than undertake an active role of conciliation initiation. It also seems that unions' willingness to resort to conciliation was increasing less rapidly than that of other interested parties.

Analysis of the causes of disputes dealt with by conciliation is subject to the same sort of difficulties as those encountered in analysing the causes of stoppages, with the additional problem that the system of classification appears to have been altered in 1973. In these circumstances we felt that there was little point in extending the analysis much beyond the traditional 'pay'–'non-pay' classification that we used in earlier chapters, although we did make a separate note of those cases involving recognition disputes.

Of the 6513 conciliation cases handled by the Ministry in the years 1961–73, 2715 (42 per cent of the total) were concerned with pay and 1889 (29 per cent) involved recognition. The remaining 1909 (29 per cent) were over other 'non-pay' matters. Of the conciliation cases where stoppages occurred, 43 per cent concerned pay, 15 per cent involved recognition and 41 per cent were over other 'non-pay' issues.

Examination of the causes of conciliated disputes revealed a good deal of year to year fluctuation but no clear trends. The number of pay disputes fell markedly in 1966–67 and 1971–72. Information was also available on the settlement rate of conciliation cases by cause. Of the 2715 pay disputes dealt with by conciliation in the period 1961–73, 77 per cent resulted in a settlement. Some 73 per cent of other non-pay disputes were settled by conciliation but only 58 per cent of conciliated recognition disputes resulted in a settlement. Distinguishing between conciliation cases involving stoppages as against those where no stoppage occurred revealed that the settlement rate was consistently higher in cases involving stoppages. However, differences in settlement rate between stoppage and non-stoppage cases cannot be taken to imply that 'militancy pays', as there is no evidence available on the terms of the settlement. It is consistent with greater degree of realisation by both parties after a stoppage of the need for an eventual settlement.

The decline in the percentage share of strikes attributable to pay disputes in 1966–7 and 1971–2 requires some explanation. The 1966–7 decline might be attributed to a reduction in the volume of bargaining in a period of 'freeze' and 'severe restraint'. It is not possible to advance an explanation of this kind again until late 1972. But it seems more likely that the 1970s fall is explicable in terms of union resistance to the informal '$n-1$' incomes policy, together with conflict over the reform of industrial relations law. Such developments created a suspicion of the government's conciliation services and a subsequent unwillingness to use them. In addition the government, in its determination both to combat inflation and to formalise industrial relations procedures, probably restricted the availability of conciliatory facilities. (Allegations of this kind were rife at the time and the operation of such a policy would account for the relative fall in the number of conciliation cases initiated by the Department of Employment in this period.)

Information on the distribution of conciliation cases by industrial sector was only available for the period 1961–72. Of the 5647 cases the metal trades accounted for 31 per cent; transport and communications 10 per cent; food, drink and tobacco 7 per cent; textiles, leather and clothing 6 per cent; and other service industries (excluding construction and transport and communication) 17 per cent. Conciliation activity had increased most rapidly in the chemicals, coal and petroleum products sector and in other manufacturing. It actually fell in shipbuilding, agriculture, forestry, and fishing, mining and quarrying, timber and furniture, and construction. Of the fifteen industry sectors all but two had a settlement rate for conciliation cases of between 66 and 73 per cent. The exceptions were shipbuilding with 79 per cent and paper, printing and publishing with 58 per cent. The predominance of the metal trades and the transport sector was not as marked as in the case of the strike series, but it is still quite clear.

The scope for conciliation activity was significantly extended on 28 February 1972 when the unfair dismissal provisions of the Industrial Relations Act 1971 came into force. Conciliation was attempted in virtually all cases. In 1972 there were 5197 completed cases of alleged unfair dismissal of which 59 per cent were dealt with through conciliation. These cases must have included some which, in earlier years, would have appeared in the redundancy and dismissals category of conciliation in industrial disputes. However, it is unlikely that there was very much overlap between the collective dispute conciliation of earlier years and the conciliation promoted by the Industrial Relations Act 1971. The great majority of the latter involved individual claims of dismissal and only a minority concerned trade unionists. The effect of this legislative change on the strike pattern is assessed later in this chapter.

ARBITRATION

The second method by which the government sought to fulfil its industrial peace-keeping role is through the provision of arbitration facilities – providing third party judgement in disputes which remain unresolved after normal procedure has been exhausted. Such judgements are not, in general, legally binding but in the great majority of cases the arbitration award does provide the basis for a settlement. Arbitration in Britain has usually been of a voluntary kind, disputes only being referred with the consent of the parties. However, there have been some instances of compulsory arbitration, principally arising out of wartime emergencies. We began with an examination of the system of voluntary arbitration and then considered the experience of compulsory arbitration.

Voluntary arbitration
Provision was made in the 1896 Conciliation Act for the appointment of single arbitrators, but a great deal of the post-war system of arbitration arose from the Industrial Courts Act 1919. Three forms of arbitration were provided for under that Act: by reference to the Industrial Court, by the appointment of one or more individuals, and by an Arbitration Board. Disputes may be reported to the Minister by or on behalf of either party to the dispute and he may, if he thinks fit, refer the dispute to arbitration where both parties agree and the normal procedural arrangements have

been exhausted. The parties have no automatic right to arbitration facilities.

The Industrial Court was set up as a standing arbitration body by the 1919 Act. Members of the Court were appointed by the Minister and consisted of independent persons and representatives of employers and workers (one or more of whom must be a woman to ensure that in disputes involving women there is a woman on the Court). The chairman of the Court was always drawn from the independent group. The Court was empowered to sit in divisions but rarely did so. The Industrial Relations Act 1971 re-titled the Court the Industrial Arbitration Board. The Employment Protection Act 1975 transferred its functions to the Central Arbitration Committee. Despite its title the Court was not a judicial body. It lacked the powers of any normal court, even to the extent that it was a matter of debate whether its decisions were legally enforceable (Wedderburn and Davies, 1969). One of the hopes expressed at its inception was that, as a standing body, it would be more consistent in its decisions and have a greater awareness of the impact of its own awards on settlements elsewhere. In practice this does not appear to have happened (Sharp, 1950). The Court seems to have paid as little attention to precedent as any *ad hoc* arbitration body.

Following the establishment of the Court it appears that it was normal practice for the Minister, when referring a case to arbitration, to make a reference to the Court unless the parties specifically sought some alternative arrangement. Among the reasons influencing the parties' preferences were that the Court usually met in London, it rarely viewed the *locus in quo*, and its reports were usually published in full by the Ministry. By contrast single arbitrators usually held their hearings on the company's premises, or in the nearest Ministry of Labour office, and their reports were confidential to the parties. Boards of Arbitration also issued their reports privately and were employed at the parties' specific request. Table 11.3 shows the number of cases dealt with by each form of arbitration in the period 1946–73.

Of the 1952 disputes arbitrated between 1946 and 1973, 964 were handled by the Industrial Court, 902 by single arbitrators and eighty-six by Boards. Industrial Court hearings fluctuated sharply in the early years of the period, although there appears to have been a rising trend up to the very early 1950s. Thereafter use of the Court declined, with the reduction being most marked in the late 1950s and 1960s. Hearings by single arbitrators followed a similar pattern to that of the Industrial Court until 1958, when a slow recovery in the popularity of this form of arbitration began. This recovery was so slow that it was not until 1973 that the 1949 peak of fifty cases per year was matched. Less than one in twenty arbitrations were handled by Boards. In the whole period the number of cases dealt with in this way only exceeded five per year on three occasions, although all of them were within the last decade.

Consideration of the annual total of arbitration hearings held under the Ministry's auspices in this period reveals a marked fall in the mid-1950s similar to that recorded in respect of conciliation. This fall was followed by a certain amount of year to year fluctuation from which no clear trend emerged – largely because the continued decline in Court hearings was offset by single arbitrator activity. Single arbitrator hearings are more likely to be concerned with local issues (Wedderburn and Davies, 1969) so this increase may simply be a reflection of an increase in the amount of local bargaining relative to that at national level. A further factor may have been a belief among the parties that *ad hoc* arbitration was less likely to be affected by incomes policy considerations than a permanent arbitration body. (This is not to suggest that the Industrial Court was affected in this way, only that it may have been thought to have been.)

Table 11.3   *Arbitration cases handled under the 1896 and 1919 Acts*

Year	By single arbitrators	By boards of arbitration	By industrial court	Total	As a percentage of non-coal stoppages
1946	44	—	39	83	9.4
1947	26	—	42	68	10.2
1948	33	1	67	101	15.7
1949	50	—	41	91	16.4
1950	25	2	38	65	13.6
1951	45	2	64	111	16.8
1952	25	4	66	95	19.3
1953	24	4	59	87	19.8
1954	24	1	54	79	15.0
1955	13	2	40	55	8.6
1956	19	5	43	67	11.7
1957	15	1	35	51	8.0
1958	21	1	34	56	8.4
1959	27	1	33	61	7.8
1960	27	4	35	66	5.7
1961	19	3	52	74	6.0
1962	23	4	41	68	5.4
1963	32	1	36	69	6.4
1964	24	—	35	59	4.0
1965	39	9	19	67	4.2
1966	43	2	22	67	4.8
1967	27	—	7	34	2.0
1968	42	2	12	56	2.6
1969	41	4	14	59	2.0
1970	48	4	9	61	0.7
1971	48	8	7	63	3.0
1972	48	17	15	80	3.5
1973	50	4	5	59	2.3

In the final column of Table 11.3 we expressed the total of arbitration cases as a percentage of the total of non-coal stoppages. In doing so we were using the stoppages series as an indicator, albeit very crude, of the volume of bargaining and the success of the normal procedural arrangements in producing peaceful settlements. It can be seen that between 1946 and 1953 arbitration cases doubled in relation to non-coal stoppages, so that by the latter date there was one arbitration case for every five stoppages. Thereafter the relative level of arbitration cases fell until by 1970 there were 140 stoppages for every arbitration hearing. After 1970 arbitration staged a small relative recovery but this appears to have owed more to the decline in the number of stoppages than to a wider acceptance of arbitration.

It might be argued that a relative decline in the number of arbitration cases was not a cause for concern as such facilities were only required when the normal procedures could not produce a settlement. If the volume of bargaining rose relative to the number of arbitration hearings, then settlements were being produced, although, judging by the rising number of stoppages, an increasing number of those settlements were being arrived at with some difficulty. In short Table 11.3 provokes two questions: Why did the number of arbitration cases not rise at anything like the same rate as the number of stoppages thereafter? Why did the number of arbitration hearings fall in the mid-1950s?

Given that these are forms of arbitration which can only be entered into voluntarily we must conclude that one or more parties became increasingly unwilling to submit disputes to this kind of settlement. But were those parties the trade unions, the employers or the Ministry, and why was arbitration regarded in a less favourable light? It is often alleged that the operation of incomes policies has created even more mistrust of arbitration than it has of conciliation. But that mistrust may be expressed by the parties themselves (who fear that the arbitrator may be unduly influenced by the government's views) or by the government itself (because it fears that the arbitrator will not pay sufficient heed to the norms of incomes policy). Direct evidence on these points is difficult to obtain but we return to them later in the chapter.

An alternative explanation of the decline in the number of arbitration cases depends on the precondition that normal procedural arrangements should have been exhausted before a dispute may be referred to arbitration. Following the Donovan analysis it might be argued that the growth in the volume of bargaining in the post-war period has derived from the growth in workplace bargaining outside of the normal procedures. Consequently any disputes which arose as a result of this bargaining would not be eligible for settlement by arbitration because the normal procedures would not have been exhausted. Such an argument could be supported by reference to the growth in the number of stoppages not known to be official which are generally thought to be unconstitutional as well.

But this argument is open to a number of objections. First, there is some doubt as to how far the Ministry insisted on the precondition being met. On its own evidence it is clear that the Minister may refer disputes to arbitration which have not exhausted procedure (Wedderburn and Davies,

1969). Secondly, the fact that a stoppage occurs in breach of procedure does not rule out the possibility that it ends on the understanding that the dispute is returned to procedure for settlement. Such a dispute would then be eligible for arbitration. Thirdly, even if the bulk of the increase in bargaining in the post-war years occurred outside the normal procedural channels it does not follow that bargaining within procedure decreased. Indeed the available evidence is to the contrary (e.g. Engineering Employers' Federation, 1966). The fall in the number of arbitration cases contrasts oddly with this development unless one believes that these procedures became much more effective in producing settlements – a belief which is not well supported by the Ministry's series of strikes known to be official. We conclude that where the precondition that normal procedural arrangements must have been exhausted before a dispute could be referred to arbitration may have served to inhibit the Ministry's willingness to intervene in some disputes, it does not explain the whole of the decline in the relative importance of arbitration as a means of dispute resolution.

In addition to the powers granted it under the 1919 Act the Industrial Court had its responsibilities increased by a number of legislative acts. These included the Road Haulage Wages Act 1938, the Civil Aviation Act 1949, the Road Traffic Act 1960, the Industrial Relations Act 1971, and the Fair Wages Resolution of the House of Commons 1946. A number of cases arose from these responsibilities but they never amounted to more than ten in any year and averages less than four a year. There appears to have been some decline in numbers since the immediate post-war years but there are so few cases that drawing conclusion is hazardous. Section 8 of the Terms and Conditions of Employment Act 1959 gave the Court certain other responsibilities but these were a direct outcome of the system of compulsory arbitration to which we now turn.

Compulsory arbitration
In 1940 a committee of the National Joint Advisory Council, set up to examine the problems of wage negotiations and strikes during the wartime emergency, recommended that the existing collective bargaining machinery should be kept intact and that any dispute which could not be settled within that machinery should be referred to the Minister of Labour who could refer the matter to compulsory arbitration. Only if the Minister failed to refer the dispute within the stipulated time limit would it be legal to undertake a strike or a lockout. In effect the recommendation was for a total ban on stoppages of work with compulsory arbitration providing an alternative sanction. It was further recommended that the wages and conditions of employment settled by negotiation or arbitration should be made binding on all employers and workers in the trade or industry concerned.

These proposals were accepted by the government and put into operation through Statutory Instrument Order No. 1305 issued under the Defence of the Realm Act. The Order provided for the establishment of the National Arbitration Tribunal (NAT) consisting of five members. Three were independent and two were chosen as representatives of employers and workers. Awards became implied terms of the individual workers' contracts and in this way could be enforced in the civil courts. In addition to the prohibition on strikes and lockouts the Order also placed an obligation upon employers in every district to observe the terms and conditions which had been settled by collective agreement or arbitration for the trade concerned in that district. Consequently two types of dispute could be reported to the Minister for reference to the Tribunal. Disputes arising from bargaining could be reported by either party to the Minister. As the term 'party' was not closely defined in the Order, non-TUC unions and unions with small memberships could report disputes. It was even possible for unorganised workers or union branches acting against the advice of their executives to invoke the Order No. 1305 procedure. In contrast, disputes over the terms and conditions of employment, which should be observed in particular cases, could only be reported to the Minister by an organisation of employers or a trade union which habitually took part in the settlement of wages and working conditions in the trade concerned. The Order also provided for the criminal prosecution of those responsible for stoppages of work in contravention of the Order. Between 1940 and 1945 there were 109 prosecutions of 6281 workers and two prosecutions of employers.

As we noted in Chapter 2 this Order did not lead to a cessation of strike activity, or even a fall in the number of stoppages. Nevertheless, after the end of the war the operation of the Order was reviewed and it was agreed that it should be renewed until 1950. No use was made of the Order's penal powers between 1945 and 1949 but in 1950 a number of gasworkers were prosecuted for strike action. In the following year a prosecution of some dockers was undertaken but they were not convicted. This use of wartime penal powers caused controversy. The government, after consultation with the NJAC, decided to abandon the system of compulsory arbitration and in August 1951 it was replaced by a system of *ex parte* arbitration.

It is difficult to assess the importance of the NAT in the cause of dispute settlement. Between 1940 and 1944 the number of cases dealt with by the NAT rose sharply to 188. Hearings then fell off for two years before rising again in 1947. In 1949 the number of cases matched that of 1944 and in 1950 over 200 cases were dealt with. By 1951, when the NAT was replaced by the Industrial Disputes Tribunal, 222 cases were handled by the two bodies.

Turner (1952) has shown that most of the NAT's cases arose from sectional claims and that most were located in small or minor industries. Many of them came from private industry, whereas cases going to the Industrial Court arose in the public sector. The significance of the NAT may best be seen by recognising that its role was essentially that of a 'long stop'. It was there to deal with disputes that the normal machinery could not resolve. Seen in this way an average of 150 cases per year would seem to suggest that the NAT was not without influence.

Given the varying strike record of the war years and the immediate post-war period, it would seem implausible to suggest that the mere existence of a system of compulsory arbitration had much impact on the frequency of stoppages from 1940 to 1951. But there is no doubt that it had a very marked effect on the form of stoppages that occurred. After all, Order 1305 had the support of the trade unions so that any stoppage which did take place was most unlikely to receive official support. (The only important strike that we could trace which did receive official support was that of the vehicle builders in 1948). The consequences of an eleven year period when virtually *all* strikes must have been unofficial are incalculable but three conclusions stand out. First, the operation of Order 1305 must have given considerable impetus to the growth of shop-floor organisation as workers mobilised to support claims outside the normal bargaining machinery. Secondly, a legal prohibition on stoppages of work must have encouraged the adoption of other sanctions, e.g. overtime bans, go-slows, etc., which were less amenable to official control. Thirdly, the conventional attitude of surprise that so many stoppages in the United Kingdom are unofficial appears in some ways ill-founded and even perverse. The surprising feature in the circumstances is surely the reappearance of official strikes in the 1950s.

In August 1951 Order 1305 was replaced by Order 1376. The most obvious effect of this change was that the legal prohibition on stoppages of work was lifted. The NAT was replaced by the Industrial Disputes Tribunal (IDT). The IDT consisted of a chairman and two 'wingmen'. Lord Terrington, who had been chairman of the NAT, took over at the IDT. To invoke the machinery a dispute had to be reported to the Minister of Labour. He had to ascertain that the dispute came within the scope of the Order, that the reporting body was entitled to do so, and that the existing procedures had been exhausted. If these conditions were satisfied the Minister was required to send the case to the IDT within fourteen days, although he could try other means of resolving it in the meantime and could impose a further period of delay if he thought it would assist a voluntary settlement.

This more cumbersome reference procedure reflected other changes on Order 1376. Access to the new machinery was restricted to organisations who were a party to the dispute, who 'habitually took part in the settlement' or could claim to represent a 'substantial proportion' of the employers or workers concerned. This change was designed to foster the formal negotiating machinery and its signatories – thus ensuring that unofficial bodies, including union 'breakaways' would be excluded.

Further support for the formal bargaining system was contained in a clause stipulating that any dispute which was the subject of a decision by existing joint arrangements, or established conciliation and arbitration machinery, could not be dealt with by the IDT.

Order 1376 also excluded disputes 'as to the employment or non-employment of any person, or as to whether any person should or should not be a member of any trade union' from the Tribunal's scope. In part this reflected the legal problems which had arisen over the NAT's right to order the reinstatement of workers (e.g. the Crowther case in 1947). But it also meant that crucial issues concerning dismissals and redundancies were denied access to the machinery. It seems likely that this denial of access served to increase the scope and volume of workplace bargaining, as workers sought to achieve settlements on these issues through other means.

One further change was that the general obligation imposed on employers to observe terms and conditions of employment 'not less favourable' than the recognised terms and conditions was not repeated in Order 1376. Instead an organisation of employers, or a trade union which 'habitually' took part in settling the recognised terms and conditions for the trade, could report an 'issue' to the Minister concerning whether or not an employer should observe the recognised terms and conditions. In other words the responsibility for securing observance was transferred from individual employers to the parties to the formal negotiating machinery. This change possibly reflected a government intention of withdrawing from the collective bargaining arena and leaving matters to the parties directly concerned.

In essence Order 1376 also provided a 'long stop' for the existing negotiating machinery, but it was a stop which could only be used if all the rules laid down were obeyed. The IDT was abolished in February 1959. In the seven and a half years of its existence it made 1270 awards, an average of 170 a year. There was some tendency for its workload to decline over the period. As the trade unions were responsible for reporting 95 per cent of its cases this decline in IDT activity must be attributed to a reduction in the unions' willingness to use it, although the number of cases reported by employers also declined. Cases were drawn from a very wide range of industries and involved a large number of workers' organisations. It would appear that the only important industries which were never involved with the IDT were those with highly developed procedures of their own – e.g. coal mining and railways. As with the NAT it is difficult to assess the significance of the IDT, partly because its importance rested more on the fact that it was there than on its own activities.

However, we would argue that its abolition was a matter of some importance and it is worth spending some time examining the alleged reasons at this point.

In the first place the arguments for abolition are an interesting reflection of contemporary attitudes in the 1950s. Secondly, the decision to abolish the IDT must be considered along with the evidence we have already noted concerning the weakening role of government in various methods of dispute resolution at this time. This evidence, when considered together with the pattern of strikes before and after abolition, constitutes a powerful argument for the suggestion that the decision to abolish the IDT constituted something in the nature of a post-war watershed.

According to the Ministry the abolition of the IDT came about because it was no longer mutually acceptable. They argued that Order 1376 had been made on the understanding that it would be reviewed as soon as either side desired this. In 1957 employers in general told the government that they could no longer support the system and it came to an end in February 1959. The Confederation of British Industry (CBI), in their evidence to the Donovan Commission, stated that they 'could not continue to support a system of compulsory arbitration which was effectively enforced against employers but not against workers'. In effect they meant that the workers had not abided by the Tribunal's decisions, whereas the employers had done so. The validity of this view was discussed by one of the authors in an earlier work (McCarthy, 1968). He found only three occasions out of a total of 1270 when attempts had been made to overturn an IDT award.

It may also be noted that our own research found one occasion when an employer successfully applied an award to those employees who were in employment when the award was made, but excluded those who entered later. Moreover, Turner (1952) quotes a case where an award was evaded by sacking all the employees and re-engaging them on their old contracts.

On this evidence it is not clear that employers were being penalised unfairly in comparison to the unions on any significant scale, or that there was any great difficulty in securing observance of the Tribunal's awards in the overwhelming majority of cases. Moreover the Transport and General Workers' Union, in their evidence to Donovan, described the situation as they saw it in a very different way:

> In 1958 it was the employer organisations which sought to secure the scrapping of the arbitration procedures that we had then, the Industrial Disputes Order 1376, and it was because of the pressures applied by the employers' organisations that this very useful piece of machinery was scrapped. At the time many employer organisations were talking about getting rid of this and fighting it out with the unions (Donovan, 1966–8, para. 4484).

But of course if the employers were adopting a more aggressive posture, and if they saw the abolition of the IDT as a stage in that process, there is considerable evidence to indicate that this was partly as a result of government pressure and not unconnected with the growing conviction of members of the government – most notably the Minister of Labour, Iain Macleod – that over-ready use of all forms of conciliation and arbitration machinery was inflationary (see Clegg and Adams, 1957; also Allen, 1954). The fact is that the government was not bound to accede, as readily as it did, to the employers desire to end the IDT – particularly if it took into account the very limited evidence available to support the employers' arguments. One is forced to conclude that, as many people best placed to know were convinced at the time, the demise of the IDT was brought about by an alliance of government and employers, united in the belief that a higher level of stoppages might be the price of a lower level of wage increases. This is not to say that the charge against the IDT could be sustained. The evidence in McCarthy (1968) suggests that IDT awards followed the general level of settlements elsewhere and did not operate as an independent factor making for increased 'wage push' inflation. But these facts were not all that well known at the time, especially to such magazines as the *Economist*, which kept up an influential and sustained argument concerning the inflationary consequences of all forms of third party involvement throughout the late 1950s and 1960s. We consider further below the effect of this action on the subsequent level of strike activity.

Although the IDT was abolished in 1959 one of its functions survived by being transferred to the Industrial Court. Under Section 8 of the Terms and Conditions of Employment Act 1959, representative organisations of workers or employers, who were party to the relevant agreement, could report a 'claim' to the Minister that an employer was not observing the recognised terms and conditions. The Minister could take such steps as seemed appropriate to find a peaceful solution but if this proved unobtainable a claim could be referred to the Industrial Court for adjudication. An award of the Court became an implied term of the individual contract of employment enforceable in the civil courts. In this very restricted form *ex parte* arbitration and legally binding awards were retained, although the crucial dispute resolution role of the IDT was abandoned.

In the fifteen years from 1959 to 1973 the Industrial Court dealt with an average of twelve cases a year brought under Section 8. In the peak years of 1966–7 the number of cases was over twenty a year – this may have reflected a search for means of avoiding the tight incomes policy which was then in operation.

INQUIRY AND INVESTIGATION

The final elements in the government's collection of peace-keeping or peace-finding devices are those of inquiry and investigation. These may be conducted through the mechanism of Courts of Inquiry or through Committees of Inquiry or Investigation.

Under the Industrial Courts Act 1919 the Minister is empowered to establish a Court of Inquiry to inquire and report to him. The report is then laid before Parliament. Consequently Courts of Inquiry are a means of informing Parliament and the public of the facts and underlying causes of a dispute. It is customary for Courts to exceed a narrow interpretation of this investigative role and to seek to resolve disputes by making recommendations. A Court of Inquiry normally consists of a chairman and such other persons as the Minister sees fit to appoint, but Courts have consisted of a

chairman acting on his own. Hearings may be held in public or private at
the Court's discretion. It is not necessary for the parties to consent to the
establishment of a Court, although it would be unusual to appoint one if
the parties indicated that it would be unhelpful. There have been instances
(e.g. the London busmen's strike of 1958 and the Local Authority
manuals' strike in 1970) when both parties have requested a Court of
Inquiry but the Minister refused to exercise his powers.

One of the authors, in an earlier analysis of the work of Courts of
Inquiry (McCarthy and Clifford, 1966), identified four sorts of dispute
where Courts might be established: those in which the majority of workers
in an industry were involved and a national strike was threatened; those
where a strike would have widespread effects, e.g. in transport; those from
which secondary effects were feared; and those which arose in areas where
such events seemed endemic.

In the period 1946–73 there were sixty-six Courts of Inquiry, an average
of two a year, although the actual range had been from six in 1967 down to
none in 1949, 1959–62, 1971 and 1973.

The Minister also has powers to set up three other sorts of Inquiry: (a) a
committee of inquiry under the 1896 Act; (b) a committee of investigation
under the 1896 Act; (c) a committee of inquiry under his general powers.
Under the 1896 Act the Minister may appoint a committee to 'inquire into
the causes and circumstances of the difference' between workmen and
employers. The term difference is not defined so the power is capable of
wide application. Usually bodies set up under this Act are called
Committees of Investigation. According to the Ministry (Ministry of
Labour, 1965) Committees of Investigation are normally used in those
cases where the public interest is not so wide and general as to require a
Court of Inquiry. The procedure of the hearings is not as formal as in a
Court and the report is not laid before Parliament. It is not clear under
what circumstances the Minister decides to appoint a Committee of Inquiry
rather than one of Investigation under the 1896 Act. On average there has
been one such committee a year in the post-war period but the popularity
of this form of dispute resolution appears to have declined. Between 1960
and 1973 there were only ten such committees and in eight out of the
fourteen years none were appointed.

The Minister also has certain general powers to establish inquiries by
virtue of his office and the Ministry has argued that the exercise of these
powers may be preferable to those of the 1896 Act in certain circumstances. These include those situations where the Minister wishes to act
jointly with another Minister, those where the inquiry is into matters which
may not be currently in dispute between the parties as the 1896 Act would
seem to require, and those where the Minister wishes that the terms of
reference should include some aspect of the national interest.

Wedderburn and Davies (1969) found that in the period 1946–66 there
had been twelve such inquiries, an average of one every two years. In the
period 1967–73 there were nine, an average of more than one a year. This
increase is probably best explained by a desire on the part of the Ministry

to find some form of machinery to deal with those situations where disputes appear to be endemic. In effect a recognition that disputes should not be regarded as simply the product of some chance combination of factors, which can be resolved on a 'one-off' basis, but rather as the product of a series of factors which have a continuing role in that situation and are likely to lead to further disputes.

In summary the various forms of inquiry and investigation have evolved beyond the simple form of a hearing and a report on the facts of the case and become, as Wedderburn and Davies point out, something much more akin to quasi-arbitration or mediation in the sense that the parties present their cases and recommendations are made for the resolution of the dispute. Over the whole period the number of inquiry and investigation cases averaged four a year. There was some tendency for the number of cases to rise in the mid- and late 1960s and a marked tendency for the number to fall in two periods, 1959–62 and 1971–3. In these latter periods cases averaged one a year, while in the remainder of the period they averaged five. The tendency for the number to increase in the 1960s might be explained by the increase in the number of disputes, as evidenced by the rising number of stoppages. Similarly, the fall in cases in the 1970s might be explained by the fall in strike frequency, although the average level was still higher than for much of the period. But this hypothesis would not account for the experience of 1959–62, when the number of cases fell while stoppages were rising. As in so many other of the government's dispute resolution mechanisms it is the events of the late 1950s and early 1960s which raise most questions.

However, before attempting to answer these questions there is a further aspect of government activity which we must consider – incomes policy. The possibility of conflict between the government's pursuit of industrial peace and observance of its incomes policies has been widely recognised. Indeed on occasion the conflict has been dramatically apparent, particularly when it was the peace-keeping role which was abandoned – e.g. in the London busmen's strike of 1958, the Local Authority manuals' strike of 1970 and the miners' strike of 1972. But our central aim is not merely to catalogue such occasions; we wish to examine the various forms of incomes policy which have been tried in order to assess their impact in the level of strike activity. An assessment of this kind must include any effect transmitted through dispute resolution mechanisms.

INCOMES POLICIES

THE POST-WAR LABOUR GOVERNMENT, 1945–51

To be able to assess the role of incomes policy on the strike pattern it is necessary to divide the period into five separate sub-periods. These relate to the policy initiatives of four successive governments. The first period is that covered by the post-war Attlee administration – i.e. 1945–51. The first point to stress is that the Attlee government inherited the wartime policy of the Churchill coalition, which had refrained from attempts to control wages directly. Under the tutelage of its extremely influential Minister of Labour, Ernest Bevin, the government reposed great trust in the common sense of employers and unions, while providing them with assistance and support through its policies of subsidies and rationing. In implementing these policies they made full use of the fact that the cost of living index was based on an outdated survey of working class expenditure (the survey had been conducted in 1912–3). By judicious use of subsidisation this index could be manipulated. This in turn provided a background against which the parties could contain wage movements within reasonable limits.

However, by 1947 it was generally agreed that the time had come to produce a more modern and representative index. This was unlikely to be so easy to manipulate. At the same time the new government was confronted by the rising cost of subsidies and the need to finance their own programme of social and economic reforms. In the face of these difficulties a ceiling was placed on the future growth in subsidies and the government voiced increasing concern about the need to ensure that wage settlements did not move too far out of line with anticipated price movements.

In February 1948 the government issued its White Paper *Personal Incomes, Costs and Prices*. The government only pledged itself to operate on personal incomes through taxation, but it stated that 'in the immediate future there was no justification for any general increase in individual money incomes'. This statement was issued without prior consultation with the TUC but a conference of union executives – after adding a number of reservations describing circumstances in which increases would be justified – accepted the policy. According to Clegg and Adams (1957) the policy had some success in that in the two and three-quarter years from January 1948 to September 1950 wage rates only rose by 6 per cent although prices rose by 12 per cent (earnings are thought to have risen in line with prices). Following the devaluation of sterling in September 1949 the government sought even more stringent wage restraint, but an attempt by the General Council of the TUC to secure an undertaking to that effect from another conference of union executives resulted in such a bare majority that it was not acted upon.

By 1950 wage restraint policies were being rejected at union conferences. The pressures leading to rejection were complex, but they included feelings of resentment that some groups of workers seemed to have been less affected by restraint than others, plus a response to the price increases resulting from devaluation and the outbreak of war in Korea.

Although the number of stoppages had fallen in 1946 and 1947 in industries other than coal mining, it seems likely that the general acceptance of wage restraint contributed to the further decline in 1948–50. This view is given some support by the pattern in coal mining which showed little decline in 1946–8 but exhibited a marked trough in 1949–50. It seems plausible to suggest that this trough was related to the incomes policy and to conclude that if the effect was strong enough to influence events in such a self-contained industry as coal mining then other industries must have been affected.

During the war the policy of subsidising basic commodities and providing compulsory arbitration as an alternative sanction to industrial action had been accompanied by a modest but continuous rise in strikes. It is difficult to conclude that in themselves these elements of economic policy were responsible for what we termed 'the post-war peace' in Chapter 2, although they no doubt made a contribution. In the absence of any other satisfactory explanation we are strongly inclined to accept that the relative freedom from strikes was much more a by-product of the widespread support for the Attlee government's economic and social reforms amongst the organised working class in general and trade union leaders in particular. Of course this support was reinforced by the need to cope with serious problems of post-war reconstruction, coupled with the maintenance and extension of wartime links between government departments and the TUC. It should also be remembered that at this time the system of independent workshop bargaining under the leadership of shop stewards was at a comparatively early stage of development. Wage bargaining was very largely national bargaining, and under the personal supervision of quasi-authoritarian leaders such as Deakin. However, Hugh Clegg, in discussion, has suggested to us a further explanation. He argues that the rise in strike activity during the war years was partly the result of the growth in workplace bargaining by an increasing number of shop stewards. But in the immediate post-war years the numbers and level of shop-floor organisations may well have declined – as the economy was restored to a peacetime footing and mobility of labour was restored with the abolition of the Control of Engagement Order. Unfortunately there appears to be insufficient evidence to allow us to decide whether shop steward numbers did move in the way this theory presupposes – although we return to the assumption behind the notion of a link between steward numbers and strikes in our final chapter. At the moment we have to record that the AEU surveys of shop steward numbers did not begin until 1947 (Marsh and Coker, 1963). It is true that the post-war reconstruction was accompanied by substantial employment shifts which might have weakened shop steward organisations. Alternatively, it might be argued that these employment shifts were likely to provoke more conflict.

THE CONSERVATIVE INTERREGNUM, 1951–5

Following the TUC's rejection of wage restraint in 1950 the Attlee government more or less abandoned all attempts at incomes policy. This was followed by a wage explosion, the substitution of the IDT for the NAT, and an upturn in strike activity. In 1951 the Labour Party lost the election and Churchill returned to office. Yet in 1952 strike activity declined and this trend continued until the last quarter of 1953.

It might be thought that a development of this sort, soon after the return of a Conservative government, goes against the explanation we have offered for the period of the 'post-war peace' from 1945 to 1950, but it must be stressed that the new administration went out of their way to emphasise that they wished to maintain close contacts with the TUC and intended to retain large parts of their predecessor's reforms – most notably in the field of welfare facilities and public ownership. However, in their 1952 budget the Conservatives introduced reductions in taxation alongside substantial cuts in food subsidies. It could be argued that the cut in food subsidies was merely an extension of policies adopted by the Attlee government, but taken together with the fact that most of their tax cuts were directed at the higher income groups it could also be said that Conservatives were beginning to move away from the broad parameters of the 'coalition' policy accepted by the previous two governments. Partly as a result the unions began to voice criticisms of budgetary and other economic policies, including the denationalisation of steel and road haulage. In the last quarter of 1953 these developments were followed by a reversal in strike trends – most notably as a result of a one day national stoppage in engineering.

One possible explanation of what was happening would be that the relationships built up between unions, government and employers since 1940 were dissolving as a result of a whole series of factors, including the determination of the government to return to a more 'market-regulated' economy. As a result there was an accumulation of differences and disagreements between the government and union leaders – e.g. in respect of subsidies, taxation policy, the abolition of direct controls and so on. Yet it is important to point out that during this period the government still continued to fulfil its traditional role as peacemaker. It intervened in a number of important disputes in late 1953 to secure settlements above the 'going rate' (Clegg and Adams, 1957). In effect it had turned away from the old policy of concensus without being too clear about what was to replace it.

CONFRONTATION AND NO WAY BACK, 1956–64

By 1956 there were signs that an alternative strategy was under way. The year began with an announcement by a number of firms that they would freeze prices for several months in the interest of containing the growing forces of inflation. This initiative was applauded by the government, and a series of speeches were made about the dangers of rising prices and wages. Meetings followed between ministers, employers and the TUC. These produced nothing more than further ministerial statements on the dangers of inflation.

In April 1956 the National Committee of the AEU passed a resolution in favour of a claim for a 'substantial' increase in wages. The following day the EEF announced that they had decided that an engineering wage claim should be resisted as such an increase would be contrary to public policy. By May the government seemed to be supporting the employers' position, while the unions were criticising the government and its failure to act directly on price increases. The nationalised industries quickly fell into line with pledges of price stability.

For a while it appeared that the government was moving towards some kind of *quid pro quo* with the unions – price stability in return for wage restraint. But no agreement was possible on the terms available and at the annual meeting of the TUC in September 1956 all forms of wage restraint were rejected. Negotiations on the wage claims in engineering and shipbuilding began in October 1956 and dragged on until March 1957 without the employers moving from their initial position of refusing to countenance any form of general increase. Following the final 'failures to agree' a national shipbuilding strike began on 16 March and a national engineering strike on 23 March. The government intervened as soon as the strikes became a real possibility with an offer of arbitration. The employers agreed but were not necessarily prepared to accept unreservedly any award. The unions rejected this offer.

Both strikes were called off on 2 April after the Minister had set up Courts of Inquiry to examine the two disputes. Their reports recommended 5 per cent increases without 'strings' or 6.5 per cent with productivity conditions. The 6.5 per cent offer provided the basis for a settlement.

These disputes were of importance partly because they were the biggest for nearly twenty-five years, but also because they arose from the government's attempt to impose an incomes policy by the threat of confrontation. As Clegg and Adams (1957) made quite clear, the employers went into the strike in the confident belief that they had the support of the government and were acting in accordance with official policy. But the government was not prepared to face the consequences of a prolonged stoppage in the wake of the Suez crisis, therefore they eventually pressurised the employers into settlements which the latter did not want.

In the event this change of tack did not add to the government's popularity or standing. The unions remained convinced that the government had conspired with the employers in an attempt to change the post-war balance of power in industrial relations. They considered that they had been able to demonstrate that the long period without industry-wide conflict had not weakened their ability to mount appropriate action. The settlement achieved was widely interpreted as an indication that 'militancy pays'.

On the other hand the government were much criticised on the employers' side, not least by the EEF, for their lack of resolve. As a result they took their first faltering steps towards a more formalised incomes policy with the institution of the Council on Productivity, Prices and Incomes under the chairmanship of Lord Cohen. The Council was asked 'to keep under review changes in prices, productivity, and the level of incomes and to report thereon from time to time'. The TUC at first gave evidence to the Council but, after the publication of its first report in February 1958, declined any further contact on the grounds that it was not impartial. More serious was the TUC's repeated rejection of all forms of wage restraint in September 1957. This led to a government decision to adopt a tough line of opposing wage increases.

Given that the private sector's attempt to resist wage increases had failed as a result of government pressure, it was inevitable that any further initiatives would have to be based, initially at least, on the public sector. The dispute that came to a head first concerned London busmen. Negotiations between the two parties broke down in January 1958. The Ministry was asked to help and at first agreed. However, after ministerial pressure the offer of conciliation was withdrawn. Ministry officials then proposed that an outside committee should be set up; both parties agreed but the proposal was blocked by the Cabinet (Wigham, 1976). The busmen then agreed to refer their claim to arbitration by the Industrial Court, but did not commit themselves to accept its findings. When the award was announced they rejected it.

An all-out strike of London busmen followed on 5 May and lasted seven weeks. The busmen received generous financial help from other unions, but appeals to widen the strike were rejected. Without external help the busmen were forced to return to work. The conclusion of the dispute was seen by many as a victory for government pay policy. A more realistic view might have been that all it showed was that there were some groups of workers who, on their own, lacked sufficient bargaining strength to maintain their claims in the face of determined government resistance. It also had catastrophic effects on the demand for bus travel and London Transport never fully recovered from the stimulus given to alternative forms of travel. (As a result they decided that they would never risk a similar confrontation in future, which helped the Transport and General Workers Union to negotiate rather more satisfactory increases during the next few years.) More importantly, the London bus strike did not indicate that the government had received either general acquiescence in its pay policy or sufficient support to be certain that it would be able to take on more powerful groups in future. Moreover, the success that was achieved was bought at the cost of a further deterioration in union–government relations.

After 1958 the confrontational aspect of government policy receded a little – although there were complaints from the printing unions that the government was siding with the printing employers in the 1959 strike over reductions in the working week. Yet during this period, according to Wigham (1976), steps were being taken inside the Ministry to undermine the independence of the conciliation service. Thus, says Wigham, the post of Chief Industrial Commissioner was abolished and it was made clear that in future the conciliation service would be expected to act as an agent of government policy, rather than as a totally independent instrument for dispute resolution. As a result conciliation officers were prevented from intervening too directly in the 1959 printing strike, although they were eventually allowed to procure outside help in the form of Lord Birkett as mediator.

This uneasy situation continued until July 1961 when the Chancellor, confronted by a balance of payments deficit, introduced a deflationary budget and announced a 'pay pause'. This involved an attempt to persuade employers not to grant any further pay increases for a limited period. Its most notable effect was in the Civil Service, where it led to the government's decision to suspend the operation of the Civil Service arbitration awards. This caused considerable controversy but there were no major stoppages over the policy, perhaps because it was not all that effective. In January 1962 the Minister of Labour announced that the 'pay pause' would finish at the end of March and be replaced by a 'guiding light' of 2.5 per cent. In the absence of any agreement or any effective back-up powers the policy was rapidly eroded.

A more successful effort to restore relations with the unions came in the field of national economic planning. Following a proposal by the Chancellor in August 1961 agreement was eventually reached on a tripartite body – the National Economic Development Council. Even though it appears that part of the price of TUC involvement was an acceptance by the government that co-operation in planning did not extend to co-operation over wage restraint, the new body did provide a lasting forum for the discussion of related issues of economic policy.

THE SECOND POST-WAR LABOUR GOVERNMENT, 1964–70

The election of a new Labour government in 1964 brought a new era of attempted co-operation in the field of incomes policy. This was exemplified in the *Declaration of Intent in Prices, Productivity and Incomes,* in which the government, the CBI and the TUC pledged themselves to a 3–3.5 per cent increase in earnings and instituted machinery and criteria to clear 'exceptional cases'. In the first phase of the new incomes policy it was interpreted in a sufficiently flexible way to avoid the danger of major confrontations – until the case of the seamen's claim which led to an all-out national strike in May 1966. While it is true that the claim was way beyond the norms of the policy, this was largely the result of the situation within the seamen's union at the time. (Essentially a new leadership was seeking to break with the over-moderate and management-orientated leadership of the past – or that was how the seamen saw the issues in dispute.) The government saw the claim as an attempt to challenge and defeat their policy. Partly as a result they allowed the dispute to develop into a major trial of strength lasting seven weeks. The result was a defeat for the union, but the fears raised concerning its effect on sterling prevented it from being seen as a victory for the government. In retrospect the physical impact of the strike does not seem to have been all that serious – trade seems to have been delayed slightly rather than lost. But exaggerated fears of its impact on the balance of payments contributed to weakening sterling and the introduction of further deflationary measures in July. These included a freeze in prices and incomes until the end of the year, together with statutory powers to enforce the policy.

At the meeting of the TUC in September this new phase of incomes policy was accepted. In October the statutory powers of enforcement were brought into operation after there had been a number of breaches of the policy. The period of freeze was accompanied by a fall in strike activity, but the deflationary measures caused a simultaneous rise in unemployment. It will be remembered that we failed to find any strong and consistent relationship between changes in unemployment and strike activity in Chapter 6. We also noted a fall in strike activity in the period 1948–50 which, we suggested, was associated with the policy of pay restraint then in operation. We think this is the case here also. It seems likely that the 1966 decline was largely due to the very considerable reduction in the volume of bargaining which resulted from the six months' freeze.

In 1967 the freeze was succeeded by a period of severe restraint under which there was to be no general increase, although a number of exceptional criteria were announced which would justify increases. The use of compulsory powers to enforce this policy was rejected by a conference of union executives in the following March. (An alternative policy – to co-ordinate major wage claims, so that they would be submitted and negotiated simultaneously, was approved but came to nothing.) Severe restraint continued to be the official policy in 1967–8 and was followed by a 'ceiling' of 3.5 per cent in 1968–9 and a norm of 2.5–4.5 per cent in 1969–70. Despite the efforts of the National Board for Prices and Incomes the policy was not successful, in the sense that most groups settled above these figures.

Of course it can be argued that incomes policies are best judged in terms of what would have happened in their absence, rather than in terms of their own objectives. But from the available evidence (e.g. Cohen, 1971, pp. 256–261) it appears that in this period the incomes policy had little beneficial effect on the wage round. Indeed it can be argued that by 1968–9 the policy had become counter-productive. However, our central interest does not lie in a precise assessment of the success or failure of particular incomes policies. Our concern is to evaluate the contribution made to the upsurge in strike activity after 1967 by the declining acceptability of the government's policies.

Here it is worth recalling that the increase in strike activity in 1951 came at the end of a similar period of pay restraint under a previous Labour government. That increase was contrary to the general trend for the period. While it may be largely explained by reference to the unusual rate of price increases, consequent on the 1949 devaluation and the Korean War-inspired commodity boom, it seems only reasonable to accept that the desire of many groups to rectify the relative inequities which occurred as a result of wage drift during the period of effective restraint contributed to the unrest.

Clegg (1971) puts forward a persuasive case for a similar effect after the 1966 freeze. He suggests that this was partly the result of conventional drift, arising out of the continuance of piecework bargaining, but it also operated in a context of expanding shop-floor bargaining of a different kind, where the size of bargaining units was susceptible to change as a result of productivity deals and where expectations were raised by knowledge of increases being gained elsewhere. Here it is particularly significant to note that the increase in strike activity after 1966 was not confined to the traditionally strike-prone groups. Occupational groups who had rarely if ever before taken militant action became involved. This suggests that some general influences were at work and that the social or economic constraints which had previously deterred these groups from strike action had become inoperative.

Two reasons may be advanced for this development. First, as Clegg stresses, the operation of the incomes policy productivity criteria undoubtedly benefitted some workers much more than others. It would be understandable if those who felt themselves disadvantaged sought to redress this situation by strike action. Secondly, the possibility of a productivity agreement – especially in the public sector – often seemed to depend on the likelihood of a strike unless a way could be found to justify a settlement substantially above the norm. Thus references often seemed to be made to the Prices and Incomes Board as a means of 'buying off' strikes (McCarthy and Liddle, 1972). Similarly, the productivity experts of the Department of Employment were often available to find the basis for a productivity agreement when the strike notices went out. It thus came to appear as if strike action, or the threat of strike action, could produce a relatively painless 'bending' of the policy. It therefore seems likely that many work groups, or their stewards, formed the conclusion that industrial action was likely to produce results which peaceful negotiations would never accomplish.

The other reason sometimes advanced for the unprecedented rise in the number of strikes towards the end of the Labour government's period of office is that it was in some way related to trade union irritation over the publication of the White Paper *In Place of Strife*. Clegg (1971) examines and rightly dismisses this view, largely on the grounds that the upsurge was well under way when the White Paper was published. A less easily testable argument is that dissatisfaction with an increasing number of different aspects of the Wilson government's policies, which included *In Place of Strife*, combined to produce growing frustration on the part of union leaders and activists. The effect of this was that they were not prepared to urge the need for restraint any longer – despite the continued presence of a Labour administration. After all, we have already concluded that support for the aims and objectives of the Attlee government played some part in securing a relatively low level of strike activity in the immediate post-war period.

All that is being said here is that during the last year or so of the Wilson government a period arose when most union leaders and activists felt unable or unwilling to perform a similar role, and that this must have had an effect. An argument of this kind helps to explain why there was an improvement in the strike pattern in the second quarter of 1970. For the pre-election atmosphere, the abandonment of the unpopular parts of *In Place of Strife*, and the acceptance of additional responsibilities in respect of strike settlement by the TUC might be expected to have worked in the opposite direction (see the following section). It is also compatible with the short-run continuance of the downward trend after the return of the Conservatives in June 1970. As we saw in 1951, there is a tendency for the trade unions to adopt a 'wait and see' attitude towards an incoming administration – even if they had hoped it would not be elected.

On balance, then, it seems that – with the possible exception of the seamen's strike – the Labour government's incomes policies did not contribute very much to an increase in strike activity until the latter part of its period in office. Even then the impact was more marked in terms of number of stoppages than workers involved or working days lost, largely because the government strove mightily to avoid major confrontations. On the other hand, and partly as a result of the trade union beliefs about the uneven and inequitable impact of the productivity criteria, some part of the increase in strike numbers was probably affected by the past application of incomes policy. But even here it must be remembered that there were other factors at work – including, for a while at least, union dissatisfaction with other aspects of the government's policies.

CONFRONTATION AND LEGAL REGULATION

The Conservatives began by denying the need for a formal incomes policy, but by the autumn of 1970 they were committed to the informal policy known as '*n* - 1'. The essence of this policy was an attempt to force down the level of successive settlements (if possible by as much as 1 per cent a settlement). Given the commitment of the government to controversial legislative change in the form of an Industrial Relations Bill that was opposed by the TUC there was no hope of an agreed policy of any kind. Moreover, since the new Prime Minister had already announced his total opposition to all forms of statutory control over pay, what the government needed could not be imposed by law. Therefore the only course open to them was to seek to set 'an example' in the public sector, and to return to the policy of restricting access to conciliation and arbitration where they had reason to believe that the results would be unduly inflationary. Thus in many ways the policy of '*n* - 1' resembled that tried by the Conservatives in 1956–61 – except that the higher rate of inflation made it impossible to propose that there should be any form of 'pay pause'.

Naturally enough the trade unions denounced this policy as one of 'confrontation' – especially during and after the first major dispute of the period which led to the Local Authority workers' stoppage of 1970. During the dispute it was widely believed that government pressure on Local Authority employers had prevented an improved offer. It was also openly admitted that the government had refused access to the usual conciliation machinery, on the grounds that the existing offer of the employers was already too high. As a result the parties were eventually forced to set up a committee of inquiry of their own without any assistance from the Department of Employment. When the inquiry recommended what the government considered to be over-generous terms their report was criticised and action taken to ensure that one member, H. A. Clegg, should not be reappointed to the chairmanship of the Civil Service Arbitration Tribunal.

There then followed a series of major disputes in the public sector which were all directly related to attempts to impose the policy of 'n - 1' (e.g. in electricity supply, the Post Office and coal mining). In the case of the Post Office the victory clearly went to the government, for the postal workers were forced to accept a settlement which was on offer before their seven week strike. In electricity supply the end result was more of a compromise – since the government eventually agreed to a Court of Inquiry under Lord Wilberforce and his report improved on the employer's offer. On the other hand the mineworkers strike, in early 1972, ended in the total defeat of the government. Once again the Department of Employment was compelled to establish a Court of Inquiry under Wilberforce and he and his colleagues more or less conceded the sum total of the miners' claim.

The policy of 'n - 1' was not only felt in the public sector. Employers in the private sector used it to justify their resistance to relatively high claims throughout 1971 and 1972 (e.g. the Ford strike of 1971, the engineering stoppages of 1972 and the building workers' strike of the same year). The effect can be seen most clearly in the net total of working days lost which exceeded thirteen million for the first time in the post-war years in 1971 and remained at this high level in 1972 (in the period 1946–70 the average net total of working days lost was less than three million per year). The number of workers involved and the number of stoppages remained at historically high levels despite the fall from 1970; in 1972 both the series resumed their upward path and showed further increases in 1973.

By the late summer of 1972 it was becoming increasingly clear that the government's hopes of reducing the rate of inflation by 'setting an example in the public sector' were not going to be met. In these conditions the government's objections to a more formal incomes policy subsided and efforts were made to reach an agreement on wage restraint. These attempts failed and in November 1972 a 90 day freeze on prices and incomes was announced. The freeze was backed by statutory powers. In January details of the prices and incomes policy were spelled out in a White Paper, which also included proposals to extend the pay freeze until the end of March and to institute a Pay Board and a Prices Commission. The TUC denied the need for either a freeze or a statutory policy, yet unions were not called upon to defy the law and most of the TUC's detailed arguments concerned the position of groups 'caught' by the freeze – i.e. those whose pay was linked with groups who had managed to obtain an increase just before the freeze was imposed. This was the position of gas workers and ancillaries in the Health Service. Disputes arising out of their postponed claims involved a loss of just about 700 000 working days. In general the net totals of strike activity during this period showed an increase in number of stoppages and workers involved but a sharp fall in days lost. This pattern is compatible with spasmodic 'unofficial' localised protests and an absence of 'formal' macro-confrontations.

After the freeze the government announced details of permitted pay movements for the following nine months, i.e. until October 1973. Virtually all unions accepted settlements within the guidelines laid down, although the formal position of the TUC remained one of outright opposition. In the following autumn the government announced a further set of guidelines, designed to last another twelve months. Once again most unions settled within the terms laid down, until the National Union of Mineworkers declared its intention to seek to restore the value of the 1972 Wilberforce award. Failure to agree on the miners' claim led to an overtime ban and government plans for a three day week. The eventual result was an all-out mining strike, a general election and a change of government; but these are matters beyond our terms of reference in terms of the time span of this study.

In summary the wages policy of 1970–2 bore a strong resemblance to that of 1956–59. There was the same attempt to forge a coalition of interest between the government and private employers; the same belief that resisting wage claims would reduce inflation; the same willingness to accept increased levels of strike activity and to subordinate the state's peacekeeping role to the anti-inflation policy.

But there were also significant differences, both in the form and the operation of the policy. The 1956–9 version was grounded on the premise that there was no cause for an all-round increase which at least implied an equality of treatment. The latter policy gave more to those who happened to be early in the wage round – which was unlikely to prove acceptable to those coming later in the same year. Further, in 1956–9 the government sought to assess the bargaining strength of the different public sector groups, and even made concessions to the railwaymen at the height of the busmen's strike rather than risk a struggle which it had serious doubts about being able to win. The government in 1970–2 coupled an inequitable policy with the belief that to make concessions to one group would result in concessions for all regardless of the merits or strengths of the different cases. This belief resulted in a confrontation with the miners, and an eventual settlement that was almost certainly well in excess of what could have been agreed before the strike started.

The wages policy of 1972–3 attempted to resolve the first of these difficulties by using statutory powers to ensure that all were limited by the same maxima (minima have never been a part of UK wages policy). The problem here was that once again the policy lacked any mechanism for dealing with exceptional cases. This caused tensions during the first phase of the policy after the freeze but no major confrontation. However, in the phases that followed it led directly to another major dispute in the mining industry. (As a result of this dispute the policy itself was swept away, along with its authors.)

CHANGE IN JUDICIAL DECISIONS AND LEGISLATIVE ACTS

From the viewpoint of their likely impact on workers and their organisations it is useful to classify both judicial and legislative changes under two heads: supportive and restrictive. We have found that these distinctions help us to assess the impact of changes in law on strike activity. But it is necessary to subdivide the first category into two further subcategories, dependent on whether the changes were designed to create support for individual workers or for trade unions. Fortunately, for the length of this chapter, the only changes deliberately designed to benefit and support trade unions in our period were those included in the 1971 Industrial Relations Act. They sought to grant a number of legal aids to trade union recognition and disclosure of information. If they had been widely utilised they might have made some impact on the number of recognition strikes and related disputes. In fact, under the terms of the 1971 Act, such supportive provisions were confined to 'registered' trade unions. Because part of the TUC campaign against the 1971 Act involved a refusal to register on the part of affiliated unions very little use was made of that part of the Act before its repeal in 1974. Therefore, in what follows, we only had to consider the influence of other Acts and legal decisions which had an impact on workers as individuals – e.g. the Contracts of Employment Act 1963 and the Redundancy Payments Act 1965. Both those acts may be regarded as 'supportive' in that they 'raised the floor' of individual rights by laying down minimum standards when dealing with issues like notice and redundancy. Parts of the 1971 Act were also supportive in this sense – i.e. in respect of unfair dismissal.

By 'restrictive' changes we mean those legal decisions or parts of the 1971 Act which have sought to place limitations on the exercise of workers' collective power – most notably through membership of and activity in trade unions (e.g. judicial decisions such as *Rookes v. Barnard* (1964), *Stratford v. Lindley* (1965), *Torquay Hotels v. Cousins* (1968) and those 'unfair industrial practices' in the 1971 legislation which had an impact on the legal limits of strike actions).

RESTRICTIVE LEGAL DECISIONS AND LEGISLATION

We deal first with the development and effect of restrictive legal decisions. Here it is significant to note that virtually all of them occurred during the later part of our period – i.e. in the mid-1960s and 1970s. There were few legal developments of substance in the 1940s and 1950s and those that did occur, such as the ending of Order 1305, were largely justified in the name of removing legal restrictions on the operation of collective bargaining, so that it could operate in its traditional manner. This view remained dominant until the late 1950s when it was used to justify the abolition of the IDT. However, by the 1960s, as Wedderburn and Davies (1969) point out, 'a new judicial attitude became apparent'. They consider that this attitude had its origins, at least in part, in increasing industrial and social concern about the assumed effects of industrial conflict together with the related problem of inflation; in effect the judges were being influenced by a growing public debate about the consequences of the 'unrestricted' legal right to industrial action as it had been developed in post-war Britain. (Of course it should be stressed that we are not primarily concerned with how far particular legal decisions were themselves a product of past strike activity; our central interest is their subsequent effect on future strike patterns.)

Wedderburn and Davies (1969) list no less than five areas of law where restrictive legal decisions impinged on presumed trade union immunities in the period before the passage of the 1971 Act. In effect most of them involved circumscriptions and limitations on the coverage and extent of key sections of the 1906 Trade Disputes Act – which most union officials believed had rendered lawful the vast majority of decisions taken by unions during the course of strike action. When the decision in *Rookes v. Barnard* appeared to undermine a crucial part of the presumed effect of the 1906 Act, the new Labour government agreed to pass the 1965 Trades Disputes Act to set this aside. In consideration of this promise the TUC agreed to co-operate in the establishment of a Royal Commission on Trade Unions and Employers' Associations under Lord Donovan. The Donovan Commission was widely expected to produce proposals for further changes in the law. Many commentators foreshadowed proposals to further 'restrict' the right to strike. Meanwhile the Conservatives published their proposals for legislative reform, entitled *A Fair Deal at Work*. They included the removal of legislative barriers to the legal enforcement of collective agreements and a narrowing of the definition of a trade dispute contained in the 1906 Act. The Donovan Commission published its report in June 1968. The Commission proposed the codification and clarification of the law on strikes but no significant reduction in the ambit of legal protection. Indeed in one or two significant respects – e.g. in relation to actions for breach of commercial contracts – Donovan proposed a clear extension of existing immunities.

In January, 1969 the government published its response to the Donovan report in the form of a White Paper: *In Place of Strife*. Virtually all Donovan's 'supportive proposals' were included, along with its suggestions for additional trade union immunity in respect of commercial contracts. However, the White Paper included three potentially 'restrictive' proposals dealing with strikes to obtain union recognition, the provision of a compulsory ballot and the so-called 'conciliation pause'. These rapidly became known as the so-called 'penal clauses' of the White Paper. The conflict within the Labour movement arising out of *In Place of Strife* is described in some detail in Jenkins (1970). It ended with the government's decision to drop its restrictive proposals in exchange for a 'solemn and binding' obligation from the TUC to assist in reducing strike activity. (But not before a protest stoppage against the White Paper by about 85 000 workers in 1969.)

Following the TUC obligation it was claimed that the TUC's General Secretary, Vic Feather, had striven mightily and to some effect to avoid and resolve a considerable number of far-reaching stoppages in the period before the government lost office. Indeed one estimate (Wedderburn, 1971) quotes a figure of two million working days 'saved' or 'avoided' as a result of Feather's efforts. In fact no details are provided and it is extremely difficult to judge the impact of the TUC's intervention at this time – especially since they usually co-operated with the Department of Employment's conciliation arm at a time when Ministers were extremely sensitive to the slightest threat of a major disruption of services or supplies during the run-up to 1970 election. On balance the most that can be said is that the TUC's intervention probably contributed something to the downturn in strike activity which emerged after the first quarter of 1970, but it is impossible to say how much.

With the return of a Conservative government in June 1970, the focus of restrictive change moved from the courts to Parliament. The Conservatives introduced a comprehensive Bill designed to promote both restrictive and supportive changes in the existing legal framework. Its restrictive aspects relied very much on *A Fair Deal at Work* – tempered by a reluctant respect for the practical objections to some of its more far-reaching proposals contained in the Donovan Report. The essence of the Bill was in proposals to restrict a range of legal immunities in respect of strike action to so called 'registered' unions and their agents. In exchange for these immunities 'registered' unions inherited a further range of responsibilities and legal liabilities – for the most part concerned with their internal government and constitutions. Unregistered unions, and their members, were made liable to a variety of actions for committing a range of 'unfair industrial practices'. It was difficult to see how an unregistered union could organise and conduct an effective strike without leaving itself open to one or another of these penalties.

The effect of the 1971 Act in action has been the subject of at least two detailed studies (Thomson and Engleman, 1975; Weekes, Mellish, Dickens and Lloyd, 1975). We do not intend to report their findings, either in general or in detail. We merely wish to draw attention to the strike activity which marked the passage of the Bill and operation of the Act and make some assessment of their consequences in terms of the overall level of activity.

During its passage through Parliament the Bill excited considerable controversy and a number of token stoppages. The Department of Employment estimated that these involved almost three million workers and the loss of a similar number of working days. However, it is difficult to judge how far these figures need to be reduced because of multiple strike acts by those involved, and it may well be that there is considerable 'double counting' in this respect.

After its enactment the effect of the Act on strikes is even more difficult to estimate. There were, of course, a number of strikes arising out of particular decisions of the National Industrial Relations' Court, which had been established to handle legal cases arising out of its provisions. The most serious of these arose in the docks and engineering industries and involved a maximum of 730 000 workers – although once again there may be multiple strike act problems involved in making these estimates – and a loss of between 750 000 and one million working days. But it may be argued that strikes of this sort are only the most evident of the Act's effects. For the most part they arose out of specific protests against particularly unpopular decisions on the part of the NIRC. What we don't know is the effect of decisions of the Court that did not produce protests of this kind. What we require is some way of estimating how far the very existence of the NIRC, and its armoury of unfair industrial practices, inhibited or increased the likelihood that the parties would resort to sanctions in the event of a disagreement.

The short answer is that questions of this kind cannot be answered in an authoritative and precise way. On the other hand, those who have studied the impact of the 1971 Act are more or less agreed that its impact on strikes was minimal. This was largely because employers did not seek to exercise their rights to proceed against trade unions or their members who tended to commit unfair industrial practices – the unfairness arose largely because they had chosen to remain 'unregistered'. Moreover, it should also be noted that the government itself did not seek to use its own limited powers to the full. And when it did – e.g. in respect of the single occasion on which the compulsory ballot power was used during a national rail strike – the result was taken to indicate that the Act had failed to prevent the continuance of the strike. In time the NIRC and its related institution, the Council for Industrial Relations (CIR), appeared to be searching for ways of not imposing their powers. As a result, by 1974 the restrictive parts of the Act were generally regarded as a failure – at best a trap to avoid, at worst a provocative nuisance. (Indeed the Director-General of the CBI was unwise enough to hint as much in an 'off the record' and much quoted answer to a question at the time of the 1974 general election). The facts were that in terms of the expectations of its supporters, and the fears of its detractors, these parts of the Act were never really tested out: very few people sought to use it to impose 'restrictions' on strike action; as a result it never came within measurable distance of either provoking strikes or preventing them.

SUPPORTIVE LEGISLATIVE CHANGES

We turn finally to the impact of 'supportive' measures in the field of individual rights. There are at least three measures that merit some consideration: the Contracts of Employment Act 1963, the Redundancy Payments Act 1965 and that part of the Industrial Relations Act 1971 which dealt with unfair dismissal. The first of these is significant for three reasons. First, because it was the first important supportive measure in our period; secondly, because it tried to formalise the employment contract; thirdly, because it was the first explicit acceptance that 'job rights' were a function of length of service. The formalisation of the employment contract arose from the requirement that employees should be given written particulars of specific terms of employment within thirteen weeks of commencement. Another part of the Act specified periods of notice related to length of service. No doubt some collective agreements contained more favourable terms for trade union members than those set out in the Act, but there is little evidence that the existence of the legislation encouraged major demands and disputes on these grounds. Moreover, few strikes have involved length of notice issues in the past, so that the mere passage of the Act cannot be said to have avoided many disputes either. The probability is that its major impact, in the field of industrial relations, has been on the granting of strike notice in the case of official strikes. Thus whereas it had been normal for manual worker unions to give strike notice of almost a week, after 1963 most unions took the view that longer periods of notice were appropriate when longer service workers were involved. Here the assumption was that if unions wished to protect their members from the allegation of action in breach of their individual employment contracts they should provide strike notice at least as long as the individual's required notice in respect of termination – a view which was 'authoritatively upheld' by the account of the legal position provided in 1968 by the Donovan Commission. It has been said that the practice of providing longer periods of notice in respect of official disputes after 1963 was sometimes a factor in deciding workers to take more immediate unofficial action, but we have no reliable evidence on this score. (Paradoxically enough subsequent legal decisions cast increasing doubt on the doctrine of 'co-terminus strike notice. It now seems clear that longer periods of notice cannot remove liability' at common law for actions for breach of the individual employment contract as a result of collective action. This is why the statutory protection of Section 13 of the Trade Union and Labour Relations Act 1974–6 was provided by the Labour government of that period. (see Wedderburn, 1980).)

The impact of our second piece of supportive legislation, the 1965 Redundancy Payments Act, has been more considerable. The Act arose out of government concern over the malutilisation of labour in the economy and a belief that one of the principal causes of such malutilisation was worker hostility to the redeployment of labour likely to result in redundancy. The aim of the Act was to encourage better utilisation of manpower by reducing worker hostility to such changes through providing compensation payments based on length of service for those who lost their jobs. The intention was not merely to facilitate the shedding of surplus labour by employers, but rather to so improve the climate of relations by guaranteeing compensation that it would be easier to introduce changes requiring reduction in the employers' requirements.

It is not our aim to assess whether the Act was successful in producing a more efficient use of manpower resources, or whether the compensation provided fully covered the redundant individual's costs. One of the authors has already contributed to a study (Parker, Thomas, Ellis and McCarthy, 1971) which dealt with this question at some length and included an examination of the industrial relations effects of the Act. The evidence presented in that study showed that in the four years after the Act was passed the average number of working days lost due to redundancy disputes was less than half that in the preceding six years. Given that stoppages for other causes increased sharply in 1966–9, that the incidence of redundancy appears to have increased, and that conditions in the external labour markets deteriorated sharply, thereby worsening the re-employment prospects of redundant workers, one might have expected losses due to redundancy disputes to have increased sharply as well. On this evidence it was apparent that the Redundancy Payments Act 1965 had had a significant effect in reducing strike losses.

However, another study of the operation and effects of the Act (Mukherjee, 1973) has suggested that this favourable view of its industrial relations consequences was ill-founded. Mukherjee argued that the average number of working days lost in the period 1960–5 was very heavily influenced by a single year – 1962. If 1962 were excluded 'the loss of days caused by redundancy disputes in the period after the introduction of the severance payments scheme becomes nearly 12% higher than it was in the years preceding the Act' (Mukherjee, 1973, p. 137).

But simply to exclude 1962 because it is large does not seem to us to be justifiable. In fact it could be argued that 1962–3 provides a more appropriate comparison with the post-1965 situation than an average of 1960–5, in that they were years of high unemployment which were more likely to provoke conflict over lay-offs. Such a comparison would indicate a fall of some 60 per cent in time lost through redundancy disputes after the Act.

A more realistic approach might be to examine the events of 1962 to see whether there were any good reasons for excluding part of all of the time lost through redundancy disputes in that year from the comparison. Such an examination revealed a token one day stoppage on the railways over redundancies which resulted in the loss of 285 000 days. It will be remembered that in other analyses we excluded token stoppages, where we felt that they obscured the pattern of events. Therefore we feel that similar exclusion was not inappropriate for this stoppage. Using Mukherjee's technique of comparing 1960–4 with 1966–70 (but *leaving in the 1962 losses*, except those arising from the rail dispute) revealed that time lost after the Act fell by 12 per cent. Similar comparisons in respect of number of strikes and workers involved (the data for which only covered 1960–9) showed reductions of 21 and 11 per cent respectively.

Margins of this kind are not perhaps large enough to be regarded as conclusive evidence that the Act had a significant effect on redundancy stoppages, but they are persuasive. This persuasiveness is heightened when one recalls that other forms of stoppage, the level of unemployment and, probably, redundancies all rose significantly after 1965.

Both of these early analyses were based on information specially provided by the Department of Employment, as stoppages over redundancy were not shown separately in its published series. However, changes in its cause classification and a published retrospective analysis allowed us to trace events since 1966. Unfortunately this new series is not compatible with the old series.

The new series gives details of the number of stoppages and days lost through redundancy disputes. The number of stoppages rose slowly between 1966 and 1969, more rapidly up to 1970 and then fell in 1972 and 1973. Days lost fell in 1967 but then rose at an accelerating rate until 1972; there was a slight fall in 1973. This pattern suggests that the 1970–1 recession was a major contributory factor to this increase in strike activity, because it raised redundancies when workers were confronted by an increasingly difficult labour market. The response to the 1966–7 recession was more muted. This may have been because the changes were less severe or because the Act became less effective as workers acquired post-redundancy experience. The long-run upward shift in unemployment after 1966 lowered the probability of redundant workers being able to find alternative employment. In these circumstances a rise in strike activity may reflect, in part, an increased reluctance to sacrifice employment for cash compensation. It should perhaps be noted that when the Redundancy Payments Act was passed it was envisaged as operating to encourage labour flexibility in a period of full employment, not in the depressed conditions which have been operative for so much of the period since then.

On balance there seems to be quite strong evidence that the Redundancy Payment Act contributed to a reduction in strike activity in the late 1960s. There is some evidence to suggest that it became less effective in the early 1970s, but this does not imply that its contribution has become insignificant.

Finally we looked at the effects of the unfair dismissal provisions of the 1971 Industrial Relations Act. The provisions only applied to those employees with at least two years service with their employer, who were not part-time or over retiring age, employed by a close relative or a very small firm (i.e. less than four employees). Such employees, if they felt that they had been unfairly dismissed, could apply, within four weeks of dismissal, to the Central Office of Industrial Tribunals. The Central Office would then arrange for the Department of Employment's conciliation officers to take up the case and see whether some voluntary settlement could be arranged. If conciliation failed the applicant was entitled to have his case heard by an Industrial Tribunal. The Tribunal, taking account of the Code of Industrial Relations Practice, had to decide whether the employer had good reason for the dismissal and whether he had acted reasonably in regarding that reason as sufficient. If the Tribunal found in the applicant's favour it could award a declaration of parties' rights, compensation up to a maximum of £4160, or it could recommend re-engagement, although it had no power to order re-engagement or re-instatement.

The operation of these provisions and their effect on industrial relations have been the subject of substantial fieldwork by Weekes *et al.*, (1975). Their evidence indicates that the majority of applicants had been employed in areas where unionism was weak or non-existent: 'Three in four claims came either from manual workers in small private firms or from white-collar workers generally . . . All the indices suggest that those areas where unions were well organised produced fewer applications of unfair dismissal.' This is reflected in the fact that in 1972–3 only 12 per cent of applicants at Tribunal hearings were represented by trade union officials. (In part this may have been influenced by trade union policy decisions not to operate the Act. Some unions took this view while others left the matter at the discretion of local officers.)

Weekes *et al.* also examined the effectiveness of the remedies available under the Act, the manner in which the Act's provisions were interpreted in the Courts and the extent to which the existence of the Act gave rise to the negotiation of new dismissal procedures by management and unions. Their conclusions on these points are as follows:

> The evidence that we have suggests that the new law hardly secured employment . . . The law's remedies for dismissal as well as its coverage remained limited. This helps explain why those working in areas where unions are strongly organised made less use of the dismissal law. At the same time this law provided only a limited inducement for employers and unions to negotiate new joint dismissal procedures, although it did cause managers to review their own procedures . . . When Donovan reported in 1968, it considered just over two hundred strikes a year over dismissals were too many. In 1973 DE figures show that there were almost four hundred strikes over dismissals and discipline.

From this it might be tempting to conclude that the unfair dismissal provision of the Act had not merely been ineffectual but counter-productive – at least in terms of improving those aspects of industrial relations which are conducted through collective bargaining. But such a conclusion would not be supported by an analysis of the relevant strike statistics on any detailed basis. The fact is that a simple comparison of the number of strikes over dismissals in the relevant periods (i.e. 1964–6 and 1973) is misleading for a number of reasons: first, the Department of Employment changed its cause classification at the beginning of 1973, so that the two series do not entirely relate to the same set of issues; secondly, the earlier figure was specially extracted from a broader category to relate solely to actual dismissals, whereas the later one included a variety of employment disputes, only some of which were disputes over alleged unfair dismissals; thirdly, to compare the average of three years with the total for one is not satisfactory.

The Department made a more appropriate series available to us. The series showed the number of stoppages and days lost through disputes over the alleged unfair dismissal of ordinary workers in the period 1966–75. (Disputes over the alleged unfair dismissal of trade union representatives are classified separately under trade union matters. Disputes over the alleged unfair dismissal of foremen are included separately under working conditions and supervision.) The series was based on the 1973 revised cause classification and is subject to the usual caveats concerning this kind of causal classification and retrospective analyses. Nevertheless, it provides the best available evidence of the impact of the Act.

Prior to 1972 (when the unfair dismissal provisions of the Act came into force) stoppages over alleged unfair dismissals of ordinary workers showed a rising trend; from 1972 onwards a downward trend was discernable. In 1968–71 stoppages over alleged unfair dismissals averaged 202 per year; in 1972–5 they fell to 141 a year. It is of course true that the gross total of stoppages showed a fall over this same period but alleged unfair dismissal stoppages fell more sharply than the general trend. In relation to the gross total of non-wage stoppages, alleged unfair dismissal stoppages accounted for 16.2 per cent of the total in 1968–71 and 12.9 per cent in 1972–75. Time lost through alleged unfair dismissal stoppages followed a similar pattern – the average annual total of days lost fell from 165 000 prior to the Act to 147 000 after its implementation. In relation to days lost through the gross total of non-wage stoppages this represented a fall from 10.1 to 7.9 per cent.

Within the totals of stoppages over alleged unfair dismissals the Department distinguished four separate reasons put forward to justify the dismissal: personal unreliability; work which was poor in quality or insufficient in amount; refusal to accept instruction of the work allotted; other offences. Following the implementation of the Act there were marked shifts in the contributions of these four reasons to the total of alleged unfair dismissal stoppages. Personal unreliability and refusal to accept the work allotted both increased their shares of the total – from 36 to 48 per cent and from 16 to 19 per cent respectively. Unfortunately it is not possible to say whether this represented an increase in employer reluctance to dismiss for the other reasons or whether employers believed that dismissals on these grounds were more likely to be judged as fair by Industrial Tribunals.

In summary both the number of stoppages and the amount of time lost over alleged unfair dismissals fell in the four years following the implementation of the Act. The reductions in strike activity were not especially large but it was not expected that the provisions would have much impact in strongly organised workplaces. Furthermore, the downward trend continued through 1974–5. (Stoppages and time lost over alleged unfair dismissals were lower in 1975 than at any time since 1966.) There are three possible reasons for this continuing downward trend. First, the coverage of the unfair dismissal provisions was extended by the Trade Union and Labour Relations Act 1974 so that the qualifying period of employment was reduced from two years to six months. Secondly, the repeal of the Industrial Relations Act in 1974 removed the constraint that some union officials felt about using Industrial Tribunals. In consequence some disputes which might otherwise have resulted in stoppages may have been handled through the statutory machinery. Thirdly, there may have been a 'learning effect'. As employers and workers gained experience of the operation of the legislation some disputes may have been avoided whilst others were dealt with through Tribunals.

SUMMARY AND CONCLUSIONS

The aim of this chapter was to examine the state's actions in respect of its traditional industrial peace-keeping role, its development of incomes policies and its initiation of new legislation in order to assess the impact of these changes, individually and collectively, on the level and form of strike activity in the post-war UK.

There are three principal means by which the government has sought to fulfil its peace-keeping obligations – conciliation, arbitration and inquiry. Records of conciliation work between 1946 and 1960 are incomplete but those available show that there was a substantial rise in conciliation cases in the immediate post-war years and then an even greater fall (54 per cent between 1953 and 1960). Interpretation of these events is complicated by the fact that we only have information on the number of settled conciliation cases and not on the total of conciliation cases, so that changes could come about either through changes in the settlement rate or through changes in the number of cases or both. Given the magnitude of the changes involved it is more likely that the total of cases changed substantially than that the settlement rate did, because otherwise one has to postulate very substantial changes in the latter and there is no particular reason to suppose that there was a change of this magnitude in the period under review. Therefore we may contrast the number of settled conciliation cases (as an index of conciliation activity) with the net total of stoppages – assuming that the latter may also be taken as a crude indication of the interaction between the volume of bargaining and the magnitude of the differences between the parties. The result is a relative fall of 80 per cent in the former during the period 1953–60. We take this to indicate a substantial decline in the relative use of official machinery for preventing and settling strikes during the period. We consider that there is ample evidence to indicate that part of this was the conscious and deliberate result of government policy. In effect the government sought to withdraw or make its services less freely available and universally acceptable to the parties. Some part of the increase in strike activity during this period may surely be put down to this fact.

After 1960 the number of settled conciliation cases rose in absolute terms, although it was not until 1970 that it exceeded the post-war peak of 1949 – indeed in relation to the net total of stoppages even the 1973 figure was below the levels which existed in the 1940s and early 1950s. Other information which became available after 1960 shows that the number of conciliation cases in which stoppages had occurred amounted to between 5 and 7 per cent of the net total of stoppages for most of the period 1961–73. The exceptional years were 1961, when it was only 4.7 per cent, and 1971 and 1973, when it was 8.0 and 9.3 per cent respectively. The majority of conciliation work concerned disputes in which no stoppage of work had occurred, although the ratio of stoppage to non-stoppage cases rose from one in five in 1961 to less than one in three in 1973.

Turning to state-sponsored voluntary arbitration we discovered a similar record of relative decline and withdrawal. As we say, arbitration can take a number of forms and to some extent they exhibit different patterns of growth and decline. Nevertheless, if we aggregate the different sorts of arbitration, we find that up to about 1960 it followed a similar pattern to conciliation – i.e. an increase in the immediate post-war years and a decline during the 1950s. After 1960 the similarity disappears, there being no upward movement in the overall number of hearings as there was in the conciliation case. As in our examination of conciliation activity, we compared the number of arbitration hearings with the net total of stoppages: 1953 emerged as the peak year with approximately one arbitration case per five stoppages; by 1960 this had fallen to one arbitration case per twenty stoppages. Thereafter, the relative decline continued, albeit more slowly, although there was a slight upturn in 1971–2 which was not maintained into 1973. We considered a number of technical arguments which might be put forward to explain this decline in the use of arbitration but none of them seemed particularly satisfactory. This led us to the conclusion that the decline was also a cause for concern.

In addition to the various forms of voluntary arbitration we drew attention to the compulsory arbitration system which operated from 1940 to 1951 and to the *ex parte* arbitration system which succeeded it and lasted until 1959. The compulsory arbitration system was accompanied by a ban on effectively all kinds of strikes and lockouts, but there seems to be little evidence that the ban had much effect on the direction of change of strike activity, although it is possible that it served to depress the overall level. We noted that, regardless of its effects on levels, the ban had had a significant impact on the form of activity as it had meant that for eleven years virtually all strikes had been unofficial and unconstitutional, because of union support for the ban and the existence of a compulsory arbitration system to deal with disputes which could not be resolved in procedure. It seems very likely that the experience and the developments of those years had played a significant part in the growth of a system of shop-floor representation accustomed to operating outside the normal bargaining procedures and prepared when necessary to adopt sanctions in cases of dispute. We suggested that in the light of this experience it might be more useful to invert the usual questions about the UK's high liability to unofficial stoppages and enquire instead why it was that official strikes made a reappearance in the 1950s.

We noted that in addition to the lifting of the ban on stoppages in 1951, the change to *ex parte* arbitration also involved a significant shift of emphasis. In effect the preservation of the existing collective bargaining machinery took precedence over the need to avoid stoppages. Nevertheless, *ex parte* arbitration was used in a wide variety of industrial and occupational circumstances with some considerable success, judging by its apparent ability to secure settlements. It was abolished in 1958 after doubtful representations by the employers which the government was willing to accept at their face value.

The final form of government intervention, its powers of inquiry and investigation, were used much less frequently than the other two, on average four times a year with an actual range between none at all and nine times a year. In the periods 1959–62 and 1971–3 there was an average of one inquiry a year compared to an average of five in the remaining years. There seem to have been no clear upward or downward trends in the use of this form of intervention, although the small number of cases and the year to year volatility render interpretation difficult. In relation to the net total of stoppages there is evidence of a sharp fall in the use of this form of dispute resolution in the late 1950s and little sign of improvement in the 1960s.

Taking all forms of state intervention together, which is not unreasonable as they constitute alternative forms of dispute resolution, reveals a number of trends which we feel are crucial to an explanation of the post-war strike pattern as it has emerged in our study. It is evident that the number of interventions rose sharply during the period of the post-war peace (i.e. 1946–8) and remained at a relatively high level until 1953 when they started to decline. This decline was momentarily halted in 1956 but then it gathered speed until reaching its all-time low in 1960 – i.e. in the end of the period we have characterised as 'the return of the strike' and at the beginning of the phase entitled 'the shop-floor movement'. During this period, the number of interventions began to increase slowly, against a background of increasing strike activity, until, at the end of our final period, and in the midst of what we have termed 'the formal challenge', interventions were actually back to their previous numerical peak in 1949. Thus the broad picture revealed is one of a relative and progressive decline in the state's role in preventing and avoiding strikes which correlated inversely with the apparent extent and size of the problem, at least until some time in the early 1960s when the trend towards abstention and decline begins to show some sign of reversal in the face of an ever growing challenge.

A similar picture is revealed by a comparison of total interventions with the number of non-coal mining stoppages. This shows a rapid relative rise in the former between 1946 and 1953 until, in the latter year, there were three cases of state intervention for every two stoppages. Between 1953 and 1960 the situation changed dramatically – by the latter date there was only one intervention for every four stoppages. This situation stabilised initially but then worsened in the late 1960s when the ratio fell to one intervention per seven stoppages. The last three years saw a significant improvement, with the ratio rising to one in three.

From this evidence we are forced to conclude that there was a causal link between the government's industrial peace-keeping activities and the level and form of stoppages. It is appreciated that much conciliation and arbitration work is concerned with disputes where stoppages have not occurred, but such activity has a useful preventative role. In cases where stoppages have occurred official intervention, on many occasions, secured the withdrawal of sanctions. Our principal concern is with events in the 1950s, when state intervention declined sharply in importance while the number of stoppages continued to rise. Our study of the Industrial Disputes Tribunal revealed that a significant cause of the fall in the Tribunal's workload was the increasing reluctance of the trade unions to refer disputes to it. But the most dramatic change in the IDT's fortunes was its abolition – an abolition brought about by the government and employers despite the obvious likelihood that it would cause an increase in the number of stoppages. The abolition of the IDT is thus important not only because of its direct effects but because it reflects the prevalent attitudes of the time. The government was seeking to reduce the rate of inflation by securing lower wage increases and, in the absence of trade union agreement to such a policy, it was prepared to accept an increase in strikes and prevent the usual conciliation and arbitration work being undertaken in case it should be construed as encouraging higher rates of settlement. This attitude of the government was reflected not only in the abolition of the IDT but also in the decline of all other forms of dispute resolution. Such a policy had two serious implications. First, at a time when the growth of shop-floor bargaining was leading to an increase in the level and spread of strikes, the government appeared to be deliberately restricting and confining the conditions under which it was prepared to intervene to procure settlements. Secondly, this withdrawal by the government, although prompted by short-term wage restraint consider-ations, was likely to undermine the long-run acceptability of its conciliation and arbitration facilities – since it was justified by reference to the government's own priorities and objectives rather than the needs of the parties themselves. In this way the 'objectivity' of the Department of Employment's services were called into question and they tended to be seen as an instrument for obtaining settlements in accordance with the incomes policy of the day. This was bound to make it more difficult for the government to perform its traditional role outside periods of tight incomes policy, or when the consequences of a particular dispute made it expedient to favour a settlement. At the same time shop stewards and their members were encouraged to conclude that settlements could best be achieved by more 'militant' methods – most obviously stoppages and other industrial sanctions.

From this it seems reasonable to conclude that the fall in the number of stoppages between 1946 and 1952 was also facilitated by the ready availability of official means of dispute resolution which the parties were willing to use. In other words, both in the post-war period and in the period that followed, the relative popularity of the government policies and objectives combined with the availability and acceptability of its techniques of disputes resolution to make a mutually reinforcing impact on the level and form of the strike pattern. Thus the return of the strike after 1952 was partly a by-product of two complementary developments. Moreover, by the late 1950s lack of support for the government's objectives had declined into outright opposition, while suspicion of their intentions in the field of dispute resolution had lead to increasing unwillingness to use them – even where they were still on offer. Of course the period 1953–6 saw a rise in non-coal stoppages of 30 per cent. In the period 1957–60 the number rose by 84 per cent. In the light of the conclusions of earlier chapters it would be absurd to argue that the greater part of this difference can be attributed to changes in the state's attitude towards dispute resolution and its primacy in relation to incomes policy. Nevertheless, we would argue that the period 1959–60 stands out as one in which there were some across the board changes arising out of a culmination of influences, many of which have been specified in some detail in earlier parts of this study. What we are arguing now is that the change in government attitudes to dispute resolution also reached some sort of turning point at about this time. It was as a combination of all these influences that there appears to have been an almost qualitative change in the post-war strike pattern, leading on to a more or less permanently higher level of activity.

We would also argue that after 1960 the attitude change was so widespread and understood that its formal reversal was unlikely to lead to any immediate improvement. Moreover, in the early 1970s a new Conservative government returned to a similar policy. From the available evidence this had a less marked effect on the volume of conciliation and arbitration activity, but it did appear to result in new restrictions being placed on traditional forms of inquiry and investigation – at least until major and prolonged strikes had the effect of changing government attitudes in particular cases.

In conclusion, on this subject, we may say that there can be no doubt that the damage done to the acceptability and availability of traditional methods of dispute resolution in our period can all be regarded as part of the search for a viable incomes policy. This brings us to the general question of the role of incomes policy in affecting strike activity.

It seems to us that all the evidence indicates that on balance incomes policy has both provoked particular strikes and done a great deal to raise the general level of strike activity. It was because of fear of inflation, and the need to move towards some form of policy to contain it, that the government decided to modify and redefine its traditional readiness to promote all forms of dispute settlement. This attitude helped to produce and prolong several major confrontations towards the end of the 1950s, but it also had a significant and insidious effect on the atmosphere and traditions of the emergent shop-floor movement of the 1950s and 1960s. Indeed the notion of confrontation reached a developed and formal expression in the 'n-1' policy. This might reasonably be said to be a form of incomes policy that relied almost exclusively on the threat of strikes, if not strikes themselves. It is difficult not to conclude that during the period of '*n* - 1' most of the increase in working days lost and much of the increase in workers involved was the direct result of the particular form of incomes policy operated by the government of the day.

But even in periods when governments have not been formally committed to confrontation in this sense, the rigidities of particular policy criteria have made it difficult for the parties to agree on the kind of settlement that might have avoided a strike – e.g. in the case of the 1966 seamen's dispute, or the second miners' strike. More important still, periods of relatively tight policy have been followed by more relaxed periods, when groups have sought to remove felt anomalies against a background of rising strike activity – e.g. in the early 1950s and late 1960s.

It should be made clear at this point that what is written above is not intended as a criticism of incomes policy *per se*. It could well be that despite its effect on strikes it was necessary to have an incomes policy of sorts throughout much of our period. We make no comment on that proposition. It is possible to argue that since 1975 – i.e. in the two years that followed the introduction of the '£6 limit' in June 1975 – we experienced a period of incomes policy where acceptable guidelines and criteria helped to avoid conflict. Once again we make no comments on this view either. All we are saying is that, in our period, on the evidence we have, the pursuit of an incomes policy seems to have had a deleterious effect on the pursuit of industrial peace. Our findings in this respect are mirrored by those of Davies (1979), although our explanations are dissimilar.

This is not to deny that there have been periods when relatively tight policies have been accompanied by reductions in strike activity – most notably in respect of strike numbers. This happened in the late 1940s and middle 1960s. Something of the sort could be discerned, so far as wage strikes were concerned, in the first period of the Heath government's statutory policy after November 1972. But in our opinion – with the exception of the late 1940s – these reductions have not been due to incomes policy itself – in the sense that the policy provided the parties with acceptable guidelines and criteria, which actually promoted compromise and helped them to avoid conflict. It has been rather that periods of this sort were regarded as temporary reductions or halts in the normal process of bargaining. (Indeed on two occasions there were actual 'freezes' or postponements for specified periods, backed by legal sanctions.) They naturally resulted in very sharp reductions in the volume of bargaining – with inevitable increases in its pace and volume afterwards. It must also not be forgotten that during their period of operation there were legal sanctions of a kind, which probably had the effect of inducing an attitude of 'wait and see' in many trade union leaders and trade union members.

Summarising what was discovered about the effect of judicial decisions and legislative changes, the firmest evidence we discovered related to supportive change in respect of individual rights. There were clear indications that the existence of the Redundancy Payments Act had an effect in containing and reducing the volume of strike activity in circumstances where it might have been expected to rise quite significantly. Similarly, the unfair dismissals legislation appears to have had a marked and continuing depressing effect on stoppages over alleged unfair dismissals of ordinary workers. On this evidence it seems that supportive legislation may play a role similar to that claimed for some incomes policies – providing the parties with acceptable guidelines and criteria which promote settlements and avoid conflicts.

In the case of restrictive legislation we found that whereas such legislation provoked a good deal of conflict while it was being considered it appeared to have been relatively unimportant in operation. The main reason for this seems to be that those granted additional rights under this part of the 1971 Act – most notably employers – failed to take them up.

12 Conclusions and Explanations

THE AIMS OF THE CHAPTER

The aim of this chapter is to draw together our findings on the pattern of UK strike activity in the period 1946–73 and to develop our interpretations and explanations of its shape and significance. We begin with a section recapitulating the main features of the pattern in each sub-period and over the period as a whole. Attention is given not only to lasting trends and persistent characteristics, but also to some of the more transient features. This is followed by five sections drawing out the implications of our findings in respect of the various factors which influenced strike activity. These sections cover the general influence of the economic environment; the role of product and labour markets; bargaining structures and institutions; management initiatives and worker responses. A further section attempts to weld these disparate influences into a more cohesive explanation.

Following this analysis we return to two more general questions which have been raised at various points in this study. Both of them continue to give rise to considerable discussion and debate by students of the subject and interested observers. The first involves a return to our starting point – the pioneering work of Kenneth Knowles and his analysis of strike activity for the period 1911–47. Here we seek to compare and contrast our findings with his, most notably from the viewpoint of what has become known as 'theory of the institutionalisation of conflict'. In one form or another this theory has attracted many distinguished adherents since Knowles wrote – most notably Ross and Hartman (1960). We argue that suitably reformulated and extended the 'institutionalisation' theory is of considerable relevance to much that has happened in Britain in the post-war period – although we prefer to call our version of the theory 'the doctrine of accommodation and containment'. Stated in summary terms this is the view that strike activity can be significantly reduced by the development of acceptable and appropriate procedures for dispute resolution.

Finally, we return to the important question of the costs and effects of strikes – where in earlier chapters we had largely negative conclusions to advance. We consider whether anything further can be said about this perennially controversial but difficult issue in the closing sections of the chapter.

THE POST-WAR STRIKE PATTERN

The most notable feature of strike activity in the post-war years was that there was not one pattern but four, i.e. the pattern seems to have changed every seven years or so. (With our last sub-period it seems that there was a further mutation in 1975, which we discuss very briefly below.) To understand the period as a whole it was necessary to recognise and pose the relevant questions concerning each sub-period. Of course strike activity showed some variation in each year, each month and even each day. But our concern was not to draw attention to the myriad changes within and between each sub-period – it was to focus upon the more widespread changes whose explanation required more general influences.

THE POST-WAR PEACE, 1946–52

The outstanding feature of this sub-period was the overall decline in the net totals of all three basic measures of strike activity – a decline which was in sharp contrast to the periods which preceded and succeeded it. Disaggregating the totals series revealed a virtually complete absence of large-scale official stoppages which left small-scale unofficial strikes as the dominant form.

Examination of the industrial distribution of stoppages over the period 1949–52 revealed that, of the thirty-six industries included in the net totals series, fifteen had experienced a rise in the number of stoppages. In these circumstances we wondered whether it was in fact accurate to describe the period as one of declining strike activity. But a number of points may be made in favour of our initial depiction. First, detailed industrial information was only available for the period 1949–52, whereas our analysis of net totals covered the period 1946–52. It is therefore quite conceivable that virtually all industries experienced a decline over the period 1946–52; for example, in the metal trades as a whole it appears that strikes fell by over half between 1946 and 1952. Secondly, further analysis of the industrial data revealed that not a single industry experienced an increase in strikes in each year of the period 1949–52; that only one industry (electrical engineering) showed a sustained rise through 1950–2, and that a further nine industries showed an increase between 1951 and 1952. To reconcile these findings with the fact that fifteen industries had an increase between 1949 and 1952 requires a reconsideration of 1951.

We have already noted that 1951 – when strike activity rose sharply – was atypical of this sub-period. Seventeen industries showed an increase in strike activity between 1950 and 1951; only one of these experienced a further rise in 1952 but in ten of them the 1952 decline did not reduce the level to that of 1949. Of the ten 'rogue' industries which showed an increase in 1951–2, only one had shown an increase in 1950–1. It is conceivable that these industries were displaying a delayed response to the factors which elsewhere had raised strikes in 1951. These 'rogue' industries were drawn from a wide range of sectors and appear to have had little in common other than a below average propensity to strike – in 1952 they accounted for 18 per cent of employees in employment but only 8 per cent of workers involved. There is little evidence to support the view that the more strike-prone industries behaved differently from the rest during this period, the general pattern of decline affected them as well.

Examination of the gross totals of strike activity revealed that coal mining was the largest single contributor to all three of the basic measures. The majority of stoppages were small, short and unofficial and arose over non-wage issues.

Three principal questions are provoked by this sub-period: Why did the net totals series show such a substantial decline on all three measures? Why were the vast majority of stoppages small, short and unofficial? Why did a minority of industries display an upward shift in strike activity in 1952? Our answers to the first two of these are closely interrelated and derive largely from the analysis of the role of government to which we return later in this chapter. In respect of the third question it seems that the industries concerned were exhibiting a delayed response to the pressures which caused a more general upturn in strike activity in 1951. Outside of these industries it seems that the factors which served to depress strike activity throughout this period continued to operate, although their influence may have been waning.

THE RETURN OF THE STRIKE, 1953–9

These years marked the beginning of the post-war rise in the net totals of strike activity and the return of official industry-wide stoppages after a twenty year absence. The net totals showed substantial increases both within the period and, in terms of workers involved and working days lost, in relation to the previous period. Although the majority of industries displayed an increase in strikes between 1953 and 1959, a quarter of the total witnessed a decline. This mixed experience was reflected in the[7] increased concentration of strike activity in the most strike-prone industries. This implied that the factors promoting stoppages were at their most powerful in the already strike-prone areas, that the 'concentration' effect was greater than the 'contagion' effect.

The gross totals of strike activity were very strongly influenced by coal mining. That industry remained pre-eminent in terms of stoppages and workers involved but was displaced from its leadership of the days lost league by shipbuilding. Wage issues became only marginally more important as a source of stoppages but substantially more important in terms of workers involved. This latter rise reflected the influence of the large official pay stoppages which took place. Such stoppages occurred in engineering, shipbuilding, printing, railways and road passenger transport. At the beginning of the period such stoppages took place largely for reasons internal to the industries concerned; by the end of the period the influence of the government in its attempts to reduce the rate of wage increases had become important. Despite these occasional large stoppages with their major effects in terms of workers involved and days lost the overwhelming majority of stoppages were small, short and unofficial. From 1955 onwards the Department included details of strike activity by region in its publications. It was difficult to draw firm conclusions from this information but it appeared that regional strike-proneness was positively associated with the incidence of coal mining and high unemployment.

Our analysis of major stoppages revealed close similarities with the net totals in respect of changes within the period and in the industrial distribution of stoppages. Regionally, there was a shift towards Scotland and the West Midlands and away from Wales and Northern Ireland. Attributed causes showed a slight increase in the proportion of wage issues – which covered a marked shift from wage disputes to claims for wage increases – and rise in the share of trade union principle disputes. We thought that the latter was largely a product of the growth in shop-floor representation.

Of the many questions thrown up by this period four were outstanding: Why was 1953 the climacteric year? Why was there a resurgence of large official stoppages over pay questions? Why did strike activity rise most strongly in the more strike-prone industries? What caused the widespread increases beyond those industries? We return to these questions in subsequent sections.

THE SHOP-FLOOR MOVEMENT, 1960–8

This period had three principal characteristics: a very substantial rise in the net totals of strike activity both within the period and in relation to the previous period; an effective absence of long drawn out, official, industry-wide stoppages; the continued growth in strike action beyond the traditionally strike-prone industries.

The year 1960 witnessed the fastest relative growth in the net total of strikes of the whole post-war period. Thereafter the growth rate slowed down but the relative significance of strike activity doubled in comparison with the previous period. Of the thirty-seven industries for which information was available all but five exhibited an increase in strike activity. The concentration of strikes in a small number of industries remained very marked but was less than in the previous period. The metal trades increased their grip on this declining share. Previously less strike-prone industries demonstrated more rapid increases than the traditional market leaders.

Despite a massive absolute decline coal mining still had more stoppages than any other industry during this period, but was supplanted in terms of workers involved by motor vehicles. In the gross totals of strike activity wage issue stoppages again increased their share of the total, but still accounted for less than half. Strike activity by region became more evenly distributed. There appeared to be some shift from small, short stoppages to larger, longer stoppages but, given the declining importance of coal mining with its pattern of very small, short strikes, it was impossible to decide whether it was merely a compositional shift or whether it reflected a real change in the nature of non-coal stoppages. It is possible that both of these changes occurred. Information on stoppages known to be official is available for 1960 onwards. It revealed that only a small minority of stoppages were known to be official, that such stoppages tended to be significantly larger and longer than others, and that they had increased less rapidly.

Analysis of major stoppages disclosed that they had increased less rapidly than other stoppages in this period and, consequently, declined in relative importance. Their industrial distribution displayed powerful 'contagion' effects. Claims for wage increases became significantly more important as an attributed cause accounting for over half of the total. Regionally, the shift away from the Celtic fringe and the South East towards the Midlands continued.

The questions raised by this analysis are several: Why did the number of stoppages rise so rapidly in 1960? Why did it continue to rise thereafter? Why were more and more industries affected by rising strike activity? What caused the virtual disappearance of prolonged large-scale stoppages? Why did major stoppages and strikes known to be official decline in relative frequency?

THE FORMAL CHALLENGE, 1969–73

This period was distinguished from its predecessors by both the magnitude and the kind of strike activity which occurred. Strike activity in volume and especially in duration was higher than at any other time in the post-war years. In addition the earlier post-war pattern of small, short, unofficial stoppages and large, official ones was supplemented by two additional forms – one of which was included in the official statistics and one of which was excluded. The included form we called 'hybrids' because we saw them as a mixture of the two earlier forms. In size they were between the small, short stoppage and the large; they were more likely to be made official than the small ones, and they frequently occurred in response to some management initiative. The excluded form were 'political' strikes, i.e. in the view of the Department of Employment they did not arise from disputes over the terms and conditions of employment. The majority of these arose out of the 1971 Industrial Relations Act. Hybrid strikes had occurred in the earlier post-war years but became much more frequent in this period; political strikes had been virtually unknown before this time.

The net totals of strike activity, especially working days lost, were significantly higher on average than in the previous period. Yet, unlike earlier periods, clear trends were less in evidence. Stoppages soared, plummetted and rose again; workers involved followed a similar pattern, although in a more staid manner, whilst days lost simply peaked and fell. The industrial concentration of strike activity was significantly lessened, confirming the impression of the previous period that strikes were rising most rapidly in the previously less strike-prone areas.

Up to 1972 coal mining continued to experience an absolute decline in stoppages so that its share of the gross total fell from 40 per cent in 1960–8 to 7 per cent in 1969–73. Prior to 1969 it had only been in exceptional years that more than half of the gross total of stoppages were attributed to wage issues, in 1969–73 every year was exceptional. The West Midlands emerged as the most strike-prone region in the country, closely followed by Wales, the North West and Scotland. Northern Ireland was the only region to experience an absolute fall in strike activity – this may not have been unconnected with the increase in other forms of unrest in that province during these years. Very small, short stoppages again declined in relative frequency, leaving us with the now familiar problem of weighing the respective contributions of 'compositional' and 'real' changes to this development. Strikes known to be official increased in relative frequency.

Major stoppages rose sharply in both absolute and relative terms. Their industrial distribution showed a wider spread than in any of the previous periods, although there was little or no reduction in their concentration in a minority of industries. Claims for wage increases rose sharply in incidence in the attributed causes of stoppages, again accounting for over half the total. The regional distribution of major stoppages paralleled that of the gross totals series with the West Midlands again to the fore.

In addition to these familiar series we noted that nearly six million workers were involved in political stoppages which resulted in the loss of at least six million days. Political protests of this kind on this scale were virtually unknown in twentieth century Britain. We argued that the factors which led to protests on such a scale could not be excluded from an explanation of the high levels of the more conventional stoppages which occurred in the same period.

The complicated events of this period involving shifts in magnitudes, characteristics and forms of strike activity proferred a multitude of questions. Among the most important of these were: What caused such rapid changes in the net totals of stoppages? Why was the 'contagion' effect further strengthened in this period? Why did stoppages known to be official and major stoppages increase in relative frequency? Why did claims for wage increases provoke so many more stoppages? What was the significance of the rise in political stoppages?

AN OVERVIEW, 1946–73

The most dramatic feature of the period as a whole was that strike activity rose almost continuously and became more widely dispersed across industries. This pattern of increasing contagion was largely a result of micro-stoppages – small, short, unofficial stoppages arising from shop-floor issues. This form of strike activity was supplemented by three others: the macro, the hybrid and the political. The latter two only rose to prominence in the last part of the period. Macro-stoppages – large, official disputes – were apparent in the late 1950s as well as at the end of our period.

Despite the pattern of increasing contagion, micro-strikes were heavily concentrated in particular industries – especially in the metal trades – although this concentration lessened over time. The changing regional pattern of stoppages probably reflects both contagion and concentration effects as well as factors connected with particular localities.

In contrast to the steady and easily discernable growth of the micro-strike, the sudden appearance and disappearance of macro-strikes took on some of the characteristics of a conjuror's prop: 'Now you see it, now you don't'. Thus after a twenty year absence the macro-strike made a reappearance in 1953 and continued to command the stage until 1959. Most of these stoppages occurred in the private sector, although the government's fumbling attempts at wage restraint were a significant influence. Between 1960 and 1970 the macro-strike virtually disappeared again – apart from the single event of the seamen's strike in 1966. Yet despite fierce competition from other forms of strike activity, macro-stoppages regained their star billing in 1970–3. This latter phase involved a much higher proportion of public sector disputes. Throughout the post-war years claims for wage increases were the most frequent attributed cause of macro-strikes.

But these latter years also witnessed the achievement of prominence by two other forms of stoppages – the hybrid and the political. The occurrence of hybrid stoppages – in contrast to more sectional disputes – may have been a reflection of changes in bargaining structures and institutions brought about in response to earlier events. In some instances stoppages may have occurred in response to management initiatives to promote change, e.g. payment system reforms. Such stoppages appear to have been more likely to receive official union support.

Despite the fact that political stoppages are excluded from the official series of strike activity, their occurrence on such a scale made it impossible to exclude them from our analysis. It is worth emphasising the relative rarity of such events – as one distinguished commentator stated 'in Britain the explicitly political strike has been so rare that I can think of only one example – and that, in 1920' (Turner, 1963). The significance of the rise in political stoppages was twofold; first, it was, we argued, quite conceivable that the feelings which produced these stoppages spilled over to raise the level of orthodox stoppages; secondly, such widespread willingness to use stoppages for overtly political ends may be taken as support for our speculation that part of the earlier rise in strike activity reflected some dissatisfaction with government policy, e.g. in 1953. (Indeed one cannot help wondering, despite the absence of any substantial evidence, whether part of the upsurge in strike activity in 1960 was in some way influenced by the third successive electoral defeat of the Labour Party in the previous year.)

Finally, our findings on the scale of strike activity in relation to the economy as a whole should be recalled. Over the whole period the net total of strike activity in terms of working days lost amounted to 0.07 per cent of potential working time. In the last few years of our period this rose to 0.20

per cent of potential working time. Even at this level time lost through stoppages was less than 6 per cent of the time lost through unemployment. Of course stoppages were not evenly spread across the economy (neither was unemployment) so that losses in some areas were much higher than these averages. The Ryder report on British Leyland revealed that in 1973–4, the worst year of the previous five, the company lost 24 million man-hours – which was equivalent to 8 per cent of the time available to the company's manual employees. (Only about 40 per cent of these losses were attributable to disputes within the company.) Against this kind of exceptional case it must be recalled that large parts of the UK economy remained effectively strike free. The reduction in the industrial concentration of strike activity meant that the aggregate figures provided a more meaningful perspective than would otherwise have been the case.

THE INFLUENCE OF THE GENERAL ECONOMIC ENVIRONMENT

Our analysis of the influence of the general economic environment fell into two parts. First, a discussion of the existing academic literature on the subject. Secondly, our own exploration of the association between strike activity and various macro-economic variables.

We felt that the existing literature was, on the whole, unsatisfactory. To explain phenomena as specific, localised and concentrated as stoppages in terms of general factors seemed inappropriate – particularly when no explanation was offered as to the absence of stoppages in wide areas of the economy, despite their exposure to the same general influences. We argued that this inappropriateness arose from failure to recognise strikes as a transient feature of the collective bargaining process. Recognition of this failure underlined the necessity of accounting for the level, scope and frequency of bargaining as a prerequisite to explaining the incidence of stoppages arising from differences between the parties to that bargaining activity. It may be plausible to suggest that macro-economic variables influence the attitude of the parties to negotiations, and perhaps their frequency as well; but this is not to show that they are likely to determine the overall level of conflict, or its distribution and form. This seems to us to be an over-simplified compression, unless it is also asserted that the structure, scope and incidence of bargaining remained constant over the relevant period.

In addition certain features of the models used also caused us disquiet. In particular, virtually all models saw workers as the initiating agents of stoppages and treated claims for wage increases as the sole cause of disputes. Yet our analysis of UK stoppages over the period 1946–73 revealed that fewer than half of all stoppages were over wage issues and that non-wage issues should not be regarded as a proxy for the former. It also seemed unrealistic to assume that managements were never the main initiating agents, particularly given the frequency of non-wage issues. Moreover, all the studies used the number of stoppages as the dependent variable – usually without any justification of this choice. In at least some of the studies it seemed that workers involved would have been a more appropriate variable in terms of the theoretical models, although with less plausible results.

Despite our misgivings about the current state of the academic art of model building in respect of strikes and the macro-economic environment, we accepted that macro-economic variables might play an influential role as background variables and that there was a certain intrinsic interest in assessing whether or not there was any consistent association between such factors and the levels of strike activity. Consequently we used multiple regression analysis to assess the nature, strength and consistency through time of the association between various macro-economic variables and levels of strike activity.

Over the period as a whole some fairly consistent findings emerged in respect of all three basic measures. The level of unemployment and the rate of change of average money earnings in the previous year were positively related to strike activity and were usually statistically significant. The rate of change of real disposable earnings was always positively related but rarely statistically significant. Other variables including changes in prices and in unemployment were usually not significant. Both the number of stoppages and the number of workers involved displayed such strong upward trends that the various macro-economic variables tended to pale into insignificance in their presence. The working days lost series was much less influenced by trends and apparently more influenced by macro-economic variables.

We checked the consistency of these relationships by estimating them over particular sub-periods. In general the estimated relationships displayed considerable instability in terms of both sign and size between sub-periods. On the quarterly data the degree of correlation was much stronger in respect of stoppages than days lost. This finding was not repeated on the annual data where there seemed to be little difference between stoppages, workers involved and days lost. The quarterly results may have been influenced by a marked seasonal pattern for stoppages which was not identified for working days lost.

Interpretation of these findings was confused by the conflicting *a priori* possibilities attaching to each variable in its influence on the negotiating parties. If unemployment rose, heralding a recession, firms might be more reluctant to concede wage increases because of concern about their ability to pass them on in price increases. On the other hand, they might feel that they were unable to face a stoppage because of the liquidity problems brought on by the recession. Similarly, it is possible that workers, concerned for their jobs, might become more reluctant to press for wage increases. Yet the recession may have resulted in such a loss of overtime earnings that the need for a large basic pay increase to maintain living standards became even more pressing. In these circumstances a rise in unemployment could be associated with a rise, fall or no change in strike activity. Indeed it is most probable that different firms would experience different effects. Given these difficulties and the variability of our findings between sub-periods we felt it would be preferable to leave any attempts at detailed interpretation of these sorts of factors until our consideration of the product and labour market influences arising out of our sectoral studies.

Before that consideration, however, we felt it worthwhile to contrast our findings with those of Knowles. Knowles concentrated on the association between the number of stoppages and various macro-economic variables. He concluded that there was a 'forward' and a 'defensive' movement effect – i.e. in the upswing of the cycle the number of stoppages rises, whereas in the downswing the number of stoppages falls, but there is an increase in size and duration.

Our own findings were in direct contradiction to these, at least in respect of the number of stoppages which rose with unemployment. But we noted that Knowles' findings were based on very large fluctuations in unemployment – between the 'over-full' employment of the war years and the massive unemployment of the Depression. The fluctuations in unemployment in our period have been much less and the average level much lower.

A similar analogy may be drawn in respect of trade union membership. From a peak just after World War I trade union membership fell continuously and dramatically until 1933 and only really recovered during World War II. Since then union membership has either been static or rising. Within this general post-war context it seems likely that strongly organised work groups have felt themselves to be relatively independent of the cyclical fluctuations which have occurred, so that previous relationships between unemployment and strike activity no longer applied. Firms would have been similarly affected, with the added factor that the very substantial growth in firm size and market concentration would have increased their ability to ignore minor fluctuations in the economy. In these circumstances it was not surprising that Knowles' findings no longer held, nor that our own findings should have suggested changing behaviour patterns within the post-war period as employers and employees adapted to their changing environment.

There was one further way in which the general economic environment may have influenced the strike pattern – indirectly through its influence on government. In Chapter 11 we stressed the influence of government actions on the strike pattern. In so far as government actions were a response to perceived changes in the economic environment, then some of the influence we ascribed to them might be more appropriately charged to economic factors.

Finally, the aspects of the post-war strike pattern on which no illumination was cast by fluctuations in the general economic environment may be recalled. Such aspects would include the vanishing and returning macro-strike, the concentration of stoppages in particular industries, the contagion process, etc. To explain those features we needed a less aggregated approach of the kind adopted in our sectoral studies. The next three sections are concerned with those findings.

THE ROLE OF PRODUCT AND LABOUR MARKET FACTORS

Our reluctance to accept the propositions or findings of the model builders in respect of the relationship between strike activity and the general economic environment did not arise from a belief that market forces were unimportant in influencing the level and form of strike activity. Moreover, each of our three sectoral studies served to emphasise the importance of product and labour market changes on the conduct of industrial relations – they also revealed that apparently similar pressures of this kind could evoke a wide range of responses.

Indeed, in this respect we frequently found that even working at industry level involved too high a degree of aggregation. In order to understand the pattern of events, and to appreciate their significance for strike activity, it was necessary to examine the manner of the change and its distribution between locations. This was especially true in docks and motor vehicles where divisions within the industries resulted in different responses to similar events.

Thus, each of the three sectors experienced a different pattern of product demand over the post-war period. The demand for coal rose rapidly in the immediate post-war years, stabilised at a high level, declined dramatically and then stabilised again. Strike activity in the industry also followed a changing pattern – decline, rise, decline – which was not related in any simple and consistent way to the changes in product demand. Yet the fluctuations in demand, in pressing the case for change in the industry and in helping to bring change about influenced the conduct of industrial relations. It is also true that stock levels were influenced by changes in demand and that these had an effect on strike action.

Simultaneously the volume of traffic through the ports has grown continuously and erratically – and so has the level of strike activity. It is true that there seemed to be little consistent relationship between the overall growth of traffic and strike activity, but major shifts in the distribution of traffic between ports did appear to be associated with rapid increases in strikes.

In motor vehicles analysis was complicated by the industry's declining competitiveness. Consequently, although the demand for new cars, nationally and internationally, grew throughout the period, production levels in the UK stabilised after 1964. Up to 1964 production levels and strike activity rose together. After 1964 strike activity continued to rise – in part spurred on by worker responses to a series of unilateral management initiatives designed to improve competitiveness.

In summary none of our three industries displayed a single consistent relationship between product market conditions and strike activity, yet in all three product market variations evoked further changes which in turn influenced the level of stoppages.

Of course product market variations affected the demand for labour but other factors also influenced labour requirements. Thus in coal mining falling demand led to a change in policy on pit closures – unprofitable as well as worked out pits were to be closed. At the same time production was to be increased in the more productive pits. This led to marked changes in the regional demand for coal mining labour. The need to improve the industry's competitiveness also led to the faster introduction of new technology. These various changes resulted in substantial productivity gains, which in turn meant that the demand for labour fell faster than the demand for its product. Yet coal mining, because it was organised on a national basis, seemed better able to accommodate these reductions in labour demand without much resort to compulsory dismissals. This dampened the conflict that inevitably arose.

The docks displayed the most consistent pattern of output growth of any of our case studies. But here a combination of new technology and changing trading patterns meant that there was a continuing decline in the demand for labour, although the severity of that decline varied markedly from port to port. While the pace of change was relatively modest the industry was able to adjust by restrictions on recruitment and some measures to encourage workers to leave the industry. When the pace quickened in the late 1960s such piecemeal policies were no longer adequate, but the fragmented structure of the industry prevented any co-ordinated response. The result was a substantial intensification of an already high level of conflict.

In motor vehicles there was a closer correspondence between changes in the demand for final product and for labour. Employment in the industry tended to rise until 1964 and then stabilised. This period of overall stability coincided with a wider geographical dispersion of employment in the industry as a result of government's regional policy. The combined effect of these changes was to make employment less secure in the face of the cyclical fluctuations. As in the docks the fragmented structure of the industry resulted in a piecemeal approach to problems which affected all of it and the result again was an intensification of conflict.

Changes in the demand for labour did not simply have implications for the overall levels of employment in these industries. Patterns of recruitment, wastage and discharge were also affected. We argued that the manner in which these changes were brought about had a strong influence on whether or not overt conflict resulted. We also drew attention to changes in overtime, short-time and earnings which also took place. In each case study we found that instability of and uncertainty about employment, hours and earnings were potent sources of conflict and that increases in instability and uncertainty were associated with increases in strike activity. One of the features which distinguished coal mining from the other industries was that in the 1960s, in the face of falling demand for its product and the consequent adjustments which were required, substantial efforts were made to reduce this instability and uncertainty through the manner in which the rundown was handled and the reform of the payment structure. It would not seem unreasonable to suppose that the decline in strike activity in that industry at that time was, in part at least, a result of those actions.

On this evidence it was impossible to draw definitive conclusions about the ways in which managements and workers would respond to any specified changes in their product or labour market conditions. Different groups appear to have responded in different ways to similar situations. The most marked difference in response was that between coal mining and the other industries – in coal mining strike activity fell dramatically in the face of events which elsewhere appear to have heightened conflict. Central to this difference were the attitudes of the parties. In coal mining joint appreciation of all the industry's problems opened the way for a common approach to their resolution. In the two private sector industries such joint appreciation was much weaker; in consequence unilateral responses were devised which were much more likely to be met by resistance. Of course in coal mining there were many factors which contributed to the parties' abilities to develop a joint agreed approach. In the other industries these factors were not present, or only in a much weaker form. However, the central point remains that where changing product and labour market conditions create problems for both sides of industry, the result may be to raise or lower the level of strike activity, depending on the solutions adopted. Changing market conditions may exert a powerful influence on strike activity, but they are not the determining factor.

BARGAINING STRUCTURES AND INSTITUTIONS

For our purposes bargaining structure is primarily a term used to define the level or levels at which negotiations took place, e.g. shop, plant, company or industry. Different bargaining structures have different implications in terms of regularity, formality, payment systems and personnel involved. This can be seen most clearly in the case of coal mining. At the beginning of the period pay bargaining in coal mining was conducted at various levels – regional, national, local and pit. Faceworkers and allied groups were paid on a piecework scheme. Constantly changing conditions in the pits provided more than adequate scope for bargaining which in turn led to a high level of small, short disputes. This system was reformed over a number of years with the objective of removing piecework and replacing it by nationally agreed and applicable time rates. The effect of changing the payment system and the pay structure in this way was to change the bargaining structure as well. Pay negotiations became the province of full-time officials and senior management meeting on a regular formal basis. The effect of changing the payment system, the pay structure and the bargaining structure was to alter the incidence, scale and duration of industrial sanctions. At the beginning of the period industry-wide action had been largely irrelevant to the needs of the more dispute-prone groups; the change in the bargaining structure meant that it was the only level at which sanctions could seriously affect the pay negotiations. Changing the bargaining structure in this way did not make industry-wide stoppages inevitable, it only made them more likely. If national negotiations had produced acceptable results, sanctions would have been redundant. Unfortunately industry-wide bargaining made it impossible to hide the real settlement rate at a time of rigorous wage restraint, which resulted in confrontation. It must be stressed that the decline in strike activity in coal mining in the 1960s was not simply a result of these factors. It must also be emphasised that, in so far as these changes did reduce the level of strike activity, they did so not merely by altering the form of bargaining. They also produced substantive terms which were preferable to those which existed before.

In our other two case studies changes in bargaining structure were harder to quantify, although some impressionistic evidence was available. In the docks and in large areas of motor vehicles the first part of the period witnessed the supplementation of industry-wide agreements by sectional bargaining – particularly over piecework rates. Such sectional bargaining appeared to increase over time, resulting in an increasing incidence of micro-strikes. (Of course there were exceptions to this pattern, notably at Ford and Vauxhall, which did not have piecework payment systems.) Later in the period management, in a number of areas, sought to change payment systems and bargaining structures in order to reduce the amount of sectional bargaining. These changes coincided with the rise to prominence of the hybrid strike.

The implication would appear to be that, by raising the bargaining level in these instances, management simply succeeded in making stoppages larger than they would have been otherwise. This was because they brought more workers into the orbit of the dispute. Explaining why these changes increased overt conflict in motor vehicles and docks, but reduced it in coal mining, appears to reinforce the argument that disputes did not arise simply because of the bargaining format. Important differences between coal mining and other industries, particularly motor vehicles, included the following factors: the changes were jointly agreed and not unilaterally imposed; the substantive terms they produced were perceived by the workers to be a significant improvement; they succeeded in dealing with the sources of conflict and not merely its appearance; the introduction of the changes themselves did not generate further conflict. In the case of the docks we recognised that the post-Devlin reforms were far-reaching and that it was possible that they would eventually lead to an improvement in industrial relations. In motor vehicles the changes introduced did little to reform the wage structure or improve job security and seem to have had little discernable effect on the level of strike activity. These contrasting experiences do not contradict our views on the significance of bargaining structure – especially from the viewpoint of its effect on the form of strike action. What they emphasize is that policies to reduce strikes are likely to be unsuccessful unless they include measures which tackle the sources of conflict.

At the heart of the Donovan Commission's explanation for the rise in British strike numbers since the early 1950s was the role of bargaining institutions – i.e. the procedures, personnel and collective organisations involved in the bargaining process. The Commission took the view that the central defect of British industrial relations was defective bargaining institutions. This explanation relied heavily on an analysis of private manufacturing – most notably the engineering industries. Here, it was argued, procedures had not been adapted to accommodate the growth in sectional bargaining and consequently failed to produce speedy and effective results. Meanwhile bargaining between shop stewards and local management had become increasingly important without achieving widespread *de jure* recognition and formal negotiating bodies on both sides had failed to incorporate these changes.

With the benefit of hindsight it may be seen that this explanation was not entirely adequate. At least three problems were left unresolved. First, the Donovan Report did not, except in the sketchiest terms, explain what brought about the growth in supplementary bargaining. Secondly, as has been said, the analysis concentrated on the engineering industry. Yet our analysis showed that there was a very substantial rise in strikes elsewhere. If the Donovan analysis were to be sustained it would be necessary to show that the conditions highlighted in engineering were widespread. Thirdly, by concentrating on the necessity of having adequate procedural arrangements, the report tended to play down the significance of substantive terms and the difficulties involved in achieving substantive agreements which are acceptable to all parties.

However, despite these difficulties it must be conceded that procedural inadequacy – when coupled with the development of shop-floor representation through shop stewards – provides a persuasive explanation of two features of the strike pattern as it developed in the 1950s and 1960s: the rise of the micro-stoppage and the contagion effect. Sectional bargaining by shop stewards entails the possibility of small-scale stoppages, whilst the growth of the shop steward system across industries helps to explain the contagion effect.

Indeed, it seems plausible to argue that in a sense procedural inadequacy and the growth of the shop steward system acted as a kind of transmission mechanism – turning the conflicts generated by the clash between worker expectations and management intentions into bargaining requirements and opportunities. And sometimes bargaining failed to provide the basis for a reconciliation, or settlement, until there had been a stoppage. But of course the transmission mechanism also had an effect on the incidence and form of stoppages – in the direction of informality, spontaneity, short duration and smallness of scale. Reform of procedures, along with other forms of bargaining change advocated by Donovan, might well be expected to have an impact on the strike pattern through bringing about a change in incidence and form – but unless complementary measures had been taken to reduce the scale of conflict any beneficial results were likely to be severely limited.

MANAGEMENT INITIATIVES AND WORKER SOLIDARITY

So far we have considered the role of economic and institutional factors – each of them relatively impersonal and more or less objectively recorded. We realise that such a focus excludes much that may help to explain parts of the strike pattern – i.e. the personalities of the parties involved, the dominant ideas of the time, the parties' perceptions of the historical background against which they operated. All these factors probably influenced behaviour and attitudes. However, it would be all too easy to say that, in the end, it was *all* a matter of personality, or attitude; and we are not saying that. It would also be somewhat disingenuous to introduce subjective factors of this kind as a causal residual – suggesting that shifts and turns in the pattern that are difficult to explain on other grounds *must* have been due to them. There is also the problem that in the broad brush approach that is an inevitable consequence of dealing with macro-data over long periods of time, it is difficult to identify many of these influences at work. Nevertheless, in our sectoral studies, we did find evidence of two particular aspects of management and worker attitudes which stood out. This section seeks to evaluate their significance.

First, particular management initiatives for change and/or reform had an impact on parts of the strike pattern. In some instances management initiatives reduced strike activity; in others they raised it; in some altered its form. Thus the actions of the National Coal Board in the late 1950s and early 1960s served, with the co-operation of the unions, to secure a massive reduction in stoppages, although the experiences of that industry in 1972–3 illustrate the limits to such actions.

In contrast the response of the docks employers to the opportunities involved in the Devlin proposals was much weaker. Their failure to foresee the effects of containerisation, and their divided response when its consequences for employment became apparent, served to prolong the crisis and exacerbate conflict. Similarly, in motor vehicles, management initiatives produced a largely negative response. Turner *et al.* have drawn attention to the spread of conflict from the Austin to the Morris factories after the formation of BMC in 1952. Similarly the creation of British Leyland in 1968 appears to have extended the orbits of coercive comparison, which in turn engendered further conflict. In the same way, management-inspired changes in payment systems and bargaining structures in motor vehicles had a mixed reception, particularly where wage structure questions were left unresolved.

One aspect of management initiatives which we neglected to study, but which might repay further examination, is the extent to which initiatives arose from detailed internal consideration of the enterprises' problems, or whether they were merely the result of a 'fashionable' movement occasioned by forces largely external to the industry – e.g. the shift away from PBR in response to incomes policy pressures. Our impressionistic judgement would be that initiatives inspired by 'fashionable' movements were less likely to be successful.

Secondly, the attitudes of workers through this period require some consideration. We have drawn attention, in the sectoral studies, to the effect of different traditions and experiences in producing different responses. Consequently, it would be an absurd over-generalisation for us to suggest that we could accurately depict the attitudes of all workers throughout our period, or even at any time within it. Yet in terms of explaining the strike pattern – in particular why increasing numbers of workers felt the necessity to strike and were confident enough to do so – we feel we must say something about changing worker attitudes.

In general unions in the UK have eschewed, or been excluded from, involvement in the initiation and formulation of management policy – even in the area of industrial relations. They have preferred to respond at the point of implementation – most typically by the formulation and present-ation of specific demands and grievances. What is required, to help account for much of the post-war strike pattern, is some explanation of the factors which transform individual workers with a grievance, which may not be all that unique, into a group with sufficient sense of solidarity to adopt sanctions to improve their bargaining position. The development of such solidarity cannot be explained simply in terms of unionisation. The overall level of unionisation did not change much over the period. Moreover, employment changes involved falling union membership in areas with strong traditions of solidarity – e.g. coal mining, railways, docks, etc. – as against rising membership in areas where the solidaristic tradition was weaker – e.g. white collar employment.

Once again there can be little doubt that the catalyst has been the development of effective shop steward systems, especially in larger plants and firms. (See Batstone, Boraston and Frenkel, 1977 and 1978, for the best recent account of the impact of shop steward systems on group activity and solidarity; also Boraston *et al.*, 1975, for an assessment of the extent to which size of plant is positively associated with the emergence of shop steward systems.)

Of course we are not suggesting that in themselves the growth of worker solidarity and shop steward systems caused the rise in strikes; what is being said is that taken together they provided the final or precipitating condition. In other words, the mere presence of more general factors – such as economic pressure, defective bargaining institutions and so on – would not in themselves have been sufficient to bring about crucial upward movement in strike activity. To this mixture there had to be added the ingredient of an effective shop steward organisation plus workers with enough sense of solidarity to think in terms of industrial action.

A further aspect of worker attitudes relates to the interaction between social restraints and behaviour. We take the view that the social consensus in the post-war period has been one of disapproval of strikes. It seems only reasonable to suppose that this aura must have served as a kind of social con-straint, and that this was strongest where strikes were least likely to occur.

But surely such a 'positive feedback' relationship was most likely to endure where strikes were also assumed to be largely ineffective – whilst other methods of protecting or advancing conditions produced acceptable results. Once the perception of stoppages, and their relative success rate, was altered – as it seemed to be during the final stages of incomes policy in our period – then workers became more willing to imitate the example of the apparently more successful strike-prone groups.

Moreover, as strikes became more widespread, because of imitative action, we would expect social restraints against such action to suffer further decline. In summary the increase in activity plotted is likely to have fed on itself: the erosion of social constraints being accompanied, in time, by the growth of demands for other restraints – i.e. restrictions on the legal rights of unions.

In this sense we see no reason to disagree with the central conclusion of Cronin (1979), in his review of the outlines of British strike pattern since 1888. As he puts it:

> The basic point to emerge from this study is that social conflict is not the manifestation of some fixed and undifferentiated quantum of discontent that expresses itself in one form or another at different points in time. Rather, social and industrial conflict are the means used by ordinary working men and women to assert their changing needs and aspirations in the face of trends and problems that even their rulers and their employers cannot control (Cronin, 1979, p. 195).

THE ROLE OF GOVERNMENT

In many respects it is in its analysis of the role of government which most clearly distinguishes this study from its predecessors. Although we have set ourselves against mono-causal explanations of all kinds, we have argued that in each sub-period there have been certain aspects of the post-war strike pattern where the reactions and policy initiatives of successive governments have been decisive.

Thus in the first sub-period our explanation of the post-war peace contained two main strands – both linked to government policy. First, the government of the day enjoyed such wide popular support for its programme of economic and social reconstruction that industrial action was eschewed to avoid hindrance to their implementation. Individual workers' feelings of loyalty were reinforced by a powerful trade union leadership, deeply committed to supporting the administration. Secondly, in the period 1948–50, this general pattern of restraint was reinforced by the introduction of a wages freeze. General acceptance of the freeze led to a substantial reduction in the volume of bargaining and the level of strike activity. These social restraints were so powerful that they continued at least until 1953, even after the demise of the administration which had engendered them.

Of course, the post-war peace was temporarily halted in 1951, but serious and continuing hostilities did not break out until the latter half of 1953. By that time the Conservative government, despite its retention of many of its predecessor's reforms, embarked on its own distinctive economic policy of tax cuts and public expenditure reductions. As we saw, these tax cuts principally benefitted the better off. Their introduction marked the end of the unspoken government–union leadership understanding on wages, with inevitable consequences for the strike pattern.

But of course the rise in strike activity post 1953 reflected a number of general influences: government attempts to impose wage restraint policies, a reduction in all forms of third party intervention in dispute resolution, and the response of the trade union leadership to the power vacuum in which they found themselves. Attempts to impose wage restraint helped to precipitate most of the major stoppages of the 1950s. The reduction in the use of third parties had a more diffuse effect, but it must be remembered that it took place during a period when the growing level of conflict would normally have dictated a development and growth of services of this kind. Withdrawal from involvement in dispute settlement not only meant that there were more and longer stoppages, but also that the government was less likely to be aware, on a day to day basis, of the kind of problems arising, and the need for action to resolve them. The abolition of the Industrial Disputes Tribunal was significant, not only because of its immediate consequences, but because it typified the government's response to the problems of the time.

Union leadership, during the post-war peace, had engaged in a mutually supportive relationship with the government that required it to discourage strike action. But in the absence of an acceptable *quid pro quo* it could no longer be expected to react in this way. If it was to maintain its position in respect of its membership it had to be seen to be giving a lead. This involved a willingness not simply to countenance, but to actively organise stoppages where they appeared to be necessary. This, in turn, resulted in the reappearance of official industry-wide stoppages after a twenty year absence.

After 1960 official industry-wide stoppages largely disappeared for a decade. A number of factors appear to have influenced that disappearance. First, the struggles of the 1950s may have exhausted the unions' appetite for confrontation on such a scale. Secondly, the growth of sectional bargaining in areas where worker solidarity was most strongly developed probably reduced the relevance of and the necessity for action on a wider scale. But we would argue that even in this sub-period the government's role was important. There was a significant improvement in government–union relations in 1962, which was associated with the abandonment of wage restraint. This improvement coincided with the unshackling of the dispute resolution services. These services appear to have been particularly effective in heading off several major official stoppages – especially after 1964 and the return of a new government.

But the new government soon began to return to more stringent forms of incomes policy, leading to the major official stoppage of the decade – that of the seamen in 1966. As we saw, the timing and duration of this stoppage owed much to the 'fine print' of the incomes policy pursued by the Wilson government of the time. Yet other possible confrontations were headed off, partly by appeals to loyalty and partly by short-term references to the National Board for Prices and Incomes.

Of course the absence of macro-stoppages in the 1960s, which it is plausible to link with changes in the policy of successive governments, is not mirrored in the micro-stoppage series. In 1960 we observed the fastest ever growth in relative strike number. But even at this level we would argue that the role of government was not without significance at various points during the decade. In the first place the withdrawal of dispute services in the late 1950s must have been having a progressive impact. By the time they were recommissioned in 1962 their credibility had been severely damaged – especially at local level. Finally, the closing years of the decade witnessed a further substantial rise in strike activity at the micro level. It has been plausibly argued by Clegg (1971) that this was largely a response to five years or so of incomes policy norms which tended to discriminate in favour of some groups more than others.

In conclusion it may be said that in the final sub-period of our study all the elements we have identified above made a reappearance, accompanied by several others. Most importantly, major confrontations arising from the 'rigid' application of incomes norms staged a revival. They differed from those of the 1950s in that a much higher proportion occurred in the public sector. In part this was a consequence of the centralised bargaining structures of that sector and of the 'high visibility' of its settlements. But it also reflected an increase in worker solidarity and a greater willingness by government to impose its policies on its own employees.

At the same time the new government returned to the policy of discouraging the use of third party dispute resolution – especially in circumstances where it seemed likely to produce settlements in excess of incomes policy. They also sought to reduce the overall rate of increase in public expenditure and launched a major initiative in the field of trade union legislation.

This last development is generally thought to have had a critical and even decisive influence on the government's own fortunes – largely because of its impact on the strike pattern. It will be remembered that in the chapter on government we sought to analyse changes in the legal framework from the viewpoint of whether or not they were concerned with individual or collective rights, and whether they were intended to be supportive or restrictive. We found that legislation which was supportive of individual rights was associated with a reduction in strike activity. After the passing of the Redundancy Payments Act in 1965 strike action over redundancies was lower than previous trends would have suggested. Similarly, after the unfair dismissal provisions of the Industrial Relations Act 1971 came into effect, strike activity over dismissals was reduced. We concluded that legislation supportive of individual rights could have a beneficial effect by reducing the scope for conflict between the parties.

But the Industrial Relations Act 1971 also included both supportive and restrictive provisions in respect of collective rights. Unfortunately the supportive provisions, e.g. on recognition, remained unused because of the TUC policy of non-co-operation with the Act. The provisions restricting collective rights were met by an unprecedented wave of protest stoppages during their enactment. After they became law they proved to be of little direct importance – if anything their effects were counter-productive. From this evidence there was little reason to suppose that further restrictive legislation would have a positive role to play in reducing the level of strike activity.

THE INTERACTION OF FACTORS INFLUENCING THE POST-WAR STRIKE PATTERN

Our principal conclusions on the factors affecting the post-war strike pattern have been set out in summary terms in the foregoing sections. The necessity of examining each set of factors separately has served to obstruct a full appreciation of the interaction of all these influences. Consequently, we thought it would be useful to end this part of the chapter with a recapitulation, in sequential terms, of the main events and our explanations for them.

In our judgement the atypical downturn in strike activity in the immediate post-war years was largely the result of the restraining influence of a union leadership operating in a context of general popular support for the Labour government's economic and social policies. The continued incidence of stoppages in some industries throughout these years, together with the events of 1951, revealed the presence of the kind of factors which, in later years, were to lead to the widespread return of the micro-stoppage. Much of the interest of this period lay in the fact that such factors were not merely quiescent but actually declined in overt significance.

In the early 1950s the atmosphere and the relationships began to alter. The Conservative administration's programme did not command the same degree of support. Personnel changes in government and in the unions replaced 'conciliators' with less accommodating men. Government calls for wage restraint to combat inflation became more strident. As part of these wage restraint manoeuvres the government retrenched on the dispute settlement front. The effects of this retrenchment were long-run, profound and unwelcome, coinciding as it did with the spread of the shop-floor challenge and the growing inadequacies of the collective bargaining machinery. The result was that strike action spread across industry, producing the contagion effect as more and more groups rejected earlier social restraints on their collective behaviour. At the same time the late 1950s was also a time of macro-strike activity – largely the product of the government's aggressive pursuit of wage restraint.

In the 1960s the generation of more and more micro-stoppages continued in the most heavily strike-prone industries. Meanwhile the less strike-prone sectors exhibited increasing signs of the contagion effect. Changing bargaining structures, growing shop-floor representation and a worsening economic climate all contributed to these developments.

Yet the growth of micro-stoppages was not paralleled by macro-stoppages – there was a reduction in the incidence of official industry-wide stoppages. A number of factors were responsible for this latter change, principal among them a more accommodating government attitude – especially after the arrival of the Wilson regime in 1964. A good deal of government effort in those years was directed to avoiding major confrontations – often on an *ad hoc* basis with consequent costs in terms of wage restraint, productivity improvements and effective bargaining reforms. Such interventions were not always successful, e.g. in the case of the seamen, but they did contribute to a significant reduction in the incidence of major stoppages.

The last years of the 1960s saw the disintegration and collapse of the government's incomes policy in a context of 'stagflation'. Against a background of rising shop steward numbers and increased worker solidarity – which may have owed something to the low level of real wage movements and the spread of legitimate orbits of coercive comparisons – the demise of the incomes policy coincided with a record wage explosion and a further rise in the level of strikes by number.

But it seems to us that it is the last three years of our period that illustrates most clearly the importance of the interplay between general economic factors and government policy. In this period unemployment, prices and earnings all rose while the government sought to impose a particularly foolish and potentially divisive incomes policy. This policy, which sought to operate by imposing a progressively decelerating settlement rate on the public sector, was compounded by the usual curtailment of dispute resolution facilities. The result was a rise in the level of conflict – most notably in the public sector, where government influence could be most easily exerted.

The statutory incomes policy which succeeded the collapse of this series of measures, after the 1972 miners' dispute, was greeted, initially at least, by acquiescence if not consent – partly because the criteria eventually chosen for the incomes norms were less severe and less discriminatory. The result was a significant reduction in losses due to pay disputes, which lasted till the second miners' strike in 1974.

Other notable features of the period included a continued high incidence of micro-stoppages and an emergence of what we termed 'hybrid stoppages' – i.e. strikes which exhibited a mixture of the characteristics of micro- and macro-strikes, including a tendency to straddle the normal boundaries between the 'official' and 'unofficial' categories. We saw these as largely a product of and response to various management initiatives – most notably changes in bargaining structures, payment systems, etc. Finally, our last sub-period contained an unprecedented series of more or less 'political' stoppages – i.e. those arising out of responses to the 1971 legislation, including one-day protests and sympathetic action at the time of the arrest of the dockers' shop stewards.

In conclusion, our views and interpretations of the strike pattern since the war may be summarised in terms of a number of broad assertions. These constitute our general explanation for the variations in incidence and scope which we have analysed. First, strikes develop when union members and officials are capable of undertaking them, and come to feel that their legitimate demands can best be carried forward in this way.

In the post-war period the growth of effective shop steward systems was the single most important factor contributing to union capacity in this respect, just as the weakening of social constraints on the shop floor was probably decisive in conditioning union members to take the view that strike action had become a legitimate instrument to use.

Secondly, given the level of union capacity and worker solidarity, a multiplicity of other factors need to be taken into account in any worthwhile explanation of the strike pattern. To begin with strikes tend to take forms that are greatly affected by the shape and form of existing bargaining structures; if structures alter, strike forms tend to change, although the incidence and consequences of strike activity may remain as before. In our period the fragmented nature of existing structures was undoubtedly the most important single factor channelling shop-floor action into unconstitutional and unofficial forms, which were for the most part small in size and of limited duration. Yet towards the end of the period management initiatives had a significant impact on bargaining structures, leading to modifications in the form of strike activity.

Thirdly, given the role of these conditioning factors, the volume and distribution of total strike activity appears to be influenced by a number of important precipitating influences. These include the net effect of general economic conditions, particular product and labour market situations and a range of more localised influences – e.g. working arrangements, traditions, the level and form of unionisation and so on. In our sectoral studies we sought to demonstrate the need to take account of each factor and their interaction. We saw that few simple general rules in respect of particular factors held across all three sectors for all periods. Even massive violations of worker expectations in respect of job rights and fair wages did not always result in stoppages, although they had a malign influence on industrial relations in certain circumstances. We also saw that management initiatives for change met with varying degrees of success, depending on the manner of their introduction and their degree of appropriateness to the problems involved.

Finally, in any total explanation we would want to stress the growing importance of government policy. Of course, it is possible to regard government initiatives – most notably those arising out of attempts to impose wage restraint – as in some sense dependent variables: political reactions to economic stimuli, which are in some way more 'fundamental' or 'basic'. We would counsel against this view. In the first place, there are several different ways in which different governments can react to similar economic constraints – including the problem of inflation containment. The record shows that these can have very different impacts on the level and form of strike activity. For this reason alone they are worth analysing separately, and being given the status of independent variables. Secondly, the forms and scope of government intervention are complex and varied. Their motivation and roots are diverse and they vary through time.

We would argue that in our period a satisfactory explanation of the shifts and turns in government policy in this field cannot be hoped for if one limits oneself to an analysis of economic factors and considerations. On the contrary, one needs to take into account a complex mesh of historical loyalties, ideological differences, plus, on more than one occasion, crude electoral calculations. (There has also been a distinct element of political incompetence, from time to time, in dealing with particular disputes.) Perhaps it would be too extreme to say that 'governments get the strikes they deserve', but at least this formulation emphasises the pervasive and at times personal influence that individual ministers and governments have exerted on parts of the post-war strike pattern.

STRIKES AND THE THEORY OF COLLECTIVE BARGAINING

The first of our two more general questions involves returning to one of the issues raised in Knowles' pioneering study of the period 1911–47: What light does our work throw on the relationship between strike activity and the development of collective bargaining?

It will be remembered that the pattern Knowles sought to explain was quite different from ours. Over his period the gross totals of strike activity showed a sharp rise in the number of stoppages, a fall in the number of workers involved and a massive drop in days lost. (The net totals series showed a similar but less extreme pattern, in particular there was only a slight rise in stoppages. As in our period coal mining displayed very marked fluctuations with stoppages rising sevenfold and days lost falling by a comparable margin.)

In accounting for these broad movements Knowles laid some stress on developments in the form and coverage of collective bargaining – in particular on developments in the trade unions and in employer–worker relations. The developments in the unions were held to have lessened their willingness to take mass strike action. Such developments included their growing heterogeneity, which reduced their sense of solidarity, and the development of welfare functions, which encouraged restraint in dispute benefit payments.

Also of importance was a sense of permanency in union institutions; full-time officials developed as negotiators, rather than strike leaders, and union executives came to exercise more control over strike funds and decisions. At the same time there was an increase in the relative importance of the TUC and a switch in issues away from pay and working conditions towards more general standards. These were said to require political rather than industrial solutions. Meanwhile there were similar changes in the structure, scope and form of collective bargaining, leading to more industry-wide agreements and the development of external procedures for conciliation and arbitration as alternatives to industrial action. Finally, Knowles noted a change in the attitudes of senior level personnel after 1926. In effect they came to search for ways of settling disputes without the need for trials of strength.

All these factors, it was held, helped to explain the reduction in workers involved and days lost during the 1920s – most notably after 1926. In effect Knowles argued that to some extent the collective bargaining system changed after World War I to accommodate to the continued presence of trade unions and the concomitant risk of industrial conflict. Another way of putting the point would be to say that the parties developed procedures and institutions to resolve the differences that arose between them without the need for overt conflict.

To account for the rise in the number of stoppages which was apparent from the mid-1930s, Knowles placed considerable emphasis on the potential divisions between officials and members – divisions whose actual realisation was reflected in the growing proportion of stoppages not known to be official. He also emphasised that the post-1926 shift in attitudes was not so strongly reflected at less senior levels.

The similarities between Knowles' findings and our own are apparent. Both studies reflect the impact of bargaining structures on the form of strikes; both emphasise worker solidarity as the *sine qua non* of strike action. In our period the development of shop steward systems recreated the conditions which had existed at the beginning of Knowles' period but could only sustain a much more sectionalised bargaining structure. The erosion of the post-1926 mentality was partly the effect of time, partly the result of changes in the attitudes of the other parties, partly a response to demands from members who had always had their suspicions of the rapprochement.

The differences between Knowles and ourselves are perhaps best illustrated by reference to a third text – that by Ross and Hartman (1960). Their international historical comparative study drew heavily on Knowles for their account of events in the UK, but their analysis lacked much of the caution and perception of the original.

Their explanation of the rising level of stoppages in the UK followed Knowles in stressing the divisions between full-time officials and their memberships, but they concluded that such stoppages were internal union protests. The implicit failure to recognise and appreciate the significance of shop steward systems in sustaining alternative bargaining structures concerned, in part, with different issues, resulted in a serious under-estimation of the likelihood of strike activity in the UK. They also emphasised the beneficial results of government support for collective bargaining, both through its encouragement of joint industrial councils and, by example, in its treatment of its own employees.

The consequences of a withdrawal of or even a reduction in such government support were not discussed. Finally, again following Knowles, but doing so in order to support their own more general thesis about the consequences of the growth in the social, industrial and political maturity of labour movements, they stressed the significance of the relationship between trade unions and the Labour Party. This relationship, it was argued, encouraged the development of objectives other than those immediately concerned with pay and conditions and provided the means by which they might be successfully pursued – thereby obviating the need for industrial action.

Again this statement had more claim to validity as an historical judgement than as a realistic appraisal of the then current or future prospects. The consequences of a perception by union members that the Labour Party was unable or unwilling to meet their objectives were ignored.

In summary Ross and Hartman, following Knowles, were primarily concerned to account for the reduction in the numbers of workers involved and in the duration of stoppages. Their explanation of these developments was in terms of 'The age and stability of unions, the sophistication of employers, the improvement of bargaining machinery, the activities of government, the political aims of the labour movement and the success of the Labour Party'. For the period it covered this explanation was substantially accurate and some of its elements retained their potency well into the post-war period. Ross and Hartman were, however, less circumspect than Knowles with regard to the significance of unofficial stoppages, and this led them to writing a premature obituary for British strike activity: 'The substance of the matter is that British labor has largely abandoned the strike as a tactical instrument in pressing its purposes.'

The next major commentary on strikes and collective bargaining in the UK was that of the Donovan Report. This commentary was in part a product of the substantial volume of research undertaken by the Commission itself, but it was also heavily influenced by the academic studies which had appeared in response to the resurgence in strike activity – e.g. the work of H. A. Turner. Having observed that British strike activity in terms of workers involved and days lost was not exceptional by international standards, the Commission focused its attention on the number of stoppages, especially on the rapid growth of unofficial stoppages outside coal mining. Its explanation of this growth relied almost exclusively on changes in bargaining structures and bargaining institutions in a context of full employment. The growth of shop steward systems had permitted the articulation of claims about job rights and fair wages which had previously passed unheard. Many such disputes arose in 'grey areas' of managerial prerogatives where it was argued that they did not come within the scope of the collective bargaining arrangements. The industry-wide procedural agreements for handling such disputes were too slow and too remote; in consequence workers adopted sanctions rather than wait upon the outcome. Their willingness to adopt sanctions was frequently reinforced by management's preparedness to reach a speedy settlement in such circumstances.

To reduce the number of stoppages Donovan proposed widespread voluntarily negotiated reforms affecting the scope, coverage and form of collective bargaining. The crucial feature of the proposals was that reform should be undertaken at the level of the individual plant or company. What was required were 'formal factory and company agreements', incorporating the realities of the shop-floor power situation into more structured and 'ordered' systems of collective bargaining. On the basis of factory and company agreements it should be possible to deal with defective payment systems and wages structures. Joint regulation at this level could also deal with problems of job security and the improvement of productivity. Above all, Donovan argued that it was only at the level of the individual plant and/or company that effective and workable dispute procedures could be negotiated.

As we saw, this analysis was not so much wrong as inadequate – given developments in the years that followed its publication. When strike activity rose again in mining, and elsewhere in the public sector, it took forms that were not anticipated by the Donovan Commission. Perhaps the Commission's failure to foresee the increased incidence of hybrid and political stoppages in the 1970s was not altogether surprising, but some change in the strike pattern might have been expected as a logical consequence of the Commission's own recommendations – e.g. a growth of larger, longer and more hybrid stoppages at plant and company level.

It is also fair to suggest that the Commission under-estimated the difficulties involved in securing voluntary reform, and failed to appreciate the influence of government policy on the strike pattern. In some ways the Donovan Report, with its emphasis on bargaining machinery and institutional factors, may be viewed as an updating of Knowles. Knowles accounted for much of the reduction of strike activity, towards the end of his period, by the development of more adequate bargaining institutions. Donovan explained the subsequent rise by suggesting that these institutions and procedures had become less adequate in a full employment situation, given the development of strong shop-floor pressures. They hoped to engineer another reduction in strikes by a further change in institutions.

In the event Donovan's hopes failed to materialise, although in terms of strike number the adoption of their proposals were not without an impact. In other circumstances they might have had a greater overall effect – but the late 1960s and early 1970s were marked by a sharp worsening of economic conditions, increasing government intervention to restrict collective rights and a greater willingness to use strike action. The resulting climate was not conducive to Donovan-type reforms, and led to a resurgence of macro-stoppages with implications for workers involved and days lost that were quite outside Donovan's experience and model of collective bargaining.

How do our findings and conclusions fit into this continuing debate? To us they appear to be more closely allied with those of Knowles than anybody else. Of course changing circumstances have led to different factors assuming greater prominence, at different points in time; but a number of continuities and similarities of approach appear to be evident. In particular both studies demonstrate the necessity for a multi-causal approach when attempting to explain variations in the national strike pattern. Both suggest that a certain caution is needed, when prescribing for substantial reductions in strike activity. Both cover long enough periods of time to uncover the dangers of extrapolating trends in respect of any of the three measures of strike activity.

There is evidence also in both studies to support the view that the form of strike activity is largely determined by bargaining structure; that inadequate or ineffective procedures increase the probability of stoppages, particularly where there is a 'learning effect' produced by more rapid and generous settlements. Of course Donovan also took a similar view in respect of micro-strike activity, but believed that more effective procedures could be relied on to reverse such trends. Our own research suggested that this would only be true if the sources of conflict were successfully tackled at the same time – as was the case for a period in the mines, but not in the docks. Otherwise, we found, there was a real likelihood that bargaining reforms would simply alter the form of strike action, leaving its incidence unaffected – e.g. in the case of the car industry. Yet we also found that even comprehensive reforms which successfully tackled internal problems and procedures could be overturned and rendered null and void by external factors. Thus it would be foolish to claim that in the absence of the 1972 national strike stoppages in coal mining would have continued to decline, or remained at their very low level. On the other hand, the wage restraint policies which provoked the 1972 strike undoubtedly helped to encourage a subsequent growth in micro-stoppages and the national strike of 1974 – for all these developments appeared to demonstrate that 'militancy pays'.

One way of summarising the view of the relationship between strikes and collective bargaining which emerges from our study might be to suggest that in itself this question is too narrow to be worth a considered reply. In practice the interaction of three factors appear to have been crucial to the explanation of post-war strike activity – bargaining machinery, substantive terms and conditions and the external environment. Explanations, or policies, which seek to rely on one or another of these to the exclusion of the others are unlikely to take us very far. On the contrary, unpropitious developments in any one of the three could be sufficient to provoke an increase in strike activity, while favourable circumstances in all three might still be insufficient to avoid a growth of conflict. As the final revisions were being made to the typescript of this book, Edwards (1982) published an article which mirrors some of these conclusions.

COSTS AND EFFECTS OF STRIKES

In Chapter 1 of this study we stressed that our concern was to depict and, in so far as we were able, to explain the pattern of strike activity in the UK. We accepted that our findings would have implications in terms of analysing the costs and effects of stoppages, but regarded such implications as secondary to our main concerns. In keeping with our principal aims we have not sought to collect further information on such' aspects of strike activity. Nevertheless, it seemed fitting to return to these questions in the final section of this study to consider what conclusions, if any, it suggested about the costs and effects of stoppages.

Discussion of the costs of stoppages raises two immediate definitional problems – costs to whom and over what period. Those bearing the costs of stoppages include the parties directly concerned – employers and workers. Others involved may include the customers and suppliers of the affected establishment(s), groups which may include large sections of the national and international communities. In most cases the costs are likely to lessen the further those involved are from the stoppage itself. The extent to which the costs spread beyond the immediate parties depends on a number of factors – i.e. the duration of the stoppage, the availability of stocks or other supplies, the level of demand and the role of the affected establishments in the production cycle. Given this variety of factors and circumstances any judgements we make must be seen as applying to the general case and not to any particular instance. The period over which the analysis of strike costs is conducted is also relevant because it admits the possibility of offset – that the losses incurred during the stoppage may be compensated by extra activity before or after the stoppage.

To regard the losses arising from strike activity as simply those incurred at the affected establishments during the stoppage itself may result in serious under- or over-estimation. If the stoppage affected a key product or service for many other firms, if no other supplies or stocks were available, if demand were high and the stoppage prolonged, then the costs would be significantly greater than simply those of struck establishments. If these circumstances were reversed, then the losses would be confined to struck establishments. Even in that case simple measurement of the stoppage might prove to be an exaggeration. If stocks were higher than required, then a stoppage might have little or no financial cost as other output-reducing methods would have been required if the stoppage had not taken place. If stocks were simply sufficient to cover the period of the stoppage, there might still be little or no loss if output could be raised after the stoppage – e.g. by overtime or higher productivity.

Given our findings on the limited extent and short duration of most strike activity in the UK, the implication of the above analysis would seem to be that direct estimates of output loss based on time loss would not be likely to under-estimate the impact of stoppages in the UK. Indeed, the result might well be the reverse. This would suggest that in 1972 – the worst year of our period, when days lost were six times greater than average – the impact of stoppages in the UK was to cause an output loss of not more than 0.25 per cent. On the same basis, reducing unemployment to an average level of 250 000 in that year would have permitted additional output equivalent to 2.5 per cent of GDP.

Against these very crude and comforting aggregate estimates three arguments may be made: that the dislocative effects of stoppages have been seriously under-estimated; that the psychological effect of stoppages on management in terms of inhibiting innovation and change has been ignored; that such global estimates ignore and consequently under-estimate the effect of stoppages where they do occur – the concentration effects.

In respect of the dislocative effects of stoppages we would stress that the capacity of strikes to affect other establishments depends on the duration of the stoppage, the availability of stock or other supplies, the level of demand and the role of the affected establishments in the production cycle. We noted earlier that UK stoppages were disproportionately concentrated in the manufacturing sector. Consequently a large proportion of their output is final output whose disruption does not have immediate disruptive consequences for other plants. We also noted earlier the tendency for UK stoppages to be small and short, which would minimise their external consequences. We would also draw attention to the apparent capacity of the UK economy in recent years largely to withstand the effects of major and prolonged stoppages of key goods and services – e.g. the miners' strikes in 1972 and 1974, the road haulage dispute in 1979 and the steel strike in 1980. These exceptional stoppages, with their far-reaching cumulative effects, did not result in output losses on the scale widely forecast for them. If the economy *can* minimise the effects of such exceptional major stoppages, then it seems likely that smaller stoppages present disproportionately fewer problems.

The psychological implications of stoppages for management were highlighted in the Donovan report: as they put it,

> If an employer forestalls a strike by making concessions in the face of threats which it might have been better to resist, or by refraining from introducing changes which he believes to be necessary in the interests of efficiency, then the economic consequences of his doing so may be more serious than those to which a strike would have given rise. . . . The upshot is that some managements lack confidence that the plans they make and the decisions they reach can be implemented rapidly and effectively or, in extreme cases, at all. . . . The economic implications are obvious and serious; the country can ill afford the crippling effect which such management attitudes are liable to have on the pace of innovation and technological change in industry.

The Commission was exercised by the occurrence of 'unpredictable', unofficial, unconstitutional stoppages. Leaving aside the problem of unpredictability (see Hyman, 1972, p. 41), there are two issues involved: How widespread are such stoppages? Do they really affect management in the way that the Commission supposed? The Commission argued that these effects were most acute in 'endemic strike situations', i.e. plants where there had been five or more officially recorded stoppages in the space of a year. According to the Ministry of Labour there were thirty-one such establishments in 1965 and twenty-seven in 1966. There were, at that time, some 80 000 establishments in the manufacturing sector plus a further substantial number in the primary and tertiary sectors. While recognising the seriousness of the situation in the strike-prone plants, and that there must have been many others where repetitive striking although not so frequent was a fact of life, one cannot help feeling that the Commission had not really established its case that 'the pace of innovation and technological advance in industry' were under serious threat from this source.

Our scepticism in this respect was strengthened by the results of a further Department of Employment survey published in November 1976. This showed that over the period 1971–3, a period of high strike activity in the manufacturing sector, where UK strike activity is disproportionately concentrated, only 0.7 per cent of establishments averaged one stoppage or more a year, accounting for 43.5 per cent of all manufacturing stoppages. In so far as repeated stoppages did leave management with severe inhibitions about introducing innovations and technological changes the effects appear likely to be confined to a very small section of industry.

The other point which should be made in respect of these 'psychological' effects is that the Commission produced no evidence to support its assertions. In these circumstances there is little to be done other than repeat the remarks of one of the authors in an earlier publication on this same issue:

> It is, at base, a matter of impression or judgement. Personally I have always thought that the Donovan Report grossly oversold the psychological deterrent effect of strikes; it has always seemed to me a managerial excuse, the first refuge of the lazy and the last ditch of the cowardly. Good managers make much more use of the more sophisticated point that all change has to be paid for in one way or another, and sometimes it is just not worth the price (McCarthy, 1970).

The last counter-argument on the cost of strikes points out that they are heavily concentrated by industry and into particular periods of time. In those particular areas and periods the costs must be much higher than our global estimates suggest. There is a substantial element of truth in this argument – although its corollary is that our global estimate exaggerates the effects of strike activity in other sectors where stoppages are effectively unknown. It also seems likely that in those areas where stoppages are relatively common the parties are aware of their likelihood and have some experience in minimising their effects. In contrast, relatively strike-free areas are more likely to be adversely affected by occasional stoppages, which may well occur because they lack the necessary experience. It may also be the case that such disputes tend to be prolonged because the parties directly concerned are less practised in handling them.

None of the above is intended to suggest that stoppages in the UK are costless or negligible. There can be little doubt that all stoppages impose costs on the parties concerned and that the more prolonged the stoppages the more substantial the costs, not only to those directly concerned and their families but also to those indirectly involved. All we sought to do was to explore the probable costs of stoppages in relation to the economy as a whole. We found that, because of their generally limited scale and duration, the costs of overall strike activity has been relatively low. Certainly, on this evidence, it is difficult to understand the almost obsessive interest of the media in stoppages, or the repeated efforts of politicians to impose additional legal restraints on strikers. But it may be argued that it is not the costs of stoppages but their effects which attract attention and concern. It is to those effects that we now turn.

In discussing the effects of stoppages one is concerned, primarily, with their effect on the terms of the settlement. But to discern the effects of strikes then requires a knowledge of the issues in dispute and an assessment of what the settlement terms would have been if a stoppage had not taken place. At first glance the latter requirements would seem to need the services of a clairvoyant, while the former, on those occasions when the parties are unable to agree on the issues, would benefit from those of Solomon. Having thus demonstrated the impossibility of the task, what follows should be regarded as a spirited attempt to make bricks without the benefit of straw or clay.

In Chapter 1 we drew attention to the interpretational difficulties associated with the Department of Employment's classification of stoppages by attributed cause. We therefore restricted ourselves to using a simple wage/non-wage issue classification. The same practice appears appropriate here. The Department's series provides the only readily available information on the issues in dispute in stoppages, but it remains subject to the usual interpretational difficulties. Another reason for using the wage/non-wage classification concerns the possibility of 'spillover effects', i.e. that the settlement terms associated with one stoppage materially influence settlements elsewhere.

It could be argued that non-wage issues – such matters as redundancy, discipline, working conditions and arrangements – are less likely to enter the orbits of coercive comparisons than are wage issues. And if it is accepted that the effects of non-wage issue stoppages are largely confined to the plants in which they originate – because they are very much the product of particular sets of circumstances which are not replicated elsewhere – then that limits the scale of the task.

In Chapter 6 we reported that, over the period as a whole, 49 per cent of the gross total of stoppages, 65 per cent of workers directly involved and 79 per cent of working days lost were concerned with wage issues. But there is little or no direct evidence available on the effect of these stoppages on the settlement terms. Our sectoral studies revealed that workers in the more highly strike-prone industries tended to receive higher wages, on average, than manual workers in other industries. In itself this reveals nothing of the effects of stoppages. Such industries – given the nature of the work, the skills required, etc. – might well have paid higher wages without such a high incidence of strikes. There was certainly no consistent tendency over time for these industries to increase their differential over less strike-prone industries.

Alternatively it could be argued that the stoppages had prevented these industries' relative advantage from being eroded. Unfortunately, in the absence of any evidence on what the level of earnings would have been if the stoppages had not occurred, it is not possible to judge between these conflicting hypotheses.

Although there is no direct evidence on the effect of stoppages in affected establishments, or of any associated 'spillover effects', there is some very indirect evidence which can be pressed into service. Some of this concerns the relative wage advantage of workers covered by collective agreements over workers not so covered. Given our view of strikes as a transient feature of collective bargaining, it could be argued that the relative wage advantage of covered over non-covered workers provides a maximum estimate of the relative wage advantage of those who can take or threaten to take strike action over those who cannot. In reality, given the small proportion of those covered by collective agreements who take strike action over wages (less than 10 per cent a year on average), and the significance of other factors in the collective bargaining process, it seems more plausible to assume that only a small proportion of the advantage provided by collective bargaining should be ascribed to strikes.

There have been a number of studies in recent years which have sought to estimate the relative wage advantage accruing to those covered by collective bargaining arrangements. The results of some of these studies and of the problems involved in such estimations have been surveyed by Metcalf (1977). These studies have suggested a relative wage advantage for adult male manual workers in the region of 20–40 per cent. If these estimates were accurate, they would provide the scope for stoppages to have had a significant effect on wages. But, as we have already noted, wages are influenced by a vast range of other factors including skill levels, education, age, plant size, degree of industry concentration, etc. In order to identify the relative wage advantage of collective bargaining it is necessary to identify the existence and significance of these other factors. Any errors on this account would result in a mis-estimation and exaggeration of the size of the relative wage advantage. Further, as Metcalf points out, the existence of multi-collinearity between the variables could result in an over-estimation of the relative wage advantage (RWA).

Given these possibilities, are there grounds for supposing that the studies quoted above significantly exaggerate the RWA? Thomson, Mulvey and Farbman (1977), in a study of bargaining structure, reported the actual unadjusted RWA for male manuals as 12 per cent; i.e. simply comparing hourly earnings of those covered by collective agreements with those not covered showed an advantage to the former of 12 per cent. Yet the majority of the other factors which influence earnings are positively associated with coverage by collective agreement; i.e. those covered are more likely to be skilled, employed in large plants in concentrated industries in conurbations, etc. This means that the crude unadjusted RWA must provide an over-estimate of the RWA gained from collective agreements.

If the 12 per cent advantage indicated by the raw data exaggerates the RWA of collective bargaining coverage, then the implication is that the RWA provided by strikes must be very small, for, given that the RWA appears to be widely spread across those covered by collective agreements, it is not possible to argue that, although their share of the total is small, strikers benefit disproportionately in their RWA. Moreover, if it were true that strikers obviously benefitted substantially by their actions, one might expect strike action to be much more widespread than has been the case. Then again, in some cases the use of strike action has been motivated by an attempt to secure wage increases similar to those gained by peaceful collective bargaining elsewhere – e.g. the postal workers' strike in 1971. In such cases strikers are acting more as the workers' rearguard than their vanguard.

But the impact of collective bargaining on wages is not confined to a stable RWA. The RWA may vary from year to year, as does the general level of wages. We may therefore ask what role, if any, strikes play in this dynamic process? Once again there is no direct evidence of the impact of stoppages themselves, or their spillover effects. In any case the extent to which money wages can be raised 'autonomously' – i.e. without the intervention of 'market forces' – is at the heart of the contemporary debate about inflation and its causes. This is not the place to attempt to decide that debate, or even to spell out our own position. Suffice it to say that on the scale that stretches between an extreme 'demand pull' view and the upper limits of 'cost push' theory, we would locate ourselves at the cost side; but not at its limit. The implication of this is that we regard it as self-evident that wages are, on occasion, raised by more than demand conditions would dictate through the forces of collective bargaining.

A certain amount of anecdotal evidence exists to support this view, but it relates to particular settlements. There is also more general evidence in respect of particular wage rounds – e.g. 1974/5 – but it does not permit any estimate to be made of the contribution of stoppages as such, as against the much more general influence of collective bargaining. Given that the general level of wages rises in response to a variety of factors of which collective bargaining is only one, and given that the greater part of collective bargaining takes place without the presence of stoppages, we find ourselves unable to accord to strike action a substantial and crucial role in the wage inflation process so far. Which is not to deny that in association with other factors, and when a number of circumstances combine to lead to a significant increase in the general wage level, particular stoppages can have a decisive effect on the pace of inflation – e.g. the miners' stoppages of 1972 and 1974.

One author, in a recent discussion of these points, remarked: 'they can then work less hard, operate more restrictive practices and are more able to "get away with" misdemeanours than if they were not unionised' (Mulvey, 1978, p. 138).

On this view the effect of collective bargaining over such issues and, by implication, the effect of stoppages, is to reduce the technical efficiency of firms, so that their output is less and/or their costs are higher than they would be in the absence of collective bargaining. But of course the assumptions underpinning such analyses include a belief in a profit-maximising and cost-minimising management, blessed with more foresight than its workforce, and always operating in a fair and equitable manner. For only if a management is cost minimising can it be relied upon to adopt the most efficient practices; unless its foresight is greater than that of its workforce it may take poor decisions which could have been avoided through collective bargaining. The exercise of prejudice, discrimination or injustice may impose avoidable costs which are inconsistent with the cost-minimising hypothesis.

Such an assumption is not one which would necessarily command universal support, so that the *a priori* hypothesis that collective bargaining *necessarily* reduces technical efficiency cannot be accepted as it stands. It seems more plausible to suppose that in some instances collective bargaining reduces technical efficiency, whereas in others – e.g. when it replaces arbitrary management decision making with due process – it may raise it. Indeed it has been argued, in a classic American work on the impact of collective bargaining on management (Slichter, Healy and Livernash, 1960), that efficient managers profit from the presence of trade unions in a firm – although they must adapt organisational structures to deal with the challenge they represent.

Meanwhile the reader may decide if he wishes that collective bargaining and, to a lesser extent, stoppages, tend to mitigate against the optimisation of technical efficiency – so long as he appreciates that a judgement of this kind depends critically on whether or not his comparisons are with the idealised world of 'perfect competition' and 'profit maximisation' or the realities of labour utilisation in the mass of non-unionised firms in Britain.

He should also remember that the effects of stoppages over wage issues are not confined to matters of technical efficiency, or even the optimum use of economic resources. They extend to the well-being of workers and the climate of industrial relations. If stoppages prevent the victimisation of a union representative or the wrongful dismissal of a worker, or if they secure safer working conditions or replace compulsory by voluntary redundancies, then their effect can be said to be to protect or enhance the dignity, self-respect and well-being of the workforce both as individuals and collectively. Unless one is prepared to countenance a massive extension of state regulation there is no effective alternative to permitting such differences to be resolved by the parties most directly involved in the manner which seems most appropriate to them.

✓ The occurrence of strikes is unfortunate, in that they usually impose some costs on all concerned. From time to time these costs may be extremely severe, and may well cancel out the gains, even to those who appear to have won. Nevertheless, they are an unfortunate necessity in that, on some occasions, their benefits – which are indispensable to a democratic society – could not be secured in any other way.

Appendix 1 Details of the Classification of Variables in the Major Strikes Series

OCCUPATIONAL DATA

As described in the text we based our occupational classification scheme on the list of major occupational groups shown in the 1971 *New Earnings Survey*. We supplemented this list by the inclusion of other occupational titles to cover specific occupational groups. Although our original classification scheme covered the whole occupational structure we found that some groups – particularly among white collar workers – were not involved in major stoppages during this period. The list set out below only covers those occupational groups which were actually involved in major stoppages.

Code no.	Occupation
25	Other foremen and supervisors
40	Draughtsmen
42	Technicians: laboratory, scientific, medical, dental
44	Other technicians
52	School teachers: secondary, primary, nursery, special
64	Ambulance men, hospital/ward orderlies
65	Other medical, dental, nursing and welfare staff
74	Authors, editors, journalists
75	Artists, musicians, photographers, entertainers, sportsmen
77	Aircrew officers, ship's officers, pilots
79	Joint stock bank officials, other bank officials
80	Clerks – all grades
86	Postmen, mail sorters, messengers
92	Shop salesmen, sales assistants, shop assistants
93	Roundsmen – retail salesmen, van salesmen
96	Insurance agents
105	Other security staff
111	Stewards, stewardesses, hostesses (air, rail, ship)
112	Waiters, waitresses, barmen, barmaids
116	Cleaners, charwomen
118	Other catering, domestic and service staff
130	Railways – drivers, motormen, 2nd men, signalmen, etc.
132	Miscellaneous other transport and communication workers
133	Bus/coach drivers and conductors
135	Lorry/van drivers
136	Deck/engine room hands, seamen, boatmen, fishermen
137	Dockers/stevedores
138	Others, inc. lightermen
139	Car delivery drivers
140	Textile spinners, doublers, twisters, winders, reelers, etc.

141	Sewing machinists
142	Tailors, cutters, dressmakers (not machinists)
145	Others, inc. dyers
151	Boilermakers, boiler shop workers and fitters
153	Compositors, typesetters
156	Crane operators
157	Fork lift truck operators
158	Furnacemen
159	Bakers, confectioners
161	Inspectors, viewers, examiners, checkers
162	Storekeepers, storemen, warehousemen
163	Packers, bottlers, canners
164	Mining workers – not coal
170	Bricklayers
171	Carpenters/joiners
172	Plumbers, pipefitters, coppersmiths
175	Heating, ventilating fitters/engineers
176	Steel erectors, benders, fixers, scaffolders
178	Electricians – building, wiring, maintenance, supply, production
179	Fitters – electric, electronic, maintenance, production, toolroom, tool/die maker, gas, maintenance engineer
180	Precision instrument makers/repairers
181	Motor vehicle fitters/mechanics
182	Radio and TV repairers/mechanics
184	Assemblers – skilled, semi-skilled and others (inc. cars)
185	Machine tool setters, setter operators
186	Machine tool operators
187	Machine operators, metal and wood, skilled and semi-skilled
189	Electroplaters
190	Moulders, coremakers
191	Pattern makers (wood and metal)
192	Platers, riveters, caulkers
193	Smiths, forgemen
194	Sheet metal workers
195	Welders
197	Telephone installers/repairers
198	Local government manual workers n.e.s.
199	Aircraft workers n.e.s.
200	Press workers, bodymakers
201	Mill men
202	Engineering and electrical engineering workers
203	Shipwrights and shipbuilders
204	Laundry workers
205	Tobacco workers
206	Film industry workers
207	Rubber workers
208	Food manufacturers
209	Market porters, slaughterers
210	Workers n.e.s.

211	Quarry workers
212	Leather and fur trade manufacturers
213	Labourers n.e.s.
214	Printing ink workers
215	Foundry workers
216	Car and vehicle industry workers n.e.s.
217	Building workers n.e.s.
218	Furniture workers, inc. upholsterers
219	Paper and printing industry workers n.e.s.
220	Stonemasons and sculptors
221	Oil refinery workers n.e.s.
222	Chemical industry workers n.e.s.
223	Brick, pottery, glass and cement industry workers n.e.s.
224	Distributive trades workers n.e.s.
300	Professional and technical staff

REGIONAL DATA

Our regional classification was based on the Standard regions set out in the Ministry of Labour *Gazette* in 1966. We supplemented this list to cover situations where stoppages affected more than one region. Details are set out below.

Region	*Area covered*
South East	Middx, Beds., Herts., Essex, Berks., Bucks., Oxon., London (GLC), Kent, Surrey, Sussex, Hants. (and Isle of Wight), Borough of Poole
East Anglia	Cambs., Hunts., Soke of Peterborough, Norfolk, Suffolk
South West	Cornwall (and Isles of Scilly), Devon, Dorset (except Poole), Glos., Somerset, Wilts.
West Midlands	Herefordshire, Salop, Staffs., Warwicks., Worcs.
East Midlands	Derbyshire (except High Peak District), Leics., parts of Holland and parts of Kesteven and City of Lincoln in Lincs., Northants, Notts., Rutland
Yorkshire and Humberside	East and West Ridings, City of York, parts of Lindsay in Lincs.
North West	Cheshire, Lancs., High Peak District of Derbyshire
Northern	Cumberland, Durham, Northumberland, Westmorland, North Riding of Yorkshire
Scotland	Whole of Scotland
Wales	Whole of Wales and Monmouthshire
Northern Ireland	Armagh, Antrim, Derry, Down, Fermanagh, Tyrone
Various	More than one English region
Great Britain	England, Scotland, Wales
United Kingdom	England, Scotland, Wales, Northern Ireland

Appendix 1

INDUSTRIAL DATA

We based our industrial classification on that used by the Department but it differs in so far as we aggregated certain sectors in order to maintain continuity despite changes in the SIC and in the Department's reporting practices.

Code No.	Industry
10	Agriculture, forestry, fishing
20	Coal mining
30	Other mining and quarrying
40	Grain milling
50	Bread, flour, confectionery, biscuits
60	Other food industries
70	Drink
80	Tobacco
90	Chemicals
100	Iron, steel and other metal manufacture
110	Non-electrical engineering
120	Electrical engineering
130	Shipbuilding
140	Motor vehicles
141	Aircraft
142	Cycles
150	Railway locos, carriages, trams, etc.
160	Carts, perambulators, etc.
170	Other metal goods
180	Textiles
190	Clothing
200	Footwear
210	Non-metalliferrous mining products
220	Furniture, timber and other wood and cork manufactures
230	Paper, board, cartons
240	Printing and publishing
250	Other manufacturing industries
260	Construction
270	Gas, electricity and water
280	Railways
290	Road passenger transport
300	Road haulage
310	Sea transport
320	Port and inland waterways
330	Other transport and communications
340	Distribution
350	Insurance, banking and finance
360	Professional and scientific services
370	Miscellaneous services
380	Public administration and defence

IMMEDIATE CAUSE OF MAJOR STOPPAGES

With the benefit of hindsight we attempted to select those issues which were of interest over the period as a whole. The list is set out below:

Cause

Wage increase claim
Other wage issue
Discipline
Redundancy
Sympathy
Demarcation
Trade union principle
Other

Appendix 2 Political Stoppages, 1969–73

All the figures given in the following list are estimates

1969
1 May   80 000–90 000 workers in protest against Labour government's proposed industrial relations reforms

1970
17 March   22 000 dockers in protest over Labour government's proposals for nationalisation of the ports
25–27   Post Office workers in protest over dismissal of the Corporation's
November   chairman; estimated 100 000–200 000 involved
8   350 000 workers against Conservative government's proposals for
December   industrial relations reform

1971
12 January   170 000–180 000 in protest against Conservatives' Industrial Relations Bill
1 March   1 250 000 in protest against Industrial Relations Bill
18 March   1 250 000 in protest against Industrial Relations Bill
23 June   100 000 in Glasgow against Conservative government's decision not to aid Upper Clyde Shipbuilders and against growing unemployment in West of Scotland
18 August   100 000 in Glasgow against reorganisation of Upper Clyde Shipbuilders and growing unemployment
24   85 000 in Scotland, the North West and London against level of
November   unemployment

1972
24–26 July   40 000 dockers and approximately 130 000 others against imprisonment of five London dockers for contempt of National Industrial Relations Court
18   55 000 engineering workers in London and South East against fine
December   imposed on AUEW by National Industrial Relations Court
20   160 000 engineering workers and 10 000 dockers against fine imposed
December   on AUEW by National Industrial Relations Court

1973
1 May   1 600 000 workers in TUC-organised protest against Government's counter-inflation policies
5 and 12   323 000 engineering and motor vehicles workers against fine imposed
November   on AUEW by National Industrial Relations Court
19 and 23   12 000 workers in Leeds and Burnley against fine imposed on AUEW
November   by National Industrial Relations Court

List of Works Cited

Allen, V. L. (1954). *Power in Trade Unions: A Study of Their Organisation in Great Britain*. London: Longmans.

Ashenfelter, O., and G. E. Johnson (1969). Bargaining theory, trade unions and industrial strike activity. *American Economic Review*, March 1969.

Bain, G. S., and R. Price (1980). *Profiles of Union Growth*. Oxford: Basil Blackwell.

Batstone, E., I. Boraston, and S. Frenkel (1977). *Shop Stewards in Action*. Oxford: Basil Blackwell.

Batstone, E., I. Boraston, and S. Frenkel (1978). *The Social Organisation of Strikes*. Oxford: Basil Blackwell.

Bean, R., and D. A. Peel (1974). A quantitative analysis of wages strikes in four industries, 1962–70. *Journal of Economic Studies*. November 1974.

Boraston, I., H. A. Clegg, and M. Rimmer (1975). *Workplace and Union*. London: Heinemann.

Brown, W. (ed.) (1981). *The Changing Contours of British Industrial Relations*. Oxford: Basil Blackwell.

Central Policy Review Staff (1975). *The Future of the British Car Industry*. London: HMSO.

Clegg, H. A. (1970). *The System of Industrial Relations in Great Britain*. Oxford: Basil Blackwell.

Clegg, H. A. (1971). *How to Run an Incomes Policy and Why We Made Such a Mess of the Last One*. London: Heinemann.

Clegg, H. A., and R. Adams (1957). *The Employers' Challenge*. Oxford: Basil Blackwell.

Cohen, C. D. (1971). *British Economic Policy 1960–69*. London: Butterworth.

Conservative Party (1968). *A Fair Deal At Work*. London: Conservative Political Centre.

Cronin, J. E. (1979). *Industrial Conflict in Modern Britain*. London: Butterworth.

Davies, R. J. (1979). Economic activity, incomes policy and strikes: a quantitative analysis. *British Journal of Industrial Relations*, July 1979.

Declaration of Intent in Prices, Productivity and Incomes (1964). London: HMSO.

Devlin, Lord (Chairman) (1965). *Final Report of the Committee of Inquiry into Certain Matters Concerning the Port Transport Industry*. London: HMSO (Cmnd 2523).

Donovan, Lord (Chairman) (1968). *Report of the Royal Commission on Trade Unions and Employers' Associations 1965–68*. London: HMSO (Cmnd 3623).

Donovan, Lord (Chairman) (1966–8). *Minutes of Evidence to the Royal Commission on Trade Unions and Employers' Associations*. London: HMSO.

Edwards, P. K. (1982). Britain's changing strike problem. *Industrial Relations Journal*, Summer 1982.

Eldridge, J. E. T. (1968). *Industrial Disputes: Essays in the Sociology of Industrial Relations*. London: Routledge.

Engineering Employers Federation (1966). Evidence to the Donovan Commission, Appendix P in *Minutes of Evidence to the Royal Commission on Trade Unions and Employers' Associations*. London: HMSO.

Goodman, J. F. B. (1967). Strikes in the United Kingdom: recent statistics and trends. *International Labour Review*, 1967.

Hyman, R. (1972). *Strikes*. London: Fontana.

Hughes, J., and R. Moore (eds) (1972). *A Special Case?* Harmondsworth, Middlesex: Penguin.

ILO (1926). *Methods of Compiling Statistics of Industrial Disputes*, Studies and reports, Series N, No. 10. Geneva: International Labour Office.

In Place of Strife (1969). London: HMSO (Cmnd 3888).

Jenkins, P. (1970). *The Battle of Downing Street*. London: Charles Knight and Co.

Knight, K. G. (1972). Strikes and wage inflation in British manufacturing industry 1950–68. *Bulletin of the Oxford Institute of Economics and Statistics*, August 1972.

Knowles, K. G. J. C. (1951). The post-war dock strikes. *Political Quarterly*, July–September 1951.

Knowles, K. G. J. C. (1952). *Strikes – A Study in Industrial Conflict: With Special Reference to the British Experience 1911–47*. Oxford: Basil Blackwell.

Kornhauser, A., R. Dubin, and A. M. Ross (eds.) (1954). *Industrial Conflict*. New York: McGraw-Hill.

Labour Research Department (various) *Labour Research: Monthly Circular of the Labour Research Department*. London: Labour Research Department.

Lane, A., and K. Roberts (1971). *Strike at Pilkingtons*. London: Fontana.

Leeson, R. A. (1973). *Strike: A Live History 1887–1971*. London: Allen and Unwin.

McCarthy, W. E. J. (1959). The reasons given for striking. *Bulletin of the Oxford University Institute of Statistics*, February 1959.

McCarthy, W. E. J. (1968). In *Three Studies in Collective Bargaining*, Research Paper no. 8 of the Royal Commission on Trade Unions and Employers' Associations. London: HMSO.

McCarthy, W. E. J. (1970). The nature of Britain's strike problem. *British Journal of Industrial Relations*, July 1970.

McCarthy, W. E. J., and B. A. Clifford (1966). The work of industrial courts of inquiry. *British Journal of Industrial Relations*, March 1966.

McCarthy, W. E. J., and R. J. Liddle (1972). The impact of the Prices and Incomes Board on the reform of collective bargaining. *British Journal of Industrial Relations*, November 1972.

McCarthy, W. E. J., and S. R. Parker (1968). *Shop Stewards and Workshop Relations*, Research Paper no. 10 of the Royal Commission on Trade Unions and Employers' Associations. London: HMSO.

McFarlane, L. J. (1981). *The Right to Strike*. Harmondsworth, Middlesex: Penguin.

Marsh, A. I., and E. E. Coker (1963). Shop steward organisation in the engineering industry. *British Journal of Industrial Relations*, June 1963.

Mayhew, K. (1979). Economists and strikes. *Oxford Bulletin of Economics and Statistics*, 41, 1979.

Mellish, M. (1972). *The Docks after Devlin*. London: Heinemann.

Metcalf, D. (1977). Unions, incomes policy and relative wages in Britain. *British Journal of Industrial Relations*, July 1977.

Ministry of Labour (1923–60). *Annual Reports*. London: HMSO.

Ministry of Labour (1961). *Industrial Relations Handbook*. London: HMSO.

Ministry of Labour (1965). Written evidence to the Donovan Commission, in

Minutes of Evidence to the Royal Commission on Trade Unions and Employers' Associations. London:HMSO.

Ministry of Labour (1966). Standard regions for statistical purposes. *Ministry of Labour Gazette*, January 1966.

Mukherjee, S. (1973). *Through No Fault of Their Own*. London: Macdonald.

Mulvey, C. (1978). *The Economic Analysis of Trade Unions*. London: Martin Robertson.

National Economic Development Office (1973). *Motors*. London: NEDO.

New Earnings Survey 1968 (1969). London: HMSO.

New Earnings Survey 1971 (1972). London: HMSO.

New Earnings Survey 1973 (1974). London: HMSO.

Office of Population, Censuses and Surveys (1974). *Workplace Industrial Relations 1972*. London: HMSO.

Office of Population, Censuses and Surveys (1975). *Workplace Industrial Relations 1973*. London: HMSO.

Parker, S. R., C. G. Thomas, N. D. Ellis and W. E. J. McCarthy (1971). *Effects of the Redundancy Payments Act*. London: HMSO.

Pencavel, J. H. (1970). An investigation in industrial strike activity in Britain. *Economica*, August 1970.

Personal Incomes, Costs and Prices (1948). London: HMSO.

Phillips, A. W. (1958). The relationship between unemployment and the rate of change of money wages in the United Kingdom 1861–1957. *Economica*, November 1958.

Prais, S. J. (1978). Strike-proneness of large plants in Britain. *Journal of the Royal Statistical Society A*, Part 3, 1978.

Rees, A. (1952). Industrial conflict and business fluctuations. *Journal of Political Economy*, October 1952.

Rochdale, Viscount (Chairman) (1962). *Report of Committee of Inquiry into the Major Ports of Great Britain*. London: HMSO (Cmnd 1824).

Ross, A. M., and P. T. Hartman (1960). *Changing Patterns of Industrial Conflict*. New York: Wiley.

Scott, W. H., E. Mumford, I. C. McGivering and J. M. Kirby (1963). *Coal and Conflict: A Study of Industrial Relations at Collieries*. Liverpool: Liverpool University Press.

Sharp, I. G. (1950). *Industrial Conciliation and Arbitration in Great Britain*. London: Allen and Unwin.

Slichter, S. H., J. J. Healy and E. R. Livernash (1960). *The Impact of Collective Bargaining on Management*, Washington, D.C.: Brookings Institute.

Smith, C. T. B., R. Clifton, P. Makeham, S. W. Creigh and R. V. Burn (1978). *Strikes in Britain*. London: HMSO.

Stewart, M. (1977). *The Jekyll and Hyde Years: Politics and Economic Policy since 1964*. London: J. M. Dent & Sons.

Thomson, A. W. J., and S. R. Engleman (1975). *The Industrial Relations Act: A Review and Analysis*. London: Martin Robertson.

Thomson, A. W. J., C. Mulvey and M. Farbman (1977). Bargaining structure and relative earnings in Great Britain. *British Journal of Industrial Relations*, July 1977.

Transport and General Workers Union (1965–8). Evidence to the Donovan Commission, in *Minutes of Evidence to the Royal Commission on Trade Unions and Employers' Associations*. London: HMSO. See para. 4484.

Turner, G. (1973). *The Leyland Papers*. London: Pan.

Turner, H. A. (1952). *Arbitration: A Study of Industrial Experience*. London: Fabian Publications.

Turner, H. A. (1963). *The Trend of Strikes*. Leeds: Leeds University Press.

Turner, H. A. (1969). *Is Britain Really Strike-prone?* London: Cambridge University Press.

Turner, H. A., and J. Bescoby (1961a). Strikes, redundancy and the demand cycle in the motor car industry. *Bulletin of the Oxford University Institute of Statistics*, May 1961.

Turner, H. A., and J. Bescoby (1961b). An analysis of post-war labour disputes in the British car manufacturing firms. *Manchester School*, May 1961.

Turner, H. A., G. Clack and G. Roberts (1967). *Labour Relations in the Motor Industry*. London: Allen and Unwin.

Wedderburn, K. W. (1971). *The Worker and the Law*. Harmondsworth, Middlesex: Penguin.

Wedderburn, K. W. and P. L. Davies (1969). *Employment Grievances and Disputes Procedures in Britain*. Berkeley: University of California Press.

Wedderburn, Lord (1980). Industrial relations and the courts. *Industrial Law Journal*, **9**, 1980.

Weekes, B., M. Mellish, L. Dickens and J. Lloyd (1975). *Industrial Relations and the Limits of the Law*. Oxford: Basil Blackwell.

Wigham, E. L. (1976). *Strikes and the Government 1893–1974*. London: Macmillan.

Wilkinson, F., and H. A. Turner (1972). The wage–tax spiral and labour militancy. In *Do Trade Unions Cause Inflation?* D. Jackson, H. A. Turner and F. Wilkinson (eds). London: Cambridge University Press.

Wilson, D. F. (1972). *Dockers: The Impact of Industrial Change*. London: Fontana/Collins.

Young, M. D., and P. Willmott (1957). *Family and Kinship in East London*. London: Routledge.

Index